We the People:
The Fourteenth Amendment
and the Supreme Court

We the People:
The Fourteenth Amendment
and the Supreme Court

MICHAEL J. PERRY

New York   Oxford

Oxford University Press

1999

Oxford University Press

Oxford   New York
Athens   Auckland   Bangkok   Bogotá   Buenos Aires   Calcutta
Cape Town   Chennai   Dar es Salaam   Delhi   Florence   Hong Kong   Istanbul
Karachi   Kuala Lumpur   Madrid   Melbourne   Mexico City   Mumbai
Nairobi   Paris   São Paulo   Singapore   Taipei   Tokyo   Toronto   Warsaw

and associated companies in
Berlin   Ibadan

Library of Congress Cataloging-in-Publication Data
Perry, Michael J.
We the people the Fourteenth Amendment and the Supreme Court / Michael J. Perry.
p.   cm.
Includes index.
ISBN 0-19-512362-X
1. United States. Constitution. 14th Amendment.   2. Civil rights—United States.
3. Political questions and judicial power—United States.   4. United States. Supreme Court.
I. Title.
KF4558 14th .P47 1999
342.73'085 — dc21   98-48865

1 3 5 7 9 8 6 4 2

Printed in the United States of America
on acid-free paper

For

JACK B. WEINSTEIN

*the judge with whom, in 1973–74,
I was greatly privileged to start
down this path*

PREFACE

I had planned to call this book *The Judicial Usurpation of Politics? The Fourteenth Amendment and the Supreme Court*. (The reader will understand, by the end of chapter 1, why I thought the title apt.) But my editor at the Oxford University Press, Thomas LeBien, suggested that the title the book now bears was a better choice. (The reader will understand, by the end of chapter 2, why Thomas preferred the latter title.) I deferred to Thomas' judgment. But not without some anxiety: As a quick visit to amazon.com will confirm, numerous books, far more than I had imagined—some famous, some not so famous—bear "We the People" as part of their title if not as the whole of it.[1]

I have focused, in this book as in most of my earlier constitutional writings, on the legitimacy vel non of certain aspects of the modern Supreme Court's Fourteenth Amendment workproduct.[2] My interest in this topic was greatly influenced by a seismic event over a quarter of a century ago, at the beginning of my final semester of law school: The Supreme Court's hugely controversial decisions, in January 1973, in the abortion cases, *Roe v. Wade* and *Doe v. Bolton*. (I discuss the cases in chapter 6). As this book reflects, my views have changed over the years. There are important continuities, but there are also important discontinuities. I am inclined to think that the latter dominate the former, though perhaps I'm not the best judge of that. For a superb study of the evolution of my constitutional jurisprudence, conjoined with insightful critical commentary, see Richard B. Saphire, "Originalism and the Importance of Constitutional Aspirations," *Hastings Constitutional Law Quarterly* 24:599–664 (1997). I am indebted to Rich Saphire not only for his generous attention to my past work, but also for his written comments on a draft of this book.

I am also grateful, for their written commentaries on all or part of this book, to several friends and colleagues or former colleagues: Kathy Abrams, Dan Conkle, Michael Curtis, Rick Kay, Pat Kelley, Gary Lawson, Beth Mertz, Wilson Parker, Dan Polsby, Steve Smith, and Ron Wright. A version of chapter 2 appeared as my contribution to Larry Alexander, ed., *Constitutionalism: Philosophical Foundations* (1998). I am grateful to the Cambridge University Press for permission to use that material here.

I am especially indebted, for their ongoing conversation with me, to Michael Curtis and Steve Smith. (Both of them disagree—sometimes strenuously—with some things I say in this book.) Michael Curtis is a wonderfully learned student of the history of the Fourteenth Amendment. His book *No State Shall Abridge: The Fourteenth Amendment and the Bill of Rights* (1986) is already a classic. Steve Smith is, among other things, a wise critic of contemporary constitutional studies, which too often consists of depressingly predictable polemical exertions masquerading as scholarship. (Has it long been so? Consider the passage by the late Robert McCloskey that I have put at the beginning of chapter 7.) The contemporary controversy about "the judicial usurpation of politics" is, as I explain in chapter 1, an important one, and I hope that in addressing the controversy—in trying to think carefully about the relevant issues—I have not succumbed to what Smith, in his important recent book, has called "the pride of reason."[3]

Finally, a word about the uncommonly decent man to whom I have dedicated this book. Jack Weinstein is one of the greatest federal trial judges of this century now ending. I cannot imagine a more wonderful way to have begun my career in the law than with Judge Weinstein, whom I was privileged to serve in my first year out of law school (1973–74). My dedication of this book to him is a small gesture of my great respect and affection for Judge Weinstein.

Winston-Salem, North Carolina   M. J. P.
January 1999

CONTENTS

We the People:
The Fourteenth Amendment
and the Supreme Court

THE FOURTEENTH AMENDMENT

1. All persons born or naturalized in the United States, and subject to the jurisdiction thereof, are citizens of the United States and of the State wherein they reside. No State shall make or enforce any law which shall abridge the privileges or immunities of citizens of the United States; nor shall any State deprive any person of life, liberty, or property, without due process of law; nor deny to any person within its jurisdiction the equal protection of the laws.

2. Representatives shall be apportioned among the several States according to their respective numbers, counting the whole number of persons in each State, excluding Indians not taxed. But when the right to vote at any election for the choice of Electors for President and Vice-President of the United States, representatives in Congress, the Executive and Judicial officers of a State, or the members of the Legislature thereof, is denied to any of the male members of such State, being twenty-one years of age, and citizens of the United States, or in any way abridged, except for participation in rebellion, or other crimes, the basis of representation therein shall be reduced in the proportion which the number of such male citizens shall bear to the whole number of male citizens twenty-one years of age in such State.

3. No person shall be a Senator or Representative in Congress, or Elector of President and Vice-President, or hold any office, civil or military, under the United States, or under any State, who, having previously taken an oath, as a member of Congress, or as an officer of the United States, or as a member of any State Legislature, or as an Executive or Judicial officer of any State, to support the Constitution of the United States, shall have engaged in insurrection or rebellion against the same, or given aid and comfort to the enemies thereof. But Congress may, by a vote of two-thirds of each House, remove such disability.

4. The validity of the public debt of the United States, authorized by law, including debts incurred for payment of pensions and bounties for services in suppressing insurrection and rebellion, shall not be questioned. But neither the United States nor any State shall assume or pay the loss or emancipation of any slave; but all such debts, obligations, and claims shall be held illegal and void.

5. Congress shall have power to enforce by appropriate legislation the provisions of this article.

1

---∞∞∞---

Introduction: "The Judicial Usurpation of Politics"

There is a dangerous tendency in these latter days to enlarge the functions of the courts, by means of judicial interference with the will of the people as expressed by the legislature. Our institutions have the distinguishing characteristic that the three departments of government are coordinate and separate. Each must keep within the limits defined by the Constitution. And the courts best discharge their duty by executing the will of the law-making power, constitutionally expressed, leaving the results of legislation to be dealt with by the people through their representatives.

Mr. Justice Harlan, dissenting, *Plessy v. Ferguson* (1896)[1]

I am about to sketch, in this introduction, a contemporary controversy about several important constitutional rulings by the Supreme Court of the United States. The rulings at issue were all handed down by the Court in the modern period of American constitutional law: the period since 1954, the year in which the Court made its historic and seminal decision in *Brown v. Board of Education*,[2] striking down racially segregated public schooling.[3] It bears mention, here at the outset, that controversy about one or more constitutional rulings by the Supreme Court—broad, deep, and persistent controversy—is not just a contemporary phenomenon. Such controversy, as students of American constitutional law well know, has been a perennial feature of American politics (as the date of this chapter's epigraph, from *Plessy v. Ferguson*, serves to illustrate). Perhaps no constitutional ruling by the Court was more controversial in its day—or more dire in its consequences—than the Court's infamous pro-slavery decision, in 1857, in *Dred Scott*.[4] Other examples, though less spectacular, are nonetheless important. Two come immediately to mind. A half century after *Dred Scott*, the Court's decision in *Lochner v. New York* (1905),[5] striking down legislation forbidding bakery owners to require or permit their employees to work more than ten hours a day or sixty hours a week, pro-

3

voked great controversy. A century after *Dred Scott* and a half century after *Lochner*, the Court's decision in *Brown v. Board of Education* provoked not merely great controversy but open defiance and loud calls for the impeachment of Chief Justice Earl Warren. (I discuss the Court's decision in *Brown* later in this book.)

Given the long history of controversy about (some of) the Court's constitutional rulings, the fact that we find such controversy in the present is not surprising. Nor is the nature of the contemporary controversy surprising: The claim at the heart of today's controversy is substantially the same claim that was at the heart of most earlier controversies about constitutional rulings by the Court—namely, that in the guise of interpreting the Constitution, the Supreme Court is actually usurping prerogatives that under the Constitution belong to one or more other branches or agencies of government.

That neither the fact nor even the nature of today's controversy about the Supreme Court is new—that such controversy is perennial in American politics—does not diminish a bit the large importance of the controversy. But it does challenge us to address the controversy, if we choose to address it at all, in a way that genuinely advances the conversation.

I

The nature of the contemporary controversy is powerfully illustrated by a symposium that appeared in November 1996 in the periodical *First Things*.[6] The title of the symposium was "The End of Democracy? The Judicial Usurpation of Politics". The constitutional rulings that the various symposiasts[7] condemned in their essays were principally rulings I address in this book: rulings, about what the Fourteenth Amendment to the Constitution of the United States forbids or requires, in cases involving sex-based discrimination, homosexuality, abortion, and physician-assisted suicide. (I also address, in this book, constitutional rulings in cases involving racial segregation and race-based affirmative action.) In their introduction to the symposium, the editors of *First Things*—in particular, Richard John Neuhaus, the editor in chief[8]—began by referring to a lower federal court's "decision favoring doctor-assisted suicide, [which] could be fatal not only to many people who are old, sick, or disabled, *but also to popular support for our present system of government.*" The editors then explained:

> This symposium addresses many similarly troubling judicial actions that add up to an entrenched pattern of government by judges that is nothing less than the usurpation of politics. The question here explored . . . is whether we have reached or are reaching the point where conscientious citizens can no longer give moral assent to the existing regime. . . . The question that is the title of this symposium is in no way hyperbolic. The subject before us is the end of democracy. . . . Perhaps the

United States, for so long the primary bearer of the democratic idea, has itself betrayed that idea and become something else. If so, the chief evidence of that betrayal is the judicial usurpation of politics.

. . . Democratic politics means that "the people" deliberate and decide [the] question[, How ought we to order our life together?] In the American constitutional order the people do that through debate, elections, and representative political institutions. But is that true today? Has it been true for, say, the last fifty years? Is it not in fact the judiciary that deliberates and answers the really important questions entailed in the question, How ought we to order our life together? Again and again, questions that are properly political are legalized, and even speciously constitutionalized. This symposium is an urgent call for the repoliticizing of the American regime.

The editors concluded their introduction with a dire evaluation of the present situation: "What is happening now is a growing alienation of millions of Americans from a government they do not recognize as theirs; what is happening now is an erosion of moral adherence to the political system."[9]

One of the contributors to the symposium was Robert Bork, whose nomination to the Supreme Court by Ronald Reagan in 1987 was rejected by the Senate. In 1989, in his best-selling book, *The Tempting of America: The Political Seduction of the Law*, Bork argued at length that section one of the Fourteenth Amendment had been, in the hands of the modern Supreme Court, an instrument of "judicial imperialism".[10] Seven years later, in his contribution to the *First Things* symposium—a contribution pointedly named "Our Judicial Oligarchy"—Bork repeated his charge: "The most important moral, political, and cultural decisions affecting our lives are steadily being removed from democratic control. . . . A majority of the [Supreme] Court routinely enacts its own preference as the command of [the Constitution]. . . . A majority of Justices have decided to rule us without any warrant in law." Bork reported, in his contribution, that his wife had accused the justices of the Court of "behaving like a 'band of outlaws.'" Bork then endorsed his wife's condemnation of the justices, saying that it was not "in the least bit extreme." He explained: "An outlaw is a person who coerces others without warrant in law. That is precisely what a majority of the present Supreme Court does. That is, given the opportunity, what the Supreme Court has always done."[11]

The *First Things* symposium provoked a strong reaction among many who generally sympathize with the socially conservative editorial sensibilities of *First Things*. Peter Berger, Walter Berns, and Gertrude Himmelfarb, three of the seven members of the periodical's editorial board, resigned. They, along with many other social conservatives, took issue with suggestions by some symposiasts to the effect that in consequence of the judicial usurpation of politics, the current "regime" had lost much of its moral authority, civil disobedience was an option to be considered seriously, and the United States was perilously close to a revolutionary situation. As Peter Steinfels reported in the *New York Times*,

Dr. Himmelfarb called the editors' hints that the United States might be reaching a revolutionary situation . . . "absurd and irresponsible" . . . Midge Decter, another member of the board, did not resign but wrote an impassioned rejoinder for the magazine's January [1997] issue. "I could hardly believe my eyes," Ms. Decter wrote. The symposium "smacks of nothing so much as the kind of careless radicalism you and I not all that long ago prayed for our country to have put behind it." Two other conservative journals, *National Review* and *The Weekly Standard*, added similar demurrers.[12]

In the February 1997 issue of the prominent "neoconservative" periodical *Commentary*, several more conservatives demurred to the *First Things* symposium.[13]

Significantly, however, none of the strong reactions to the symposium by social conservatives, several of which (like Midge Decter's) were published in a continuation of the symposium in the January 1997 issue of *First Things*, rejected the symposium's central argument that in the modern period of American constitutional law, and especially recently, the judiciary—in particular, the United States Supreme Court—has been engaged in the usurpation of politics. To the contrary, they *affirmed* that argument, notwithstanding their distaste for other aspects of the symposium. For example, in resigning from the editorial board of *First Things*, Gertrude Himmelfarb wrote that she "entirely agree[s] with those contributors [to the symposium] who maintain that the judiciary has vastly exceeded its proper powers and that this is a very serious problem for our polity."[14]

Shortly after the *First Things* symposium was published, many other socially conservative critics of the Court were quick to join the chorus of condemnation.[15] For example, Linda Bowles, a nationally syndicated columnist, wrote that "[t]oday, the greatest threat to the freedom of the American people is not some external enemy but their own government. . . . [T]he greatest enemy in America to a government of, by and for the people is . . . the judiciary. . . . The provisions of the Constitution are 'amended' by interpretation and selectively applied as a function of the collective ideological biases of whoever happens, at any point in time, to be sitting on the Supreme Court. . . . The Constitution no longer protects us. It has become, in the hands of the unaccountable, power-corrupted judges, an instrument of our oppression."[16] It bears mention that such comments are not confined to newspaper columnists, whose oversimplification and polemicization of difficult, politically charged issues is perhaps unremarkable. Similar comments, bereft of nuance, are not uncommon even among those who, by virtue of training and profession, know, or should know, how complicated the issues really are. Consider, for example, these statements by my former colleague at the Northwestern University Law School, Steven Calabresi: "Bill Clinton's judges . . . have been unwilling to follow the Constitution in a number of very important cases. And . . . when they chose not to follow the Constitution, they have all too often replaced it with radical and unpopular left-wing social policy. . . . [These] justices and judges are working quietly to impose a radical Mc-Governite legislative agenda on the country. . . . The last two years have seen an increasingly large number of [judicial] opinions that are contemptuous of the beliefs, values, and prerogatives of the American people *as well as of the democratic process itself.*"17

Let's put aside the hyperbole that characterizes some of the preceding passages (which, like most hyperbole, sheds more heat than light). Indeed, let's put aside even the most extreme (and least plausible) claims in the preceding passages—the claims about one or more recent constitutional rulings being "fatal . . . to popular support for our system of government"; about "the growing alienation [in consequence of one or more recent constitutional rulings] of millions from a government they do not recognize as theirs[,] an erosion of moral adherence to the political system"; about the Constitution having "become, in the hands of the . . . power-corrupted judges, an instrument of our oppression"; and so on. Even without such extreme claims, a grave charge remains—a charge mainly about several modern rulings by the Supreme Court about what the Fourteenth Amendment forbids or requires. Listen to the social conservatives whose responses to the first installment of the *First Things* symposium were published in the January 1997 issue of the magazine:18

- William Bennett: "[O]n many of the most important issues of our time, the courts are acting in remarkably inappropriate and injurious ways. . . . We need to do a better job educating citizens about how the modern-day Supreme Court is improperly intruding into issues of birth, marriage, and death . . ."
- Midge Decter: "One certainly cannot deny that the Court has usurped powers rightly belonging to the political process, nor can one in all sanity deny that it has been using those powers to reach extraconstitutional and illegitimate decisions . . ."
- James Dobson: "On the most essential matters of human life and conscience, the courts have systematically invalidated the will of the people . . . by constructing a jurisprudence that leaves no doubt they intend to continue ruling by judicial fiat for the foreseeable future."
- Mary Ann Glendon: "[T]he judiciary has steadily usurped power over matters that the Constitution wisely left to ordinary political processes."

The charge, in short, is that in the name of the Constitution, and especially in the name of the Fourteenth Amendment, the judiciary—in particular, the United States Supreme Court—has usurped important aspects of American politics, thereby seriously compromising the democratic character of American government. As the editors of *First Things* put it in the January 1997 issue, "The Supreme Court . . . has increasingly arrogated to itself the legislative and executive functions of government."

On July 4, 1997, about forty persons issued a statement endorsing and amplifying the charge that the Supreme Court has usurped our politics.19

The group included several persons who had contributed to the *First Things* symposium;[20] indeed, Richard John Neuhaus, the principal organizer of the symposium, and Charles Colson, a participant, convened the group that drafted the statement. The group also included John Cardinal O'Connor of New York, twelve other bishops and archbishops of the Catholic Church, Theodosius, Primate of the Orthodox Church in America, and the heads of several evangelical churches and church-related organizations. In their proclamation—the title of which, "We Hold These Truths: A Statement of Christian Conscience and Citizenship", made reference to the Declaration of Independence—the religious leaders and other signatories wrote that "on this Fourth of July, our attention must be directed to the role of the courts in disordering our liberty." They explained:

> Our nation was constituted by agreement that "we the people," through the representative institutions of republican government, would deliberate and decide how we ought to order our life together. In recent years that agreement has been broken. The Declaration [of Independence] declares that "governments are instituted among men, deriving their just powers from the consent of the governed." In recent years, however, power has again and again been wielded, notably by the courts, without the consent of the governed.

In support of their "judicial usurpation" claim, those who signed the July 4th statement, like the *First Things* symposiasts before them, pointed to several Fourteenth Amendment decisions by the Supreme Court, especially the Court's decision in *Roe v. Wade*:[21] "The most egregious instance of such usurpation of power is the 1973 decision of the Supreme Court in which it claimed to have discovered a 'privacy' right to abortion and by which it abolished, in what many constitutional scholars have called an act of raw judicial power, the abortion law of all 50 states." Citing, in addition to *Roe v. Wade*, the Court's rulings in some other Fourteenth Amendment cases—including the Court's controversial 1996 decision striking down a Colorado constitutional amendment that (in the Court's view) discriminated against homosexuals[22]—the statement declared that the Supreme Court has embarked on a "course of hostility to democratic self-government."

The *First Things* symposium and the kindred July 4th statement provide an especially useful point of departure for the principal inquiry I pursue in this book: Has the modern Supreme Court, in the name of the Fourteenth Amendment, usurped prerogatives and made choices that properly belong to the electorally accountable representatives of the American people; if so, to what extent has the Court done so? I cannot examine, in this book, every area of modern Fourteenth Amendment doctrine. (Still less can I examine here many important areas of constitutional doctrine—doctrines concerning federalism,[23] for example, or those concerning the separation of powers[24]—based on parts of the Constitution other than the Fourteenth Amendment.) The principal constitutional conflicts on which I focus—all of which have been resolved by the Court, at least in part, and at least for a time, on the basis of a claim about what the Fourteenth Amendment does or does not forbid or require—are the conflicts over racial segregation, race-based affirmative action, sex-based discrimination, homosexuality, abortion, and physician-assisted suicide. Again, constitutional rulings about sex-based discrimination, homosexuality, abortion, and physician-assisted suicide were the principal examples given by the *First Things* symposiasts in support of their "judicial usurpation" charge.

II

By way of setting the stage for the chapters that follow, I now want to do two things. First, I want to clarify the central claim about the modern Supreme Court that the *First Things* symposiasts were making; I want to do so by distinguishing their claim—let's call it "the *First Things* claim"—from a different claim with which the *First Things* claim might be confused. Second, I want to refine the *First Things* claim by disaggregating it into three distinct claims.

The implausible claim with which the *First Things* claim might be confused is that the modern Supreme Court has been acting illegitimately because it has been resolving *political* issues rather than *constitutional* ones. I have addressed elsewhere, at length, the distinction between "constitutional" issues and "political" issues—and, more generally, between "law", including constitutional law, and "politics"; and I have explained why the law/politics distinction, though superficially appealing, is deeply flawed.[25] For present purposes, I want only to emphasize that the *First Things* claim does not assert, presuppose, or entail any such distinction. The serious distinction, as the *First Things* claimants seem to understand, is between those political—that is, political-moral-issues about which the Constitution is silent, and whose resolution is therefore left solely to ordinary politics, and those political-moral issues about which the Constitution is vocal, if not necessarily articulate, and whose resolution is therefore committed, in our constitutional tradition, ultimately to the Supreme Court. (An example of an issue of the latter sort: the legitimacy of a municipal regulation making it difficult for pro-life activists to communicate their anti-abortion views to pregnant women on their way into an abortion clinic.[26]) Consider, with respect to this distinction, Mary Ann Glendon's statement, which I quoted earlier: "[T]he judiciary has steadily usurped power over matters that the Constitution wisely left to ordinary political processes." Glendon does not deny, in this passage, that (to paraphrase Glendon) there are matters that the Constitution (wisely) did *not* leave to ordinary political processes. Moreover, there is no reason to believe that a legal scholar as distinguished and astute as Glendon would deny that in addressing matters, in resolving issues, that the Constitution did not leave to ordinary political processes, the Court is resolving issues that are, whatever else they are, issues of political morality; or that she would deny that, as I explain in the next chapter, Supreme Court justices must make choices, in resolving some of these difficult political-moral issues, about which they (and others) can reasonably differ among themselves. Glendon's claim—the *First Things* claim—is simply that there are many "matters that the Constitution wisely left to ordinary political processes" and that the modern Court has illegitimately taken some of these matters away from those processes; it has illegitimately addressed matters, it has illegitimately resolved issues of political morality, that are *none of the Court's proper business—none of the business that the Constitution, rather than leaving solely to ordinary politics, has committed ultimately to the Court.*

I now want to refine the *First Things* claim by disaggregating it into three distinct claims.

- By charging the Court with "the judicial usurpation of politics", one might mean that in the name of the Constitution, the Court has imposed a norm on the popularly elected branches of government that was never established as a part of the Constitution by "We the people of the United States". The Preamble to the Constitution states: "*We the people of the United States, in Order to form a more perfect Union, establish Justice, insure domestic Tranquility, provide for the common defence, promote the general Welfare, and secure the Blessings of Liberty to ourselves and our Posterity, do ordain and establish this Constitution for the United States of America.*"
- As I explain in chapter 2, however, some norms have become, for us, "the people of the United States" now living, constitutional bedrock *even if they were never established as a part of the Constitution by "We the people"*. (I write "We the people", throughout this book, rather than "We the People", because in the original text of the Constitution, which I am quoting, the first letter of "people" is lowercase.) One such norm dictates that the national government may not discriminate on any basis on which the states are forbidden to discriminate by the Fourteenth Amendment; the national government, therefore, may not discriminate on a racist basis. (The Fourteenth Amendment applies only to the states, not to the national government.) Few if any persons argue that the Court ought not to continue to enforce such "bedrock" norms. A more serious "judicial usurpation" charge, therefore, is that the Court has imposed a norm that not only was never established as a part of the Constitution by "We the people", but that, moreover, is not constitutional bedrock for us, the people of the United States now living.
- Finally, by charging the Court with "the judicial usurpation of politics", one might mean only that in the course of reaching its decision, the Court failed to enforce a constitutional norm—a norm that was estab-

lished as a part of the Constitution by "We the people" or, at least, that is now a part of our constitutional bedrock—in an appropriately deferential manner: a manner appropriately deferential to another part of the government—a state legislature, for example—which is entitled (so the argument goes) to proceed on the basis of its own understanding of what the norm forbids or requires, so long as that understanding is not unreasonable.

I develop each of these three different senses of "judicial usurpation"— each of these three different "judicial usurpation" claims—more fully in subsequent chapters. Here I want only to caution that throughout our discussion, clarity requires that we take care to identify which of the three different "judicial usurpation" claims is on the table.

In whatever version, the charge that the modern Supreme Court has usurped our politics ought not to be taken lightly. Alas, the charge that the Court has usurped our politics is so long-standing, familiar, and predictable that the temptation, in some quarters, is to yawn—or even sneer—at the charge. But however long-standing, familiar, and predictable, the charge is very credible and deeply troubling to many of our fellow citizens, as the *First Things* symposium powerfully confirms. We owe it to them, and to ourselves, to confront the charge and evaluate it with great care. The truth, after all, is at stake, and with it, the quality of American political discourse. Moreover, the practical importance of the controversy is great: The claim that one or more of the modern Court's principal Fourteenth Amendment rulings were "remarkably inappropriate and injurious", "extraconstitutional and illegitimate", and so on, is a claim about what the Court should henceforth do, or not do, in the name of the Fourteenth Amendment, and what the Court henceforth does, or does not do, in the name of the Fourteenth Amendment will have profound effects on central aspects of the lives of countless persons. Indeed, constitutional rulings about abortion and physician-assisted suicide are, for some, matters of life and death.

III

An overview of the chapters that follow, and a summary of my principal conclusions, might be useful to the reader.

Chapter 2. What Is "the Constitution"? (And Other Fundamental Questions). Has the modern Supreme Court usurped our politics? In particular, has the Court resolved important political-moral issues that are none of the Court's proper business—none of the business that *the Constitution* has committed to the Court? Has it resolved such issues not on the basis of *the Constitution* but on some other, pseudo-constitutional basis? If one wants to pursue such an inquiry, one must first address three fundamental questions: What is "the Constitution"? What does it mean to interpret the Constitution? Is the Supreme Court supreme in interpreting the Constitution? I take up these and related questions in chapter 2, thereby providing the foundation for the rest of the book.

Chapter 3. The Fourteenth Amendment: What Norms Did "We the People" Establish? The constitutional issues I examine in this book, concerning such matters as homosexuality and abortion, have each been resolved by the Supreme Court on the basis of a claim about what the Fourteenth Amendment forbids or requires. Which of those issues, if any, understood as Fourteenth Amendment issues, have been resolved—which have been resolved on the basis of the Fourteenth Amendment—as they should have been resolved? One cannot fully answer that question without first inquiring what norms "We the people"—through their elected representatives, of course—established in adding the Fourteenth Amendment to the Constitution of the United States. This is not to say that the Supreme Court should *never* resolve a constitutional conflict, qua *constitutional* conflict, on the basis of a norm not established by "We the people". (I argue in chapter 2 that the Court should *sometimes* resolve a constitutional conflict on the basis of such a norm.) It is just to recognize that, as I emphasize in chapter 2, if one wants to argue that a governmental action—for example, a state law—violates the Constitution, the least controversial basis on which to do so, in American constitutional culture, is a norm established as a part of the Constitution by "We the people". Certainly the least problematic basis on which the Supreme Court can rely in ruling that governmental action is unconstitutional is such a norm. In chapter 3, I inquire what norms "We the people" established in making the Fourteenth Amendment a part of the Constitution. This inquiry has persistently failed to generate a consensus among students of the history of the Fourteenth Amendment. So it bears emphasis that, as I explain in the final section of chapter 3, even if I am wrong about the norms "We the people" established in bequeathing us the Fourteenth Amendment, my error would have few if any practical implications for the arguments I make in chapters 4 through 6. Nonetheless, the historical inquiry I pursue in chapter 3 is an important component of our effort to understand and evaluate the role the modern Supreme Court has played in interpreting the Fourteenth Amendment.

Chapter 4. The Fourteenth Amendment and Race: Segregation and Affirmative Action. With the necessary foundation and relevant historical background now in place, I turn to the various Fourteenth Amendment rulings that are the principal subject matter of this book: the modern Court's rulings about racial segregation, race-based affirmative action, sex-based discrimination, homosexuality, abortion, and physician-assisted suicide. I begin, in chapter 4, with the rulings that address the central concern of the Fourteenth Amendment: racial discrimination. I inquire whether in outlawing the creation or maintenance by government of racial segregation, or in erecting high barriers to reliance by government on race-based affirmative action, the Supreme Court can be understood to have usurped our politics.

- *Racial segregation.* Even now, almost half a century after the Court, in *Brown v. Board of Education*, struck down racially segregated public schooling, some scholars insist that *Brown* was wrongly decided—that however morally repugnant racial segregation was (and is), the Court's decision in *Brown* was nonetheless a usurpation of our politics.[27] I conclude in chapter 4 that neither the Court's decision in *Brown* nor its kindred decisions in many later cases—decisions outlawing the creation or maintenance by government of racial segregation—can fairly be said to have "usurped" our politics on any plausible understanding of the usurpation claim.
- *Affirmative action.* My evaluation of the Court's decisions concerning affirmative action is more complicated and not easily summarized. I conclude that, in one respect, the Court has not usurped our politics in erecting high barriers to reliance by government on race-based affirmative action: As I explain in chapter 4, the Court's approach to affirmative action—its erecting high barriers—can be understood as warranted by a conjunction of two norms, one of which was established by "We the people", the other of which, though never established by "We the people", has become a part of our constitutional bedrock. I also conclude, however, that, in another respect, the Court's approach to affirmative action *does* involve a usurpation: The Court's failure to proceed in a deferential manner—a manner deferential to a legislature's or other policymaking body's *reasonable* judgment that a particular instance of affirmative action satisfies the applicable constitutional requirement—is troubling and can fairly be said to usurp our politics.

Chapter 5. Beyond Race: Sex and Sexual Orientation. In the 1970s, the Supreme Court moved beyond racially discriminatory laws and began to outlaw some laws, policies, and other government action that discriminated on the basis of sex. Was that move a judicial usurpation? Is it a usurpation for the Court to do what, in the name of the Fourteenth Amendment, it now does: disfavor all (government-sponsored) discrimination based on sex and outlaw most instances of such discrimination? In 1996, in a case that outraged many social conservatives, the Court struck down a newly adopted Colorado constitutional amendment that, in the Court's view, discriminated against homosexuals in violation of the Fourteenth Amendment. In what sense, if any, was the Court's action a usurpation of our politics? In what sense would it be a usurpation for the Court to disfavor discrimination against homosexuals the way it now disfavors discrimination against women, namely, by subjecting it to a strict standard of review—a standard that is often lethal? In chapter 5, I explain why it was legitimate for the Court, in enforcing the Fourteenth Amendment, to move beyond discrimination based on race to discrimination based on sex. The Court's move beyond race to sex was not a usurpation of our politics, on any plausible understanding of the usurpation claim. I then explain why it would not be illegitimate—it would not be a usurpation—for the Court now to move beyond race and sex to sexual orientation. Indeed, the serious question, as I suggest at the end of chapter 5, is not whether it would be a judicial usurpation of our politics for the Supreme Court to move beyond discrimination against women to discrimination against homosexuals. (It would not.) The serious question is whether it would be an illegitimate judicial capitulation to our politics—in particular, to our prejudices—for the Court to refuse to make that move.

Chapter 6. Further Beyond: Abortion and Physician-Assisted Suicide. No constitutional decision by the Supreme Court in the modern period of American constitutional law has been more controversial—certainly none has been more persistently controversial—than the Court's 1973 ruling in the abortion cases, *Roe v. Wade*[28] and *Doe v. Bolton*,[29] that no state may outlaw abortion in the period of pregnancy prior to the time at which the fetus becomes "viable" (i.e., "[capable] of meaningful life outside the mother's womb").[30] Even after a quarter of a century, the legitimacy of the Court's decision in the abortion cases is widely contested. In recent years, physician-assisted suicide has become, like abortion, the focus of great moral, political, and constitutional controversy in the United States. In June 1997, in the physician-assisted suicide cases, *Washington v. Glucksberg*[31] and *Vacco v. Quill*,[32] the Court ruled—all nine justices agreed—that states are free to outlaw physician assistance in suicide even if the person requesting the physician's assistance is mentally competent and terminally ill. I conclude, in chapter 6, that the Court's decision in the physician-assisted suicide cases was exactly right. I also conclude that considerations substantially identical to those that led the Court to decide the physician-assisted suicide cases the way it did should have led the Court, twenty-four years earlier, to a different decision—a narrower decision—in the abortion cases. The Court's ruling in the abortion cases, as I explain in chapter 6, was unduly broad and is fairly understood, therefore, as a judicial usurpation of American politics.

Chapter 7. Concluding Reflections. In the final chapter, I summarize the conclusions I reach in chapters 4 through 6, comment briefly on the constitutional "theory" that underlies my arguments in chapters 4 through 6, and suggest what is, in my judgment, the productive way to continue the conversation about judicial usurpation.

2

——∞∞∞——

What Is "the Constitution"?
(And Other Fundamental Questions)

Several of the most divisive *moral* conflicts that have beset us Americans in the period since the end of World War II have been transmuted into *constitutional* conflicts—conflicts about what the Constitution of the United States forbids—and resolved as such. The most prominent instances include the conflicts over racial segregation, race-based affirmative action, sex-based discrimination, homosexuality, abortion, and physician-assisted suicide, each of which has been resolved—at least in part, and at least for a time—on the basis of a claim about what the Fourteenth Amendment does or does not forbid.[1] Which of the conflicts, if any, understood as *constitutional* conflicts, have been resolved as they should have been resolved; that is, which have been resolved on the basis of *the Constitution* as they should have been resolved? If one wants, as I do, to pursue that inquiry, one must first answer three questions: What is "the Constitution"? What does it mean to interpret the Constitution? Is the Supreme Court supreme in interpreting the Constitution? Although this chapter is, then, preparatory, the questions I address here—*connected* questions—are fundamental.

I. What Is "the Constitution"?

A. *Constitutional Text v. Constitutional Norms*

The referent of the phrase "the Constitution of the United States" is sometimes the text—the writing—that we call the Constitution of the United States. But the referent is sometimes—indeed, often—"the supreme Law of the Land". (Article VI of the Constitution states: "This Constitution . . . shall be the supreme Law of the Land . . .") That there is no disagreement about what sentences the Constitution-in-the-first-sense (the constitutional text) contains[2] does not mean that there is no disagreement about what norms the Constitution-in-the-second-sense (the supreme law) comprises. Hereafter, when I mean to refer to the Constitution-in-the-first-sense, I will say "the constitutional text"; when I mean to refer to the Constitution-in-the-second-sense, I will say "the Constitution".

What norms does the Constitution comprise?[3] The first part of the constitutional text—the Preamble—declares: "We the people of the United States . . . do ordain and establish this Constitution for the United States of America."[4] In American constitutional culture, few if any persons (even, remarkably, few if any constitutional theorists) disagree that the Constitution comprises at least some directives issued by—that is, some norms "ordained and established" by—"We the people". More to the point, few disagree that the Constitution comprises some such norms partly because the norms were "ordained and established" by "We the people".[5] It is now a convention—an axiom—of American constitutional culture that "We the people of the United States" not only "do ordain and establish this Constitution for the United States of America" but *may* ordain and establish it. This is not to say that *only* "We the people" may establish norms as constitutional. More about that later.[6]

What directives have "We the people" issued, what norms have they established? When "We the people", through their elected representatives, add words to the constitutional text, they do so for the purpose of issuing—and, in that sense, establishing—one or more constitutional directives. The constitutional text, in each and all of its various parts, is the yield of political acts of a certain sort: acts intended to establish not merely particular configurations of words but, ultimately, particular norms, namely, the norms that "We the people" understood—or would have understood, had they been engaged, had they been paying attention—the particular configurations of words to communicate. Does anyone really believe that were *we* to add words to the constitutional text in our day, it might be a political act of a different sort: an act intended to establish not, ultimately, a particular norm but merely a particular configuration of words? If not, why would anyone believe that when *they* added words to the constitutional text in their day, they acted to establish merely a particular configuration of words? Establishing, in a political or legal document, a norm to govern the future—unlike establishing, in such a document, merely a particular configuration of words—is a recognizably human act. "[I]t is hard to think of any recommendation for a regime of law created by the 'interpretation' of disembodied words that have been methodically severed from the acts of mind that produced them."[7] Therefore, the norm (or norms) that "We the people" established, in adding a particular configuration of words to the constitutional text, is the norm they understood (or would have understood) their words to communicate. They did not establish a norm they would not have understood their words to communicate. In what sense would "We the people of the United States . . . ordain and establish this Constitution for the United States of America" if the norm they are deemed to have established is one they would not have understood their words to communicate?[8]

B. Why Bow to Old Constitutional Directives? And Why Issue New Ones?

I said that few if any persons disagree that the Constitution comprises some directives issued by "We the people of the United States". The "people of the United States" who did "ordain and establish" the Constitution in 1787–89—and the Bill of Rights in 1789–91—are long dead. So, too, are the people who amended the Constitution in the aftermath of the Civil War. Why, then, should *we*, the people of the United States *now living*, accept constitutional directives issued by persons long dead as *our* "supreme Law of the Land"?[9] Some directives comprised by the Constitution, including some of the oldest ones, are directives that we, the people of the United States now living, should want to be a part of our Constitution if they were not a part of it already. In the view of some of us, however, not every directive that is a part of our Constitution should be a part of it.[10] Why should those of us who believe that a directive should not be a part of our Constitution bow to the directive—that is, bow to it unless and until we succeed in disestablishing the directive in a constitutionally ordained way? Put another way, why should we follow the convention established by the directive? Why shouldn't we follow a different, competing convention—one not established by the Constitution but, nonetheless, more to our liking?

We might try to change the existing convention by amending the Constitution in a constitutionally ordained way—for example, in the way ordained by Article V.[11] But to pursue that strategy is to follow a convention established by the Constitution. The question at hand, however, is whether we should follow a convention not established by the Constitution that competes with a constitutionally established convention. Why should we do *that*? Why should those of us who believe that a directive should not be a part of our Constitution bow to the directive unless/until it is disestablished in a constitutionally ordained way? Why shouldn't we (or our representatives) try to disestablish the directive in a way that is not constitutionally ordained? (But, in *what* way that is not constitutionally ordained?) Indeed, why shouldn't we try to establish a new constitutional directive in a way that is not constitutionally ordained?

The most basic reason for bowing to a constitutional directive, unless/until it is disestablished in a constitutionally ordained way, is practical. "Contracts are generally backed by external sanctions; constitutions are more nearly backed by default, by the difficulty of recoordinating on an alternative arrangement. . . . [O]nce we have settled on a constitutional arrangement, it is not likely to be in the interest of some of us then to try to renege on the arrangement. And this is generally true not because we will be coerced to abide if we choose not to but because we generally cannot do better than to abide. To do better, we would have to carry enough others with us to set up an alternative, and that will typically be too costly to be worth the effort."[12] Trying to disestablish a constitutional directive, or to establish a new one, *in a way that is not constitutionally ordained* would be an exemplary instance of "try[ing] to renege on the arrangement." Because to succeed in that effort "we would have to carry enough others with us to set up an alternative, and that will typically be too costly to be worth the effort", it is not surprising that there is no significant support—nor, absent a severe constitutional crisis, is there ever likely to be such support—for disestablishing or establishing a constitutional directive in an other than constitutionally ordained way. Those of us who believe that an existing directive should not be a part of our Constitution usually have no option but to bow to the directive (unless/until it is disestablished in a constitutionally ordained way), because "we generally cannot do better than to [do so]." Similarly, those of us who believe that a directive should be a part of our Constitution usually have no option but to bow to the fact that the directive is not a part of our Constitution (unless/until it is established in a constitutionally ordained way), because "we generally cannot do better than to [do so]."[13] This is not to deny, however, that in truly extraordinary circumstances (e.g., a revolution, a civil war, or a great depression) some of us could disestablish a directive, or could establish one, in an other than constitutionally ordained way.[14] For example, Bruce Ackerman has argued—persuasively, in my view—that the Fourteenth Amendment was neither proposed by Congress nor ratified by the states in full accord with the requirements of Article V.[15] (Ackerman's project is not to challenge the constitutional status of the Fourteenth Amendment, but to demonstrate that the ways in which "We the people of the United States . . . do ordain and establish this Constitution for the United States of America" are sometimes different from, and more complex than, those authorized by Article V.) Moreover, it is almost certainly the case that in at least a few instances Supreme Court justices have disestablished a directive, or have established one, or have done both. More about this state of affairs in subsection C of this section.

We can disestablish a constitutional directive, in a constitutionally ordained way, without establishing (issuing) a new directive in its place. However, some day we might want to establish a constitutional directive (whether or not in place of an existing one). What reasons might we have for wanting to establish the directive as a *constitutional* directive—for wanting to establish it, that is, not, or not merely, by means of an ordinary statute, but by means of a constitutional amendment?

Whereas a statute typically may be revised or repealed by a legislative majority, national constitutions typically require much more than a legislative majority to amend the constitution. According to Article V of the Constitution, for example, "The Congress, whenever two thirds of both Houses shall deem it necessary, shall propose Amendments to this Constitution, or, on the Application of the Legislatures of two thirds of the several States, shall call a Convention for proposing Amendments, which, in either Case, shall be valid to all Intents and Purposes, as Part of this Constitution, when ratified by the Legislatures of three fourths of the several states, or by Conventions in three fourths thereof, as the one or the other

Mode of Ratification may be proposed by the Congress. . . ."[16] For us to establish a directive by means of a constitutional amendment, then, is for us to try to make it especially difficult, both for ourselves at a later time and for our political descendants at a much later time, to disestablish the directive. Opting for the constitutional strategy rather than for, or merely for, the statutory one is to decree that the directive may be disestablished, not by a legislative majority acting through the ordinary politics of legislative revision, but only by a supermajority acting through the extraordinary politics of constitutional amendment.[17]

What reasons might we have for wanting to make it so difficult to disestablish a directive? We might be skeptical about the capacity of our ordinary, majoritarian politics to safeguard the directive adequately, especially during politically stressful times when the directive might be most severely challenged. We might fear that at some time in the future, we who are so enthusiastic about the directive—for example, a directive expressly limiting the power of government—might lose our political dominance and that those who take our place might be hostile to the directive. We might fear too that even if we hold on to our political dominance, our political representatives, over whom we exert imperfect control, might fail to safeguard the directive adequately. In short, we might distrust—we might lack faith in—our (future) politics.

Not that there aren't other reasons for pursuing the constitutional strategy. For example, a political community might need to establish, or to reestablish, its basic institutions, institutional arrangements, and practices, so that its day-to-day politics might then begin, or begin again, to operate. Or it might want to remove certain issues from the agenda of its ordinary politics because it fears, not that its politics cannot be trusted to resolve the issues, but that a contest about how they should be resolved might tear or even destroy the bonds of community.[18] Even when a political community has already established its basic institutions, institutional arrangements, and practices, however, and even when it has no reason to fear that a contest about how a certain issue should be resolved might tear, much less destroy, the bonds of community, the community might be skeptical about the capacity of its ordinary, majoritarian politics, especially during stressful times, to safeguard adequately a directive the community deems important. In a federal political community, like our own, such skepticism might focus, at one time, less on the capacity of the politics of the states to safeguard a directive than on the capacity of the politics of the national government to do so. At another time, it might focus more on the capacity of the politics of the states, or of some of them.

C. What Norms Does the Constitution Comprise?

Again, few if any persons disagree that the Constitution comprises some directives established by "We the people" (and that it comprises some such norms partly because they were "ordained and established" by "We the people"). However, that the Constitution comprises some such norms does not entail that it comprises *only* such norms. As I now explain, few constitutional scholars disagree that the Constitution comprises at least some fundamental norms that were probably never established by "We the people". (Although few scholars disagree that the Constitution comprises at least some such norms, whether one or another norm was established by "We the people" is often a matter of controversy—as is the question whether one or another norm not so established is nonetheless a part of the Constitution.)

Under what circumstances, if any, is it legitimate for the Supreme Court to strike down as unconstitutional a law or other governmental action on the basis of a norm that, in the Court's view, is not part of the Constitution that has been "ordained and established" by "We the people of the United States" through their political representatives—that is, a norm that no generation of "We the people" understood, or would have understood, themselves to be establishing in putting particular words into the text of the Constitution? In our constitutional culture, it would be extremely difficult to justify such an action. It is widely accepted among us that "We the people of the United States"—not "We the justices of the Supreme Court"—should "ordain and establish" the Constitution of the United States.[19] By what right, then, would the Court impose on government—whether on the national government or on state government—a norm that in its view no generation of "We the people" had ever established?[20]

The issue, however, is rarely so simple. Assume that, a generation or even longer ago, the Supreme Court struck down as unconstitutional a law or other governmental action on the basis of a norm that, in the view of the Court today, is no part of the Constitution ordained and established by "We the people". It doesn't matter, to the inquiry I want to pursue here, whether the past Court based its decision on an honest but mistaken view about what norm the text of a constitutional provision was understood to establish, or on a pretense—a lie—about what norm the provision was understood to establish, or on an unreasonable specification of an indeterminate constitutional norm,[21] or even on a theory of constitutional adjudication according to which the Court may enforce, in the name of the Constitution, norms that no one, past or present, could fairly understand any language in the Constitution to communicate. Assume further that in the view of the Court today the old ruling was wrong because it was not warranted by—it was not based on—any norm established by "We the people". Under what circumstances, if any, should the Court today acquiesce in the old ruling rather than overrule it? Few constitutional scholars or jurists—not even Robert Bork or Antonin Scalia— insist that the Court should never acquiesce in old constitutional rulings it believes to have been wrong; the disputed question is when—under what conditions—the Court should do so.[22]

I don't mean to provide an exhaustive answer here, but this much is clear: If, over time, the premise decreed by the old, wrong (at the time) ruling has become such a fixed and widely affirmed and relied-upon (by us the people of the United States now living[23]) feature of the life of our political community that the premise is, for us, bedrock, then the premise has achieved a virtual constitutional status;[24] it has become a part of our fundamental law—the law that is constitutive of ourselves as a political community of a certain sort. Such a premise, therefore, ought not now to be overturned by the Court. Even Robert Bork—who, in the *First Things* symposium, charged the Supreme Court with usurping our politics[25]— has acknowledged that some mistaken constitutional precedents "have become so embedded in the life of the nation, so accepted by the society, so fundamental to the private and public expectations of individuals and institutions, that the result should not be changed now."[26] (Because Article V's processes of constitutional amendment are supermajoritarian, for the Court to overturn such a premise would be for it to empower a minority to impede the reestablishment of the premise as a part of our constitutional law. Perhaps ultimately the minority would fail, but, given the reality of so much of our politics—logrolling, sound bites, demagoguery, and so on—one couldn't be sure.) Moreover, after declining to overturn such a premise, the Court should not treat the premise as a sport and refuse to go further.[27] By hypothesis, we are talking about a premise that has achieved a virtual constitutional status, that has become a part of our fundamental law. It would be anomalous, therefore, for the Court to refuse to weave the premise into the fabric of the constitutional law that, in its "common law" mode, the Court develops over time.[28]

What premises would satisfy the condition articulated in the preceding paragraph? What premises are constitutional bedrock for us the people of the United States now living—and would remain so even if all of us who pay attention to such things came to be persuaded not only that the premises were never established by "We the people" but also that the premises were not warranted by—that they could not be derived from— any norm established by "We the people"?

- Consider, for example, the premise that the privileges and immunities —the rights and freedoms—protected against the national government by the Bill of Rights are protected against state government by the Fourteenth Amendment. It has been controversial whether that or any similar premise was established by the Fourteenth Amendment. (I discuss the controversy briefly in chapter 3.) Even if we were to discover tomorrow that, contrary to what some scholars believe the historical record shows[29] and to what the Court's rulings have long affirmed, the premise was not so established—that the generation of "We the people" that made the Fourteenth Amendment a part of the Constitution did not understand the Amendment to communicate any such premise —the premise is now constitutional bedrock for us; no Court either would or should overturn it.[30]

- Consider in particular the premise that not only the national government, but state government too, may not establish religion or prohibit the free exercise thereof or abridge the freedom of speech or the freedom of the press. It is at least somewhat controversial whether, even if the Fourteenth Amendment made (i.e., was meant to make) applicable to the states the norms, or some of the norms, made applicable to the national government by the Second through Eighth Amendments of the Bill of Rights, the Fourteenth Amendment made the norms of the First Amendment applicable to the states.[31] But even if we were to discover tomorrow that, contrary to what some scholars believe the historical record shows[32] and to what the Court's rulings have long affirmed, the Fourteenth Amendment did not "incorporate" the First Amendment, thereby making its norms applicable to the states, the premise that First Amendment norms are applicable to the states—that no state may establish religion or prohibit the free exercise thereof or abridge the freedoms of speech and of the press—is constitutional bedrock for us the people of the United States now living; no Court would or should overturn it.
- Finally, consider the premise that whatever antidiscrimination norm is applicable to state government under the Fourteenth Amendment is applicable to the national government as well. The Supreme Court has hung this premise on the due process provision of the Fifth Amendment, which states that "[n]o person shall be . . . deprived of life, liberty, or property, without due process of law . . ."[33] However, it is implausible that the due process provision of the Fifth Amendment—which, unlike the Fourteenth, applies to the national government—was understood by the generation of "We the people" that made the Fifth Amendment a part of the Constitution (the founding generation) to communicate any antidiscrimination norm, *much less the same antidiscrimination norm established by a later generation of "We the people" when they made the Fourteenth Amendment a part of the Constitution.*[34] I argue in chapter 4 that a historically accurate reading of the Ninth Amendment, mediated by a modest judicial strategy for determining what unenumerated rights against the national government are "retained by the people", warrants subjecting the national government to the same antidiscrimination norm to which state government is subject under the Fourteenth Amendment.[35] But even if we were to discover tomorrow that no constitutional norm established by "We the people" warrants doing so, the premise that the same antidiscrimination norm that applies to state government also applies to the national government is now constitutional bedrock and no Court would or should overturn it.

Whatever other premises satisfy the condition I've sketched here,[36] the three fundamental premises just listed, if not established by "We the people" and even if not warranted by any norm established by "We the people", surely would satisfy it.

I mean the condition articulated here to be a sufficient condition for the Court acquiescing in mistaken constitutional precedent, not a necessary condition. I am agnostic about whether it should also be a necessary condition.[37] It does seem to me that the condition is appropriately stringent. Nonetheless, there would doubtless be self-serving and implausible, even frivolous, claims to the effect that a premise is, for us the people of the United States now living, constitutional bedrock and ought not to be overturned by the Court.[38] But that even most such claims would be implausible does not entail that no such claim would be compelling. One might doubt that the premises to which I referred in the preceding paragraph are "mistaken" constitutional precedents. But whether or not they are—and, so, even if they are—mistaken, the premises are, for us the people of the United States now living, constitutional bedrock.

Although, as I have said, the Constitution comprises norms established by "We the people" (and not subsequently disestablished by them) in a constitutionally ordained way, it comprises neither every such norm nor only such norms. Both as a description of our practice and as a prescription for the continuance of the practice, the Constitution also comprises premises that, *whether or not any generation of "We the people" meant to establish them in the Constitution, and, so, even if no generation of "We the people" meant to establish them,* have become such fixed and widely affirmed and relied-upon (by us the people of the United States now living) features of the life of our political community that they are, for us, constitutional bedrock—premises that have, in that sense, achieved a virtual constitutional status, that have become a part of our fundamental law, the law constitutive of ourselves as a political community of a certain sort. Moreover, if such a premise is inconsistent with a norm established in the past by "We the people" (and not subsequently disestablished by them) in a constitutionally ordained way, the premise has, in our practice, lexical priority.[39]

II. What Does It Mean to Interpret the Constitution?

A. Interpreting the Constitutional Text

If one wants to argue that a governmental action—for example, a state law—violates the Constitution, the least controversial basis on which to do so, in American constitutional culture, is a norm established as a part of the Constitution by "We the people". Certainly the least problematic basis on which the Supreme Court can rely in invalidating a governmental action is such a norm. (As I mentioned earlier, it is widely accepted among us that "We the people of the United States"—not "We the justices of the Supreme Court"—should "ordain and establish" the Constitution of the United States.) "We the people", through their representatives, sometimes added words to the constitutional text that, even after more than two hundred years, succeed in communicating, without much interpretive inquiry by readers of the words, the norm that "We the people" understood the words to communicate and, through their representatives, meant to establish. Two such provisions are the part of Article I, section three, that states that "[t]he Senate of the United States shall be composed of two Senators from each State" and the part of Article II, section one, that states that "neither shall any person be eligible to that Office [of President] who shall not have attained to the Age of thirty-five Years". Thus, we may say that the sentence "The Senate of the United States shall be composed of two Senators from each State" is a part of the constitutional text and the norm that the Senate of the United States shall be composed of two senators from each state is a part of the Constitution. To say (as I did in § I.A) that the constitutional text is not identical to the Constitution is not to say that every provision of the constitutional text must undergo a significant interpretive inquiry—that every provision must be decoded or translated —if we are to discern what norm the provision was understood to communicate.

Sometimes, however, constitutional language does not communicate, without significant interpretive inquiry, the norm that "We the people" understood (or would have understood) it to communicate; sometimes a constitutional provision is, if not opaque, at least vague or, especially, ambiguous and so must be clarified. (The unintelligibility of a text is not necessarily either-or; it can be, and often is, a matter of degree.) Concomitantly, sometimes we readers of a constitutional provision can reasonably disagree, even after significant interpretive exertions, about what norm "We the people" understood a provision to communicate. Consider, for example, that part of the First Amendment that forbids government to "prohibit[] the free exercise [of religion]".[40] It is safe to assume that the free exercise language was not understood to communicate a norm forbidding government to prohibit each and every imaginable religious practice. (One need not concoct frightening hypotheticals about human sacrifice to dramatize the point. One need only point, for example, to the refusal of Christian Science parents to seek readily available lifesaving medical care for their gravely ill child.[41]) What norm, then, was the free exercise language understood to communicate? The language is ambiguous about what directive "We the people" meant to issue, what norm they meant to establish. Was it a norm forbidding government to engage in prohibitory action that discriminates against religious practice—that is, that disfavors religious practice *as such*: as *religious* practice, practice embedded in and expressive of one or more religious beliefs?[42] Or was it a broader norm, one that forbids, in addition to prohibitory action that discriminates against religious practice, at least some prohibitory action that, although nondiscriminatory, nonetheless impedes religious practice?[43] The position of five justices of the Supreme Court, in 1990, was that the free exercise language represents a norm that forbids only discriminatory action. The position of the remaining four justices—and of the Congress that, in 1993, passed the Religious Freedom Restoration Act and of the president who signed it into law—was that the free exercise norm also forbids some nondiscriminatory action that impedes religious practice.[44]

Consider next section one of the Fourteenth Amendment, which states, among other things, that "[a]ll persons born or naturalized in the United States, and subject to the jurisdiction thereof, are citizens of the United States and of the State wherein they reside" and that "[n]o State shall make or enforce any law which shall abridge the privileges or immunities of citizens of the United States".[45] We the people of the United States now living cannot discern what norm "We the people" then living understood the privileges or immunities language to communicate without strenuous interpretive inquiry, because we cannot know, without such inquiry, what the particular generation of "We the people" who put the language into the Constitution—the generation that had just lived through the Civil War and the abolition of slavery—understood the phrase "the privileges or immunities of citizens of the United States" to mean. We need to pursue a clarification of the language, which, by itself, is ambiguous about what norm they, through their representatives, meant to establish. Does the privileges or immunities norm they established protect only the privileges and immunities that persons who are citizens of the United States are due under the law, including the Constitution, of the United States?[46] Or does it protect not only those privileges and immunities but also all the privileges and immunities that persons who are citizens of the United States are due under the law of the state "wherein they reside"? Or does it protect, if not all the privileges and immunities citizens are due under the law of their state, at least some of them—and, if so, which ones?[47]

And whatever privileges and immunities are protected by the privileges or immunities norm that "We the people" established, what kind or kinds of state legislation does the privileges or immunities norm established by "We the people" protect the protected privileges and immunities from or against: laws that discriminate on a racist basis? laws that discriminate on the basis of color, whether or not the discrimination is "racist"? some other kinds of discriminatory laws, too? what kinds?[48] And who—what class of persons—does the norm protect: just citizens of the United States (all of whom are also citizens of the state wherein they reside) or all persons? (The very same sentence that contains the privileges or immunities language also contains this language: "[N]or shall any State deprive *any person* of life, liberty, or property, without due process of law; nor deny to *any person* within its jurisdiction the equal protection of the laws" (emphasis added).) The language of the privileges or immunities provision is undeniably limited to the privileges and immunities *of* such citizens (whatever those privileges and immunities are). But the language does not preclude the possibility that the norm the language was understood to communicate is not limited *to* such citizens. As John Ely has put the point: "'No State shall make or enforce any law which shall abridge the privileges or immunities of citizens of the United States' *could* mean that only citizens are protected in their privileges or immunities, but it surely doesn't have to. It could just as easily mean that there is a set of entitlements, 'the privileges and immunities of citizens of the United States,' which states are not to deny to anyone. In other words, the reference to citizens may define the class of rights rather than limit the class of beneficiaries."[49]

Sometimes, therefore, it will be necessary for us readers of the text of a constitutional provision to engage in a difficult historical inquiry into what norm the provision was understood to communicate by the generation of "We the people" that (through its representatives) put the provision into the Constitution. It is simply not true of every constitutional provision, even though it is true of many, that the question of the norm the provision was understood to communicate can usefully be answered by a statement of what the provision says. Referring to Article II, section one, of the Constitution, which states that "[n]o person except a natural born Citizen . . . shall be eligible to the Office of President", John Ely has observed that "[u]nless we know whether 'natural born' meant born to American parents on the one hand or born to married parents on the other, we don't know what the ratifiers thought they were ratifying and thus what we should recognize as the constitutional command."[50]

Interpreting the text of a constitutional provision, in the sense of inquiring what norm "We the people" (probably) understood, or would have understood, the provision to communicate—and therefore what norm they meant to establish—has sometimes been confused with a different inquiry, namely, what the generation of "We the people" that established a constitutional norm would have believed to be the correct way of resolving, on the basis of the norm, a conflict that besets us today, a conflict that implicates the norm.[51] What they would have believed to be the correct way of resolving our conflict is not irrelevant, because knowing what they would have believed might help us discern better than we otherwise could the precise contours of the norm they (through their representatives) established; in particular, it might help us discern how wide their norm is, or how narrow. What finally matters, however, is not what they would have believed to be the correct way of resolving (on the basis of their norm) our conflict, but what norm they established. After all, if "We the people" in the past would have believed X to be the correct answer, on the basis of a norm they issued, to a conflict that besets us today, they might have been mistaken about the contextual requirements of the norm, just as we today might be mistaken about the contextual requirements of a norm.

Sometimes readers of the text of a constitutional provision will have to mine historical materials that are scant or equivocal or both in their effort to discern what norm the provision was (or would have been) understood to communicate by the generation of "We the people" that (through its representatives) put the provision into the Constitution.[52] As students of American constitutional law are well aware, readers who pursue such an inquiry, even readers who pursue it altogether dispassionately, might end up disagreeing among themselves—*reasonably* disagreeing—about what norm the provision was understood to communicate. There seems to be ample room, with respect to some parts of the Constitution, for reasonable disagreement about what norms the provisions were understood to communicate.[53] I return to this point in § III.B, in discussing the Supreme Court's role in constitutional adjudication.

Two paragraphs back, I began: "Interpreting the text of a constitutional provision, *in the sense of inquiring what norm 'We the people' (probably) understood, or would have understood, the provision to communicate—and therefore what norm they meant to establish* . . ." One can "interpret" the text of a constitutional provision in a different sense of the term, however: One can inquire what norm the provision in question is now taken to represent—or what norm it shall hereafter be taken to represent. The conjunction of two factors makes it virtually inevitable that the Supreme Court will "interpret" some provisions of the Constitution in the second sense of the term rather than in the first sense. First, there is the fact that, as I explained in § I.C, some premises have achieved the status of constitutional bedrock even if the premises are not part of, and are not warranted by, the Constitution "ordained and established" by "We the people". Second, there is the textualist sensibility of American constitutional culture, which Andrezj Rapaczynski has described: "[J]udges sometimes admit that constitutional interpretation is sensitive to historical evolution and that history adds a 'gloss' on the text. But they never admit to deriving the authority for their decisions from outside the constitutional text. . . . Instead, any new result is unfailingly presented as a new and better *interpretation* of the text itself. . . . This behavior of judges is very significant because it expresses their belief that purely noninterpretive [i.e., nontextualist] review would constitute an abuse of their power and undermine the legitimacy of judicial review. In this belief, moreover, they are very likely to be right."[54] It ought not to be surprising, given the textualist sensibility of American constitutional culture, that even when the Supreme Court believes that a premise that has become constitutional bedrock for us was not established by, and is not warranted by any norm established by, "We the people", the Court will nonetheless refer the premise to some provision of the Constitution. The Court will impute the premise to some linguistically opportune piece of the constitutional text—to some configuration of words that the Court believes or hopes will bear the imputed meaning—which thereafter is taken by the Court to represent the premise. Consider a prominent example of this phenomenon: Whatever the "original" understanding of the due process language of the Fifth Amendment, for example—whatever norm(s) the generation of "We the people" that put that language into the Constitution understood the language to communicate/establish—the language is now deemed to represent a fundamental premise that no one, not even Supreme Court justices, can reasonably believe was any part of the original understanding of the language, namely, that the same anti-discrimination norm that applies to state government under the Fourteenth Amendment applies to the national government under the Fifth.[55] (At this point, the reader might want to consider the "thought experiment" presented at the end of chapter 3.)

B. Interpreting (Specifying) the Constitution

I said that interpreting the text of a constitutional provision—in the sense of inquiring what norm the provision was understood to communicate—should not be confused with inquiring what the generation of "We the people" that established a constitutional norm would have believed to be the correct way of resolving, on the basis of the norm, a conflict that besets us today. There is something else that interpreting the text of a constitutional provision should not be confused with: "specifying" (as I call it) a constitutional norm *in the context of a conflict in which the norm is implicated but in which it is also indeterminate*. Just as the constitutional text is not identical to the Constitution, so too interpretation of the constitutional text is not identical to interpretation of the Constitution—that is, of the norms that the Constitution ("the supreme Law of the Land") comprises.

Assume that we agree—or, at least, that we accept for the sake of argument—that the relevant constitutional norm is X. For present purposes, it suffices to say that X is determinate in the context of a conflict that implicates it if persons who agree about both (1) what the relevant facts of the conflict—the "adjudicative" facts—are[56] and (2) what the other relevant legal norms, if any, are and what the implications of those other norms are for the conflict, cannot *reasonably* disagree with one another about how, given X, the conflict should be resolved. Similarly, X is indeterminate—more precisely, *under*determinate[57]—in the context of a conflict that implicates it if persons who agree about (1) and (2) *can* reasonably disagree with one another about how, given X, the conflict should be resolved. (Indeterminacy is not either-or; it is a matter of degree.) That X is determinate in the context of one or more conflicts does not mean that it is not indeterminate in the context of one or more other conflicts. If X is indeterminate in the context of a conflict that implicates it, then X must be "specified" in that context.

The process of "specifying", in a particular context, a norm implicated but also indeterminate in the context is the process of deciding what the norm, in conjunction with all the other relevant considerations, should be construed to require in that context. It is the process of "shaping" the norm, of rendering the norm determinate in the context of a conflict in which it is implicated but (until specified) indeterminate. Whereas the process of applying a determinate norm is basically deductive, the process of specifying an indeterminate norm is basically nondeductive. A specification "of a principle for a specific class of cases is not a deduction from it, nor a discovery of some implicit meaning; it is the act of setting a more concrete and categorical requirement in the spirit of the principle, and guided both by a sense of what is practically realizable (or enforceable), and by a recognition of the risk of conflict with other principles or values. . . ."[58] The challenge of specifying an indeterminate constitutional norm, then, is the challenge of deciding how best to achieve, how best to "instantiate", in the context of a particular conflict, the political-moral value (or values) at the heart of the norm;[59] it is the challenge of discerning what way of achieving that value, what way of embodying it, best reconciles all the various and sometimes competing interests of the political community at stake in the conflict. What Anthony Kronman has said of the process of "judgment" aptly describes the process of specifying an indeterminate norm. Such specification is a species of judgment.

> Good judgment, and its opposite, are in fact most clearly revealed in just those situations where the method of deduction is least applicable, where the ambiguities are greatest and the demand for proof most obviously misplaced. To show good judgment in such situations is to do something more than merely apply a general rule with special care and thoroughness, or follow out its consequences to a greater level of detail. Judgment often requires such analytic refinement but does not consist in it alone. That this is so is to be explained by the fact that we are most dependent on our judgment, most in need of *good* judgment, in just those situations that pose genuine dilemmas by forcing us to choose between, or otherwise accommodate, conflicting interests and obligations whose conflict is not itself amenable to resolution by the application of some higher-order rule. It is here that the quality of a person's judgment comes most clearly into view and here, too, that his or her deductive powers alone are least likely to prove adequate to the task.[60]

Although courts are not the only governmental institutions that face the challenge of specifying indeterminate legal norms, courts do often face the challenge. "[A] court asked to apply a rule must decide in light of information not available to the promulgators of the rule, what the rule should mean in its new setting. That is a creative decision, involving discretion, the weighing of consequences, and, in short, a kind of legislative judgment. . . ."[61]

The fact of legal indeterminacy—and the need, therefore, for specification—is one thing, its value another: Why might a political community, or its representatives, want to establish an indeterminate norm (a norm indeterminate in a significant number of the contexts that implicate it)? Why not issue only determinate norms? Discussing the matter of rules—in particular, legal rules—H.L.A. Hart emphasized that "a feature of the human predicament . . . that we labour under . . . whenever we seek to regulate, unambiguously and in advance, some sphere of conduct by means of general standards to be used without further official directions on particular occasions . . . is our relative ignorance of fact . . . [and] our relative indeterminacy of aim."[62] Given that "feature of the human predicament", it makes sense that many legal (and other) norms are relatively indeterminate. "If the world in which we live were characterized only by a finite number of features, and these together with all the modes in which they could combine were known to us, then provision could be made in advance for every possibility. We could make rules, the application of which to particular cases never called for a further choice. Everything could be known, and for everything, since it could be known, something could be done and specified in advance by rule. . . . Plainly this world is not our world. . . . This inability to anticipate brings with it a relative indeterminacy of aim."[63] The point is not that (relatively) determinate norms cannot be achieved.[64] The point, rather, is that determinacy ought not always to be a goal.[65] To achieve determinacy is sometimes "to secure a measure of certainty or predictability at the cost of blindly prejudging what is to be done in a range of future cases, about whose composition we are ignorant. We shall thus succeed in settling in advance, but also in the dark, issues which can only reasonably be settled when they arise and are identified."[66] We who "do ordain and establish this Constitution for the United States of America" have long understood Hart's point. Some norms comprised by the Constitution are "not rules for the passing hour," as Cardozo put it, "but principles for an expanding future. Insofar as it deviates from that standard, and descends into details and particulars, [a constitution] loses its flexibility, the scope of interpretation contracts, the meaning hardens. While it is true to its function, it maintains its power of adaptation, its suppleness, its play."[67]

I now want to return to—and, against the background of what I have said in this subsection, rehearse and amplify—a point I emphasized in the preceding subsection: Interpreting the text of a constitutional provision—in the sense of inquiring what norm the provision was understood to communicate—should not be confused with inquiring what the generation of "We the people" that established a constitutional norm would have believed to be the correct way of resolving, on the basis of the norm, a conflict that besets us today. We may say, using the language of "intention" and speaking of legal texts more broadly, that trying to discern what norm they who enacted a legal text meant or "intended" the text to communicate—which is presumably the norm that, in enacting the text, they intended to establish—should not be confused with trying to discern how they would have resolved a particular conflict, or wanted it to be resolved, on the basis of the norm they intended to establish. How the enactors would have resolved a particular conflict, or wanted it to be resolved, on the basis of the norm they established is a different question, the answer to which is relevant only to the extent it sheds light on the answer to the question of the norm they intended their text to communicate.[68]

Now, one might try to deflect this point by asserting that the norm they intended to establish, and the text to communicate, just *is* that each and every particular conflict be resolved *just as they would have resolved it.* Put another way, one might assert that what the enactors intended is that their enactment have just those legal effects that they would have "de-

scribe[d] [to be] the enactment's legal effects in each possible circumstance."[69] (The reference, presumably, is to what they, believing what *they*
believed, mistakes included, and valuing what *they* valued, would have described to be the enactment's legal effects in each possible circumstance;
if the reference were to what they, believing what *we* believe and valuing
what *we* value, would have described to be the enactment's legal effects in
each possible circumstance, then "they" would not be they.) In our political-
legal culture, however, this is a wildly implausible construal of what those
who enact legal texts often understand themselves to be doing (intend-
ing); as the statements by Neil MacCormick, Richard Posner, and H.L.A.
Hart that I have quoted in this subsection illustrate, it is an implausible
construal of what many legal norms are taken to be—even by those who
establish the norms.[70] (This is not to deny that *some* legal norms—norms
that are determinate in virtually every context in which the norms are implicated—can be so described. But, *pace* H.L.A. Hart, it is not plausible to
describe all legal norms—least of all, all constitutional norms, that way.)
"Lon Fuller, Henry Hart and Albert Sacks, and Reed Dickerson have all
argued persuasively that the intended general meaning of statutory language is not reducible to the set of specifically intended applications of
that statutory language."[71] Nor is it reducible to the set of applications of
the statutory language that the enactors *would have* described to be the enactment's legal effects in each possible circumstance. "[L]egislative intent
is best understood as the intent to adopt directive language with a particular general meaning and to bring about the consequences flowing from
the consistent application of that general meaning in particular circumstances."[72]

None of this is to deny that the norm they intended to establish, and
the text to communicate, includes at its core that one or more conflicts be
resolved just as they would have resolved them. It is not to deny that a
central part of what the enactors intended is that *with respect to some cases—
"paradigm" or "exemplary" cases*—their enactment have just those legal effects
that they would have "describe[d] [to be] the enactment's legal effects" in
those cases. But this is a far cry from saying that the sum total of what the
enactors intended is that their enactment have just those legal effects that
they would have "describe[d] [to be] the enactment's legal effects" in *each
and every possible case that might arise and implicate their enactment*. A piece of
Hart's discussion is in point here:

> When we are bold enough to frame some general rule of conduct (e.g. a
> rule that no vehicle may be taken into the park), the language used in
> this context fixes necessary conditions which anything must satisfy if it is
> to be within its scope, and certain clear examples of what is certainly
> within its scope may be present to our minds. They are the paradigm,
> clear cases (the motor-car, the bus, the motor-cycle); and our aim in leg-
> islating is so far determinate because we have made a certain choice. We
> have initially settled the question that peace and quiet in the park is to be
> maintained at the cost, at any rate, of the exclusion of these things. On

the other hand, until we have put the general aim of peace in the park into conjunction with those cases which we did not, or perhaps could not, initially envisage (perhaps a toy motor-car electrically propelled) our aim is, in this direction, indeterminate. We have not settled, because we have not anticipated, the question which will be raised by the unenvisaged case when it occurs: whether some degree of peace in the park is to be sacrificed to, or defended against, those children whose pleasure or interest it is to use these things. When the unenvisaged case does arise, we confront the issues at stake and can then settle the question by choosing between the competing interests in the way which best satisfies us. In doing so we shall have rendered more determinate our initial aim, and shall incidentally have settled a question as to the meaning, for the purpose of this rule, of a general word.[73]

I don't want to mount an argument here about how many norms comprised by the Constitution are indeterminate in many contexts in which they are implicated. For present purposes, I am content to observe that it is not unreasonable to believe that at least some of our most important constitutional norms are indeterminate in a significant number of the contexts that implicate them. (Recall, in that regard, Cardozo's observation that many of our constitutional norms are "not rules for the passing hour, but principles for an expanding future."[74]) Consider, for example, that part of the First Amendment that forbids government to prohibit "the free exercise of religion".[75] According to the Congress of the United States, which in 1993 passed the Religious Freedom Restoration Act, and to the president of the United States, who signed it into law, the free exercise language was meant to communicate, whatever else it was meant to communicate, a norm to this effect: "Government shall not substantially burden a person's exercise of religion even if the burden results from a rule of general applicability, . . . [unless] application of the burden to the person (1) is in furtherance of a compelling governmental interest and (2) is the least restrictive means of furthering that compelling governmental interest."[76] There is sometimes ample room for reasonable disagreement about whether, in a particular context, a governmental interest is "compelling"—about whether, taking into account all the relevant particularities of context, the interest is sufficiently important—and even about whether a state action "is the least restrictive means . . ."

Let the European Court of Human Rights make the point in its own context. Article 10 of the European Convention for the Protection of Human Rights and Fundamental Freedoms provides in relevant part:

> 1. Everyone has the right to freedom of expression. This right shall include freedom to hold opinions and to receive and impart information and ideas without interference by public authority and regardless of frontiers. . . .
> 2. The exercise of these freedoms, since it carries with it duties and responsibilities, may be subject to such formalities, conditions, restric-

tions or penalties as are prescribed by law and are necessary in a democratic society, . . . for the protection of health or morals . . .[77]

In a famous case involving a claim that the United Kingdom had violated Article 10 of the European Convention, the European Court of Human Rights stated, in a voice reminiscent of James Bradley Thayer's:[78]

> 48. These observations apply, notably, to Article 10 § 2. In particular, it is not possible to find in the domestic law of the various Contracting States a uniform European conception of morals. The view taken by their respective laws of the requirements of morals varies from time to time and from place to place, especially in our era which is characterised by rapid and far-reaching evolution of opinions on the subject. By reason of their direct and continuous contact with the vital forces of their countries, State authorities are in principle in a better position than the international judge to give an opinion on the exact content of these requirements as well as on the "necessity" of a "restriction" or "penalty" intended to meet them. . . . [I]t is for the national authorities to make the initial assessment of the reality of the pressing social need implied by the notion of "necessity" in this context.
>
> Consequently, Article 10 § 2 leaves to the Contracting States a margin of appreciation. This margin is given both to the domestic legislator ("prescribed by law") and to the bodies, judicial amongst others, that are called upon to interpret and apply the laws in force. . . .

To say that among different states or countries, or even among persons from the same state or country, there is sometimes ample room for a reasonable difference in judgments about one or more matters that the relevant law makes determinative is not to say that anything goes; it is not to say that every difference in judgments about such matters is necessarily reasonable. Thus, the European Court of Human Rights went on to declare:

> 49. Nevertheless Article 10 § 2 does not give the Contracting States an unlimited power of appreciation. The [European] Court [of Human Rights] is empowered to give the final ruling on whether a "restriction" or "penalty" is reconcilable with freedom of expression as protected by Article 10. The domestic margin of appreciation thus goes hand in hand with a European supervision. Such supervision concerns both the aim of the measure challenged and its "necessity" . . .[79]

*   *   *

Since 1973, when the Supreme Court decided the abortion cases,[80] there has been an unending explosion of academic writing both about what it means and, especially, about what it *should* mean, above all for the Court, to "interpret" the Constitution.[81] Much of the writing is weakened by its failure to attend to two very different senses of constitutional "interpretation". It is marred by its failure to heed the fundamental distinction between, on the one hand, "interpreting" a constitutional *text*, in the sense of trying to discern what norm the text represents and, on the other, "interpreting" a constitutional *norm*, in the sense of determining what shape to give the norm in the context of a conflict in which the norm is implicated but in which it is also indeterminate. I argued, in § I.A, that with respect to the constitutional text, the question "What norm does this piece of the text—this provision—represent?" is often the question "What norm was this provision understood to communicate by the 'We the people' whose representatives put the provision into the Constitution?" But even if one rejects that argument, the fact remains that there is an important difference between, first, interpreting a *text* in the sense of *trying to discern what norm a text represents* and, second, interpreting a *norm* in the sense of *determining what shape to give an indeterminate norm in the context of a particular conflict*.[82] (Again, interpreting the constitutional text should not be confused with interpreting, in the sense of specifying, one or more of the norms the Constitution comprises.) Note that disagreement about what norm, X or Y, a provision represents can coexist with agreement about how both X and Y should be shaped (specified) in the context at hand, and that agreement about what norm a provision represents (X) can coexist with disagreement about how X should be shaped in the context at hand.

One might try to challenge, in two steps, the distinction on which I am insisting here: first, by identifying my distinction with, or by otherwise assimilating it to, the familiar dichotomy between "understanding" a law and then "applying" the law, now understood, to resolve a case; second, by responding, with Hans-George Gadamer, that "[u]nderstanding . . . is always application."[83] However, the distinction on which I am insisting here is not—nor does it presuppose, entail, or even track—the problematic dichotomy that Gadamer rightly challenged: the distinction between, on the one hand, understanding a legal norm and, on the other, "applying" the norm—in the sense of "bringing it to bear"—in adjudicating a particular conflict. That distinction is not my distinction. Indeed, the second half of my distinction—the act of determining what shape to give an indeterminate norm in the context of a particular conflict—presupposes that the Gadamerian insight is accurate. It presupposes that there is no difference between understanding the meaning—the *contextual* meaning—of a legal norm and "applying" the norm, bringing it to bear, in the case at hand; to do the latter just *is* to determine (to "specify") the contextual meaning of the norm.

The first half of my distinction—the act of trying to discern what norm a legal text represents—simply recognizes that some legal texts (not all, but some) are initially unintelligible (opaque, vague, ambiguous, etc.), in the sense that it is not initially clear to readers of the text what norm the text represents. (Like indeterminacy, unintelligibility is not either-or but a matter of degree.) If it is not clear what norm a legal text represents, a court (assuming for the moment that a court is the relevant reader of the text) must translate or decode the text: A court must identify, or try to identify, the norm the text represents. *Before* the norm the text represents can be "understood"/"applied"—which, *pace* Gadamer, is one move, not two—the norm the text represents must be identified.[84] As I explained in

§ I.A, it is simply not true of every constitutional provision, even though it is true of many, that the question of the norm the provision represents can usefully be answered by a repetition of what the text says.[85]

III. Is the Supreme Court Supreme—And, If So, How Deferential Ought It to Be, If Deferential at All— in Interpreting the Constitution?

A. Is the Supreme Court Supreme?

Justice Brennan wrote that "[t]he genius of the Magna Carta, as well as its longevity, lay partly in its creation of a device for resolving grievances and compelling the Crown to abide by the committee of barons' decision. Paper promises whose enforcement depends wholly on the promisor's goodwill have rarely been worth the parchment on which they were inked."[86] To be as effective as possible, the constitutional strategy for establishing norms must include one or more enforcement mechanisms. (This is especially true with respect to those norms the constitutionalization of which presupposes a realistic skepticism about majoritarian politics.) For us, a principal such mechanism has been the practice of judicial review[87]—but not because we believe what only the historically uninformed could believe, namely, that the justices of the Supreme Court of the United States, or any of our other judges, are necessarily or invariably better than any other public officials at safeguarding constitutional norms. Judicial review is simply one way, albeit a very important one, of trying to protect constitutional norms when other ways, and other officials, might have failed to do so. Sometimes judicial review itself fails.

One might want to inquire (as I have elsewhere) whether "We the people" ever established the practice of judicial review in a constitutionally ordained way.[88] But that is not, for us the people of the United States now living, a live question. Judicial review has been a bedrock feature of our constitutional order almost since the beginning of our country's history.[89] Nor is it a live question, for us, whether judicial review is, all things considered, a good idea. It would be startling, to say the least, were we Americans to turn skeptical about the idea of judicial review—an American-born and -bred idea that, in the twentieth century, has been increasingly influential throughout the world.[90] For us, the live questions about judicial review are about how the power of judicial review should be exercised. To endorse the idea and the practice of judicial review, however, is not necessarily to endorse the doctrine of judicial supremacy.

As I explained in § II.A of this chapter: There is ample room for reasonable disagreement about what norms some parts of the constitutional text were understood to communicate (e.g., the privileges or immunities language of the Fourteenth Amendment). But even if there were little if any room for *reasonable* disagreement about such a matter, there would be disagreement. As I explained in § II.B: There is ample room for reasonable disagreement about how some norms comprised by the Constitution should be specified in some of the contexts that implicate them. But, again, even if there were little if any room for *reasonable* disagreement about such a matter, there would be disagreement. Both disagreements about what norm a provision of the constitutional text was understood to communicate and disagreements about how one of our constitutional norms should be specified in a particular context are disagreements about what the Constitution forbids.

Article III of the Constitution anoints the Supreme Court of the United States as the arbiter of disagreements between itself and any state judiciary about what any national law, including the Constitution, forbids.[91] As a practical matter, the position of the Supreme Court about what a national law forbids will prevail over any competing position of the legislature or of the governor of any state (as well as over the competing position of the judiciary of any state) so long as the executive branch of the national government is willing to stand behind the ruling of the Supreme Court.[92] (I am assuming here that in any such dispute, any state actor—for example, the governor—can be sued in a case that will eventually be decided, even if only on appeal, on the basis of the Supreme Court's position.) As it happens, however, the Constitution comprises no norm anointing any branch of the national government as the arbiter of disagreements between itself and any other branch of the national government about what a national law—including "the supreme Law of the Land"—forbids. Contrary to what many citizens might believe—and, indeed, contrary to what some justices of the Supreme Court have seemed to believe[93]—the constitutional text does not state that the Supreme Court of the United States is to be the arbiter of such disagreements, nor does the Constitution comprise any norm to that effect.[94] Of course, a constitution could designate the judicial branch of government (or another branch) as the arbiter of some or all such disagreements, but ours does not do so.

Over time, however, an expectation has emerged, yielding a practice that has what we may call a "quasi-constitutional" status in American politics: In American constitutional culture, the firm expectation is that the legislative and executive branches of the national government will each refrain from doing anything the Supreme Court says the Constitution forbids them to do, and they will each do anything the Court says the Constitution requires them to do, even when they disagree with the Court's position about what the Constitution forbids or what it requires.[95] Why has this expectation emerged? Certainly not because we the people of the United States believe that the position of a majority of the justices on the Supreme Court about what norm a constitutional provision should be taken to represent, or about how a constitutional norm should be specified, is necessarily or invariably superior to the position of a majority of the members of Congress or to the position of the President. Rather, this expectation has emerged mainly for two connected reasons.

First, we have come to believe that it is desirable—because less messy and more productive for our political life—that different political institutions and actors not interminably struggle with one another over their different understandings of what the Constitution forbids (or requires), some acting on the basis of one understanding, others on the basis of another, competing understanding. Accordingly, we believe that, in general, one institution of government should have the power to settle, as a *practical* matter, disruptive controversies about what the Constitution forbids; one institution should have the power to determine, as a *practical* matter, what the Constitution forbids.[96] (This is not to say that one institution should have the power to determine, as an *intellectual* or *theoretical* matter, what the Constitution forbids. Practical assent—assent in practice or action—is one thing; intellectual assent is something else altogether. That there is, or might be, a need for the former does not entail that there is an equal need, or indeed any need, for the latter.)

Second, we have come to believe—at least, many of us have—that, in general, the Supreme Court is the institution least to be feared and most to be trusted in determining, as a *practical* matter, the minimum boundaries of what the Constitution forbids.[97]

The *minimum* boundaries, it bears emphasis, not the maximum. Again, the firm expectation that has emerged is that the legislative and executive branches of the national government will each refrain from doing anything the Supreme Court says the Constitution forbids them to do, even if they disagree with the Court's position about what the Constitution forbids. But it is not inconsistent with this expectation for Congress either (a) to decline to enact legislation based on its view that some constitutional norm forbids it to do *more* than the Court says the norm does or (b) to enact legislation based on its view that some constitutional norm requires it to do *more* than the Court says the norm does. Nor, moreover, is it inconsistent with this expectation for Congress, in enacting legislation pursuant to its responsibility under section five of the Fourteenth Amendment to enforce the provisions of the Amendment, to conclude that some constitutional norm forbids (or requires) state government to do *more* than the Court says the norm does. (According to section five, "The Congress shall have power to enforce this [amendment] by appropriate legislation.) It is relevant that because every norm applicable to state government under section one of the Fourteenth Amendment is also applicable to the national government under one or another other constitutional provision, for Congress to conclude that some norm applicable to state government under the Fourteenth Amendment forbids (or requires) state government to do more than the Court says the norm does is for Congress to conclude that *its own power*, too, is more limited than the Court says it is, not less limited. There is certainly much less, if any, reason to fear Congress—much less, if any, reason not to trust it— when the constitutional boundaries it sets on its own power are stricter, when they are larger, than those the Court has set.[98] Similarly, there would be less, if any, reason for skepticism about the president's understanding of what the Constitution forbids or requires him to do—or about a state legislature's or a state governor's understanding of what the Constitution forbids or requires it or him to do—if that understanding were to yield stricter/larger limits on his or its own power than those the Court has decreed.[99]

In the period since the end of World War II, we Americans have succeeded in exporting our practice of judicial supremacy to many parts of the world. Several countries now accord their judiciaries similar supremacy in deciding what their constitutions forbid.[100] Moreover, the European Court of Human Rights is accorded supremacy in deciding what the European Convention for the Protection of Human Rights and Fundamental Freedoms forbids.[101] The belief that, on balance and in general, a well-functioning judiciary is the least to be feared and the most to be trusted —especially in deciding what the authoritative provisions regarding human rights forbid—is waxing in global influence,[102] not waning, and it seems unlikely that the belief will relax its grip, at least for long, on American constitutional culture. Nonetheless, the belief is a highly contingent one; we cannot rule out the possibility of a future in which the belief comes to seem, to a growing number of us, untenable. Indeed, the belief already seems untenable to some of us.[103]

To say that the Supreme Court serves as the arbiter of disputes between itself and one or both of the other branches of the national government about what the Constitution forbids is not to say that the Court should never conclude that the Constitution commits resolution of a conflict about what some provision of the Constitution forbids to a branch of the national government other than itself.[104] Nor is it to say that, as the arbiter of such disputes, the Court (when it does not conclude that the Constitution commits resolution of the conflict to another branch of government) should never defer to another branch's position about what the Constitution forbids. (In the next two subsections, I take up the question of the propriety of deference by the Court to another branch's judgments about what the Constitution forbids.) Moreover, nothing I have said here is meant to deny that, under the Constitution, every citizen of the United States, including every citizen who is an official of the national government or of a state government, may persist in disagreeing, as vigorously as she thinks appropriate, with a constitutional decision of the Supreme Court even long past the point where it is clear that the Court will not soon, if ever, change its mind.

Finally, it bears emphasis that neither Congress nor the President is constitutionally (much less morally) obligated to defer to the Court's constitutional decisions about what the Constitution forbids. The practice of deferring to such decisions is, as I said, merely "quasi-constitutional". It is best understood as a *presumptive* practice—a practice appropriate for circumstances both constitutionally and morally ordinary. In a circumstance neither constitutionally nor morally ordinary, it might be appropriate for Congress or the President (or both) not to defer to the Court. As I said earlier, to endorse the idea and the practice of judicial review is not necessarily to endorse the doctrine of judicial supremacy. When Abraham Lincoln delivered his First Inaugural Address on March 4, 1861, the circumstances were undeniably both constitutionally and morally extraordinary: "[I]f the policy of the government upon vital questions affecting the whole people is to be irrevocably fixed by decisions of the Supreme Court . . . the people will have ceased to be their own rulers, having to that extent practically resigned their Government into the hands of that eminent tribunal."[105] Lincoln had in mind, of course, the Supreme Court's infamous decision in *Dred Scott v. Sandford*.[106]

I said that the Court must decide when to defer to another branch's judgment about what the Constitution forbids. Because in a circumstance neither constitutionally nor morally ordinary, it might be appropriate for Congress or the President (or both) not to defer to the Court, Congress and the President must decide when to defer to the Court[107]—although, again, the practice that has emerged is one of deference, a practice so long-standing and so sensible as to be, in ordinary circumstances, bedrock. (Not that the practice couldn't evolve in the direction of less deference.) As I said, the Constitution could designate the Supreme Court (or another branch) as the arbiter of some or all interbranch disagreements about what the Constitution forbids. Such a state of affairs would be less ambiguous than the state of affairs that now prevails. But perhaps we are better off that the constitutional text does not state and that the Constitution is not to the effect that the Court (or another branch) is to be the arbiter. Perhaps the present, less well defined arrangement—in which the Court must decide when to defer to one or both of the other branches and, as a constitutional matter, it remains open to each of the other branches to decide when extraordinary circumstances warrant its not deferring to the Court—yields constitutional decisions that are generally less divisive and destabilizing than the decisions a different, more hierarchical arrangement might yield. Perhaps.

In circumstances both constitutionally and morally ordinary, the Supreme Court of the United States serves, at least for now, as the arbiter of disagreements between itself and one or both of the other branches of the national government about what the Constitution forbids.[108] Undeniably, this is an awesome responsibility. I said, in the preceding paragraph, that the Court must decide when to defer. How large a role ought the Court to play, or how small—put another way, how active a role ought it to play, or how passive, *how deferential*—in serving as the arbiter of disagreements between itself and one or both of the other branches about what the Constitution forbids?

B. How Deferential Ought the Court to Be in Interpreting the Constitutional Text?

Again, there is ample room for reasonable disagreement about what norms some parts of the constitutional text were understood to communicate. How large a role ought the Supreme Court to play, or how small a role, when it is a party to such a disagreement; in particular, ought the Court to play a deferential role? That is, how deferential ought the Court to be in interpreting the constitutional text?[109] Assume, for example, that according to a majority of the Court, the text of a particular constitutional provision was probably understood to communicate norm X, but that according to a different view that prevailed in Congress, the provision was probably understood to communicate norm Y. Ought the majority to defer to Congress' view? It is unrealistic to expect the Court to defer to Congress' view if in its opinion that view is not merely wrong but, all things considered, unreasonable. Moreover, an intellectually arrogant or politically willful justice might not be able to discern the distinction between thinking that Congress' view is wrong and thinking that it is unreasonable. Imagine, however, that in the majority's opinion, Congress' view, though wrong, is not unreasonable. Ought the Court to defer? The twofold point I want to emphasize here is that, first, it is perilous to generalize and, second, many considerations are relevant. In particular:

- How confident is the majority that it is right and Congress, wrong; that is, how close is the majority to thinking that Congress is not merely wrong, but unreasonable?
- How thoroughly has Congress considered the issue? (How has it done so—by means of what processes?) To the extent Congress has thoroughly considered the issue, the case for the Court deferring is stronger; to the extent it has not done so, the case is weaker.
- Is Congress' view likely distorted (and, if so, to what extent) by its interest in avoiding the broader limitation that norm X would place on Congress' power to act? Or, instead, does norm Y place a broader limitation on government's, including Congress', power to act? If the former, Congress is saying that the Constitution forbids (or requires) government to do *less* than the Court says it forbids, and the case for the Court deferring is weaker. If the latter, Congress is saying that the Constitution forbids (or requires) government to do *more* than the Court says it forbids, and the case for judicial deference is stronger.[110]
- Which norm, X or Y, is more attractive, in the majority's view, as a matter of political morality? (Relatedly, which norm is more attractive, in the majority's view, as a matter of the judicial role that enforcement of the norm would require of the Court?[111]) If X, the case for the Court deferring is, in its view, weaker; if Y, the case is stronger.

C. How Deferential Ought the Court to Be in Interpreting (Specifying) the Constitution?

Even if only a few norms comprised by the Constitution are indeterminate —indeterminate in many of the contexts that implicate them—this fundamental question remains: How large a role ought the Supreme Court to play, or how small—how active a role, or how passive—in specifying indeterminate constitutional norms?[112] In particular, ought the Court to play a primary role, or only a secondary, deferential role of the sort recommended by James Bradley Thayer more than a century ago?[113] That is, how deferential ought the Court to be in specifying the Constitution? (Recall here the "margin of appreciation" doctrine developed by the European Court of Human Rights.[114]) Assume, for example, that according to a majority of the Court, the best or optimal specification of a particular constitutional norm is *X* and that, given *X*, a particular national law is unconstitutional. Assume further that according to the view that prevailed in Congress, the appropriate specification of the norm is *Y* and that, given *Y*, the national law is not unconstitutional. Ought the Court to defer to Congress' view? As before, it is unrealistic to expect the Court to defer to Congress' view if in its opinion that view is not merely wrong but, all things considered, unreasonable. And as before, an intellectually arrogant or politically willful justice might not be able to discern the distinction between thinking that Congress' view is wrong and thinking that it is unreasonable.[115] Imagine, however, that in the majority's opinion, Congress' view, though wrong, is not unreasonable. Ought the Court to defer? Again, many considerations—similar considerations—are relevant.

* How close is the Court to thinking that Congress is not merely wrong, but unreasonable?
* How thoroughly has Congress considered the issue?
* Is Congress' view likely distorted by its interest in avoiding the broader limitation that specification *X* would place on Congress' power to act?
* Is the norm one that Congress is arguably better positioned to specify than the judicial branch—for example, a norm establishing not a "negative" right to be free from some governmental overreaching (perhaps in conjunction with a liberty to engage in some activity) but a "positive" entitlement "to governmental assistance to meet basic material needs"?[116]
* Is the question which specification, *X* or *Y*, is best or optimal a question that Congress' political processes can be trusted to handle fairly and well?[117] Or is it one that, perhaps because the norm is "unusually vulnerable to majority sentiment",[118] the politically independent Court is more likely, all things considered, to handle fairly and well?

Just as it is perilous to generalize about when the Court ought to defer to Congress' or the President's view about what norm the text of a particular constitutional provision was understood to establish, it is perilous to generalize about when the Court ought to defer to Congress' view about the best or optimal specification of an indeterminate constitutional norm.[119]

We can pursue much the same inquiry—to much the same conclusion—with respect to a state law and a state legislature. The relevant considerations are the same, and it is no less perilous to generalize about when the Court ought to defer to a state legislature's (not unreasonable) view, as distinct from Congress' view, about the best or optimal specification of an indeterminate norm.[120]

Perilous though the enterprise is, I do want to gesture in the direction of one generalization. In *Democracy and Distrusts*,[121] John Ely did not address the question of the role the Court ought to play in specifying indeterminate constitutional norms. Ely's concern was mainly with the different question of the unenumerated rights the judiciary—in particular, the Supreme Court—may legitimately enforce as constitutional rights (if any). Nonetheless, Ely's answer is relevant to our question. In 1991, Ely characterized the essential argument of *Democracy and Distrust* as follows: "[P]ublic issues generally should be settled by a majority vote of [sane adults] or their representatives. . . ."[122] But, Ely continued, public issues of three sorts are sensibly resolved—resolved as *constitutional* issues—principally by the judiciary:

> (1) the question whether, "where a majority of such persons [sane adults or their representatives] votes to exclude other such persons from the [political] process or otherwise to dilute their influence on it", it may do so;
> (2) the question whether, "where such a majority enacts one regulatory regime for itself and another, less favorable one, for one or another minority", it may do so; and
> (3) the question whether, where such a majority makes a political choice that implicates a "side constraint" with a certain pedigree, the choice violates the side constraint: a side constraint that, because it is "sufficiently important (and vulnerable to majority sentiment)", was designated by a supermajority "in a constitutional document and thereby render[ed] . . . immune to displacement by anything short of a similar supermajority vote in the future."[123]

Ely then explained: "[P]recisely because of their tenure, courts are the appropriate guardians of at least exceptions (1) and (2)".[124] Ely added, with respect to exception (3)—which, unlike exceptions (1) and (2), concerns enumerated rights, not unenumerated ones—that on "the supposition that no right is to be thus designated *unless it is unusually vulnerable to majority sentiment*", courts are the appropriate guardians of exception (3) as well.[125] Finally, Ely wrote: "What does not follow from anything said above, or in my opinion from anything sensible said ever, is that judges are also to be given a license to create or 'discover' further rights, not justified by exceptions (1) or (2) nor ever constitutionalized by a supermajority, and protect them as if they had been."[126]

Whether or not one agrees with Ely's position about the (only) unenumerated rights the Court may enforce (exceptions (1) and (2)), one could agree with his position about the enumerated rights the Court may enforce (exception (3)) and yet insist that if and to the extent any such right is indeterminate, the Court should play only a secondary role—a Thayerian role—in specifying it. One could say, in that regard, that answering the question of the best or optimal specification of an indeterminate constitutional right—the best or optimal specification, that is, of a constitutional norm establishing and protecting an indeterminate right—requires many "judgment calls" (as Ely has described them),[127] and that as long as the judgment calls implicit in the challenged governmental action are not unreasonable, the Court should defer to them. Nonetheless, Ely's argument lends support to the position that as a comparative matter, as an issue in the allocation of competencies, the judiciary—not least, the federal judiciary—is institutionally well suited to play the primary role in specifying any right- or liberty-regarding norm it is charged with enforcing *if our historical experience suggests that the norm is "unusually vulnerable to majority sentiment"*. To settle for our elected representatives, and not the judiciary, playing the primary role in specifying such a norm is probably to settle for many specifications that, even if "not unreasonable" for purposes of Thayer's minimalist approach to constitutional adjudication, are nonetheless suboptimal: specifications that fail to give the important constitutional value at stake—the value privileged by the norm—its full due.

(A word of clarification is in order. My comments here are directed at the situation in which the Court faces a choice between two not unreasonable specifications of a right- or liberty-regarding norm that our history has shown to be "unusually vulnerable to majority sentiment": the Court's own, more generous specification of the norm—more generous to the principal beneficiaries of the norm—and another branch's less generous specification. It is a different situation altogether, of course, if the Court faces a choice between its own, less generous specification of a right- or liberty-regarding norm and another branch's more generous specification. That the Court should not defer, à la Thayer, to another branch's less generous specification of such a norm does not entail that it should not defer to another branch's more generous specification *if the Court concludes that that more generous specification is a reasonable one*. In particular, there might be little if any reason for the Court to insist on a specification of a right- or liberty-regarding norm less generous than the specification that Congress, in exercising its responsibility under section five of the Fourteenth Amendment to enforce the provisions of the Amendment, is willing to embrace. Least of all should the Court do so if *both* of the other two branches of the national government—Congress in enacting a law and the President in signing it—are in agreement in embracing a specification of a right- or liberty-regarding norm more generous than the specification that the Court has embraced or is inclined to embraced.)

Of course, that the Supreme Court chooses to exercise the principal responsibility for specifying some indeterminate constitutional norm does not preclude the possibility that in exercising that responsibility the Court will, on occasion, act too timidly, or with insufficient sensitivity or vigilance, thereby failing to give the constitutional value at stake its full due. But that possibility does not begin to support the argument that the Court should exercise only a secondary responsibility, that it should pursue only the Thayerian approach to the specification of the norm. Even if in exercising the principal responsibility the Court occasionally acts too timidly— even if usually it acts too timidly—the American political community is no worse off than it would be if the Court were to exercise a secondary responsibility *as a matter of course*, habitually deferring to political judgments that, while arguably reasonable for purposes of Thayer's approach, nonetheless give the constitutional value less than its full due. The Supreme Court's sorry record of failing to take free exercise claims very seriously comes to mind here.[128] But, as Doug Laycock has emphasized: "Some of the time, judicial review will do some good. Judges did nothing for the Mormons, but they may have saved the Jehovah's Witnesses and the Amish. If judges can save one religious minority a century, I consider that ample justification for judicial review in religious liberty cases."[129]

For a depressing example of the kind of suboptimal specification the Thayerian approach might well affirm, consider the political judgment to which Thayer's most prominent judicial disciple, Felix Frankfurter, deferred in *West Virginia State Board of Education v. Barnette*,[130] in which he, and he alone, dissented from the Supreme Court's decision striking down a public school regulation that compelled students, including Jehovah's Witnesses who conscientiously objected on religious grounds, to salute the American flag and recite the Pledge of Allegiance. It was, Frankfurter insisted, a judgment "upon which men might reasonably differ. . . . And since men may so reasonably differ, I deem it beyond my constitutional power to assert my view of the wisdom of this law against the view of the State of West Virginia."[131] As Frankfurter's Thayerian performance in *Barnette* illustrates, because legislatures so rarely make political choices about whose constitutionality men and women may *not* reasonably differ, the Thayerian approach to the specification of any constitutional norm effectively marginalizes the norm—virtually to the point of eliminating it—insofar as constitutional adjudication is concerned. It is not obvious, therefore, why one would advocate the Thayerian approach to the specification of a norm unless one thought that the norm *should be* marginalized.

Now, one might think that some norms should be marginalized because mechanisms other than constitutional adjudication—political as distinct from judicial mechanisms—are adequate, more or less, to the protection of the norms: namely, norms regarding the allocation of power, whether between the national government and the governments of the states[132] or between the legislative and executive branches of the national government. One might also think that some right- or liberty-regarding norms are relatively unimportant, or at least inappropriate to a constitution that is to be judicially enforced, and should therefore be marginalized. But it is not obvious why one would want to marginalize any right- or liberty-regarding norm—that is, why one would support the Thayerian approach to the specification of any such norm—that one thought was relatively important, and appropriate to a constitution, unless one concluded that, overall, political mechanisms were somehow adequate to protect the norm. However, our history suggests that such a conclusion is doubtful with respect to at least some right- or liberty-regarding norms.

Jeremy Waldron has argued that judicial review—judicial review in the sense of according the judiciary supremacy in deciding what a constitution forbids—is deeply problematic as a matter of political morality.[133] The final two paragraphs of Waldron's "right-based critique of constitutional rights" suggest the problem he sees:

> If we are going to defend the idea of an entrenched Bill of Rights put effectively beyond revision by anyone other than the judges, we should try and think what we might say to some public-spirited citizen who wishes to launch a campaign or lobby her [representative] on some issue of rights about which she feels strongly and on which she has done her best to arrive at a considered and impartial view. She is not asking to be a dictator; she perfectly accepts that her voice should have no more power than that of anyone else who is prepared to participate in politics. But—like her suffragette forbears—she wants a vote; she wants her voice and her activity to count on matters of high political importance.
>
> In defending a Bill of Rights, we have to imagine ourselves saying to her: "You may write to the newspaper and get up a petition and organize a pressure group to lobby [the legislature]. But even if you succeed, beyond your wildest dreams, and orchestrate the support of a large number of like-minded men and women, and manage to prevail in the legislature, your measure may be challenged and struck down because your view of what rights we have does not accord with the judges' view. When their votes differ from yours, theirs are the votes that will prevail." It is my submission that saying this does not comport with the respect and honor normally accorded to ordinary men and women in the context of a theory of rights.[134]

Waldron's rejection of the idea of "an entrenched Bill of Rights put effectively beyond revision by anyone other than the judges" might not be extreme in the context of, say, English political-legal culture, which has never known such a Bill of Rights and even now is wary about creating one. But Waldron's position *is* extreme in the context of a political-legal culture like ours, because, even though we do not always agree about what some of its provisions forbid, we generally revere our entrenched Bill of Rights.[135] (That Waldron's argument is extreme in the context of American political-legal culture does not entail that his argument is not, in that context, thoughtful or important. It is both.) Nonetheless, Waldron's argument can be borrowed to support three claims that are not extreme in the context of American political-legal culture. (That none of the three claims is extreme does not entail that none of them is controversial.)

- A constitution should comprise few if any indeterminate norms.
- The appropriate *practice* of judicial review, in the case of indeterminate constitutional norms, is Thayerian.[136]
- It is a good thing that the legislative and executive branches are not constitutionally obligated to defer to the judicial branch's beliefs about what the Constitution forbids, including its beliefs about the best or optimal specification of an indeterminate constitutional norm.

That Waldron's argument lends support to these three claims does not mean that we should accept the claims. I do accept, partly on the basis of considerations like those Waldron highlights, the first and third claims. At least, I am inclined to agree both that constitution-makers should be cautious about including indeterminate norms in a constitution (which is not to say that they should never do so) and that it is a good thing that Congress and the President are, as I noted in § III.A, constitutionally free not to defer to the Supreme Court's beliefs about what the Constitution forbids. (This is not to say that the legislative and executive branches should not accord the judiciary supremacy—i.e., *presumptive* supremacy; it is not to deny that in circumstances both constitutionally and morally ordinary, the legislative and executive branches should defer.) But we should not accept the second claim, in my view. Neither total abstinence from the non-Thayerian practice of judicial review nor total indulgence in it is appropriate. Here, as elsewhere, there is a more moderate choice—a "middle way". In the case of at least a few indeterminate constitutional norms, the practice of judicial review should be non-Thayerian. Which norms? As I have suggested: important right- or liberty-regarding norms that our history has shown to be "unusually vulnerable to majority sentiment".[137]

Admittedly, the position I am recommending here—non-Thayerian judicial review for important right- or liberty-regarding norms "unusually vulnerable to majority sentiment"—is embedded in speculative and therefore highly contestable judgments about the likely consequences of alternative ways of allocating political power. (What position in the area is not so embedded, at least in part?) Still, in the context of the United States today, the position I am recommending here resolves any doubt about the appropriate judicial role in protecting such norms—which is, of course, an easy doubt to have, given the difficulty of the issue—in a politically realistic direction, namely, toward privileging more generous rather than less generous specifications of the norms. "Non-Thayerian judicial review for important right- or liberty-regarding norms 'unusually vulnerable to majority sentiment'" comes at least as close as any competing position to satisfying Bickel's famous criteria—or so it seems to me:

> The search must be for a function which might (indeed, must) involve the making of policy, yet which differs from the legislative and executive

functions; which is peculiarly suited to the capabilities of the courts; which will not likely be performed elsewhere if the courts do not assume it; which can be so exercised as to be acceptable in a society that generally shares Judge [Learned] Hand's satisfaction in a "sense of common venture"; which will be effective when needed; and whose discharge by the courts will not lower the quality of the other departments' performance by denuding them of the dignity and burden of their own responsibility.[138]

The disagreement between Waldron and American political-legal culture about whether an entrenched Bill of Rights is a good thing is no more susceptible to definitive resolution than the issue between a thoroughgoing Thayerian and me about how deferential a role the Court should play in connection with certain right- or liberty-regarding norms. What Bickel said about judicial review is relevant both to the difference between Waldron and American political-legal culture and to the difference between a thoroughgoing Thayerian and me: "It will not be possible fully to meet all that is said against judicial review. Such is not the way with questions of government. We can only fill the other side of the scales with countervailing judgments on the real needs and the actual workings of our society and, of course, with our own portions of faith and hope. Then we may estimate how far the needle has moved."[139]

In many constitutional cases—even cases in which the question of the norm the relevant provision represents cannot usefully be answered by a repetition of what the provision says—an identification of the norm the provision represents will be unnecessary: The Supreme Court will *already* have identified, *in an earlier case now deemed authoritative*, the norm the provision represents. Moreover, if the applicable constitutional norm (or norms) is indeterminate, the Court might *already* have begun, in earlier cases, the process of specifying the norm—a process that, if it has been going on for a long time, will have yielded a substantial body of constitutional doctrine, much of which will not be in question but will be deemed authoritative. In the cases in which the applicable constitutional doctrine is itself indeterminate—as, at the margin, constitutional doctrine typically is—the challenge will be to develop that doctrine further. In that sense, the challenge will be to shape further the norm that is both the warrant for and the foundation of the doctrine. The specification of an indeterminate constitutional norm is, then, a temporally extended process, the judicial version of which is analogous to the ongoing judicial development of—including the occasional revision of—the "common law".[140] Of course, a principal aim in the judicial development of any area of law, including any area of constitutional law, is to fashion doctrine that is both internally coherent and at least not inconsistent with other doctrines of equal legal status, especially other doctrines in the same neighborhood.

3

The Fourteenth Amendment: What Norms Did "We the People" Establish?

As I said at the beginning of the preceding chapter, several of the most divisive moral conflicts that have beset us Americans since the end of World War II have been transmuted into constitutional conflicts—conflicts about what the Constitution of the United States forbids—and resolved as such. The particular constitutional conflicts I examine in this book—over racial segregation, race-based affirmative action, sex-based discrimination, homosexuality, abortion, and physician-assisted suicide—are, in the main, conflicts about what the Fourteenth Amendment forbids. What Raoul Berger wrote in 1977, in *Government by Judiciary: The Transformation of the Fourteenth Amendment*, is no less true today: "Because the [Fourteenth] Amendment . . . furnishes the chief fulcrum for [the Supreme Court's] control of controversial policies, the question whether such control is authorized by the Constitution is of great practical importance."[1]

Some constitutional scholars—most famously, perhaps, Robert Bork —have concurred in Berger's unequivocal judgment that the Fourteenth Amendment authorizes little if any "such control". (Berger has delivered that judgment in many venues, but nowhere more prominently than in *Government by Judiciary*.) In 1989, in *The Tempting of America: The Political Seduction of the Law*, Bork argued at length that section one of the Fourteenth Amendment has been, in the hands of the modern Supreme Court, an instrument of "judicial imperialism".[2] In 1996, citing recent Fourteenth Amendment decisions by the Court, Bork declared that "[t]he most important moral, political, and cultural decisions affecting our lives are being steadily removed from democratic control."[3] According to Bork, the justices of the Supreme Court have been "behaving like a 'band of outlaws.' . . . An outlaw is a person who coerces others without warrant in law. That is precisely what a majority of the present Supreme Court does. That is, given the opportunity, what the Supreme Court has always done."[4] Referring mainly to Fourteenth Amendment decisions, the editors of the periodical in which Bork's 1996 essay appeared commented on "troubling judicial actions that add up to an entrenched pattern of government by judges that is nothing less than the usurpation of politics. . . . Again and again, questions that are properly political are legalized, and even speciously constitutionalized."[5]

The constitutional conflicts I examine in this book have each been resolved—at least in part, and at least for a time—on the basis of a claim about what the second sentence of section one of the Fourteenth Amendment forbids. Which of those conflicts, if any, understood as Fourteenth Amendment conflicts, have been resolved—which have been resolved on the basis of the Fourteenth Amendment—as they should have been resolved? One cannot fully answer that question, or evaluate claims like those pressed by Berger and Bork and many others, without first ascertaining what norms "We the people" established, or probably established, in making the second sentence of section one of the Fourteenth Amendment a part of the Constitution of the United States. This is not to say that the Supreme Court should never resolve a constitutional conflict, qua *constitutional* conflict, on the basis of a norm not established by "We the people"; I argued in the preceding chapter that the Court should sometimes resolve a constitutional conflict on the basis of such a norm.[6] It is just to recognize that, as I said in the preceding chapter, if one wants to argue that a governmental action—for example, a state law—violates the Constitution, the least controversial basis on which to do so, in American constitutional culture, is a norm established as a part of the Constitution by "We the people". Certainly the least problematic basis on which the Supreme Court can rely in ruling that governmental action is unconstitutional is such a norm.

Let me rehearse a basic point from the preceding chapter. In American constitutional culture, few if any persons disagree that the norms the Constitution consists of include at least some directives issued by—that is, some norms "ordained and established" by—"We the people" and, moreover, that the Constitution consists of some such norms partly because the norms were "ordained and established" by "We the people". What directives have "We the people" issued, what norms have they established? As I remarked in the preceding chapter, when "We the people", through their elected representatives, put words into the text of the Constitution, they do so for the purpose of issuing—and, in that sense, establishing—one or more constitutional directives. The text of the Constitution, in each and all of its various parts, is the yield of political acts of a certain sort: acts intended to establish, not merely particular configurations of words, but, ultimately, particular norms, namely, the norms that "We the people" understood—or would have understood, if they had been engaged, if they had been paying attention—the particular configurations of words to communicate. Therefore, the norm (or norms) that "We the people" established, in putting a particular configuration of words into the text of the Constitution, is the norm they understood (or would have understood) their words to communicate. They did not establish a norm they would not have understood their words to communicate.

What norms did "We the people" understand—that is, what norms did they *probably* understand—the second sentence of section one of the Fourteenth Amendment to communicate? (I mean that question to include the question: What norms would they have understood the sentence to communicate, if they had been paying attention? Many of "the people" *were* paying attention, but inevitably not all were.) Put another way: What norms did "We the people" (probably) establish in making the second sentence of section one of the Fourteenth Amendment a part of the text of the Constitution?[7]

I

The basic features of the historical background of the Fourteenth Amendment are neither disputed not unfamiliar. For present purposes, a bare sketch is sufficient.

In 1863, President Abraham Lincoln, exercising his power as Commander in Chief of the Union forces to strengthen the Union's side in the Civil War, issued the Emancipation Proclamation,[8] declaring an end to slavery in the United States.[9] Two years later, after the Civil War had ended, the Thirteenth Amendment proclaimed that "[n]either slavery nor involuntary servitude, except as a punishment for crime whereof the party shall have been duly convicted, shall exist within the United States, or any place subject to their jurisdiction." In the former Confederate states, however, the subordinated position of the ex-slaves was maintained by the infamous Black Codes. In Mississippi, for example, an 1865 law provided:

> . . . every civil officer shall, and every person may, arrest and carry back to his or her legal employer any freedman, free negro, or mulatto who shall have quit the service of his or her employer before the expiration of his or her term of service without good cause. . . .
>
> . . . if any freedman, free negro or mulatto, convicted of any of the misdemeanors provided against in this act, shall fail or refuse for the space of five days after conviction, to pay the fine and costs imposed, such person shall be hired out by the sheriff or other officer, at the public outcry, to any white person who will pay said fine and all costs, and take the convict for the shortest time.[10]

"Other provisions of some of the Black Codes barred Blacks from any business except 'husbandry' without obtaining a special license, or forbade them from renting or leasing land except in towns and cities."[11] In 1872, in the *Slaughter-House Cases*, the Supreme Court recounted the story of the Black Codes:

> Among the first acts of legislation adopted by several of the States [were] laws which imposed upon the colored race onerous disabilities and bur-

dens, and curtailed their rights in the pursuit of life, liberty, and property to such an extent that their freedom was of little value, while they had lost the protection which they had received from their former owners from motives both of interest and humanity.

They were in some States forbidden to appear in the towns in any other character than menial servants. They were required to reside on and cultivate the soil without the right to purchase or own it. They were excluded from many occupations of gain, and were not permitted to give testimony in the courts in any case where a white man was a party. It was said that their lives were at the mercy of bad men, either because the laws for their protection were insufficient or were not enforced.[12]

The Civil Rights Act of 1866 was directed against the Black Codes. Section one of the Act provided, in relevant part:

[A]ll persons born in the United States and not subject to any foreign power, excluding Indians not taxed, are hereby declared to be citizens of the United States; and such citizens, of every race and color, without regard to any previous condition of slavery or involuntary servitude, except as punishment for a crime whereof the party shall have been duly convicted, shall have the same right, in every State and Territory of the United States, to make and embrace contracts, to sue, be parties, and give evidence, to inherit, purchase, lease, sell, hold, and convey real and personal property, and to full and equal benefit of all laws and proceedings for the security of person and property, as is enjoyed by white citizens, and shall be subject to like punishment, pains, and penalties, and to none other, any law, statute, ordinance, regulation, or custom, to the contrary notwithstanding.[13]

President Andrew Johnson had vetoed the 1866 Civil Rights Act partly on the ground that the Congress lacked constitutional power to enact it. (Many in Congress disagreed; they thought that Congress had ample power under section two of the Thirteenth Amendment, according to which Congress has "power to enforce this [amendment] by appropriate legislation."[14]) The Congress—the Thirty-ninth Congress—overrode the veto and then, leaving nothing to chance, proposed the Fourteenth Amendment, which, when ratified two years later, in 1868, not only constitutionalized the 1866 Act but also removed any doubt about congressional power to enact legislation like the 1866 Act.[15]

The relevant provision of the Fourteenth Amendment, for present purposes, is section one, which consists of two sentences, the first of which states: "All persons born or naturalized in the United States, and subject to the jurisdiction thereof, are citizens of the United States and of the State wherein they reside." That sentence was understood to "overturn[] the Dred Scott decision by making *all persons* born within the United States and subject to its jurisdiction citizens of the United States."[16] The crucial second sentence of section one—the sentence that is the constitutional basis of the various constitutional rulings I examine in this book—states: "No State shall make or enforce any law which shall abridge the privileges or immunities of citizens of the United States; nor shall any State deprive any person of life, liberty, or property, without due process of law; nor deny to any person within its jurisdiction the equal protection of the laws." Whatever else it was understood to do, that sentence was understood—by those who proposed it, by those who ratified it, and by "We the people" in whose name the sentence was proposed and ratified—to constitutionalize the 1866 Act and thereby place the Act beyond repeal by a later Congress.[17] Section five of the Fourteenth Amendment states: "The Congress shall have power to enforce, by appropriate legislation, the provisions of this article." That sentence was understood to affirm Congress' power to enact, not merely the 1866 Act, but other, kindred acts that a future Congress might want to enact.[18]

II

Again, what norms did "We the people" establish in making the second sentence of section one of the Fourteenth Amendment a part of the text of the Constitution? In the aftermath of the Civil War, it quickly became clear that a state could, and the former Confederate states did, oppress the ex-slaves, and others, in three basic ways. As it happens, each of the three basic parts of the second sentence of section one responds to one of the three basic ways (each part responds to a different way) state actors might be inclined to oppress ex-slaves and others.

"No State shall . . . deprive any person of life, liberty, or property, without due process of law"

First, state actors—for example, a county sheriff and his deputies, perhaps in conjunction with private actors—could act "outside the law" to achieve their goals by damaging or destroying a person's property, by detaining or imprisoning a person, or by injuring or even killing a person (or by threatening to do such things). Such lawless acts of terror could be and were directed not only against ex-slaves but against other citizens and noncitizens too—for example, Southern whites who had remained loyal to the Union or Northern whites traveling in the South after the Civil War. Given this historical context, and given too the ordinary meaning of the words, there is no reason to doubt that "We the people" understood the due process language of the Fourteenth Amendment ("No State shall . . . deprive any person of life, liberty, or property, without due process of law") to communicate a norm that forbids state actors to engage in such acts of terror. The norm protects not just ex-slaves (of whom there are now none), but all citizens, and not just all citizens, but all persons. Under the due process norm established by "We the people", state actors intent on depriving any person of life, liberty, or property may do so, if at all, not extrajudicially or otherwise "outside the law", but only pursuant to "due process of law".

"Due process of law" was understood to refer principally to the process of law that, under state law, is due ordinary citizens. As the 1866 Civil Rights Act put it: "[C]itizens [of the United States], of every race and color, . . . shall have the same right, in every State and Territory of the United States, . . . to full and equal benefit of all laws and proceedings for the security of person and property, *as is enjoyed by white citizens*, . . . any law, statute, ordinance, regulation, or custom, to the contrary notwithstanding" (emphasis added). It is less clear whether "due process of law" was understood to refer to more "process of law" than just the process due ordinary (i.e., white) citizens under state law. But whatever the outer bounds of the original understanding of "due process of law", the Supreme Court has long been of the view that both the Fifth Amendment due process norm, which applies to the national government, and the Fourteenth Amendment due process norm, which applies to state government, require more process than government might happen to provide.[19] Because there is often disagreement about whether the procedural protection government has provided in depriving a person of life, liberty, or property is the process of law that is "due", or is all the process that is "due", courts—and ultimately the Supreme Court—often have to decide whether the kind or amount of process government has provided is "due process of law".[20]

One question remains: Whether or not "due process of law" was understood to refer to more process of law than just the process due ordinary citizens under state law, was it understood to refer to more than just process; was "due process of law" understood to refer to more than just procedural protections? John Harrison has reported that "[b]y the time the Fourteenth Amendment was proposed, significant authority existed at the state level for the proposition that the due process clauses forbade direct legislative confiscations of property."[21] (Similarly, Stephen Siegel has observed that "[t]he only historical investigation of the original scope of the Fifth Amendment Due Process Clause that found an intent to govern the law's substance limited that intent to invalidating laws working a taking of property."[22]) Harrison then states:

> That support, however, does not buttress the notion that "nor shall any person be deprived of life, liberty, or property, without due process of law" meant "no person shall be forbidden to do something by a law that interferes with the fundamental right to liberty." With regard to deprivations of liberty, the framers of the Fourteenth Amendment appear to have agreed with the framers of the Fifth Amendment[:] The phrase "deprived of liberty" referred to physical restraint and 'due process of law' referred to procedure.[23]

Raoul Berger earlier reached substantially the same conclusion.[24] So far as I am aware, the historical materials bearing on the question of the original understanding of the due process language of section one do not tell against the Berger/Harrison conclusion.

"No State shall . . . deny to any person within its
jurisdiction the equal protection of the laws"

Now, a second but closely related way a state could, and the former Confederate states did, oppress the ex-slaves and others: State actors could stand idly by while private actors damage or destroy a person's property or detain, kidnap, or injure or even kill a person; they could refuse to investigate or prosecute such acts of terror under the various laws designed to protect the life, liberty, or property of persons. "[T]he wave of Klan lynchings and private violence undeterred and unpunished by the state that characterized the post–Civil War era is the paradigmatic equal protection violation, not Jim Crow laws and segregated schools."[25] Given this historical context, and given too the ordinary meaning of the words, there is no reason to doubt that "We the people" understood the equal protection language of the Fourteenth Amendment ("No State shall . . . deny to any person within its jurisdiction the equal protection of the laws") to communicate a norm that forbids state actors to turn a blind eye to such "private" acts of terror.[26] Like the due process norm, this norm protects not just ex-slaves, but all citizens, and not just all citizens, but all persons.[27] It protects them by requiring states to give to them the very same protection ("equal protection") given to ordinary citizens and others—the same protection "of the laws". What laws? At a minimum, laws designed to protect life, liberty, or property—in the words of the 1866 Civil Rights Act, "laws and proceedings for the security of person and property".[28]

The equal protection norm would be ineffectual if it did not forbid states to make or enforce protective laws (laws designed to protect life, liberty, or property) that themselves discriminate against nonwhites or other persons. Consider, for example, a law making it a crime to steal from, or to kill, white persons, but no crime, or a lesser crime, to steal from, or to kill, nonwhite persons. Consider, too, a law making it easier to obtain a criminal conviction against nonwhites than against whites—a law, for example, like that ruled unconstitutional in *Strauder v. West Virginia*,[29] excluding nonwhites from grand and petit juries. (Laws that make it more difficult to obtain a criminal conviction are protective laws of a sort: such laws, and the criminal process such laws establish, exist at least partly to protect the life, liberty, or property of the accused—as indeed the Court in *Strauder* was quick to recognize.[30] In that sense, such laws are, in the words of the 1866 Civil Rights Act, "laws and proceedings for the security of person and property".) As a practical matter, then, the equal protection norm must be construed not only to forbid states to deny the equal protection of protective laws, but also to forbid them to make or enforce racially or otherwise invidiously discriminatory protective laws.[31] Moreover, there is a firm historical basis for such a construction if, as John Harrison has suggested, the equal protection provision was understood to govern not only the administration of protective laws, but also their content:

It is likely that the clause also governs the content of protective laws. The Civil Rights Act of 1866 gave blacks the full and equal benefit of all laws and proceedings for the security of persons and property. This is critical for equal protection, for one way of depriving someone of the benefit of a law would be to pass another law that took the benefit away. Thaddeus Stevens said that the amendment required that whatever law protected the white should protect the black equally, a point that goes to the substance of the laws. Similarly, Bingham's initial draft was understood to affect the content of laws when it spoke of equal protection. . . . The Equal Protection Clause thus . . . probably also imposes the equality requirement on the substance of a category of laws that was, in the nineteenth century, of fundamental importance.[32]

The particular historical circumstance that occasioned the Fourteenth Amendment was the concentrated effort by the former Confederate states, in the aftermath of the Civil War, to maintain, often by means of lawless violence, the subordinated position of Americans of African ancestry. (In the *Slaughter-House Cases* the Court referred to "the one pervading purpose found in [the Thirteenth, Fourteenth, and Fifteenth Amendments], lying at the foundation of each, and without which none of them would have been even suggested; we mean the freedom of the slave race, the security and firm establishment of that freedom, and the protection of the newly-made freeman and citizen from the oppressions of those who had formerly exercised unlimited dominion over him."[33]) Unlike the 1866 Civil Rights Act, however, which was directed specifically at discrimination against nonwhites, in the form of the Black Codes, the due process and equal protection provisions were cast broadly enough that there is little if any reason to doubt that they were understood to communicate norms that transcend the historical circumstance that occasioned the Fourteenth Amendment. There is no reason to doubt that if a state were to deprive any person of life, liberty, or property without due process of law for reasons wholly unrelated to the effort to maintain the subordinated position of Americans of African ancestry or of any other racial group, the state would nonetheless violate the due process norm established by "We the people". Nor is there any reason to doubt that if, for reasons wholly unrelated to the effort to maintain the subordinated position of African Americans or of any other racial group, a state were to deny any person within its jurisdiction the equal protection of the laws designed to protect life, liberty, or property, the state would nonetheless violate the equal protection norm.

I said that, in the original understanding, the laws to which "the equal protection of the laws" referred were, *at a minimum*, "protective" laws: laws designed to protect a person's life, liberty, or property—in the words of the 1866 Civil Rights Act, "laws and proceedings for the security of person and property". Some students of the history of the Fourteenth Amendment in effect drop the "at a minimum"; they contend that according to the original understanding of the equal protection language, the *only* laws the equal protection of which no state may deny are *protective* laws: A state may neither deny to any person within its jurisdiction the equal protection of any *protective* law—any law designed to protect life, liberty, or property—nor make or enforce any *protective* law that is racially or otherwise invidiously discriminatory.[34] However, some other scholars argue for a broader view of the laws to which, in the original understanding, "the equal protection of the laws" referred—a broader view of the laws the equal protection of which (according to the original understanding) no state may deny.[35] A recent instance of such an argument is an article, in 1997, by Melissa Saunders, who contends that the equal protection language was understood

> to nationalize a constitutional limitation on state action developed by the state courts in the first half of the nineteenth century: the doctrine against "special" or "partial" laws, which forbade the state to single out any person or group of persons for special benefits or burdens without an adequate "public purpose" justification. . . . [A] majority of the Republicans who participated in the framing and ratification of the Fourteenth Amendment understood its Equal Protection Clause to do nothing more than nationalize the antebellum doctrine against partial or special laws. . . . The Court's famous dictum that 'the equal protection of the laws is a pledge of the protection of equal laws' is thus not a 'textual sleight of hand,' as Professor Harrison alleges, but an accurate translation of what the clause meant to those who framed and ratified it."[36]

Saunders adds, in a footnote: "I do not contend, of course, that this was the *only* reading of the clause held by those who participated in its framing and ratification; there were certainly those who saw it differently. My argument is simply that the *dominant* understanding among the framers and ratifiers was that the clause wrote this developing state law doctrine into the federal Constitution . . ."[37]

Saunders' argument is controversial.[38] But whether or not the equal protection language was understood (in Saunders' words) to "nationalize the antebellum doctrine against partial or special laws"—and, so, even if the language was not so understood—the privileges or immunities language, as I explain later in this chapter, was understood to do substantially just that (among other things). If Saunders is right about the original understanding of the equal protection language and I am right about the original understanding of the privileges or immunities language, we may say that "the Equal Protection Clause overlaps the Privileges or Immunities Clause to a significant extent."[39] If, however, only one of us is right, we may say that the sentence that contains both the privileges or immunities language and the equal protection language—the second sentence of section one of the Fourteenth Amendment—was understood to accomplish (whatever else it was understood to accomplish) what I believe the privileges or immunities language was understood to accomplish and what Saunders believes the equal protection language was understood to accomplish. Therefore, this argument about how broadly, or narrowly, the equal protection language was originally understood—about whether the language, in the original understanding, referred just to "protective" laws or, more generally, to *any* law that allocates a benefit or a burden—is largely inconsequential as a practical matter if at least one of us is right.[40]

> *"No State shall make or enforce any law which shall abridge the privileges or immunities of citizens of the United States"*

The due process norm established by "We the people" speaks to the possibility of lawless state action; the equal protection norm, to the possibility of state complicity in (by deliberately not protecting against) lawless private action. What possibility does the privileges or immunities norm speak to? The final basic way a state could, and the former Confederate states did, oppress the ex-slaves and others: By means of legislation denying to some of its citizens one or more "privileges" (or "freedoms to") or "immunities" ("freedoms from") that other of its citizens—its ordinary citizens—enjoyed. For example, a state could deny to some of its citizens, and some states did deny to them, "the same right . . . to make and embrace contracts, to sue, be parties, and give evidence, to inherit, purchase, lease, sell, hold, and convey real and personal property . . . *as is enjoyed by white citizens . . .*" (These words, though not the italicization, are from the 1866 Civil Rights Act.) Few if any observers now doubt that "We the people" understood the privileges or immunities language of the Fourteenth Amendment ("No State shall make or enforce any law which shall abridge the privileges or immunities of citizens of the United States") to communicate a norm limiting the power of states to do such a thing. Still, it is far from clear precisely what norm "We the people" meant to establish in making the privileges or immunities language a part of the Constitution; it is far from clear precisely what limit they meant to impose on the states.

III

Consider three related questions: (1) *What* is protected? (2) *Who* is protected? (3) Protected *from or against what*? With respect to the due process norm established by "We the people", the general answer to these three questions is relatively clear: The norm protects (1) the life, liberty, and property (2) of all persons (3) mainly against lawless state action. With respect to the equal protection norm, too—the equal protection norm established by "We the people"—the general answer is relatively clear: The norm protects (1) the life, liberty, and property (2) of all persons (3) mainly against state complicity in lawless private action. But with respect to the privileges or immunities norm established by "We the people", there has been significant disagreement about the answer to each of the three questions. Consider the first question. Although everyone can agree that the privileges or immunities norm established by "We the people" protects "the privileges and immunities of citizens of the United States", it has been a matter of controversy what privileges and immunities "We the people" understood "the privileges and immunities of citizens of the United States" to refer to; therefore, it is a matter of controversy what privileges and immunities are protected by the privileges or immunities norm established by "We the people". It has also been a matter of controversy whom the privileges or immunities provision was understood to protect: all persons? or only "citizens of the United States" (each of whom is also a citizen of the state wherein he or she resides)? Finally, it has been a matter of controversy what kind or kinds of state legislation the privileges or immunities provision was understood to protect the protected privileges and immunities (whatever they are) and the protected parties (whoever they are) against: racially discriminatory laws? some other kinds of discriminatory laws, too? what other kinds?

What Is Protected?

Let's begin with the "what is protected" question, which has generated enormous controversy. What privileges and immunities did "We the people" understand "the privileges and immunities of citizens of the United States" to refer to? There are two polar possibilities and also some intermediate possibilities. (One of the intermediate possibilities, in my judgment, is correct—as I will explain.) At one extreme, they might have understood the phrase to refer just to the privileges and immunities that persons who are citizens of the United States are due under national law—under the law, including the Constitution, of the United States. At the other extreme, they might have understood the phrase to refer to *all* the rights, *all* the privileges and immunities, that persons who are citizens of the United States—all of whom are also, under the first sentence of section one of the Fourteenth Amendment, citizens "of the State wherein they reside"—are due, *not just under national law, but also under the law of the state in which they reside.*[41]

In 1872, just four years after the Fourteenth Amendment became a part of the Constitution, a majority of the justices in the *Slaughter-House Cases* argued that the first polar possibility was the right answer.[42] As Richard Aynes noted in 1994, however, "everyone agrees" that the *Slaughter-House* majority was mistaken.[43] Indeed, the majority's mistake was so egregious as to make one wonder whether it was willful. Charles Black has aptly described the majority's opinion in the *Slaughter-House Cases* as "one of the most outrageous actions of our Supreme Court."[44]

The very structure of section one makes it very likely that the phrase was understood to refer to a larger set of rights than the *Slaughter-House* majority claimed: A focus only "on the rights of national citizenship . . . ignore[s] the state citizenship guaranteed by the first sentence of Section 1 and therefore provide[s] at most an incomplete account of the citizenship

rights protected by the clause."[45] Harrison continues: "The natural interpretation of the text is that the privileges and immunities of citizens of the
United States include the privileges and immunities of both of the citizenships that the Constitution confers. . . . We are . . . justified in reading
the Fourteenth Amendment as including positive law rights of state citizenship within the scope of the privileges and immunities of citizens."[46]

But we have much more than the bare structure of section one. The
historical record—in particular, the congressional statements from the
spring and summer of 1866 that are reproduced in the *Congressional Globe*
(39th Congress, 1st Session)—make abundantly clear that "We the people" understood "the privileges and immunities of citizens of the United
States" to refer to a larger set of rights than the *Slaughter-House* majority
claimed.

> Contrary to the Supreme Court's holding in the *Slaughter-House Cases*,
> advocates of the Fourteenth Amendment never implied that Section 1
> guaranteed only those privileges and immunities peculiar to national cit-
> izenship, in contradistinction to some different set of privileges peculiar
> to state citizenship. Section 1, which made them citizens of the State in
> which they resided, necessarily embraced the privileges and immunities
> of that status as well. A citizen was a citizen, and advocates of Section 1 in-
> tended to cloak every citizen with all the traditional privileges and im-
> munities of that status. Republicans fretted continuously that Southern
> states systematically denied blacks the privileges and immunities of citi-
> zenship. They would not have adopted a guarantee that only prevented
> those states from abridging a limited number of privileges and immuni-
> ties, derived solely from their status as citizens of the United States.
> Again, the critics understood that Section 1 was intended to protect citi-
> zens in the exercise of all the privileges and immunities of citizenship,
> whether they derived from the state or the nation.[47]

As the 1866 Civil Rights Act attests, and as the historical record abundantly confirms, the generation that gave us the Fourteenth Amendment
—"We the people" and, in particular, their representatives in the Thirty-
ninth Congress—were obviously and understandably focused on particular privileges and immunities, especially the fundamental rights to life and
to liberty and basic rights of property and of contract. As William Nelson
has written, "No one who sat in Congress or in the state legislatures that
dealt with the Fourteenth Amendment doubted that section 1 was designed to put to rest any doubt about the power of the national government to protect basic common law rights of property and contract. While
there were doubts about the extent to which the section protected basic
rights, there was no doubt that it extended some protection to them."[48]
From the fact that the people who gave us the Fourteenth Amendment
were undeniably focused on particular privileges and immunities that citizens, or some citizens,[49] are due under the law of the state in which they
reside, the inference is sometimes drawn—by Raoul Berger, Earl Maltz,
and Patrick Kelley, for example—that the privileges or immunities norm

established by "We the people" protects not each and every privilege or immunity that (some) citizens are due under the law of the state in which they reside, but only a subset of such privileges and immunities, namely, those rights pertaining to life, liberty, property, and contract that at the time the Fourteenth Amendment was proposed and ratified were believed to be "fundamental" or "natural" rights.[50] The Berger/Maltz/Kelley position represents one of the intermediate possibilities—one that, in my view, is mistaken. (I will refer to this as "the Berger position" or "the Berger reading", because Raoul Berger presented and defended the position in 1977, before Earl Maltz or Patrick Kelley began to address the issue.)

Although rights pertaining to life, liberty, property, and contract are certainly protected by the privileges or immunities norm established by "We the people", I have been unable to discern any reason in the historical record—in particular, in the congressional statements reproduced in the *Congressional Globe*—for concluding that the phrase "the privileges or immunities of citizens of the United States" was understood to exclude all other rights that citizens, or some citizens, are due under the law of the state in which they reside. (True, the phrase was generally understood not to refer to so-called "political" privileges—in particular, the right to vote. I discuss that fact below.) That the people who gave us the Fourteenth Amendment were focused on particular privileges and immunities certainly does not entail that they meant to protect only such privileges and immunities. Moreover, it strains credulity to insist that "We the people" and their representatives deliberately left the former Confederate states constitutionally free to discriminate against nonwhites—free to marginalize the newly freed slaves, who had just been granted citizenship as a matter of federal constitutional right, free to turn them into second-class citizens—with respect to whatever privileges and immunities a state might then or later choose to bestow on its ordinary (i.e., white) citizens that were not embodiments or instantiations of those rights believed at the time the Fourteenth Amendment was proposed and ratified to be "fundamental" rights. Such a reading of the central point of the privileges or immunities provision is implausible in part because it is so deeply counterintuitive. In the context of the profound—indeed, revolutionary—transformation they were spearheading, and indeed understood themselves to be spearheading, and given the forces against which they were contending, it would have been stupidly shortsighted for "We the people" and their representatives to have left the former Confederate states—the states that had established the Black Codes—free to subordinate nonwhites (and disfavored others) with respect to state-law-created privileges and immunities that were non-"fundamental".[51] Significantly, the historical record simply fails to support the sad proposition that they did so. To have done so would have been for them to have left the states free to make nonwhites second-class citizens—free to make nonwhites a lower caste of citizens. We are justified in concluding that they did not leave the states free to make nonwhites a lower caste of citizens, because we know that section one of the Fourteenth Amendment was understood and meant to "[strike] down [not only] the constitutionally-mandated system of caste with respect to citizenship of the United States erected by the Court in *Dred Scott* [but also] constitutionally-permitted systems of caste with re-spect to state citizenship . . ."[52] Section one of the Fourteenth Amendment requires every state to treat nonwhites as citizens fully equal to whites (subject to the proviso that, as I explain below, section one, in an act of po-litical compromise, stopped short of requiring a state to give nonwhite cit-izens the vote or other "political" privileges).

Again, this is not to deny that the people who gave us the Fourteenth Amendment were focused on particular privileges and immunities, espe-cially the fundamental rights to life and to liberty and basic rights of prop-erty and of contract. But to infer from that fact that the privileges or im-munities norm established by "We the people" protects only some subset of all the positive law rights of state citizenship imputes to the people who gave us the Fourteenth Amendment an utterly bewildering failure of in-sight and/or commitment. The much more plausible conclusion, which the historical record amply supports, is that—with the exception of "po-litical" privileges, like the right to vote—the privileges or immunities norm established by "We the people" protects not merely some privileges and immunities that citizens are due under the law of their state, but each and every such privilege and immunity (as well as each and every privi-lege and immunity they are due under national law). Congressional state-ments in the *Globe* do support the claim that the phrase "the privileges and immunities of citizens of the United States" was understood to refer —and to refer centrally—to rights pertaining to life, liberty, property, and contract, but those statements do *not* support the very different claim that the phrase was understood to refer to a *closed* set of rights that *excluded* any other, new privileges and immunities that a state might fashion and dis-tribute to (some of) its citizens. To the contrary, those statements, some of which I reproduce below,[53] support the claim that the phrase was under-stood to refer to an *open* set that *included* any (nonpolitical) privileges and any immunities that a state might create and distribute to its citizens.

The claim is supported by much more than a few congressional state-ments, however. According to Eric Foner, who is the leading historian of the Reconstruction era, "too many attempts by legal scholars to ascertain the 'original intent' of the Fourteenth Amendment rely on a handful of se-lected quotations from Congressional debates rather than the full histori-cal context of Republican ideology and its evolution in the Civil War era."[54] What do "the full historical context of Republican ideology and its evolution in the Civil War era" show? Foner's conclusion merits quotation in full:

> Republicans did not deny one Democrat's description of the [Four-teenth] Amendment as "open to ambiguity and . . . conflicting construc-tions." The debate abounded in generalities such as "the fundamental

rights of citizens," and Republicans rejected calls to define these with precision. Unlike the [1866] Civil Rights Act, which listed numerous rights a state could not abridge, the Amendment used only the broadest language. Clearly, Republicans proposed to abrogate the Black Codes and eliminate any doubts as to the constitutionality of the Civil Rights Act. Yet to reduce their aims to this is to misconstrue the difference between a statute and a constitutional amendment. Some amendments, dealing with narrow, immediate concerns, can be thought of as statutes writ large; altering one aspect of national life, they leave the larger structure intact. Others are broad statements of principle, giving constitutional form to the resolution of national crises, and permanently altering American nationality. The Fourteenth Amendment was a measure of this kind. In language that transcended race and region, it challenged legal discrimination throughout the nation and changed and broadened the meaning of freedom for all Americans.

On the precise definition of equality before the law, Republicans differed among themselves. Even moderates, however, understood Reconstruction as a dynamic process, in which phases like "privileges and immunities" were subject to changing interpretation. They preferred to allow both Congress and the federal courts maximum flexibility in implementing the Amendment's provisions and combating the multitude of injustices that confronted blacks in many parts of the South. The final version, it should be noted, was far stronger than Bingham's earlier proposal directly granting national lawmakers the power to enforce civil rights, for this would become a dead letter if Democrats regained control of the House or Senate. Now, discriminatory state laws could be overturned by the federal courts regardless of which party dominated Congress. (Indeed, as in the Civil Rights Act, Congress placed great reliance on an activist federal judiciary for civil rights enforcement—a mechanism that appeared preferable to maintaining indefinitely a standing army in the South, or establishing a permanent national bureaucracy empowered to oversee Reconstruction.)[55]

The position I have just been criticizing, the Berger position, represents one of the intermediate possibilities—intermediate between the two polar possibilities identified above. John Harrison's position represents another intermediate possibility. In contrast to the position I am defending here (which represents a third intermediate possibility), John Harrison has concluded that the privileges or immunities norm established by "We the people" does not protect *all* the nonpolitical rights that citizens, or some citizens, are due under the law of their state, but only some such rights. Whereas for Raoul Berger, Earl Maltz, Patrick Kelley, and some others, the rights protected by the privileges or immunities norm are only those rights pertaining to life, liberty, property, and contract that at the time the Fourteenth Amendment was proposed and ratified were believed to be "fundamental" or "natural" rights, for Harrison the protected rights are only those "that constitute citizenship rights". Harrison writes: "[T]he central task [in bringing the privileges or immunities norm to bear] is distinguishing between those aspects of the positive law that constitute citizenship rights and those that do not." Then, distinguishing his position from the Berger position, Harrison adds: "The task is not easy, but it is not as difficult as an inquiry into [what are and what are not] natural rights."[56] Further along, Harrison states: "The Privileges or Immunities Clause forbids abridgment of the privileges or immunities of citizens, not of any other kind of rights."[57]

Harrison's position is no more plausible than the Berger position—and for the very same reasons. According to the Harrison position, a state would not violate the privileges or immunities norm if it were to create and allocate a right among its citizens on a racist basis—giving the right to some citizens, but, for racist reasons, denying it to other citizens—so long as the right in question was not a "citizenship right". Thus, a state may marginalize and subordinate some of its citizens on a racist basis, it may treat them as second-class members of the political community, according to Harrison's position, so long as it does so with respect to rights that are not "citizenship rights" (whatever such rights are). A reprise of comments I made earlier in response to the Berger position is in order: It is not plausible to think that "We the people" and their representatives deliberately left the former Confederate states constitutionally free to discriminate against nonwhites—free to marginalize the newly freed slaves, who had just been granted citizenship as a matter of federal constitutional right, free to turn them into second-class citizens—with respect to whatever privileges and immunities a state might then or later choose to bestow on its ordinary (i.e., white) citizens that were not what Harrison calls "citizenship rights". Like the Berger reading, such a reading of the central point of the privileges or immunities provision is implausible in part because it is so deeply counterintuitive. In the context of the profound transformation they were spearheading, and of the forces against which they were contending, it would have been stupidly shortsighted for "We the people" and their representatives to have left the former Confederate states free to subordinate nonwhites (and disfavored others) with respect to state-law-created privileges and immunities that were not "citizenship rights". Though different from the Berger reading, the Harrison reading is like the Berger reading in imputing to the people who gave us the Fourteenth Amendment a bewildering failure of insight and/or commitment. (If Harrison were to define "citizenship rights" so broadly that any (non-political) right a state creates and distributes to (some of) its citizens would qualify as a "citizenship right", then the difference between Harrison's position and mine would be merely verbal.)

That Harrison feels constrained to embrace a position with such unattractive implications is especially puzzling in light of the fact that in his essay Harrison quotes several passages from the historical record that support the claim—my claim—that the privileges or immunities norm established by "We the people" protects not merely some privileges (i.e., nonpolitical privileges) and immunities that (some) citizens are due under the law of the state in which they reside, but every privilege and immunity they are due under such law. Consider, for example, the following passages. Significantly, not a single one of the passages makes any distinction whatsoever between, on the one side, a set of rights, due (some) citizens under the law of their state, *that are protected by the privileges or immunities norm* and, on the other, a different set of such rights *that are not so protected.*

- Representative Giles Hotchkiss, Republican of New York and a member of the Joint Committee, said that a principal point of the proposed Amendment was "to provide that no State shall discriminate between its citizens and give one class of citizens greater rights than it confers upon another. . . . [The object is] to provide [protection] against a discrimination to the injury or exclusion of any class of citizens in any State from the privileges which other classes enjoy . . ."[58]

- "Representative Henry Raymond, Republican of New York, explained that Section 1 'secures an equality of rights among all the citizens of the United States.' When he introduced the Fourteenth Amendment in the Senate, Senator [Jacob] Howard [of Michigan] said that Section 1 'established equality before the law,' and that '[w]ithout this principle of equal justice to all men . . . , there is no republican government.' This doctrine of general equality meant, as Thaddeus Stevens put it, that 'the law which operates upon one man shall operate *equally* upon all.' . . . As Senator Howard explained, the purpose of the Fourteenth Amendment was . . . to 'abolish[] all class legislation in the States and [do] away with the injustice of subjecting one caste of persons to a code not applicable to another.' "[59]

- "A clear explanation [of the meaning of the privileges or immunities provision] was given by then-Senator Boutwell a few years after the Amendment passed. To determine a citizens rights under the clause, he said, we

    > see what the rights and privileges and immunities of citizens of the State generally are under the laws and constitution of the State. . . . The Government of the United States can take the humblest citizen in the State of Ohio who by the constitution or the laws of that State may be deprived of any right, privilege, or immunity that is conceded to the citizens of that State generally, and lift him to the dignity of equality as a citizen of that State . . . ."[60]

- In February 1872, Senator Matthew Hale Carpenter of Wisconsin, in support of civil rights legislation that he was introducing, said about the Fourteenth Amendment privileges or immunities norm:

    > If no State can make or enforce a law—and law in this connection includes State constitutions, common law, statutes, and usages in such State—to abridge the rights of any citizen it must follow that the privileges and immunities of all citizens must be the same. If my privileges are not equal to those of the senator from Maine, then mine are abridged. This no State can do.[61]

• In December 1873, Representative Benjamin Butler of Massachusetts, chairman of the House Judiciary Committee, said in connection with civil rights legislation that he was introducing "that the Constitution forbade discrimination with respect to ordinary civil rights, such as those of riding on a railroad or attending a common school:

> [T]he result of the late war has been that every person born on the soil, or duly naturalized, is a citizen of the United States, entitled to all the rights, privileges, and immunities of a citizen. All legislation, therefore, that seeks to deprive a well-behaved citizen of the United States of any privilege or immunity to be enjoyed, and which he is entitled to enjoy in common with other citizens, is against constitutional enactment.

Although [that Butler was talking about equality] would have been obvious from the inclusion of cemeteries and public schools, he made it explicit: 'No State has a right to pass any law which inhibits the full enjoyment of all the rights she gives to her citizens by discriminating against any class of them provided they offend no law.' "[62]

Given passages like these—passages that Harrison features in his essay—it is curious that Harrison feels compelled to conclude that the privileges or immunities norm protects only *some* nonpolitical rights that citizens, or some citizens, are due under the law of their state. Harrison acknowledges that "[t]he task [of distinguishing between those aspects of the positive law that constitute citizenship rights and those that do not] is not easy . . ."[63] Because the privileges or immunities norm established by "We the people" protects *all* the nonpolitical rights that states create and allocate among their citizens, and not merely some such rights, Harrison's "not easy" task is, happily, not necessary. There is little if any reason in the historical record to doubt that, like the privileges and immunities language, the privileges or immunities norm that the language was understood to communicate—the privileges or immunities norm that "We the people" established—protects not just *some* nonpolitical privileges and immunities that citizens are due, but *each and every* such privilege and immunity they are due, including each and every privilege or immunity they are due under the law of their state. Again, this is not to deny that the historical record reveals that the representatives of "We the people" were focused on some privileges and immunities much more than on others: those pertaining to life, liberty, property, and contract. But, again, the record does not support the proposition that the privileges or immunities provision was understood to refer to a *closed* set of rights that *excluded* any other, new privileges and immunities that a state might fashion and distribute to (some of) its citizens. Indeed, passages like those set forth above—as well as what Foner has called "the full historical context of Republican ideology and its evolution in the Civil War era"—support the claim that the provision was understood to refer to an *open* set that *included* any (nonpolitical) privileges and any immunities that a state might create and allocate among its citizens. As Justice Bradley declared in his dissenting opinion in the *Slaughter-House Cases*, "[c]itizenship of the United States ought to be, and, according to the Constitution, is, a sure and undoubted title to equal rights in any and every State of this Union, subject to such regulations as the legislature may rightfully prescribe." It is not just *some* rights that must be "equal", but *all* rights—that is, all (nonpolitical) privileges and immunities a state might create and allocate among its citizens. My citizenship is scarcely equal to yours if a state may deny to me, because of the color of my skin, one or more privileges or immunities that it grants to you.

Those who, like Berger, Maltz, Kelley, and Harrison, argue that the privileges or immunities norm established by "We the people" protects only some subset of all the nonpolitical rights that states create and allocate among their citizens typically rely on this fact: At the time the Fourteenth Amendment was proposed and ratified, the privileges *and* immunities provision of Article IV of the Constitution—which the historical record reveals to have been something of a precursor of the privileges *or* immunities provision of the Fourteenth Amendment[64]—was not understood to protect all the rights that states create and allocate among their citizens, but only some of them.[65] The privileges and immunities provision of Article IV states: "The citizens of each state shall be entitled to all privileges and immunities of citizens in the several states." This provision was understood to protect citizens of one state who are temporarily in another state from some discrimination against them by the other state in favor of the state's own citizens. However, it seems obvious that a state should not be obligated to spend its scarce resources, material or financial, on citizens of another state temporarily in the state. A state should be permitted to spend its scarce resources only on its own citizens. After all, the citizens of a state are the "owners" of the state's resources; their relationship to those resources is "proprietary". Not surprisingly, then, the "privileges" to which the privileges and immunities provision of Article IV refers were understood, in the first half of the nineteenth century and at the time of the Fourteenth Amendment, not to include legal entitlements to a state's scarce resources.[66]

At its core, the privileges or immunities norm of the Fourteenth Amendment protects nonwhite citizens of a state from (some) discrimination against them in favor of the state's white citizens. A state should *not* be permitted to spend its scarce resources only on its white citizens. (*All* the citizens of a state, nonwhite as well as white, female as well as male, and so on, are, as citizens of the state, the "owners" of the state's material resources.) Moreover, from the perspective of the people who gave us the Fourteenth Amendment, no consideration supported permitting a state to spend its scarce resources only on its white citizens. There is no good reason to believe that "We the people" understood the "privileges" to which the privileges or immunities provision of the Fourteenth Amendment refers not to include legal entitlements to a state's scarce resources.

(This is not to deny that in the 1860s, before the dawn of the welfare state, such entitlements were rare, and that because they were rare, they were certainly not uppermost in the minds of the people who gave us the Fourteenth Amendment. Uppermost in their minds, again, were the fundamental rights to life and to liberty and basic rights of property and of contract.) The more limited understanding of "privileges" in the context of the privileges and immunities provision of Article IV makes no sense at all in the crucially different context of the privileges or immunities provision of the Fourteenth Amendment. The proposition that because legal entitlements to a state's scarce resources were understood by the people who gave us the Fourteenth Amendment not to be among the "privileges" to which Article IV refers, such entitlements must have been understood (by those who gave us the Fourteenth Amendment) not to be among the "privileges" to which the Fourteenth Amendment refers, conspicuously fails to take account of the profound difference between the kind of discrimination at which Article IV was aimed (discrimination by a state against citizens of another state) and the kind of discrimination at which the Fourteenth Amendment was aimed (discrimination by a state against some of its own citizens). Again, the much more plausible conclusion, which the historical record does not come close to disconfirming, is that the privileges or immunities norm established by "We the people" protects not merely some nonpolitical privileges and some immunities that citizens, or some citizens, are due under the law of their state, but all such privileges and immunities—including privileges in the form of entitlements to a state's scarce material or financial resources.

The intermediate possibility—the position—that is, in my judgment, most likely correct is broader than either the one advanced by Berger, Maltz, and Kelley or the one advanced by Harrison. It holds that the privileges or immunities norm established by "We the people" protects all the privileges and immunities that a state distributes to its citizens, or to some of them, *with the exception of "political" privileges, like the right to vote*. Why should we conclude that the right to vote and other political rights are not protected by the privileges or immunities norm established by "We the people"? Why are only nonpolitical rights—albeit, all nonpolitical rights —protected? The generation of "We the people" that adopted the Fourteenth Amendment apparently understood the phrase "the privileges or immunities of citizens of the United States" not to refer to so-called political privileges; in particular, they understood it not to refer to the right or freedom to vote, which we consider to be one of the most important "citizen" rights or privileges of all. "[N]ineteenth-century usage concerning political participation confirms the close connection between privileges and immunities and civil rights: neither was thought to extend to political rights, such as voting or serving on juries. Political rights were commonly distinguished from civil rights, and only a subset of the citizens had the right to participate politically. . . . Most Republicans agreed that neither civil rights nor privileges and immunities included political rights, and legal usage generally appears to have reflected this approach."[67] Not that some Republican leaders—like Senator Jacob Howard of Michigan, who introduced the Fourteenth Amendment in the Senate—did not want to extend the right to vote to freedmen. They did, but despaired that a constitutional provision to that effect would be ratified.[68] In an act of compromise with that state of affairs, congressional sponsors of the Fourteenth Amendment explicitly exempted so-called political (v. civil) privileges from the protection of section one.[69] In our effort to discern the shape of the privileges or immunities norm that "We the people" probably established, we may not (however much we might want to) ignore that compromise. (Again, the language of the phrase "the privileges . . . of citizens of the United States" did not conceal the compromise from "We the people".) Because the right to vote was excluded from protection, it was understood that a further constitutional amendment would be necessary to protect the right to vote against denial or abridgment based on race.[70] As it turned out, that further amendment was the Fifteenth, which was ratified in 1870, just two years after the Fourteenth Amendment was ratified. Section one of the Fifteenth Amendment declares: "The right of citizens of the United States to vote shall not be denied or abridged by the United States or by any State on account of race, color, or previous condition of servitude."

Therefore, the privileges or immunities norm established by "We the people" does not protect *every* right that (some) citizens are due under the law of the state in which they reside; in particular, it does not protect the right to vote or other political rights. Nonetheless, although the historical record supports the position that the protection of the privileges or immunities norm established by "We the people" stops short of "political" rights—in particular, the right to vote—the record does *not* support the position that the norm's protection stops short of any other, "nonpolitical" rights. The protection of the privileges or immunities norm established by "We the people" extends to every *nonpolitical* right that a state creates and distributes to citizens, or to some of them; the norm protects every state-law–created *nonpolitical* right.[71] A political compromise led to the exclusion of political rights from the protection of the Fourteenth Amendment, but no such compromise led to the exclusion of any other rights—of any nonpolitical rights—from the protection of section one.

Over time the right to vote has assumed a status in American political-legal culture profoundly different from the status it had at the time the Fourteenth Amendment was proposed and ratified.[72] The right to vote is now widely regarded not as a merely "political" right that is only a creature of state or local law, but as a fundamental right due all the law-abiding citizens (above a certain age) of a country. Both the international law of human rights and, closer to home, the trajectory of constitutional amendments since the ratification of the Fourteenth Amendment are unmistakable reflections of that fact. Indeed, given the trajectory of constitutional amendments since the ratification of the Fourteenth, that the privileges or immunities norm established by "We the people" does not protect the right to vote (or other political rights) has limited practical significance. The right to vote (and, inferentially, the allied right of access to the ballot) is now protected by several constitutional amendments other than the Fourteenth. Three different constitutional amendments over the course of 101 years all speak of "the right of citizens of the United States to vote". In addition to the Fifteenth, there is the Nineteenth Amendment (1920), according to which "[t]he right of citizens of the United States to vote shall not be denied or abridged by the United States or by any State on account of sex", and the Twenty-sixth Amendment (1971), according to which "[t]he right of citizens of the United States, who are eighteen years of age or older, to vote shall not be denied or abridged . . . on account of age."[73] As John Ely has observed: "Excluding the Eighteenth and Twenty-First Amendments—the latter repealed the former—six of our last ten constitutional amendments have been concerned precisely with increasing popular control of government. And five of those six—the exception being the . . . Seventeenth—have extended the franchise to persons who had previously been denied it."[74]

I have argued here that the privileges or immunities norm established by "We the people" protects all the rights that citizens are due—that is, all the nonpolitical rights they are due—under the law of their state. But, again, some others argue that the norm protects only some state-law–created privileges and immunities—for example, those that embody or instantiate rights, or aspects of rights, believed at the time the Fourteenth Amendment was proposed and ratified to be "fundamental" or "natural" rights (which is the Berger reading), or those that are "citizenship rights" (the Harrison reading). Although, for the reasons I have indicated, the former position is more plausible than any position of the latter sort, let's assume, for the sake of argument, that a position of the latter sort—either the Berger position or the Harrison position—has a plausibility roughly equal to the plausibility of the former position (my position). Now, consider this question: Which position should get the benefit of the doubt? Isn't it the position according to which the privileges or immunities norm established by "We the people", by forbidding states to allocate not just some but *any* privileges or immunities among its citizens on a racist basis, affirms—or, at least, comes closer to affirming—the full and equal humanity of *all* citizens, *nonwhite as well as white*? Why would anyone think the benefit of the doubt should go to the position that leaves the states free to marginalize some of its citizens, free to turn them into second-class citizens, by distributing some privileges or immunities to its citizens on a racist basis?[75] (As I explain later in this chapter, whatever else it protects the protected privileges and immunities, *whatever they are*, from, the privileges or immunities norm established by "We the people" forbids states to allocate protected privileges or immunities among its citizens on a racist basis.)

Who Is Protected?

Let's now turn to the second of our three basic questions: Whom did "We the people" understand the privileges or immunities provision to protect—all persons or just citizens? There is an interesting difference between, on the one side, the language of the due process and equal protection provisions of the Fourteenth Amendment and, on the other, the language of the privileges or immunities provision: The former speaks of "any person", but the latter speaks of "citizens": "citizens of the United States". The privileges or immunities language is undeniably limited to the privileges and immunities *of* "citizens of the United States" (whatever those privileges and immunities are), and there is no reason to doubt that the protection of the privileges or immunities norm the language was understood to communicate is also limited to such privileges and immunities. But the privileges or immunities language does not preclude the possibility that the protection of the privileges or immunities norm the language was understood to communicate is not limited *to* citizens. As John Ely has put the point: "'No State shall make or enforce any law which shall abridge the privileges or immunities of citizens of the United States' *could* mean that only citizens are protected in their privileges or immunities, but it surely doesn't have to. It could just as easily mean that there is a set of entitlements, 'the privileges and immunities of citizens of the United States,' which states are not to deny to anyone. In other words, the reference to citizens may define the class of rights rather than limit the class of beneficiaries."[76] Ely's conclusion: "Since everyone seems to agree that such a construction would better reflect what we know of the purpose, and since it is one the language will bear comfortably, it is hard to imagine why it shouldn't be followed."[77]

Ely says that "everyone seems to agree". He also says that "[i]t seems to be generally agreed that no conscious intention to limit the protection of the [privileges or immunities] clause to citizens appears in the historical records."[78] Ely to the contrary notwithstanding, however, it is *not* generally agreed that "no conscious intention . . . appears in the historical records."[79] In particular, Earl Maltz and John Harrison, in separate articles, have presented an impressive argument that whereas the due process language and the equal protection language were each understood to communicate a norm protecting all persons, aliens no less than citizens, the privileges or immunities language was understood to communicate a norm protecting only citizens.[80] The Maltz/Harrison reading imputes to the original understanding of section one of the Fourteenth Amendment the position that although with respect to one's life, to one's liberty, and to the property one already owns, everyone, including aliens, merits the same "protection of the laws", including the same "process of law", due citizens, not everyone merits *all* the same privileges and immunities due citizens—in particular, and for example, aliens do not merit precisely the same privileges of buying, owning, and selling real property due citizens. (This is not to say that a state may not extend to aliens precisely the same such privileges due citizens.) "The framers clearly believed that aliens were entitled to *some* rights; at the same time, however, they carefully noted and preserved the distinction between aliens and citizens. . . . The absolute right to real property . . . derived from citizenship; thus, the rights of aliens in this regard were often restricted by the states."[81]

Protected from What?

Now, the final of our three related questions: What kind or kinds of state legislation does the privileges or immunities norm established by "We the people" protect the protected privileges and immunities (whatever they are) and the protected parties (whoever they are) from or against: laws that discriminate on a racist basis? laws that discriminate on the basis of color, whether or not the discrimination is "racist"? some other kinds of discriminatory laws, too? what kinds?

Let's start with the word "abridge". The Fourteenth Amendment forbids states to make or enforce laws that "abridge" the privileges or immunities of citizens of the United States. Other amendments forbid states to "deny or abridge" one or another right. The Fifteenth Amendment, for example, states that "[t]he right of citizens of the United States to vote shall not be denied or abridged by the United States or by any State on account of race, color, or previous condition of servitude." Is it significant that the Fourteenth Amendment says "abridge" rather than "deny or abridge"? According to the *Oxford English Dictionary*, the range of reference of "abridge", in the nineteenth century no less than today, was sufficiently broad to include "deprive"; therefore, to say that a state may not "abridge" a right is tantamount to saying that a state may not "deny or abridge" it. A state "abridges" a right if the state "deprives" someone of it altogether; a state also "abridges" a right if, less drastically, the state merely "lessens" or "diminishes" the right.[82] So, in inquiring about the kind(s) of state action protected against by the privileges or immunities norm established by "We the people", one should not put any weight on the fact that the privileges or immunities language says "abridge" rather than "deny or abridge". Given the range of reference of "abridge", it made sense to say "abridge" rather than "deny or abridge". "Abridge" was enough: Both laws that "deny" a privilege (or immunity) of citizens of the United States and laws that "diminish" or "lessen" the privilege "abridge" the privilege. Michael Curtis has reached substantially the same conclusion on the basis of his careful review of the relevant legislative materials: "'Abridge' . . . was simply an intensive form of the prohibition of any denial, so the concept reached partial denials as well as total denials."[83]

Again, what kind(s) of state action does the privileges or immunities norm established by "We the people" protect the protected privileges and immunities and the protected parties against? The norm undeniably forbids every state to allocate any privilege or immunity among its citizens—

giving the privilege or immunity to some, denying it to others—on a racist basis. Thus, the norm forbids every state to give a right to make contracts or to own property, for example, to its white citizens while denying the right to its nonwhite citizens. (Recall that whatever else it did, the second sentence of section one constitutionalized the 1866 Civil Rights Act.) For a state to allocate such a right among its citizens on the basis of their skin color—as the former Confederate states did under their Black Codes—is certainly for the state to allocate the right among its citizens on a racist basis. As a real-world matter, what else but a racist ideology could explain a color-based allocation of such a right? But, did "We the people" understand the privileges or immunities language to communicate a norm (i.e., did they establish a norm) forbidding more than racist allocation of rights (and immunities)?[84] Although the historical record leaves the answer unclear, it is safe to assume that the privileges or immunities language was not understood to communicate a norm forbidding states ever to treat any of their citizens less favorably than others in distributing protected privileges and immunities—for example, by bestowing privileges on adults not bestowed on children, or by bestowing privileges on those with medical degrees not bestowed on those without. (When I say, here and elsewhere, "protected" privileges and immunities, I mean those privileges and immunities ("the privileges and immunities of citizens of the United States"), whatever they are, that are protected by the privileges or immunities norm established by "We the people".) Should we conclude, then, that the privileges or immunities norm established by "We the people" does no more than forbid states to deny to any of their nonwhite citizens any protected privilege or immunity enjoyed by their white citizens or to lessen or diminish any of their nonwhite citizens' enjoyment of any such privilege or immunity relative to their white citizens' enjoyment of the privilege or immunity? Should we conclude, at least, that the norm does no more than forbid states ever to treat any of their citizens less favorably than others in distributing protected privileges and immunities, if the basis of the less favorable treatment is racist? This conclusion is quite problematic. Again, there is no reason to doubt that the due process and equal protection norms established by "We the people" transcend the particular historical circumstance that occasioned their establishment. State action wholly unrelated to the effort to maintain the subordinated position of African Americans or of any other racial group can violate the due process norm, and such state action can also violate the equal protection norm. It seems likely, therefore, that the same thing is true of the privileges or immunities norm—that state action wholly unrelated to the effort to maintain the subordinated position of African Americans or of any other racial group can violate the privileges or immunities norm. After all, one and the same sentence—the second sentence of section one of the Fourteenth Amendment—represents all three norms.

William Nelson's important work on the history of the Fourteenth Amendment is instructive here: "While equality for blacks was surely the central concern of the [fourteenth] amendment's framers and ratifiers, it was never their sole and exclusive concern. Those who discussed the amendment were aware of its implications for other groups, such as Chinese, Indians, women, and religious minorities. Moreover, there is no doubt that the proponents of the amendment meant to protect yet another group—namely, Northern whites who were migrating to the South after the Civil War and were threatened with potentially discriminatory legislation at the hands of Southern states and localities."[85] Nelson neglects to mention here that proponents of the Fourteenth Amendment also meant to protect yet another group of whites: Southern whites who were against secession and remained loyal to the Union, many of whom even fought on the Union side in the Civil War.[86] (Returning Southern whites were often called "refugees—that is to say the loyal white men who have fled their homes because of the rebellion".[87]) As Alfred Avins concluded: "If the first section [of the Fourteenth Amendment] had been confined to racial discrimination, one of the major objects of congressional solicitude in submitting the fourteenth amendment [namely, the Southern whites who had been loyal to the Union] would have been left out. It is therefore clear once again that if racial discrimination were deemed to have a special condemnation, under the fourteenth amendment, an important group, of equal concern with Negroes to the framers, could not benefit from it. This is strong evidence that no such primacy was given to racial discrimination."[88]

The following interchange during congressional discussion of the proposed Fourteenth Amendment is additional evidence that the privileges or immunities language was understood to communicate a norm forbidding discrimination (in the allocation of protected privileges and immunities) more broadly than just discrimination against nonwhites—or even just discrimination based on racism:

> On February 27, [1866,] Robert Hale of New York asked whether the amendment would remove all legal disabilities that most states then imposed on married women. No, replied Thaddeus Stevens, not if all wives were treated alike; "where all of the same class are dealt with in the same way, there is no pretense of inequality." Hale did not hesitate to close the trap into which Stevens had fallen. "Then by parity of reasoning it would be sufficient if you extended to one negro the same rights you do to another, but not those you extend to a white man." Hale voted for the amendment anyway, in spite of the fact that he never got a convincing answer to his objections.[89]

The most significant thing about this interchange, for present purposes, is what Hale's question to Stevens did *not* presuppose and what Stevens' answer to Hale did *not* assert: namely, that the Fourteenth Amendment, if it governs more than discrimination against nonwhites, governs no more than discrimination based on racism, and, therefore, discrimination against women, whether women generally or some subset, such as married women, does not even implicate, much less violate, the Amendment.

Indeed, John Harrison has reported that "Hale's point in the colloquy with Stevens . . . was that equality extended beyond racial equality, that it forbade discrimination on grounds other than race, such as marital status or possibly sex."[90]

It seems an unavoidable conclusion, then, that, like the due process and equal protection norms, the privileges or immunities norm established by "We the people" transcends the historical circumstance that occasioned the Fourteenth Amendment. State action wholly unrelated to the effort to maintain the subordinated position of African Americans or of any other racial group can violate the privileges or immunities norm, just as such state action can violate the due process and equal protection norms. The privileges or immunities norm established by "We the people" does more than just forbid states to allocate the privileges and immunities "of citizens of the United States" on a racist basis. But how much more? What discrimination (in the allocation of protected privileges and immunities) beyond racist discrimination does the privileges or immunities norm forbid? Listen to William Nelson:

> A theory that the state should treat all people equally cannot mean that the state may never treat two people differently, for such a theory would mean the end of all law. In order to sustain a principle of equality under law—the principle for which the framers of the Fourteenth Amendment were striving, it is necessary to have some theory about when discrimination is appropriate and when it is not.
>
> In their efforts to elaborate a theory of equality, statesmen of the generation which framed and ratified the Fourteenth Amendment faced [a difficult issue] that continue[s] to plague Fourteenth Amendment analysis today. [The issue], once they moved beyond obviously defective racial criteria, was to distinguish classifications that would be reasonable under the amendment from those that would be arbitrary. . . .
>
> In dealing with the . . . issue, the congressional proponents of the Fourteenth Amendment were always able to specify whether a particular classification was reasonable or arbitrary. But they were persistently unable to elaborate how their conclusions were derived from or compelled by their more general theory; they simply knew an arbitrary exercise of power when they saw one.[91]

There is no reason to believe that "We the people" were any less confused than their congressional representatives about what criteria, "beyond obviously defective racial criteria," would be impermissible under the privileges or immunities norm that was in the process of being established in their name. There is no reason to believe, that is, that they were any less confused than their representatives about precisely what norm was being established. The best we can do, given that confusion, is try to articulate the norm that best captures what "We the people" and their representatives seem to have been getting at. Put another way, the best we can do is try to construct the norm that best reflects what "We the people" and their representatives were seeking to achieve in making the privileges or immunities provision a part of the Constitution. The norm that best captures what they seem to have been getting at—that best reflects what they were seeking to achieve—is, in my view, a tripartite norm.

First. Clearly, they meant to ban more discrimination than just racist (or, more broadly, race-based) discrimination. No less clearly, they did not mean to ban all discrimination (in the allocation of protected privileges and immunities). What discrimination—what discriminatory laws—did they ban? It captures at least a part of what they were getting at—indeed, the central part—to say that they banned any discriminatory law based on the view that those against whom the discrimination operates are "innately" or "inherently" or "by nature" degraded or defective human beings, if human beings at all. Recall that at the foundation of the slaveholder's ideology was the conviction that the slaves were not true or full human beings, just as at the foundation of Nazi ideology was the conviction that Jews were not true or full human beings but only pseudo-humans.[92] There are countless other examples, because unfortunately such thinking is quite common across both space and time. For example, in India there is even today a "'tenacious and widespread' belief in the inherent inferiority of lower castes and untouchables . . ."[93] Richard Rorty has written about another contemporary example: "Serbian murderers and rapists do not think of themselves as violating human rights. For they are not doing these things to fellow human beings, but to *Muslims*. They are not being inhuman, but rather are discriminating between the true humans and the pseudohumans. The Serbs take themselves to be acting in the interests of true humanity by purifying the world of pseudo-humanity."[94] Rorty then observes: "[The Serbs] are making the same sort of distinction as the Crusaders made between the humans and the infidel dogs, and the Black Muslims make between humans and blue-eyed devils. [Thomas Jefferson] was able both to own slaves and to think it self-evident that all men are endowed by their creator with certain inalienable rights. He had convinced himself that the consciousness of Blacks, like that of animals, 'participates more of sensation than reflection.' Like the Serbs, Mr. Jefferson did not think of himself as violating *human* rights."[95]

Second. Recall not only the Northern whites who migrated to the former Confederate states after the Civil War, but also the Southern whites who were against secession and remained loyal to the Union, many of whom even fought on the Union side in the Civil War. It captures another, complementary part of what "We the people", through their representatives, were getting at to say that they banned any discriminatory law based on disapproval of and hostility toward a constitutionally protected choice, like the choice of a Southern white during the Civil War to remain loyal to the Union.

Third. Finally, there is ample evidence in the historical record that they were pervasively concerned about, and meant to forbid, "arbitrary" as distinct from "reasonable" exercises by a state of its "police power". (Predictably and understandably, they were not always clear about which was which; and there is no reason to think that if they had been presented with a series of hypothetical cases, they would always have been in full agreement with one another about which was which.) In particular, Republican proponents of the Fourteenth Amendment explained that although section one was not meant to prevent the states from regulating protected privileges or immunities, states could do so only "for the public good in a reasonable fashion."[96] It therefore captures a remaining part—and the most general part—of what they were getting at to say that they banned arbitrary or unreasonable discrimination, in this sense: discrimination—differential treatment—not reasonably designed to accomplish a legitimate governmental purpose. As the Supreme Court put the point at the end of the nineteenth century: "[E]very exercise of the police power must be reasonable, and extend only to such laws as are enacted in good faith for the promotion of the public good, and not for the annoyance or oppression of a particular class."[97]

In my judgment, then, the fundamental antidiscrimination norm that best reflects and meets the various concerns that inspired "We the people", in the person of their representatives, to make the second sentence of section one of the Fourteenth Amendment a part of the Constitution— the articulation of the norm that best captures the fundamental point or trajectory of "We the people"'s antidiscrimination project—is complex:

> No state may make or enforce any law that denies to some of its citizens, or otherwise lessens or diminishes their enjoyment of, any protected privilege or immunity enjoyed by other of its citizens, if the differential treatment
>
> (1) is based on a view to the effect that the disfavored citizens are not truly or fully human—that they are, at best, defective, even debased or degraded, human beings; or
>
> (2) is based on hostility to one or more constitutionally protected choices; or, finally,
>
> (3) is otherwise not reasonably designed to accomplish a legitimate governmental purpose.

(As I noted earlier, Melissa Saunders argues that what I have presented here as part (3) was widely understood to be the principal meaning of the equal protection language: differential treatment by a state of persons within its jurisdiction—in Saunders parlance, "'partial' or 'special' laws"—must be designed to accomplish a legitimate governmental purpose. As Saunders puts it, the equal protection norm forbids "the state to single out any person or group of persons for special benefits or burdens without an adequate 'public purpose' justification."[98] As I said earlier in this chapter, little if anything of practical importance depends on whether the norm—no differential treatment that is not designed to accomplish a legitimate governmental purpose—is a part of the original understanding of the equal protection language of the Fourteenth Amendment or, instead, a part of the original understanding of the privileges or immunities language (or, indeed, a part of the original understanding of both texts). In either case, the norm is a part of the original understanding of the second sentence of section one of the Fourteenth Amendment.)

I have difficulty discerning a more plausible articulation—a more plausible representation or construction—of what "theory about when discrimination is appropriate and when it is not"[99] they were groping towards. But perhaps that's due to some dearth of imagination—or of judgment—on my part. If you, dear reader, believe that there is a more plausible articulation, please identify it.[100] As it happens, the Supreme Court enforces, albeit in the name of "equal protection",[101] a norm substantially identical to the one I have articulated here.[102]

Note that parts (1) and (2) of the articulated norm are specifications, they are particular instantiations, of the most general part, part (3): A state law does not "regulate for the public good in a reasonable fashion"—it is not "reasonably" designed to accomplish a legitimate governmental purpose—if it is based either (1) on a view to the effect that the disfavored citizens are not truly or fully human or (2) on hostility to one or more constitutionally protected choices. Assume, however, that a state law is based neither on a view to the effect that the disfavored citizens are not truly or fully human nor on hostility to one or more constitutionally protected choices. When does such a law fail to regulate for the public good in a reasonable fashion; when does it fail to be reasonably designed to accomplish a legitimate governmental purpose? I pick up that question in chapter 6;[103] for now, I want to address only a particular instance of the question.

The Fourteenth Amendment and the Bill of Rights

The particular instance I want to address here concerns the important issue of the applicability of (some of) the Bill of Rights to the states under the Fourteenth Amendment:[104] Should any state law regulating a protected privilege or immunity be deemed to regulate "for the public good in a reasonable fashion" *if the law, were it a national law, would violate a privilege or an immunity of citizens—a "freedom to" or a "freedom from" of citizens—protected by the Bill of Rights?* Consider, for example, a law forbidding every person to disseminate any publication criticizing the Black Codes, racial segregation, or antimiscegenation policy. Such a law, if enacted by the national government, would violate the First Amendment's ban on laws abridging the freedom of the press. Consider, too, a law forbidding every person to teach Americans of African ancestry to read the Bible. Such a law, if enacted by the national government, would violate not only the First Amendment's ban on laws abridging the freedoms of speech and of the press but also its ban on laws abridging the free exercise of religion.

Notice that both laws in the preceding paragraph apply not just to some persons, but to every person; they govern the behavior not just of some persons, but of *every* person *without regard to race, sex, etc.* It bears emphasis here, therefore, that laws that treat some persons differently from others on the basis of a trait, like race or sex, are not the only laws that entail differential treatment. Indeed, every law entails differential treatment. Thus, no law is immune to challenge on the basis of part (3) of the norm I have articulated above. Imagine a law that requires every person to wear a protective helmet when riding on a motorcycle and subjects any person who fails to do so to a fine and/or punishment. Even though the law applies not just to some persons (e.g., women) but to every person, the law treats some persons differently from others. It does so on the basis, not of a trait, like sex, but of an act: the act of wearing a protective helmet when riding on a motorcycle. Just as some laws treat some persons differently from others depending on whether or not, for example, they are women, the motorcycle law treats some persons differently from others depending on whether they have worn a protective helmet when riding on a motorcycle. Those who obey the requirement to wear a protective helmet are treated differently from those who disobey; they are treated better, they are left alone. Pursuant to part (3) of the antidiscrimination norm articulated above, we can inquire: Is a law punishing the act of not wearing a protective helmet when riding on a motorcycle, while leaving alone those who do wear a protective helmet, a regulation "for the public good in a reasonable fashion"? Is the law—the differential treatment—"reasonably" designed to achieve a legitimate governmental purpose? Similarly, is a law punishing the act of disseminating a publication criticizing the Black Codes (etc.), while leaving alone those who do not do so, including those who disseminate a publication defending the Black Codes, a regulation for the public good in a reasonable fashion? Is a law punishing the act of teaching the recently freed slaves to read the Bible (while leaving alone those who do not do so) a regulation "for the public good in a reasonable fashion"?

According to Michael Kent Curtis and Akhil Amar, the privileges or immunities provision was understood to protect against state law (whatever else it was understood to protect against the states) all the rights (freedoms) of citizens that are protected against national law by the Bill of Rights (e.g., the freedom of speech);[105] moreover, it was understood to protect them (against the states) from the same range of laws from which they are protected (against the national government) by the Bill of Rights.[106] If Curtis and Amar (and others[107]) are right, then, insofar as the original understanding of the privileges or immunities provision is concerned, the answer to the question I posed two paragraphs back is this: No state law regulates "for the public good in a reasonable fashion"—no state law is "reasonably" designed to accomplish a legitimate governmental purpose—if the law, were it a national law, would violate a right of citizens protected by the Bill of Rights.

Put another way: If Curtis and Amar are right, then we may say that "We the people", through their representatives, constitutionalized not only the general requirement that no state regulate a protected privilege or immunity except "for the public good in a reasonable fashion", but also a particular understanding, a particular specification, of the requirement: that no state law that, were it a national law, would violate a right of citizens protected by the Bill of Rights is a regulation "for the public good in a reasonable fashion". Recall our third question about the privileges or immunities provision: "Protected from what?" The privileges or immunities provision was understood (if Curtis and Amar are right) to protect from, among other things, state lawmakers making and enforcing policies that, under the Bill of Rights, national lawmakers may not make or enforce.

The following point bears emphasis, at least to students of the original meaning of the Fourteenth Amendment: Contrary to what participants in debates about the original meaning of the privileges or immunities provision generally assume, one can believe *both* that the privileges or immunities norm established by "We the people" is nothing more than an antidiscrimination norm *and* that the privileges or immunities norm is the instrument that makes Bill-of-Rights rights (e.g., the freedom of speech) applicable to the states—and applicable in the same way they are applicable to the national government. We do not need to resort, therefore, to anything like Akhil Amar's "two-tiered" approach to the privileges or immunities language of the Fourteenth Amendment:

> The language of the privileges or immunities clause can be understood as . . . two-tiered. [John] Harrison's central textual argument is that the word "abridge" can be read to prohibit mere discrimination in the allocation of state-created rights . . . Where only state-law–created rights are at stake, this is a plausible—perhaps the most plausible—reading of the word "abridge." But where rights specified and declared by We the People in Our Constitution are at stake, the best understanding of the word "abridge" in Section One surely comes from its fundamental rights counterpart in the First Amendment, whose language Section One so carefully tracks. . . . Plainly, the Amendment's framers meant to prevent a state from abridging speech critical of the Black Codes, even where the state "evenhandedly" abridges the rights of all speakers, white and black, Southern and Northern.[108]

Amar seems to have in mind that only laws treating persons differently on the basis of traits like white/black, Southern/Northern, entail differential treatment. But, as I have explained, even laws that "evenhandedly" apply to every person without regard to race, sex, etc., entail differential treatment. Contrary to what Amar suggests, a legislative ban on speech critical of the Black Codes, although evenhanded in *some* respects, is *not* evenhanded in *all* respects: Those who condemn the Black Codes are treated differently from—they are treated worse than—those who do not; in particular, they are treated worse than those who praise the Black Codes. Amar's "two-tiered" approach is therefore unnecessary; the one-tiered antidiscrimination approach sketched here reaches even laws, like a ban on speech critical of the Black Codes, that "evenhandedly" apply to every person.[109]

Though powerful, the argument that the Fourteenth Amendment was understood and meant to protect against state law the rights of citizens protected against national law by the Bill of Rights, and to protect them in substantially the same way they are protected by the Bill of Rights, remains controversial.[110] However, the controversy ought not to obscure the fact that even if Curtis' and Amar's historical claims were tomorrow thoroughly discredited, it would nonetheless remain constitutional bedrock for us the people of the United States now living, as I indicated in chapter 2, that the rights of citizens (or, at least, the most important of them) that are protected against national law by the Bill of Rights are protected against state law by the Fourteenth Amendment, and protected from the same range of laws from which they are protected (against the national government) by the Bill of Rights. The Supreme Court would not dream of trying to alter that state of affairs.

Nor, indeed, should the Court try to alter it, even if the Court were tomorrow to become persuaded that that state of affairs is not warranted by any constitutional norm established by "We the people". Consider the claim that the privileges or immunities provision was not understood to protect against state law—and that therefore the privileges or immunities norm established by "We the people" does not protect against state law—any of the privileges or immunities protected against national laws by the Bill of Rights. That claim, even if not demonstrably false, is by no reasonable standard of historical judgment more likely accurate than the competing claim for which Curtis, Amar, and others have contended. The question arises, then, what nonhistorical reasons might influence the Court to incline in favor of the former claim rather than in favor of the latter? The political-moral reasons for inclining in favor of the former claim are less than obvious: Is it better, as a matter of political morality, that state laws *not* be subject to the norms regarding religious liberty, for example, or to those regarding the freedoms of speech and of the press, to which national laws are subject under the First Amendment? One might be tempted to think that if state lawmaking is to be subject to such limitations, it is better that it be subject to them not under the national Constitution, but only under the state's own constitution. Charles Black, in his inimitably elegant way, has made the decisive objection to that position: "[W]ithout such a corpus of national human rights law good against the States, we ought to stop saying, 'One nation indivisible, with liberty and justice for all,' and speak instead of, 'One nation divisible and divided into fifty zones of political morality, with liberty and justice in such kind and measure as these good things may from time to time be granted by each of these fifty political subdivisions.'"[111]

IV

It is now time to summarize. What norms did the generation of "We the people" that made the second sentence of section one of the Fourteenth Amendment a part of the text of the Constitution establish in doing so? That is, what norms did they understand, or probably understand—or, what norms would they (probably) have understood—the second sentence to communicate?

"No State shall . . . deprive any person of life, liberty, or property, without due process of law . . ." In making this language a part of the Constitution, "We the people" established a norm forbidding state actors to damage or destroy a person's life, liberty, or property extrajudicially or otherwise "outside the law". Under the due process norm established by "We the people", state actors may deprive a person of life, liberty, or property, if at all, only pursuant to "due process of law", which, whatever else it might have been understood to refer to, was understood to refer to the process of law (in the words of the 1866 Civil Rights Act, to the "laws and proceedings for the security of person and property") that, under state law, is due ordinary citizens and others.

"No State shall . . . deny to any person within its jurisdiction the equal protection of the laws." In making this language a part of the Constitution, "We the people" established a norm requiring state actors to give to every person within the state's jurisdiction the very same protection ("equal protection") that, under state law, is due ordinary citizens and others—the same protection "of the laws". What laws? At a minimum, laws designed to protect life, liberty, or property—in the words of the 1866 Civil Rights Act, "laws and proceedings for the security of person and property". Relatedly, the equal protection norm they established also forbids states to make or enforce protective laws that are themselves racially or otherwise invidiously discriminatory.

"No State shall make or enforce any law which shall abridge the privileges or immunities of citizens of the United States . . ." In making this language a part of the Constitution, "We the people" understood themselves to be protecting not all persons, but only citizens, and they understood themselves to be protecting citizens not only with respect to all the privileges and immunities that citizens enjoy under the law, including the Constitution, of the United States, but also with respect to all the (nonpolitical) privileges and all the immunities that citizens, or some citizens, enjoy under the law of the state in which they reside—that is, with respect to all the (nonpolitical) rights that states distribute to their citizens. From what did they understand the protected privileges and immunities to be protected? I have suggested that the privileges or immunities norm established by "We the people" protects the protected privileges and immunities against, most generally, any state law that does not regulate "for the public good in a reasonable fashion"—that is not "reasonably" designed to accomplish a le-

gitimate governmental purpose. In particular, the norm forbids enactment or enforcement of any racist state law or other state law based on the
view that the disfavored citizens are not truly or fully human—that they
are, at best, defective, debased, or degraded human beings. In the United
States, after the Civil War and ratification of the Fourteenth Amendment,
no state law based on the view that the disfavored citizens are not truly or
fully human may be deemed to regulate for the public good in a reasonable fashion.

V

I explained at the beginning of this chapter the point of pursuing the historical inquiry that has engaged us here: The constitutional conflicts I examine in the remaining chapters of this book have each been resolved—
at least in part, and at least for a time—on the basis of a claim about what
the Fourteenth Amendment forbids; one cannot fully address the question which of those conflicts, if any, have been resolved on the basis of the
Fourteenth Amendment as they should have been resolved, without first
trying to ascertain what norms "We the people" established in adding the
text of the Fourteenth Amendment—in particular, the second sentence of
section one—to the text of the Constitution of the United States. As my
discussion in this chapter illustrates, however, there is an enduring and
(because enduring) unnerving dissensus among students of the history of
the Fourteenth Amendment about precisely what norms "We the people"
(through their representatives) established in adding section one to the
constitutional text.

Undeniably, the inquiry is difficult; indeed, one may fairly wonder
whether the inquiry isn't largely futile. In reviewing William Nelson's *The
Fourteenth Amendment: From Political Principle to Judicial Doctrine*, Judith
Baer wrote: "To say that we fourteenth amendment mavens disagree
among ourselves about the framers' meaning is a considerable understatement. The extremes of opinion are represented on the right by Raoul
Berger's insistence that section 1 of the amendment had only the 'clearly
understood and narrow' purpose of putting the Civil Rights Act of 1866
beyond the reach of presidential veto; and on the left by those of us who
assert that 'the amendment both applies the Bill of Rights to the states and
guarantees equality together with other unspecified rights.'"[112] Baer concluded her review by observing that "[l]ooking for a balanced, moderate
interpretation of the fourteenth amendment, Nelson finds it. It is there to
be found among the rich, copious records, just as the broad and narrow
readings are there to be found."[113] John Harrison has sounded a similar
note: "Although both groups produce a great many words, students of the
Fourteenth Amendment are at a disadvantage compared to the infinitely
large collection of monkeys who set out to produce *Hamlet* by typing ran-

dom keystrokes. The monkeys are bound to produce their tragedy. But
. . . Fourteenth Amendment scholars are unlikely to come up with a
canonical account of . . . the original meaning of the amendment . . ."[114]

In light of Baer's and Harrison's salutary warnings about the difficulty
of the inquiry, let's assume, for the sake of argument, that I am just one
more sadly mistaken student of the history of the Fourteenth Amendment;[115] at least, let's assume that the effort to ascertain what Fourteenth
Amendment norms were established *is* largely futile. What practical implications follow for my arguments in the remaining chapters of this
book?[116] The answer: few, if any. The reason for this perhaps startling
reply is this: Whatever narrow antidiscrimination norm "We the people"
established, in adding section one of the Fourteenth Amendment to the
constitutional text—and, indeed, even if they had established *no* antidiscrimination norm—the following broad antidiscrimination norm, which
is the norm most relevant to and supportive of my arguments in the remaining chapters, has nonetheless become constitutional bedrock for
us:[117]

> Government may not treat any person or group of persons less well than
> another person or group, if the differential treatment is based on a view
> to the effect that the disfavored persons are not truly or fully human—
> that they are, at best, defective, even debased or degraded, human be-
> ings—or if the differential treatment is otherwise arbitrary, in the sense
> of not reasonably designed to accomplish a legitimate governmental pur-
> pose.

Note that this antidiscrimination norm is broader in two distinct ways
than any antidiscrimination norm "We the people" established when,
through their representatives, they added section one of the Fourteenth
Amendment to the constitutional text. First, the norm governs every instance of differential treatment, and not just those instances that touch,
that diminish or deny, a privilege or an immunity that is a member of a
limited set of privileges and immunities—the set, for example, of *nonpolitical* privileges and immunities. Second, the norm, as I explain in the
next chapter, applies to government generally, including the national government, and not just to state government.

The broad antidiscrimination norm articulated in the preceding paragraph became a part of our constitutional bedrock in the period after
World War II, because, in that post-Holocaustal period, the true and full
humanity of *every* person (including, therefore, *every* citizen) emerged as
a fundamental axiom of American political morality. No law (or other governmental action) that violated this axiom—no law based on the view that
a black person, for example, or a Jew, or a woman, is not truly, fully
human—could any longer be adjudged consistent with "the supreme
Law of the Land". (Of course, there could be, and was, disagreement
about whether one or another law was based on such a view.)

As I have explained in my book *The Idea of Human Rights*, the first part of the idea of human rights—an idea to which we, as a people, are now deeply committed—is the proposition that each and every person (black as well as white, Jew as well as Christian, woman as well as man, and so on) is truly, fully human.[118] This proposition is variously expressed: Every human being is "sacred", is "inviolable", has "infinite worth and dignity", has "equal moral worth", and so on. The proposition that all human beings are sacred (inviolable, etc.) is, for many persons, a religiously based tenet. However, many persons who are not religious believers embrace the proposition as a fundamental principle of morality. The proposition is an axiom of many secular moralities as well as a fundamental principle, in one or another version, of many religious moralities. (As Ronald Dworkin has observed: "We almost all accept . . . that human life in all its forms is *sacred*. . . . For some of us, this is a matter of religious faith; for others, of secular but deep philosophical belief."[119]) Indeed, the proposition that every human being is sacred is axiomatic for so many secular moralities that many secular moral philosophers have come to speak of "the moral point of view" as the view according to which "every person [has] some sort of equal status".[120] Bernard Williams has noted that "it is often thought that no concern is truly moral unless it is marked by this universality. For morality, the ethical constituency is always the same: the universal constituency. An allegiance to a smaller group, the loyalties to family or country, would have to be justified from the outside inward, by an argument that explained how it was a good thing that people should have allegiances that were less than universal."[121]

Recall, from chapter 2, the textualist sensibility of American constitutional culture.[122] It ought not to be surprising, given this sensibility, that, whatever narrow antidiscrimination norm was established by the generation of "We the people" that bequeathed us the Fourteenth Amendment, the Supreme Court came to refer the broad antidiscrimination norm articulated above (as the norm applies to *state* government) to section one of the Fourteenth Amendment. The language of section one can bear that meaning; it can bear the weight of the broad antidiscrimination norm. Moreover, the history of the Fourteenth Amendment makes it clear that section one was at least partly an antidiscrimination provision—that whatever else section one was meant to do, it was meant to achieve and protect, against the states, a fuller measure of equality for a particular group of Americans, a group that had long been regarded and treated as less than truly, fully human.

So: Even if I *am* just one more mistaken student of the history of the Fourteenth Amendment—or, even if the effort to ascertain what Fourteenth Amendment norms were established *is* largely futile—this much is clear: The broad antidiscrimination norm articulated above is now a part of our fundamental law; it is now constitutional bedrock for us. In inquiring whether the constitutional conflicts I examine in the remaining chapters of this book—the conflicts over racial segregation, race-based affirmative action, sex-based discrimination, homosexuality, abortion, and physician-assisted suicide—have been resolved as they should have been resolved, let us remember that if a judicial resolution of a constitutional conflict is mandated by the antidiscrimination norm articulated above, then in no plausible sense of the "judicial usurpation" claim can that resolution be said to be a judicial usurpation of our politics. As I explained in chapter 1, the serious charge of judicial usurpation is that the judiciary has imposed on our politics a norm that not only was never established as a part of the Constitution by "We the people", *but that, moreover, is not constitutional bedrock for us, the people of the United States now living.*

*   *   *

Afterthought: A Thought Experiment

Assume, for the sake of argument, that the following premise was not established by, and is not warranted by any constitutional norm that was established by, "We the people": No state may allocate *any* privilege or immunity among its citizens—giving it to some, denying it to others—on a racist basis. That a state may not allocate any privilege or immunity among its citizens on a racist basis is one of those premises that, even if not warranted by any norm established by "We the people", the Supreme Court neither would nor should overturn: The premise is, for us the people of the United States now living, constitutional bedrock. But let's travel back to a time *before* the premise became constitutional bedrock—indeed, to a time *before* the premise was even accepted into the constitutional law of the United States; and, for the sake of argument, let's assume that those scholars are right who claim that the privileges or immunities norm established by "We the people" protects only *some* privileges and immunities, namely, those that were believed at the time the Fourteenth Amendment was proposed and ratified to be the "fundamental" rights of citizens.

- Now, imagine that you are a justice of the Supreme Court of the United States at some time after two moral premises, P1 and P2, have been accepted into the constitutional law of the United States. P1 holds that it is morally wrong for government to allocate certain privileges and immunities among its citizens on a racist basis: those believed at the time the Fourteenth Amendment was proposed and ratified to be "fundamental" rights. According to the assumption we are making here, "We the people" accepted P1 into the constitutional law of the United States in making the privileges or immunities norm of the Fourteenth Amendment a part of the Constitution. P2 holds that it is morally wrong for government to allocate a certain privilege among its citizens on a racist basis, namely, the right to vote. (P1 and P2 are, fundamentally, and whatever else they are, *moral* premises.) "We the people" accepted P2 into the constitutional law of the United States in adopting the Fifteenth Amendment, section one of which declares: "The right of citizens of the United States to vote shall not be denied or abridged by the United States or by any State on account of race, color, or previous condition of servitude."

- Imagine further that you and your colleagues on the Court are faced with the opportunity, in a case or series of cases, to accept into the constitutional law of the United States the further moral premise (P3) that it is wrong for government to allocate *any* privilege or immunity—any benefit or burden—among its citizens on a racist basis.
- Imagine finally that you doubt that P3 was ever established by "We the people". (Pursuant to the assumption we are making here, "We the people" did not establish P3 in making the privileges or immunities provision a part of the Constitution.)

Would it be morally wrong for you, in conjunction with your colleagues, to take the step of accepting P3 into the constitutional law of the United States?[123]

It is relevant, is it not, that, *given that P1 and P2 have already been accepted into—given that they are already a bedrock part of—the constitutional law of the United States,* accepting P3 into the constitutional law of the United States would be a relatively marginal step? It is true that such judicial action, even though relatively marginal, would go beyond any constitutional norm established by "We the people". (At least, that is our assumption here.) It is also true that such judicial action, even though relatively marginal, might not be supported by a majority of "We the people". But neither of those two data entails that the action would be morally wrong. Note that P3 represents a fundamental human right. Although that datum does not entail that your accepting P3 into the constitutional law of the United States would be morally right, it is relevant, is it not?

Suppose that, because P3 was widely acknowledged to represent a fundamental human right, P3 became—and that you had good reason to expect that it would become—constitutional bedrock soon after you and your colleagues accepted it into the constitutional law of the United States. Suppose further that it is now widely agreed—and that you had good reason to expect that it would be widely agreed—that the moral legitimacy of American government and the moral quality of various governmental policies and acts were significantly enhanced in virtue of P3 having become a part of the constitutional law of the United States. Why might one want to claim that *nonetheless* it was morally wrong for you (and your colleagues) to accept P3 into the constitutional law of the United States? On the basis of a rule according to which judges may not accept into the constitutional law of the United States moral premises they believe not to be warranted by any constitutional norm established by "We the people"? Even if such a rule is a constituent of American political-moral culture, it is far from obvious that as a constituent of American political-moral culture, the rule is absolute or unconditional rather than merely presumptive. If the rule is presumptive, not unconditional, why wasn't the presumption overcome in the case of P3? And if not in the case of P3, in what imaginable case *would* the presumption be overcome?

True, Supreme Court justices take an "Oath . . . to support this Constitution". (As do many other public officials. Article VI directs that "[t]he Senators and Representatives before mentioned, and the members of the several State Legislatures, and all executive and judicial officers, both of the United States and of the several States, shall be bound by Oath or Affirmation, to support this Constitution . . .") Putting aside the question what "this Constitution" means, however, promise-keeping is not generally thought to be, any more than truth-telling, one's highest moral duty in each and every situation in which one might find oneself. One cannot rule out the possibility of truly extraordinary circumstances in which the Court would act appropriately, even admirably, were it to pretend that there is a traditional legal foundation, in the form of a constitutional norm established by "We the people", for a constitutional decision or rule *even when it doubts that there is any*. The question of the morality of such judicial action would be far from simple in circumstances where, for example, the very political survival of the nation—or, for many persons, the fundamental moral legitimacy of government—was at stake.[124] Indeed, the question of the moral legitimacy of such judicial action would be far from simple even in some less dramatic circumstances.[125]

In any event, my "what if" inquiry is merely academic. First, P3 is warranted by a conjunction of two constitutional norms established by "We the people": the privileges or immunities norm established by "We the people" protects, against racist discrimination, all the nonpolitical privileges and all the immunities—it protects all the nonpolitical rights—that citizens, or some citizens, are due under the law of the state in which they reside; and the Fifteenth Amendment protects, against racist discrimination, the right to vote and, inferentially, other political rights, like the right to be a candidate for public office. Second, whether or not warranted by any constitutional norm (or norms) established by "We the people"—and, so, even if *not* warranted by any such norm—P3 is, for us the people of the United States now living, constitutional bedrock; the Court neither would nor should overturn it.

4

The Fourteenth Amendment and Race: Segregation and Affirmative Action

The most important initiative undertaken by the Supreme Court of the United States in the period since the end of World War II was its effort, most famously in the seminal case of *Brown v. Board of Education* (1954),[1] to abolish governmental racism: racist laws and other kinds of racist governmental action, including policies aimed at creating and/or maintaining racial segregation. (Charles Black described *Brown* as "the decision that opened our era of judicial activity."[2]) Was the Supreme Court's effort to abolish governmental racism justified by any constitutional norm (or norms) established by "We the people of the United States"? If some aspects of constitutional doctrine forbidding governmental racism are not justified by any such norm, are they justified nonetheless—that is, justified as *constitutional* doctrine—on some other basis? Or was the Court's effort to abolish governmental racism an instance of "the judicial usurpation of politics"?

One of the most controversial initiatives undertaken by the Supreme Court in the contemporary period is its effort to restrict the extent to which government may rely on policies of race-based "affirmative action": policies that, to ameliorate the present effects of past racist acts and/or for some other, nonracist reason (e.g., to increase the racial diversity and hence overall effectiveness of an urban police department), give a preference—in hiring, for example, or in admission to a state university—to members of a racial minority. Is the Court's effort to restrict reliance by government on race-based affirmative action—is the Court's erecting high barriers to such reliance—justified by any constitutional norm established by "We the people of the United States"? If not, is contemporary constitutional doctrine restricting government reliance on affirmative action justified nonetheless—justified as a *constitutional* doctrine—on some other basis? Or is its effort to restrict government reliance on affirmative action an instance of the Court's usurpation of our politics?

To forestall misunderstanding, two clarifications are in order. First, I do not mean to suggest that the Court's effort to abolish governmental racism has been as thoroughgoing as it could have been. Undeniably, the

Court could have done more. (The serious and controverted question is whether, all things considered, it *should* have done more. I have addressed that question elsewhere.[3]) Second, both the Court's effort to abolish governmental racism and its effort to restrict government reliance on affirmative action have been based, not on the (antidiscrimination) norm the Court believes the privileges or immunities provision of the Fourteenth Amendment to represent, but on the norm it believes the equal protection provision to represent. (In the case of the national government, to which the Fourteenth Amendment does not apply, the Court has relied on a norm it believes the due process provision of the Fifth Amendment represents. The Fifth Amendment, unlike the Fourteenth, applies to the national government. I criticize the Court's reading of Fifth Amendment due process later in this chapter.) This is at least partly because an early misreading by the Court of the privileges or immunities provision yielded a privileges or immunities norm that was largely useless.[4] The Court has never had much incentive to correct its misreading, however, because at about the same time the Court misread the privileges or immunities provision, the Court began relying on what is arguably a misreading (i.e., a historically inaccurate reading) of the equal protection provision—albeit a *compensating* misreading: a misreading that yielded an equal protection norm that forbids all those instances of governmental racism that the privileges or immunities provision, accurately read, would have forbidden.[5] Given these misreadings, I should emphasize that my principal concern in this chapter is not whether a constitutional ruling that the Court has referred to one piece of constitutional text should have been referred instead to a different piece. (This is surely an exceedingly minor question where both pieces of the text are, after all, part of one and the same sentence: the second sentence of section one of the Fourteenth Amendment.) Indeed, my principal concern is not even whether a constitutional ruling that the Court has based on one constitutional norm should have been based instead on a different norm. Rather, my principal concern is whether a constitutional ruling, like the Court's ruling in *Brown v. Board of Education* that a state may not create or maintain one set of schools for white students and another set for nonwhite students, is justified on the basis of *any* constitutional norm—in particular, on any constitutional norm established by "We the people". Although a right answer for the right reasons is better than a right answer for the wrong reasons, a right answer for the wrong reasons is still better, if fidelity to the Constitution is our aim, than a wrong answer.[6]

As I reported in chapter 3, Melissa Saunders has mounted an argument that the Court's reading of the equal protection language of the Fourteenth Amendment is, contrary to what I said in the preceding paragraph, historically accurate, not inaccurate.[7] Saunders' historical argument is problematic.[8] But if we assume that Saunders is right, what follows for my argument in this chapter? Little if anything of practical importance depends on whether Saunders is right or I am right about the original meaning of the equal protection provision. Saunders' position and mine converge on this proposition: Whether the equal protection language or, instead, the privileges or immunities language is the textual vehicle by which they did it, "We the people", in adding the second sentence of section one of the Fourteenth Amendment to the constitutional text, established as a part of the Constitution the antidiscrimination norm I refer to below as the privileges or immunities norm.

Moreover, there would be few if any practical implications even if, contrary to what both Saunders and I have argued, "We the people" had established no antidiscrimination norm, because, as I explained in the final section of the preceding chapter, the antidiscrimination norm I believe them to have established is now constitutional bedrock for us even if the generation of "We the people" that bequeathed us the Fourteenth Amendment did not establish it. Indeed, the antidiscrimination norm that is now a part of our constitutional bedrock—the antidiscrimination norm I articulated in the final section of the preceding chapter—is, as I explained in the preceding chapter, broader than any antidiscrimination norm we may plausibly believe "We the people" (through their representatives) to have established when they added section one of the Fourteenth Amendment to the constitutional text.[9]

I. Segregation

Recall, from chapter 3, that whatever else it forbids, the privileges or immunities norm established by "We the people" centrally forbids a state from making or enforcing any law that allocates a privilege (i.e., a "nonpolitical" privilege) or an immunity among its citizens on a racist basis. (In *Loving v. Virginia*, the 1967 case in which it ruled that antimiscegenation laws are unconstitutional, the Supreme Court stated: "The clear and central purpose of the Fourteenth Amendment was to eliminate all official state sources of *invidious* racial discrimination in the States."[10]) Now, consider a typical instance of governmental racism: a state law or other state rule that bestows a privilege on its white citizens (or perhaps on all white persons) but not on its nonwhite citizens (or other nonwhite persons), and that does so at least partly based on the view that the disfavored nonwhites are, *because they are nonwhite*, less worthy or deserving than the favored whites. Consider, too, a state law or other state rule that imposes a burden on its nonwhite citizens (and other nonwhite persons) but not on its white citizens (or other white persons), and that does so at least partly based on the view that disfavored nonwhites are, *as such*, less worthy or deserving. Both laws violate the privileges or immunities norm established by "We the people"; the former law allocates a privilege among the state's citizens on a racist basis, the latter law allocates an immunity—an immunity from the burden imposed by the law—on a racist basis. Therefore, the Supreme Court's invalidation of such laws is undeniably justified—indeed, required—by a norm established by "We the people".

But what about government policies aimed at creating and/or maintaining racial segregation: Is the Court's invalidation of those policies justified by the privileges or immunities norm established by "We the people"? Is it so clear that those policies violate that norm—or, indeed, any constitutional norm? This inquiry arises in part because some members of the generation of "We the people" that established the privileges or immunities norm and the other Fourteenth Amendment norms would not have believed that all such policies—for example, a law forbidding interracial marriage, or a law creating one set of schools for white students and another set for students of African ancestry—were inconsistent with any norm they established. Some scholars have relied on that fact to argue that the Court's decision in *Brown v. Board of Education*, in which the Court ruled that the maintenance by a state (or by a subdivision of the state, like a public school district) of one set of schools for white students and another set for nonwhite students violated the Fourteenth Amendment, was not justified by any Fourteenth Amendment norm established by "We the people".[11] Indeed, Michael McConnell has reported "that in the fractured discipline of constitutional law, there is something very close to a consensus that *Brown* was inconsistent with the original understanding of the Fourteenth Amendment, except perhaps at an extremely high and indeterminate level of abstraction."[12]

That consensus, however—if it any longer survives—is mistaken. For a state to allow a white student who satisfies all the nonracial criteria to attend a school while disallowing a nonwhite student who satisfies all the nonracial criteria to attend the school, and to do so even partly for one or more reasons of the sort for which systems of racial segregation are invariably maintained—that is, for white-supremacist reasons—is for the state to allocate a privilege among its citizens (the privilege of attending the school) on a racist basis.[13] (Not that the legitimacy of the Court's ruling in *Brown* was in doubt for us, the people of the United States now living.[14] The premise that states may not allocate privileges or immunities among their citizens on a racist basis is constitutional bedrock for us, whether or not any constitutional norm established by "We the people" warranted the Supreme Court accepting the premise into the constitutional law of the United States.[15] As I argued in chapter 3, however: Whatever else it forbids, the privileges or immunities norm established by "We the people" forbids every state to allocate privileges or immunities among its citizens on a racist basis.) More broadly, for a state to allow a white person who satisfies all the nonracial criteria to be in a particular place—for example, to occupy an available seat near the front of a bus—while disallowing a nonwhite person who satisfies all the nonracial criteria to occupy such a seat, and to do so even partly for white-supremacist reasons, is for the state to allocate a privilege among its citizens (the privilege of sitting near the front of the bus) on a racist basis. Similarly, for a state to allow a white person who satisfies all the nonracial criteria to enter into a contract with a public carrier to occupy an available seat near the front of a bus while disallowing a nonwhite person who satisfies all the nonracial criteria to enter into such a contract, and to do so even partly for white-supremacist reasons, is for the state to allocate a privilege among its citizens (the privilege of entering into such a contract) on a racist basis. Thus, the Court's notorious ruling, in 1896, in *Plessy v. Ferguson*,[16] that Louisiana did not violate the Fourteenth Amendment by requiring the separation of the races in railway cars, represents a failure—a conspicuous and reprehensible failure, as Justice Harlan emphasized in his prophetic dissent[17]—to protect the Constitution.[18]

Similarly, for a state to allow a white person who satisfies all the nonracial criteria to marry the white person she wants to marry, while disallowing a nonwhite person who satisfies all the nonracial criteria to marry the white person she wants to marry, and to do so even partly on the basis of the white-supremacist ideology that invariably underlies antimiscegenation laws, is for the state to allocate a privilege among its citizens— the privilege of marrying the white person one wants to marry, if one wants to marry a white person—on a racist basis. The analysis is the same if we focus on the fact that an antimiscegenation law allows a nonwhite person who satisfies all the nonracial criteria to marry the nonwhite person she wants to marry, while disallowing a white person who satisfies all the nonracial criteria to marry the nonwhite person she wants to marry; given that focus, however, the privilege being allocated on a racist basis is the privilege of marrying the nonwhite person one wants to marry, if one wants to marry a nonwhite person. Thus, the Supreme Court's decision in *Loving v. Virginia*,[19] striking down antimiscegenation legislation as violative of the Fourteenth Amendment, no less than the Court's decision in *Brown*, was warranted by a constitutional norm established by "We the people".[20]

Michael McConnell has acknowledged that at the time the Fourteenth Amendment was proposed and ratified, "the practice of school segregation was widespread in both Southern and Northern states, as well as in the District of Columbia, . . . and almost certainly enjoyed the support of a majority of the population even at the height of Reconstruction."[21] McConnell goes on to demonstrate, however, "that there was genuine debate and uncertainty about [the constitutionality of school segregation] throughout [the Reconstruction] period."[22] Indeed, McConnell argues that "school segregation was understood during Reconstruction to violate the principles of equality of the Fourteenth Amendment."[23] Even if one concludes that McConnell's argument is overstated,[24] it is simply not true that all the members of the generation of "We the people" that established the privileges or immunities norm of the Fourteenth Amendment would have been surprised to learn that the norm directs a state not to make or enforce a law creating one set of schools for white students and another set for students of African ancestry. Nonetheless, some of them would have been surprised. Why? Suffice it to say that, then as now, one can be mistaken about some of the implications of a norm, including a constitutional norm, to which one professes commitment. Moreover, it might be politically expedient, then as now, to be mistaken about the politically inexpedient implications of a constitutional norm to which one professes commitment.[25] In any event, government policies aimed at creating and/or maintaining racial segregation (e.g., laws that create one set of schools for white students and another set for students of African ancestry) or racial separation (e.g., laws that forbid interracial marriage), no less than other kinds of governmental racism, violate the privileges or immunities norm established by "We the people".[26]

More precisely, racist laws, rules, and policies violate that norm if they are the laws, rules, or policies of a state. If they are the laws, rules, or policies not of a state government, however, but of the national government, they do not violate the Fourteenth Amendment, which by its very terms applies only to *state* action. ("No *state* shall make or enforce any law which shall abridge the privileges or immunities of citizens of the United States; nor shall any *state* deprive any person of life, liberty, or property, without due process of law; nor deny to any person within its jurisdiction the equal protection of the laws" (emphasis added).) According to the Court, racist laws, rules, and policies of the national government violate the due process norm of the Fifth Amendment, which, like the other norms of the first eight amendments ("the Bill of Rights") to the Constitution of the United States, applies to laws and other actions of the national government. Indeed, it is now the Court's view that whatever discrimination violates the Fourteenth Amendment if performed by a state government, violates Fifth Amendment due process if performed by the national government.[27]

After telling the states, in *Brown v. Board of Education*, that the Fourteenth Amendment prohibited them from maintaining one set of schools for white students and another set for students of African ancestry, the Court stated, in the companion case to *Brown*, *Bolling v. Sharpe*: "In view of our decision that the Constitution prohibits the states from maintaining racially segregated public schools, it would be unthinkable that the same Constitution would impose a lesser duty on the Federal Government."[28] (*Bolling* involved racially segregated schools maintained by the District of Columbia, which, as a subdivision of the national government, is not subject to the Fourteenth Amendment.) Although in *Bolling* the Court relied on the Fifth Amendment due process provision in ruling that the Constitution did not "impose a lesser duty on the Federal Government", the Court did not impute an antidiscrimination norm to the Fifth Amendment due process provision just to meet the exigencies of *Bolling*. About ten years earlier, in *Hirabayashi v. United States*[29] and *Korematsu v. United States*,[30] the Court had first relied on an antidiscrimination reading of the Fifth Amendment due process provision to assess the constitutionality of action of the national government discriminating, during World War II, against Americans of Japanese ancestry.[31]

A fundamental problem with the Court's antidiscrimination reading of the Fifth Amendment due process provision is that nothing in the historical record suggests that the due process language of the Fifth Amendment ("No person shall . . . be deprived of life, liberty, or property, without due process of law") was understood to impose an antidiscrimination norm on the national government. The due process norm established the generation of "We the people" responsible for the Fifth Amendment (and for the rest of the Bill of Rights) does not forbid racially discriminatory laws or other discriminatory laws or other governmental action; rather, it simply requires that governmental actors not damage or destroy a person's—*any* person's—life, liberty, or property extrajudicially or otherwise "outside the law". Under the Fifth Amendment due process norm established by "We the people", governmental actors may deprive a person of life, liberty, or property, if at all, only pursuant to "due process of law", which, whatever other process of law they might have understood it to refer to, "We the people" understood to refer to the process of law to which citizens[32] and other persons are entitled under the law of the land. Supreme Court decisions invalidating laws and other acts of the national government on the ground that they are discriminatory (unlike its decisions invalidating acts of the national government on the ground that they deprive a person of life, liberty, or property without the process of law to which the person is entitled) are clearly not justified by the Fifth Amendment due process norm established by "We the people".[33] Are those decisions justified on the basis of any other norm established by "We the people"?

They are justified on the basis of the Ninth Amendment, which states: "The enumeration in the Constitution, of certain rights, shall not be construed to deny or disparage others retained by the people." (The Ninth Amendment, like the other nine amendments of the first ten amendments to the Constitution, is concerned with limits on the power of the national government.) Assuming a commitment by the Supreme Court to act modestly in the exercise of the awesome power of judicial review, how ought the Court to determine what other (i.e., unenumerated) constitutional rights against the national government are "retained by the people"? An appropriately modest strategy, in my view, is for the Court to say that

- if an established constitutional norm *already* protects a right against state government,
- and if, because the right is a human right (or at least is widely recognized to be such), it cannot reasonably be maintained that the right ought to be protected *only* against state government,
- then the right is one of those "other" rights against the national government that, *pace* the Ninth Amendment, are "retained by the people."

This is a very modest judicial strategy for determining what other constitutional rights against the national government are retained by the people. Indeed, it is hard to think of how the Court could act more modestly *short of simply abdicating altogether any responsibility for determining what other constitutional rights against the national government are retained by the people.* According to this strategy, a judge may not conclude that a right against the national government is retained by the people unless, first, the right is *already* protected against state government by an established constitutional norm and, second, the right is, or at least is widely recognized to be, a human right, such that it cannot reasonably be maintained that the right ought to be protected *only* against state government. There would probably be at most only a few occasions on which this strategy for identifying rights retained by the people could in good faith be used to challenge, much less invalidate, action of the national government. (This should make people happy who are wary about multiplying the occasions of judicial review.) But, surely, *Bolling v. Sharpe* was one such occasion. If, as the Court stated in *Bolling*, "it would be unthinkable that the same Constitution would impose a lesser duty on the Federal Government", the Ninth Amendment was (and remains) a much more plausible textual basis for rejecting the "unthinkable" than was the due process language of the Fifth Amendment.[34]

What if it were the case, however, that no constitutional norm—neither the Fifth Amendment due process norm nor any other norm—established by "We the people", including the Ninth Amendment, warranted the premise that the same prohibition on discrimination that applies to state government under the Fourteenth Amendment also applies to the national government? I am arguing here that, as it happens, it is *not* the case that no norm established by "We the people" warrants the premise. The Ninth Amendment supports the premise that the same prohibition on discrimination that applies to state government under the Fourteenth Amendment (whatever the precise content of that prohibition might be) also applies to the national government; it applies to the national government under the Ninth Amendment. But what if one disagrees (as some do) with the reading of the Ninth Amendment on which I am here relying—a reading according to which the Ninth Amendment term "rights" was understood by "We the people" to mean, whatever else it might have been understood by them to mean, substantially what we today understand the term to mean?[35]

I suggested, in chapter 2, that even if no norm established by "We the people" warranted the premise in question, the premise would nonetheless be constitutional bedrock for us the people of the United States now living. The Supreme Court would not overturn the premise—nor should it, even if the Court were to awake tomorrow morning gripped by the conviction that neither the Fifth Amendment due process norm nor any other constitutional norm established by "We the people" warranted the premise. In particular, now that "We the people", by making the Fourteenth and Fifteenth Amendments a part of the Constitution, have admitted into the constitutional law of the United States the moral proposition (for it surely is, whatever else it is, a *moral* proposition) that it is wrong for state government to discriminate against any of its citizens on a racist basis, there would be no good reason for the Court to exclude from the constitutional law of the United States the further but connected moral proposition that it is wrong for *the national government, too,* to discriminate against any of its citizens on a racist basis. As the Universal Declaration on Human Rights and many other international human rights documents affirm, the fundamental immorality of government discriminating against any of its citizens on a racist or any similar (e.g., sexist) basis does not depend on the level of government doing the discriminating. The case for the Supreme Court overturning the premise that is now constitutional bedrock for us—the premise that the same prohibition on discrimination that applies to state government under the Fourteenth Amendment also applies to the national government—would be far from obvious. Isn't the constitutional law of the United States better than it would otherwise be—*morally* better—in virtue of including that premise? Who would argue that if neither the Fifth Amendment due process norm nor any other norm established by "We the people" warranted the premise, the Court should now, at this late date, overturn the premise, that it should now evict the premise from the constitutional law of the United States? Indeed, one might want to adapt my "what if" inquiry from the preceding chapter[36] to suggest that it would not have been morally wrong for Supreme Court justices to accept the premise into the constitutional law of the United States even if they had doubted that any constitutional norm established by "We the people" warranted their doing so.[37]

In any event, my argument here is that a historically accurate reading of the Ninth Amendment,[38] mediated by the modest judicial strategy I have outlined, supports applying to the national government the same prohibition on discrimination that applies to state government; it supports subjecting the national government to the same antidiscrimination norm to which state government is subject under the Fourteenth Amendment.[39]

The Supreme Court's effort to abolish governmental racism, including its effort to abolish policies aimed at creating and/or maintaining racial segregation, was justified by constitutional norms established by "We the people of the United States". That effort, therefore, was not a judicial usurpation of our politics, on any plausible understanding of the "usurpation" claim. To the contrary, because the Court's effort was required by constitutional norms established by "We the people", it would have been an illegitimate judicial capitulation to our prejudices had the Court failed to do what it could to abolish governmental racism.

Assume, however, that I am wrong; assume that the Court's effort to abolish governmental racism was not justified by any constitutional norm established by "We the people". The Court's effort was nonetheless justified by t... ...ation norm—the broad norm I articulated in the final sec... ...ding chapter, which applies to government generally, a... ...te government—that in the post–World War II period h... ...rt of our constitutional bedrock. In no plausible sense of ... ...rpation" claim, therefore, can the Court's effort be said t... ...udicial usurpation of our politics. The serious charge o... ...tion, as I explained in chapter 1, is that the judiciary has ... ...r politics a norm that not only was never established as ... ...nstitution by "We the people", but that, moreover, is n... ...bedrock for us, the people of the United States now livin...

Now l... ...uestion whether the Court's effort to restrict government ... ...native action—its erecting high barriers to such reliance—... ...ny norm established by "We the people", or by any norm ... ...me a part of our constitutional bedrock, or whether, instead, that effort is fairly judged to be a "judicial usurpation of politics".

II. Affirmative Action

For government to rely on policies of race-based "affirmative action" is for it to rely on policies that, to ameliorate the present effects of past racist acts and/or for some other, nonracist reason (e.g., to increase the racial diversity and hence overall effectiveness of an urban police department), give a preference—in hiring, for example, or in admission to a state university—to members of a racial minority.[40] Such affirmative action is a deeply divisive issue in the United States. "Proponents regard the continuation of affirmative action as a litmus test of our nation's commitment to racial justice. Opponents see it as an unacceptable violation of the ideal of equality of opportunity, and the principle that government should treat its citizens in a color-blind fashion."[41] There is a large literature addressing the question whether reliance on affirmative action, including (indeed, especially) reliance by government, is *morally* permissible.[42] The different question I want to address here is whether government reliance on race-based affirmative action is *constitutionally* permissible.[43]

Recall, again, that whatever else it forbids, the privileges or immunities norm established by "We the people" centrally forbids a state from making or enforcing any law that allocates a (nonpolitical) privilege or an immunity among its citizens on a racist basis. Recall, more generally, the complex antidiscrimination norm that best reflects and meets the various concerns that inspired "We the people", in the person of their representatives, to make the second sentence of section one of the Fourteenth Amendment a part of the Constitution.[44] As I articulated the norm in the preceding chapter:

No state may make or enforce any law that denies to some of its citizens, or otherwise lessens or diminishes their enjoyment of, any protected privilege or immunity enjoyed by other of its citizens, if the differential treatment

(1) is based on a view to the effect that the disfavored citizens are not truly or fully human—that they are, at best, defective, even debased or degraded, human beings; or

(2) is based on hostility to one or more constitutionally protected choices; or, finally,

(3) is otherwise not reasonably designed to accomplish a legitimate governmental purpose.

Recall, finally, that the national government, too, no less than a state government, is constitutionally forbidden to allocate privileges or immunities on a racist basis—or, more broadly, to engage in any discrimination that, under the Fourteenth Amendment, no state may engage in.

In relying on (policies of) affirmative action, does government allocate a privilege among its citizens on a racist basis—or on any other basis that violates part (1) of the norm articulated in the preceding paragraph (or that violates the kindred, broader norm that became a part of our constitutional bedrock in the period after World War II)? That is, does government give the privilege to some and deny it to others, because, or partly because, those to whom the privilege is denied are believed to be, because of their race or for any other reason, inferior human beings—that is, defective, even debased or degraded human beings—and therefore less worthy or deserving than they would otherwise be? Or, does government give the privilege to some and deny it to others, because, or partly because, those to whom the privilege is given are believed to be, because of their race or for any other reason, inferior human beings? An affirmative answer to either question is implausible. If government reliance on affirmative action is morally and/or constitutionally problematic, it is not because government is allocating a privilege among its citizens on a racist basis or on any other basis that violates part (1) of the articulated norm (or that violates the kindred, broader norm that became a part of our constitutional bedrock in the post–World War II period).[45] Some (but not all) critics of race-based affirmative action are admirably quick to concede this point and move on. Jeremy Rabkin is a recent example: "It is perfectly true—and pointless to deny—that affirmative action does not injure whites in the same way that the old discrimination injured minorities. Reverse discrimination does not stamp disappointed white candidates with a stigma of inferiority or signal that minority individuals cannot bear to mix with them."[46]

It seems equally clear that in relying on race-based affirmative action, government does not violate part (2) of the articulated norm: Such reliance is not "based on hostility to one or more constitutionally protected choices." Does government violate part (3) of the norm? Is government reliance on affirmative action reasonably designed to accomplish a legitimate governmental purpose? Or, to use a different, but equivalent, formulation:[47] Is such reliance an instance of regulation "for the public good in a reasonable fashion"? The typical purposes of such reliance—to ameliorate the present effects of past racist acts and/or to achieve some other, nonracist goal—are not illegitimate. Even the most vigorous judicial critics of government-sponsored affirmative action programs allow that such programs are sometimes animated by "the most admirable and benign of purposes".[48] Indeed, why *would* anyone think it illegitimate for government to aim at bringing about, for example, a more racially diverse and hence more effective urban police department? Or increased participation by members of a racial minority in some part of economic or social life from which members of the minority remain disproportionately and persistently absent—a state of affairs that threatens social and political unity?

The fundamental constitutional objection to government relying on affirmative action has not been that the characteristic goals of such reliance constitute "illegitimate governmental purposes". Rather, the fundamental objection has been that as a race-based or race-conscious instrument, affirmative action is, in government's hands, an unconstitutional means—or, at least, a presumptively unconstitutional means—even if the end or ends be worthy. In that sense, the fundamental objection has been that government reliance on affirmative action violates, or presumptively violates, part (3) of the norm: that, all things considered—in particular, all *costs* considered—such reliance is, at least presumptively, not a "reasonable" regulation for the public good. Why might one believe this? Why does the Supreme Court believe it? (The Court's position, as we'll see, is that it is *presumptively* unconstitutional for government to rely on race-based affirmative action, in this sense: Government may not do so unless government can demonstrate to the Court's satisfaction that its reliance is "necessary" to achieve a "compelling" governmental purpose.)

It is well established, as we have seen, that neither state government nor the national government may distribute benefits or burdens even partly on a racist basis. Recall the Court's statement in *Loving v. Virginia*: "The clear and central purpose of the Fourteenth Amendment was to eliminate all official state sources of *invidious* racial discrimination in the States."[49] However, to distribute a benefit or a burden on, or partly on, the basis of race—to use race as a criterion of selection in distributing a benefit or a burden—is not *necessarily* to distribute the benefit or the burden on an "invidious" (i.e., racist) basis, because there might be a nonracist reason for using race as a criterion of selection. Accordingly, and as it has acknowledged, the Supreme Court has never ruled that it is always unconstitutional for government to distribute benefits or burdens on the basis of race.[50]

Two members of the present Court, however, have espoused such a position: Justices Antonin Scalia and Clarence Thomas. According to Jus tices Scalia and Thomas, government may never use race as a criterion of selection in distributing a benefit or a burden, *even to advantage a racial minority for a nonracist reason*; government must always act in a "color-blind" way. That a racial criterion of selection is not "invidious" is, according to the Scalia-Thomas position, constitutionally irrelevant. In Justice Scalia's view, "under our Constitution there can be no such thing as either a creditor or a debtor race. . . . In the eyes of government, we are just one race here. It is American."[51] According to Justice Thomas, "[t]hat [affirmative action] programs may have been motivated, in part, by good intentions cannot provide refuge from the principle that under our Constitution, the government may not make distinctions on the basis of race. As far as the Constitution is concerned, it is irrelevant whether a government's racial classifications are drawn by those who wish to oppress a race or by those who have a sincere desire to help those thought to be disadvantaged."[52]

The fundamental problem with the Scalia-Thomas position, which goes well beyond what the Court stated in *Loving*, and which every other member of the Court has rejected, is that no norm established by "We the people" supports the position. The available historical evidence fails to support the proposition that the generation of "We the people" that made the Fourteenth Amendment a part of the Constitution understood the Amendment to ban laws (or other governmental actions) based on race without regard to whether the laws were racist.[53] True, the Civil Rights Act of 1866[54] did ban certain laws (and other governmental actions) based on race. Section one of the Act provided, in relevant part, that citizens of the United States, "of every race and color, without regard to any previous condition of slavery or involuntary servitude, except as punishment for a crime whereof the party shall have been duly convicted, shall have the same right, in every State and Territory of the United States, to make and embrace contracts, to sue, be parties, and give evidence, to inherit, purchase, lease, sell, hold, and convey real and personal property, and to full and equal benefit of all laws and proceedings for the security of person and property, *as is enjoyed by white citizens*, and shall be subject to like punishment, pains, and penalties, and to none other, any law, statute, ordinance, regulation, or custom, to the contrary notwithstanding." (Emphasis added.) As I explained in the preceding chapter, however, the banned laws and practices were conspicuously racist; there was no plausible nonracist explanation for them. It ignores the context of the 1866 Civil Rights Act to invoke the Act in support of the proposition that the generation of "We the people" that made the Fourteenth Amendment a part of the Constitution might have understood and indeed wanted the Amendment to ban certain laws and practices based on skin color *without regard to whether the laws and practices were racist*; such an argument ignores the undeniable if, for some, inconvenient fact that, as I reported in the preceding chapter, the 1866 Act was directed specifically against a variety of prominently racist laws and other slavery-like practices commonly known as the Black Codes.[55] Although morally appealing to many persons, the Scalia-Thomas position is no part of the Constitution that has been ordained and established by "We the people of the United States".[56]

As I said, no member of the Supreme Court other than Justices Scalia and Thomas supports the position that government's use of race as a criterion of selection is always unconstitutional. But although more permissive than the Scalia-Thomas position, the Court's position is not permissive. According to the Court, government's use of race as a criterion of selection in distributing a benefit or a burden, though not always actually unconstitutional, is always *presumptively* unconstitutional—unconstitutional *unless* government can demonstrate to the Court's satisfaction that its use of race as a criterion of selection is "necessary" to achieve a "compelling" governmental purpose.[57] In that sense, government's use of race as a criterion of selection in distributing a benefit or a burden is always constitutionally disfavored, *even when the use of race as a criterion of selection is aimed at advantaging a racial minority for a nonracist reason.* Why? It is one thing to disfavor the use of race as a criterion of selection in a law or other governmental action that *disadvantages* a racial minority; it is another thing altogether to use race as a criterion of selection in a law (or other governmental action) that *advantages*—and indeed that was designed to advantage—a racial minority.

Let's begin by considering why the Court disfavors the use of race as a criterion of selection in laws that disadvantage a racial minority.[58] As a real-world matter, for government to use race as a criterion of selection in distributing a benefit or a burden, *denying the benefit to members of a racial minority or imposing the burden on them*, has virtually always been for government to distribute the benefit or the burden on a racist basis. Understandably, therefore, the Court's practice, in the modern period of American constitutional law, has been to regard as suspicious any use of race as a criterion of selection in a law that disadvantages a racial minority. In the Court's practice and parlance, race is a "suspect classification"—that is, a suspect basis of classification. Suspected of what? The Court suspects that the use of race as a criterion of selection in a law that disadvantages a racial minority is a racist act: an act based on a view to the effect that because of their race, the disadvantaged minority are not truly or fully human—that they are, at best, defective, even debased or degraded, human beings. Accordingly, the Court presumes that the use of race as a criterion of selection in a law that disadvantages a racial minority is in fact racist, and therefore unconstitutional, unless government can defeat the presumption by showing that its use of race as a criterion of selection is "necessary" to satisfy a "compelling" governmental interest.[59] That is the sense in which the use of race as a criterion of selection in a law that disadvantages a racial minority is constitutionally disfavored: The Court will subject such use of race to the most demanding "standard of review", it will subject it to "strict scrutiny" (or, as the Court said in 1995, "the strictest judicial scrutiny"[60]); that is, the Court will inquire whether the use of race as a criterion of selection is necessary to satisfy a compelling gov-

ernmental interest. Such scrutiny is the Court's shrewd, practical way of
ferreting out, indirectly or by proxy, what might otherwise be the hidden
racist rationale for a law: If the use of race as a criterion of selection in a
law that disadvantages a racial minority is not necessary to satisfy a compelling governmental interest, then the *real* reason for the law, the *actual*
basis for the use of race as a criterion of selection in the law, is almost certainly racist. As the Court recently put it, "the purpose of strict scrutiny is
to 'smoke out' illegitimate uses of race by assuring that the legislative body
is pursuing a goal important enough to warrant use of a highly suspect
tool. The test also insures that the means chosen 'fit' this compelling goal
so closely that there is little or no possibility that the motive for the classification was illegitimate racial prejudice or stereotype."[61] (In the modern
period—the period since 1954—the Court has never concluded that the
use of race as a criterion of selection in a law that disadvantaged a racial
minority was necessary to satisfy a compelling governmental interest. It
has thus been said that with respect to the use of race as a criterion of selection in laws that *disadvantage* a racial minority, strict scrutiny is "strict
in theory, but fatal in fact".[62])

In terms of the likelihood that a law (or other governmental action) is
racist, there is a world of difference between, on the one side, the use of
race as a criterion of selection in a law that disadvantages a racial minority
and, on the other, the use of race as a criterion of selection in a law designed to advantage a racial minority. This crucial point was pressed by
Justice John Paul Stevens, dissenting from the Court's judgment in
Adarand Constructors, Inc. v. Pena, a 1995 affirmative action case.

> [The Court] assumes that there is no significant difference between a de-
> cision by the majority to impose a special burden on the members of a
> minority race and a decision by the majority to provide a benefit to cer-
> tain members of that minority notwithstanding its incidental burden on
> some members of the majority. In my opinion that assumption is unten-
> able. There is no moral or constitutional equivalence between a policy
> that is designed to perpetuate a caste system and one that seeks to erad-
> icate racial subordination. Invidious discrimination is an engine of op-
> pression, subjugating a disfavored group to enhance or maintain the
> power of the majority. Remedial race-based preferences reflect the op-
> posite impulse: a desire to foster equality in society. . . .
>
>   . . .
> . . . [The Court disregards] the difference between a "No Trespass-
> ing" sign and a welcome mat. It would treat a Dixiecrat Senator's deci-
> sion to vote against Thurgood Marshall's confirmation in order to keep
> African Americans off the Supreme Court as on a par with President
> Johnson's evaluation of his race as a positive factor. It would equate a law
> that made black citizens ineligible for military service with a program
> aimed at recruiting black soldiers. An attempt by the majority to exclude
> members of a minority race from a regulated market is fundamentally
> different from a subsidy that enables a relatively small group of newcom-
> ers to enter that market.[63]

Nonetheless, a majority of the Court ruled in *Adarand* that the use of race as a criterion of selection is disfavored—it is subject to the most demanding standard of review, to strict scrutiny—even in a law designed to advantage a racial minority or, more generally, in any affirmative action law. (Not every affirmative action law is designed to advantage a racial minority. The point of an affirmative action law aimed at increasing the racial diversity of an urban police department, for example, might be only to create a more effective police department, not to advantage a racial minority.)

> [A]ny person, of whatever race, has the right to demand that any governmental actor subject to the Constitution justify any racial classification subjecting that person to unequal treatment under the strictest judicial scrutiny. . . . [A]ll racial classifications, imposed by whatever federal, state, or local governmental actor, must be analyzed by a reviewing court under strict scrutiny. In other words, such classifications are constitutional only if they are narrowly tailored measures that further compelling governmental interests.[64]

Why insist, as the Court now does, that the use of race as a criterion of selection is disfavored (i.e., subject to strict scrutiny) even in an affirmative action law? The rationale for disfavoring the use of race as a criterion of selection in a law that disadvantages a racial minority—namely, the probability and suspicion that the law is racist—cannot serve as the rationale for disfavoring the use of race as a criterion of selection in an affirmative action law or program, which, whatever else it is, and however morally or even constitutionally problematic one might believe it to be, is not a racist act. As Justice Stevens observed in *Adarand*, "It is one thing to question the wisdom of affirmative action programs . . . It is another thing altogether to equate the many well-meaning and intelligent lawmakers and their constituents—whether members of majority or minority races—who have supported affirmative action over the years, to segregationists and bigots."[65] One of the Court's principal statements in *Adarand*—that "[t]he guarantee of equal protection cannot mean one thing when applied to one individual and something else when applied to a person of another color"[66]—is both unresponsive and conspicuously unhelpful: No one disputes that "the guarantee of equal protection" centrally means the same thing applied to a white person as it does applied to a nonwhite person, namely, that no person, *whatever his or her color*, is to suffer racist discrimination at the hands of government; the disputed question is whether, if government-sponsored affirmative action—whether in general or a particular instance of it—is neither racist nor reasonably suspected of being racist, the Court should rule that government-sponsored affirmative action is nonetheless constitutionally disfavored.[67] "[D]iscriminating against whites in order to humiliate and subjugate them would be just as wrong as discriminating against blacks for the same purpose. . . . But it is not plausible to equate preferences under affirmative action with the malign and crippling discriminati............ .ormer regimes of racial oppression."[68] Or, as Stephen ....e point: "[W]hatever the source of racism, to count it the s............, to say that two centuries of struggle for the most basic of ....been mostly about freedom from racial categorization rat...........reedom from racial oppression, is to trivialize the lives a...........hose who have suffered under racism."[69] The question ....s it appropriate for the Court to disfavor—in particular, ...t based on any norm established by "We the people" for th...........vor—government reliance on affirmative action?[70]

Let's proceed in this ....tifying the various reasons one might have—one who is ....or even in the grip, consciously or not, of "racially selectiv...........indifference"[71]—for being wary about, and perhaps even ....ernment relying on race-based affirmative action progran............ five reasons seem to predominate:

- First, government-spons............ action delays the arrival of the day when the color of one's skin is no longer seen to be a morally relevant factor. As the Court put it in 1993: "Racial classifications of any sort pose the risk of lasting harm to our society. They reinforce the belief, held by too many for too much of our history, that individuals should be judged by the color of their skin."[72] Justice Brennan made the same point earlier, in 1977: "[E]ven in the pursuit of remedial objectives, an explicit policy of assignment by race may serve to stimulate our society's latent race consciousness, suggesting the utility and propriety of basing decisions on a factor that ideally bears no relationship to an individual's worth or needs."[73] Justice Scalia lent his voice to the point in 1995: "To pursue the concept of racial entitlement—even for the most admirable and benign of purposes—is to reinforce and preserve for future mischief the way of thinking that produced race slavery, race privilege and race hatred."[74]
- Second, by leading some to believe that many members of a racial minority need special breaks if they are to succeed, or at least if they are to achieve a position from which they have a better chance of succeeding, government-sponsored affirmative action can and does serve to reinforce the view that in general members of the racial minority are naturally inferior to others in one or more respects (e.g., intellectually).[75] This is a view that, in one or another form, can infect members of the racial minority as well as others, sapping their self-esteem.[76]
- Third, by denying certain important opportunities (economic, educational, etc.) to persons partly because of their race, government-sponsored affirmative action offends the emergent popular view that the opportunities open to one ought not to depend on the color of one's skin or on one's ethnic ancestry.
- Fourth, government-sponsored affirmative action can and does pro-

voke racial resentment and precipitate racial division (in part because it offends the view that the opportunities open to one ought not to depend on the color of one's skin or on one's ethnic ancestry).[77]

- Fifth, if government is free to sponsor affirmative action programs, then we must endure a troubling racial politics: A proposed program of affirmative action then becomes a political objective to be won or lost, and inevitably the political alliances and battle lines will be defined at least partly along racial lines, thereby threatening to exacerbate racial divisions and tensions.[78]

Now, which of these reasons, if any, counts as a *constitutionally relevant reason* for the Court disfavoring, by subjecting to strict scrutiny, government reliance on affirmative action? That government-sponsored affirmative action delays the arrival of the day when the color of one's skin is no longer seen to be a morally relevant factor; that it can serve to reinforce the (racist) view that in general members of the racial minority are naturally inferior to others in one or more respects; that it offends the view that the opportunities open to one ought not to depend on the color of one's skin or on one's ethnic ancestry; that it can provoke racial resentment and precipitate racial division; that it can lead to a politics in which racial or ethnic alliances and divisions are prominent; these are all reasons for government to be cautious, even wary, about relying on affirmative action. But none of them entails that government-sponsored affirmative action violates any constitutional norm established by "We the people".

Citizens of all colors can and do reasonably disagree among themselves about whether, all things considered (including the five reasons listed above), government-sponsored affirmative action is a good thing or a bad thing. (One recent poll suggests that 11 percent of African Americans favor "outright abolition" of affirmative action.[79]) Sometimes the disagreement is about government-sponsored affirmative action in general; sometimes it is about a particular instance of such affirmative action. Why shouldn't such reasonable if vigorous disagreements remain, in our democracy, within the exclusive jurisdiction of ordinary politics, for resolution by the electorally accountable representatives of the people?[80] So long as a particular instance of government-sponsored affirmative action does not violate any norm that has been established by "We the people", by what right does the Supreme Court of the United States take upon itself the authority to declare that a particular instance of government-sponsored affirmative action is constitutionally impermissible?

In chapter 2, I noted that few if any persons disagree that the norms the Constitution consists of include some directives established by "We the people" (and that it includes some such norms partly because they were "ordained and established" by "We the people"). However, that the Constitution consists of some such norms does not entail that it consists *only* of such norms. As I explained in chapter 2, few constitutional scholars disagree that the Constitution consists of at least some fundamental norms that were never (or probably never) established by "We the people": namely, political-moral norms that have become such fixed and widely affirmed and relied-upon (by us the people of the United States now living) features of the life of our political community that the norms are now, for us, constitutional bedrock; norms that have become a part of our fundamental law—the law that is constitutive of ourselves as a political community of a certain sort.[81] Let's assume, for the sake of discussion, that the Court's doctrinal hostility to government-sponsored affirmative action—its practice of subjecting government reliance on affirmative action to strict scrutiny, striking down such reliance as unconstitutional if in the Court's view the affirmative action program in question is not necessary to satisfy what the Court deems to be a sufficiently compelling governmental interest—is not warranted by, that it is not grounded in, any norm established by "We the people". That the Court's doctrinal hostility to government-sponsored affirmative action is not warranted by any norm established by "We the people" leaves open the possibility that the Court's doctrinal hostility to government-sponsored affirmative action *is* warranted by a norm that, although not established by "We the people", has nonetheless become constitutional bedrock for us.

The norm that government may not—absolutely, unconditionally, unqualifiedly may not—allocate opportunities on the basis of race, which is substantially the norm embraced by Justices Scalia and Thomas, certainly has not become constitutional bedrock for us.[82] To the contrary, that norm is widely and deeply controversial among us and is rejected by the many Americans who support government-sponsored affirmative action. A powerful case can be made, however, that a different though related norm *has* become constitutional bedrock for us: that government *ordinarily* ought not to allocate opportunities even partly on the basis of race; indeed, that government *presumptively* may not allocate opportunities even partly on the basis of race; specifically, government may do so only if, first, allocating opportunities partly on the basis of race is aimed at achieving, and substantially achieves, a compelling goal and, second, there is no other way of achieving that goal or, at least, of achieving it to substantially the same extent. This norm does seem to have become constitutional bedrock for us; significantly, this norm is accepted even by many Americans who support government-sponsored affirmative action. Relatively few Americans think it morally proper for government to allocate opportunities even partly on the basis of race if doing so is not aimed at achieving, or does not actually achieve, a compelling goal, or if there is a racially neutral way of achieving the goal. (Needless to say, no racist goal is morally or constitutionally legitimate, much less compelling.)

Why has this norm taken such hold in the American political community? Why has this norm become (if it has become) constitutional bedrock for us? The answer is not difficult to discern. The norm is nourished by a deep moral (and, for some, religious) conviction that has been growing among us and indeed throughout the world: that the color of one's skin (or one's ethnic ancestry) is simply and radically irrelevant to one's status as a human being.[83] In particular, the norm—the presumption against government-sponsored affirmative action, the insistence that government may rely on affirmative action only if certain relatively strict conditions are satisfied—reflects an understandable concern that however well-intentioned an affirmative action program might be, the various unintended social costs of government-sponsored affirmative action are serious and ought not to be discounted. I listed the most serious such costs above, in specifying five reasons one might have for wariness about government-sponsored affirmative action. The most relevant of those costs here is the first one,[84] namely, the fact that "generalizations about race, however positive, harm their subjects by perpetuating one of the most oppressive features of their stigmatization: to be seen primarily as representatives of a group rather than as individuals."[85] In the aftermath of recent ethnic and tribal conflict in places like Bosnia and Rwanda—deadly and even genocidal conflict—we should hesitate to discount the magnitude of such a cost. If the norm that government *presumptively* should not allocate opportunities even partly on the basis of race has become constitutional bedrock for us, then even if it were not warranted by any constitutional norm established by "We the people", the Court's doctrinal hostility to government-sponsored affirmative action would be no more an example of "the judicial usurpation of politics" than other constitutional doctrines that, though not warranted by norms established by "We the people", are nonetheless warranted by norms that have become a part of our constitutional bedrock.

In the preceding sentence, I said "even if it were not warranted". I suggested, three paragraphs back, that for the sake of discussion we assume that the Court's doctrinal hostility to government-sponsored affirmative action is not warranted by any norm established by "We the people". Let's now release that assumption. It is far from clear that the Court's doctrinal hostility is not warranted by any constitutional norm established by "We the people". Indeed, the Court's doctrinal hostility can quite plausibly be understood as warranted by a constitutional norm that was established, or probably established, by "We the people", namely, part (3) of the antidiscrimination norm articulated earlier in this chapter: Given the various social costs of government relying on race-based affirmative action, and given that those costs are undeniably substantial, it arguably makes sense for the Court to rule, as in substance it has done, that such reliance is, *presumptively*, not a "reasonable" regulation for the public good, it is not "reasonably" related to the public good; such reliance is not a "reasonable" regulation for the public good *unless the reliance satisfies strict scrutiny, unless it is "necessary" to achieve a "compelling" governmental purpose.* The Court's underlying point is this: Given that the social costs of government relying on affirmative action are great, unless the benefit or benefits of such reliance are also great—in the Court's language, unless government reliance on affirmative action is necessary to achieve a compelling governmental interest—the benefits are not proportionate to the costs. Instead, the costs are disproportionate to the benefits, and, therefore, government reliance on affirmative action is unreasonable.

In any event, the norm that government ordinarily ought not to allocate opportunities even partly on the basis of race—that it ought not to do so in the absence of quite extraordinary circumstances—seems not only to have achieved a virtually axiomatic status in the American political community, but also to have become constitutional bedrock for us. Therefore, the Court's approach to affirmative action—its erecting high barriers to reliance by government on race-based affirmative action—can be understood as warranted not only by a norm that was established as a part of the Constitution by "We the people" but also, and independently, by a different norm that, though never established by "We the people", has become a part of our constitutional bedrock. Indeed, the Court's approach to affirmative action is even more strongly warranted by a conjunction of the two norms than by either of them alone. The conjunction of the two norms yields what is substantially the Court's approach to affirmative action: Government may not rely on race-based affirmative action—such reliance, which involves differential treatment based on race, is not a "reasonable" regulation for, it is not "reasonably" related to, the public good—*unless the reliance, the race-based differential treatment, satisfies strict scrutiny, unless it is "necessary" to achieve a "compelling" governmental purpose.* The serious question, then, is not whether the Court should subject government reliance on affirmative action to—not whether the Court should test it by—"strict scrutiny", but what goals the Court should deem sufficiently important ("compelling") to satisfy strict scrutiny.[86]

The goal of minimizing the present effects of past or present racial injustice is deemed compelling by the Supreme Court. The Court is surely right: that goal *is* compelling.[87] Nonetheless, the danger lurks that arguments invoking the goal might become so all-encompassing as to swallow the presumption against government-sponsored affirmative action. Understandably, therefore, the Court has carefully delimited the arguments of that sort it will accept. In *Shaw v. Hunt*, the Court wrote:

> A State's interest in remedying the effects of past or present racial discrimination may in the proper case justify a government's use of racial distinctions. For that interest to rise to the level of a compelling state interest, it must satisfy two conditions. First, the discrimination must be identified discrimination. While the States and their subdivisions may take remedial action when they possess evidence of past or present discrimination, they must identify that discrimination, public or private, with some specificity before they may use race-conscious relief. A generalized assertion of past discrimination in a particular industry or region is not adequate because it provides no guidance for a legislative body to determine the precise scope of the injury it seeks to remedy. . . . Second, the institution that makes the racial distinction must have had a strong

basis in evidence to conclude that remedial action was necessary, before it embarks on an affirmative-action program.[88]

Owen Fiss has written that "[t]he compensatory justice rationale [for affirmative action] . . . falters because of the lack of identity between the victims of the wrong and the recipients of the preferential treatment, and between the perpetrators of the wrong and those who bear the cost of the remedy. The rationale also leaves unexplained why a plus in the allocative process . . . is the appropriate compensation for the wrongs of the past."[89] The way in which the Court has delimited the minimizing-the-present-effects-of-racial-injustice arguments that it will accept meets the concern about "why a plus in the allocative process . . . is the appropriate compensation for the wrongs of the past": A "plus" in a particular allocative process (e.g., the construction industry in Chicago) is a fitting response to a past "negative" in that same process. However, there is no denying that "the lack of identity between the victims of the wrong and the recipients of the preferential treatment" makes government reliance on affirmative action as a way of responding to racial injustice a "second-best" response. It does not follow, however, that a second-best response is worse than no response at all. In a society that has been and to some extent remains permeated by racism, and that persists in the grip of racial division and distrust, "no response" can reasonably be thought much worse, symbolically and otherwise, than a second-best response. Finally, that there is a regrettable lack of identity "between the perpetrators of the wrong and those who bear the cost of the remedy" is yet another reason that government should rely on a particular program of affirmative action as a way of minimizing the present effects of racial injustice, if at all, only if there is no other way of achieving that morally compelling goal, or of achieving it to substantially the same extent.

Reviewing, in a recent case, the Supreme Court's affirmative action jurisprudence, Judge Richard Posner observed that the Court has not decided whether any other goals—and goals beyond that of minimizing the present effects of racial injustice—are sufficiently important to justify government reliance on affirmative action. "That question remains open in the Supreme Court."[90] Posner then offered his own view: "A judge would be unreasonable to conclude that no other consideration except a history of discrimination could ever warrant a discriminatory measure unless every other consideration had been presented to and rejected by him. . . . It is not as if the rectification of past discrimination has a logical or equitable priority over other legitimate goals that [affirmative action] might serve."[91] According to Posner, "the law-enforcement and correctional settings [are] the very clearest examples of cases in which departures from racial neutrality are permissible" in order to achieve a racially diverse work force that can function optimally in environments—the inner city, for example, or a prison—that are predominantly or at least disproportionately nonwhite.[92] Posner (joined by two other judges) then ruled, on behalf of the United States Court of Appeals for the Seventh Circuit, that a race-based hiring preference that the administrators of a county boot camp gave to a black male applicant for a lieutenant's job did not violate the requirement of equal protection.

> The black lieutenant is needed because the black inmates are believed unlikely to play the correctional game or brutal drill sergeant and brutalized recruit unless there are some blacks in authority in the camp. This is not just speculation, but is backed up by expert evidence that the plaintiffs did not rebut. The defendants' experts—recognized experts in the field of prison administration—did not rely on generalities about racial balance or diversity; did not, for that matter, defend a goal of racial balance. They opined that the boot camp . . . would not succeed in its mission of pacification and reformation with as white a staff as it would have if a black male had not been appointed to one of the lieutenant slots. For then a security staff of less than 6 percent black (4 out of 71), with no male black supervisor, would be administering a program for a prison population almost 70 percent black in a prison the staff of which is expected to treat the inmates with the same considerateness, or rather lack of considerateness, that a marine sergeant treats recruits at Parris Island.[93]

Judge Posner's decision seems quite sensible. But what happens when we move beyond "the law-enforcement and correctional settings" that are, according to Posner, "the very clearest examples of cases in which departures from racial neutrality are permissible"?[94] For example, may a state university give a race-based preference to applicants in order to achieve a more racially diverse student body? In particular, should a more racially diverse student body be deemed a "compelling" governmental interest? In 1996, in a controversial decision, *Hopwood v. Texas*, the United States Court of Appeals for the Fifth Circuit, ruling that the University of Texas School of Law "may not use race as a factor in law school admissions",[95] answered this question in the negative.[96] According to the court, a more racially diverse student body is not a compelling goal: "The use of race, in and of itself, to choose students simply achieves a student body that looks different. Such a criterion is no more rational on its own terms than would be choices based upon the physical size or blood type of applicants."[97]

If the goal of the race-based admissions practice challenged in *Hopwood* were "achieving a more racially diverse student body", understood as an end in itself, it would be hard to fault the court's claim that the goal was not compelling. Indeed, it would be hard to see the point of the goal, understood as an end in itself. A more plausible characterization of the goal is "achieving among its students the sort of social (experiential) and intellectual diversity that will greatly enrich the university experience for all students". When it asked the Supreme Court to reverse the lower court's decision in *Hopwood*, the University of Texas School of Law emphasized the importance of "the mix of viewpoints, opinions, talents, and experiences that enrich the university and facilitate its mission."[98] Such social and intellectual diversity is a compelling goal for any university, public no less than private.

> In a widely circulated report in 1996, Neil Rudenstine, president of Harvard University, justified Harvard's commitment to [such] diversity . . . by invoking John Stuart Mill, who stressed the value of bringing "human beings in contact with persons dissimilar to themselves, and with modes of thought and action unlike those with which they are familiar." A diverse student body, argued Rudenstine, is as much an "educational resource" as a university's faculty, library, and laboratories. Consequently, Harvard takes great pains to assure that its admission process results in such a student body.[99]

The problem with the admissions practice invalidated in *Hopwood* was not that the goal, understood in the way I'm suggesting, was not compelling, but that the means the University of Texas School of Law relied on to achieve the goal—giving applicants for admission a plus based simply on the color of their skin or their ethnic ancestry—was not only not necessary to achieve the goal, but was ill suited to achieve it.[100] Ill suited, that is, unless one accepts a problematic assumption about which the court was understandably skeptical, namely, "that a certain individual possesses characteristics by virtue of being a member of a certain racial group. This assumption . . . does not withstand scrutiny. 'The use of a racial characteristic to establish a presumption that the individual also possesses other, and socially relevant, characteristics, exemplifies, encourages, and legitimizes the mode of thought and behavior that underlies most prejudice and bigotry in modern America.'"[101] As Robert Fullinwider recently put the point: "Although it is very popular these days to talk about 'group perspectives,' it is also dubious to talk this way. Women don't share a single perspective, even on matters of gender. Blacks don't share a single perspective, even on matters of race. When someone claims to represent a 'group perspective,' that construction is mostly a construction of the claimer (and of like-minded persons), privileging certain propositions about society, justice, and the group's interests."[102]

A more effective, if less mechanical,[103] admissions practice would aim to achieve a greater degree of social and intellectual diversity among its students by relying less heavily on standardized test scores[104] and emphasizing various factors other than the color of one's skin—factors whose function as proxies does not "exemplify, encourage, and legitimize the mode of thought and behavior that underlies most prejudice and bigotry in modern America." To mention just a few examples:[105] Is the applicant from an economically disadvantaged family? (Contrary to what some have suggested,[106] application of this criterion, in conjunction with other racially neutral criteria, need not lead to a "whiteout".[107]) Did the applicant's parents go to college?[108] *Is the applicant a member of a group that his-*

torically has been the object of systematic public (legal) and private vilification, dis-crimination, subordination, and exclusion?[109] It bears emphasis that this third factor, which is arguably an especially relevant and appealing considera-tion in the law school admissions process, is racially neutral: Racial groups are not the only ones that historically have been the object of systematic public and private vilification, discrimination, etc. Religious groups, too, have suffered that distinction—as have homosexuals and others. That members of (some) racial and ethnic minorities would, of course, be among the principal beneficiaries of the third factor does not entail that the factor is not racially neutral.[110]

In Judge Posner's case, government reliance on a benign racial pref-erence was necessary to give the boot camp experiment a chance of suc-ceeding. In *Hopwood v. Texas,* by contrast, giving applicants for admission a plus based simply on the color of their skin or their ethnic ancestry was not only not necessary to achieve the kind of diversity that is most com-pelling in a university context—social (experiential) and intellectual di-versity—but was ill suited to achieve it, *or at least less well suited than alter-natives that do not rely on the color of one's skin as a rough proxy for other, nonracial characteristics or factors.* If we assume that the admissions process was in fact aimed at a different kind of diversity—as one judge in *Hop-wood* put it, "increas[ing] the percentage of black faces and brown faces in that year's entering class"[111]—the problem is that for many persons, in-cluding the judges in *Hopwood,* that goal is not only not compelling, but puzzling and unappealing, even troubling. President Clinton is no op-ponent of affirmative action; his rhetorical counter to opponents of affir-mative action has been "Mend it, don't end it." But even on Clinton's watch, the Office of the Solicitor General of the U.S. Department of Jus-tice has acknowledged, in a legal brief submitted to the Supreme Court in an affirmative action case, that "[a] simple desire to maintain diversity for its own sake . . . is not a permissible basis for taking race into account . . . under the Constitution. When race is used to foster diversity, [gov-ernment] 'must seek some further objective, beyond the mere achieve-ment of diversity itself.' Equally important, [government] must produce convincing evidence demonstrating a connection between diversity and the objective sought to be furthered; such a connection may not be merely asserted."[112]

Let's accept, as a given, what a majority of the Supreme Court has de-creed: that government's use of race as a criterion of selection, even when aimed at advantaging a racial minority for a nonracist reason, is subject to the requirement that the racial criterion be "necessary" to satisfy a "com-pelling" governmental interest. I now want to raise a question about how deferentially ought the Court to apply this requirement: Ought the Court to ask whether *it* believes that the racial criterion is necessary to achieve a compelling governmental purpose? Or ought the Court to ask, instead, only whether the legislators or other governmental actors who chose to use the racial criterion could reasonably believe that the criterion was necessary to achieve a compelling governmental purpose?

The claim that the Court is "usurping politics" might be the claim that the Court is enforcing as constitutional a norm that "We the people" never established as constitutional. Even if true, however, this claim is little troubling if the norm the Court is enforcing as constitutional is one that has become constitutional bedrock for us the people of the United States now living.[113] It would be a much more serious matter, however, and would constitute a troubling "usurpation of politics", if the Court were enforcing as constitutional a norm that not only was never established by "We the people" but also is not constitutional bedrock for us. I want to focus now, however, on another, more subtle (but nonetheless troubling) way in which the Court can "usurp politics": by refusing to give other governmental actors an appropriate latitude to make and implement their own reasonable judgments about whether one or another policy choice is consistent with the relevant constitutional norm or norms. (Recall here my discussion, in chapter 2: "How deferential ought the Court to be in interpreting (specifying) the Constitution?"[114]) This possibility raises an important question about the Court's approach to judicial review of government-sponsored affirmative action.

The answer to the question about how deferentially the Court ought to apply the requirement that government's use of a racial criterion be necessary to achieve a compelling governmental purpose is relatively easy if government's use of a racial criterion operates to deny something good to, or to impose something bad on, a racial minority. The Court should be suspicious about a race-based law (or other governmental act) that disadvantages a racial minority—suspicious that the law is, at bottom, a racist act. The Court should not only subject the racial criterion in such a law to "strict scrutiny" but do so aggressively, not deferentially, by inquiring if it, the Court itself, believes that the racial criterion is necessary to achieve a compelling governmental purpose. This is in fact the practice the Court has followed; moreover, it is the practice the Court should follow, according to the conventional wisdom, which is sound, that the Court has a special role to play in guarding against racist governmental acts, in part by aggressively ferreting out such acts.

The answer to the question of deference is more difficult, however, if government's use of a racial criterion does not operate to disadvantage a racial minority. Again, there is no reason to suspect that government-sponsored affirmative action is a racist act, and the question arises, therefore, why the Court shouldn't simply inquire whether the legislators or other governmental actors who choose to use the racial criterion could reasonably believe that the criterion was necessary to achieve a compelling governmental interest. It seems a safe assumption that there is sometimes room for a reasonable difference in judgments about whether or not one or another goal is sufficiently important ("compelling") to justify a particular instance of government-sponsored affirmative action—and perhaps even about whether a racial criterion is necessary to achieve the goal. Let's assume that, given the various costs of government relying on a racial criterion even when doing so does not operate to disadvantage a racial minority and is not a racist act, it makes sense for the Court to insist that government not use race as a criterion of selection even for the purpose of advantaging a racial minority unless the racial criterion is necessary to achieve a compelling governmental purpose. Still, the question remains whether the Court shouldn't defer to government's judgment that the racial criterion is necessary to achieve a compelling governmental purpose by asking, not whether it (the Court) agrees with government's judgment, but only whether the judgment is a reasonable one. So far as I can tell, no member of the Supreme Court has identified this question, much less addressed it. Every member of the Court seems unreflectively to assume that if the constitutional requirement is that government avoid reliance on affirmative action unless such reliance is necessary to achieve a compelling governmental purpose, the relevant question for the Court is whether the Court itself believes that government reliance on affirmative actin is necessary to achieve a compelling governmental purpose.

Consider, for example, an instance of congressional reliance on a program of affirmative action. What reason or reasons might the Court have for refusing to defer to Congress' judgment, in choosing to rely on the program of affirmative action, that a racial criterion is necessary to satisfy a compelling governmental purpose, if Congress' judgment, though not uncontroversial, is nonetheless reasonable? And, especially, if Congress has thoroughly considered the issue? Is there some reason to doubt Congress' capacity to weigh the competing considerations appropriately? (A statement by Justice Stevens in *Adarand* is relevant here: "If the legislature is persuaded that its [affirmative action] program is doing more harm than good to the individuals it is designed to benefit, then we can expect the legislature to remedy the problem. *Significantly, this is not true of a government action based on invidious discrimination.*"[115]) Indeed, in a political climate that has often been hostile to affirmative action, isn't it much more likely that a majoritarian political institution like the Congress of the United States will bend over backward *not* to sponsor programs of affirmative action than that it will lightly or casually sponsor them? Recall, in that regard, that in 1996 the California electorate—the most ethnically diverse electorate in the United States—approved Proposition 209.[116]

So, those who, like the *First Things* symposiasts, are exercised about "the judicial usurpation of politics" ought to consider the possibility that an aspect of the Supreme Court's doctrinal hostility to affirmative action—namely, the Court's *nondeferential* enforcement of the "necessary to achieve a compelling governmental purpose" requirement—is a problematic instance of such usurpation. That possibility is especially troubling, if the Court's lack of deference is not only inappropriate but undermines efforts by Congress and other governmental and nongovernmental actors to abolish racism and its tragic effects. The question is therefore important and even urgent: What reasons are there, if any, for the Court to privilege its own answer to the central question here ("is the racial criterion necessary to achieve a compelling governmental purpose?") over Congress' (or a state legislature's, or a city's, etc.) answer, if Congress' answer, though different from the one a majority of the Court would give if it were considering the issue de novo, is nonetheless one the Court cannot plausibly deny is reasonable?[117]

Even if the answer to that question is that there are no such reasons, the Court's doctrinal hostility to government-sponsored affirmative action is still not in the same "usurping politics" league as Justice Scalia's and Justice Thomas' unyielding opposition to any and all instances of government-sponsored affirmative action—an opposition (it bears repeating) warranted *neither* by any constitutional norm established by "We the people" *nor* by any norm that has become constitutional bedrock for us. As Justice Ginsburg, with an eye on the Scalia-Thomas position, cautioned in her dissenting opinion in *Adarand*, "The divisions in this difficult case should not obscure the Court's recognition of the persistence of racial inequality *and a majority's acknowledgement of Congress' authority to act affirmatively, not only to end discrimination, but also to counteract discrimination's lingering effects.*"[118]

III. Conclusion

Let's now return to the issues I raised at the beginning of this chapter. Again, the most important initiative undertaken by the Supreme Court of the United States in the modern period of American constitutional law was arguably its effort to abolish governmental racism: racist laws and other kinds of racist governmental action, including policies aimed at creating and/or maintaining racial segregation. In the first part of this chapter, I explained that, contrary to what some critics of the Supreme Court have recently suggested, the Court's attack on public policies aimed at creating and/or maintaining racial segregation was no "usurpation of politics" but was justified—indeed, required—by two constitutional norms established by "We the people of the United States": the privileges or immunities norm of the Fourteenth Amendment and, insofar as racist action by the national government is concerned, the Ninth Amendment. I also explained that even if I am wrong—even if the Court's attack on public policies aimed at creating and/or maintaining racial segregation was not justified by any constitutional norm established by "We the people"—the Court's efforts were nonetheless required by the broad antidiscrimination norm that in the period after World War II had become an important part of our constitutional bedrock.

One of the most controversial initiatives undertaken by the Supreme Court in the contemporary period is its effort to restrict the extent to which government may rely on policies of race-based affirmative action. In the second part of this chapter, I argued that, in one respect, the Court has not usurped our politics in erecting high barriers to government reliance on affirmative action. The Court's approach to affirmative action can be understood as warranted by a conjunction of two norms, one of which was established by "We the people", the other of which, though never established by "We the people", has become constitutional bedrock for us. The former norm requires differential treatment by government to be "for the public good in a reasonable fashion". According to the latter norm, government ordinarily ought not—it ought not in the absence of truly extraordinary circumstances—to allocate opportunities even partly on the basis of race. The conjunction of the two norms yields the Court's approach to affirmative action, which, in substance, is this: Because government reliance on race-based affirmative action entails various, substantial social costs, government may not rely on race-based affirmative action—such reliance, which involves differential treatment based on race, is not a "reasonable" regulation for, it is not "reasonably" related to, the public good—*unless the reliance, the race-based differential treatment, satisfies strict scrutiny, unless it is "necessary" to achieve a "compelling" governmental purpose*. Even if, contrary to what I have argued, "We the people" never established the former norm, the latter norm alone, as I noted earlier in this chapter, grounds the Court's approach to affirmative action.

I also argued, however, that, in another respect, the Court's approach to affirmative action *is* usurpative, it *does* involve a usurpation. Whether the "necessary to achieve a compelling governmental purpose" requirement should apply to government reliance on race-based affirmative action is distinct from the question whether the Court should apply the requirement nondeferentially; moreover, that the requirement should apply (if it should) does not entail that the Court should apply it nondeferentially. It is difficult to discern any warrant for the Court applying the requirement nondeferentially. In the absence of such a warrant, the Court's failure to enforce the applicable requirement in a deferential manner—a manner deferential to a legislature's or other policymaking body's *reasonable* judgment that a particular instance of affirmative action *is* necessary to achieve a compelling governmental purpose—is troubling and can fairly be said to usurp our politics.

5

————✕✕✕————

Beyond Race: Sex and Sexual Orientation

History, Stephen said, is a nightmare from which I am trying to awake.

James Joyce, *Ulysses* [1]

Students of the history of the Fourteenth Amendment disagree among themselves about precisely what racially discriminatory state laws (and other racially discriminatory state action) section one of the Fourteenth Amendment was understood and meant to forbid. (I explored that disagreement in chapter 3.) They agree, however, that section one was understood and meant to forbid *some* racially discriminatory state laws; they agree, in particular, that section one was meant to forbid *at least* the kinds of racially discriminatory state laws and practices—the Black Codes— outlawed by the Civil Rights Act of 1866. Racial discrimination was a core concern of section one of the Fourteenth Amendment.

In the 1970s, the Supreme Court moved beyond racially discriminatory laws (and kindred laws discriminating on the basis of ethnicity or nationality) and began to outlaw some laws, policies, and other government action that discriminated on the basis of sex.[2] In what sense, if any, is it a usurpation of our politics for the Court, in the name of the Fourteenth Amendment,[3] to do what it now does: disfavor, by subjecting to a strict standard of review, all (government-sponsored) discrimination based on sex and outlaw most instances of such discrimination?[4]

In 1996, in a case that outraged many social conservatives, the Court struck down a newly adopted Colorado constitutional amendment that, in the Court's view, discriminated against homosexuals in violation of the Fourteenth Amendment. In what sense, if any, was it a usurpation of our politics for the Court to do so? In what sense would it be a usurpation for the Court to disfavor discrimination against homosexuals the way it now disfavors discrimination against women, namely, by subjecting it to a strict standard of review—a standard that is often lethal?

In the preceding chapter, I addressed two main issues: the legitimacy of the Court outlawing (in the name of the Fourteenth Amendment) state-created or -maintained racial segregation, and the legitimacy of its erecting high barriers to government reliance on race-based affirmative action. In this chapter, too, I address two main issues. The first issue concerns something the Court already does, namely, disfavor all discrimination based on sex and outlaw most instances of it. The second issue concerns something that the Court has been urged by some to do: disfavor discrimination against homosexuals the way it disfavors discrimination against women. Was it illegitimate—was it a usurpation of our politics—for the Court, in the name of the Fourteenth Amendment, to move beyond race to sex? Would it be illegitimate—would it be a usurpation—for the Court now to move beyond race and sex to sexual orientation?

I. Sex-Based Discrimination

First, a clarification. The question is not whether section one of the Fourteenth Amendment—in particular, the second sentence of section one—was understood and meant to protect women. The due process and equal protection norms established by "We the people" each protect all persons, and women are persons. The privileges or immunities norm established by "We the people" protects at least all citizens, and women as well as men are citizens. The question is what section one—especially the privileges or immunities norm—protects women (and others) from. Whatever else it protects them from, the privileges or immunities norm protects all those whom it protects, including women, from at least some discrimination—for example, racist discrimination. The disputed question is whether the privileges or immunities norm established by "We the people" also protects women from discrimination against them *as women*: Does the privileges or immunities norm protect women (and others) from sexist discrimination? (If, like the Supreme Court, one reads the equal protection provision, rather than the privileges or immunities provision, to supply the relevant norm,[5] the disputed question is whether, in addition to protecting women from, for example, racist discrimination, the equal protection norm also protects them from sexist discrimination.)

Undeniably, the generation of "We the people" that (through their representatives) made the Fourteenth Amendment a part of the Constitution did not believe—in particular, their representatives did not believe—that the Amendment rendered legislative or other governmental distinctions based on sex constitutionally problematic. (They did not believe—not many of them, at any rate—that distinctions based on sex were morally problematic.) They did not understand themselves to have established as a part of the Fourteenth Amendment a norm that called into question legislative or other governmental distinctions based on sex. It is

therefore not surprising that even after ratification of the Fourteenth
Amendment, the conventional judicial wisdom remained that sex-based
distinctions were not constitutionally (or morally) problematic. In the
Slaughter-House Cases, for example, which were decided, in 1872, just four
years after ratification of the Fourteenth Amendment was complete, the
Court wrote: "To [citizens of the United States], everywhere, all pursuits,
all professions, and all avocations as are open without other restrictions
than such are imposed equally upon all others of the same age, *sex*, and
condition."[6] Eight years later, in striking down a law that restricted jury
service to "white male persons who are twenty-one years of age [or older]
and who are citizens of this State", the Court said: "We do not say [that] a
State may not prescribe the qualifications of its jurors, and in so doing
make discriminations. It may confine the selection to *males,* to freeholders,
to citizens, to persons within certain ages, or to persons having educational qualifications."[7] Consider, too, Justice Bradley's now-notorious
opinion in *Bradwell v. Illinois*, in which the Court ruled that Illinois could
exclude women from admission to the bar. (The Court announced its decision in *Bradwell* on April 15, 1873, just one day after the Court announced its decision the *Slaughter-House Cases*.) Bradley declared: "The
natural and proper timidity and delicacy which belongs to the female sex
evidently unfits it for many of the occupations of civil life. . . . The para-
mount mission and destiny of woman are to fulfill the noble and benign
offices of wife and mother. This is the law of the Creator."[8] Such senti-
ments were not confined to the judiciary. Consider, for example, the following information, recited in a 1996 Supreme Court opinion:

> Dr. Edward H. Clarke of Harvard Medical School, whose influential
> book, Sex in Education, went through 17 editions, was perhaps the most
> well-known speaker from the medical community opposing higher edu-
> cation for women. He maintained that the physiological effects of hard
> study and academic competition with boys would interfere with the de-
> velopment of girls' reproductive organs. See E. Clarke, Sex in Education
> 38–39, 62–63 (1873); id. at 127 ("identical education of the two sexes is
> a crime before God and humanity, that physiology protests against, and
> that experience weeps over"); see also H. Maudsley, Sex in Mind and in
> Education 17 (1874) ("It is not that girls have not ambition, nor that they
> fail generally to run the intellectual race [in coeducational settings], but
> it is asserted that they do it at a cost to their strength and health which
> entails life-long suffering, and even incapacitates them for the adequate
> performance of the natural functions of their sex."); C. Meigs, Females
> and Their Diseases 350 (1848) (after five or six weeks of "mental and ed-
> ucational discipline," a healthy woman would "lose . . . the habit of men-
> struation" and suffer numerous ills as a result of depriving her body for
> the sake of the mind).[9]

Again, the generation of "We the people" that made the Fourteenth
Amendment a part of the Constitution did not believe that the Amendment rendered legislative or other governmental distinctions based on sex

constitutionally problematic; they did not understand themselves to have established, as a part of the Fourteenth Amendment, a norm that called into question legislative or other governmental distinctions based on sex. Does this fact entail that the modern Court's disfavoring of discrimination against women is a usurpation of our politics? We do not believe that the fact, if it is a fact, that they did not understand themselves to have established a norm that called into question racially segregated public schooling or antimiscegenation legislation entails that the Court's outlawing of state-created or -maintained racial segregation was a usurpation of our politics. Why, then, should we believe that the fact that they did not understand themselves to have established a norm that called into question legislative or other governmental distinctions based on sex entails that the Court's disfavoring of discrimination against women, and its outlawing of most instances of such discrimination, constitute a usurpation of our politics? The determinative question is not what many or even most members of the generation of "We the people" that made the Fourteenth Amendment a part of the Constitution believed or didn't believe about the constitutionality, under the Fourteenth Amendment, of racially segregated public schooling, antimiscegenation legislation, or (state-sponsored) discrimination based on sex. The determinative question is whether a norm that "We the people", through their representatives, established as a part of the Constitution of the United States is finally consistent or inconsistent with racially segregated public schooling, antimiscegenation legislation, or discrimination based on sex. The generation that made the Fourteenth Amendment a part of the Constitution might have been right in believing what they did about the implications of the Amendment's antidiscrimination norm for racially segregated public schooling, antimiscegenation legislation, or discrimination based on sex. But they might have been wrong. They were not infallible. (Moreover, as I remarked in chapter 4, not only can one be mistaken about some of the implications of a norm, including a constitutional norm, to which one professes commitment, but it might be politically expedient to be mistaken, or at least agnostic, about the politically inexpedient implications of a constitutional norm to which one professes commitment.) We who, generations later, are charged with enforcing their antidiscrimination norm are not infallible either: We might be wrong in believing what we do about the implications of the norm for racially segregated public schooling, antimiscegenation legislation, or discrimination based on sex.[10] But we might be right—even when what we believe about the implications of the norm is different from what they believed. In any event, the determinative inquiry is not what they believed about the implications of the norm they established. The determinative inquiry is twofold: First, what norm did they establish? Second, what are the implications of the norm they established for the matter at hand, what does the norm require with respect to the matter at hand? Even so severe a critic of the modern Supreme Court as Hadley Arkes, who is one of the *First Things* symposiasts who charged the Court with judicial usurpation, acknowledges the point. In commenting approvingly on the Court's decision, in *Loving v. Virginia*,[11] striking down antimiscegenation legislation, Arkes writes:

> Senator Lyman Trumbull, one of the managers of the [Fourteenth] Amendment, had assured his colleagues that there was nothing in the Amendment that would overturn the laws on miscegenation in the separate States. As Trumbull reasoned, those statutes would not violate [the Amendment] because they bore equally on blacks and whites: they barred whites from marrying blacks, as they barred blacks from marrying whites. We would not take that view of the matter today, and not merely because "times have changed." It might be as apt to say that times have changed precisely because we have come to understand, in a more demanding, rigorous way, the principle that bars discriminations based on race.
>
> To put the matter another way, it is possible for jurists and legislators in our own day to find, in the principles behind the Fourteenth Amendment, an understanding that was not shared by the men who enacted the Amendment.[12]

What Fourteenth Amendment norm did "We the people" establish that might be implicated, if not violated, by discrimination against women (i.e., by discrimination against women *as women*)—and, more generally, by any kind of discrimination based on sex, including discrimination that disadvantages men? Several pages of discussion in chapter 3 are relevant here.[13] Let me quote the conclusion to that discussion:

> [T]he fundamental antidiscrimination norm that best reflects and meets the various concerns that inspired "We the people", in the person of their representatives, to make the second sentence of section one of the Fourteenth Amendment a part of the Constitution—the articulation of the norm that best captures the fundamental point or trajectory of "We the people"'s antidiscrimination project—is complex:
>
>> No state may make or enforce any law that denies to some of its citizens, or otherwise lessens or diminishes their enjoyment of, any protected privilege or immunity enjoyed by other of its citizens, if the differential treatment
>>
>> (1) is based on a view to the effect that the disfavored citizens are not truly or fully human—that they are, at best, defective, even debased or degraded, human beings; or
>>
>> (2) is based on hostility to one or more constitutionally protected choices; or, finally,
>>
>> (3) is otherwise not reasonably designed to accomplish a legitimate governmental purpose.

It's easy to see that part (1) of this antidiscrimination norm is implicated (and sometimes violated) by discrimination against women; part (1) is implicated by singling out women (or some women) and treating them differently, and less well, than men (or some men). Moreover, the antidiscrimination norm that, as I explained in the final section of chapter 3, is now a part of our constitutional bedrock is implicated by discrimination against women. Recall, for example, Illinois' exclusion of women from the bar, and many colleges' and universities' exclusion of women from their student bodies. We can now see what was obscure to most members of the generation that gave us the Fourteenth Amendment: Many instances of discrimination against women are based on a view to the effect that being male is normative, that Man is the fully human, the exemplary human, and that by contrast women are not fully human, they are, at best, defective human beings. This is so even when that view is dressed up, as it typically was, as a solicitous concern for the health of a woman's reproductive capacity, for example, or for her divinely ordained role as wife and mother. That such dressings were (and are) often sincere is beside the point: Such dressings are now inexplicable except as rationalizations—self-deluding rationalizations—for a view, an ideology, of women as somehow less than fully human. We can see this, and *should* see it, even if the generation that gave us the Fourteenth Amendment did not. Discrimination against women is commonly rooted, if not in a conscious, explicit affirmation of women as morally inferior, at least in a deeply, culturally ingrained view of women as properly subordinate to men—of women "as persons who [should] play a supportive role to men and to the [social] structure [men] have built and maintain with that support."[14] In 1975, in *Stanton v. Stanton*, the Supreme Court referred to "the role-typing society has long imposed" on women and to the normative view that "the female [is] destined solely for the home and the rearing of the family, and only the male for the marketplace and the world of ideas".[15] (Michael Levin's statement is a conspicuous example of such a view: "In the human species Man is the aggressor and Woman the accepter."[16]) David Richards has rehearsed the classical and medieval antecedents of such an ideology and commented on the modern-day influence of those classical sources:

> Aristotle . . . place[d] women below men but above slaves, so that considerations of equal justice (with men) do not apply to women . . . The Aristotelian view, absorbed into Christian theoretical thought by St. Thomas, was confirmed for Christian and Jewish thought by scripture as well. . . .
> Such an ancient and powerful tradition of thought has understandably led to a common conception of women as not being moral persons in the full sense. . . . [W]omen are supposed incapable of full public life in the world of work and politics; accordingly, on paternalistic grounds women are by law or convention denied the right to participate in that world, or are given that right in special areas on terms of special protections not afforded men.[17]

Even today, an ideology implicit in much of American culture—and sometimes explicit—is "that the man is the 'norm' for being human while the woman is an 'auxiliary,' someone defined exclusively by her relationships to men."[18] According to this ideology, "the one sex . . . is superior to the other in the very order of creation or by the very nature of things."[19]

Many supporters of sex-based differential treatment no doubt sincerely believe, like many in the generation that gave us the Fourteenth Amendment, that what often explains and even necessitates such differential treatment is not the view that being male is normative, that Man is the fully human, but only the view that women are "different but equal"— different from men but equal to them in moral worth. Along these lines, Steven Smith has remarked, in correspondence, that claiming—as some "traditionalists" have, and do, of women—that one or another group of persons "is deficient in some particular quality is not equivalent to saying that [the members of the group are] less than fully human."[20] Smith concludes that it is a mistake, therefore, to think that sex-based differential treatment based on such a claim about women presupposes that women are less than fully human. He also notes that traditionalist supporters of sex-based differential treatment do not say, and do not understand themselves to be implying, that women are less than fully human.

Smith is right that claiming that one or another group of persons—for example, bald men—is deficient in some particular quality is not necessarily to say that the members of the group are less than fully human. But it is also true that claiming that one or another group of persons is deficient in some particular quality might well be to say that the members of the group are less than fully human, especially if the claim is part of an effort to justify the social or political subordination (if not the extermination) of the group. To claim, for example, that African Americans, or Jews, are deficient in reason, or in the capacity for moral judgment, or in whatever it takes to navigate the more esteemed public callings of life—and to make that claim as part of an effort to justify the social or political subordination of African Americans, or of Jews—is to say that African Americans, or Jews, are less than fully human. (Thomas Jefferson "was able both to own slaves and to think it self-evident that all men are endowed by their creator with certain inalienable rights. He had convinced himself that the consciousness of Blacks, like that of animals, 'participates more of sensation than reflection.' Like the Serbs, Mr. Jefferson did not think of himself as violating *human* rights. The Serbs take themselves to be acting in the interests of true humanity by purifying the world of pseudohumanity."[21]) Similarly, to claim that women are deficient in reason, or in the capacity for moral judgment, or in whatever it takes to navigate the more esteemed public callings of life—and to make that claim as part of an effort to justify the social or political subordination of women—is to say that women are less than fully human. At least, given everything we have learned about the ways in which, across space and time, women have been subordinated, and about the various rationalizations that have been offered for that subordination,[22] it seems naive in the extreme to doubt that the claim that women are deficient in reason, etc.—presented as part of an effort to justify limiting the opportunities of women as a group relative to those of men as a group—is *pro tanto* the claim that being male is normative, that Man is the exemplary human.[23]

Consider this: "Even the New England Freedmen's Society said in

1865 [in support of racially segregated education] that 'while we do not admit the absolute inferiority of any race . . . there can yet be no question that races, like nations and individuals, have their peculiarities. All elements are present, but they are blended in different proportions. In the negro race we believe the poetic and emotional qualities predominate, rather than the prosaic, mechanical, and merely intellectual powers.'"[24] (Recall here the outrageous statement by the majority in *Plessy v. Ferguson*: "Laws permitting, and even requiring, [the separation of the two races] in places where they are liable to be brought into contact *do not necessarily imply the inferiority of either race to the other* . . . The most common instance of this is connected with the establishment of separate schools for white and colored children . . . [T]he enforced separation of the two races [does not] stamp[] the colored race with a badge of inferiority."[25]) Does the fact that the New England Freedmen's Society (like the majority in *Plessy*) did not accept that its position was racist mean that we, almost a century and a half later, should deny that the Society's position—presented in justification of limiting the educational opportunities of "negroes" as a group relative to those of whites as a group—imputed to Americans of African descent a lesser, an inferior, humanity? Why, then, should we doubt that when similar things are said about women as a group ("the poetic and emotional qualities predominate, rather than the prosaic, mechanical, and merely intellectual powers")—in justification of limiting the opportunities of women as a group relative to those of men as a group—a lesser humanity is being imputed to women, even if those who say such things about women do not see the demeaning import of their position? Obviously, those who say such things about women, like those who say such things about a racial minority, have a powerful interest—they have a huge investment—in not seeing the demeaning import of their position. Note that "[w]hatever the articulated beliefs regarding 'different but equal' roles of women and men, women's gender-assigned roles have invariably been subordinate, passive, and/or restricted to the private sphere."[26] Are we to believe this state of affairs to be a mere coincidence?

So: The antidiscrimination norm is implicated, and sometimes—indeed, often—violated, by discrimination against women. Hereafter, when I say "the antidiscrimination norm", I do not, because I need not, distinguish between the version of the norm I believe to have been established by "We the people" and the broader version that, as I explained in chapter 3, is now constitutional bedrock for us *even if no version was established by "We the people"*. Each version suffices for purposes of the arguments I make in this chapter.

To say that a particular instance of discrimination against women implicates the antidiscrimination norm is not to say that the discrimination actually violates the norm. It might be the case—*might* be—that there is a nonsexist explanation for the discrimination. But how is the Court to separate the wheat from the chaff, the innocent from the guilty? Recall, from the preceding chapter, how the Court deals with a similar problem posed by discrimination against members of a racial minority:

> As a real-world matter, for government to use race as a criterion of selection in distributing a benefit or a burden, *denying the benefit to members of a racial minority or imposing the burden on them*, has virtually always been for government to distribute the benefit or the burden on a racist basis. Understandably, therefore, the Court's practice, in the modern period of American constitutional law, has been to regard as suspicious any use of race as a criterion of selection in a law that disadvantages a racial minority. In the Court's practice and parlance, race is a "suspect classification"—that is, a suspect basis of classification. Suspected of what? The Court suspects that the use of race as a criterion of selection in a law that disadvantages a racial minority is a racist act: an act based on a view to the effect that because of their race, the disadvantaged minority are not truly or fully human—that they are, at best, defective, even debased or degraded, human beings. Accordingly, the Court presumes that the use of race as a criterion of selection in a law that disadvantages a racial minority is in fact racist, and therefore unconstitutional, unless government can defeat the presumption by showing that the use of race as a criterion of selection is "necessary" to satisfy a "compelling" governmental interest. That is the sense in which the use of race as a criterion of selection in a law that disadvantages a racial minority is constitutionally disfavored: The Court will subject such use of race to the most demanding "standard of review", it will subject it to "strict scrutiny" (or, as the Court recently put it, "the most rigid scrutiny"); that is, the Court will inquire whether the use of race as a criterion of selection is necessary to satisfy a compelling governmental interest. Such scrutiny is the Court's shrewd, practical way of ferreting out, indirectly or by proxy, what might otherwise be the hidden racist rationale for a law: If the use of race as a criterion of selection in a law that disadvantages a racial minority is not necessary to satisfy a compelling governmental interest, then the *real* reason for the law, the *actual* basis for the use of race as a criterion of selection in the law, is almost certainly racist.[27]

The Court deals with discrimination that disadvantages women in an analogous way and for an analogous reason. Indeed, the Court deals with any (state-sponsored) discrimination based on sex—including discrimination that disadvantages men[28]—in an analogous way and for an analogous reason. Given the practical difficulty of discerning if a particular instance of singling out women for worse treatment than men receive, or men for worse treatment than women receive, is based on a sexist view of women's and men's relative worth or capacity as human beings—and given, too, the prevalence of sexist ideology even in contemporary American culture and the importance, therefore, of a healthy suspicion about the real (v. the asserted) rationale for singling out women or men for worse treatment[29]—it makes sense for the Court to do what it does, namely, disfavor discrimination based on sex by presuming that such discrimination violates the applicable norm. Pursuant to the Court's approach, any singling out, any differential treatment, based on sex will be adjudged unconstitutional unless the Court is persuaded that the rationale for the singling out—the rationale for drawing a line based on sex rather than on some other, less suspicious basis—satisfies a strict standard of justification. As the Court, per Justice Sandra Day O'Connor, put it in *Mississippi University for Women v. Hogan*, "[T]he party seeking to uphold a statute that classifies individuals on the basis of their gender must carry the burden of showing an 'exceedingly persuasive justification' for the classification. . . . The burden is met only by showing at least that the [sex-based singling out] serves 'important governmental objectives and . . . [is] substantially related to the achievement of those objectives.' "[30] No sexist rationale for discrimination based on sex satisfies the strict standard. In particular, no governmental objective is constitutionally legitimate, much less "important", if it presupposes that sex is a determinant of a person's status or worth as a human being: "Although the test for determining the validity of a gender-based classification is straightforward, it must be applied free of fixed notions concerning the roles and abilities of males and females. Care must be taken in ascertaining whether the statutory objective itself reflects archaic and stereotypic notions. Thus, if the statutory objective is to exclude or 'protect' members of one gender because they are presumed to suffer from an inherent handicap or to be innately inferior, the objective itself is illegitimate."[31]

In *Hogan*, the Court left no doubt that the principal function of strict scrutiny in the context of discrimination based on sex—to "smoke out" the suspected sexist rationale for an instance of such discrimination—is substantially the same as the function of strict scrutiny in the context of discrimination on the basis of race. Recall the Court's statement, in *Adarand*, about the function of strict scrutiny of differential treatment based on race: "[T]he purpose of strict scrutiny is to 'smoke out' illegitimate uses of race by assuring that the legislative body is pursuing a goal important enough to warrant use of a highly suspect tool. The test also insures that the means chosen 'fit' this compelling goal so closely that there is little or no possibility that the motive for the classification was illegitimate racial prejudice or stereotype."[32] Now, compare the Court's earlier, similar statement in *Hogan* about the function of strict scrutiny of differential treatment based on sex:

> If the State's objective is legitimate and important, we next determine whether the requisite direct, substantial relationship between objective and means is present. The purpose of requiring that close relationship is to assure that the validity of a classification is determined through reasoned analysis rather than through the mechanical application of traditional, often inaccurate assumptions about the proper roles of men and women. The need for the requirement is amply revealed by reference to the broad range of statutes already invalidated by this Court, statutes that rely upon the simplistic, outdated assumption that gender could be sued

as a "proxy for other, more germane bases of classification" . . . to establish a link between objective and classification.[33]

In the preceding chapter, I explained why it was not a "judicial usurpation" of our politics, on any plausible understanding of the usurpation claim, for the modern Supreme Court to outlaw, in the name of the Fourteenth Amendment, state-created or -maintained racial segregation. Now we can see why it is no "judicial usurpation" for the Court to outlaw sexist laws and practices. For the Court to disfavor all (government-sponsored) discrimination based on sex, by subjecting it to a strict standard of review, a strict scrutiny, and for the Court to outlaw most instances of such discrimination, is for the Court to enforce a norm that was established as a part of the Constitution—as a part of the Fourteenth Amendment—by "We the people". It was legitimate, therefore, for the Court to move beyond race to sex. Indeed, it was more than legitimate: The Court was obligated to move beyond race to sex by its special responsibility for protecting the Constitution—the constitutional norms—that "We the people" have ordained and established.

Moreover, even if I am wrong in thinking that in the cases under discussion the Court is enforcing a norm that was established by "We the people"—even if no antidiscrimination norm was established by "We the people"—an antidiscrimination norm nonetheless became a part of our constitutional bedrock; indeed, the antidiscrimination norm that became a part of our constitutional bedrock, as I explained in the final section of chapter 3, is broader than any antidiscrimination norm that was arguably established by the generation that bequeathed us the Fourteenth Amendment. This broad norm (as I explained in chapter 3) became constitutional bedrock in the post–World War II era, in part because of the horrific lessons of the war and, especially, of the Holocaust. The norm centrally forbids government to treat any person or group of persons less well than another person or group on the basis of the view that the disfavored persons (nonwhites, women, Jews, etc.) are not truly or fully human—that they are, at best, defective, even debased or degraded, human beings. Because this norm became constitutional bedrock for us in the postwar era, it was not a judicial usurpation of our politics for the modern Court to enforce the norm—or, in enforcing the norm, to move beyond race to sex. That the Supreme Court brings to bear on our politics a norm that was not established as a part of the Constitution by "We the people" does not entail that the Court is usurping our politics; as I explained in chapter 1, there is no judicial usurpation unless, in addition, the norm the Court brings to bear is not constitutional bedrock for us, the people of the United States now living.

I just concluded that it was no judicial usurpation for the modern Court to move beyond race to sex. Some critics of the Court, however, disagree. Consider, in that regard, the firestorm that greeted the Supreme Court's decision, in 1996, in *United States v. Virginia*,[34] also known as "the

VMI case". Virginia did not permit women to enroll as cadets at the Virginia Military Institute. The Court did not rule that the Fourteenth Amendment forbade Virginia from maintaining a single-sex institution of higher learning, military or otherwise.[35] The Court ruled only that Virginia could not maintain a single-sex educational opportunity for young men *while at the same time failing to provide a truly comparable opportunity for young women*. By a vote of seven to one, the Court concluded that Virginia had failed to justify, under the applicable standard of review, its refusal to provide interested and otherwise qualified young women with substantially the same educational opportunity that it happily provided interested and qualified young men. (Justice Clarence Thomas abstained from participating in the case because his son was a cadet at The Citadel, "[a]nother famous Southern institution [that] has existed as a state-funded school of South Carolina since 1842."[36]) The Court reasoned that "[a] purpose genuinely to advance an array of educational options . . . is not served by VMI's historic and constant plan—a plan to 'affor[d] a unique educational benefit only to males.' However 'liberally' this plan serves the State's sons, it makes no provision whatever for her daughters. That is not *equal* protection."[37] It is a significant indicator of the weakness of Virginia's position in the case that even Chief Justice William H. Rehnquist, a judicial conservative who had dissented from many of the Court's previous constitutional rulings against sex-based discrimination, agreed that Virginia had failed to justify its discriminatory treatment of women. "The difficulty with [Virginia's] position is that the diversity benefited only one sex; there was single-sex public education available for men at VMI, but no corresponding single-sex public education available for women."[38]

The conspicuous weakness of Virginia's position in the VMI case—a weakness evidenced by the lopsided, seven-to-one vote in the case—mattered to Chief Justice Rehnquist and six other Supreme Court justices, but it did not matter to angry, would-have-been justice Robert Bork. In his best-selling book, *Slouching Towards Gomorrah: Modern Liberalism and the American Decline*, Bork greeted the Court's decision with this fevered response: "The Court continues to use [the Fourteenth Amendment] to take basic cultural decisions out of the hands of the people. Culture is made by the fiat of a majority of nine lawyers [i.e., the nine Supreme Court justices] and forced upon the nation. No more egregious example can be found than the decision in *United States v. Virginia* that the Virginia Military Institute, the state's only single-sex school, now must admit women."[39] One could have said, with as much plausibility—or as little—that in outlawing racially segregated public schools and antimiscegenation legislation, "the Court uses the Fourteenth Amendment to take basic cultural decisions out of the hands of the people. Culture is made by the fiat of a majority of nine lawyers and forced upon the nation."[40]

Later in 1996, in his contribution to the *First Things* symposium, Bork declared: "This last term of the Supreme Court brought home to us with fresh clarity what it means to be ruled by an oligarchy. The most important moral, political and cultural decisions affecting our lives are steadily being removed from democratic control. . . . A majority of the Court routinely enacts its own preference as the command of our basic document. . . . This last term was unusually rich in examples." Bork then gave, as one of his examples, the Court's decision in the VMI case, where, he charged, the Court "adopted the radical feminist view that men and women are essentially identical . . ."[41] This is an egregiously mistaken reading of the Court's opinion in the VMI case, where in the body of its opinion, and not merely in a footnote, the Court, per Justice Ruth Bader Ginsburg, emphasized: "'Inherent differences' between men and women, we have come to appreciate, remain cause for celebration . . ."[42] That doesn't sound like the Court adopting "the radical feminist view that men and women are essentially identical". The Court did go on to say that, although a cause for celebration, the differences between men and women are not a cause "for denigration of the members of either sex or for artificial constraints on an individual's opportunity. Sex classifications . . . may not be used, as they once were, to create or perpetuate the legal, social, and economic inferiority of women."[43] Is such a statement what Bork means by "a majority of the Court routinely enact[ing] its own preference as the command of our basic document"? What antidiscrimination norm, in Bork's view, did "We the people" establish as a part of the Fourteenth Amendment? What antidiscrimination norm, in Bork's view, is now a part of our constitutional bedrock (if indeed Bork believes that *any* general antidiscrimination norm is constitutional bedrock for us)? Recall, from chapter 1, that in his contribution to the *First Things* symposium, Bork reported that his wife had accused the justices of the Court of "behaving like a 'band of outlaws.'" It was "[w]hen the VMI decision came down," Bork explained, that his wife delivered her accusation. Recall, too, that Bork endorsed his wife's condemnation of the justices, saying that it was not "in the least bit extreme." He explained: "An outlaw is a person who coerces others without warrant in law. That is precisely what a majority of the present Supreme Court does. That is, given the opportunity, what the Supreme Court has always done."[44]

A no less angry attack on the Court's decision in the VMI case was mounted by a furious Justice Antonin Scalia, who not only dissented from the Court's ruling but maligned it. (Scalia was the only justice to dissent, although Justice Thomas surely would have dissented had he participated in the case. In Robert Bork's judgment, "Only Justices Antonin Scalia and Clarence Thomas attempt to give the Constitution the meaning it had for those who adopted it."[45]) Anticipating Bork's criticism, Scalia charged in his dissenting opinion that "this most illiberal Court has embarked on a course of inscribing one after another of the current preferences of the society (and in some cases only the countermajoritarian preferences of the society's law-trained elite) into our Basic Law."[46] What did Justice Scalia say about the constitutionality of VMI's exclusion of women? According to Scalia, "longstanding national traditions [are] the primary determinant of what the Constitution means."[47] He explained, in dissent, that "'when a practice not expressly prohibited by the text of the Bill of Rights bears the endorsement of a long tradition of open, widespread, and unchallenged use that dates back to the beginning of the Republic, we have no proper basis for striking it down.' The same applies, *mutatis mutandi*, to a practice asserted to be in violation of the post–Civil War Fourteenth Amendment."[48] Therefore, reasoned Scalia, VMI's exclusion of women was constitutionally permissible. Doesn't Scalia's approach lend support to, if not indeed yield, the proposition that in 1954 the Court should not have struck down the practice of racially segregated public schooling (or, later, the practice of outlawing interracial marriages)? Racially segregated public schooling, after all, was a practice not expressly prohibited by the text of the Fourteenth Amendment that bore the endorsement of a long tradition of open, widespread, and largely unchallenged use that dated back to the time of the Fourteenth Amendment and earlier.

Scalia emphasized, in the VMI case, that "all the federal military colleges—West Point, the Naval Academy at Annapolis, and even the Air Force Academy, which was not established until 1954—admitted only males for most of their history. Their admission of women in 1976 . . . came not by court decree, but because the people, through their elected representatives, decreed a change." According to Scalia, "the tradition of having government-funded military schools for men is . . . well rooted in the traditions of this country . . ." Although "[t]he people may decide to change [that] tradition . . . through democratic processes", the conclusion that the tradition violates the Fourteenth Amendment "is not law, but politics-smuggled-into-law."[49] In 1945, would it have been, "not law, but politics-smuggled-into-law" to conclude that a racially segregated West Point violated the Constitution? According to Scalia's deferential-to-the-traditions-of-this-country approach, wouldn't it have been a judicial usurpation of our politics for the Court to rule, in 1945, that West Point, or VMI, or The Citadel, could not, consistently with the Constitution, exclude nonwhites? Wasn't it a judicial usurpation, according to Scalia's approach, for the Court to declare, in 1954, that racially segregated public schooling violated section one of the Fourteenth Amendment? Doesn't Scalia's approach dictate that a departure from a traditional practice like racially segregated public education should have been made, not by the Court in the course of constitutional adjudication, but only by the people, through their elected representatives, in the course of ordinary lawmaking. We can imagine someone, in 1954, anticipating Scalia's approach by insisting: "Although the people may decide to abolish the tradition of racially segregated public schooling through democratic processes, the conclusion that the tradition violates the Fourteenth Amendment is not law, but politics-smuggled-into-law." Indeed, as I pointed out in the preceding chapter, there are even today some who steadfastly maintain that the Court's decision in *Brown v. Board of Education*[50] was, to use Scalia's term, "politics-smuggled-into-law". Consider, for example, Lino Graglia's claim, in 1994, forty years after the Court's decision in *Brown*, that racially segregated public schooling "was held unconstitutional, in *Brown*, . . . for no other reason than that the justices had a different policy preference and were willing to have their preference prevail."[51] Does Scalia, like Graglia, believe that the Court's decision in *Brown* was politics-smuggled-into-law?

It is axiomatic, in American constitutional culture, that the Court has a special responsibility to protect, by enforcing, the norms comprised by the Constitution. As I explained in chapter 2, this responsibility, though axiomatic, leaves room for disagreement among the justices of the Court, and others, about how deferentially the Court should exercise its responsibility, both in deciding whether a norm is a part of the Constitution and, if a constitutional norm is indeterminate in the context at hand, in specifying, or shaping, the norm. Nonetheless, it is difficult to see how Scalia's approach can be squared with the Court's obligation to enforce, even if only deferentially, constitutional norms. Does Justice Scalia think that the Court's obligation contains an escape clause, according to which the Court can and indeed should defer to "We the people"'s belief that a norm they established does not forbid one or another practice *whether or not the belief is mistaken—and, so, even if the belief is palpably mistaken*? (It is scarcely surprising that in the VMI case, seven members of the United States Supreme Court, including Chief Justice Rehnquist, refused to follow their brother Scalia's complacently "traditionalist" approach to enforcement of the Fourteenth Amendment.[52]) Or is it that Scalia denies that any antidiscrimination norm—either one that might have been established by "We the people" or one that might now be constitutional bedrock for us—is even implicated, much less violated, by discrimination based on sex?

II. Discrimination against Homosexuals

The Court's decision in *Romer v. Evans*,[53] striking down a newly adopted Colorado constitutional amendment that, in the Court's view, discriminated against homosexuals in violation of the Fourteenth Amendment, was at least as controversial as its decision in the VMI case. (The Court announced its decision in *Romer* in May 1996, just one month before the Court announced its decision in the VMI case. Recall Robert Bork's lament that the 1995–96 Term of Court "brought home to us with fresh clarity what it means to be ruled by an oligarchy.") I have just explained why it was legitimate for the Court, in enforcing the Fourteenth Amendment, to move beyond discrimination based on race to discrimination based on sex. The Court's move beyond race to sex was not a usurpation of our politics, on any plausible understanding of the usurpation claim. Would it be legitimate for the Court now to move beyond race and sex to sexual orientation? Or would such a move, as some have insisted, constitute a judicial usurpation? (Does the Supreme Court's decision in *Romer*, as some fear and others hope, signal that the Court has already begun to move beyond race and sex to sexual orientation?) Up to now, I have inquired whether certain constitutional doctrines that the modern Supreme Court has fully articulated and that seem firmly in place—doctrines about racial segregation, race-based affirmative action, and discrimination based on sex—do or do not constitute a judicial usurpation of our politics, in any plausible sense of the usurpation claim. The inquiry now is whether a constitutional doctrine that the Court has not (yet) articulated—a doctrine disfavoring discrimination against homosexuals the way that discrimination against women is disfavored, namely, by subjecting it to a strict standard of review—would or would not constitute a usurpation of our politics.

As before, a clarification is in order. The question is not whether section one of the Fourteenth Amendment—in particular, the second sentence of section one—protects (i.e., was understood and meant to protect) homosexuals. The due process and equal protection norms established by "We the people" each protect all persons, and homosexuals are persons. The privileges or immunities norm established by "We the people" protects at least all citizens, and homosexuals as well as heterosexuals are citizens. The question is what section one—especially the privileges or immunities norm—protects homosexuals (and others) from. Whatever else it protects them from, the privileges or immunities norm protects all those whom it protects, including homosexuals, from at least some discrimination—for example, racist discrimination. The disputed question is whether the privileges or immunities norm established by "We the people" protects homosexuals from discrimination against them *as homosexuals*. (If, like the Supreme Court, one reads the equal protection provision, rather than the privileges or immunities provision, to supply the relevant norm,[54] the disputed question is whether, in addition to protecting homosexuals from, for example, racist discrimination, the equal protection norm also protects homosexuals from discrimination against them as homosexuals.)

What laws (and other official actions) discriminate against homosexuals—that is, discriminate against homosexuals *as such*? Let's proceed analogically, by asking what laws discriminate against black persons (as such), or against women (as such). Clearly, a law discriminates against persons who are black if it treats them differently, and less well, than it would treat them if they were not black. But, undeniably, a law also discriminates against black persons, even though by its terms the law applies to, and disadvantages, persons without regard to their color, if the law would not have been enacted but for the purpose of preventing black persons from doing something, or at least of making it more difficult for black persons to do something, that (a majority of) the lawmakers believe it undesirable for black persons, *because they are black persons,* to do, or less desirable for them than for white persons to do—for example, work, or work in such large numbers, for the police department. Imagine, in that regard, a hiring test that a disproportionately large number of black persons fail, deployed for the purpose of minimizing the number of black employees in the police department.[55] Similarly, a law discriminates against women if it treats them less well than it would treat them if they were men. But, of course, a law also discriminates against women, even though by its terms the law disadvantages persons without regard to their sex, if the law would not have been enacted but for the purpose of preventing women from doing something (or at least of making it more difficult for them to do something) that the lawmakers believe it undesirable for women, *because they are women,* to do, or less desirable for them than for men to do— for example, hold certain jobs. Imagine a veteran's preference scheme test that a disproportionately large number of women cannot claim, deployed for the purpose of minimizing the number of women in certain civil service positions.[56] Finally, a law discriminates against homosexuals if it treats them less well than it would treat them if they were heterosexuals. But a law also discriminates against homosexuals, even though by its terms the law disadvantages persons without regard to their sexual orientation, if the law would not have been enacted but for the purpose of preventing homosexuals from doing something that the lawmakers believe it undesirable for homosexuals, *because they are homosexuals,* to do, or less desirable for them than for heterosexuals to do.

Now, imagine a law that outlaws all sex outside of marriage: all sexual activity between (or among) persons not married to one another. Whatever constitutional problems it might present, if indeed it would present any, this law does not treat homosexuals less well than it would treat them if they were heterosexual, because it applies to every person without regard to his or her sexual orientation: No person, whatever his or her sexual orientation, may engage in any sexual activity with another person, whatever his or her sexual orientation, unless they are married to one another. The law does not treat a homosexual who is engaging in sexual activity with someone to whom she is not married less well than it would treat her if she were a heterosexual engaging in sexual activity with someone to whom she is not married. (Later in this chapter, I address the question whether it is unconstitutional for a state to refuse to recognize same-sex unions. But for now, assume that a state's refusal to recognize same-sex unions does not violate the Fourteenth Amendment.) Imagine, by contrast, a law that outlaws all same-sex sexual activity: all sexual activity between persons of the same sex. Now, one might say something to this effect: "This law does not treat homosexuals less well than it would treat them if they were heterosexual, because it applies to every person without regard to his or her sexual orientation: No person, no matter what his or her sexual orientation, may engage in any sexual activity with another person of the same sex, whatever his or her sexual orientation. The law does not treat a homosexual who is engaging in sexual activity with someone of the same sex less well than it would treat her if she were a heterosexual engaging in sexual activity with someone of the same sex." Strictly speaking, this response is accurate. But the law nonetheless discriminates against homosexuals (as such) if, as is surely the case, the law, which by its terms applies to persons without regard to their sexual orientation, would not have been enacted but for the purpose of preventing homosexuals from doing something (or at least of making it more difficult for them to do something) that the lawmakers believed it undesirable for homosexuals, because they are homosexuals, to do, namely, live lives in fulfillment of their sexual desire: the sexual desire that they have as homosexuals—indeed, the sexual desire that is constitutive of them as homosexuals.[57]

The serious claim is not that laws that discriminate against homosexuals are ipso facto unconstitutional. Just as the fact that a law discriminates against black persons, or against women, does not entail that the law violates the Fourteenth Amendment, that a law discriminates against homosexuals does not entail that the law violates the Fourteenth Amendment. The serious claim is that, like laws that discriminate against black persons, or against women, laws that discriminate against homosexuals should be disfavored—*constitutionally* disfavored, disfavored *under the Fourteenth Amendment*. Again, let's proceed analogically. As I explained in the preceding chapter, the Supreme Court disfavors, by subjecting to a strict standard of review, laws that discriminate against black persons because the Court understands that most such laws are based on a view, an ideology, that violates the antidiscrimination norm and that therefore every such law should be strictly scrutinized to make sure that it is not in fact based on such a view. (Recall that the antidiscrimination norm forbids government to treat one group less well than another based on a view to the effect that members of the former group are not truly or fully human—that they are, at best, defective, even debased or degraded, human beings. Again, when I say "the antidiscrimination norm", I need not distinguish between the version of the norm I believe to have been established by "We the people" and the broader version that is now constitutional bedrock for us even if no version was established by "We the people", because each version suffices for purposes of the position I defend here.) Similarly, and as I explained earlier in this chapter, the Court disfavors laws that discriminate against women because the Court understands that most such laws are based on an ideology that violates the antidiscrimination norm and that therefore every such law should be strictly scrutinized to make sure that it is not in fact based on such a view. Laws that discriminate against homosexuals should be disfavored, by being subjected to a strict standard of review, because most such laws are based on an ideology that violates the antidiscrimination norm, and therefore every such law should be strictly scrutinized to make sure that it is not in fact based on such a view. That laws discriminating against homosexuals are typically based on an ideology that offends the antidiscrimination norm scarcely seems a radical proposition. Consider, in that regard, Richard Posner's observation that statutes which criminalize homosexual behavior express *an irrational fear and loathing of a group that has been subjected to discrimination, much like that directed against the Jews, with whom indeed homosexuals—who, like Jews, are despised more for who they are than for what they do—were frequently bracketed in medieval persecutions.* The statutes thus have a quality of invidiousness missing from statutes prohibiting abortion or contraception. The position of the homosexual is difficult at best, even in a tolerant society, which our society is not quite; and it is made worse, though probably not much worse, by statutes that condemn the homosexual's characteristic methods of sexual expression as vile crimes . . . There is a gratuitousness, an egregiousness, a cruelty, and a meanness about [such statutes].[58]

Posner's comment was occasioned by the Supreme Court's five-to-four decision, in 1986, in *Bowers v. Hardwick*, ruling that the Fourteenth Amendment did not prevent Georgia from criminalizing "consensual homosexual sodomy".[59] The majority opinion placed substantial weight on the proposition that "[p]roscriptions against [homosexual] conduct have ancient roots."[60] Not surprisingly, the Court failed to note that proscriptions embedded in racist views and proscriptions embedded in sexist views—proscriptions that the modern Court, in the name of the Fourteenth Amendment, had disestablished—also had ancient roots.[61] In the opinion of the slim majority that prevailed in *Bowers*, although a state may not, under the Fourteenth Amendment, adopt a negative attitude to a person's being black, or a woman, a state *may* adopt a negative attitude toward homosexual sexual desire; in particular, it may act on the basis of the proposition that it is immoral for one to live a life in fulfillment of the sexual desire that one has as a homosexual. Was *Bowers v. Hardwick* rightly decided? Would it have been a judicial usurpation of our politics for the Court to decide that Georgia, by targeting not all nonmarital sexual desire, but only a *homosexual's* sexual desire, was acting in violation of the Fourteenth Amendment?

Assume that a state, under the Fourteenth Amendment, may target all nonmarital sexual desire. Assume, that is, that a state may outlaw all sexual activity outside of marriage. (Such a law would reach sexual activity without regard to whether it was same-sex or other-sex.) Assume further that in reforming its laws, a state has repealed its law against sexual activity outside of marriage but has left on the books its law against same-sex sexual activity. (Or assume, equivalently for constitutional purposes, that a state no longer enforces, or even threatens to enforce, its law against sexual activity outside of marriage but that it sometimes enforces, or at least sometimes threatens to enforce, its law against same-sex sexual activity.) It does not follow that because a state may outlaw sexual activity outside of marriage, a state may also take the lesser step of outlawing nonmarital sexual activity between two persons (a man and a woman) of different races while leaving unregulated nonmarital sexual activity between two persons (a man and a woman) of the same race. Such a law would be no less unconstitutional than the antimiscegenation law struck down by the Court in *Loving v. Virginia*.[62] Similarly, that a state may outlaw sexual activity outside of marriage does not entail that it may also take the lesser step of outlawing sexual activity between two persons of the same sex while leaving unregulated nonmarital sexual activity between two persons of the opposite sex.

It is true that engaging in sexual activity, including same-sex sexual activity, is typically something one chooses to do, whereas being black, or a woman, or having homosexual sexual desire, is not something one chooses. But that difference is beside the present point. That sexual activity is (typically) an object of human choice does not entail that a state may outlaw—and, in fact, a state may not outlaw—nonmarital sexual activity between two persons of different races while leaving unregulated nonmarital sexual activity between two persons of the same race. Nor does it entail that a state may outlaw sexual activity between two persons of the same sex while leaving unregulated nonmarital sexual activity between two persons of the opposite sex. As I explained earlier, by outlawing sexual activity between two persons of the same sex while leaving unregulated nonmarital sexual activity between a man and a woman, a state undeniably discriminates against homosexuals. But, again, to discriminate against homosexuals—or against blacks, or women—is not *necessarily* to violate the Fourteenth Amendment. Whether discrimination against blacks or women or homosexuals violates the Fourteenth Amendment depends on what the basis of the discrimination is; it depends on whether the discrimination can be explained—justified—in terms that rebut the inference that the basis of the discrimination is constitutionally illicit. The serious question, therefore, is not whether outlawing same-sex sexual activity while leaving unregulated (nonmarital) sexual activity between a man and a woman, a state discriminates against homosexuals. (It does.) The serious question is whether in discriminating against homosexuals in that way, a state acts in violation of the Fourteenth Amendment.

Consider, with respect to that question, an important decision, in 1993, by the Supreme Court of Kentucky. In *Commonwealth [of Kentucky] v. Wasson*,[63] the Kentucky Supreme Court said: "Certainly, the practice of [sodomy] violates traditional morality. But so does the same act between heterosexuals, which activity is decriminalized. Going one step further, *all* sexual activity between consenting adults outside of marriage violates our traditional morality." The court then put the central constitutional question: "The issue here is not whether sexual activity traditionally viewed as immoral can be punished by society, *but whether it can be punished solely on the basis of sexual preference.* . . . The question is whether a society that no longer criminalizes adultery, fornication, or [sodomy] between heterosexuals, has a rational basis to single out homosexual acts for different treatment."[64] The Kentucky Supreme Court went on to conclude—correctly, in my view—that Kentucky had failed to justify its differential treatment of homosexuals:

The Commonwealth [of Kentucky] has tried hard to demonstrate a legitimate governmental interest justifying a distinction [between homosexuals and heterosexuals], but it has failed. Many of the claimed justifications are simply outrageous: that "homosexuals are more promiscuous than heterosexuals, . . . that homosexuals enjoy the company of children, and that homosexuals are more prone to engage in sex acts in public." The only proffered justification with superficial validity is that "infectious diseases are more readily transmitted by anal sodomy than by other forms of sexual copulation." But this statute is not limited to anal copulation, and this reasoning would apply to male-female anal intercourse the same as it applies to male-male anal intercourse. . . .

In the final analysis we can attribute no legislative purpose to this statute except to single out homosexuals for different treatment for indulging their sexual preference by engaging in the same activity heterosexuals are now at liberty to perform. . . . We need not sympathize, agree with, or even understand the sexual preference of homosexuals in order to recognize their right to equal treatment before the bar of criminal justice.[65]

(Because the Kentucky Supreme Court based its decision on the state constitution, its decision was not vulnerable to reversal by the United States Supreme Court.)

By failing to offer a persuasive explanation for its differential treatment of homosexuals, Kentucky failed to rebut the inference that its differential treatment of homosexuals was based on what Justice Stevens, in a dissenting opinion in *Bowers v. Hardwick*, decried as "the habitual dislike for, or ignorance about," homosexuals.[66] Kentucky failed to rebut the inference that its discrimination against homosexuals was based on what Judge Posner described as "an irrational fear and loathing of a group that . . . like Jews, are despised more for who they are than for what they do . . ." As history teaches, "an irrational fear and loathing" of *any* group "more for who they are than for what they do" has tragic consequences. The irrational fear and loathing of homosexuals—that is, the fear and loathing of them *more for who they are than for what they do*—is no exception. There is, for example, the horrible phenomenon of "gay bashing". "The coordinator of one hospital's victim assistance program reported that 'attacks against gay men were the most heinous and brutal I encountered.' A physician reported that injuries suffered by the victims of homophobic violence he had treated were so 'vicious' as to make clear that 'the intent is to kill and maim' . . ."[67] Consider, too, that, as "[a] federal task force on youth suicide noted[,] because 'gay youth face a hostile and condemning environment, verbal and physical abuse, and rejection and isolation from family and peers,' young gays are two to three times more likely than other young people to attempt and to commit suicide."[68]

Discrimination against homosexuals based on "an irrational fear and loathing" of them—a fear and loathing of them "more for who they are than for what they do"—plainly violates the Fourteenth Amendment imperative that no state discriminate against any group on the basis of a view to the effect that members of the disfavored group are not truly or fully human, that they are, at best, defective, even debased or degraded, human beings. *Bowers v. Hardwick*, therefore, was wrongly—very wrongly—decided. It would not have been a judicial usurpation of our politics, on any plausible understanding of the usurpation claim, for the Court to have ruled that in targeting homosexuals—that is, in targeting not all nonmarital sexual desire, but only a homosexual's sexual desire—Georgia was violating the Fourteenth Amendment. To the contrary, it was an unjustified denigration of our Constitution for the Court to rule that Georgia's targeting of homosexuals was consistent with the Fourteenth Amendment. Significantly, when the Court ruled, in *Romer v. Evans*, that a newly adopted Colorado constitutional amendment discriminated against homosexuals in violation of the Fourteenth Amendment, the Court did not see fit even to mention, much less try to distinguish, its decision a decade earlier in *Bowers*. The Court's decision in *Romer*, coupled with its stunning silence about *Bowers*, suggests that *Bowers*, if not already dead, is very near death.[69]

Let's consider the Court's decision in *Romer*. In their bans on discrimination in housing, employment, education, and some other areas, the cities of Aspen, Boulder, and Denver each included discrimination against homosexuals (as such). This did not sit well with many Coloradans. In 1992, a majority of the Colorado voters who participated in a statewide referendum adopted a proposed amendment—"Amendment 2", as it was called in the referendum—to the state constitution. Amendment 2 declared:

> No Protected Status Based on Homosexual, Lesbian, or Bisexual Orientation. Neither the State of Colorado, through any of its branches or departments, nor any of its agencies, political subdivisions, municipalities or school districts, shall enact, adopt, or enforce any statute, regulation, ordinance or policy whereby homosexual, lesbian or bisexual orientation, conduct, practices or relationships shall constitute or otherwise be the basis of or entitle any person or class of persons to have or claim any minority status, quota preferences, protected status or claim of discrimination. This Section of the Constitution shall be in all respects self-executing.

In other words, Amendment 2 instructed the cities of Aspen, Boulder, and Denver that they could no longer ban discrimination against homosexuals (with respect to housing, employment, education, etc.). Indeed, not even the Colorado legislature could, under Amendment 2, enact a ban on discrimination against homosexuals.

Litigation ensued, and eventually the Colorado Supreme Court declared that Amendment 2 violated the Fourteenth Amendment to the U.S. Constitution. The United States Supreme Court affirmed the judgment of the Colorado Supreme Court.[70] A majority of the Court reasoned that Amendment 2 violated the Fourteenth Amendment because was it "born of animosity towards [homosexuals]. 'If the constitutional conception of "equal protection of the laws" means anything, it must at the very least mean that a bare . . . desire to harm a politically unpopular group cannot constitute a *legitimate* governmental interest.' "[71]

Justice Scalia, in an impassioned dissent that spoke for himself, Chief Justice Rehnquist, and Justice Thomas, was quick to attack the majority's reasoning at its most vulnerable point:

> The constitutional amendment here is not the manifestation of a " 'bare . . . desire to harm' " homosexuals, but is rather a modest attempt by seemingly tolerant Coloradans to preserve traditional sexual mores against the efforts of a politically powerful minority to revise those mores through use of the laws. That objective, and the means chosen to achieve it, are not only unimpeachable under any constitutional doctrine hitherto pronounced . . . ; they have been specifically approved by . . . this Court.
>
> In holding that homosexuality cannot be singled out for disfavorable treatment, the Court contradicts a decision, unchallenged here, pronounced only ten years ago [i.e., *Bowers v. Hardwick*] . . . If [, as the Court ruled in *Bowers*,] it is constitutionally permissible for a State to make homosexual conduct criminal, surely it is constitutionally permissible for a State to enact other laws merely *disfavoring* homosexual conduct. As the Court of Appeals for the District of Columbia Circuit has aptly put it: "If the Court [in *Bowers*] was unwilling to object to state laws that criminalize the behavior that defines the class, it is hardly open . . . to conclude that state sponsored discrimination against the class is invidious. After all, there can hardly be more palpable discrimination against a class than making the conduct that defines the class criminal."[72]

As Scalia went on to point out, nothing in the Fourteenth Amendment presents a state with an all-or-nothing choice: either criminalize homosexual sexual activity or act as if such activity is not immoral. A state may, as Colorado did, conclude that an activity, though morally problematic, ought nonetheless to be decriminalized. "[T]he society that eliminates criminal punishment for homosexual acts does not necessarily abandon the view that homosexuality is morally wrong and socially harmful; often, abolition simply reflects the view that enforcement of such criminal laws involves unseemly intrusion into the intimate lives of citizens."[73]

Scalia was right, as even some of those who celebrated the Court's decision in *Romer*, like Ronald Dworkin, acknowledged: If the Fourteenth Amendment does not prevent a state from criminalizing homosexual sexual activity, if it does not prevent a state from punishing those who have been duly convicted of engaging in homosexual sexual activity, the Fourteenth Amendment certainly does not prevent the people of a state from taking the lesser step of saying, in their constitution, that homosexual sexual activity is immoral and that no public policies shall be adopted or enforced that presuppose otherwise. As Dworkin put the point: "Scalia was right, in his biting dissent, that the combination of the result in [*Romer*] and the result in *Bowers* is ludicrous: practicing homosexuals can be jailed but not put at an electoral disadvantage—having to amend a constitution to get legislation they want—that many other groups, including people who favor prayer in schools, suffer."[74] No wonder the majority in *Romer* studiously avoided even mentioning the Court's decision in *Bowers v. Hardwick*.

That Scalia was right about the fundamental inconsistency of the Court's decision in *Romer* with its earlier decision in *Bowers* does not entail that the former decision, rather than the latter one, was wrong. I have explained why *Bowers* was wrongly decided. And for the same reason that *Bowers* was wrongly decided, *Romer* was rightly decided—though not rightly reasoned. The Court in *Romer* should simply have overruled its earlier decision in *Bowers* in the course of explaining that discrimination against homosexual persons *because they are homosexual* violates the Fourteenth Amendment *if the discrimination cannot be defended in terms that rebut the inference that the discrimination is based on the irrational fear and loathing of homosexuals*.

It bears emphasis that a law that embodies the judgment, for example, that *all* sex outside of marriage is immoral, *including sex between a man and a woman no less than between two persons of the same sex*, might not be grounded even partly in the irrational fear and loathing of homosexuals. Similarly, a law that embodies the traditional Roman Catholic position that *all* deliberately nonprocreative genital acts are immoral, *including such acts between a man and a woman no less than between two persons of the same sex*, might not be grounded even partly in the irrational fear and loathing of homosexuals.[75] It is surely the case that some of the Coloradans who supported Amendment 2, perhaps many of them, did so not because they harbor any fear or loathing of homosexuals but because they believe that all sex outside of marriage is immoral, including sex between a man and a woman no less than between two persons of the same sex. Perhaps it is even the case that some Coloradans supported Amendment 2 because they believe that all deliberately nonprocreative genital acts are immoral, including such acts between a man and a woman, even between a husband and wife, no less than between two persons of the same sex. Such Coloradans will want to insist that *their* support of Amendment 2 was not based on any fear or loathing of homosexuals, and that to contend otherwise is to impute to them, imperially and falsely, a hatred of homosexuals they simply do not have. As Robert Nagel has written, in a thoughtful article about the political effort to add Amendment 2 to the Colorado Constitution: "There is the obvious but important possibility that one can 'hate' an individual's behavior without hating the individual."[76]

The problem, however, is that Amendment 2 was not directed against, for example, all sex outside of marriage. Imagine a law directed against, not all nonmarital sex, but just nonmarital sex between two (or more) persons of different "races"—between a white person and a black person, for example, or between an Aryan and a Jew. Whatever the supporters of the law say about their reasons for supporting it, and indeed whatever the supporters of the law actually believe about their reasons for supporting the law, the fact is that the existence of the law is not fully explicable without reference to the racism that the law represents and embodies. Now imagine a law directed against, not all nonmarital sex, but just nonmarital sex between two persons of the same sex. Whatever the supporters of the law say about their reasons for supporting it, and indeed whatever the supporters of the law actually believe about their reasons for supporting the law, the existence of the law is not fully explicable without reference to homophobia—to a devaluing of the humanity of homosexuals. Again, this is not to deny that the existence of a *different* law might be fully explicable even in the absence of any homophobia—in particular, a law that embodies the judgment that *all* nonmarital sex is immoral, or a law that embodies the traditional Roman Catholic position that *all* deliberately nonprocreative genital acts are immoral. But, as the Kentucky Supreme Court concluded in *Wasson*, the existence of law that targets just homosexuals seems finally inexplicable on a non-homophobic basis—it seems finally inexplicable without reference to a culture in which homosexuals are devalued more for who they are than for what they do—even if some supporters of the law sincerely insist that they hate, or otherwise disvalue, only the sin, not the sinner.

I said that the existence of a law directed against just nonmarital sex between two persons of the same sex is not fully explicable without reference to a devaluing of the humanity of homosexuals—to the vision of homosexuals not merely as different humans but as lesser humans, as inferior humans, as defective, even degraded, humans. Let me explain. Why would a majority of the citizens of a state, or of their elected representatives, accept the proposition, not that all persons who engage in nonmarital sex, or all persons who engage in deliberately nonprocreative genital activity, should not be protected from discrimination, but that only homosexuals should not be protected, *unless the citizens or their representatives were, to some degree, in the grip of fear and loathing of homosexuals more for who they are than for what they do*? It is extremely difficult to discern the point of distinguishing between, on the one side, the morality of sexual lovemaking between two persons of the opposite sex (who are not married to one another) and, on the other, the morality of sexual lovemaking between two persons of the same sex. What reason might one have for wanting to outlaw or otherwise regulate the latter lovemaking *but not the former*? Rosemary Ruether has explained that for those who disagree, as of course the vast majority of Americans do, with the traditional Roman Catholic position that all deliberately nonprocreative genital acts are immoral,

> it is no longer possible to argue that sex/love between two persons of the same sex cannot be a valid embrace of bodily selves expressing love. If sex/love is centered primarily on communion between two selves *rather than on biologistic concepts of procreative complementarity*, then the love of two persons of the same sex need be no less than that of two persons of the

opposite sex. Nor need their experience of ecstatic bodily communion be less valuable.[77]

This is not to say that with respect to sexual activity, heterosexual or homosexual, anything goes. The point, rather, is that for one who is not in the grip of some degree of fear and loathing of homosexuals, the morality or immorality of sexual activity does not depend on whether the sexual activity is between two persons of the opposite sex or between two persons of the same sex. Margaret Farley—who is Roman Catholic, a member of a religious order, the Gilbert L. Stark Professor of Christian Ethics at Yale University, and a former president of the Society of Christian Ethics—has developed the point:

> My answer [to the question of what norms should govern same-sex relations and activities] has been: the norms of justice—the norms which govern all human relationships and those which are particular to the intimacy of sexual relations. Most generally, the norms are respect for persons through respect for autonomy and rationality; respect for relationality through requirements of mutuality, equality, commitment, and fruitfulness. More specifically one might say things like: sex between two persons of the same sex (just as two persons of the opposite sex) should not be used in a way that exploits, objectifies, or dominates; homosexual (like heterosexual) rape, violence, or any harmful use of power against unwilling victims (or those incapacitated by reason of age, etc.) is never justified; freedom, integrity, privacy are values to be affirmed in every homosexual (as heterosexual) relationship; all in all, individuals are not to be harmed, and the common good is to be promoted.

Farley then adds that "[t]he Christian community will want and need to add those norms of faithfulness, forgiveness, of patience and hope, which are essential to any relationships between persons in the Church."[78]

My principal point here is, in a sense, cultural-anthropological: Even though some supporters of a law against just nonmarital sex between two persons of different races might sincerely insist that they hate only the sin, not the sinner, it is implausible to think that such a law might emerge in a cultural milieu that was not pervasively racist. Similarly, even though some supporters of a law against just nonmarital sex between two persons of the same sex sincerely insist that they hate only the sin, not the sinner, it is extremely difficult to imagine, in a cultural milieu that is not pervasively homophobic—that does not pervasively regard the homosexual not merely as a different human but as a lesser, inferior, defective human—the maintenance of such a law, as distinct from a law, for example, against *all* sex outside of marriage, heterosexual as well as homosexual. Just as a law that targets nonmarital sex between two persons of different races is rooted in and expresses the racism in a culture, a law that targets nonmarital sex between two persons of the same sex is rooted in and expresses the homophobia in a culture.

Analogously, a law, like Amendment 2, that, among all persons who engage in sex outside of marriage, leaves just homosexuals politically and legally defenseless against actions that target them, that discriminate against them as such, seems based on—it seems rooted in and expressive of—the irrational fear and loathing of homosexuals. (For a homosexual to be politically and legally defenseless against actions that discriminate against him *as a homosexual* is not to be politically or legally defenseless against actions that discriminate against him as, for example, a black person, or a Jew.) Amendment 2 is a way of enabling, by removing legal impediments to discrimination, not against all persons who engage in nonmarital sex, but only against homosexuals. Amendment 2 endorses the proposition, not that all persons who engage in nonmarital sex should not be protected from discrimination against them as such, but that homosexuals should not be protected—legally protected—from discrimination against them as such. Why, among all persons who engage in sex outside of marriage, leave only homosexuals politically and legally defenseless, especially when, among all persons who engage in nonmarital sex, it is precisely homosexuals, not heterosexuals, who are most likely to be vilified and most in need of protection from discrimination? The inference seems inescapable that Amendment 2 is based on the fear and loathing of homosexuals more for who they are than for what they do. As the Court said in *Romer*, "[l]aws of the kind now before us raise the inevitable inference that the disadvantage imposed is born of animosity toward the class of persons affected."[79]

A similar, corroborating conclusion was reached in an important case, *Vriend v. Alberta*, decided by the Supreme Court of Canada on April 2, 1998.[80] The province of Alberta had on its books a law called the Human Rights, Citizenship and Multiculturalism Act, which outlawed discrimination in certain domains (public accommodations, employment practices, etc.) on any of several listed bases, including race or color, ancestry, place of origin, religious beliefs, sex, physical disability, mental disability, age, or marital status. But the Act did not outlaw discrimination on the basis of sexual orientation. This omission was not inadvertent; as the court explained, "[d]espite repeated calls for its inclusion sexual orientation has never been included in the list of those groups protected from discrimination." The court concluded—indeed, *unanimously* concluded—that the omission, in the Act, of sexual orientation as a prohibited basis of discrimination violated section 15(1) of the Charter of Rights and Freedoms (which, in Canada, has constitutional status). Section 15(1) states, in relevant part: "Every individual is equal before and under the law and has the right to the equal protection and equal benefit of the law without discrimination . . . ." The court reasoned that an "implicit message was conveyed by the exclusion," namely,

> that gays and lesbians, unlike other individuals, are not worthy of protection. This is clearly an example of a distinction which demeans the individual and strengthens and perpetuates the view that gays and lesbians

are less worthy of protection as individuals in Canada's society. The potential harm to the dignity and perceived worth of gay and lesbian individuals constitutes a particularly cruel form of discrimination.

. . .

In excluding sexual orientation from the [Act's] protection, the Government has, in effect, stated that "all persons are equal in dignity and rights", except gay men and lesbians. Such a message, even if it is only implicit, must offend s. 15(1), the "section of the *Charter*, more than any other, which recognizes and cherishes the innate human dignity of every individual". This effect, together with the denial to individuals of any effective legal recourse if they are discriminated against on the ground of sexual orientation, amount to a sufficient basis on which to conclude that the distinction created by the exclusion from the [Act] constitutes discrimination [in violation of s. 15(1)].

In *Vriend v. Alberta*, the plaintiff had been dismissed from his position by the president of a college pursuant to the college's policy on homosexual practice. Bear in mind that in ruling that Alberta was obligated by the Charter to prohibit a college or other employer from discriminating against employees on the basis of sexual orientation, the court was not saying that Alberta was obligated to prohibit an employer from dismissing employees for engaging in nonmarital sexual activity—only that Alberta was obligated to prohibit an employer from discriminating against homosexuals in implementing such a policy. A policy against all nonmarital sexual activity, heterosexual as well as homosexual, is one thing; a policy against just homosexual sexual activity is something else.

Because Alberta failed to explain its exclusion of sexual orientation as a prohibited basis of discrimination in terms that rebutted the strong inference that the exclusion was based on a devaluing of homosexuals, the Canadian Supreme Court's unanimous conclusion that the exclusion violated section 15(1) of the Charter was correct. Similarly, because Colorado failed to explain Amendment 2 in terms that rebutted the strong inference that Amendment 2 was based, to some degree, on a devaluing of homosexuals, on a fear and loathing of homosexuals more for who they are than for what they do, Amendment 2 violated the Fourteenth Amendment.[81] *Romer*, therefore, was rightly decided—though, again, Scalia was right that the Court's decision in *Romer* was inconsistent with its earlier decision in *Bowers v. Hardwick*. Although a right answer for the right reasons is better than a right answer for the wrong reasons, a right answer for the wrong reasons is still better, if fidelity to the Constitution is our aim, than a wrong answer.

The Court's decision in *Romer v. Evans* outraged many social conservatives, beginning with Justice Scalia himself. The passionate contempt with which Scalia dissented in *Romer* equaled the passionate contempt with which he would dissent, a month later, in the VMI case. At the conclusion of his dissent in *Romer*, Scalia charged that "[t]oday's opinion has no foundation in American constitutional law, and barely pretends to. The people of Colorado have adopted an entirely reasonable provision . . . Striking it down is an act, not of judicial judgment, but of political will."[82] Other social conservatives, off the Court, were quick to follow Scalia's lead in condemning the Court's decision in *Romer*.[83] (Robert Bork, for example, wrote that "[t]here is no logical or constitutional foundation for the majority's decision in *Romer v. Evans*."[84]) But their condemnations were just as mistaken as Scalia's. Although, as I acknowledged, Scalia was right about the inconsistency of the Court's decision in *Romer* with its decision in *Bowers*, he was quite wrong that the former decision "has no foundation in American constitutional law . . ." Again, the Court's decision in *Romer* is rooted firmly in one of the most well-established and important norms of modern American constitutional law: the Fourteenth Amendment imperative that no state discriminate against any group on the basis of a view to the effect that members of the disfavored group are not truly or fully human—that they are, at best, defective, even debased or degraded, human beings.

I believe, and argued in chapter 3, that such a norm was established by "We the people" when they made the Fourteenth Amendment a part of our Constitution in the late 1860s. But whether or not I am right about that doesn't matter, because even if I am wrong, even if no such norm was established, it is nonetheless true—it is, I think, undeniable—that, in the wake of World War II and, especially, of the Holocaust, an even broader antidiscrimination than any "We the people" might have established became a part of our constitutional bedrock. One might want to argue that *Romer* was wrongly decided because, contrary to what I have contended here, Amendment 2 did *not* violate the norm in question. But whether or not Amendment 2 violated the norm, the norm is, for us the people of the United States now living, constitutional bedrock, as I explained in the final section of chapter 3.

Because (in my judgment) the Court's decision in *Romer* was rooted firmly in that bedrock norm, its decision was no judicial usurpation of our politics—the outrage of many social conservatives to the contrary notwithstanding. (Again, that the Supreme Court brings to bear on our politics a norm that was not established as a part of the Constitution by "We the people" does not entail that the Court is usurping our politics; there is no judicial usurpation unless, in addition, the norm the Court brings to bear is not a part of our constitutional bedrock.) Nor would it be a usurpation of our politics, on any plausible understanding of the usurpation claim, for the Supreme Court to move beyond discrimination against women to discrimination against homosexuals. That is, it would not be a judicial usurpation for the Court to disfavor discrimination against homosexuals the way it now disfavors discrimination against women, namely, by subjecting it to a strict standard of review. As I said earlier, the serious claim is not that laws that discriminate against homosexuals are ipso facto unconstitutional, but that laws that discriminate against homosexuals should be disfavored, because such laws, like laws that discriminate against women, or against blacks, are typically based on an ideology that violates the antidiscrimination norm that is constitutional bedrock for us, and therefore every such law should be strictly scrutinized to make sure that it is not in fact based on such a view.

I now want to comment on the constitutional dimension of an issue that has been fiercely contested in the culture wars[85] of the last several years: homosexual marriage. The literature addressing this controversial issue has quickly become voluminous.[86] My discussion here will be very brief.[87]

A state's refusal to extend legal recognition to same-sex unions—its refusal to recognize such unions as exemplifying a relationship like traditional marriage in certain crucial respects—should be adjudged unconstitutional, pursuant to the approach I have defended in this chapter, unless that refusal can be explained (justified) in terms that rebut the inference that the refusal is embedded in a view of homosexuals, an ideology of homosexuality, that violates our bedrock antidiscrimination norm.[88] (It is a non sequitur to conclude from the fact that a same-sex union cannot be a marriage in the traditional sense either that such a union is necessarily immoral or that a state's refusal to recognize such a union is necessarily constitutional.) In a society, like our own, in which it is widely agreed that not all deliberately nonprocreative genital acts are immoral, it is difficult to discern any such explanation. (Recall here the two statements I quoted a few pages back, one by Rosemary Ruether, the other by Margaret Farley.[89]) This is so even if in a different society—one in which a critical mass of citizens did accept the traditional Roman Catholic position that all deliberately nonprocreative genital acts are immoral—there might be such an explanation.[90]

Consider two efforts at explanation. First: God forbids homosexual relations, as the Bible reveals. For reasons I have developed elsewhere, this thoroughly religious explanation is deservedly problematic, as a sole basis of political choice, under the imperative, applicable to the states under the Fourteenth Amendment, that government not establish religion.[91] In any event, it is fanciful to suppose that this explanation would be offered either to the citizens of a state or to the Supreme Court as the *sole* justification for a state's refusal to recognize same-sex unions. What other, secular explanation/justification might be offered? Consider Roger Scruton's argument (as summarized by Roderick Hills):

> [O]ne might reasonably believe that men and women have different and complementary sexual "temperaments" such that sexual relationships between members of different sexes will be more psychologically satisfactory than relationships between members of the same sex. Scruton argues that men tend to be more sexually predatory and promiscuous than women; while women seek permanence in their sexual relationships, men tend to seek adventure. Therefore, if men form sexual relationships with other men rather than with women, those relationships will tend to have shorter duration and a greater concentration on physical self-

gratification than heterosexual relationships. If one assumes that these characteristics are undesirable, then one might conclude that at least male homosexuality is undesirable.[92]

Martha Nussbaum has explained why we should be wary of Scruton's argument.[93] But even if, for the sake of discussion, we credit Scruton's argument, there are serious problems with invoking it in an effort to justify a state's refusal to recognize same-sex unions:

- The position doesn't support a state's refusal to recognize woman-woman unions.
- That in general man-woman unions might be "more psychologically satisfactory" than man-man unions is not a reason for refusing to recognize man-man unions if those who form such unions are typically incapable of forming man-woman unions.
- That man-man sexual relationships are, whether for biological reasons like those Scruton suggests or for some other reasons, more transitory than man-woman sexual relationships is hardly a ground for refusing to recognize the man-man unions of those who are proclaiming to the world their commitment to their union as a kind of marriage—as a life-long union of faithful love—and seeking public affirmation of their union as such.[94]

As I said, it is extremely difficult, in our society, to discern any explanation for a state's refusal to recognize same-sex unions that rebuts the inference that the refusal is based on a view of homosexuals that violates the antidiscrimination norm.

Richard Posner has suggested that he finds the "argument for recognizing homosexual marriage quite persuasive"—but only as a policy argument "addressed to a state legislature."[95] Posner is deeply skeptical that the Supreme Court should

> compel[ ] every state in the United States to adopt a radical social policy that is deeply offensive to the vast majority of its citizens and that exists in no other country in the world, and to do so at the behest of an educated, articulate, and increasingly politically effective minority that is seeking to bypass the normal political process for no better reason than impatience, albeit an understandable impatience. . . . [For the Court to do so] would be an unprecedented example of judicial immodesty. The well-worn epithet "usurpative" would finally fit.[96]

Posner would prefer to "[l]et a state legislature or activist (but elected, and hence democratically responsive) state court adopt homosexual marriage as a policy in one state, and let the rest of the country learn from the results of its experiment. That is the democratic way . . ."[97] Whether one sides with Posner here surely depends in large part on whether one believes it is possible to discern any credible explanation (justification) for a state's refusal to recognize same-sex unions that rebuts the inference that the refusal is embedded in an ideology that violates the antidiscrimination norm. In my judgment, it is exceedingly difficult—difficult to the point of impossible—to discern any such explanation in a society in which it is widely agreed that not all deliberately nonprocreative genital acts are immoral. If—*if*—that is your judgment too, how attractive is Posner's position?

Posner anticipates the response that his position is so weak-kneed that had the Court accepted it in *Brown v. Board of Education* or in *Loving v. Virginia*, the Court would not have struck down racially segregated public schooling or antimiscegenation legislation. Posner's reply: "When the Supreme Court moved against public school segregation, it was bucking a regional majority but a national minority (white southerners). When it outlawed the laws forbidding racially mixed marriages, only a minority of states had such laws on their books."[98] Presumably, then, Posner believes that had a national majority approved of racially segregated public schooling, the Court should not have struck it down, and that had a majority of states had antimiscegenation legislation on their books, the Court should not have struck it down. (Does Posner believe that *Plessy v. Ferguson* was rightly—i.e., prudentially—decided?) But is it not powerfully relevant— even if not, as a practical matter, determinative—that even if a national majority had approved of racially segregated public schools, such schools would nonetheless have violated the Fourteenth Amendment—and that even if a majority of states had had antimiscegenation legislation on their books, such legislation would nonetheless have violated the Fourteenth Amendment?

Continuing to insist that his knees are strong, Posner suggests that the Court's ruling in *Roe v. Wade*[99] was not "usurpative"—or, at any rate, was *less* usurpative than a ruling requiring the states to recognize same-sex unions would be—because the Supreme Court "created a right of abortion against a background of a rapid increase in the number of lawful abortions."[100] Even if that "rapid increase" is not overstated, it is undeniable that, forced to choose between the Court's ruling in *Roe v. Wade* and a ruling by the Court requiring the states to recognize same-sex unions, most Americans who are outraged by the former ruling and would be outraged by the latter ruling would point to the former ruling, not the latter, as the greater of the two evils and, more important, as the greater usurpation—indeed, as the truly exemplary usurpation, the defining usurpation—of our politics by the Supreme Court in the modern period of American constitutional law. More about that in the next chapter, where I discuss *Roe v. Wade*.

Observing that "no other country in the world authorizes [same-sex unions]," and suggesting that "this is a datum that should give pause to a court inclined to legislate in the name of the Constitution[,]" Posner concludes: "One would have to have more confidence in the power of reason than I do to decide novel issues of constitutional law . . . to be willing to ignore what the people affected by the issues think about them."[101] It is easy to accept the counsel—because it is a wise, if obvious, counsel—that if a majority of Americans does not believe that a particular practice is unconstitutional, the Supreme Court should think long and hard before concluding that the practice is unconstitutional, especially if a plausible constitutional argument supports the position of the majority. It is much harder to accept the different counsel that the Court should defer to the position of the majority even if at the end of the day, after having thought very long and very hard about the matter, the Court concludes that no plausible constitutional argument supports the majority's position and that the practice is indeed unconstitutional.

I do not mean to discount the difficulty of the following question, which Posner's remarks occasion: If the Supreme Court were eventually to become persuaded that a state's refusal to extend legal recognition to same-sex unions violates the Fourteenth Amendment, would the fact that a majority of Americans does not see it that way—that a majority of Americans opposes legislation extending such recognition to same-sex unions —excuse the Court's failure to say what, in its judgment, the Fourteenth Amendment requires? Put more starkly—but not, I think, inaccurately: Does the fact that a majority of Americans opposes legislation extending legal recognition to same-sex unions excuse the Court's failure to enforce the constitutionally protected human rights of homosexuals?[102] The issue here is not the judicial usurpation of politics, but the judicial capitulation to politics. Is the latter somehow less problematic, in our constitutional democracy, than the former?

We began this section of the chapter by asking whether it would be a judicial usurpation of our politics for the Supreme Court to move beyond sex to sexual orientation—beyond discrimination against women to discrimination against homosexuals.[103] I have argued here that a bedrock constitutional norm requires the Court to make that move. The serious question is whether it would be an illegitimate judicial capitulation to our politics—to our prejudices—for the Court to fail to make the move. The serious question is whether, by failing to make the move, the Court wouldn't illegitimately compromise the bedrock constitutional imperative that no state discriminate against any group on the basis of a view to the effect that members of the disfavored group are not truly or fully human, that they are, at best, defective, even debased or degraded, human beings.

On May 3, 1954, precisely two weeks before it handed down its historic decision in *Brown v. Board of Education*,[104] the United States Supreme Court issued its opinion in *Hernandez v. Texas*.[105] This passage from the Court's opinion in *Hernandez*—which, like its opinion in *Brown*, was a unanimous opinion written by Chief Justice Earl Warren—is a fitting conclusion to this chapter:

> Throughout our history differences in race and color have defined easily identifiable groups which have at times required the aid of the courts in securing equal treatment under the laws. But community prejudices are not static, and from time to time other differences from the

community norm may define other groups which need the same protection. Whether such a group exists within a community is a question of fact. When the existence of a distinct class is demonstrated, and it is further shown that the laws, as written or as applied, single out that class for different treatment not based on some reasonable classification, the guarantees of the Constitution have been violated.[106]

6

—⊶⊷⊶—

Further Beyond: Abortion and Physician-Assisted Suicide

On January 22, 1973, in *Roe v. Wade*, the Supreme Court of the United States decreed that under the Fourteenth Amendment, no state may outlaw abortion in the period of pregnancy prior to the time at which the fetus becomes "viable", that is, "[capable] of meaningful life outside the mother's womb."[1] (In January 1998, on the eve of the twenty-fifth anniversary of *Roe v. Wade*, the *New York Times* reported that because of advances "in neonatology, most experts place the point of fetal viability at 23 or 24 weeks."[2] Although, according to the Court's decree, a state may outlaw abortion in the post-viability period of pregnancy, it must provide an exception for any abortion "necessary to preserve the life or health of the mother."[3]) No constitutional decision by the Supreme Court in the modern period of American constitutional law has been more controversial—certainly none has been more persistently controversial—than the Court's ruling in *Roe*. Even after more than a quarter of a century, the legitimacy of the Court's decision is widely and furiously contested.[4] By contrast, in 1979, twenty-five years after the Court's decision in *Brown v. Board of Education*,[5] the legitimacy of the Court's ruling in *Brown* was largely undisputed.[6]

It is no secret that the principal critics of the Court's decision in *Roe* have been "pro-life" on the question whether abortion should be a crime. The most powerful critique of the decision, however, was written not by such a person, but by someone who announced, in his critique, that as a legislator he would vote to decriminalize abortion: John Hart Ely. Notwithstanding that as "a legislator I would vote for a statute very much like the one the Court ends up drafting",[7] Ely's unequivocal judgment—delivered in April 1973, just three months after the Court decided *Roe*—was that the Court's ruling in *Roe* is "a very bad decision[,] . . . because it is bad constitutional law, or rather because it is *not* constitutional law and gives almost no sense of an obligation to try to be."[8] Ely is not the only liberal constitutional scholar who charged that the Court's decision in *Roe* was illegitimate.[9] In 1976, Archibald Cox, who served as solicitor general of the United States under Presidents Kennedy and Johnson, complained that in *Roe*

151

the Court failed to establish the legitimacy of the decision by articulating a precept of sufficient abstractness to lift the ruling above the level of a political judgment . . . Nor can I articulate such a principle—unless it be that a State cannot interfere with individual decisions relating to sex, procreation, and family with only a moral or philosophical State justification: a principle which I cannot accept or believe will be accepted by the American people.[10]

In 1979, another liberal constitutional scholar, Gerald Gunther, wrote that although "*Brown v. Board of Education* was an entirely legitimate decision[,] . . . I have not yet found a satisfying rationale to justify *Roe v. Wade* . . . on the basis of modes of constitutional interpretation I consider legitimate."[11] So, one need be neither "pro-life" nor a conservative constitutional scholar to conclude that *Roe v. Wade* constitutes one of the greatest—and, therefore, one of the worst—judicial usurpations of American politics in the period since World War II.

I

Was the Supreme Court's decision in *Roe* a judicial usurpation—and, if so, in what way? There are two possibilities. (Recall, from chapter 1, my disaggregation of the usurpation claim into three distinct claims, only two of which are serious claims.[12]) The Court's ruling that state legislation outlawing pre-viability abortion is unconstitutional is fairly characterized as a judicial usurpation of our politics if the ruling can be grounded neither in any norm established by "We the people" nor in any norm that has become constitutional bedrock for us. Even if, however, the Court's ruling *can* be grounded in a norm established by "We the people" or one that has become a part of our constitutional bedrock, the ruling is nonetheless a judicial usurpation of our politics—it is nonetheless an act of judicial imperialism—if in the course of reaching its decision the Court failed to enforce the applicable constitutional norm in an appropriately deferential manner: a manner appropriately deferential to the state legislature's *reasonable* judgment that the legislation in question satisfies the applicable constitutional norm.

Does state legislation outlawing (pre-viability) abortion even implicate (much less violate) any norm established by "We the people"? The answer is yes, but only *if*, as I argued in chapter 3, the reasonableness requirement is a component of the antidiscrimination norm that "We the people" established as a part of the Fourteenth Amendment—the requirement that no state treat some less well than others unless the differential treatment is reasonably designed to accomplish a legitimate governmental purpose.[13] Does state legislation outlawing abortion implicate any norm that has become constitutional bedrock for us? Again, the answer is yes *if*, as I claimed in the final section of chapter 3, the reasonableness requirement is a component of the antidiscrimination norm that has become a part of our constitutional bedrock. (Anti-abortion legislation does not seriously implicate, much less violate, any other constitutional norm.[14]) Because not everyone will agree that the reasonableness requirement was established by "We the people" or even that it is now a part of our constitutional bedrock, let us assume, for the sake of discussion, that the requirement has constitutional status and then see where the assumption leads: Is legislation outlawing abortion reasonably designed to accomplish a legitimate governmental purpose? Or, to use a different, but equivalent, formulation: Does such legislation "regulate for the public good in a reasonable fashion"?[15]

I can anticipate this response: "Legislation outlawing abortion—unlike, for example, legislation based on race—is not 'differential treatment' and therefore is not subject to the requirements of the antidiscrimination norm." It is true that a legislative ban on abortion applies not just to some persons, but to all persons (or so we may assume): No one—black or white, male or female, etc.—may participate in (the act of) abortion. Nonetheless, legislation outlawing abortion *is* an instance of "differential treatment". Let me proceed analogically by rehearsing a point I made in chapter 3:[16] Laws that treat some persons differently from others on the basis of a trait, like race or sex, are not the only laws that entail differential treatment. Indeed, every law entails differential treatment. Thus, no law is immune to challenge on the basis of the antidiscrimination norm. Imagine a law that requires every person to wear a protective helmet when riding on a motorcycle and subjects any person who fails to do so to a fine and/or punishment. Even though the law applies not just to some persons (e.g., women) but to every person, the law treats some persons differently from others. It does so on the basis, not of a trait, like sex, but of an act: the act of wearing a protective helmet when riding on a motorcycle. Just as some laws treat some persons differently from others depending on whether or not, for example, they are women, the motorcycle law treats some persons differently from others depending on whether they have worn a protective helmet when riding on a motorcycle. Those who obey the requirement to wear a protective helmet are treated differently from the way that those who disobey are treated; they are treated better, they are left alone. Pursuant to the component of the antidiscrimination norm articulated above, we can inquire: Is a law punishing the act of not wearing a protective helmet when riding on a motorcycle, while leaving alone those who do wear a protective helmet, a regulation "for the public good in a reasonable fashion"? Is the law—the differential treatment—"reasonably" designed to achieve a legitimate governmental purpose?

Similarly, even though it applies not just to some persons but to every person, legislation outlawing abortion *is* an instance of "differential treatment". Such legislation treats some persons differently from others, not on the basis of a trait, like sex, but on the basis of an act: participation in abortion. Legislation outlawing abortion treats some persons differently from others depending on whether they have participated in abortion. Those who obey the command not to participate are treated differently from the way that those who disobey are treated; they are treated better, they are left alone. Legislation outlawing abortion is therefore subject to the requirements of the antidiscrimination norm. Pursuant to the antidiscrimination norm, the question arises: Is a law punishing participation in abortion, while leaving alone those who do not participate, a regulation "for the public good in a reasonable fashion"? Is the law—the differential treatment—"reasonably" designed to achieve a legitimate governmental purpose?

When does a law—*any* law—fail to regulate for the public good in a "reasonable" fashion? When is a law not "reasonably" designed to achieve a legitimate governmental purpose? (Assume, for the sake of discussion, that the law is not based on a view to the effect that the disfavored citizens are not truly or fully human. A law so based would violate a different, more specific, part of the antidiscrimination norm—the part with which we were concerned in the preceding chapter.) There are three generic possibilities.

- First, the law is aimed at achieving a "good" or "benefit" that cannot plausibly be characterized as "public"; it is aimed at serving an "interest" that is no part of government's proper business and therefore cannot plausibly be said to be a "legitimate governmental interest".
- Second, although the law is aimed at a genuinely "public" good or benefit, although it is aimed at serving a legitimate governmental interest, the law fails in its aim; it fails to serve, to any extent, the legitimate governmental interest at which it is aimed.
- Third, although the law is aimed at serving a legitimate governmental interest, and although the law succeeds in serving that interest to some extent, the costs imposed by the law on those the law regulates are so out of proportion to the benefits achieved by the law that the law is not a "reasonable" regulation for the public good; it is not "reasonably" designed to serve a legitimate governmental interest. The law is unreasonable because the costs of the law are too disproportionate to its benefits.

Now, which possibility, if indeed any of them, is realized by legislation outlawing abortion? Certainly not the first: No one can fairly claim— moreover, the Court in *Roe* did not claim—that legislation outlawing abortion is not aimed at serving a legitimate governmental interest. The protection of the life of a human fetus—no less, for example, than the protection of the life of an Alaskan wolf—is undeniably a legitimate governmental interest. (As the Court put the point in *Roe*: "[A state] has [an] important and legitimate interest in protecting the potentiality of human life."[17]) Nor is the second possibility realized by legislation outlawing abortion: There is no reason to doubt that legislation outlawing abortion succeeds, to some extent, in protecting the lives of human fetuses, even though it also fails, to some extent, in protecting them. All criminal prohibitions fail, to some extent.

That leaves the third possibility: Are the costs visited by legislation outlawing abortion on those the legislation regulates so out of proportion to the benefits achieved by the legislation that the legislation does not regulate for the public good in a "reasonable" fashion, it is not "reasonably" designed to serve a legitimate governmental interest? Is legislation outlawing abortion unreasonable because the costs of such legislation are too disproportionate to the benefits?

What costs does legislation outlawing abortion visit on those the legislation regulates—in particular, on women who want to have an abortion—and how great are those costs? The Court in *Roe* answered just this question, and it did so accurately. Referring to "a women's decision whether or not to terminate her pregnancy", the Court wrote:

> The detriment that the State would impose upon the pregnant woman by denying this choice altogether is apparent. Specific and direct harm medically diagnosable even in early pregnancy may be involved. Maternity, or additional offspring, may force upon the woman a distressful life and future. Psychological harm may be imminent. Mental and physical health may be taxed by child care. There is also the distress, for all concerned, associated with the unwanted child, and there is the problem of bringing a child into a family already unable, psychologically and otherwise, to care for it. In other cases, as in this one, the additional difficulties and continuing stigma of unwed motherhood may be involved.[18]

Did the Court overstate the costs? Richard Posner has suggested that the Court *understated* the costs: "No effort is made to dramatize the hardships to a woman forced to carry her fetus to term against her will. The opinion does point out that 'maternity, or additional offspring, may force upon the woman a distressful life and future,' and it elaborates on the point for a few more sentences. But there is no mention of the woman who is raped, who is poor, or whose fetus is deformed. There is no reference to the death of women from illegal abortions."[19]

Legislation outlawing abortion imposes great costs on pregnant women who want to have an abortion. ("Let us not underestimate what is at stake: Having an unwanted child can go a long way toward ruining a woman's life."[20]) Legislation outlawing abortion is very different, in that regard, from, say, legislation requiring one to wear a protective helmet when riding on a motorcycle, or a public school dress code regulating what a student may wear to class. Commanding a woman to forgo the abortion that she wants is commanding her to do something that will profoundly affect the shape of her life for years to come, perhaps for the rest of her life.

However, that the costs of legislation outlawing abortion are undeniably great does not entail that the costs are out of proportion to the benefits achieved by the legislation; it does not conclude the question whether the costs are disproportionate to the benefits. But that the costs of legislation outlawing abortion are great *does* mean that the benefit or benefits achieved by the legislation must be great too, lest the costs be so disproportionate to the benefits that the legislation fails to regulate for the public good in a "reasonable" fashion. The Court in *Roe* was therefore right to insist that because the magnitude of the costs is great, the magnitude of the public benefit secured by the legislation must be great, too. The latter must be proportionate to—commensurate with—the former. As the Court put it, legislation outlawing abortion "may be justified only by a 'compelling state interest,' . . . [and] must be narrowly drawn to express only the legitimate state interests at stake."[21]

(Whereas in some contexts, as we've seen, "strict scrutiny"—the "compelling state interest" test—functions to vindicate or dissipate the Court's suspicion about the actual, as distinct from the asserted, basis of a particular instance of differential treatment,[22] in other contexts, like the present one, the test serves a different function: to establish whether or not a particular instance of differential treatment achieves the proportionality that is an essential ingredient of "reasonable" regulation.[23])

The principal public good or benefit—the principal "legitimate governmental interest"—achieved by legislation outlawing abortion is, of course, protecting fetal life (i.e., protecting the lives of human fetuses). Here, then, is the crucial constitutional question: Is this benefit proportionate to the costs of the legislation, such that we can say that the legislation is a "reasonable" regulation for the public good? (Assume that we are talking here about legislation that exempts from its ban on abortion any abortion necessary to save the life of the mother or to protect her physical health from a serious threat of grave and irreparable harm.) Obviously, not everyone will give the same answer to this question. Those who minimize the importance of protecting fetal life—perhaps because they minimize the value or worth of fetal life—will conclude confidently that the benefit is not proportionate to the costs. Those who attach overriding importance to the protection of fetal life—because they attach overriding importance to the worth of fetal life—will conclude confidently that the benefit is not merely proportionate to the costs, but overwhelms them. Others, however, will find the question excruciatingly difficult; of these, some will conclude, but not confidently, that the benefit outweighs the costs, and others, that the costs outweigh the benefit.

I said that the crucial question is whether the benefit is proportionate to the costs of the legislation. Not quite. The crucial question *for the Supreme Court* is slightly, but importantly, different: Can a state legislature reasonably—plausibly—conclude that the benefit is proportionate to the costs? Put another way, can a state legislature reasonably conclude that legislation outlawing abortion is warranted by a compelling state interest; can it reasonably conclude that a compelling state interest necessitates the legislation? Why is *that* the crucial question for the Court? Because if a state legislature *can* reasonably conclude that the benefit is proportionate to the costs—if it can reasonably conclude that legislation outlawing abortion is warranted by a compelling state interest—then it is simply willful for the Court to say that the legislation is not a "reasonable" regulation for the public good and therefore violates the Fourteenth Amendment. Unless the justices of the Supreme Court mean to arrogate to themselves the legislative function, unless they mean to usurp the legislative function, the issue for a justice, under the component of the antidiscrimination norm that is relevant here, is not whether he or she would conclude that the benefit is proportionate to the costs, but only whether in his or her judgment a state legislature can reasonably conclude that the benefit is proportionate to—commensurate with—the costs. The office of the Court, under the "reasonableness" component of the antidiscrimination norm, is not to make legislative judgments de novo, but only to determine if the legislative judgment at issue is a reasonable one—whether the legislation in dispute is a "reasonable" regulation for the public good. Justice Souter discerned the point in his concurring opinion in *Washington v. Glucksberg*, one of the two physician-assisted suicide cases we examine later in this chapter:

> [J]udicial review . . . has no warrant to substitute one reasonable resolution of the contending positions for another, but authority to supplant the balance already struck between the contenders only when it falls outside the realm of the reasonable. . . . [It is] essential to the discipline of substantive due process review [to understand] the basic need to account for the two sides in the controversy and to respect legislation within the zone of reasonableness. . . . It is no justification for judicial intervention merely to identify a reasonable resolution of contending values that differs from the terms of the legislation under review. It is only when the legislation's justifying principle, critically valued, is so far from being commensurate with the individual interest as to be arbitrarily or pointlessly applied that the statute must give way. Only if this standard points against the statute can the individual claimant be said to have a constitutional right.[24]

Note that under the Supreme Court's own reasoning in *Roe*, a state legislature can reasonably conclude that the benefit of protecting post-viable fetal life is proportionate to the costs of doing so—it can reasonably conclude that legislation outlawing post-viability abortion is warranted by a compelling state interest (so long as an exception is made to preserve both the life and the health of the mother). The question then becomes: Can a state legislature also reasonably conclude that the benefit of protecting *pre-viable* fetal life is proportionate to the costs of doing so—can it reasonably conclude that legislation outlawing pre-viability abortion is warranted by a compelling state interest? This, I think, is an easy question: Yes, a state legislature *can* reasonably conclude that the benefit is proportionate to the costs, just as it can reasonably conclude that the benefit is not proportionate to the costs. (As John Ely emphasized in his critique, it is difficult to the point of impossible to understand why "viability" should be thought the constitutionally relevant point, such that outlawing pre-viability abortion violates the Fourteenth Amendment but outlawing post-viability abortion does not.[25]) Although not everyone would do so—and, let us assume, although it is not unreasonable for anyone to decline to do so—it is not unreasonable for the legislature to attach overriding importance both to the worth of all human life, *including pre-viable unborn human life,* and therefore to the importance of protecting pre-viable fetal life. Certainly nothing in the Constitution of the United States makes it problematic for a state legislature to do this. It is certainly no less reasonable for a state legislature to *include* pre-viable unborn human life within the circle of the human community—to count the pre-viable unborn as subjects of justice—than for the legislature to *exclude* pre-viable unborn human life from the circle, to decline to count the pre-viable unborn as subjects of justice. Robert George has written that "[o]pponents of abortion . . . view all human beings, including the unborn . . . , as members of the community of subjects to whom duties in justice are owed . . . The real issue of principle between supporters of abortion . . . and opponents . . . has to do with the question of who are subjects of justice." In George's view, "The challenge to the orthodox liberal view of abortion . . . is to identify nonarbitrary grounds for holding that the unborn . . . do not qualify as subjects of justice." George then adds: "Frankly, I doubt that this challenge can be met."[26] Whether or not the challenge can be met, it is certainly no less reasonable—it is certainly not arbitrary—for a state legislature to "view all human beings, including the unborn . . . , as members of the community of subjects to whom duties in justice are owed" than for it to decline to do so. The serious question, as George's comment suggests, is whether it isn't arbitrary to hold that the pre-viable unborn are not subjects of justice.[27]

In *Roe*, the Court rejected Texas's contention that "life begins at conception and is present throughout pregnancy, and that, therefore, the State has a compelling interest in protecting that life from and after conception." The Court said that "[w]e need not resolve the difficult question of when life begins. . . . [T]he judiciary, at this point in the development of man's knowledge, is not in a position to speculate as to the answer."[28] But the proper question was not what answer the judiciary, or anyone else, would give, but only whether Texas wasn't constitutionally free to give the answer it did. That others would give a different answer—or no answer—is beside the point. (As John Ely wrote, "[t]he problem with *Roe* is not so much that [the Court] bungles the question it sets itself, but rather that it sets itself a question the Constitution has not made the Court's business."[29]) The Court went on to say that "we do not agree that, by adopting one theory of life, Texas may override the rights of the pregnant woman that are at stake."[30] But, as Richard Epstein appropriately responded: "It makes no sense to hold in conclusionary terms that 'by adopting one the-

ory of life, Texas may [not] override the rights of the pregnant woman
that are at stake.' That formulation of the issue begs the important question because it assumes that we know that the woman's rights must prevail
even before the required balance takes place. We could as well claim that
the Court, by adopting another theory of life, has decided to override the
rights of the unborn child."[31] The crucial question was this: *Why* wasn't
Texas free—free as a *constitutional* matter, free *under the Fourteenth Amendment*—to proceed on the basis of the assumption that a pre-viable unborn
child is no less a subject of justice than a post-viable unborn child or a
born child? The Court did not address that question—or, if it matters, addressed it only in the most conclusory terms. (Again, Ely: "The Court
grants that protecting the fetus is an 'important and legitimate' governmental goal, and of course it does not deny that restricting abortion pro-
motes it. What it does, instead, is simply announce that that goal is not
important enough to sustain the restriction."[32]) If the right answer is
that Texas and other states *are* constitutionally free to proceed on the basis
of the assumption that a pre-viable unborn child is a subject of justice,
then the pregnant woman does not have "at stake" the right against a state
that the Court had in mind, because there is no such right: a constitutional right to noninterference by the state with her decision to have an
abortion.[33]

To assert (for that is all the Court did: assert) that there is no room for
reasonable, and indeed conscientious, differences in judgment here—
that no legislator can reasonably conclude that in saving (pre-viable) fetal
life to the extent it does, anti-abortion legislation is proportionate to the
(great) costs of the legislation—is, in a word, ridiculous. (The point is not
that one cannot reasonably conclude that anti-abortion legislation does
not satisfy the proportionality requirement; the point, rather, is that one
cannot reasonably think that it is unreasonable to conclude that the legislation *does* satisfy the requirement.) There are, in contemporary American society, large differences in judgment about whether the benefit secured by anti-abortion legislation is proportionate to the (great) costs of
the legislation, and those differences in judgment divide persons of
reason and conscience on the one side from persons of reason and conscience on the other. (Not that everyone who supports anti-abortion legislation—or everyone who opposes it—is a person of reason and conscience.) To deny that those large differences are reasonable is to be in a
state of denial about the daunting complexity of the question of the
morality of abortion.

A state legislature can reasonably conclude that the benefit of legislation outlawing (pre-viability) abortion is proportionate to the costs of the
legislation; it can reasonably conclude that the legislation is warranted by
a compelling governmental interest. Therefore, such legislation is a reasonable regulation for the public good. It is implausible—indeed, it is
willful—to conclude otherwise.

II

But the matter does not end there. Assume that, as I argued in the preceding section, the kind of anti-abortion legislation at issue here—legislation that exempts from its ban one important category of abortion, namely, abortion necessary to save the mother's life or to protect her physical health from a serious threat of grave and irreparable harm—satisfies the reasonableness component of the antidiscrimination norm. This does not entail that such legislation does not violate a different constitutional norm—or a different component of the same norm. In particular, it might be the case that a state legislature's failure to exempt from its ban certain *other* categories of abortion (e.g., abortion in cases where the pregnancy is a consequence of rape) discriminates against women in violation of the central component of the antidiscrimination norm.[34] Recall that according to the central component of the norm, no state may disfavor some citizens relative to others based on a view to the effect that the disfavored citizens are not truly or fully human—that they are, at best, defective, even debased or degraded, human beings. In the preceding chapter, I argued that for a state to discriminate against women—for it to disfavor women relative to men—is almost always for the state to violate the central component of the antidiscrimination norm.

As I've indicated, many constitutional scholars who are attracted to the bottom line in *Roe*—the deregulation of abortion—have acknowledged the failure of the Court in *Roe* to justify that result as a constitutional requirement. A few such scholars have tried to construct a justification that succeeds in doing what the Court's opinion in *Roe* failed to do. The most common such efforts argue that anti-abortion legislation is a species of unconstitutional discrimination against women.[35] I myself developed such an argument, first in 1988, then, more elaborately, in 1994.[36] I will explain why such arguments, if they work at all, work only to a very limited extent. But first, I want to present the argument I mounted in 1994:[37]

*   *   *

A law or policy whose adverse effect is visited only or mainly on nonwhites is an expression of what Paul Brest has called "racially selective sympathy and indifference"[38] if it would not have been enacted or adopted if its adverse effect were visited only or mainly or even equally on whites. A hypothetical example of such a policy: A state's decision not to fund research aimed at finding a cure for sickle-cell anemia, *if* that decision would not have been made—if, instead, a decision to fund such research would have been made—but for the fact that the disease afflicts primarily nonwhites. Such a decision singles out nonwhites for worse treatment than whites (would) receive, notwithstanding that some whites are victimized by the decision, namely, those who have, or will have, sickle-cell anemia. A law or policy should be deemed to violate the antidiscrimination norm if it is an expression of racially selective sympathy and indifference, because such sympathy and indifference is rooted in a sensibility according to which (some) nonwhites have not merely a different but a lesser humanity. Such sympathy and indifference represents, therefore, the very racist ideology that may not, under the antidiscrimination norm, be a predicate for state laws or other state action.

Similarly, a law or policy whose adverse effect is visited only or mainly on women is an expression of sex-selective sympathy and indifference if it would not have been enacted or adopted if its adverse effect were visited only or mainly or even equally on men. An example of such a policy: A state's decision to outlaw abortions even in cases of rape, *if* that decision would not have been made—if, instead, a decision to allow such abortions would have been made—but for the fact that the condition (pregnancy due to rape) afflicts only women. Such a decision singles out women for worse treatment than men (would) receive. A law or policy should be deemed to violate the antidiscrimination norm if it is an expression of sex-selective sympathy and indifference, because such sympathy and indifference is rooted in a sensibility according to which women have not merely a different but a lesser humanity. Such sympathy and indifference represents, therefore, the very sexist ideology that may not, under the antidiscrimination norm, be a predicate for state laws or other state action.

In *Personnel Administrator of Massachusetts v. Feeney*, the Supreme Court wrote: "'Discriminatory purpose,' however, implies more than intent as volition or intent as awareness of consequences. . . . It implies that the decisionmaker . . . selected or reaffirmed a particular course of action at least in part 'because of,' not merely 'in spite of,' its adverse effects upon an identifiable group. Yet nothing in the record demonstrates that this preference for veterans was originally devised or subsequently re-enacted because it would accomplish the collateral goal of keeping women in a stereotypic and predefined place in the Massachusetts Civil Service."[39] However, that a law was enacted, not because of its adverse effect on women, but in spite of it, does not preclude the possibility that the law would not have been enacted (or maintained) were the law's adverse effect visited equally on men. It does not preclude the possibility that the law would not have been enacted "in spite of its adverse effect" were the law's adverse effect visited equally on men. Therefore, that a law was enacted in spite of its adverse effect on women, not because of it, cannot conclude the matter. However difficult the inquiry, the Court should ask if the law would have been enacted were its adverse effect visited equally on men. If the law would not have been enacted were its adverse effect visited equally on men, the law is an expression of sex-selective sympathy and indifference and should be understood to violate the antidiscrimination norm.

To conclude that a legal restriction on a particular category of abortion—for example, abortion in cases of rape—would not have been enacted were its adverse effect visited equally on men and that the restriction is therefore an expression of sex-selective sympathy and indifference does not presuppose or entail that each and every person who supports the restriction would not do so but for sex-selective sympathy and indifference. But to acknowledge, as we should, that some people who support the restriction are not in the grip of sex-selective sympathy and indifference is not to deny the possibility that the restriction is virtually inconceivable in a world in which the phenomenon of sex-selective sympathy and indifference was absent, or in which the costs of the restrictions were visited equally on men. With respect to restrictions on some categories of abortion, if we remove the support of the legislators whose support for the restrictions is partly an expression of their sex-selective sympathy and indifference, there is very likely inadequate remaining support to enact the restrictions or even to maintain them on the books.

Michael McConnell has observed that "[g]iven the inconvenience (albeit unequal) of unintended parenthood to both men and women, it is inconceivable that even the most sexist of legislatures would pass an antiabortion law if it were not for a good faith concern for fetal life."[40] But McConnell's observation misses the point: That "a good faith concern for fetal life" is a *necessary* condition for enactment of legal restrictions on abortion does not entail that it is *sufficient* condition for enactment of every such restriction; there is good reason to believe that sex-selective sympathy and indifference is a necessary (though, by itself, not sufficient) condition for enactment of restrictions on some categories of abortion.[41] At any rate, a judge can reasonably conclude that in a world happily bereft of sex-selective sympathy and indifference, there would not be a critical mass of political support for enacting or maintaining legislation forbidding a woman to abort, for example, a pregnancy caused by rape or incest, or a pregnancy that, if it proceeds, will yield a severely deformed infant destined to live a short and painful life.

A judge who takes the time to inform herself and who conscientiously concludes that a legal restriction on a particular category (or categories) of abortion would almost certainly not have been enacted if the adverse effect of the restriction were visited on men equally with women, should conclude as well that the restriction, as an expression of sex-selective sympathy and indifference, violates the antidiscrimination norm. It is simply not possible to discern any explanation, much less justification, for what we are assuming the judge has found to be true — namely, that were its adverse effect visited equally on men, the restriction would not have been enacted, that, in that sense, the restriction is an expression of sex-selective sympathy and indifference — other than an ideology that may not, under the antidiscrimination norm, be a predicate for state laws or other state action.

Richard Posner misconceives the point, which is not that judges should strike down laws "just because *some* of the supporters of [the] laws

. . . had bad motives."[42] "Some" supporters is not enough. A judge must conclude not merely that some political support for the restriction at issue, but a critical mass of such support, is rooted in sex-selective sympathy and indifference. A judge should strike down a restriction, as a violation of the antidiscrimination norm, only if she concludes that but for sex-selective sympathy and indifference, the restriction would not exist—that the restriction, in that sense, is an expression of, that it expresses or embodies, such sympathy and indifference.

Admittedly, such counterfactual judgments—"this restriction would not exist were its adverse effect visited equally on [whites, men, etc.]"—are difficult to make, and no court should make them casually. But that is not to say that the inquiry should not be undertaken. (John Ely has written that "it will be next to impossible for a court responsibly to conclude that a position was affected by an unconstitutional motivation whenever it is possible to articulate a plausible legitimate explanation for the action taken. But what does that prove? Only that it often will not be possible responsibly to conclude that the challenged action was the product of unconstitutional motivation, not that the inquiry should not be undertaken."[43]) Such judgments are not impossible to make, after all. (Michael McConnell has conceded that the pregnancy exclusion upheld by the Court in *Geduldig v. Aiello*[44] was probably an expression of sex-selective sympathy and indifference.[45]) Of course, not every judge will agree that a legal restriction on a particular category of abortion—or, indeed, a restriction on *any* category of abortion, other than the category no sane person wants to restrict anyhow, namely, abortion necessary to save the mother's life—is an expression of sex-selective sympathy and indifference. But it seems disingenuous to deny that a judge can conclude, in good faith and with good reason, that a restriction on at least *some* categories of abortion is very likely an expression of such sympathy and indifference.[46]

* * *

That, then, is the antidiscrimination argument I presented in 1994. Now I want to explain why such arguments—antidiscrimination arguments for the result decreed by the Court in *Roe v. Wade*—can bear, at most, only a relatively small part of the weight that is typically put on them.

In the companion case to *Roe*—*Doe v. Bolton*[47]—the Supreme Court invalidated a modern Georgia abortion statute that, while restrictive, was nonetheless more moderate than the much older Texas legislation invalidated in *Roe*. As the Court put it,

> The Texas statutes under attack here are typical of those that have been in effect in many States for approximately a century. The Georgia statutes, in contrast, have a modern cast and are a legislative product that . . . obviously reflects the influences of recent attitudinal change, of ad-

vancing medical knowledge and techniques, and of new thinking about an old issue.[48]

The Texas legislation exempted only one category of abortion: abortion "for the purpose of saving the life of the mother."[49] The Georgia statute, by contrast—which was enacted in 1968 and "patterned upon the American Law Institute's Model Penal Code"[50]—exempted three categories: "(1) [a] continuation of the pregnancy would endanger the life of the pregnant woman or would seriously and permanently injure her health; or (2) [t]he fetus would very likely be born with a grave, permanent, and irremediable mental or physical defect; or (3) [t]he pregnancy resulted from forcible or statutory rape."[51] The Court was "assured by [Georgia] at reargument that . . . the statute's reference to 'rape' was intended to include incest."[52]

In *Roe* and *Doe*, the Court ruled that states may not outlaw *any* category of (pre-viability) abortion. An antidiscrimination argument of the sort presented above, however, would have justified, at most, a ruling that states may not outlaw *some* categories of abortion—namely, those categories exempted by the Georgia statute. It is, I think, implausible—it is wishful thinking—to conclude that restrictive abortion statutes like Georgia's would not have existed but for sex-selective sympathy and indifference. It does not seem improbable that in some states, in 1973, there would have been a critical mass of support for a statute like Georgia's even in the absence of sex-selective sympathy and indifference. *At least, because one simply cannot speculate with much confidence about whether or not there would have been a critical mass of support for a statute like Georgia's even in the absence of sex-selective sympathy and indifference, the premise that there would not have been a critical mass of support would have been an inappropriate basis for a constitutional decision, least of all a constitutional decision about a deeply divisive moral issue of such great difficulty as abortion.* Thus, the Court's 1973 ruling that states may not outlaw *any* category of abortion cannot be salvaged by the kind of antidiscrimination argument presented above.

Although a different ruling—that states may not outlaw *some* categories of abortion—might have been more defensible, the political process had already begun to repeal legal restrictions on the relevant categories. Statutes like Georgia's were on the way to becoming the norm.[53] As the Court noted in *Roe*, "[f]ourteen States have adopted some form of the ALI [American Law Institute] statute." Indeed, "[b]y the end of 1970, four other States had repealed criminal penalties for abortions performed in early pregnancy by a licensed physician, subject to stated procedural and health requirements."[54] Various data suggest that the trend would almost certainly have continued. Consider, for example, that in 1967, the American Medical Association gave its support to exceptions like the three enumerated above, and that five years later, in 1972, the American Bar Association did the same.[55] Even some mainline religious denominations were heading in that direction. In 1992, for example, when delegates to the national legislative convention of the Presbyterian Church (U.S.A.) voted to take a more "conservative" position on abortion, both the majority report (which called abortion "an option of last resort" and was adopted by a vote of 434 to 121) and the minority report (which called abortion "unjustified and a sin before God") "would permit abortion in circumstances such as rape, incest, a threat to the mother's life or threat of a serious fetal deformity."[56] In January 1998, twenty-five years after the Court's rulings in *Roe* and *Doe*, the *New York Times* reported that although the American people had grown more skeptical about the moral propriety of abortion, "[s]upport remained overwhelming . . . for women who sought abortions because they had been raped, their health was endangered, or there was a strong chance of a defect in the baby."[57]

Would a more limited ruling by the Court in *Roe*—to the effect that states may not outlaw *some* categories of (pre-viability) abortion—have been more defensible than the Court's actual, broader ruling that states may not outlaw *any* categories of abortion? Imagine that the Supreme Court had ruled only that states were constitutionally required to exempt from their bans on abortion—they were constitutionally disabled from outlawing—three categories of abortion: (1) abortion necessary to save the mother's life or to protect her physical health from a serious threat of grave and irreparable harm; (2) abortion in cases of rape or incest; and (3) abortion in cases where, to use the ALI's language, "[t]he fetus would very likely be born with a grave, permanent, and irremediable mental or physical defect or a threat of serious fetal deformity." Would such a limited ruling have been a judicial usurpation of politics? This question does not yield to a confident answer. One's answer depends on whether one finds persuasive the sort of antidiscrimination argument presented above—an argument that relies on impossible-to-verify counterfactual inquiry that, although it can be pursued in good faith, is also vulnerable to manipulation, whether deliberate or unconscious, to reach whatever result one desires. My own answer is that such a limited ruling would not have been a judicial usurpation: It is very likely, in my judgment, that few if any states, in the absence of sex-selective sympathy and indifference, would outlaw any of the three categories of abortion listed above. (Precisely because it relies on counterfactual speculation, my answer will look to some like little more than a willful ipse dixit.) But whatever one's answer, the fact remains that the Court's 1973 ruling was not so limited.

The Court's actual ruling in *Roe* was quite broad: States are constitutionally disabled from outlawing any and all abortions in the pre-viability period of pregnancy, including those millions of abortions every year that are not covered by any of the three categories listed in the preceding paragraph. Was that broader ruling a judicial usurpation of politics? The answer, I think, is yes. Again, the Court's ruling in *Roe* (and *Doe*) is not supported by the sort of antidiscrimination argument presented above; the ruling is not justified by any argument based on the central component of the antidiscrimination norm. (The serious question is whether even the

more limited ruling I have asked the reader to imagine would be sup-
ported/justified by such an argument.) Nor, as I explained in the preceding section of this chapter, was the ruling the yield of an appropriately deferential application of the reasonableness component of the norm. The
Supreme Court's broad ruling in *Roe v. Wade* was, as John Ely and many
others have argued in the last quarter of a century, a judicial usurpation of
American politics. At least, it is surely much more plausible to insist that
the Court's broad ruling in *Roe* was a judicial usurpation than it is to deny
it. Listen, in that regard, to no less committed and vigorous an advocate
of women's constitutional rights than Justice Ruth Bader Ginsburg, who,
in 1985, while a judge on the United States Court of Appeals for the District of Columbia Circuit, wrote:

> *Roe*, I believe, would have been more acceptable as a judicial decision
> if it had not gone beyond a ruling on the extreme [Texas] statute before
> the Court. The political process was moving in the 1970s, not swiftly
> enough for advocates of quick, complete change, but majoritarian insti-
> tutions were listening and acting. Heavy-handed judicial intervention
> was difficult to justify and appears to have provoked, not resolved, con-
> flict.[58]

III

Roe v. Wade was decided in 1973. In 1992, in *Planned Parenthood of South-
eastern Pennsylvania v. Casey*,[59] the issue addressed by the three Supreme
Court justices who, as the crucial "swing" votes on the issue, would deter-
mine whether or not the Court's ruling in *Roe* would survive—Sandra
Day O'Connor, Anthony Kennedy, and David Souter—was not whether
Roe was rightly decided in 1973, but whether it would be right to overrule
Roe in 1992. In their joint opinion, Justices O'Connor, Kennedy, and
Souter concluded that it would be wrong for the Court to overrule *Roe*.
The votes of Justices O'Connor, Kennedy, and Souter, together with the
vote of Justice Blackmun (who authored the opinion of the Court in *Roe*)
and the vote of Justice Stevens, each of whom argued that *Roe* was rightly
decided,[60] were just enough to support the Court's five-to-four ruling in
Casey that "the essential holding of *Roe v. Wade* should be retained and
once again affirmed."[61] If the O'Connor-Kennedy-Souter conclusion was
sound, then we can say that although (or, if one prefers, "even if") the
Court's decision in *Roe* was a judicial usurpation, the Court's decision in
Casey not to overrule its decision in *Roe* was not a reprisal of that earlier
usurpation but only a judicially fitting response to an invitation, many
years later, to overrule *Roe*. But was their conclusion sound?

I explained in chapter 2 that some constitutional rulings that were not,
when made, justifiable on the basis of any norm established by "We the
people" have nonetheless become constitutional bedrock for us.[62] Did the

Court's ruling in *Roe v. Wade* portend or even help to precipitate change(s) in American culture such that nineteen years later, in 1992, the proposition that government should not outlaw pre-viability abortion, or some proposition grounding that proposition, had become politically-morally axiomatic for us and a part of our constitutional bedrock? Hardly. In the interval between *Roe* and *Casey*, the American people had understandably become accustomed—some of them happily accustomed, others of them unhappily—to the availability of legal abortion. (The Court's affirmance of *Roe* in June 1992, followed by the election of Bill Clinton as President in November 1992, made critics of *Roe* resigned to the political reality that legal abortion would remain available for a long time to come.) But whether the Fourteenth Amendment *really* prevented the states from outlawing (pre-viability) abortion—and whether, even if they were constitutionally free to outlaw abortion, states should do so, and if they should do so, to what extent they should do so—remained, in 1992, deeply and widely contested constitutional and political-moral issues in the United States. If, then, Justices O'Connor, Kennedy, and Souter were right to conclude, in *Casey*, that the Court should not overrule *Roe*, it was not because by 1992 the proposition that government should not outlaw pre-viability abortion (or some proposition grounding that proposition) had become constitutional bedrock for us. That proposition had not become a part of our constitutional bedrock, and Justices O'Connor, Kennedy, and Souter did not suggest that it had.

Why, then, did the three justices conclude that it would be wrong for the Court in *Casey* to overrule *Roe*? (Recall that unlike Justices Blackmun and Stevens, Justices O'Connor, Kennedy, and Souter did not claim that *Roe v. Wade* had been rightly decided in the first place.) Their fundamental argument—the argument but for which their affirmance of *Roe* would make no sense at all—was that by 1992 so many persons had become so accustomed to the availability of legal abortion, that for the Court suddenly to change direction and now permit states to recriminalize abortion would prove too costly: The recriminalization of abortion, they argued, would frustrate the expectations and threaten the way of life of too many persons—especially of too many women who had made fundamental choices in their lives based on the assumption that whatever reproductive choices they might later want to make, or feel constrained by personal circumstances to make, including the choice of abortion, would be immune to governmental interference.[63] For the O'Connor-Kennedy-Souter argument to be persuasive, one must believe that the costs of recriminalizing abortion dominate the benefits of resuming the protection of fetal life by recriminalizing abortion. (If the benefits of resuming the protection of fetal life are proportionate to the costs of recriminalizing abortion, why not permit the states that want to do so to recriminalize abortion?) However, just as neither the Fourteenth Amendment nor any other part of the Constitution warranted, or required any state to accept, a calculus according to which, in 1973, the costs of making abortion unlawful outweighed the benefits of protecting fetal life by doing so, so too neither the Fourteenth Amendment nor any other part of the Constitution warranted, or required any state to accept, a calculus according to which, in 1992, the costs of making abortion unlawful—that is, of making it unlawful *again*, after a hiatus of nineteen years—dominated the benefits of resuming the protection of fetal life by doing so. Therefore, those who are convinced that the Court's ruling in *Roe* was a judicial usurpation of politics have little if any reason to concur in the O'Connor-Kennedy-Souter opinion that "the essential holding of *Roe v. Wade* should [have been] retained and once again affirmed."

And, indeed, in reading their joint opinion in *Casey*, one may fairly conclude that Justice O'Connor, Kennedy, and Souter were far from convinced that the Court's ruling in *Roe* was a judicial usurpation; to the contrary, they were conspicuously coy about whether, in their judgment, it was a judicial usurpation. (Perhaps they were comfortably agnostic about the issue and preferred a course that did not require them to take a stand. That would not have been a surprising preference for any of them to have had: Who among them would have wanted to risk concluding that the Court's decision in *Roe* had *not* been a judicial usurpation after all? Justices O'Connor and Kennedy were appointed by President Reagan; Justice Souter, by President Bush. Recall that Ronald Reagan nominated Anthony Kennedy to the Supreme Court when Reagan's nomination of Robert Bork was rejected by the Senate. The Court in *Casey* would have overruled *Roe* had it been Justice Bork voting rather than Justice Kennedy.) By contrast, Chief Justice Rehnquist and Justice Scalia wrote opinions in *Casey* that leave no doubt whatsoever that in their view (and in the view of Justices White and Thomas, who joined Rehnquist's and Scalia's opinions), *Roe v. Wade* is one of the most disturbing judicial usurpations of American politics in the twentieth century.[64]

IV

Physician-assisted suicide has become, like abortion, the focus of great moral and political controversy in the United States (and elsewhere[65]). A voluminous literature has been produced, just in the last few years, addressing questions about the circumstances, if any, under which it is morally permissible for one to commit suicide—and, in particular, about the circumstances, if any, under which it is morally permissible for a physician to assist one to commit suicide.[66] Moreover, physician-assisted suicide has become, again like abortion, the focus of great constitutional controversy. The principal constitutional question—May a state, under the Fourteenth Amendment, ban physician assistance in (committing) suicide if the person requesting the physician's assistance is both mentally competent to request the assistance and terminally ill?—ended up before the

Supreme Court of the United States in two cases: *Washington v. Glucksberg*[67] and *Vacco v. Quill*.[68]

Before the Court announced its decision, in June 1997, some of those who had been charging the Court with usurping politics feared that the Court would once again do so—this time, by ruling that no state may outlaw physician assistance in suicide if the person requesting the physician's assistance is mentally competent and terminally ill, thereby removing from the agenda of every state's politics the question *whether* to outlaw physician assistance in suicide. Indeed, the editors of the *First Things* symposium I discussed in chapter 1[69] called attention to the Court's then-forthcoming decision in the physician-assisted suicide cases by writing, in the very first paragraph of their introduction to the symposium, that a "decision favoring doctor-assisted suicide . . . could be fatal not only to many people who are old, sick, or disabled, but also to popular support for our present system of government."[70] The editors and many other anxious Court watchers were no doubt relieved when, on June 26, 1997, the Court ruled that states are free, under the Fourteenth Amendment, to outlaw physician assistance in suicide even if the person requesting the physician's assistance is mentally competent and terminally ill.[71] Did the Court decide the physician-assisted cases correctly? Would the decision that the editors of *First Things* feared have been a judicial usurpation of politics?

Like legislation outlawing abortion, legislation forbidding physicians and others to assist anyone to commit suicide is an instance of "differential treatment", even though it applies not just to some persons but to every person. Such legislation treats some persons differently from others, not on the basis of a trait, like sex, but on the basis of an act: assisting someone to commit suicide. Legislation outlawing such activity treats some persons differently from others depending on whether they have assisted in suicide. Those who obey the command not to assist anyone to commit suicide are treated differently from the way that those who disobey are treated; they are treated better, they are left alone. Legislation outlawing assistance (including physician assistance) in suicide is therefore subject, like legislation outlawing abortion, to the requirements of the antidiscrimination norm. Under the relevant part of the norm—the reasonableness component—the question arises: Does a law that punishes assistance in suicide, while leaving alone those who do not assist in suicide, regulate for the public good in a reasonable fashion? Is the law—the differential treatment—reasonably designed to achieve a legitimate governmental purpose?

Recall the three generic ways in which differential treatment might fail to regulate for the public good in a reasonable fashion.[72] Which of the three possibilities, if any of them, is realized by legislation outlawing assistance in suicide? Not the first: No one can fairly claim that such legislation is not aimed at serving legitimate governmental interests—for example, the protection of human life. (I list the various governmental interests below.) Nor is the second possibility realized by such legislation: There is no reason to doubt that legislation outlawing assistance in suicide succeeds, to some extent, in serving the various interests it is meant to serve; such legislation succeeds, for example, in protecting human life. That leaves only the third possibility: that the costs visited by the legislation on those the legislation regulates so dominate the benefit(s) of the legislation that the legislation does not regulate for the public good in a "reasonable" fashion, it is not "reasonably" designed to serve a legitimate governmental interest.

Legislation of the sort in question doesn't outlaw just physician assistance in suicide; it outlaws assistance in suicide, including physician assistance. But the issue on the table concerns the constitutionality of a state's failure to exempt from its general ban a particular species of assistance in suicide: physician assistance where the person requesting the assistance is mentally competent and terminally ill. So, the relevant question is this: Are the costs visited by legislation outlawing (inter alia) *physician* assistance in suicide on those the legislation regulates—in particular, on mentally competent, terminally ill persons who want to commit suicide and need assistance to do so—so out of proportion to the benefits achieved by the legislation, that the legislation does not regulate for the public good in a "reasonable" fashion, it is not "reasonably" designed to serve a legitimate governmental interest? Is such legislation unreasonable because the costs of the legislation are too disproportionate to the benefits?

Imagine a patient who has lost the ability to move about, whose sight and hearing, if they remain at all, are marginal, whose bodily functions are uncontrollable, who is dependent on others for the smallest things, and who, because of the large doses of sedatives needed to ameliorate chronic pain, is in an extremely lethargic, barely alert state. For a terminally ill person to be in such a condition and not to be able to end his or her life sooner rather than later—not to be able to exert some control over the way or the time his or her earthly life will end, not to be able to, in the phrase that many advocates of physician-assisted suicide use, "die with dignity"—is certainly no small matter. The situations of the patient-plaintiffs in *Gluckberg* and *Quill*, all of whom died while their cases were pending, are sadly illustrative.[73] The costs that a ban on physician assistance in suicide visits on mentally competent, terminally ill persons who want to commit suicide and need assistance to do so are undeniably great.

That the costs are great, however, does not entail that the costs are out of proportion to the benefits achieved by the ban; it does not conclude the question whether the costs are disproportionate to the benefits. But that the costs are great does mean that the benefit or benefits achieved by the legislative ban must be great too, lest the costs be so disproportionate to the benefits that the legislation fails to regulate for the public good in a "reasonable" fashion. In the physician-assisted suicide cases, therefore, the Supreme Court should have insisted that because the magnitude of the costs is great, the magnitude of the public benefit secured by the legislation must be great, too. The latter must be proportionate to—commensurate with—the former. As in *Roe v. Wade*, the Court should have said that a ban on physician assistance in suicide (i.e., in cases of mentally competent, terminally ill persons) is subject to strict scrutiny—that such a ban "may be justified only by a 'compelling state interest,' . . . [and] must be narrowly drawn to express only the legitimate state interests at stake."[74] In *Washington v. Glucksberg*, however, the Court declined to review the challenged state action under such a demanding standard of review. Instead, the Court inquired only whether "Washington's assisted-suicide ban [was] rationally related to legitimate governmental interests."[75] Justice Souter, concurring in the Court's judgment but not in its analysis, correctly responded that given the magnitude of the costs such a ban imposes on mentally competent, terminally ill persons, "a State may not rest on threshold rationality or a presumption of constitutionality, but may prevail only on the ground of an interest sufficiently compelling to place within the realm of the reasonable a refusal to recognize the individual right asserted."[76] The Court's misstep was ultimately inconsequential, however, because, as I explain below, the Court should have reached the same conclusion it did—that Washington's ban on physician-assisted suicide is constitutional—even under the appropriate, strict standard. Indeed, Justice Souter reached just that conclusion under what he termed "careful scrutiny".[77]

A ban on physician-assisted suicide serves several important governmental interests. The Court, in *Glucksberg*, listed five.

- First, the ban protects human life. "Washington has an 'unqualified interest in the preservation of human life.' The State's prohibition on assisted suicide, like all homicide laws, both reflects and advances its commitment to this interest."[78]
- Second, the ban protects the depressed from suicide. The New York State Task Force on Life and the Law, whose analysis the Court highlighted in its opinion, "expressed its concern that, because depression is difficult to diagnose, physicians and medical professionals often fail to respond adequately to seriously ill patients' needs. Thus, legal physician-assisted suicide could make it more difficult for the State to protect depressed and mentally ill persons . . ."[79]
- Third, the ban protects the elderly, the disabled, and the poor, some of whom might, if physician-assisted suicide were legal, be pressured to commit suicide.

> [T]he State has an interest in protecting vulnerable groups—including the poor, the elderly, and disabled persons—from abuse, neglect, and mistakes. . . . We have recognized . . . the real risk of subtle coercion and undue influence in end-of-life situations. Similarly, the New York Task Force warned that "legalizing physician-assisted suicide would pose profound risks to many individuals who are ill and vulnerable. . . . The risk of harm is greatest for the many individuals in our society whose auton-

omy and well-being are already compromised by poverty, lack of access to good medical care, advanced age, or membership in a stigmatized social group." . . . If physician-assisted suicide were permitted, many might resort to it to spare their families the substantial financial burden of end-of-life health-care costs.

The State's interest here goes beyond protecting the vulnerable from coercion; it extends to protecting disabled and terminally ill persons from prejudice, negative and inaccurate stereotypes, and "societal indifference." The State's assisted-suicide ban reflects and reinforces its policy that the lives of terminally ill, disabled, and elderly people must be no less valued than the lives of the young and healthy, and that a seriously disabled person's suicidal impulses should be interpreted and treated the same way as anyone else's.[80]

- Fourth, the ban protects "the integrity and ethics of the medical profession."[81] The Court noted that "the American Medical Association, like many other medical and physicians' groups, has concluded that '[p]hysician-assisted suicide is fundamentally incompatible with the physician's role as healer.' . . . And physician-assisted suicide could, it is argued, undermine the trust that is essential to the doctor-patient relationship by blurring the time-honored line between healing and harming."[82]
- Fifth, "the State may fear that permitting assisted suicide will start it down the path to voluntary and perhaps even involuntary euthanasia."[83] Referring to *Physician-Assisted Suicide and Euthanasia in the Netherlands*, the Court wrote:

> This study suggests that, despite the existence of various reporting procedures, euthanasia in the Netherlands has not been limited to competent, terminally ill adults who are enduring physical suffering, and that regulation of the practice may not have prevented abuses in cases involving vulnerable persons, including severely disabled neonates and elderly persons suffering from dementia. . . . The New York Task Force, citing the Dutch experience, observed that "assisted suicide and euthanasia are closely linked," and concluded that the "risk of . . . abuse is neither speculative nor distant." Washington, like most other States, reasonably ensures against this risk by banning, rather than regulating, assisted suicide.[84]

Here, then, is the crucial constitutional question: Can a state legislature reasonably conclude that the foregoing five interests are, cumulatively, sufficiently important to warrant a ban on physician-assisted suicide? Again, the issue for a judge, under the reasonableness component of the antidiscrimination norm, is not whether he or she would conclude that the benefits of legislation are proportionate to the costs, but only whether in his or her judgment a state legislature can reasonably conclude that the benefits are proportionate to—commensurate with—the costs. As I explained earlier in this chapter, the office of the Court, in pursuing the reasonableness inquiry, is not to make legislative judgments de novo, but only to determine if the legislative judgment at issue is a reasonable one—whether the legislation in dispute is a "reasonable" regulation for the public good. As I have already noted, Justice Souter made the point in his concurring opinion in *Glucksberg*: "It is no justification for judicial intervention merely to identify a reasonable resolution of contending values that differs from the terms of the legislation under review. It is only when the legislation's justifying principle, critically valued, is so far from being commensurate with the individual interest as to be arbitrarily or pointlessly applied that the statute must give way."[85]

It is clear to the point of undeniable that a state legislature can reasonably conclude that one or more of the governmental interests listed above are sufficiently important to provide the requisite constitutional warrant for a legislative ban on physician-assisted suicide—as, indeed, all nine justices in *Glucksberg* acknowledged. Therefore, Supreme Court was right to decide that states are free, under the Fourteenth Amendment, to ban physician-assisted suicide even if the person requesting the physician's assistance is mentally competent and terminally ill.

V

Today, most states explicitly permit a physician, in limited circumstances, to honor a mentally competent patient's request to withhold or withdraw life-sustaining treatment. Consider, for example, the State of Washington, whose policy is like that of most other states: "It has always been a crime to assist a suicide in the state of Washington. . . . At the same time, Washington's Natural Death Act, enacted in 1979, states that the 'withholding or withdrawal of life-sustaining treatment' at a patient's direction 'shall not, for any purpose, constitute a suicide.'"[86] In a footnote in *Glucksberg*, the Court reported:

> Under Washington's Natural Death Act, "adult persons have the fundamental right to control the decisions relating to the rendering of their own health care, including the decision to have life-sustaining treatment withheld or withdrawn in instances of a terminal condition or permanent unconscious condition." In Washington, "[a]ny adult person may execute a directive directing the withholding or withdrawal of life-sustaining treatment in a terminal condition or permanent unconscious condition," and a physician who, in accordance with such a directive, participates in the withholding or withdrawal of life-sustaining treatment is immune from civil, criminal, or professional liability.[87]

I explained above why a ban on assisted suicide is, like a ban on abortion, an instance of "differential treatment", even though it applies not just to some persons but to every person. Those who obey the command not to assist anyone to commit suicide are treated differently from the way that those who disobey are treated; they are treated better, they are left alone. (Therefore, a ban on assisted suicide, like a ban on abortion, must regulate for the public good in a reasonable fashion; understood as an instance of differential treatment, the ban must be reasonably designed to achieve a legitimate governmental purpose.) In a state that, like Washington, bans assisted suicide, including physician-assisted suicide, physicians (and others) who assist a person to commit suicide are treated differently not only from physicians (and others) who do not assist a person to commit suicide. They are also treated differently from physicians who honor a mentally competent patient's request to withhold or withdraw life-sustaining treatment. The latter differential treatment, no less than the former, is subject to the requirements of the antidiscrimination norm.

Assume that, as I argued above, there is a constitutionally adequate justification for a state to treat physicians who assist a patient to commit suicide differently (less well) from physicians who do not. It does not follow that there is necessarily a constitutionally adequate justification for a state to treat physicians who assist a patient to commit suicide differently from physicians who, at a patient's request, withhold or withdraw life-sustaining treatment, thereby hastening the patient's death. That the former differential treatment satisfies the requirements of the antidiscrimination norm does not entail that the latter does so as well. (That there is a good reason to treat *A* differently from *B* does not entail that there is a good reason to treat *A* differently from *C*.) Under the reasonableness component of the norm, the question arises: Does a state that punishes physicians who assist a patient to commit suicide, while leaving alone physicians who, at a patient's request, withhold or withdraw life-sustaining treatment, thereby hastening the patient's death, regulate for the public good in a reasonable fashion? Is the state's policy—banning one course of action that hastens the death of a patient while tolerating another course of action that also hastens the death of a patient—reasonably designed to achieve a legitimate governmental purpose? Or is the policy arbitrary, because it rests on an arbitrary distinction?

That was the question addressed by the Court in the second of the two physician-assisted suicide cases, *Vacco v. Quill*, which involved a challenge to New York's ban on physician-assisted suicide. "In New York, as in most States, it is a crime to aid another to commit or attempt suicide, but patients may refuse even lifesaving medical treatment."[88] All nine justices in *Quill* agreed that the particular differential treatment at issue there was a reasonable regulation. As Chief Justice Rehnquist explained, in the opinion of the Court: "[T]he distinction between assisting suicide and withdrawing life-sustaining treatment, a distinction widely recognized and endorsed in the medical profession and in our legal traditions, is both important and logical; it is certainly rational."[89] The distinction to which the Court referred is, of course, the familiar distinction between "killing" and "allowing to die"; it is, as the Court put it, "the distinction between letting a patient die and making the patient die."[90] As the Court noted, the laws of most jurisdictions in the United States today rely on the distinction,[91] and the principal representative of the medical profession itself in the United States, the American Medical Association,

> emphasizes the "fundamental difference between refusing life-sustaining treatment and demanding a life-ending treatment." American Medical Association, Council on Ethical and Judicial Affairs, Physician-Assisted Suicide, 10 Issues in Law & Medicine 91, 93 (1994); see also American Medical Association, Council on Ethical and Judicial Affairs, Decisions Near the End of Life, 267 JAMA 2229, 2230–2231, 2233 (1992) ("The withdrawing or withholding of life-sustaining treatment is not inherently contrary to the principles of beneficence and Nonmaleficence," but assisted suicide "is contrary to the prohibition against using the tools of medicine to cause a patient's death"); New York State Task Force on Life and the Law, When Death Is Sought: Assisted Suicide and Euthanasia in the Medical Context 108 (1994) ("[Professional organizations] consistently distinguish assisted suicide and euthanasia from the withdrawing or withholding of treatment, and from the provision of palliative treatments or other medical care that risk fatal side effects"); Brief for the American Medical Association et al. as *Amici Curiae* 18–25.[92]

It also merits mention that, in addition to most state lawmakers and most doctors, many religious traditions have embraced the distinction.[93]

It risks understatement to say that it would have been incredibly arrogant for the Supreme Court to have declared that the distinction between "letting a patient die and making the patient die"—and the related distinction between "refusing life-sustaining treatment and demanding a life-ending treatment"—are so ephemeral that any state policy that relies on such distinctions is an arbitrary, not a reasonable, regulation for the public good. It is not my purpose here to argue that the distinction between "letting a patient die and making the patient die" is in fact morally relevant and that one is therefore mistaken to believe that it is not morally relevant. (In the voluminous literature on physician-assisted suicide that has been produced in the last few years, there have been numerous defenses of the moral relevance of the distinction between "killing" and "allowing to die".[94]) The point, rather, is that even if one can reasonably believe that the distinction is not morally relevant—or, at least, that the distinction bears much less moral weight than it is sometimes thought to bear—it is not unreasonable, it is not arbitrary, for others to believe that the distinction *is* morally relevant, even morally determinative.[95]

VI

Did the Supreme Court decide the physician-assisted cases correctly? It did. (Significantly, the vote was nine to nothing.) Would the decision that the

First Things editors and symposiasts feared have been a judicial usurpation of politics? It would have been. The Court acknowledged the point, in the last paragraph of its opinion in *Glucksberg*: "Throughout the Nation, Americans are engaged in an earnest and profound debate about the morality, legality, and practicality of physician-assisted suicide. Our holding permits this debate to continue, as it should in a democratic society."[96]

That Americans are engaged in the "earnest and profound debate" to which the Court referred seems clear.[97] As the Court observed earlier in its opinion, "[p]ublic concern and democratic action are . . . sharply focused on how best to protect dignity and independence at the end of life, with the result that there have been many significant changes in state laws and in the attitudes these laws reflect. Many States, for example, now permit 'living wills,' surrogate health-care decisionmaking, and the withdrawal or refusal of life-sustaining medical treatment."[98] (The Court then added: "At the same time, however, voters and legislators continue for the most part to reaffirm their States' prohibitions on assisting suicide."[99]) As a part of the ongoing national discussion, the New York State Task Force on Life and the Law studied the matter of physician-assisted suicide. "[T]he Task force unanimously concluded [in 1994] that '[l]egalizing assisted suicide and euthanasia would pose profound risks to many individuals who are ill and vulnerable. . . . [T]he potential dangers of this dramatic change in public policy would outweigh any benefit that might be achieved.'"[100] By contrast, the people of Oregon, in a statewide referendum on November 4, 1997, approved a law ("the Oregon Death with Dignity Act") permitting "doctors to prescribe a lethal dose of drugs to a terminally ill patient who has made a written request to die."[101] The *New York Times* reported:

> As recently as 15 years ago, doctors were prosecuted for withdrawing life-support systems from dying patients, even at the behest of a family. Today in Oregon, after a surprisingly strong vote that takes one state to the frontier of medical ethics, doctors can begin helping terminally ill patients kill themselves.
>
> The vote reflects how far and how fast public opinion, at least in this state, has moved on an issue once considered taboo.
>
> There was little ambiguity in the Oregon vote. In a huge turnout, perhaps the biggest in 34 years, about 60 percent of this state's voters rebuffed an attempt to repeal the nation's first assisted-suicide law. The law, which was passed in 1994 by 51 percent to 49 percent, had been held up by court challenges.[102]

It is an indication of how over the top some constitutional scholars are—Ronald Dworkin is the most conspicuous example—that, on the basis of constitutional arguments that are, at best, tenuous, they would have the Supreme Court of the United States preempt the American people's "earnest and profound debate about the morality, legality, and practicality of physician-assisted suicide."[103] They would have Supreme Court justices substitute their own judgment for the judgment of, for example, the New York Task Force on Life and the Law, "an ongoing, blue-ribbon commission composed of doctors, ethicists, lawyers, religious leaders, and interested laymen [that] was convened in 1984 and commissioned with 'a broad mandate to recommend public policy on issues raised by medical advances.'"[104] A unanimous Supreme Court acted appropriately in resisting what amounted to a plea, by Ronald Dworkin and others, to usurp American politics in the name of a controversial judgment about the political morality of laws banning physician-assisted suicide, a judgment that many persons committed to the Constitution of the United States—in particular, to the Fourteenth Amendment—can and do reasonably reject. (Anthony Kronman has referred to "extravagant claims of the kind that Dworkin makes about the relationship of law and morality."[105]) It bears mention that Dworkin delivered his plea to the Court after he had already failed to persuade policymakers in Great Britain and, later, in New York to endorse his position on physician-assisted suicide.[106] That Dworkin failed to move the political process either in Great Britain or in New York does not mean that—and there is little if any reason to believe that—ordinary politics is incapable of handling the issue of physician-assisted suicide in a reasonable fashion. (Not that every state will take the same path. New York and Oregon, for example, have not taken the same path.) As Justice O'Connor explained in her concurring opinion in Glucksberg:

> Every one of us may at some point be affected by our own or a family member's terminal illness. There is no reason to think the democratic process will not strike the proper balance between the interests of terminally ill, mentally competent individuals who would seek to end their suffering and the State's interests in protecting those who might seek to end life mistakenly or under pressure. As the Court recognizes, States are presently undertaking extensive and serious evaluation of physician-assisted suicide and other related issues.[107]

(Instead of "the" proper balance, Justice O'Connor should have written "a" proper balance. There is no reason to assume that only one balance is proper—reasonable—here. Not every state need take the same path.)

VII

Now, by way of conclusion, let us revisit *Roe v. Wade* and its companion case, *Doe v. Bolton*.

"Let democracy do its work." If some such refrain was fitting in the physician-assisted suicide cases, why not in the abortion cases too? It is difficult to see why it was less usurpative for the Court to rule that states may not ban *any* category of pre-viability abortion than it would have been for the Court to rule that states may not ban physician-assisted suicide. That, and why, it would have been a judicial usurpation for the Court to rule that states may not ban physician-assisted suicide helps us understand that, and why, it was a judicial usurpation for the Court to rule the way it did—that is, the *broad* way it did—in the abortion cases.[108] In *Roe* and *Doe*, no less than in *Glucksberg* and *Quill*, it would have been accurate for the Court to say: "Throughout the Nation, Americans are engaged in an earnest and profound debate about the morality, legality, and practicality of [abortion]. Our holding permits this debate to continue, as it should in a democratic society."[109] In *Roe* and *Doe* no less than in *Glucksberg* and *Quill*, it would have been accurate for the Court to say: "[T]here have been many significant changes in state laws and in the attitudes these laws reflect." (Recall that by 1973, when *Roe* and *Doe* were decided, the political process had already begun to repeal legal restrictions on some categories of abortion. As the Court noted in *Roe*, "[f]ourteen States have adopted some form of the ALI statute. By the end of 1970, four other States had repealed criminal penalties for abortions performed in early pregnancy by a licensed physician, subject to stated procedural and health requirements."[110]) And, in *Roe* and *Doe* no less than in *Glucksberg* and *Quill*, it would have been accurate for the Court to say: "Every one of us may at some point be affected by a family member's [unwanted pregnancy]. There is no reason to think the democratic process will not strike a proper balance between the interests of [pregnant women] who would seek to end their [pregnancy] and the State's interests in protecting [unborn human life]. States are presently undertaking extensive and serious evaluation of [abortion]."

Early in this chapter I said that state legislation outlawing abortion implicates a norm established by "We the people" *if*, as I argued in chapter 3, the reasonableness requirement is a component of the antidiscrimination norm that "We the people" established as a part of the Fourteenth Amendment—the requirement that a state not treat some less well than others unless the differential treatment is reasonably designed to accomplish a legitimate governmental purpose. I also said that such legislation implicates a norm that has become constitutional bedrock for us *if*, as I claimed in the final section of chapter 3, the reasonableness requirement is a component of the antidiscrimination norm that has become a part of our constitutional bedrock. Of course, not everyone will agree that the reasonableness requirement was established by "We the people" or even that it is now a part of our constitutional bedrock. So I suggested that, for the sake of discussion, we assume that the requirement has constitutional status and see where the assumption leads. This is where it has led: Legislation that bans abortion—but that, like the Georgia statute struck down in *Doe v. Bolton*, exempts certain narrow categories of abortion—is reasonably designed to accomplish a legitimate governmental purpose. The Supreme Court's decision to the contrary over a quarter of a century ago, in *Roe v. Wade* and *Doe v. Bolton*, was a usurpation of politics. Listen, again, to then-Judge Ginsburg: "*Roe* . . . would have been more acceptable as a judicial decision if it had not gone beyond a ruling on the extreme [Texas] statute before the Court. The political process was moving in the 1970s, . . . majoritarian institutions were listening and acting. Heavy-handed judicial intervention was difficult to justify and appears to have provoked, not resolved, conflict."[111]

7

❦

Concluding Reflections

American constitutional history has been in large part a spasmodic running de-
bate over the behavior of the Supreme Court, but [in almost two centuries] we
have made curiously little progress toward establishing the terms of this war of
words, much less toward achieving concord. . . . [T]hese recurring constitu-
tional debates resemble an endless series of re-matches between two club-boxers
who have long since stopped developing their crafts autonomously and have
nothing further to learn from each other. The same generalizations are
launched from either side, to be met by the same evasions and parries. Famil-
iar old ambiguities fog the controversy, and the contestants flounder among
them for a while until history calls a close and it is time to retire from the arena
and await the next installment. In the exchange of assertions and counter-
assertions no one can be said to have won a decision on the merits, for small at-
tempt has been made to arrive at an understanding of what the merits are.

Robert G. McCloskey, *The Modern Supreme Court*[1]

The *First Things* symposiasts and many others, as I explained in chapter 1,
have charged that in the modern period of American constitutional law,
the Supreme Court of the United States has usurped our politics. Is the
charge accurate? The answer I have provided in this book is only partial:
I have focused only on Fourteenth Amendment issues—and only on a few
such issues.[2] Nonetheless, the issues on which I have focused are among
the most important and controversial in the modern period; moreover,
they are, with a single exception, issues on which those who have recently
charged the Court with judicial usurpation have themselves focused. Here
is a brief summary of the conclusions I have reached in this book.

1. In outlawing racially segregated public schooling and other instances of government-created or -maintained racial segregation,
   the Court did not usurp our politics.
2. In subjecting government reliance on race-based affirmative action
   to a strict standard of review, the Court has not acted inappropri-

ately; but the Court's nondeferential stance—its nondeferential application of the standard—can fairly be said to usurp our politics: The Court should, but does not, inquire whether a legislature's (or other policymaking institution's) judgment that a particular instance of affirmative action satisfies the standard—whether a legislature's judgment that a particular instance of affirmative action is necessary to achieve a compelling governmental purpose—is reasonable; if in the Court's view the legislature's judgment is reasonable, the Court should defer to the judgment.

3. In moving beyond discrimination based on race to discrimination based on sex—in commencing to disfavor discrimination based on sex—the Court did not usurp our politics.

4. It is not clear whether the Court is now prepared to move beyond discrimination against women to discrimination against homosexuals, but the Court would not usurp our politics were it to make that move; indeed, so long as it fails to make the move, the Court capitulates to our prejudices, unjustifiably compromising the central meaning—the antidiscrimination meaning—of the Fourteenth Amendment.

5. As John Ely saw right away, and as some other liberal constitutional scholars eventually acknowledged—including, in 1985, then-Judge Ruth Ginsburg—the Court's broad ruling in the abortion cases (*Roe v. Wade* and *Doe v. Bolton*) was a usurpation of our politics.

6. The Court's refusal to strike down the laws against physician-assisted suicide that were challenged in *Washington v. Glucksberg* and *Vacco v. Quill* was correct; had it accepted the invitation of Ronald Dworkin & Co. to invalidate the laws, the Court would have usurped our politics.

I said that the issues on which I have focused here are, with a single exception, issues on which those who have recently charged the Supreme Court with judicial usurpation have themselves focused. The single exception: The social conservatives who have charged the Court with judicial usurpation—for example, the *First Things* symposiasts—have not focused on, much less criticized, the Court's nondeferential, usurpative stance with respect to government reliance on race-based affirmative action. Surely one reason for this is that these critics of the modern Court are typically opposed to affirmative action and are therefore resistant to seeing the Court's stance as usurpative—just as, for example, many who support abortion rights are resistant to seeing the Court's aggressively broad ruling in the abortion cases as usurpative.

Of course, I don't expect everyone who has charged the Court with judicial usurpation—or even many who have done so—to embrace all the conclusions I have reached here. But I do hope that, at least, I have clarified the kinds of questions that the disputants in the argument about judicial usurpation should address. Consider, for example, discrimination against homosexuals. Why might one think that for the Court to disfavor such discrimination would be for it to usurp our politics?

- Because in making the Fourteenth Amendment a part of the Constitution, "We the people" (through their political representatives) never established an antidiscrimination norm? And, further, because no antidiscrimination norm has ever become constitutional bedrock for us?
- Or because discrimination against homosexuals does not even implicate, much less violate, either the antidiscrimination norm that "We the people" established (if they did) or the antidiscrimination norm that is now a part of our constitutional bedrock (if one is)? (If an antidiscrimination norm forbids only racist discrimination, then discrimination against homosexuals does not implicate the norm—i.e., it does not raise a serious question under the norm.)
- Or because discrimination against homosexuals, even if it implicates an antidiscrimination norm that has constitutional status, rarely if ever violates the norm? (Assume that an antidiscrimination norm forbids not just racist discrimination but any discrimination that, like racist discrimination, presupposes the lesser humanity of those who are the objects of the discrimination. That discrimination against homosexuals raises a question under the norm does not entail that a particular instance of discrimination against homosexuals actually violates the norm; it does not entail that a particular instance of such discrimination in fact presupposes the lesser humanity of homosexuals.)

Addressing questions like these is a productive way—I am tempted to say that it is *the* productive way—to continue the conversation about judicial usurpation.[3]

But it is certainly not the only way to continue the conversation. One might prefer to challenge, or at least to question, the constitutional "theory" presupposed by my doctrinal arguments in this book: the set of premises on which my arguments rest. Any argument about how the Supreme Court should resolve a constitutional conflict necessarily presupposes a constitutional theory, even if the presupposed theory is not systematized—indeed, even if it is unreflective and finally self-contradictory. Richard Posner has argued recently that constitutional scholarship should abandon constitutional theory in favor of social science.[4] But it is a mistake to think that critical constitutional scholarship can do without constitutional theory. (Not that there isn't need, in constitutional scholarship, for more and better social science; Posner has some interesting things to say about that.) We should make our presuppositions explicit and reflect on them when our presuppositions are or might be controversial. Moreover, it is inevitable that some of us will be driven to clarify and critically examine our presuppositions when they are or might be controversial. "'Theory' . . . is what erupts when what was once silently agreed to in a community becomes disputed, forcing its members to formulate and defend assumptions that they previously did not even have to be aware of."[5]

In chapter 2, I presented and defended the premises—the "theory"—on which my doctrinal arguments in chapters 4 through 6 rest.[6] With my doctrinal arguments in chapters 4 through 6 now behind us, I want to emphasize three connected premises from chapter 2.

But, first, let me pause to emphasize what precisely is at issue here and what is not. The issue is not whether the Constitution of the United States is the best possible constitution for us today—for us, the people of the United States now living. (We can all imagine a constitution that is at least marginally better, though we will disagree among ourselves about what a better constitution would look like.) Nor is the issue whether we are morally obligated to be loyal or faithful to—in particular, to obey—the Constitution, in whole or in part.[7] (I did explain, in chapter 2, why as a *practical* matter—not as a *moral* matter—we should generally abide constitutional directives that old and even dead generations of "We the people" have issued.[8]) The issue—our question-in-chief—is much more mundane than that: In issuing its rulings about racial segregation, race-based affirmative action, sex-based discrimination, homosexuality, and abortion, has the Supreme Court, in the guise of interpreting section one of the Fourteenth Amendment, usurped prerogatives that under the Constitution belong to one or more other branches or agencies of government? Recall, from chapter 1, Mary Ann Glendon's statement of the point: "[T]he judiciary has steadily usurped power over matters that the Constitution wisely left to ordinary political processes." Glendon's claim—and, indeed, the claim of the *First Things* symposiasts generally—is that the modern Supreme Court has removed from "ordinary political processes" many "matters that the Constitution wisely left to ordinary political processes." Specifically, the claim is that the Court has resolved many issues of political morality that are none of the Court's proper business, in this sense: they are none of the business that the Constitution, rather than leaving solely to ordinary politics, has committed ultimately to the Court.

Now, the three connected premises, from chapter 2, that I want to emphasize here.

- The Constitution comprises directives issued by—norms established by—"We the people" (acting through their political representatives) and not subsequently disestablished by them.
- The Constitution also comprises norms that, even if they were never established by "We the people", have nonetheless become constitutional bedrock for us the people of the United States now living. (As a part of our constitutional bedrock, such norms are lexically prior to norms of the former sort.)
- Relatedly, to interpret the constitutional text (i.e., some part of it)—really to interpret it and not just to engage in some other performance in the guise of interpreting it—is to (try to) discern either the norm (or norms) that "We the people", in adding the text to the existing constitutional text, meant to establish or the bedrock norm that the text (under the pressure of what I called, in chapter 2, the textualist sensi-

bility of American constitutional culture) has come to represent. (I distinguished, in chapter 2, between two different senses of "interpretation": first, interpreting the constitutional text in an effort to discern/identify the norm represented by the text; second, interpreting—"specifying"—a constitutional norm that is implicated, but that is also underdeterminate, in the context at hand.)

One is certainly free to make, and some constitutional theorists do make, one or another version of the following twofold argument:

- The Constitution also comprises—or, at least, it should be understood to comprise—norms that (a) do not fall into either of the two categories indicated above (i.e., norms established by "We the people" and norms that, even if they were not established by "We the people", have nonetheless become constitutional bedrock for us) and, moreover, (b) are not simply specifications of norms that do fall into one of those two categories.
- As a matter of American political morality, it is legitimate for electorally unaccountable judges to divine those norms and then bring them to bear against the electorally accountable branches and agencies of government.

In the context of the constitutional culture we Americans actually have, however, as distinct from the context of the constitutional culture some constitutional theorists fantasize us to have, any such argument is an obviously and exceedingly vulnerable position from which to engage those, like Mary Ann Glendon and the other *First Things* symposiasts, who make the judicial usurpation charge. Any such argument is destined to enjoy at most scant support in American constitutional culture.[9] (Learned Hand's famous comment comes to mind here: "For myself it would be most irksome to be ruled by a bevy of Platonic Guardians, even if I knew how to choose them, which I assuredly do not."[10]) Were a skilled advocate—a skilled rhetorician or polemicist—to make such an argument about the content of our Constitution in a debate before an audience of informed lay citizens whose ideological diversity was roughly representative of the ideological diversity of the American people as a whole—and were he faced, on the other side, by an equally skilled advocate—he would not come close to winning a show of hands at the end of the debate. Instead, and understandably, he would be dismissed by most of the audience as a result-oriented advocate. Richard Posner is exactly right about how result-driven academic constitutional theory typically is.[11]

Now imagine an argument at another extreme: an argument to the effect that even if a norm—for example, the antidiscrimination norm I articulated in the final section of chapter 3—does in fact fall into one of the two categories indicated above, it is nonetheless illegitimate for the Supreme Court to enforce the norm against the electorally accountable branches and agencies of government.[12] Given the shape of American constitutional culture, any such argument is an obviously and exceedingly vulnerable position from which to charge the Court with "usurping" our politics. After all, it is widely agreed in American constitutional culture—indeed, it is virtually axiomatic—that, however much we might disagree about the outer limits of the Court's proper role, the Court's central responsibility is to protect norms that fall into one of the two categories indicated above. To enforce such norms is not a usurpation. To fail to enforce them is an abdication.

None of this is to deny that we can imagine, and even desire, a constitutional culture different from our own. We can imagine, for example, a constitutional culture in which the people affirm their judges not only as protectors of their constitution but even as originators of it—as originators of basic constitutional norms. We can also imagine a constitutional culture in which electorally unaccountable judges are expected to play, and in fact play, little or even no role in protecting the constitution.[13] But neither the former constitutional culture nor the latter is American constitutional culture.

This brings me back to an earlier point. I hope I have succeeded in clarifying the kinds of questions that, given the constitutional culture we Americans actually have, those who charge the Supreme Court with the usurpation of politics should be addressing. For example: In making the Fourteenth Amendment a part of the Constitution, didn't "We the people" (through their representatives) establish an antidiscrimination norm? Whether or not they did—and, so, even if they did not—isn't it nonetheless the case that, in the post-Holocaustal period, an antidiscrimination norm became constitutional bedrock for us? Doesn't discrimination against homosexuals implicate either the antidiscrimination norm that "We the people" established (if they did) or the antidiscrimination norm that is now a part of our constitutional bedrock (if one is)? If so, don't at least some instances of discrimination against homosexuals violate the authoritative antidiscrimination norm? Again, addressing these and kindred questions is, I think, the most productive way, in American constitutional culture, to continue the conversation about judicial usurpation. It is also, I think, the most promising way to escape the relentless judgment by Robert McCloskey that I quoted at the beginning of this chapter.

In any event, addressing these and kindred questions is the way I have sought, in this book, to advance the perennial conversation about judicial usurpation. It is the way I have sought to engage the perennial, and grave, charge that the modern Supreme Court has usurped our politics.

NOTES

Preface

1. Some better known recent examples: Bruce Ackerman, *We the People: Foundations* (1993); Bruce Ackerman, *We the People: Transformations* (1998); Forrest McDonald, *We the People: The Economic Origins of the Constitution* (1992); Theodore J. Lowi et al., *We the People: An Introduction to American Politics* 1997).

2. My earlier constitutional writings include two books: Michael J. Perry, *The Constitution, the Courts, and Human Rights* (1982); Michael J. Perry, *The Constitution in the Courts: Law or Politics?* (1994). I have focused, in other writings, mainly on two other topics: first, the proper role of morality, including religious morality, in the politics and law of a liberal democracy like the United States; and, second, the relation of religion to morality. See Michael J. Perry, *Morality, Politics, and Law* (1988); Michael J. Perry, *Love and Power* (1991); Michael J. Perry, *Religion in Politics* (1997); Michael J. Perry, *The Idea of Human Rights* (1998).

3. See Steven D. Smith, *The Supreme Court and the Pride of Reason* (1998).

Chapter 1

1. 163 U.S. 537, 558.

2. 347 U.S. 483.

3. See Charles L. Black, Jr., Decision According to Law 33 (1981) (describing *Brown* as "the decision that opened our era of judicial activity"). See also William J. Brennan, Jr., "Why Have a Bill of Rights?" 9 Oxford J. Legal Studies 425, 430–31 (1989).

4. In *Dred Scott v. Sandford*, 60 U.S. (19 How.) 393—surely the single most infamous case in American constitutional law—the Supreme Court ruled that under the Constitution, Congress lacked power to outlaw slavery in the federal territories and that "a man of African descent, whether a slave or not, was not and could not be a citizen of a State or of the United States." Slaughter-House Cases, 83 U.S. (16 Wall.) 36, 73 (1872). See Robert P. George, "The Tyrant State," First Things, November 1996, at 39, 40: "[T]he Supreme Court of the United States, in a ruling that helped to precipitate the Civil War, held in *Dred Scott v. Sandford* that blacks were noncitizens—and, for all practical purposes, nonpersons—possessed of no rights that white people must respect." On *Dred Scott*, see Don E. Fehrenbacher, The Dred Scott Case: Its Significance in American Law and Politics (1978). For a shorter commentary, see Don E. Fehrenbacher, "Dred Scott v. Sandford, 19 Howard 393 (1857)," in 2 Encyclopedia of the American Constitution 584 (Leonard W. Levy, Kenneth L. Karst, & Dennis J. Mahoney eds., 1986).

5. 198 U.S. 45.

6. The November 1996 installment of the symposium, along with a subsequent installment (from the January 1997 issue of *First Things*) and many other, related pieces, have been reprinted in a book: The End of Democracy? The Judicial

Usurpation of Politics (Mitchell S. Muncy ed., 1997). The book also contains an extensive new contribution by Richard John Neuhaus, editor in chief of *First Things* and principal organizer of the symposium. For yet a further extension of the symposium, see "Conference on Judicial Usurpation," 44 Loyola L. Rev. 83–133 (1998) (contributions by Russell Hittinger, Robert P. George, and Richard J. Neuhaus).

7. The contributors to the November 1996 installment of the symposium were Hadley Arkes, Robert Bork, Charles Colson, Robert George, and Russell Hittinger.

8. Neuhaus is "a former Lutheran pastor and political radical who is now a neoconservative Roman Catholic priest in the Archdiocese of New York . . ." Peter Steinfels, "Beliefs," New York Times, Dec. 14, 1996, 1, p. 11.

9. The quoted passages (emphasis added) appear at pp. 18–20 of the November 1996 issue of *First Things*.

10. Robert H. Bork, The Tempting of America: The Political Seduction of the Law 180 (1989). See also Robert H. Bork, Slouching Towards Gomorrah: Modern Liberalism and the American Decline, ch. 6 ("The Supreme Court as an Agent of Modern Liberalism") (1996). I have commented critically on Bork's views elsewhere. See Michael J. Perry, The Constitution in the Courts: Law or Politics? (1994).

11. The quoted passages appear at pp. 21–23 of Bork's contribution to the *First Things* symposium.

12. Steinfels, n. 8. For more on the controversy among social conservatives sparked by the *First Things* symposium, see Editorial, "First Things First," National Review, Nov. 11, 1996, at 16; "On the Future of Conservatism: A Symposium," Commentary, February 1997, at 14–43. See also Jacob Heilbrun, "Neocon v. Theocon," New Republic, Dec. 30, 1996, at 20. All of this material—and much more—is reprinted in The End of Democracy, n. 6.

13. Contributions to the *Commentary* symposium are reprinted in id.

14. Himmelfarb's letter of resignation was published in the January 1997 issue of *First Things* and is reprinted in id.

15. See the extensive bibliography compiled in The End of Democracy?, n. 6, at 269–81.

16. Linda Bowles, "What Constitution?," Chicago Tribune, Dec. 11, 1996, 1, p. 27.

17. Steven G. Calabresi, "Out of Order," Policy Review, September–October 1996, at 14, 21 (emphasis added). For a less polemical, more measured statement, see Steve G. Calabresi, "Textualism and the Countermajoritarian Difficulty," 66 George Washington L. Rev. 1356 (1998).

18. The following comments all appeared in the January 1997 issue of *First Things*, under the heading: "The End of Democracy? A Discussion Continued", and all are reprinted in The End of Democracy?, n. 6.

19. The statement is reprinted at pp. 51–54 of the October 1997 issue of *First Things*.

20. Charles Colson, James Dobson, Robert George, Mary Ann Glendon, Russell Hittinger, and Richard John Neuhaus.

21. 410 U.S. 113 (1973).

22. Romer v. Evans, 517 U.S. 620, 116 S. Ct. 1620 (1996). I discuss the Court's decision in *Romer* in chapter 5.

23. Concerning, that is, the constitutionally proper relationship between the national ("federal") government and the governments of the states.

24. Concerning, that is, the constitutionally proper relationship among the

three coordinate and coequal branches of the national government: the legislative, the executive, and the judicial branches.

25. See Perry, n. 10, especially pp. 3–14 & 192–204.

26. See Madsen v. Women's Health Center, Inc., 512 U.S. 753 (1994).

27. See, e.g., Lino A. Graglia, "Constitutional Interpretation," 44 Syracuse L. Rev. 631, 637 (1994); Richard E. Morgan, "Coming Clean About *Brown*," City Journal, Summer 1996, at 42. See also Richard John Neuhaus, "Coming Clean About *Brown*," First Things, February 1997, at 62–63 (calling attention to and commenting favorably on "an important article by Richard E. Morgan, the William Nelson Cromwell Professor of Constitutional Law and Government at Bowdoin College").

28. 410 U.S. 113.

29. 410 U.S. 179.

30. Roe v. Wade, 410 U.S. at 163.

31. 117 S. Ct. 2258.

32. 117 S. Ct. 2293.

Chapter 2

1. Claims about what the Constitution forbids (or does not forbid) are also claims about what the Constitution requires (or does not require). To say that the Constitution forbids government to do *X* is to say that it requires that government not do *X*; to say that the Constitution requires government to do *X* is to say that it forbids government not to do *X*. If the Constitution neither forbids nor requires government to do *X*, then it permits government to do *X*.

2. Well, almost no disagreement. In 1789, Congress proposed this constitutional amendment: "No law varying the compensation for the services of the Senators and Representatives shall take effect, until an election of Representatives shall have intervened." In 1992—over two hundred years later!—the thirty-eighth state voted to ratify the proposed amendment, which Congress then declared "valid . . . as part of the Constitution of the United States." One may fairly wonder whether completion of the process of ratifying the (alleged) Twenty-seventh Amendment was legally valid—and whether, therefore, the constitutional text really contains the language of the Amendment. See, e.g., William Van Alstyne, "What Do You Think About the Twenty-Seventh Amendment?" 10 Constitutional Commentary 9 (1993).

3. Steven Smith has asked a "fundamental, and ultimately ontological, question: What *is* a principle? Where, or in what form, can a principle be said to exist, or to be real?" Steven D. Smith, "Idolatry in Constitutional Interpretation," 79 Virginia L. Rev. 583, 621 (1993). If we talk, as I think we should, not in terms of constitutional "principles", but in terms of constitutional "directives" or "norms"—the directives constitution makers issue, the norms they establish—Smith's ontological inquiry seems puzzling. "What is a directive or norm?" In its central case, a directive or norm is simply a direction, an imperative, issued by one person (or persons) to another: for example, "Do not abridge the freedom of speech." With respect to such imperatives, the serious question is not "Where can a directive (or norm) be said to exist?" A serious question is: Did P in fact issue the directive she is claimed to have issued, or did she issue a different directive—or perhaps no directive? Another serious question: What does the directive require us to do in *this* context, in which the directive is, as directives sometimes are, underdeterminate?

4. The Preamble states, in its entirety, that "We the people of the United States, in Order to form a more perfect Union, establish Justice, insure domestic Tranquility, provide for the common defence, promote the general Welfare, and secure the Blessings of Liberty to ourselves and our Posterity, do ordain and establish this Constitution for the United States of America."

5. As I explained in the introduction to this book, I write "We the people" rather than "We the People" because in the original text of the Constitution, which I am quoting, the first letter of "people" is lowercase.

6. See § I.C. Moreover, American constitutional history reveals that it is not only "We the people" who do in fact establish norms as constitutional. See id.

7. Steven D. Smith, "Law Without Mind," 88 Michigan L. Rev. 104, 119 (1989).

8. Richard Kay has emphasized, over the course of several essays, much the same point I am making here:

> There may be plausible theories of government and judicial review which demote the authority of both intention and text, but it is hard to see what the political rationale would be for a theory that elevates a text for reasons unrelated to the people and circumstances which created it.

Richard S. Kay, "Adherence to the Original Intentions in Constitutional Adjudication: Three Objections and Responses," 82 Northwestern U. L. Rev. 226, 234 (1988).

> [T]o the extent we would bind ourselves, in whole or in part, to rules inferred from mere marks and letters on paper without reference to the will of the human beings who selected those marks and letters, we enter a regime very foreign to our ordinary assumptions about the nature of law.

Richard S. Kay, "Original Intentions, Standard Meanings, and the Legal Character of the Constitution," 6 Constitutional Commentary 39, 50 (1989).

> The influence of the Constitution is the consequence of continuing regard not for a particular assortment of words, but for the authority and sense of a certain constituent act. . . . [To deem authoritative the words of a constitutional provision] independently of the intentional act which created them is to disregard exactly that which makes the text demand our attention in the first place. That the words will bear some different meaning is purely happenstance. Without their political history, the words of the Constitution have no more claim on us than those of any other text.

Richard S. Kay, "The Bork Nomination and the Definition of 'The Constitution'," 84 Northwestern U. L. Rev. 1190, 1193 (1990).

Paul Campos' work is also quite relevant to the point I am making here. See Paul Campos, "Against Constitutional Theory," 4 Yale J. L. & Humanities 279 (1992); Paul Campos, "That Obscure Object of Desire: Hermeneutics and the Autonomous Legal Text," 77 Minnesota L. Rev. 1065 (1993); Paul Campos, "Three Mistakes About Interpretation," 92 Michigan L. Rev. 388 (1994).

9. The "people" who ordained and established the Constitution and Bill of Rights at the end of the nineteenth century and the "people" who amended the Constitution after the Civil War consisted mainly of white males. The question why we the people now living should accept constitutional directives issued by persons

long dead as our "supreme Law of the Land" has a special urgency, therefore, for those of us who are not white males. See James MacGregor Burns, The Vineyard of Liberty 392 (1982): "Every new state admitted after 1819 restricted voting to whites. Only five New England states—Massachusetts, Rhode Island, Maine, New Hampshire, and Vermont—provided for equal voting rights for black and white males." Cf. id. at 364: "Some suffrage restrictions fell during the Jeffersonian era . . . and during the War with England. . . . Property requirements were replaced by taxpaying requirements, which in turn gradually faded away. . . . 'Well before Jackson's election most states had lifted most restrictions on the suffrage of white male citizens or taxpayers.'"

10. See, e.g., "Constitutional Stupidities Symposium," 12 Constitutional Commentary 139–225 (1995) (twenty essays on "the stupidest provision of the United States Constitution").

11. I quote Article V later in this subsection.

12. Russell Hardin, "Why a Constitution?" in The Federalist Papers and the New Institutionalism 100, 102, 113 (Bernard Grofman & Donald Wittman eds., 1989).

13. Whether the processes of constitutional amendment provided for by Article V are the only constitutionally legitimate way to amend our Constitution—whether they are the only constitutionally ordained processes of constitutional amendment—is a matter of controversy. On this, and on many other interesting questions about constitutional amendment, see the rich collection of essays in Sanford Levinson, ed., Responding to Imperfection: The Theory and Practice of Constitutional Amendment (1995). See also Lawrence Lessig, "What Drives Derivability: Responses to *Responding to Imperfection*," 74 Texas L. Rev. 839 (1996) (reviewing the Levinson collection); Frank I. Michelman, "Thirteen Easy Pieces," 93 Michigan L. Rev. 1297 (1995) (reviewing the Levinson collection); Henry Paul Monaghan, "We the People[s], Original Understanding, and Constitutional Amendment," 96 Columbia L. Rev. 121 (1996).

It is implausible to suggest that constitutionally ordained processes of constitutional amendment are the only *morally* legitimate way to alter our Constitution. On this issue, too, see the Levinson collection. See also Richard S. Kay, "Comparative Constitutional Fundamentals," 6 Connecticut J. International L. 445 (1991). Cf. Richard S. Kay, Book Review, 7 Constitutional Commentary 434, 440–41 (1990): "No matter how far they transgress existing rules, successful constitutional conventions, like those of 1787–89, are unlikely to be perceived as outlaws. If they prosper, they will be founders."

In the conclusion to *The Constitution in the Courts*, I suggested a modification in the practice of judicial review under which the Congress and the President, acting together in their legislative capacity, would play a larger role, not in amending our Constitution, but in shaping indeterminate constitutional norms. See Michael J. Perry, The Constitution in the Courts: Law or Politics? 197–201 (1994). Perhaps they—and, especially, "We the people"—should play a larger role, too, in amending the Constitution, as Bruce Ackerman has suggested. See Bruce Ackerman, We the People: Foundations 54–55 (1991); Bruce Ackerman, We the People: Transformations, ch. 13 (1998). Or, perhaps they shouldn't: "Article V is part of a Constitution that reflects a considered attempt to slow down change, and it has been so understood from the very beginning of our constitutional history. In our time, this policy may be a wise one." Monaghan, supra this n., at 177.

14. Not that there might not be costs to our doing so. A second practical reason

for bowing to constitutional directives that we believe should not be a part of our Constitution, unless/until they are disestablished in a constitutionally ordained way, is that if and to the extent we were not to do so, if and to the extent we were to disestablish constitutional directives in an other than constitutionally ordained way—or if and to the extent we were to condone violations of constitutional directives—we would risk diminishing our own power. Someday we might want to issue a constitutional directive. By maintaining a culture of fidelity to constitutional directives that have not been disestablished in a constitutionally ordained way, including directives issued by persons long dead, we make it more likely that a constitutional directive issued by *us* will be obeyed (unless/until it is disestablished in a constitutionally ordained way) even when *we* are long dead.

15. See Ackerman, We the People: Transformations, n. 13, chs. 4–8.

16. Indeed, a constitution can forbid that one or more of its parts be amended at all. It has been suggested that the Constitution of Germany, because it "declares that certain fundamental principles are immune to constitutional amendment," exemplifies "absolute entrenchment". Anupam Chander, "Sovereignty, Referenda, and the Entrenchment of a United Kingdom Bill of Rights," 101 Yale L. J. 457, 462 & n. 30 (1991). See Bruce Ackerman, The Future of Liberal Revolution 110–11 (1992) (commenting on the German practice of absolute entrenchment). The Constitution of Japan arguably immunizes some of its parts against amendment in providing, in Article 11, that "[t]he people shall not be prevented from enjoying any of the fundamental human rights. These fundamental human rights guaranteed to the people by this Constitution shall be conferred upon the people of this and future generations as eternal and inviolate rights." Similarly, Article 98 provides: "The fundamental human rights by this Constitution guaranteed to the people of Japan are fruits of the age-old struggle of man to be free; they have survived the many exacting tests for durability and are conferred upon this and future generations in trust, to be held for all time inviolate."

17. The "may" is the may of legality, not of politics or of morality. See n. 13. Cf. Chander, n. 16, at 462: "An absolutely entrenched [constitutional norm] is . . . (as are all other parts of an existing legal regime) vulnerable to revolution."

We might be tempted to think that the constitutional strategy for establishing a directive differs from the statutory strategy in another basic respect, in that constitutions, unlike statutes, typically declare themselves to be "the supreme law"—and that therefore to opt for the constitutional strategy is to decree that the directive is lexically prior to statutory and other nonconstitutional law, including subsequently enacted law. (Article VI of the Constitution states that "[t]his Constitution . . . shall be the supreme Law of the Land . . ." Article 98 of the Japanese Constitution states: "This Constitution shall be the supreme law of the nation and no law, ordinance, imperial prescript or other act of government, or part thereof, contrary to the provisions hereof, shall have legal force or validity.") But a legislature may decree in a statute establishing a directive that the directive is lexically prior to subsequently enacted statutory law in this sense and to this extent: "A court is not to give effect to any future statute enacted by this legislature to the extent the statute, in the court's judgment, violates the directive established by this statute, *unless such future statute explicitly states that a court is to give it effect even if in the court's judgment the statute violates the directive established by this statute.*" See Chander, n. 16, at 463: "One common type of manner and form entrenchment requires that all contrary legislation contain an explicit declaration of its intent to override the entrenched rule." Canada has pursued, in its Charter of Rights and Freedoms, such a strategy. See Perry, The Constitution in the Courts, n. 13, at 197–98. Even if a legislature may, in one session, enact such a decree, however, the legislature presumably may, in a later session, repeal the decree. See Julian N. Eule, "Temporal Limits on the Legislative Mandate: Entrenchment and Retroactivity," 1987 American Bar Foundation Research J. 379. What is most distinctive about the constitutional strategy, then, is less the supremacy of constitutional law than the extreme difficulty of amending a constitution.

18. For an "outline of some of the reasons for entrenching institutional arrangements and substantive rights", see Cass R. Sunstein, "Constitutionalism and Secession," 58 U. Chicago L. Rev. 633, 636–43 (1991).

19. See Thomas B. McAffee, "*Brown* and the Doctrine of Precedent: A Concurring Opinion," 20 Southern Illinois U. L. Rev. 99, 100 (1995):

> [O]ur constitutional order is based on a moral vision that humans have rights which they do not forfeit when joining civil society. At the same time, we recognize that the people are the supreme judiciary as to the content of those rights when they engage in the sovereign act of creating or amending the Constitution, a document which will in various ways define and limit those rights. There is no way out of this tension—our natural law aspirations must inevitably play themselves out through some system of human decision-making, and historically we have believed that the popular sovereignty manifest in the constitution-making process is likely to yield superior results to rule by judges or a system in which each individual becomes the judge of his own obligations to enacted law.

20. It would be especially difficult to justify the Court's imposing on government, in the name of the Constitution, a norm that no one, past or present, could fairly read any language in the Constitution to represent. As Justice William Brennan explained in his Hart Lecture at Oxford:

> But if America's experience demonstrates that paper protections are not a sufficient guarantor of liberty, it also suggests that they are a necessary one, particularly in times of crisis. Without a textual anchor for their decisions, judges would have to rely on some theory of natural right, or some allegedly shared standard of the ends and limits of government, to strike down invasive legislation. But an appeal to normative ideals that lack any mooring in the written law . . . would in societies like ours be suspect, because it would represent so profound an aberration from majoritarian principles. . . . A text . . . helps tether [judges'] discretion. I would be the last to cabin judges' power to keep the law vital, to ensure that it remains abreast of the progress in man's intellect and sensibilities. Unbounded freedom is, however, another matter. One can imagine a system of governance that accorded judges almost unlimited discretion, but it would be one reminiscent of the rule by Platonic Guardians that Judge Learned Hand so feared. It is not one, I think, that would gain allegiance in either of our countries.

William J. Brennan, Jr., "Why Have a Bill of Rights?" 9 Oxford J. Legal Studies 425, 432 (1989). Recalling that Chief Justice John Marshall's justification for the practice of judicial review, in *Marbury v. Madison*, appealed to the writtenness of the Constitution (see Marbury v. Madison, 5 U.S. (1 Cranch) 137, 177 (1803)), Michael Moore has commented that "[j]udicial review is easier to justify if it is exercised with reference only to the written document. . . . By now, the object of [constitutional] interpretation should be clear: it is the written document. Hugo Black was right, at least, about this. Black's Constitution—the one he was so fond of pulling out of his pocket—is our only Constitution." Michael S. Moore, "Do We Have an Unwritten Constitution?" 63 Southern California L. Rev. 107, 122, 123 (1989). See id. at 121–23. See also n. 54 & accompanying text.

21. I discuss the "specification" of indeterminate constitutional norms in § II.B.

22. See, e.g., Robert Bork, The Tempting of America: The Political Seduction of the Law 155–59 (1989); Antonin Scalia, A Matter of Interpretation: Federal Courts and the Law 139–40 (1997). But see Gary S. Lawson, "The Constitutional Case against Precedent," 15 Harvard J. L. & Public Policy 23 (1994). For a critical comment on Gary Lawson's position, see McAffee, n. 19, at 101–3.

23. Or, at least, by those of us—policymakers, religious leaders, editorial writers, politically engaged citizens, etc.—who concern ourselves with such things.

24. Cf. Frederick Schauer, "Amending the Presuppositions of a Constitution," in Levinson, n. 13, at 145, 156–57 (presenting a hypothetical in which "[t]he small *c* constitution would . . . have been amended by virtue of [an] amendment to the ultimate rule of recognition, even though it could also be accurately said that the large *C* Constitution had not been validly amended according to its own terms").

25. See ch. 1, n. 11 & accompanying text.

26. Bork, n. 22, at 158. According to Tom McAffee, the Supreme Court "ought to be especially reluctant to overrule precedent that is: (1) proven and long-established; (2) the product of the carefully considered judgment of all three branches of the government; and (3) based upon the fundamental values of the sovereign people. Under such circumstances, the least that can be said is that the case for the impropriety of the original constitutional judgment should be overwhelming before [the] Court should even decide whether to overrule such a precedent." McAffee, n. 19, at 104. See also Peter B. McCutcheon, "Mistakes, Precedent, and the Rise of the Administrative State: Toward a Constitutional Theory of the Second Best," 80 Cornell L. Rev. 1 (1994).

27. Cf. Lawson, n. 22, at 33 n. 27 (wondering whether "the irrevocable enshrinement of errors through precedent should compel the self-conscious creation of errors in subsequent cases").

28. See n. 140.

29. See ch. 3, n. 110 & accompanying text.

30. Cf. Charles L. Black, Jr., " 'One Nation Indivisible': Unnamed Human Rights in the States," 65 St. John's L. Rev. 17, 55 (1991): "[W]ithout such a corpus of national human rights law good against the States, we ought to stop saying, 'One nation indivisible, with liberty and justice for all,' and speak instead of, 'One nation divisible and divided into fifty zones of political morality, with liberty and justice in such kind and measure as these good things may from time to time be granted by each of these fifty political subdivisions.' "

31. The First Amendment states: "Congress shall make no law respecting an establishment of religion, or prohibiting the free exercise thereof; or abridging the freedom of speech, or of the press; or the right of the people peaceably to assemble, and to petition the government for a redress of grievances." That section one of the Fourteenth Amendment was meant to protect against state government the privileges and immunities of citizens already protected against the national government by the Bill of Rights, if true, would not entail that the First Amendment

was meant to protect any privileges or immunities of citizens against the national government. Jay Bybee has recently argued that the First Amendment, unlike the Second through Eighth Amendments, was not meant to protect any privileges or immunities of citizens, but only to make explicit a congressional disability, a lack of legislative power on the part of Congress ("Congress shall make no law . . ."). See Jay S. Bybee, "Taking Liberties with the First Amendment: Congress, Section 5, and the Religious Freedom Restoration Act," 48 Vanderbilt L. Rev. 1539 (1995). See also Steven D. Smith, Foreordained Failure: The Quest for a Constitutional Principle of Religious Freedom, chs. 2–3 (1995).

32. See, e.g., ch. 3, n. 7.

33. See, e.g., Bolling v. Sharpe, 437 U.S. 497 (1954); Adarand Constructors, Inc. v. Pena, 515 U.S. 200 (1995).

34. See ch. 4, section I. By itself, the Fifth Amendment, which became a part of the Constitution in 1791, applies only to the national government. The Fourteenth Amendment, which became a part of the Constitution in 1868, applies only to state government.

35. See id.

36. Cf. McCutcheon, n. 26 (noting that the "unconstitutional" administrative state is now beyond judicial overruling).

37. For efforts to articulate criteria that should inform a theory of precedent, see—in addition to McAffee, whom I quote in n. 26—Michael J. Gerhardt, "The Role of Precedent in Constitutional Decisionmaking and Theory," 60 George Washington L. Rev. 68 (1991); Henry P. Monaghan, "Stare Decisis and Constitutional Adjudication," 88 Columbia L. Rev. 144 (1988).

38. Cf. Planned Parenthood of Southeastern Pennsylvania v. Casey, 505 U.S. 833, 854–69 (1992) (op'n of O'Connor, Kennedy, & Souter, JJ.).

39. I am skeptical about how accurately we can generalize either about how such "nonconstitutional" premises emerge in our constitutional law or about how, when they do emerge, some of them eventually survive to become constitutional bedrock. I suspect that we can only particularize. But cf. Ackerman, We the People: Foundations, n. 13; Ackerman, We the People: Transformations, n. 13.

40. The First Amendment states, in relevant part, that "Congress shall make no law respecting an establishment of religion, or prohibiting the free exercise thereof . . ." According to the constitutional law of the United States, however, neither any branch of the national government nor state government may establish religion or prohibit the free exercise thereof. For a discussion, see Michael J. Perry, Religion in Politics 10–12 (1997).

41. See, e.g., Lundman v. McKown, 530 N.W.2d 807 (Minnesota 1995). See also Caroline Frasier, "Suffering Children and the Christian Science Church," Atlantic Monthly, April 1995, at 105.

42. Discussing "a distinction that is implicit in the idea of 'persecution'" and that the Court in *Church of the Lukumi Babalu Aye, Inc. v. City of Hialeah* (508 U.S. 520 (1993)) "repeatedly tried to articulate", Steve Smith has explained: "The distinction is between measures that 'target' a religion *on religious grounds* and because it is objectionable *as* a religion and, on the other hand, measures that 'target' a religion only by prohibiting a practice of the religion that is objectionable *on independent or nonreligious grounds*." Steven D. Smith, "Free Exercise Doctrine and the Discourse of Disrespect," 65 U. Colorado L. Rev. 519, 563 (1994). See id. at 563–68.

43. For an extended presentation and defense of the latter position, see

Michael W. McConnell, "The Origins and Historical Understanding of Free Exercise of Religion," 103 Harvard L. Rev. 1309 (1993); Michael W. McConnell, "Free Exercise Revisionism and the *Smith* Decision," 57 U. Chicago L. Rev. 1109 (1990). See also Kurt T. Lash, "The Second Adoption of the Free Exercise Clause: Religious Exemptions Under the Fourteenth Amendment," 88 Northwestern U. L. Rev. 1106 (1994). McConnell's historical argument has been criticized. See Gerard V. Bradley, "Beguiled: Free Exercise Exemptions and the Siren Song of Liberalism," 20 Hofstra L. Rev. 245 (1991); Philip A. Hamburger, "A Constitutional Right of Religious Exemption: An Historical Perspective," 60 George Washington L. Rev. 915 (1992). See also William P. Marshall, "The Case Against the Constitutionally Compelled Free Exercise Exemption," 40 Case Western Reserve L. Rev. 357, 375–79 (1989–90).

44. In *Employment Division, Oregon Department of Human Resources v. Smith*, Justice Scalia wrote, for himself and four other members of the Court, that "if prohibiting the exercise of religion . . . is . . . merely the incidental effect of a generally applicable and otherwise valid provision," the free exercise norm, without regard to whether the refusal to exempt the religious practice in question serves an important public interest, has not been violated. Employment Division, Department of Human Resources of Oregon v. Smith, 494 U.S. 872, 878 (1990). Three members of the Court joined a statement by Justice O'Connor that the accommodation position should not have been rejected by the majority. See 494 U.S. at 892–903. The majority's position provoked so many interested persons off the Court that an unprecedented alliance of groups, from the American Civil Liberties Union on the one side to the "religious right" on the other, joined forces to lobby Congress to undo the decision. The alliance was successful. Congress enacted, in 1993, the Religious Freedom Restoration Act (RFRA), Public Law 103–141, 42 U.S. Code 2000bb. Section three of the Act states: "Government shall not substantially burden a person's exercise of religion even if the burden results from a rule of general applicability, [unless] . . . it demonstrates that application of the burden to the person (1) is in furtherance of a compelling governmental interest; and (2) is the least restrictive means of furthering that compelling governmental interest." (After the Court's decision in *Smith*, which involved Oregon's failure to exempt the religious use of peyote from its ban on the ingestion of hallucinogenic substances, Oregon passed a law making it lawful to use peyote in connection "with the good faith practice of a religious belief" or association "with a religious practice." Oregon Revised Statutes § 475.992(5)(a)&(b) (1991).)

On RFRA, see Thomas C. Berg, "What Hath Congress Wrought? An Interpretive Guide to the Religious Freedom Restoration Act," 39 Villanova L. Rev. 1 (1994); Scott C. Idleman, "The Religious Freedom Restoration Act: Pushing the Limits of Legislative Power," 73 Texas L. Rev. 247 (1994); Douglas Laycock & Oliver S. Thomas, "Interpreting the Religious Freedom Restoration Act," 73 Texas L. Rev. 209 (1994); "Symposium: The Religious Freedom Restoration Act," 56 Montana L. Rev. 1–294 (1995).

In June 1997, the Supreme Court ruled that in enacting RFRA, Congress exceeded the scope of its power under section five of the Fourteenth Amendment. See City of Boerne v. Flores, 117 S. Ct. 2157 (1997). Three lower federal courts had ruled to the contrary. See Flores v. City of Boerne, Texas, 73 F.3d 1352 (5th Cir. 1996); Sasnett v. Sullivan, 65 USLW 2115 (7th Cir. 1996); Belgard v. Hawaii, 883 F. Supp. 510 (D Hawaii 1995). At the time of the Court's ruling, scholarly opinion was divided. Those who argued that RFRA is unconstitutional include:

Bybee, n. 31, at 1624–32; Daniel O. Conkle, "The Religious Freedom Restoration Act: The Constitutional Significance of an Unconstitutional Statute," 56 Montana L. Rev. 39 (1995); Christopher L. Eisgruber & Lawrence G. Sager, "Why the Religious Freedom Restoration Act Is Unconstitutional," 69 New York U. L. Rev. 437 (1995); Eugene Gressman & Angela C. Carmella, "The RFRA Revision of the Free Exercise Clause," 57 Ohio State L. J. 65 (1996); Marci A. Hamilton, "The Religious Freedom Restoration Act: Letting the Fox into the Henhouse Under Cover of Section Five of the Fourteenth Amendment," 16 Cardozo L. Rev. 357 (1994); William W. Van Alstyne, "The Failure of the Religious Freedom Restoration Act Under Section 5 of the Fourteenth Amendment," 46 Duke L. J. 291 (1996). For arguments that RFRA is constitutional, see Douglas Laycock, "RFRA, Congress, and the Ratchet," 56 Montana L. Rev. 145, 152–70 (1995); Bonnie I. Robin-Vergeer, "Disposing of the Red Herrings: A Defense of the Religious Freedom Restoration Act," 69 Southern California L. Rev. 589 (1996). For an argument that RFRA is constitutional and, in particular, that the Supreme Court's decision in *Boerne* was wrong, see Michael W. McConnell, "Institutions and Interpretations: A Critique of *City of Boerne v. Flores,*" 111 Harvard L. Rev. 153 (1997). See also David Cole, "The Value of Seeing Things Differently: Boerne v. Flores and Congressional Enforcement of the Bill of Rights," 1997 Sup. Ct. Rev. 31 (1998). For a collection of essays on the Court's decision, see "Symposium: Reflections on *City of Boerne v. Flores,*" 39 William & Mary L. Rev. 601–960 (1998).

45. The second sentence of section one of the Fourteenth Amendment provides, in its entirety, that "[n]o State shall make or enforce any law which shall abridge the privileges or immunities of citizens of the United States; nor shall any State deprive any person of life, liberty, or property, without due process of law; nor deny to any person within its jurisdiction the equal protection of the laws."

46. This was the position of the majority in the *Slaughter-House Cases*. See Slaughter-House Cases, 83 U.S. (16 Wall.) 36 (1873). But see Richard L. Aynes, "Constricting the Law of Freedom: Justice Miller, the Fourteenth Amendment, and the *Slaughter-House Cases,*" 70 Chicago-Kent L. Rev. 627, 627 & n. 4 (1994) (noting that "everyone agrees" that the majority's position in the *Slaughter-House Cases* was wrong).

47. I address all these questions in chapter 3.

48. I address these questions, too, in chapter 3.

49. John Hart Ely, Democracy and Distrust: A Theory of Judicial Review 25 (1980). I address the who-is-protected question in chapter 3.

50. Id. at 16.

51. For a discussion of the confusion, see Perry, The Constitution in the Courts, n. 13, at 42–46.

52. For a helpful discussion of how—on the basis of what sources—to pursue such an inquiry, see Steven G. Calabresi & Saikrishna B. Prakash, "The President's Power to Execute the Laws," 104 Yale L. J. 541, 550–59 (1994).

53. Consider, for example, the vigorous debate about what norm the free exercise language of the First Amendment was understood to communicate. See, on one side of the debate, McConnell, "The Origins and Historical Understanding of Free Exercise of Religion," n. 43; McConnell, "Free Exercise Revisionism and the *Smith* Decision," n. 43. McConnell acknowledges, however, that the historical record does not speak unequivocally. See McConnell, "The Origins and Historical Understanding of Free Exercise of Religion," n. 43, at 1511–13; McConnell, "Free Exercise Revisionism and the *Smith* Decision," n. 43, at 1117. Indeed, one could

plausibly conclude, as some scholars have, that McConnell's position is wrong. See note 43.

54. Andrezj Rapaczynski, "The Ninth Amendment and the Unwritten Constitution: The Problems of Constitutional Interpretation," 64 Chicago-Kent L. Rev. 177, 192 (1988). See n. 20.

55. See n. 34.

56. By "adjudicative" facts, I mean the facts of the case (e.g., who did what, and where and when she did it), as distinct from "legislative" facts, facts that transcend the case (e.g., what will likely happen to our society if we let this kind of speech go unregulated).

57. See Lawrence B. Solum, "On the Indeterminacy Crisis: Critiquing Critical Dogma," 54 U. Chicago L. Rev. 462 (1987).

58. Neil MacCormick, "Reconstruction After Deconstruction: A Response to CLS," 10 Oxford J. Legal Studies 539, 548 (1990). Where I have used the term "specification", MacCormick uses the Latin term *determinatio*, borrowing it from John Finnis. "John Finnis has to good effect re-deployed St Thomas' concept of *determinatio*; Hans Kelsen's translators used the term 'concretization' to much the same effect." Id. (Citing J.M. Finnis, "On the Critical Legal Studies Movement," 30 American J. Jurisprudence 21, 23–25 (1985), and Hans Kelsen, The Pure Theory of Law 230 (1967).)

59. Put another way, it is the challenge of deciding how best to avoid the political-moral *disvalue* at the heart of the norm.

60. Anthony T. Kronman, "Living in the Law," 54 U. Chicago L. Rev. 835, 847–48 (1987).

In *The Federalist* No. 37, James Madison commented on the need, in adjudication, for specification: "All new laws, though penned with the greatest technical skill and passed on the fullest and most mature deliberation, are considered as more or less obscure and equivocal, until their meaning be liquidated and ascertained by a series of particular discussions and adjudications." The Federalist Papers 229 (Clinton Rossiter ed., 1961). Cf. Kim Lane Scheppele, Legal Secrets 94–95 (1988): "Generally in the literature on interpretation the question being posed is, What does a particular text (or social practice) *mean*? Posed this way, the interpretive question gives rise to an embarrassing multitude of possible answers, a cacophony of theories of interpretation. . . . [The] question that (in practice) is the one actually asked in the course of lawyering and judging [is]: what . . . does a particular text mean *for the specific case at hand*?"

In *Truth and Method*, Hans-Georg Gadamer commented on the process of specification both in law and in theology:

> In both legal and theological hermeneutics there is the essential tension between the text set down—of the law or of the proclamation—on the one hand and, on the other, the sense arrived at by its application in the particular moment of interpretation, either in judgment or in preaching. A law is not there to be understood historically, but to be made concretely valid through being interpreted. Similarly, a religious proclamation is not there to be understood as a merely historical document, but to be taken in a way in which it exercises its saving effect. This includes the fact that the text, whether law or gospel, if it is to be understood properly, i.e., according to the claim it makes, must be understood at every moment, in every particular situation, in a new and different way. Understanding here is always application.

Hans-Georg Gadamer, Truth and Method 275 (1975).

61. Richard A. Posner, "What Am I? A Potted Plant?" New Republic, Sept. 28, 1987, at 23, 24. Cf. Benjamin N. Cardozo, The Nature of the Judicial Process 67 (1921): "[W]hen [judges] are called upon to say how far existing rules are to be extended or restricted, they must let the welfare of society fix the path, its direction and its distance."

62. H.L.A. Hart, The Concept of Law 128 (2d ed. 1994).

63. Id.

64. They can. One way to do so, writes Hart, "is to freeze the meaning of the rule so that its general terms must have the same meaning in every case where its application is in question. To secure this we may fasten on certain features present in the plain case and insist that these are both necessary and sufficient to bring anything which has them within the scope of the rule, whatever other features it may have or lack, and whatever may be the social consequences of applying the rule in this way." Id. at 129.

65. This is not to say that determinacy ought never to be a goal: "To escape this oscillation between extremes we need to remind ourselves that human inability to anticipate the future, which is at the root of this indeterminacy, varies in degree in different fields of conduct . . ." Id. at 130–31. See id. at 130 et seq.

66. Id. at 129–30.

67. Cardozo, n. 61, at 83–84.

68. See Richard Kay, "American Constitutionalism," in Constitutionalism: Philosophical Foundations 16, 31–32 (Lawrence A. Alexander ed., 1998): "Since the principal feature of constitutionalism is its employment of fixed, a priori rules, constitutional interpretation cannot be a direction to decide individual controversies over the use of public power in whatever way is thought would be most congenial to the constitutional enactors. Such disputes are to be resolved, rather, by reference to the constitutional *rules*. Recourse to the original intentions is proper in determining the content of those rules. Once the intended scope of the rules is decided, however, the relevance of the original intentions is exhausted."

69. Larry Alexander, "All or Nothing at All? The Intentions of Authorities and the Authority of Intentions," in Law and Interpretation: Essays in Legal Philosophy 357, 370 (Andrei Marmor ed., 1995). But see n. 68.

70. Much of the discussion in Alexander's essay, id., seems to me to proceed on the basis of this implausible construal.

71. Patrick J. Kelley, "An Alternative Originalist Opinion for *Brown v. Board of Education*," 20 Southern Illinois U. L. Rev. 75, 76 (1995).

72. Id. Kelley continues:

Thus, although the intended general meaning is fixed by legislative action and does not thereafter change, the set of factual applications of that fixed general meaning may expand or contract with the application of the fixed general meaning to changed circumstances. New situations, unheard of at the time the statute was enacted, may fall squarely within the fixed intended meaning. Later changes in the institutions existing at the time the statute was enacted may alter the later application of the fixed statutory meaning to those institutions. So the fact that no one at the time it was adopted thought that the Fourteenth Amendment affected segregated public schools is not controlling in the two-step process of first, determining the intended general meaning of constitutional language; and second, applying that fixed general meaning to particular current factual situations.

Id. (It is doubtful that "no one at the time it was adopted thought that the Fourteenth Amendment affected segregated public schooling." See Michael W. McConnell, "Originalism and the Desegregation Decisions," 81 Virginia L. Rev. 947 (2995); Michael W. McConnell, "The Originalist Justification for *Brown*: A Reply to Professor Klarman," 81 Virginia L. Rev. 1937 (1995).)

73. Hart, n. 62, at 128–29. Cf. Paul Brest, "The Misconceived Quest for the Original Understanding," 60 Boston U. L. Rev. 204, 216–217 (1980) (paragraphs rearranged):

> The extent to which a clause may be properly interpreted to reach outcomes different from those actually contemplated by the adopters depends on the relationship between a general principle and its exemplary applications. A principle does not exist wholly independently of its author's subjective, or his society's conventional exemplary applications, and is always limited to some extent by the applications they found conceivable. Within these fairly broad limits, however, the adopters may have intended their examples to constrain more or less. To the intentionalist interpreter falls the unenviable task of ascertaining, for each provision, how much more or less.
>
> What of a case where the adopters viewed a certain punishment as not cruel and unusual? This is not the same as saying that the adopters "intended not to prohibit the punishment." For even if they expected their laws to be interpreted by intentionalist canons, the adopters may have intended that their own views not always govern. Like parents who attempt to instill values in their child by both articulating and applying a moral principle, they may have accepted, or even invited, the eventuality that the principle would be applied in ways that diverge from their own views. The adopters may have understood that, even as to instances to which they believe the clause ought or ought not to apply, further thought by themselves or others committed to its underlying principle might lead them to change their minds. Not believing in their own omniscience or infallibility, they delegated the decision to those charged with interpreting the provision. If such a motivation is plausible with respect to applications of the clause in the adopters' contemporary society, it is even more likely with respect to its application by future interpreters, whose understanding of the clause will be affected by changing knowledge, technology, and forms of society.

74. See n. 67. Cf. Richard A. Posner, The Problems of Jurisprudence 131 (1990): "In many cases the conventional materials will lean so strongly in one direction that it would be unreasonable for the judge to go in any other. But in some they will merely narrow the range of permissible decision, leaving an open area within which the judge must perforce attempt to decide the case in accordance with sound policy—in those grand symbolic cases that well up out of the generalities and ambiguities of the Constitution . . .—while paying due heed to the imprudence of trying to foist an idiosyncratic policy conception or social vision on a recalcitrant citizenry."

75. The First Amendment states, in relevant part: "Congress shall make no law respecting an establishment of religion, or prohibiting the free exercise thereof . . ." This and the other commands of the First Amendment are now taken to apply not only to the legislative branch of the national government, but also to the executive

and judicial branches. Moreover, the commands are understood to apply not only to the national government, but also to state government. See Perry, Religion in Politics, n. 40, at 10–12.

76. See n. 44.

77. In its entirety, § 2 of Article 10 states:

> The exercise of these freedoms, since it carries with it duties and responsibilities, may be subject to such formalities, conditions, restrictions or penalties as are prescribed by law and are necessary in a democratic society, in the interests of national security, territorial integrity or public safety, for the prevention of disorder or crime, for the protection of health or morals, for the protection of the reputation or rights of others, for preventing the disclosure of information received in confidence, or for maintaining the authority and impartiality of the judiciary.

For the European Convention, see Ian Brownlie ed., Basic Documents on Human Rights 326 (1992).

78. See James Bradley Thayer, "The Origin and Scope of the American Doctrine of Constitutional Law," 7 Harvard L. Rev. 129 (1893). See generally "One Hundred Years of Judicial Review: The Thayer Centennial Symposium," 88 Northwestern U. L. Rev. 1–468 (1993).

79. Handyside Case, European Court of Human Rights, 1976, Ser. A, No. 24, 1 EHRR 737. (The European Convention on the Protection of Human Rights and Fundamental Freedoms contains several provisions with provisos substantially identical to Article 10 § 2. See Article 8 (protecting one's "right to respect for his private and family life, his home and his correspondence"), Article 9 (protecting "the right to freedom of thought, conscience, and religion"), and Article 11 (protecting "the right to peaceful assembly and to freedom of association with others").)

Similar examples can be drawn from the international law of human rights. (A national political community can agree to remove certain choices or options from the agenda of its politics by ratifying legal norms established in conventional international law.) For example, Article 18 of the International Covenant on Civil and Political Rights (ICCPR) provides in relevant part: "Everyone shall have the right to freedom of thought, conscience, and religion. This right shall include the freedom to have or adopt a religion or belief of his choice, and freedom, either individually or in community with others and in public or private, to manifest his religion or belief in worship, observance, practice or teaching." Article 18 further states: "Freedom to manifest one's religion or beliefs may be subject only to such limitations as are prescribed by law and are necessary to protect public safety, order, health, or morals of the fundamental rights and freedoms of others." There is sometimes ample room for reasonable disagreement about what, in a particular context, "the public morals" require—or about what, in a particular context, is "necessary to protect public safety, order, health, or morals". (For the ICCPR, see Brownlie, supra this n., at 125. The United States ratified the ICCPR, including Article 18, in 1992.)

On the "margin of appreciation" doctrine in the European Convention system, see Henry J. Steiner & Philip Alston, eds., International Human Rights in Context: Law, Politics, Morals 626–36 (1996).

80. Roe v. Wade, 410 U.S. 113 (1973); Doe v. Bolton, 410 U.S. 179 (1973).

81. This book continues my contribution to the enterprise. My other (and, in

some cases and to some extent, recanted) contributions include: The Constitution, the Courts, and Human Rights (1982); "The Authority of Text, Tradition, and Reason: A Theory of Constitutional 'Interpretation'," 58 Southern California L. Rev. 551 (1985); Morality, Politics, and Law, ch. 6 (1988); and The Constitution in the Courts: Law or Politics? (1994). For an insightful critical commentary on the course of my work in constitutional theory, see Richard B. Saphire, "Originalism and the Importance of Constitutional Aspirations," 24 Hastings Constitutional L. Q. 599 (1997).

82. Philip Bobbitt's presentation of six types of constitutional argument implicitly collapses the important difference between discerning what norm the text of a constitutional provision represents and deciding what shape to give an indeterminate constitutional norm in a particular context. See Philip Bobbitt, Constitutional Fate: Theory of the Constitution (1982); Philip Bobbitt, Constitutional Interpretation (1991). The very same thing is true of Richard Fallon's presentation of "the five types of argument that generally predominate in constitutional debate." See Richard H. Fallon, Jr., "A Constructive Coherence Theory of Constitutional Interpretation," 100 Harvard L. Rev. 1189 (1987). (The quoted language appears at p. 1194.) Although Richard Posner, too, ignores the distinction between discerning what norm a constitutional norm represents and deciding what shape to give an indeterminate constitutional norm in a particular context, Posner's writings in support of a "pragmatist" approach to constitutional adjudication are best understood, in my view, as supporting a pragmatist approach to the question of what shape to give, in a particular context, an indeterminate constitutional norm—or, at least, to the question of what shape to give an indeterminate constitutional doctrine (indeterminate in the context at hand) that is the yield of earlier judicial efforts to give shape to such a norm. See, e.g., Richard A. Posner, "Bork and Beethoven," 42 Stanford L. Rev. 1365 (1990); Richard A. Posner, "What Has Pragmatism to Offer Law?," 63 S. California L. Rev. 1653 (1990).

83. Gadamer, n. 60, at 275. For the complete passage in which Gadamer's statement appears, see n. 60.

84. For an argument that, contrary to what I claim, my position here *is* contrary to Gadamer's insight, see Frederick Mark Gedicks, "Conservatives, Liberals, Romantics: The Persistent Quest for Certainty in Constitutional Interpretation," 50 Vanderbilt L. Rev. 613 (1997). For a hermeneutical position substantially consistent with my own, see Michael Herz, "Rediscovering Francis Lieber: An Afterword and Introduction," 16 Cardozo L. Rev. 2107 (1995).

85. See Perry, The Constitution in the Courts, n. 13, at 34–35.

86. Brennan, n. 20, at 426.

87. "Judicial review" is the name for the judicial practice of inquiring if an act or failure to act violates the Constitution of the United States. On the origins of the term "judicial review", see Robert Lowry Clinton, *Marbury v. Madison* and Judicial Review 7 (1989): "'Judicial review,' as a term used to describe the constitutional power of a court to overturn statutes, regulations, and other governmental activities, apparently was an invention of law writers in the early twentieth century. Edward S. Corwin may have been the first to coin the phrase, in the title of an article in the 1910 *Michigan Law Review*." Clinton's reference is to Edward S. Corwin, "The Establishment of Judicial Review," 9 Michigan L. Rev. 102 (1910).

88. See Perry, The Constitution in the Courts, n. 13, at 24–27.

89. See Charles L. Black, Jr., Structure and Relationship in Constitutional Law 71 (1969): "[J]udicial review of Acts of Congress for federal constitutionality . . .

rests also on the visible, active, and long-continued acquiescence of Congress in the Court's performance of this function. The Court now confronts not a neutral Congress nor a Congress bent on using its own constitutional powers to evade the Court's mandates, as some state legislatures have tried (and as Congress very clearly could succeed in doing, in many cases, if it were so minded), but rather a Congress which has accepted, and which by the passage of jurisdictional and other legislation has facilitated, this work of the Court." See also Sylvia Snowiss, Judicial Review and the Law of the Constitution x (1990): "I do not offer this [historical] reinterpretation as a way of attacking or defending the [modern] institution of judicial review. I share the prevailing view that judicial authority over legislation has by now generated sufficient support to be unaffected by assessments of original intent."

90. Consider, to cite but one example, albeit a very important one, the European Court of Human Rights. For recent developments, see Anthony Lester, "Radical Reform of the Enforcement Procedures of the European Convention," 8 Interrights Bulletin 25 (1994); Jeremy McBride, "A New European Court of Human Rights," 8 Interrights Bulletin 47 (1994).

91. For the argument, which invokes Article III of the Constitution, see Justice Story's persuasive opinion for the Court in *Martin v. Hunter's Lessee*, 14 U.S. (1 Wheat.) 404 (1816). Cf. Alexander M. Bickel, The Least Dangerous Branch: The Supreme Court at the Bar of Politics 12–13 (2d ed. 1986).

Article VI of the Constitution states that it "shall be the supreme Law of the Land; and the Judges in every State shall be bound thereby, any thing in the Constitution of Laws of any State to the Contrary notwithstanding." But this provision leaves room for a state judiciary to oppose its own view of what the Constitution forbids—to the Supreme Court's view (even if the Court's view is endorsed by one or even by both of the other branches of the national government). The state judiciary's view will not stand, because, under Article III of the Constitution, the Supreme Court gets to reverse any state judiciary's interpretation of national law it believes to be incorrect.

92. See n. 95.

93. See, e.g., Cooper v. Aaron, 358 U.S. 1, 18 (1958) (unanimous op'n). For a persuasive critical comment on the relevant aspect of the Court's opinion in *Cooper v. Aaron*, see Robin-Vergeer, n. 44, at 643–50.

94. See Michael Stokes Paulsen, "The Most Dangerous Branch: Executive Power to Say What the Law Is," 83 Georgetown L. J. 217 (1994); Gary Lawson & Christopher D. Moore, "The Province and Duty of the President: The Executive Power of Constitutional Interpretation" (unpublished ms., 1995). See also Robin-Vergeer, n. 44. But cf. Van Alstyne, n. 44.

95. Similarly, the firm expectation, in American constitutional culture, is that the executive branch of the national government will stand behind a constitutional ruling of the Supreme Court—even one with which the officers of the executive branch, including the President, might disagree—that is being resisted by the state against whom the ruling has gone. In *Cooper v. Aaron*, n. 93, the justices of the Court understood this.

96. For an interesting elaboration of the point, see Larry Alexander & Frederick Schauer, "On Extrajudicial Constitutional Interpretation," 110 Harvard L. Rev. 1359 (1997).

97. Cf. Christopher L. Eisgruber, "The Most Competent Branches: A Response to Professor Paulsen," 83 Georgetown L. J. 347, 371 (1994): "Considera-

tions related to stability, individual rights, and judicial competence provide compelling justification for much (though not all) of the respect routinely accorded the judiciary. In particular, Paulsen's Euclidean logic supplies no ground for doubting two core tenets of the modern doctrine of judicial supremacy: the states may not flout the Supreme Court's interpretations of the Constitution, and the President is almost always (perhaps simply always) bound to comply with and enforce judicial mandates rendered in good faith."

98. Cf. Richard John Neuhaus, "The Anatomy of a Controversy," in The End of Democracy? The Judicial Usurpation of Politics 173, 257–58 (Mitchell S. Muncy ed., 1997) (supporting a large congressional authority under section five of the Fourteenth Amendment to interpret the Amendment).

99. Significantly, Congress wrote the Religious Freedom Restoration Act (RFRA) to apply to the national government no less than to state government. (As applied to the laws and acts of the national government, RFRA has been held constitutional. See Equal Employment Opportunity Commission v. Catholic University of America, 83 F.3d 455 (D.C. Cir. 1996); In re Young, 141 F.3d 854 (8th Cir. 1998).) Given this, and given Congress' clear responsibility under section five of the Fourteenth Amendment to enforce the provisions of the Amendment, the Court should have deferred to—it should have upheld the constitutionality of—RFRA, if Congress' interpretation of the free exercise language of the First Amendment was a reasonable one. For an argument along these lines, see McConnell, "Institutions and Interpretations," n. 44. See also Cole, n. 44. In any event, RFRA did not violate what the Court had determined to be the minimum boundaries of what the Constitution forbids. However, in ruling recently that RFRA is unconstitutional, the Court has said that the Constitution forbade Congress to enact RFRA, and, given the "firm expectation" stated at the beginning of the paragraph accompanying this note, that is very likely the end of the matter— at least for now.

100. See David M. Beatty, ed., Human Rights and Judicial Review: A Comparative Perspective (1994).

101. See n. 90.

102. Cf. Jon Elster, "Majority Rule and Individual Rights," in On Human Rights: The Oxford Amnesty Lectures 1993 175 (Stephen Shute & Susan Hurley eds., 1993).

103. See, e.g., Allan C. Hutchinson, Waiting for Coraf: A Critique of Law and Rights (1995); Robert F. Nagel, Judicial Power and American Character: Censoring Ourselves in an Anxious Age (1994). Cf. Mary Becker, "Conservative Free Speech and the Uneasy Case for Judicial Review," 64 U. Colorado L. Rev. 975 (1993).

104. On the so-called political question doctrine, see Louis Henkin, "Is There a 'Political Question' Doctrine?" 85 Yale L. J. 597 (1976); Martin H. Redish, "Judicial Review and the Political Question," 79 Northwestern U. L. Rev. 1031 (1985); Robert F. Nagel, "Political Law, Legalistic Politics: A Recent History of the Political Question Doctrine," 56 U. Chicago L. Rev. 643 (1989).

105. Abraham Lincoln, First Inaugural Address (Mar. 4, 1861), reprinted in Inaugural Addresses of the Presidents of the United States from George Washington 1789 to George Bush 1989, S. Doc. No. 10, 101st Cong., 1st Sess. 133, 139 (1989).

106. 19 How. 393 (1857). See Don E. Fehrenbacher, The Dred Scott Case: Its Significance in American Law and Politics (1978).

107. Cf. Alexander & Schauer, n. 96, at 1383: "Given the inadvisability of designing a decision procedure around one case that might never be repeated, it is
better to treat *Dred Scott* as aberrational, recognizing that officials can always override judicial interpretations if necessary, especially if they are willing to suffer the
political consequences."

108. For a defense of substantially this position, see id.

109. For further discussion, see Perry, The Constitution in the Courts, n. 13,
ch. 4.

110. Given that Congress wrote the Religious Freedom Restoration Act to limit
the power not only of state government, but of the national government as well,
including Congress' own power, the case that the Court should have deferred to
RFRA is stronger than it would have been. (The case for the Court deferring to
RFRA was very strong indeed, in my view, given two additional factors: first, Congress has a clear responsibility under section five of the Fourteenth Amendment to
enforce the provisions of the Amendment; second, Congress' interpretation of the
free exercise language of the First Amendment was not unreasonable. For arguments along these lines, see McConnell, "Institutions and Interpretations," n. 44;
Cole, n. 44.) If Congress had written RFRA to apply only to state government, the
case for the Court deferring would have been weaker. Cf. Laycock, "RFRA, Congress, and the Ratchet," n. 44, at 164 (explaining that the approach Laycock defends "is effectively limited to rules that Congress is willing to impose on itself, because if Congress violates the rule it enacts for the states, that is almost conclusive
evidence that Congress does not really think that its enacted rule is constitutionally required").

111. See Perry, The Constitution in the Courts, n. 13, at 84–86 (discussing the
influence of Justice Scalia's conception of proper judicial role on his interpretation
of the free exercise language of the First Amendment).

112. I have discussed this issue at length elsewhere. See id., ch. 6.

113. See n. 78.

114. See nn. 77–79 & accompanying text.

115. Of course, different persons—different judges—might well draw the
boundaries of "the reasonable" in different places. What I am referring to here is
not an algorithm of choice, but a judicial stance, a judicial attitude. Although, at
the limit, some judge might always or almost always draw the boundaries of "the
reasonable" so that they are substantially congruent with "what I, the judge, believe", I think most of us recognize the arrogance, the dogmatism, in that. There
will be some occasions, perhaps many, on which we want to say to our interlocu-
tors: "I disagree with you. I think you are wrong. Nonetheless, I have to admit
that your position is not unreasonable."

116. In commenting on the suggestion that the Constitution be read "to recognize that governmental assistance to meet basic material needs is a constitutional right", Terrance Sandalow writes:

> I have already suggested that there is little in our constitutional tra-
> dition to warrant such a reading and much to argue against it. Even if
> that difficulty is waived, however, the question remains whether courts
> are competent to undertake the responsibility that Sager would assign
> them. Governmental budgets call for the resolution of intractable issues,
> requiring not only choices from among the innumerable demands upon
> the public fisc, but judgments about the levels of taxation the citizenry

will accept and the economic effects of both taxation and the proposed expenditures. Responding to these issues requires access to technical resources unavailable to judges and a breadth of perspective that judges, just because they are politically unaccountable, necessarily lack. The demands upon the treasury that Sager would authorize judges to make, to put the latter point somewhat differently, would necessarily be the product of tunnel vision.

Terrance Sandalow, "Social Justice and Fundamental Law: A Comment on Sager's Constitution," 88 Northwestern U. L. Rev. 461, 467 (1993).

117. Herbert Wechsler's argument about "the political safeguards of federalism" is relevant here. See Herbert Wechsler, "The Political Safeguards of Federalism," in Principles, Politics, and Fundamental Law 49 (Herbert Wechsler, 1961). See also Jesse H. Choper, Judicial Review and the National Political Process: A Functional Reconsideration of the Supreme Court, ch. 4 (1980). For dissents from the position defended by Wechsler and the kindred position defended by Choper, see Steven G. Calabresi, "'A Government of Limited and Enumerated Powers': In Defense of *United States v. Lopez*," 94 Michigan L. Rev. 752 (1995); John C. Yoo, "The Judicial Safeguards of Federalism," 70 Southern California L. Rev. 1311 (1997).

118. See n. 125 & accompanying text.

119. For one who accepts an "originalist" approach to constitutional interpretation, the question whether the judiciary should play a primary role or only a secondary, Thayerian one in cases arising under the United States Constitution could be answered by the Constitution. Listen, in that regard, to Gary Lawson, who wrote in his review of my book: "[W]hile Professor Perry is entirely correct that originalism and minimalism are logically distinct concepts, he does not explore the possibility that originalism can resolve the minimalism/nonminimalism debate. Does 'the judicial power of the United States,' as originally understood in 1789, carry with it an understanding of the judicial role that compels either minimalism or nonminimalism as a strategy for [the specification of indeterminate constitutional norms]?" Gary Lawson, "Recommended Reading: Michael J. Perry's *The Constitution in the Courts: Law or Politics?*" The Federalist Paper, July 1994, at 9–10. Gary has raised a fair question and identified an important inquiry. Let me just say that I remain deeply skeptical that a constitutional consensus was ever achieved about the best answer, all things considered, to the minimalism/nonminimalism question.

120. Is there, with respect to state action, a need for a nationally uniform specification of any indeterminate norm that is part of the Constitution of the United States? I don't see it. Imagine this scenario: At Time 1, the legislature in State A declined to enact a law, because it believed that the law would be inconsistent with the best or optimal specification of a relevant but indeterminate norm in the United States Constitution; at Time 2, the legislature in State B enacted the law that the legislature in State A declined to enact, because, unlike the legislature in State A, the legislature in State B believed that the law would not be inconsistent with the best specification of the norm in question; at Time 3, the Supreme Court, on the ground that State B's specification is not unreasonable, declined to invalidate State B's law; at Time 4, the legislature in State A, after reconsidering the matter, reaffirmed its original view and so declined to enact the law. Why is the persistence of a disagreement between the two state legislatures, about the best

specification of the norm in question, a problem—much less a problem the Court needs to resolve?

121. See n. 49.

122. John Hart Ely, "Another Such Victory: Constitutional Theory and Practice in a World Where Courts Are No Different from Legislatures," 77 Virginia L. Rev. 833, 834 n. 4 (1991).

123. Id.

124. Id.

125. Id. at 834 n. 4 (emphasis added).

126. Id.

127. Ely, Democracy and Distrust, n. 49, at 103.

128. See John T. Noonan, Jr., "The End of Free Exercise," 42 DePaul L. Rev. 567 (1992).

129. Douglas Laycock, "The Benefits of the Establishment Clause," 42 DePaul L. Rev. 373, 376 (1992).

130. 319 U.S. 624 (1943).

131. 319 U.S. at 666–67 (1943).

132. See n. 117.

133. See Jeremy Waldron, "A Right-Based Critique of Constitutional Rights," 13 Oxford J. Legal Studies 18 (1993); Jeremy Waldron, "Freeman's Defense of Judicial Review," 13 Law & Philosophy 27 (1994). See also Jeremy Waldron, "Precommitment and Disagreement," in Alexander, ed., Constitutionalism, n. 68, at 271.

134. Waldron, "A Right-Based Critique of Constitutional Rights," n. 133, at 50–51.

135. Cf. Mark V. Tushnet, Red, White, and Blue: A Critical Analysis of Constitutional Law 4 (1988): "Judicial review is an institution designed to meet some difficulties that arise when one tries to develop political institutions forceful enough to accomplish values goals and yet not so powerful as to threaten the liberties of the citizenry."

136. Cf. Jeremy Waldron, Book Review, 90 J. Philosophy 149, 153 (1993) (reviewing Bruce Ackerman, We the People: Foundations (1991)):

> Even if one concedes the superior authority of Ackerman's higher law making, one is left unsure why it should be the special function of the courts to interpret that legislation. Judicial review becomes politically most important in cases where citizens disagree among themselves about the best way of understanding some constitutional provision. . . . [W]e were all enthusiastically in favor of the free exercise of religion, [for example,] but now in the cold light of morning we have to work out how it is to fit in with public-education policy. Surely on Ackerman's account, this is a problem for normal politics—the phase of the democratic process that alone is capable of working out how various aspects of public policy fit together. . . . Once the people begin disagreeing among themselves about how to interpret their own past acts of higher law making, it is unclear why any particular interpretation of that heritage should be able to trump any other simply because it is endorsed by five judges out of nine. Ackerman asks, "Isn't it better for the Court to represent the *absent* People by forcing our elected politicians/statesmen to measure their statutory conclusions against the principles reached by those who

have most successfully represented the People in the past?" But that game is up once there is disagreement about the meaning of those principles: then all we have is our present legislation, measured against two or more contrary interpretations of our past.

137. My point is not that with respect to every other indeterminate constitutional norm, the practice of judicial review should always be Thayerian. As I said, it's perilous to generalize. My point is only that with respect to certain norms, the practice should always be non-Thayerian.

138. Bickel, n. 91, at 24.

139. Id.

140. For a discussion of the "common law" mode of constitutional decision-making, see David A. Strauss, "Common Law Constitutional Interpretation," 63 U. Chicago L. Rev. 877 (1996); see also David A. Strauss, "Tragedies Under the Common Law Constitution," in Constitutional Stupidities, Constitutional Tragedies 235, 236 (William N. Eskridge, Jr. & Sanford Levinson eds., 1998).

Chapter 3

1. Raoul Berger, Government by Judiciary: The Transformation of the Fourteenth Amendment 1 (1977).

2. Robert H. Bork, The Tempting of America: The Political Seduction of the Law 180 (1989).

3. Robert H. Bork, "Our Judicial Oligarchy," First Things, November 1996, at 21. The two Fourteenth Amendment decisions cited by Bork (both of which I discuss in chapter 5): Romer v. Evans, 517 U.S. 620, 116 S. Ct. 1620 (1996); United States v. Virginia, 518 U.S. 515, 116 S. Ct. 2264 (1996).

4. Id. at 23.

5. Editors, "The End of Democracy? The Judicial Usurpation of Politics," First Things, November 1996, at 18.

6. See ch. 2, section I.C.

7. My colleague and friend Michael Curtis tells me that the story I sketch in this chapter—like the stories some others (e.g., Charles Fairman, Raoul Berger, William Nelson, and John Harrison) have told—fails adequately to account for the fundamental importance, to many of those who bequeathed us the Fourteenth Amendment, of protecting certain Bill-of-Rights privileges and immunities, especially the allied freedoms of speech and of the press, against the states by means of the privileges or immunities clause of section one of the Amendment. In correspondence, Michael has written to me:

> Many accounts of the history of the Fourteenth Amendment and the legal meaning of its first section begin with the Civil Rights Act of 1866. But a wider focus is required for understanding. For more than thirty years before the 1866 framing of the Fourteenth Amendment the nation had been racked by controversy over slavery. One of the most prominent and continuing controversies was the issue of whether anti-slavery speech was legitimate any where in the nation, and particularly in the South. Southern states had passed laws making anti-slavery expression criminal and, unsuccessfully, demanded similar laws in the North. In the mid 1830s Northern mobs had made repeated attempts to silence abolitionists; private violence also faced opponents of slavery in the South. In

response to these developments, more and more opponents of slavery insisted that all Americans were or should be protected by the national constitution's guarantees of civil liberty throughout the nation and against state action. A reading of the congressional debates from 1859–1866 shows a large number of Republicans expressed this view, including very prominent leaders of the party. While Republicans explicitly claimed a number of Bill of Rights liberties were national rights belonging to all American citizens, they particularly emphasized freedom of speech, press, religion, the right to bear arms, due process, and the freedom from unreasonable searches and seizures.

From the beginning of the nation it was common to refer to liberties such as freedom of speech and press as "privileges" or "immunities" of American citizens. As the controversy over anti-slavery speech intensified, so did references to rights such as free speech, press, and religion as "privileges" of American citizens which protected them from hostile state action throughout the nation. The phrase "laws for the security of person and property" which appears in the Civil Rights Bill was also commonly used to refer to liberties or "privileges" such as those in the Bill of Rights. For people who believed that the Bill of Rights contained rights of Americans which no state could abridge, the phrase "laws for the security of person and property as enjoyed by white citizens" would include such rights. Once this fact is understood, statements about the correspondence between the Civil Rights Act and the Fourteenth Amendment can be seen to have a different meaning—at least to a great many people. In addition, of course, one needs to recall that the newly freed slaves were being denied the right to bear arms, to speak, and to hold religious meetings by some Black Codes. In the view of many Republicans, such laws were suspect on two grounds—they denied basic constitutional liberties to which the newly freed slaves as American citizens were entitled and they denied equality.

So when, in the Thirty-ninth Congress, Jacob Howard read privileges of citizens of the United States to include Bill of Rights liberties which no state should henceforth abridge, he was explaining the words in a way that was consistent with very widespread usage of the words over the past thirty years of the struggle against slavery. Many Republican congressmen thought that Bill of Rights guarantees, property interpreted, should limit the states (under the privileges and immunities clause of Article IV according to some, or the guarantee of republican government, or otherwise). So what Howard said would not have seemed as much of an innovation as it in fact was. The orthodox judicial interpretation was that the Bill of Rights limited only the Federal Government.

It is also true that many believed that a right to equality at least in certain fundamentals was a right of American citizens, and some found this right also in Article IV. The orthodox interpretation of Article IV, of course, was that it protected temporary out of state visitors from discrimination in certain fundamental interests. Because of the similarity of the language of the inter-state and Fourteenth Amendment privileges or immunities clause, it is natural that some have suggested that the Fourteenth Amendment was also merely an equality provision—though one of a very different sort.

Because so many people are involved in the framing and ratification of the Fourteenth Amendment, no theory, whatever it is, can reconcile all the divergent strands to come up with a universally shared or even universally shared lowest common denominator understanding of the meaning, for example, of the privileges or immunities clause. The most that one can hope to do is to look at the wide sweep of the history that shaped the clause, at common contemporary word usage, and at the legal philosophy held by Republicans and come to a global conclusion as to which reading is the most likely. No account of the history of the Fourteenth Amendment which simply begins with the Civil Rights Bill debate in 1866 can purport to do this.

Correspondence, dated Aug. 25, 1998, on file with author. Quoted with permission of Michael Curtis.

The cases and doctrines I discuss in chapters 4 through 6 of this book do not implicate the question whether the Fourteenth Amendment was understood and meant to make Bill-of-Rights privileges and immunities, in whole or in part, applicable to the states. (For an excellent discussion of the historical controversy, see Pamela Brandwein, "Dueling Histories: Charles Fairman and William Crosskey Reconstruct 'Original Understanding'," 30 Law & Soc'y Rev. 289 (1996).) I nonetheless discuss the question, briefly, near the end of this chapter.

In any event, Michael Curtis is a formidable student of the history of the Fourteenth Amendment. His work is an essential complement to the account I give in this chapter. See Michael Kent Curtis, No State Shall Abridge: The Fourteenth Amendment and the Bill of Rights (1986). See also Michael Kent Curtis, "The 1859 Crisis over Hinton Helper's Book, *The Impending Crisis*: Free Speech, Slavery, and Some Light on the Meaning of Section One of the Fourteenth Amendment," 68 Chicago-Kent L. Rev. 1113 (1993); Michael K. Curtis, "Resurrecting the Privileges or Immunities Clause and Revising the *Slaughter-House Cases* Without Exhuming *Lochner*: Individual Rights and the Fourteenth Amendment," 38 Boston College L. Rev. 1, 82–85 (1996); Michael Kent Curtis, "The Curious History of Attempts to Suppress Antislavery Speech, Press and Petition in 1835–37," 89 Northwestern U. L. Rev. 785 (1996); Michael Kent Curtis, "The 1837 Killing of Elijah Lovejoy by an Anti-Abolition Mob: Free Speech, Mobs, Republican Government, and the Privileges of American Citizens," 44 UCLA L. Rev. 1109 (1997).

8. 12 Statutes 1268 (1863).

9. See David Donald, Lincoln Reconsidered 137–38 (2d ed. 1966):

The ability to face reality means a willingness to change with events. Lincoln willingly admitted that his opinions and his actions were shaped by forces beyond his control. His shifting position on emancipation clearly illustrates his flexibility. At first Lincoln and his administration were committed to the Crittenden Resolution, declaring that the purpose of the war was simply to restore the Union without disturbing slavery at all. Then the pressures for emancipation began mounting. By 1862 American diplomats warned that only a firm antislavery stand would check the pro-Confederate sympathies of France and England. Northern governors bluntly told the President that their antislavery young men were unwilling to enlist in an army still legally bound to preserve the hated institution. Military leaders like General Grant demanded more men and pointed to the large number of Negroes who would willingly serve for their freedom.

As events moved, so moved the President. He was not going to act blindly, he assured a group of antislavery churchmen; there was certainly no point in issuing proclamations that "must necessarily be inoperative, like the Pope's bull against the comet." But he did act when ends and means were fitted, and the Emancipation Proclamation was a master-piece of political sagacity. Lincoln rightly regarded the Proclamation as his chief claim to historical fame, but he was always careful to insist that it was a product of circumstances. He had responded to the changing times. In 1864 he wrote to an admirer: "I claim not to have controlled events, but confess plainly that events have controlled me."

10. Quoted in William Cohen & Jonathan D. Varat, eds., Constitutional Law: Cases and Materials 22 (10th ed. 1997).

11. Id.

12. 83 U.S. (16 Wall.) 36, 70 (1872). For a fuller description of the Black Codes, see Richard Bardolph, The Civil Rights Record: Black Americans and the Law, 1849–70, at 25 (1970) (quoted in Patrick J. Kelley, "An Alternative Original-ist Opinion for *Brown v. Board of Education*," 20 Southern Illinois L. Rev. 75, 79–80 (1995)).

13. 14 Statutes 27 (1866).

14. See, e.g., Congressional Globe, 39th Congress, 1st Session, 474, 941 (1866) (remarks of Senator Lyman Trumbull of Illinois, who authored the Act and man-aged it in the Senate). See also John Harrison, "Reconstructing the Privileges or Immunities Clause," 101 Yale L. J. 1386, 1389 n. 13 (1992): "Those Republicans who thought that the [1866] Act was constitutional without the amendment relied mainly on Congress' power to eliminate badges of slavery under the 13th Amend-ment. This was the theory espoused by the Act's author, Senator Lyman Trumbull of Illinois."

15. See William E. Nelson, The Fourteenth Amendment: From Political Prin-ciple to Judicial Doctrine 104 (1988); Harrison, "Reconstructing the Privileges or Immunities Clause," n. 14, at 1397. Raoul Berger has argued that the second sentence was understood to do *nothing but* constitutionalize the 1866 Act. See Berger, n. 1.

Bruce Ackerman has argued—persuasively, in my view—that the Fourteenth Amendment was neither proposed by Congress nor ratified by the states in full ac-cord with the requirements of Article V of the Constitution. See Bruce Ackerman, We the People: Transformations, chs. 4–8 (1998). Nonetheless, it is constitutional bedrock for us the people of the United States now living that the Fourteenth Amendment is a part of the Constitution of the United States. As I said in chapter 2, Ackerman's project is not to challenge the constitutional status of the Fourteenth Amendment, but to demonstrate that the ways in which (in the words of the Pre-amble to the Constitution) "We the people of the United States . . . do ordain and establish this Constitution for the United States of America" are sometimes differ-ent from, and more complex than, those authorized by Article V.

Given that the Fourteenth Amendment was neither proposed nor ratified by the states in full accord with the requirements of Article V, one may fairly doubt whether—or, at least, to what extent—"We the people" did indeed "ordain and establish" the Fourteenth Amendment. Still, because it is settled that the Four-teenth Amendment is a part of the Constitution, we can and should ask how "We the people" understood, or would have understood, the text of the Amendment that was added to the Constitution in their name.

16. Slaughter-House Cases, 83 U.S. (16 Wall.) 36, 73 (1872). In *Dred Scott v. Sandford*, 60 U.S. (19 How.) 393 (1857)—surely the single most infamous case in American constitutional law—the Supreme Court ruled, inter alia, that "a man of African descent, whether a slave or not, was not and could not be a citizen of a State or of the United States. . . . That [the] main purpose [of the first sentence of section one of the Fourteenth Amendment] was to establish the citizenship of the negro can admit of no doubt. The phrase, 'subject to its jurisdiction' was intended to exclude from its operation children of ministers, consuls, and citizens or subjects of foreign States born within the United States." 83 U.S. (16 Wall.) at 73. On *Dred Scott*, see Don E. Fehrenbacher, The Dred Scott Case: Its Significance in American Law and Politics (1978). For a shorter commentary, see Don E. Fehrenbacher, "Dred Scott v. Sandford, 19 Howard 393 (1857)," in 2 Encyclopedia of the American Constitution 584 (Leonard W. Levy, Kenneth L. Karst, & Dennis J. Mahoney eds. 1986).

17. See n. 15.

18. Although sections two, three, and four of the Fourteenth Amendment are no longer operative, they—especially sections two and three—bear on the question of how "We the people" understood, or would have understood, section one of the Amendment. The text of the entire Fourteenth Amendment appears in this book following the table of contents.

19. For an early case, see Murray's Lessee v. Hoboken Land & Improvement Co., 59 U.S. (18 How.) 272, 276 (1856): "It is manifest that it was not left to the legislative power to enact any process which might be devised. The [due process clause of the Fifth Amendment] is a restraint on the legislative as well as on the executive and judicial powers of government, and cannot be so construed as to leave congress free to make any process 'due process of law,' by its mere will." (As Justice Scalia has pointed out, this case "involv[ed] the constitutionality of a *procedure* whereby property was seized, without trial, to satisfy a debt allegedly owed to the government." Antonin Scalia, A Matter of Interpretation: Federal Courts and the Law 143 n. 23 (1997).) For a case involving state action, see Hurtado v. California, 110 U.S. 516, 534 (1884). (In *Hurtado*, the Court also ruled that Fourteenth Amendment due process imposes the same procedural requirements on state government that Fifth Amendment due process imposes on the national government.)

20. See generally Mathews v. Eldridge, 424 U.S. 319 (1976).

21. John C. Harrison, "Utopia's Law, Politics' Constitution," 19 Harvard J. L. & Public Policy 917, 923 (1996).

22. Stephen A. Siegel, "The Federal Government's Power to Enact Color-Conscious Laws: An Originalist Inquiry," 92 Northwestern U. L. Rev. 477, 528–29 (1998) (citing Robert E. Riggs, "Substantive Due Process in 1791," 1990 Wisconsin L. Rev. 941, 977–87).

23. Harrison, "Utopia's Law, Politics' Constitution," n. 21, at 921, 923 (passages rearranged). See id. at 921–23.

24. See Berger, n. 1, at 193–214.

25. Robin West, "Toward an Abolitionist Interpretation of the Fourteenth Amendment," 94 West Virginia L. Rev. 111, 139 (1991).

26. Richard Aynes has collected several passages from the congressional debates that support this claim. See Richard L. Aynes, "Constitutional Considerations: Government Responsibility and the Right Not to Be a Victim," 11 Pepperdine L. Rev. 63, 81–84 (symposium issue, supp. to v. 11, 1984).

27. This point seems obvious enough, but early on the Court emitted some noises to the contrary. See Slaughter-House Cases, 83 U.S. (16 Wall.) 36, 81 (1872); Strauder v. West Virginia, 100 U.S. 303, 306, 307 (1880). Soon thereafter, however, the Court embraced the point. See Barbier v. Connolly, 113 U.S. 27 (1885); Yick Wo v. Hopkins, 118 U.S. 356 (1886).

28. See Harrison, "Reconstructing the Privileges or Immunities Clause," n. 14, at 1390 & 1433–51. Harrison writes:

> [T]he Equal Protection Clause's function as the basis of the [1866 Civil Rights] Act rests on a piece of textual sleight of hand familiar from *Yick Wo v. Hopkins*, which asserts that "the equal protection of the laws" means "the protection of equal laws." [118 U.S. 356, 369 (1886).] If that seems obvious to us, it is because custom has run a groove in our minds. By shifting the focus from "protection" to "laws," the *Yick Wo* maneuver draws our attention away from the embarrassing fact that the subject of the Equal Protection Clause is protection. That word suggests either the administration of the laws or, if it is about their content, laws that protect as opposed to laws that do other things. In order for the clause to be a requirement of equality in everything the states do, the word "protection" must simply drop out, so that the text would read "equal laws" rather than "the equal protection of the laws."

Id. at 1390. Alfred Avins' position seems substantially the same. See Alfred Avins, "The Equal 'Protection' of the Laws: The Original Understanding," 12 New York L. Forum 385, 424 (1966): "It was not until the Republican majority was, under political pressure, forced to find a way of justifying the constitutionality of the Civil Rights Act of 1875 that, for the first time, the theory was developed and expounded that the word 'protection' in the Equal Protection Clause meant 'benefit,' and that this clause conferred anything more than the same remedies for preexisting rights." But see Melissa Saunders, "Equal Protection, Class Legislation, and Colorblindness," 96 Michigan L. Rev. 245, 291 (1997): "It may be true that the sponsors of the Civil Rights Act of 1875 did not rest it on the Equal Protection Clause until after the Supreme Court's decision in the *Slaughter-House Cases*. But Senator Morton first advanced his theory that the Equal Protection Clause was a general prohibition against unequal laws in February of 1872, more than a year before the Supreme Court handed down that decision in April of 1873. The theory that the 'equal protection of the laws' means 'the protection of equal laws' did not, in any event, originate with Morton; it was deeply embedded in American legal and political thought long before he spoke." For criticism of Saunders' historical argument, see Bret Boyce, "Originalism and the Fourteenth Amendment," 33 Wake Forest L. Rev. 909, 969–70 n. 304 (1998).

29. 100 U.S. 303 (1879).

30. See id. at 308–9. See also n. 71.

31. See Kelley, n. 12, at 86–89.

32. Harrison, "Reconstructing the Privileges or Immunities Clause," n. 14, at 1448, 1450. See also Speech of Senator Howard, May 23, 1866, Congressional Globe, 39th Congress, 1st Session, 2766 (1866):

> [The equal protection clause] abolishes all class legislation in the States and does away with the injustice of subjecting one caste of persons to a code not applicable to another. It prohibits the hanging of a black man

for a crime for which the white man is not to be hanged. It protects the black man in his fundamental rights as a citizen with the same shield which it throws over the white man. Is it not time, Mr. President, that we extend to the black man, I had almost called it the poor privilege of the equal protection of the law? Ought not the time to be now passed when one measure of justice is to be meted out to a member of one caste while another and a different measure is meted out to the member of another caste, both castes being alike citizens of the United States, both bound to obey the same laws, to sustain the burdens of the same Government, and both equally responsible to justice and to God for the deeds done in the body?

Senator Jacob Howard of Michigan introduced the Fourteenth Amendment in the Senate, and Representative John A. Bingham of Ohio, Howard's ally, introduced the Amendment in the House.

33. 83 U.S. (16 Wall.) 36, 71 (1872).

34. See, in addition to John Harrison and Alfred Avins (see n. 28), David P. Currie, The Constitution in the Supreme Court: The First Hundred Years 1789–1888, at 349 & n. 143, 350 n. 148 (1985); Earl A. Maltz, "The Concept of the Equal Protection of the Laws: A Historical Inquiry," 22 San Diego L. Rev. 499 (1985).

35. My colleague Michael Curtis is one such scholar. See Curtis, "Resurrecting the Privileges or Immunities Clause and Revising the *Slaughter-House Cases* Without Exhuming *Lochner*: Individual Rights and the Fourteenth Amendment," n. 7, at 82–85 (1996).

36. Saunders, n. 28, at 247–48, 292, 293.

37. Id. at 292 n. 209.

38. See Boyce, n. 28, at 969–70 n. 304.

39. Harrison, "Reconstructing the Privileges or Immunities Clause," n. 14, at 1450. For a discussion of the overlap, see id. at 1450–51.

40. But what about the fact that the equal protection language mentions "persons" and the privileges or immunities language mentions only "citizens"? See n. 81.

41. And perhaps even under some "natural" law. See n. 50.

42. See 83 U.S. (16 Wall.) 36, 73–80 (1872).

43. Richard L. Aynes, "Constricting the Law of Freedom: Justice Miller, the Fourteenth Amendment, and the *Slaughter-House Cases*," 70 Chicago-Kent L. Rev. 627, 627 & n. 4 (1994). For a passionate critique of the *Slaughter-House Cases*, see Charles L. Black, Jr., A New Birth of Freedom: Human Rights, Named and Unnamed 41–85 (1997).

44. Id. at 89.

45. Harrison, "Reconstructing the Privileges or Immunities Clause," n. 14, at 1395. Cf. Siegel, n. 22, at 137: "[T]he specific reason for writing the Citizenship Clause [i.e., the first sentence of section one] was to define who had the benefit of the second sentence's Privileges or Immunities Clause. The Citizenship Clause was an afterthought; the Fourteenth Amendment could have been, and almost was, enacted without it."

46. Harrison, "Reconstructing the Privileges or Immunities Clause," n. 14, at 1416, 1419–20. See id. at 1415:

[A]lthough Section 1 recognizes that there are separate citizenships of the states and the United States, the Amendment does not divide those citizenships, but staples them together. Every citizen of the United States who resides in a state is a citizen of that state and therefore has the privileges and immunities of state citizenship by operation of the Constitution. This makes the possession of the rights of state citizenship into a right of national citizenship. . . . It is thus virtually impossible to avoid the conclusion that . . . "[a]s a citizen of the United States, the first right of the citizen of the State is that he shall enjoy all the privileges and immunities of a citizen of the State."

Cf. Douglas G. Smith, "Citizenship and the Fourteenth Amendment," 34 San Diego L. Rev. 681, 687 (1997): "Although a distinction may have been made between citizenship of a state and citizenship of the United States, that does not mean that there existed no single conception of the meaning of the term 'citizen' and the accompanying privileges and immunities of citizenship."

As it happens, Harrison, while rejecting the *Slaughter-House* majority's embrace of one of the two polar possibilities, does not himself embrace the other polar possibility. Instead, Harrison defends one of the intermediate possibilities. Harrison's claim is that not all the rights that states create and distribute to their citizens are protected, but only what Harrison calls "citizenship rights". This is a false claim, as I explain later in this chapter.

47. James E. Bond, No Easy Walk to Freedom: Reconstruction and the Ratification of the Fourteenth Amendment 256–57 (1997).

48. Nelson, n. 15, at 163.

49. *Pace* the 1866 Civil Rights Act, which section one of the Fourteenth Amendment was understood and meant to constitutionalize, the privileges or immunities norm established by "We the people" protects not just privileges and immunities that, under the law of a state, *all* citizens of the state are due; it protects even privileges and immunities that, under the law of a state, only some citizens of the state—for example, *white* citizens—are due. If section one of the Fourteenth Amendment means anything, it means that in distributing protected privileges and immunities (whatever they are) to its citizens, no state may construct, implicitly or otherwise, a hierarchy of citizens, some of whom are more equal than others. By bestowing privileges or immunities only on themselves, the politically dominant white citizens of a state imply that they are the *real* citizens of the state, the *true* citizens, the *primary*, the *exemplary*, the *first-class* citizens. A privilege or an immunity of *white* citizens is, if it is one of the privileges or immunities protected by section one of the Fourteenth Amendment, the privilege or immunity of *all* citizens, *nonwhite as well as white*.

50. See Berger, n. 1, at 20–51. See also Earl M. Maltz, "A Dissenting Opinion to Brown," 20 Southern Illinois L. Rev. 93 (1995); Kelley, n. 12, at 83–85.

John Harrison has opted for the "positive law" reading of the privileges or immunities language over the "natural law" or "natural rights" reading. See Harrison, "Reconstructing the Privileges or Immunities Clause," n. 14, at 1419. Earl Maltz, by contrast, has opted for the "natural rights" reading. See Earl M. Maltz, Civil Rights, the Constitution, and Congress, 1863–69, 1–5, 93–96 (1990). See also Douglas G. Smith, "The Privileges and Immunities Clause of Article IV, Section 2: Precursor of Section 1 of the Fourteenth Amendment," 34 San Diego L. Rev. 809 (1997); Douglas G. Smith, "Natural Law, Article IV, and Section One of the Fourteenth Amendment," 47 American U. L. Rev. 351 (1997). But it is a mistake to think that one has to choose between the two readings. One can believe,

and at least some of the people who gave us the Fourteenth Amendment did believe—probably many of them did—that citizens are due certain privileges and
immunities not simply under positive (enacted) law, but also, even especially,
under some "natural" law, which positive law embodies and thereby protects or
should embody and protect. (Harrison understands the point. See Harrison, "Reconstructing the Privileges or Immunities Clause," n. 14, at 1419 n. 138.) See Kelley, n. 12, at 84 (commenting on "natural law theories"):

> A provision in the Pennsylvania Constitution elaborates this ideal clearly:
>   All men are born free and independent, and have certain inherent
>   and indefeasible rights, among which are those of enjoying and
>   defending life and liberty, or acquiring, possessing, and protecting
>   property and reputation, and of pursuing their own happiness.
> These fundamental natural rights were summarized by Chancellor Kent
> as follows: "[t]he right of personal security, the right of personal liberty,
> and the right to acquire and enjoy property." In formulating their cri-
> tique of slavery the Republicans recurred to this basic American view of
> fundamental natural rights of all human beings. . . . The Republican
> position . . . was based on the principle that blacks as human beings
> ought to have those inherent rights of all men.

51. How revolutionary was the transformation that they understood themselves to be spearheading? See n. 55. Cf. Eric L. McKitrick, "A Hero of Antislavery,"
New York Rev., Nov. 14, 1996, at 46: "[B]y 1860 most people in the North had
come sufficiently to see Southern slavery as an abomination that they were prepared to support a major act of challenge. . . . The people of the North were now
prepared to elect to the presidency a man who had in various ways made known
his conviction that slavery was bad and was doomed to extinction. They would do
so in the face of grim advance warnings from all over the South that a Lincoln victory would be met by resistance *in extremis*, to the point of the Union's breakup—
to the point, even, of blood."

52. Smith, "Citizenship and the Fourteenth Amendment," n. 46, at 808.

53. See text accompanying nn. 59–63.

54. Eric Foner, Reconstruction: America's Unfinished Revolution, 1863–1877
257 n. 53 (1988). See id. at 257:

> [T]he aims of the Fourteenth Amendment can only be understood within
> the political and ideological context of 1866: the break with the Presi-
> dent, the need to find a measure upon which all Republicans could unite,
> and the growing consensus within the party around the need for strong
> federal action to protect the freedmen's rights, short of the suffrage. De-
> spite the many drafts, changes, and deletions, the Amendment's central
> principle remained constant: a national guarantee of equality before the
> law. Some critics, indeed, played on racial fears to charge that no state
> could henceforth regulate the rights not merely of blacks, but of Indians,
> Chinese, even Gypsies. ("I have lived in the United States now for many
> a year," declared one Republican Senator, "and really I have heard more
> about Gypsies within the past two or three months than I have heard be-
> fore in my life.") But the principle of equal civil rights was now so widely
> accepted in Republican circles, and had already been so fully discussed,
> that compared with the now-forgotten disqualification and representa-
> tion clauses, the first section inspired relatively little discussion. It was "so

just," a moderate Congressman declared, "that no member of this House can seriously object to it."

55. Id. at 257–58. See also Eric Foner & Olivia Mahoney, America's Reconstruction: People and Politics After the Civil War 80 (1995).

56. Harrison, "Reconstructing the Privileges or Immunities Clause," n. 14, at 1452.

57. Id. at 1454.

58. Congressional Globe, 39th Congress, 1st Session, 1095 (1866), quoted in Harrison, "Reconstructing the Privileges or Immunities Clause," n. 14, at 1408.

59. Id. at 1412–13.

60. Id. at 1423.

61. Congressional Globe, 42d Congress, 2d Session, 762 (1872), quoted in Harrison, "Reconstructing the Privileges or Immunities Clause, n. 14, at 1426.

62. Id. at 1428–29 & n. 173.

63. See n. 56.

64. See generally Smith, "The Privileges and Immunities Clause of Article IV, Section 2," n. 50; Smith, "Natural Law, Article IV, and Section One of the Fourteenth Amendment," n. 50. In his speech in the Congress on May 23, 1866, Senator Howard, who introduced the proposed Fourteenth Amendment in the Senate and was the senator principally responsible for shepherding it there, quoted Justice Bushrod Washington's opinion in *Corfield v. Coryell* (6 F. Cas. 546 (C.C.E.D. Pa. 1823)), which concerned the privileges and immunities provision of Article IV: "[The protected privileges and immunities include] those privileges and immunities . . . which belong of right to the citizens of all free Governments. . . . They may . . . be all comprehended under the following general heads: protection by the Government, the enjoyment of life and liberty, with the right to acquire and possess property of every kind, and to pursue and obtain happiness and safety, subject nevertheless to such restraints as the Government may justly prescribe for the general good of the whole." Speech of Senator Howard, May 23, 1866, n. 32, at 2765.

65. See Harrison, "Reconstructing the Privileges or Immunities Clause," n. 14, at 1454–55.

66. See Smith, "The Privileges and Immunities Clause of Article IV, Section 2," n. 50, at 885. See also Corfield v. Coryell, 6 F. Cas. 546 (C.C.E.D. Pa. 1823) (No. 3230).

67. Harrison, "Reconstructing the Privileges or Immunities Clause," n. 14, at 1417. See, e.g., Speech of Senator Howard, May 23, 1866, n. 32, at 2766.

68. See, e.g., id.

69. See, e.g., id. Another and crucial part of the compromise: section two of the Fourteenth Amendment. See n. 18. "In a compromise between Radical and moderate positions on black suffrage, [the Fourteenth Amendment] did not give blacks the right to vote, but threatened to reduce the South's representation in Congress if black men continued to be denied the ballot." Foner & Mahoney, America's Reconstruction: People and Politics After the Civil War, n. 55, at 79.

For further support of the proposition that the right to vote was exempted from the protection of section one, see Berger, n. 1, at 52–98; Timothy Bishop, "The Privileges or Immunities Clause of the Fourteenth Amendment: The Original Intent," 79 Northwestern U. L. Rev. 142, 151–57 (1984); Maltz, Civil Rights, the Constitution, and Congress, 1863–69, n. 50, at 118–20. Cf. John Harrison, "If the Eye Offend Thee, Turn Off the Color," 91 Michigan L. Rev. 1213, 1216 (1993): "As originally proposed, the 1866 [Civil Rights] Act included a general ban on race discrimination with respect to 'civil rights or immunities' as well as a specific list of rights with respect to which discrimination was forbidden. After the Senate passed the bill, Republicans in the House expressed the fear that the general language might be thought to include political rights, especially suffrage. The bill was amended to eliminate the offending phrase and passed over President Johnson's veto."

70. Although I bow to convention in using the word "race" here, I concur in K. Anthony Appiah's critique of the idea of "race". See K. Anthony Appiah, "Race, Culture, Identity: Misunderstood Connections," in Color Consciousness: The Political Morality of Race 30 (K. Anthony Appiah & Amy Gutman, 1996).

71. Including, for example, a criminal defendant's right not to have members of his race excluded, because of their race, from the pool from which the jury is to be selected. See Harrison, "Reconstructing the Privileges or Immunities Clause," n. 14, at 1463:

> In *Strauder v. West Virginia*, [100 U.S. 303 (1880),] the Supreme Court held that a black defendant could not be convicted by a jury from which all blacks had been excluded. [The Court apparently relied on the equal protection norm. See 100 U.S. at 305–12.] Such a law would not abridge the privileges or immunities of the potential juror because jury service is a political and not a civil right. The Court, however, rested its decision on the rights of the defendant. Justice Strong argued that a criminal defendant received unequal protection when he faced a jury that had been selected from a pool containing no members of his race. Although the issue is not easy, the result was probably right under both the Privileges or Immunities and Equal Protection Clauses, which overlap on this point. The difficult question is whether and when the race of the jury counts as part of the legal treatment afforded the defendant. I think that it did in *Strauder*. Certainly jury-composition rules can constitute immunities. Blacks could not be tried by juries deliberately drawn from conviction-prone groups.

I agree that the result in *Strauder* was right under the equal protection norm as well as under the privileges or immunities norm. But it was also right under the due process norm, because the law at issue in *Strauder* denied black defendants some of the "process of law"—in particular, of an important procedural protection—that ordinary (i.e., white) citizens were "due" and enjoyed. It seems unremarkable that one and the same law might violate two or more constitutional norms, especially two or more *related* norms—for example, that a law might *both* deprive someone of life, liberty, or property without due process of law *and at the same time* deny her the equal protection of the laws.

72. At the time the Fourteenth Amendment was proposed and ratified, state or local law determined who could vote, and under the laws of every state, and even putting aside citizens who were minors, not even all white citizens could vote. In particular, white citizens who were female could not vote. Only (some) male citizens could vote.

73. Moreover, according to the Twenty-fourth Amendment, "The right of citizens of the United States to vote in any primary or other election for President or Vice-President, or for Senator or Representative in Congress, shall not be denied or abridged by the United States or by any State by reason of failure to pay any poll tax or other tax."

74. See John Hart Ely, Democracy and Distrust: A Theory of Judicial Review 7 (1980). Moreover, further protection of the rights to vote and of access to the ballot—protection of the sort the Supreme Court has based on section one of the Fourteenth Amendment (see, e.g., Reynolds v. Sims, 377 U.S. 533 (1964); Harper v. Virginia Board of Elections, 383 U.S. 663 (1966); Williams v. Rhodes, 393 U.S. 23 (1968); Kramer v. Union Free School District No. 15, 395 U.S. 621 (1969))—could reasonably have been derived from that part of Article IV, section four, of the Constitution guaranteeing "to every State in the Union a Republican Form of Government . . ." (Cf. Gerald Gunther, Constitutional Law 842 n. 2 (12th ed. 1991).) Preserving and protecting the right to vote, after all, is the heart of preserving and protecting—and, in that sense, of "guaranteeing"—a republican form of government. We can see this clearly now even if our constitutional forebears could have seen it only dimly at best. As both the trajectory of our last several constitutional amendments and the international law of human rights disclose, we now understand the right to vote to be a fundamental constituent—perhaps *the* fundamental constituent—of representative democracy (a.k.a "republican form of government"). Moreover, a vigorous judicial role in doing the "guaranteeing" scarcely seems radical. "Unblocking stoppages in the democratic process is what judicial review ought preeminently to be about, and denial of the vote seems the quintessential stoppage." Ely, this n., at 117.

75. The "thought experiment" at the end of this chapter is relevant at this point.

76. Ely, n. 74, at 25.

77. Id.

78. Id. at 25.

79. See, e.g., Maltz, Civil Rights, the Constitution, and Congress, 1863–69, n. 50, at 96–102 (clause meant to be limited to citizens). Cf. Nelson, n. 15, at 52 (noting an interpretation according to which "what ultimately became section 1 was designed to give constitutional stature to a basic distinction in mid-nineteenth-century American law between the rights of aliens and the rights of citizens"). But see Berger, n. 1, at 215–20 (clause not meant to be limited to citizens); cf. Earl M. Maltz, "The Constitution and Nonracial Discrimination: Alienage, Sex, and the Framers' Ideal of Equality," 7 Constitutional Commentary 251, 262 (1990) (disputing Berger's position).

80. See id. at 257–65; Harrison, "Reconstructing the Privileges or Immunities Clause," n. 14, at 1442–46.

81. Maltz, "The Constitution and Nonracial Discrimination," n. 79, at 264 & 271. It bears mention that even if the intended beneficiaries of the privileges or immunities provision are only citizens, this need not have significant practical consequences: As I explained years ago, the modern Supreme Court's solicitude for aliens is best justified, not on the basis of the equal protection norm, on which the Court has tended to rely, or on the basis of any other part of section one, but on the basis of the supremacy clause of Article VI of the Constitution. See Michael J. Perry, "Modern Equal Protection: A Conceptualization and Appraisal," 79 Columbia L. Rev. 1023, 1060–65 (1979). For a serendipitous but more elaborate development of the point, see two student works published at about the same time: Note, "The Equal Treatment of Aliens: Preemption or Equal Protection?" 31 Stanford L. Rev. 1069 (1979); Note, "State Burdens on Resident Aliens: A New Preemption Analysis," 89 Yale L. J. 940 (1980).

82. See 1 Oxford English Dictionary 43 (2d ed. 1989).

83. Curtis, "Resurrecting the Privileges or Immunities Clause and Revising the *Slaughter-House Cases* Without Exhuming *Lochner*," n. 1, at 49. See id. at 47–50.

84. Or, forbidding more than color-based allocations? In the next chapter, in discussing affirmative action, I consider the claim that the Fourteenth Amendment forbids states to allocate rights among their citizens on the basis of their skin color *without regard to whether the allocation is "racist"*.

85. Nelson, n. 15, at 163.

86. Eric Foner has discussed the fascinating subject of Southerners who were against secession and loyal to the Union. See Foner, Reconstruction: America's Unfinished Revolution, n. 54, at 11–18. Foner writes, for example, that "secret Union societies flourished in the Ozark mountains of northern Arkansas, from which 8,000 men eventually joined the federal army." Id. at 13.

87. Congressional Globe, 39th Congress, 1st Session, 516 (1866) (statement of Rep. Eliot).

88. Alfred Avins, "Fourteenth Amendment Limitations on Banning Racial Discrimination: The Original Understanding," 8 Arizona L. Rev. 236, 246 (1967). Cf. Michael R. Belknap, Federal Law and Southern Order: Racial Violence and Constitutional Conflict in the Post-Brown South 11 (1987): "Congress had written the Fourteenth Amendment following hearings at which its Joint Committee on Reconstruction took extensive testimony about the refusal of southern states to punish private wrongs against blacks, carpetbaggers, and unionists."

89. Judith A. Baer, "Making Moderation an End in Itself: William Nelson's *Fourteenth Amendment*," 15 L. & Social Inquiry 321, 335 (1990).

90. Harrison, "If the Eye Offend Thee, Turn Off the Color," n. 69, at 1228.

91. Nelson, n. 15, at 138–39. Cf. id. at 80: "Americans in 1866, like Americans of today, could all agree upon the rightfulness of equality only because they did not agree on its meaning, and their political leaders, unlike the managers of the modern bureaucratic state, were content to enact the general principle rather than its specific applications into law."

92. See Johannes Morsink, "World War Two and the Universal Declaration," 15 Human Rights Q. 357, 363 (1993).

93. Barbara Crosette, "Caste May Be India's Moral Achilles' Heel," New York Times, Oct. 20, 1996, at E3 (reporting on a new study by Human Rights Watch titled *Children in Bondage*).

94. Richard Rorty, "Human Rights, Rationality, and Sentimentality," in On Human Rights: The Oxford Amnesty Lectures 1993 111, 112 (Stephen Shute & Susan Hurley eds., 1993) (passages rearranged). See also id. at 125.

95. Id. at 112.

96. See Nelson, n. 15, at 150 (emphasis added):

> [The proponents of the Fourteenth Amendment did not effectively] explain how national enforcement of principles designed to affect nearly every aspect of human endeavor could be limited so as not to undermine the plenary lawmaking power of the states. The most cogent explanation was that the Fourteenth Amendment would not, in and of itself, create rights, but would leave that task to state law; the amendment's sole restriction on state legislative freedom would lie in its requirement that the states confer equal rights on all.
>
> But not all of the amendment's proponents accepted this view. Consistently with their antislavery heritage, some Republicans claimed that

the amendment did more than protect rights equally; it protected absolutely certain fundamental rights such as those specified in the Bill of Rights and those given by common law to enter contracts and to own property. This absolute rights interpretation involved the Republican proponents of the amendment in a serious difficulty, however, because congressional assumption of plenary legislative jurisdiction over basic rights threatened to deprive state legislatures of their authority over the rights. Republicans protested, of course, that they did not intend the Fourteenth Amendment to have this effect, and a few tried to explain why it would not. They urged that, although section 1 would prohibit states from impairing the enjoyment of fundamental rights, states would remain free to regulate those rights *for the public good in a reasonable fashion.*

97. Plessy v. Ferguson, 163 U.S. 537, 550 (1896). See also Gulf, Colorado & Santa Fe Railroad Co. v. Ellis, 165 U.S. 150 (1897), 155 (classification "must always rest upon some difference which bears a reasonable and just relation to the act in respect to which the classification is proposed, and can never be made arbitrarily and without any such basis"); Mugler v. Kansas, 123 U.S. 623, 661 (1887) ("If . . . a statute purporting to have been enacted to protect the public health, the public morals, or the public safety, has no real or substantial relation to those objects, . . . it is the duty of the courts to so adjudge, and thereby give effect to the Constitution").

98. Saunders, n. 28, at 247–48.

99. See text accompanying n. 91.

100. As I emphasize in the next chapter, the available historical evidence fails to support the proposition that the generation of "We the people" that made the Fourteenth Amendment a part of the Constitution understood the Amendment to ban laws (or other governmental actions) based on skin color without regard to whether the laws were racist. See, e.g., Andrew Kull, The Color-Blind Constitution vii (1992): "[T]he evidence I adduce tends strongly to refute [the contention that] the Fourteenth Amendment was intended by its framers to require color blindness on the part of government . . ." True, the Civil Rights Act of 1866 did ban certain laws (and other governmental actions) based on skin color. See n. 13 & accompanying text (in particular, the "as is enjoyed by white citizens" language). However, the banned laws and practices were conspicuously racist; there was no plausible nonracist explanation for them. It ignores the context of the 1866 Civil Rights Act to invoke the Act in support of the proposition that the generation of "We the people" that made the Fourteenth Amendment a part of the Constitution might have understood and indeed wanted the Amendment to ban certain laws and practices based on skin color *without regard to whether the laws and practices were racist*; such an argument ignores the undeniable if, for some, inconvenient fact that, as I reported earlier in this chapter, the 1866 Act was directed specifically against a variety of prominently racist laws and other slavery-like practices commonly known as the Black Codes. Michael Curtis has reported that Senator Lyman Trumbull of Illinois, who authored the Act and "managed [it] in the Senate[,] referred to *the discriminatory Black Codes* and said, 'The purpose of the [Civil Rights] Bill . . . is to destroy *all these discriminations and to carry into effect the [Thirteenth] Amendment.'*" Curtis, "Resurrecting the Privileges or Immunities Clause and Revising the *Slaughter-House Cases* Without Exhuming *Lochner*," n. 7, at 38 (emphasis added).

For an example of someone who seems to argue that the Fourteenth Amendment was meant to ban certain laws and practices based on skin color *without regard to whether the laws and practices were racist*, see Harrison, "If the Eye Offend Thee, Turn Off the Color," n. 69, at 1234 (contending that section one of the Fourteenth Amendment was meant to ban all "discrimination", including all "race discrimination", albeit "only with respect to a limited set of rights—the privileges and immunities of citizens and the protection of the laws").

101. See ch. 4.

102. See, e.g., City of Cleburne v. Cleburne Living Center, 473 U.S. 432 (1985).

103. See ch. 6.

104. See n. 7.

105. See Akhil R. Amar, "The Bill of Rights and the Fourteenth Amendment," 101 Yale L. J. 1193, 1197 (1992): "This synthesis, which I call 'refined incorporation,' begins with [Justice Hugo] Black's insight that *all* of the privileges and immunities of citizens recognized in the Bill of Rights became applicable to the states by dint of the Fourteenth Amendment. But not all of the provisions of the original Bill of Rights were indeed rights of citizens. Some instead were at least in part rights of states, and as such, awkward to incorporate *fully* against states."

106. See (in addition to the article by Amar cited in the preceding note) the works by Michael Kent Curtis cited in note 7 of this chapter.

107. Among contemporary students of the Fourteenth Amendment, Curtis and Amar are not alone. Earl Maltz, for example, has concluded that "there can be little doubt that the privileges and immunities clause was [meant] to [protect] *some* of the Bill of Rights. Republicans had constantly complained that slave-state governments had denied opponents of slavery freedom of speech, and both [Representative John A.] Bingham [of Ohio] and Governor Jacob Cox of Ohio referred directly to these concerns during arguments over ratification. Bingham also mentioned the right to teach the Bible—a clear appeal to the religion clauses. Thus, the evidence impressively demonstrates that the basic guarantees of the First Amendment were understood to be included in the concept of privileges and immunities." Maltz, Civil Rights, the Constitution, and Congress, 1863–69, n. 50, at 117. Maltz continues that "[o]ther values from the Bill of Rights also figured prominently in the Reconstruction-era debates", including the Fifth Amendment's "no taking of property without just compensation", the Second Amendment's "right to keep and bear arms", and the Eighth Amendment's "no cruel or unusual punishments". Id. "In short, one can only conclude that contemporaries must have understood the privileges and immunities clause to embody most of the Bill of Rights, and they probably viewed the first eight amendments as incorporated in their entirety." Id. at 117–18. See also Foner, Reconstruction: America's Unfinished Revolution, n. 54, at 258–59; Richard L. Aynes, "On Misreading John Bingham and the Fourteenth Amendment," 103 Yale L. J. 57 (1993).

108. Amar, n. 105, at 1231 n. 174 (commenting on John Harrison's effort to discern the privileges or immunities norm established by "We the people": Harrison, "Reconstructing the Privileges or Immunities Clause," n. 14).

109. Amar's two-tiered approach is problematic as well as unnecessary. As Doug Smith has put the point: "[The] protection afforded the peculiarly 'national' privileges and immunities of citizenship should not differ from that afforded those privileges and immunities traditionally within the regulatory control of the state

governments since all of the privileges and immunities of citizens of the United States flow from an individual's status as a citizen *of the United States*." Smith, "Citizenship and the Fourteenth Amendment," n. 46, at 804 n. 402.

110. See, e.g., Raoul Berger, Government by Judiciary: The Transformation of the Fourteenth Amendment 155–97 (2d ed. 1997); Bond, n. 47, at 252–74. See also Bork, "Our Judicial Oligarchy," n. 3, at 23 ("the [Supreme] Court invented the theory that the Bill of Rights limit[s] states as well as the federal government"); Lino A. Graglia, "'Interpreting' the Constitution: Posner on Bork," 44 Stanford L. Rev. 1019, 1033–34 (1992) ("there is very little basis for the implausible proposition that the States that ratified the Fourteenth Amendment understood that it would 'incorporate' the Bill of Rights, making its restrictions applicable to the states"). For an excellent discussion of the historical controversy, and a listing of key players, see Brandwein, n. 1.

111. Charles L. Black, Jr., "'One Nation Indivisible': Unnamed Human Rights in the States," 65 St. John's L. Rev. 17, 55 (1991).

112. Baer, n. 89, at 324. Professor Baer cites, "on the right", Raoul Berger's *Government by Judiciary: The Transformation of the Fourteenth Amendment* (1977) and Chester J. Antieau's *The Original Understanding of the Fourteenth Amendment* (1981) and, "on the left", Michael Kent Curtis' *No State Shall Abridge: The Fourteenth Amendment and the Bill of Rights* (1986) and her own *Equality Under the Constitution: Reclaiming the Fourteenth Amendment* (1983). Baer, this n., at 324.

113. Id. at 341. For a fuller statement of Professor Baer's position about the difficulty of retrieving the original understanding of a constitutional provision, see Judith A. Baer, "The Fruitless Search for Original Intent," in Judging the Constitution: Critical Essays on Judicial Lawmaking 49 (Michael W. McCann & Gerald L. Houseman eds., 1989).

114. Harrison, "If the Eye Offend Thee, Turn Off the Color," n. 69, at 1213.

115. On "law office" history, see Mark Tushnet, "Interdisciplinary Legal Scholarship: The Case of History-in-Law," 71 Chicago-Kent L. Rev. 909 (1996). See also Morgan Cloud, "Searching Through History; Searching for History," 63 U. Chicago L. Rev. 1707 (1996). Eric Foner, on whom I rely at a crucial point in my argument, is certainly no law-office historian. See nn. 54–55 & accompanying text.

116. That so formidable a student of the history of the Fourteenth Amendment as my colleague Michael Kent Curtis is skeptical about important aspects of my argument in this chapter is reason enough for me to ask what implications follow from the fact that I might be wrong in this chapter, if indeed any implications follow, for my arguments in the remaining chapters of this book.

117. "I have reached bedrock and this is where my spade is turned." Ludwig Wittgenstein, Philosophical Investigations, sec. 217 (1953).

118. See Michael J. Perry, The Idea of Human Rights, ch. 1 (1998).

119. Ronald Dworkin, "Life Is Sacred. That's the Easy Part," New York Times Magazine, May 16, 1993, at 36. Cf. Ronald Dworkin, Life's Dominion: An Argument About Abortion, Euthanasia, and Individual Freedom 25 (1993) ("sacred" is often used in a theistic sense, but it can be used in a secular sense as well).

120. James Griffin, Well-being: Its Meaning, Measurement, and Moral Importance 239 (1987).

121. Bernard Williams, Ethics and the Limits of Philosophy 14 (1985). Cf. Samuel Brittan, "Making Common Cause: How Liberals Differ, and What They Ought to Agree On," Times Lit. Supp., Sept. 20, 1996, at 3, 4:

[P]erhaps the litmus test of whether the reader is in any sense a liberal or not is Gladstone's foreign-policy speeches. In [one such speech,]
taken from the late 1870s, around the time of the Midlothian campaign,
[Gladstone] reminded his listeners that "the sanctity of life in the hill vil-
lages of Afghanistan among the winter snows, is as inviolable in the eye of
almighty God as can be your own . . . that the law of mutual love is not
limited by the shores of this island, is not limited by the boundaries of
Christian civilization; that it passes over the whole surface of the earth,
and embraces the meanest along with the greatest in its unmeasured
scope." By all means smile at the oratory. But anyone who sneers at the
underlying message is not a liberal in any sense of that word worth preserving.

122. See ch. 2, section II. A.

123. Morally wrong—or morally right—from *whose* moral perspective? Isn't
the relevant and indeed determinative perspective for a judge faced with the question whether to accept such a premise—or whether to join with other judges in fa-
cilitating its acceptance—into the constitutional law of the United States *the judge's
own moral perspective*? If the question is, for a judge, a moral question, isn't it silly to
think that the judge would or even should resolve it on the basis of a morality not
her own—on the basis, that is, of *someone else's* morality? This is not to deny that
a judge's own morality might and hopefully does include norms concerning what
she should and should not do *in her role as a judge*—norms that are plausible in the
context of American political-moral culture. Still, there is little if any reason to
think that there is but a single set of such norms plausible in the context of American political-moral culture, and that according to that single set of norms, it
would necessarily be immoral for a judge to accept into the constitutional law of
the United States such a premise: a premise correctly believed by the judge never
to have been established by "We the people".

124. The fundamental moral legitimacy of government in the United States
was at stake for very many persons in *Brown v. Board of Education*. Cf. Steven D.
Smith, "Brown v. Board of Education: A Revised Opinion," 20 Southern Illinois U.
L. J. 41 (1995) (defending the Court's ruling in *Brown v. Board of Education* as justified not in ordinary constitutional-legal terms but in extraordinary political-
moral terms; and urging that the Court's action in *Brown* not be (mis)understood
as a model for ordinary judicial review). However, the Court's decision in *Brown*
can be defended on the basis of a constitutional norm established by "We the people". See ch. 4, section I.

125. Commenting on a hypothetical "statute making it a crime for any person
to remove another person's gall bladder, except to save that person's life", John Ely
has written that "[i]t is an entirely legitimate response to the gall bladder law to
note that it couldn't pass and refuse to play any further. In fact it can only deform
our constitutional jurisprudence to tailor it to laws that couldn't be enacted, since
constitutional law appropriately exists for those situations where representative
government cannot be trusted, not those where we know it can." Ely, n. 74, at 183.
On what Justice Ely might be tempted to do in morally extraordinary circumstances, see id. (contemplating the possibility of "staying on the bench and engaging in a little judicial civil disobedience"). On what Justice Ackerman would do in
such circumstances, see Bruce Ackerman, We the People: Foundations 10–16
(1991) (rejecting "rights foundationalism").

Chapter 4

1. 347 U.S. 483. I bow to convention in using the word "race" at various points in this chapter, and elsewhere in this book, but the term "skin color" would generally be more accurate. For an illuminating critique of the idea of "race", see K. Anthony Appiah, "Race, Culture, Identity: Misunderstood Connections," in *Color Consciousness: The Political Morality of Race* 30 (K. Anthony Appiah & Amy Gutman, 1996). See also *Houston Contractors Association v. Metropolitan Transit Authority of Harris County*, 984 F. Supp. 1027, 1029 (S.D. Tex. 1997) ("Race is politics not biology"); Walter Benn Michaels, "Autobiography of an Ex-White Man: Why Race Is Not a Social Construction," Transition, Issue 73, 122, 143 (1998) ("whiteness is not—like class—a social construction. It is instead—like phlogiston—a mistake"). It bears mention here that in its Draft Statement on "Race" (1997), the American Anthropological Associaton has declared:

> The [human] species is not divided into exclusive genetically distinct, homogeneous groupings similar to subspecies, as the concept of "race" implies. All human groups share many features with other groups, and it is impossible to draw rigid boundaries around them. Genetically there are greater differences between indivduals within a group popularly defined as a race than there are between two "races". There are no pure "races," and no groups are physically, intellectually or morally superior, or inferior, to others.

2. Charles L. Black, Jr., Decision According to Law 33 (1981). See also William J. Brennan, Jr., "Why Have a Bill of Rights?" 9 Oxford J. Legal Studies 425, 430–31 (1989). As Gerard Lynch has written, "to most lawyers of my generation, *Brown* is a touchstone for constitutional theory fully as powerful as *Lochner* was for a previous generation." Gerard Lynch, Book Review, 63 Cornell L. Rev. 1091, 1099 n. 32 (1983). See also Gregory Bassham, Original Intent and the Constitution: A Philosophical Study 105 (1992) ("The acid test of originalism, as indeed of any theory of constitutional adjudication, is its capacity to justify what is now almost universally regarded as the Supreme Court's finest hour: its decision in *Brown v. Board of Education*"); Mark V. Tushnet, Reflections on the Role of Purpose in the Jurisprudence of the Religion Clauses," 27 William & Mary L. Rev. 997, 999 n. 4 (1986) ("For a generation, one criterion for an acceptable constitutional theory has been whether that theory explains why [*Brown*] . . . was correct"). But see John Harrison, "Reconstructing the Privileges or Immunities Clause," 101 Yale L. J. 1385, 1463 n. 295 (1992): "I do not think that my theory of the 14th Amendment stands or falls with [its ability to accommodate the Court's decision in *Brown*]. Man is not the measure of all things, as Socrates replied to the Sophists, and neither is Brown v. Board of Educ., 347 U.S. 483 (1954). An interpretation of the Constitution is not wrong because it would produce a different result in *Brown*."

3. See Michael J. Perry, "The Disproportionate Impact Theory of Racial Discrimination," 125 U. Pennsylvania L. Rev. (1977); Michael J. Perry, "Modern Equal Protection: A Conceptualization and Appraisal," 79 Columbia L. Rev. 1023, 1036–42 (1979).

4. See Richard L. Aynes, "Constricting the Law of Freedom: Justice Miller, the Fourteenth Amendment, and the *Slaughter-House Cases*," 70 Chicago-Kent L. Rev. 627 (1994).

5. For the historically accurate reading of the equal protection provision, see ch. 3.

6. A terminological clarification might be helpful here. I do not use the terms constitutional "provision" and constitutional "norm" as different ways of saying the same thing. When I say, for example, "the equal protection *provision*", I mean this text or language: "No state shall . . . deny to any person within its jurisdiction the equal protection of the laws." In the parlance of chapter 2: In saying "the equal protection *provision*", I refer to a part of the constitutional text. By contrast, in saying "the equal protection norm established by 'We the people'", I refer to a part of the Constitution; I mean the norm that "We the people" (probably) understood (or would have understood) the equal protection provision to communicate—which, as I explained in chapter 2 we should take to be the norm that "We the people" established in making the equal protection provision a part of the constitutional text.

7. See Melissa L. Saunders, "Equal Protection, Class Legislation, and Color-blindness," 96 Michigan L. Rev. 245 (1997).

8. See Bret Boyce, "Originalism and the Fourteenth Amendment," 33 Wake Forest L. Rev. 909, 969–70 n. 304 (1998).

9. See ch. 3, section V.

10. 388 U.S. 1, 10 (1967) (emphasis added).

11. Recent examples include: Richard A. Posner, "Bork and Beethoven," 42 Stanford L. Rev. 1365, 1374 (1990); Lino A. Graglia, "Constitutional Interpretation," 44 Syracuse L. Rev. 631, 637 (1994); Richard E. Morgan, "Coming Clean About *Brown*," City Journal, Summer 1996, at 42. See also Michael J. Perry, The Constitution, the Courts, and Human Rights 1–2 (1982). (I later saw the light. See Michael J. Perry, "*Brown, Bolling*, and Originalism," 20 Southern Illinois L. Rev. 53 (1995).)

12. Michael W. McConnell, "Originalism and the Desegregation Decisions," 81 Virginia L. Rev. 947, 952 (1995).

13. Thus, Lino Graglia, Richard Morgan, and Richard Posner are simply wrong in their judgments about the Court's ruling in *Brown*. See n. 11.

John Harrison has written: "Schools financed by general taxation are very probably a privilege of citizens." Harrison, "Reconstructing the Privileges or Immunities Clause," n. 2, at 1462–63. But it makes no difference whether or not the schools—or any other public benefit, like a public park or a public beach—are financed by general taxation. Suppose a hugely wealthy benefactor gives a state all the money it needs to provide its (young) citizens with a free elementary and secondary public education. If the state then proceeds (with the blessing of the benefactor) to give access to such an education to its white citizens—an education wholly unsupported by taxation—it may not deny such access to its nonwhite citizens, because notwithstanding the fact that it is unsupported by taxation, access to a free public education is a privilege that the state is bestowing on (some of) its citizens, and under the privileges or immunities norm established by "We the people", no state may distribute a privilege or immunity to its citizens on a racist basis. Cf. John Harrison, "Equality, Race Discrimination, and the Fourteenth Amendment," 13 Constitutional Commentary 243 & n. 4 (1996) (suggesting that "public education is a privilege of state citizenship within the meaning of the Privileges or Immunities Clause").

14. See n. 2.

15. See ch. 3, section V.

16. 163 U.S. 537 (1896).

17. See 163 U.S. at 552–64.

18. For a critical comment on the Court's decision in *Plessy*, see McConnell, "Originalism and the Desegregation Decisions," n. 12, at 1120–31.

19. 388 U.S. 1 (1967).

20. Even Hadley Arkes, one of the *First Things* symposiasts who charged the modern Supreme Court with judicial usurpation, has acknowledged the point. See Hadley Arkes, "Scalia Contra Mundum," 21 Harvard J. L. & Public Policy 231, 241–42 (1997).

21. McConnell, "Originalism and the Desegregation Decisions," n. 12, at 955–56. See also Daniel A. Farber, William N. Eskridge, Jr., & Philip P. Frickey, eds., Constitutional Law: Themes for the Constitution's Third Century 82, 83 (1993).

22. McConnell, "Originalism and the Desegregation Decisions," n. 12, at 956. See also Farber et al., n. 21, at 82–83.

23. McConnell, "Originalism and the Desegregation Decisions," n. 12, at 1140.

24. See Michael W. McConnell, "The Asymmetricality of Constitutional Discourse," in Integrity and Conscience 300, 312 (Ian Shapiro & Robert Adams eds., 1998): "[M]y thesis has [not] been conclusively established. As with most interesting issues, there are plausible arguments on both sides. But I think enough has been said to show that the historical case for *Brown* is based on more than 'wishful' thinking or 'self-deception'." For responses to McConnell's argument, see Raoul Berger, "The 'Original Intent'—As Perceived by Michael McConnell," 91 Northwestern U. L. Rev. 242 (1996); Michael J. Klarman, "*Brown*, Originalism, and Constitutional Theory: A Response to Professor McConnell," 81 Virginia L. Rev. 1881 (1995); Earl M. Maltz, "Originalism and the Desegregation Decisions—A Response to Professor McConnell," 13 Constitutional Commentary 223 (1996). For McConnell's replies to Karman and Maltz, see Michael W. McConnell, "The Originalist Justification for *Brown*: A Reply to Professor Klarman," 81 Virginia L. Rev. 1937 (1995); Michael W. McConnell, "Segregation and the Original Understanding: A Reply to Professor Maltz," 13 Constitutional Commentary 233 (1996). See also McConnell, "The Asymmetricality of Constitutional Discourse," this n., at 307–12. For a suggestion that McConnell's history is of the "law office" variety, see Mark Tushnet, "Interdisciplinary Legal Scholarship: The Case of History-in-Law," 71 Chicago-Kent L. Rev. 909 (1996).

25. Cf. Farber et al., n. 21, at 145 (relying on Herbert Hovenkamp, "Social Science and Segregation Before *Brown*, 1985 Duke L. J. 624): "In the nineteenth century, even 'progressives,' such as the Radical Republicans who pushed through the Fourteenth Amendment, often believed that the white race was different and superior to the black race and that 'mixing of the races' was a bad idea mainly because it would lead to interracial marriages, which were widely considered to produce defective children and even to 'dilute' the white race." Cf. Louisiana [Catholic] Bishops, "Racism's Assumption That Some Are Superior," 26 Origins 526 (1997): "Contemporary scientific research on the degree of genetic variations in people indicates that almost all genetic diversity is accounted for by variations *within* populations rather than by differences *between* populations. Individual variations in human DNA profiles overwhelm any interpopulation differences, no matter how the populations are ethnically or racially classified. Therefore, the superiority or inferiority of races cannot be sustained by genetics." The position of the Louisiana Catholic Bishops is substantially identical to the position articulated in the Draft Statement on "Race" 1997) of the American Anthropological Association, which I quoted in n. 1.

26. Cf. McConnell, "Originalism and the Desegregation Decisions," n. 12, at 1101: "It is widely agreed among originalists [of whom McConnell is one of the most respected] that the intentions or understandings of the framers regarding a specific issue, while informative, are not ultimately authoritative, for it is their understanding of the constitutional principles embodied in the constitutional provision—not their analysis of a particular legal phenomenon—that is controlling." (I have emphasized this point earlier in this book. See ch. 2, section II.B.)

27. See, e.g., Adarand Constructors, Inc. v. Pena, 515 U.S. 200, 213 et seq. (1995). According to the Court, racist laws, rules, and policies of state government violate the equal protection norm of the Fourteenth Amendment. However, the Court's position involves a misreading—a *compensating* misreading—of the text of the equal protection provision. See n. 5.

28. 347 U.S. 497, 500 (1954).

29. 320 U.S. 81 (1944).

30. 323 U.S. 214 (1944).

31. The Court's decision in *Korematsu* is notorious. In a dissenting opinion, Justice Murphy argued that the military exclusion order at issue in *Korematsu* "goes over 'the very brink of constitutional power' and falls into the ugly abyss of racism." Murphy then claimed that in sustaining the order, the majority had participated in "the legalization of racism." Id. at 242.

In Adarand Contructors, Inc. v. Pena, 515 U.S. 200, 213 (1995), the Court noted that "[t]hrough the [early] 1940s, this Court had routinely taken the view in non-race-related cases that, '[u]nlike the Fourteenth Amendment, the Fifth contains no equal protection clause and it provides no guaranty against discriminatory legislation by Congress.'" By the mid-1970s, the Court's position was that the Fifth Amendment not only provides a "guaranty" against discriminatory congressional legislation and other discriminatory action by the national government, but that it provides the very same protection against such action that the Fourteenth Amendment provides against discriminatory state action. "[I]n 1975, the Court stated explicitly that 'this Court's approach to Fifth Amendment equal protection claims has always been precisely the same as to equal protection claims under the Fourteenth Amendment.'" 515 U.S. at 218.

32. Or *some* citizens: *white* citizens.

33. See John C. Harrison, "Utopia's Law, Politics' Constitution," 19 Harvard J. L. & Public Policy 917, 921–22 (1996):

> [Ronald] Dworkin locates the requirement that the national government comply with the abstract principles of liberty and equality in the Fifth Amendment Due Process Clause . . . Dworkin apparently means to assert that "deprived of liberty" means "subject to a law forbidding certain conduct," and that "without due process of law" means "not on the basis of morally illegitimate governmental decisions."
>
> The Fifth Amendment was proposed by the First Congress in 1789 and came into effect through state ratifications in 1791. The phrase "deprived" of liberty referred to physical restraint and "due process of law" referred to procedure. The claim that anyone thought at the time that the clause meant what Dworkin says it meant lacks historical support. Fifth Amendment substantive due process is nonsense as a matter of the original understanding, and Fifth Amendment general equality is nonsense on stilts.

See also id. at 922–23.

34. John Hart Ely, too, has concluded that "[h]ope for responsible application of an [antidiscrimination] concept to the federal government may . . . lie, if anywhere, in . . . the Ninth Amendment." John Hart Ely, Democracy and Distrust: A Theory of Judicial Review 33 (1980). In addition to the modest Ninth Amendment strategy I have recommended here, consider the complementary strategy I have sketched elsewhere:

> [T]he command of the First Amendment is directed only at *Congress*— and even then only at congressional *legislation*. [The First Amendment begins with the words "Congress shall make no law . . ."] Is there a basis in . . . the Constitution for extending the command of the First Amendment beyond Congress to the other two branches of the national government? " 'Congress' does not on its face refer to the president, the courts, or the legions that manage the Executive Branch, and 'law' only arguably includes administrative orders or congressional investigations. Freedom of political association, which (without serious controversy) has been held to be fully protected, is not even mentioned in the document . . . It requires a theory to get us where the courts have gone." [Ely, this note, at 105.] Is there such a "theory"? The Ninth Amendment states: "The enumeration in the Constitution, of certain rights, shall not be construed to deny or disparage others retained by the people." If the Constitution protects a right to a fundamental human freedom, like the freedom of religion or the freedom of speech, against one branch of the national government (e.g., Congress), perhaps a right to that freedom against the other two branches ought to be deemed an unenumerated constitutional right "retained by the people"—*unless* there is a reason for concluding that the freedom, even though it is already constitutionally protected against the one branch of the national government, ought not to be constitutionally protected against the other two branches.

Michael J. Perry, Religion in Politics: Constitutional and Moral Perspectives 10–11 (1997) (passages rearranged).

35. Thomas McAffee has argued that the Ninth Amendment term "rights" was understood to mean something other than what we today understand the term to mean. See Thomas B. McAffee, "The Original Meaning of the Ninth Amendment," 90 Columbia L. Rev. 1215 (1990); Thomas B. McAffee, "The Bill of Rights, Social Contract Theory, and the Rights 'Retained' by the People," 16 Southern Illinois L. J. 267 (1992); Thomas B. McAffee, "Prolegomena to a Meaningful Debate on the 'Unwritten Constitution' Thesis," 61 U. Cincinnati L. Rev. 107 (1992). See also Thomas B. McAffee, "A Critical Guide to the Ninth Amendment," 69 Temple L. Rev. 61 (1996). In my view, the historical record does not contravene the claim that the term "rights" was understood to mean substantially what we today understand the term to mean, *even if it was also understood to mean something else*. See Michael J. Pery, The Constitution in the Courts: Law or Politics? 63–68 (1994). See also Randy E. Barnett, ed., The Rights Retained by the People: The History and Meaning of the Ninth Amendment (1989); Randy E. Barnett, ed., The Rights Retained by the People: The History and Meaning of the Ninth Amendment, vol. 2 (1993).

McAffee properly bears the burden of proof with respect to the proposition that the Ninth Amendment term "rights" was understood to mean something completely different from what we today take to be the term's principal meaning. See Richard S. Kay, "Adherence to the Original Intentions in Constitutional Adjudication: Three Objections and Responses," 82 Northwestern U. L. Rev. 226, 235 (1988): "Certainly when most readers agree that a particular clause or phrase means one thing, the burden of persuasion ought to be on the advocate of some other meaning. Such a presumption is fully consistent with [the originalist approach to constitutional interpretation] and a convenient rule of administration." See also Michael W. McConnell, "Free Exercise Revisionism and the *Smith* Decision," 57 U. Chicago L. Rev. 1109, 1115–16 (1990) (discussing the free exercise provision): "While we cannot rule out the possibility that the term 'prohibiting' might impliedly be limited to laws that prohibit the exercise of religion in a particular way—that is, in a discriminatory fashion—we should at least begin with the presumption that the words carry as broad a meaning as their natural usage."

36. See the "thought experiment" at the end of chapter 3.

37. It bears repeating that in American constitutional culture, any justification of a basic constitutional premise—even of one that is, for us, bedrock—must be, at bottom, textualist. As I noted in chapter 2, American constitutional culture includes a textualist sensibility: "[J]udges sometimes admit that constitutional interpretation is sensitive to historical evolution and that history adds a 'gloss' on the text. But they never admit to deriving the authority for their decisions from outside the constitutional text. . . . Instead, any new result is unfailingly presented as a new and better *interpretation* of the text itself. . . . This behavior of judges is very significant because it expresses their belief that purely noninterpretive [i.e., nontextualist] review would constitute an abuse of their power and undermine the legitimacy of judicial review. In this belief, moreover, they are very likely to be right." Andrezj Rapaczynski, "The Ninth Amendment and the Unwritten Constitution: The Problems of Constitutional Interpretation," 64 Chicago-Kent L. Rev. 177, 192 (1988).

Therefore, if it were the case that no norm established by "We the people" warranted the premise that the same prohibition on discrimination that applies to state government under the Fourteenth Amendment also applies to the national government, the Court would nonetheless need a textual hook on which to hang the premise. Whatever the original understanding of the language of the Ninth Amendment (see n. 35), given the meaning that the language will bear—given the meaning that can be imputed to the language—the Ninth Amendment is one obvious choice for the textual hook on which to hang the premise. In chapter 2, I said that "[i]t does not seem especially problematic, as a political-moral matter, for the Court to refer a premise never established by 'We the people' to a linguistically opportune provision of the Constitution—a provision that will bear the meaning in question, even if the provision was not understood to have that meaning by the generation of 'We the people' that put the provision into the Constitution—*if the premise is truly constitutional bedrock for us the people of the United States now living.* Can't we all agree that it is better to cultivate, by accommodating, the textualist sensibility of American constitutional culture, thereby maintaining rather than relaxing the sensibility as a restraint on the awesome power of judicial review?" Ch. 2, section II.A.

38. See n. 35.

39. For a thoughtful, critical comment on my Ninth Amendment rationale for the Court's decision in *Bolling v. Sharpe*, see Stephen A. Siegel, "The Federal Government's Power to Enact Color-Conscious Laws: An Originalist Inquiry," 92 Northwestern U. L. Rev. 477, 536–41 (1998).

40. The definition of "affirmative action" I employ for the purposes of this chapter is narrower than some. "'Affirmative action' means many different things. Among them: outreach to broaden the pool of eligible individuals to include more members of specific groups; targeted or compensatory training to upgrade the qualifications of individuals in these groups; goals and timetables to measure progress; preferences; set-asides; and actual quotas." William A. Galston, "An Affirmative Action Status Report: Evidence and Options," 17 Philosophy & Public Policy 2 (Special Issue, Winter/Spring 1997).

41. "The Affirmative Action Debate," 17 Philosophy & Public Policy 1 (Special Issue, Winter/Spring 1997) (quoting Glenn Loury).

42. For a recent discussion, see "The Affirmative Action Debate," 17 Philosophy & Public Policy 2–38 (Special Issue, Winter/Spring 1997) (articles by William A. Galston, Robert K. Fulliwinder, Judith Lichtenberg & David Luban, David Wasserman, and Owen M. Fiss).

43. Not that morality—political morality—and constitutionality are entirely separate realms.

44. See ch. 3, section III.

45. See nn. 68–69 & accompanying text. See also J.M. Balkin, "The Constitution of Status," 106 Yale L. J. 2313, 2352–53 (1997):

> Admission preferences that attempt to increase the number of historically disadvantaged minorities . . . do not single out whites as social inferiors.
> . . .
> [They] clearly do not send the message that racial minorities are superior human beings by virtue of their identity. Whites may grumble that blacks and other minorities are getting "special treatment," but they would hardy view these preferences as a governmental assertion that blacks have higher social status or have a greater share of positive qualities and social esteem. To the contrary, so powerful are the social meanings of race and ethnicity in this country that affirmative action preferences often create the opposite social meaning among whites. They see these preferences as further evidence of the inferiority and unworthiness of racial and ethnic minorities.

46. Jeremy Rabkin, "Private Preferences: Why Affirmative Action Won't Disappear Anytime Soon," American Spectator, November 1998, 62, 63.

47. See ch. 3, n. 96 & accompanying text.

48. See Adarand Constructors, Inc. v. Pena, 515 U.S. 200, 239 (1995) (Scalia, J., concurring in part and concurring in the judgment).

49. 388 U.S. 1, 10 (1967) (emphasis added).

50. See Shaw v. Reno, 509 U.S. 630, 642 (1993): "This Court has never held that race-conscious state decisionmaking is impermissible in *all* circumstances." See generally Andrew Kull, The Color-Blind Constitution (1992).

51. Adarand Constructors, Inc. v. Pena, 515 U.S. 200, 239 (1995) (Scalia, J., concurring in part and concurring in the judgment).

52. See id. at 240. (Thomas, J., concurring in part and concurring in the judgment). Remarkably, Justice Thomas said in his opinion that he believes that there is a "'moral [and] constitutional equivalence' . . . between laws designed to subjugate a race and those designed to foster some current notions of equality." In Justice Thomas' view, the discrimination involved in government-sponsored affirmative action "is just as noxious as discrimination inspired by malicious prejudice." Id.

53. See, e.g., Kull, n. 50, at vii: "[T]he evidence I adduce tends strongly to refute [the contention that] the Fourteenth Amendment was intended by its framers to require color blindness on the part of government . . ." See also Jed Rubenfeld, "Affirmative Action," 107 Yale L. J. 427, 429–32 (1997) (presenting statutory evidence contemporaneous with the framing and ratifying of the Fourteenth Amendment that the Amendment was not understood to require color blindness on the part of government).

54. 914 Statutes 27 (1866).

55. For a brief recounting of all this, see ch. 3, section I. Michael Curtis has reported that Senator Lyman Trumbull of Illinois, who authored the Act and "managed [it] in the Senate[,] referred to *the discriminatory Black Codes* and said, 'The purpose of the [Civil Rights] Bill . . . is to destroy *all these discriminations and to carry into effect the [Thirteenth] Amendment.*'" Michael Kent Curtis, "Resurrecting the Privileges or Immunities Clause and Revising the *Slaughter-House Cases* Without Exhuming *Lochner*: Individual Rights and the Fourteenth Amendment," 38 Boston College L. Rev. 1, 38 (1996) (emphasis added).

For an example of someone who seems to argue that the Fourteenth Amendment was meant to ban certain laws and practices based on skin color *without regard to whether the laws and practices were racist*, see John Harrison, "If the Eye Offend Thee, Turn Off the Color," 91 Michigan L. Rev. 1213, 1234 (1993) (contending that section one of the Fourteenth Amendment was meant to ban all "discrimination", including all "race discrimination", albeit "only with respect to a limited set of rights—the privileges and immunities of citizens and the protection of the laws").

56. As Frank Easterbrook has observed, "[Justice Scalia's approach to the question of the constitutionality of affirmative action] reduces judicial *discretion* but increases judicial *power* relative to the other branches." Judge Easterbrook continues: "It is the claim of judicial power that must be justified; although a reduction in judicial discretion is desirable, we do not get there unless the scope of the authority has first been established." Frank Easterbrook, "Abstraction and Authority," 59 U. Chicago L. Rev. 349, 377 (1992). Cf. Kull, n. 50, at 124: "If we ought to refuse to let judges distinguish the reasonable from the unreasonable racial classification it is largely because history, *Plessy* [*v. Ferguson*, 163 U.S. 537 (1896)] included, shows that the courts are not to be trusted on the subject and that we would be better off with a per se prohibition. If on the other hand, when all is said and done, we are willing or even relieved to let judges decide these matters, then [Justice] Harlan's syllogism [in *Plessy*] falls, and much of the argument for a color-blind Constitution falls with it."

57. See n. 64.

58. As the Court observed in 1995, most of its racial discrimination cases have "involved classifications burdening groups that have suffered discrimination in our society. In 1978, the Court confronted the question whether race-based governmental action designed to *benefit* such groups should also be subject to 'the most rigid scrutiny'." Adarand Constructors, Inc. v. Pena, 515 U.S. 200, 218 (1995). The 1978 case was *Regents of University of California v. Bakke*, 438 U.S. 265.

59. See, e.g., McLaughlin v. Florida, 379 U.S. 184, 191–92 (1964); Loving v. Virginia, 388 U.S. 1, 11 (1967).

60. See n. 64.

61. Adarand Constructors, Inc. v. Pena, 515 U.S. 200, 226 (1995). Referring to the Court's 1967 decision in *Loving v. Virginia*, 388 U.S. 1, but in a statement that applies no less to the Court's decision in *Adarand*, Andrew Kull has written: "[B]y 1967, if not before, the Court had concluded that it would be unwise to accept the

restrictions that a color-blind Constitution would place on its power to pick and choose among racial classifications. In place of a rule of color blindness, *Loving* announced a pledge of the Court's assiduous oversight of the politics of race." Kull, n. 50, at 171. See id. at 164–81.

62. See Adarand Constructors, Inc. v. Pena, 515 U.S. 200, 237 (1995). See also id. at 275 (Ginsburg, J., dissenting, joined by Breyer, J.) (suggesting that strict scrutiny should be " 'fatal' for classifications burdening groups that have suffered discrimination in our society" but not for affirmative-action programs).

63. Adarand Constructors, Inc. v. Pena, 515 U.S. 200, 243, 245 (1995) (Stevens, J., dissenting, joined by Ginsburg, J.). See also Shaw v. Hunt, 517 U.S. 899, 116 S. Ct. 1894, 1907 (1996) (Stevens, J., dissenting, joined by Ginsburg & Breyer, JJ.): "[T]he Court's aggressive supervision of state action designed to accommodate the political concerns of historically disadvantaged minority groups is seriously misguided. A majority's attempt to enable the minority to participate more effectively in the process of democratic governance should not be viewed with the same hostility that is appropriate for oppressive and exclusionary abuses of political power."

64. Id. at 227. In Wittmer v. Peters, 87 F.3d 916, 918 (7th Cir. 1996), Judge Richard Posner wrote: "While we may assume that a practice that is subject to the skeptical, questioning, beady-eyed scrutiny that the law requires when public officials use race to allocate burdens or benefits is not illegal per se, it can survive that intense scrutiny only if the defendants show that they are motivated by a truly powerful and worthy concern and that the racial measure they have adopted is a plainly apt response to that concern. They must show that they had to do something and had no alternative to what they did. The concern and the response, moreover, must be substantiated and not merely asserted."

65. Adarand Constructors, Inc. v. Pena, 515 U.S. 200, 247 n. 5 (1995) (Stevens, J., dissenting, joined by Ginsburg, J.).

66. Id. at 218 (quoting Justice Powell's statement in Regents of University of California v. Bakke, 438 U.S. 265, 289–90 (1978) (speaking for himself and Justice White)).

67. In its opinion in *Adarand*, the Court offered this explanation for subjecting government-sponsored affirmative action to strict scrutiny:

> Absent searching judicial inquiry into the justification for such race-based measures, there is simply no way of determining what classifications are "benign" or "remedial" and what classifications are in fact motivated by illegitimate notions of racial inferiority or simple racial politics. Indeed, the purpose of strict scrutiny is to "smoke out" illegitimate uses of race by assuring that the legislative body is pursuing a goal important enough to warrant use of a highly suspect tool. The test also insures that the means chosen "fit" this compelling goal so closely that there is little or no possibility that the motive for the classification was illegitimate racial prejudice or stereotype.

515 U.S. 200, 226 (1995). But see 515 U.S. at 245–46 (Stevens, J., dissenting, joined by Ginsburg, J.):

> The Court's explanation for treating dissimilar race-based decisions as though they were equally objectionable is a supposed inability to differentiate between "invidious" and "benign" discrimination. But the

term "affirmative action" is common and well understood. Its presence in everyday parlance shows that people understand the difference between good intentions and bad. As with any legal concept, some cases may be difficult to classify, but our equal protection jurisprudence has identified a critical difference between state action that imposes burdens on a disfavored few and state action that benefits the few "in spite of" its adverse affects on the many.

Cf. Rubenfeld, n. 53, at 439: "[T]he idea that the proponents of affirmative action programs are 'in fact motivated' by 'illegitimate notions of racial inferiority' is so implausible that the Court has never taken it seriously."

68. Robert K. Fullinwider, "Civil Rights and Racial Preferences: A Legal History of Affirmative Action," 17 Philosophy & Public Policy 9, 19 (Special Issue, Winter/Spring 1997).

69. Stephen L. Carter, "When Victims Happen to Be Black," 97 Yale L. J. 420, 433–34 (1988).

70. See Rubenfeld, n. 53, at 428:

[T]he Court's recent affirmative action decisions have consummated a remarkable but unremarked-upon transformation in the entire analytic structure of heightened scrutiny doctrine. One powerful function of strict scrutiny has always been that of "smoking out" invidious purposes masquerading behind putatively legitimate public policy. But under today's affirmative action doctrine, strict scrutiny has become altogether different. It has become a cost-benefit test measuring whether a law that falls (according to the Court itself) squarely within the prohibition of the equal protection guarantee is justified by the specially important social gains that it will achieve.

See also David Chang, "Discriminatory Impact, Affirmative Action, and Innocent Victims: Judicial Conservatism or Conservative Justices?" 91 Columbia L. Rev. 790, 831 (1991):

Concern for the "innocent white victim" of affirmative action addressed explicitly in *Wygant* [*v. Jackson Board of Education*, 476 U.S. 267 (1986)] as a basis for invalidating an affirmative action program is implicitly reflected in the conditions that [several justices] develop in [*Richmond v. J. A. Croson Co.*, 488 U.S. 469 (1980)] for restrictively defining when the purpose of redressing the effects of past racial discrimination is permissible. These conditions have nothing to do with determining whether the government acted because of impermissible racial animus, favoritism, or stereotype. They have everything to do with whether individual justices view the state's redefinition of policies allocating public goods as wise or "fair." Political conservatism, rather than judicial conservatism, pervades the Court's restrictions on legislative discretion to redress the effects of past racial discrimination.

71. On "racially selective sympathy and indifference", see Paul Brest, "Foreword: In Defense of the Antidiscrimination Principle," 90 Harvard L. Rev. 1 (1976).

72. Shaw v. Reno, 509 U.S. 630, 657 (1993). In *Shaw v. Reno*, the Court wrote: "Racial classifications with respect to voting carry particular dangers. Racial gerrymandering, even for remedial purposes, may balkanize us into competing racial

factions; it threatens to carry us further from the goal of a political system in which race no longer matters—a goal that the Fourteenth and Fifteenth Amendments embody, and to which the Nation continues to aspire. It is for these reasons that race-based districting by our state legislatures demands close judicial scrutiny." 509 U.S. at 657. For the Court's most recent statements about "race-based districting", see Shaw v. Hunt, 517 U.S. 899, 116 S. Ct. 1894 (1996); Bush v. Vera, 517 U.S. 952, 116 S. Ct. 1941 (1996).

73. United Jewish Organizations of Williamsburg, Inc. v. Carey, 430 U.S. 144, 173 (1977) (Brennan, J., concurring in part).

74. Adarand Constructors, Inc. v. Pena, 515 U.S. 200, 239 (1995) (Scalia, J., concurring in part and concurring in the judgment).

75, See id. at 229 (majority op'n): " '[E]ven though it is not the actual predicate for this legislation, a statute of this kind inevitably is perceived by many as resting on an assumption that those who are granted this special preference are less qualified in some respect that is identified purely by their race. Because that perception . . . can only exacerbate rather than reduce racial prejudice, it will delay the time when race will become a truly irrelevant, or at least insignificant, factor.'" (Quoting Justice Stevens' dissenting opinion in Fullilove v. Klutznick, 448 U.S. 448, 545 (1980).)

76. See Adarand Constructors, Inc. v. Pena, 515 U.S. 200, 241 (1995) (Thomas, J., concurring in part and concurring in the judgment):

> [T]here can be no doubt that racial paternalism and its unintended consequences can be as poisonous and pernicious as any other form of discrimination. So-called "benign" discrimination teaches many that because of chronic and apparently immutable handicaps, minorities cannot compete with them without their patronizing indulgence. Inevitably, such programs engender attitudes of superiority or, alternatively, provoke resentment among those who believe that they have been wronged by the government's use of race. These programs stamp minorities with a badge of inferiority and may cause them to develop dependencies or to adopt an attitude that they are "entitled" to preferences.

77. See United Jewish Organizations v. Carey, 430 U.S. 144, 174 (1977) (Brennan, J., concurring in part). The racial resentment/division is exacerbated if and to the extent some of the beneficiaries of an affirmative action program are seen to be relatively advantaged in their material (and related) circumstances as compared to some of those who are, or might be, "victimized" in consequence of the program—for example, the upper-middle-class African American student who in consequence of an affirmative action program easily gets into a highly desirable state university as compared to the working-class white student who, perhaps in consequence of the affirmative action program, must settle for a less prestigious state institution. See n. 108.

78. In *Adarand*, the Court expressed a concern about racial politics in this passage: "Absent searching judicial inquiry into the justification for such race-based measures, there is simply no way of determining what classifications are 'benign' or 'remedial' and what classifications are in fact motivated by illegitimate notions of racial inferiority *or simple racial politics*." 515 U.S. 200, 226 (1995) (emphasis added).

79. Galston, n. 40, at 6.

80. See n. 115 & accompanying text.

81. See ch. 2, section I.C.

82. But cf. Houston Contractors Association v. Metropolitan Transit Authority

of Harris County, 984 F. Supp. 1027, 1029 (S.D. Tex. 1997): "Race is politics not biology. . . . Because race is inescapably arbitrary, basing governmental action on race offends the American Constitution."

83. For example, in his introduction to a symposium on "Race and the Law", Douglas Kmiec wrote that "[i]n the Catholic, if not larger Judeo-Christian tradition, race is morally irrelevant. We are all created in God's image, and therefore skin color tells us nothing about an individual's intellectual, spiritual, or moral worth." Douglas W. Kmiec, "Foreword: The Abolition of Public Racial Preference —An Invitation to Private Racial Sensitivity," 11 Notre Dame J. L., Ethics & Public Policy 1, 1 (1997). In a footnote, Kmiec presented two quotes:

> "God created man in his own image, in the image of God he created him, male and female he created them." Genesis 1:27 (New International Version). "God's word in Genesis announces that all men and women are created in God's image; not just *some* races and racial types, but *all* bear the imprint of the Creator and are enlivened by the breath of His one Spirit." National Conference of Catholic Bishops, "Brothers and Sisters to Us," para. 7 (Nov. 14, 1979).

Id. at 1 n. 1.

84. See nn. 72–74 & accompanying text.

85. David Wasserman, "Diversity and Stereotyping," 17 Philosophy & Public Policy 32, 34 (Special Issue, Winter/Spring 1997). In his interesting essay, Wasserman discusses the way in which "generalizations about the experience or perspective of minority candidates for faculty positions function as ideological straitjackets." The quoted language is at p. 34 of Wasserman's essay.

86. For an argument, however, that the Court ought not to subject government reliance on affirmative action to strict scrutiny, see Rubenfeld, n. 53.

87. But see Houston Contractors Association v. Metropolitan Transit Authority of Harris County, 984 F. Supp. 1027, 1036 (S.D. Tex. 1997): "Posturing about historic wrongs as a cloak for new arbitrary power does not do justice. The solution to racism is not more racism."

88. 517 U.S. 899, 116 S. Ct. 1894, 1902–3 (1996) (internal quotes omitted).

89. Owen Fiss, "Affirmative Action as a Strategy of Justice," 17 Philosophy & Public Policy 37 (Special Issue, Winter/Spring 1997).

90. Wittmer v. Peters, 87 F.3d 916, 918 (7th Cir. 1996).

91. Id. at 919.

92. Id. at 919.

93. Id. at 920.

94. The Office of the Solicitor General of the U.S. Department of Justice wrote, in an amicus curiae supporting affirmance in *Piscataway Township Board of Education v. Taxman* (U.S. Supreme Court, No. 96–679), that

> [T]here are some circumstances—not presented by this case—in which an employer should be permitted to demonstrate that taking race into account for nonremedial purposes is narrowly tailored to further a compelling interest. For example, if an undercover officer is needed to infiltrate a racially homogeneous gang, a law enforcement agency must have the flexibility to assign an officer of the same race to that task. Against the backdrop of racial unrest, a diverse police force may be essential to secure

the public support and cooperation that is necessary for preventing and solving crime. Prison institutions may find it impossible to cope with racial tensions without an integrated work force. And school districts may responsibly conclude that a diverse faculty is essential to dispel students' stereotypes and promote mutual understanding and respect. The careful, tailored use of race to serve similarly compelling goals would satisfy the Constitution's strict scrutiny standard.

Brief at 8–9. See also id. at 18–23. But, *what* goals are "similarly compelling"? Indeed, is "a [racially] diverse faculty"—or a racially diverse student body—as essential as a racially diverse police force?

(The Piscataway Township Board of Education was persuaded to drop its appeal of the case (which it lost in the court below; see Taxman v. Board of Education, 91 F.3d 1547 (3d Cir. 1996)) while the case was pending before the Supreme Court. The groups that persuaded the Board of Education to drop its appeal—and that supplied the money the Board of Education needed to pay damages to the plaintiff, Sharon Taxman—were all supporters of affirmative action who feared that the Court's decision in the case would have been adverse to affirmative action programs everywhere. See Larry Reibstein, "A Tactical Retreat in a Race Case: Civil-Rights Leaders Buy Themselves Out of a Bind," Newsweek, Dec. 1, 1997, at 40.)

95. 78 F.3d 932, 935 (5th Cir. 1996).

96. *Hopwood* has attracted a great deal of attention. See, e.g., Ellis Cose, "The Color Bind," Newsweek, May 12, 1997, at 58; S.C. Gwynne, "Back to the Future," Time, June 2, 1997, at 48. On the consequences of the court's ruling in *Hopwood* and of California's Proposition 209 (see n. 116), see Jerome Karabel, "Reclaiming the High Ground: Can Affirmative Action Survive?" Tikkun, September/October 1997, at 29:

> Thanks to the University of California and the University of Texas, we now have our first glimpse of what a post-affirmative action America might look like. At the University of Texas Law School, in recent years the nation's leading supplier of minority lawyers, the number of African Americans in the entering class has plummeted from 21 last year to three this fall. At UC Berkeley's Boalt School of Law, the figures are even more startling: only 14 black students were admitted (compared to 75 last year), and not one plans to attend. Boalt will, however, have one entering African American this year—a student accepted last year who deferred admission. As Amy Wallace of the *Los Angeles Times* pointed out, this will leave Boalt with the same number of blacks in the entering class as the University of Mississippi in 1962.

97. 78 F.3d at 945.

98. Robert K. Fullinwider, "Diversity and Affirmative Action," 17 Philosophy & Public Policy 26 (Special Issue, Winter/Spring 1997).

99. Id.

100. Indeed, this is substantially what one of the three judges in *Hopwood* said. See id. at 962, 966 (Wiener, J., specially concurring). For a defense of the "illsuited" point, see Fullinwider, "Diversity and Affirmative Action," n. 98.

101. Id. at 946 (quoting Richard A. Posner, "The DeFunis Case and the Constitutionality of Preferential Treatment of Racial Minorities," 1974 Sup. Ct. Rev. 12 (1974)).

102. Fullinwider, "Diversity and Affirmative Action," n. 98, at 31. See Wasserman, n. 85, at 34 et seq. (discussing the way in which "generalizations about the experience or perspective of minority candidates for faculty positions [and minority candidates for other positions, including places in a student body] function as ideological straitjackets").

103. Cf. Cose, n. 96, at 59: "Heavy dependence on test scores . . . is typical of selective law schools—as well as of medical schools and elite universities. And without some form of affirmative action, many blacks and Latinos who currently get into such institutions are certain to be excluded."

104. Or by relying on different standardized tests: ones designed to test "practical" intelligence and "creative" intelligence as well as "analytical" intelligence. See Ethan Bronner, "Colleges Look for Answers to Racial Gaps in Testing," New York Times, Nov. 8, 1997, at A1, A8: "[Arguing] that current standardized tests measure a specific, static kind of intelligence when there are, in fact, several different kinds[,] Professor [Robert J.] Sternberg [of Yale University] has created a model of a three-pronged intelligence, analytical, creative, and practical, and says that when students take the intelligence tests he designed, high scorers are more racially and ethnically diverse."

105. For presentation and discussion of a fuller list, see Fullinwider, "Diversity and Affirmative Action," n. 98, at 27 (age, region, political affiliation, nation, occupation, urban v. rural upbringing, historical experience, religion, military service, special aptitudes and skills).

106. See Cose, n. 96, at 59:

> Serious researchers dismiss the notion that affirmative action based on socioeconomic status can be much of a substitute. A wide-ranging statistical analysis by Thomas Kane of Harvard's Kennedy School of Government demonstrates what critics have long assumed: since so many poor whites and poor Asians do relatively well on standardized tests, class-based but colorblind affirmative action is more likely to help them than it is to assist poor blacks and poor Latinos—at least as long as selective schools put so much stock in tests.

See also Clarence Page, "Texas Finds a Creative Way to Retain Diversity," Chicago Tribune, June 1, 1997, at § 1, p. 23: "This year a panel of sociologists advising the Texas education commissioner predicted that substituting income or any other socioeconomic factors would just about cut current black and Latino enrollment in half. The problem is that, yes, there are a lot of poor, struggling white and Asian people, too. In fact, there are quite a few more poor white people than poor black people in America, although you'd never guess it from watching most television newscasts." Cf. Galston, n. 40, at 8: "As Glenn Loury notes, 'In 1990 black high school seniors from families with annual incomes of $70,000 or more scored an average of 854 on the SAT, compared with average scores of 855 and 879 respectively for Asian-Americans and white seniors whose families had incomes between $10,000 and $20,000 per year.'"

107. See Richard D. Kahlenberg, "In Search of Fairness: A Better Way," Washington Monthly, June 1998, at 26. (Kahlenberg criticizes the Kane study mentioned in the preceding note.) For a discussion of the effectiveness *vel non* of class-based affirmative action in enhancing the racial diversity of a student body—a discussion focused especially on the UCLA Law School's class-based affirmative action program that Kahlenberg writes about—see the articles by Deborah Mala-

mud and Richard Sander in the December 1997 issue (47:4) of the *Journal of Legal Education*.

108. "Writing in his [1996] book, *Not All Black and White: Affirmative Action and American Values*, Christopher Edley [a Harvard law professor who is himself an African American] puts one of the standard challenges this way: 'Imagine a college admissions committee trying to decide between the white daughter of an Appalachian coal miner's family and the African-American son of a successful Pittsburgh neurosurgeon. Why should the black applicant get preference over the white applicant?'" Fullinwider, "Civil Rights and Racial Preferences," n. 68, at 17.

109. In many contexts, weighting this third factor would contribute to the goal the importance of which Owen Fiss has emphasized: "eradicat[ing] caste structure by altering the social standing of . . . any group currently subordinated in society." Fiss, n. 89, at 37–38. Fiss explains: "By giving members of [subordinated groups] a greater share of the prized positions of society, we improve the relative positions of [the groups] and, in so doing, make a small but determined contribution to eliminating the caste structure." Id. at 37. But cf. Galston, n. 40, at 4 (commenting on "what Seymour Martin Lipset has characterized as 'growing differentiation' within the black community"):

> On one side, there is now a burgeoning black middle class; on the other, there are the ghetto poor, economically and socially isolated from the rest of society. These poor people belong primarily to two groups: single mothers and their minor children, and young men who have dropped out of both high school and the labor force.
>
> As numerous scholars have argued, affirmative action programs have not had significant positive consequences for the bulk of the ghetto poor, nor are they likely to. The reason is straightforward: these programs work most effectively when they remove barriers to opportunity for those who possess the credentials to succeed of who are strongly motivated to acquire them within established norms and institutions.

110. Cf. Hopwood v. Texas, 78 F.3d at 948: "In sum, the use of race to achieve a diverse student body, whether as a proxy for permissible characteristics, simply cannot be a state interest compelling enough to meet the steep standard of strict scrutiny. *These latter factors may, in fact, turn out to be substantially correlated with race, but the key is that race itself not be taken into account.*" (Emphasis added.)

For the response of the Texas legislature to the court's ruling in *Hopwood*, see Gwynne, n. 96, at 48:

> In Texas, . . . a group of minority state senators threatened to cut off funding for the University of Texas if it did not find a way to maintain minority enrollment, and the legislature just passed a bill that attempts to redress the problem by requiring state universities to automatically admit students in the top 10% of their high school classes and allowing the universities to consider "a variety of other factors" in assessing the top 15% to 25%. [Those other factors include academic record, socioeconomic status, linguistic ability, and family background.] Some schools, such as the state-owned University of Houston law school, encourage applicants to write about their family background as a way around the requirement that the application contain no "race" box to check.

Clarence Page has discussed and defended Texas' response to *Hopwood* in Page, n. 106. At the conclusion of his discussion, Page writes:

> [S]chools need more than a simple shift from racial preferences to geographic preferences in state university admissions. They also need to produce black and Latino graduates whose basic cognitive skills are adequate to compete at the mainstream college level. To meet that challenge, another affirmative action battleground, the University of California, is proposing a multimillion-dollar effort to mentor students in some of the state's poorest school districts. Even Ward Connerly, the black conservative, University of California regent who led last year's successful Proposition 209 ballot campaign to outlaw racial preferences, favors such outreach efforts. So do I. So should you.

111. 78 F.3d at 966 (Wiener, J., concurring).
112. Brief, n. 94, at 16.
113. See ch. 2, section I.C.
114. See id., section III.C.
115. Adarand Constructors, Inc. v. Pena, 515 U.S. 200, 247 n. 5 (1995) (Stevens, J., dissenting, joined by Ginsburg, J.) (emphasis added). See also Shaw v. Hunt, 517 U.S. 899, 116 S. Ct. 1894, 1922 (1996) (Stevens, J., dissenting, joined by Ginsburg & Breyer, JJ.):

> It is, of course, irrelevant whether we, as judges, deem it wise policy to create majority-minority districts as a means of assuring fair and effective representation to minority voters. We have a duty to respect Congress' considered judgment that such a policy may serve to effectuate the ends of the constitutional Amendment that it is charged with enforcing. We should also respect North Carolina's conscientious effort to conform to that congressional determination. Absent some demonstration that voters are being denied fair and effective representation as a result of their race, I find no basis for this Court's intervention into a process by which federal and state actors, both black and white, are jointly attempting to resolve difficult questions of politics and race that have long plagued North Carolina. Nor do I see how our constitutional tradition can countenance the suggestion that a State may draw unsightly lines to favor farmers or city dwellers, but not to create districts that benefit the very group whose history inspired the Amendment that the Voting Rights Act was designed to implement.

116. See California Ballot Pamphlet, General Election, Nov. 5, 1996 (enacted as California Constitution, art. I, § 31). Cf. Coalition for Economic Equity v. Wilson, 110 F.3d 1431 (9th Cir. 1997) (ruling that Proposition 209 does not violate the Fourteenth Amendment), cert. denied, 118 S. Ct. 397 (1997).
117. My suggestion that the Supreme Court (and other courts) should proceed more deferentially in the context of affirmative action than a majority of the Court seems inclined to proceed draws support from something Bob Nagel has written:

> [W]hen a society must act in some significant degree of ignorance, when it must gamble for or against a policy as significant as affirmative action, it makes sense to minimize the risks. It makes sense, that is, to proceed in many small, experimental ways. It makes sense to proceed in ways that

we can easily abandon or reverse. Institutionally, this means that affirmative action policies should be decided as far as possible at the local level. And, because courts do not easily reverse direction, it means such policies should not be decided by the courts. It makes no difference to this analysis whether a liberal judge is striking down the California Civil Rights Initiative or a conservative judge is striking down the Texas Law School's admissions program. In either case, judges are writing on constitutional stone when they quite literally do not know what they are doing.

Robert F. Nagel, "Utilitarianism Left and Right: A Response to Professor Armour," 68 U. Colorado L. Rev. 1201, 1207 (1997).

118. 515 U.S. 200, 273 (Ginsburg, J., dissenting, joined by Breyer, J.) (emphasis added). Justice Ginsburg went on to say:

Those effects, reflective of a system of racial caste only recently ended, are evident in our workplaces, markets, and neighborhoods. Job applicants with identical resumes, qualifications, and interview styles still experience different receptions, depending on their race. White and African-American consumers still encounter different deals. People of color looking for housing still face discriminatory treatment by landlords, real estate agents, and mortgage lenders. Minority entrepreneurs sometimes fail to gain contracts though they are the low bidders, and they are sometimes refused work even after winning contracts. Bias both conscious and unconscious, reflecting traditional and unexamined habits of thought, keep up barriers that must come down if equal opportunity and nondiscrimination are ever genuinely to become this country's law and practice.

Given this history and its practical consequences, Congress surely can conclude that a carefully designed affirmative action program may help to realize, finally, the "equal protection of the laws" the Fourteenth Amendment has promised since 1868.

Id. at 273–74.

Chapter 5

1. James Joyce, Ulysses 40 (Penguin ed., 1969).

2. In the late 1960s, the Court began to outlaw some instances of discrimination based on one's status as an "illegitimate" child. In the 1970s, the Court began to outlaw some instances of discrimination based on one's status as an alien. I discussed both developments in an article published in 1979: Michael J. Perry, "Modern Equal Protection: A Conceptualization and Appraisal," 79 Columbia L. Rev. 1023, 1056–60 (illegitimacy), 1060–65 (alienage).

3. And, insofar as national laws and policies are concerned, in the name of the Fifth Amendment.

4. For an important recent discussion of several relevant cases, see Kathryn Abrams, "The Constitution of Women," 48 Alabama L. Rev. 861 (1997) (the inaugural Hugo Black Lecture at the University of Alabama School of Law).

5. See ch. 3, n. 98 & accompanying text.

6. 83 U.S. (16 Wall.) 36, 110 (1872) (emphasis added).

7. Strauder v. West Virginia, 100 U.S. 303, 310 (1880) (emphasis added).

8. 83 U.S. (16 Wall.) 130, 141 (1873) (Bradley, J., joined by Swayne & Field, JJ., concurring in the judgment).

9. United States v. Virginia, 518 U.S. 515, 116 S. Ct. 2264, 2277 n. 9 (1996). I discuss *United States v. Virginia* later in this chapter.

10. We might be wrong, too, in imputing to them the norm that we do. And the fact that the norm we are imputing to them leads us to strike down laws and practices that they almost certainly would not have struck down is certainly reason enough to go back to the drawing board to check our math—to go back and see whether the norm that we are imputing to them is the norm that, all things considered, is most plausibly imputed to them. But even if, after checking our math, we conclude that the norm we are imputing to them is indeed the norm that is most plausibly imputed to them, we might nonetheless be wrong in believing what we do about the implications of the norm for some law or practice.

11. 388 U.S. 1 (1967).

12. Hadley Arkes, "Scalia Contra Mundum," 21 Harvard J. L. & Public Policy 231, 241–42 (1997).

13. See ch. 3, pp. 71–77.

14. Carter Heyward & Suzanne Hiatt, "The Trivialization of Women," 38 Christianity and Crisis 158, 160 (1978).

15. 421 U.S. 7, 14–15 (1975).

16. Michael Levin, "Vs. Ms.," in Sex Equality 216, 217–18 (J. English, ed., 1977), quoted by Kenneth L. Karst, "Foreword: Equal Citizenship Under the Fourteenth Amendment," 91 Harvard L. Rev. 1, 4 (1977) (categorizing Levin's statement as "Neanderthal").

17. David A.J. Richards, The Moral Criticism of Law 174 (1977). On Aquinas' view of women, see Paul J. Weithman, "Complementarity and Equality in the Political Thought of Thomas Aquinas," 59 Theological Studies 277 (1998).

18. United States Catholic Bishops, "Fourth Draft/Response to the Concerns of Women for Church and Society," 22 Origins 221, 224 (1992). Cf. Peter Steinfels, "Pastoral Letter on Women's Role Fails in Vote of Catholic Bishops," New York Times, Nov. 19, 1992, at A1 (letter too liberal for some bishops, too conservative for others, failed to achieve required two-thirds support of bishops).

19. United States Catholic Bishops, n. 18, at 224. "This error and the sinful attitudes it generates represent, in fact, a radical distortion of the very order of creation. Unjust discrimination of this sort, whether subtle or overt, distorts interpersonal relations and adversely affects the social patterns and the modes of communication that influence day-to-day life in our world." Id.

20. Steven D. Smith, Letter to Michael J. Perry, Apr. 7, 1998. Quoted with permission.

21. Richard Rorty, "Human Rights, Rationality, and Sentimentality," in On Human Rights: The Oxford Amnesty Lectures 1993 111, 112 (Stephen Shute & Susan Hurley eds., 1993).

22. See, e.g., n. 19 & accompanying text.

23. We can now see this, though only relatively few members of the generation who, through their representatives, established the norm were able to see it. Not that none of them saw it: Even in the 1860s—and earlier—there were insightful and articulate feminists in America. See, e.g., Elizabeth Ann Bartlett, Liberty, Equality, Sorority: The Origins and Interpretation of American Feminist Thought: Frances Wright, Sarah Grimke, and Margaret Fuller (1994); Sylvia D. Hoffert, When Hens Crow: The Woman's Rights Movement in Antebellum America (1995).

24. Rogers M. Smith, "The Inherent Deceptiveness of Constitutional Discourse: A Diagnosis and Prescription," in Integrity and Conscience 218, 252 n. 25 (Ian Shapiro & Robert Adams eds., 1998) (quoting material presented in Robert C. Morris, Reading, 'Riting, and Reconstruction: The Education of Freedmen in the South, 1861–1870 (1981)).

25. Plessy v. Ferguson, 163 U.S. 537, 544, 551 (1896) (emphasis added).

26. Margaret A. Farley, "Sexism," New Catholic Encyclopedia (Supplement), vol. 17, 604 (1979).

27. Ch. 3, pp. 101–2 (footnotes omitted).

28. See n. 30.

29. For a fuller statement and defense of the point, see Perry, "Modern Equal Protection," n. 2, at 1052–54.

30. 458 U.S. 718, 724 (1982).

31. Id. at 724–25. In *Hogan*, the Court remarked:

> Rather than compensate for discriminatory barriers faced by women, MUW's policy of excluding males from admission to the School of Nursing tends to perpetuate the stereotyped view of nursing as an exclusively women's job. By assuring that Mississippi allots more openings in its state-supported schools to women than it does to men, MUW's admissions policy lends credibility to the old view that women, not men, should become nurses, and makes the assumption that nursing is a field for women a self-fulfilling prophecy.

Id. at 729–30.

32. Adarand Constructors, Inc. v. Pena, 515 U.S. 200, 226 (1995). But this is not the function of strict scrutiny in every context in which it is used. See ch. 6, p. 156. Indeed, contrary to what the Court's statement in *Adarand* suggests, it is not the function of strict scrutiny even in the context of race-based affirmative action. See ch. 4, pp. 103–8.

33. 458 U.S. at 725–26.

34. 518 U.S. 515, 116 S. Ct. 2264.

35. The Court made it clear that it was not questioning the constitutionality, under the Fourteenth Amendment, of state-sponsored single-sex schools. See, e.g., id. at 2276 n. 7 & 2276–77 & n. 8. But cf. Christopher H. Pyle, "Women's Colleges: Is Segregation by Sex Still Justifiable After *United States v. Virginia?*" 77 Boston U. L. Rev. 209 (1997) (answering in the negative).

36. Id. at 2293 (Scalia, J., dissenting).

37. Id. at 2279.

38. Id. at 2290 (Rehnquist, C.J., concurring in the judgment).

39. Robert H. Bork, Slouching Towards Gomorrah: Modern Liberalism and the American Decline 108 (1996).

40. Even today, as I reported in the preceding chapter, some critics of the modern Court do make that claim. See, e.g., Lino A. Graglia, "Constitutional Interpretation," 44 Syracuse L. Rev. 631, 637 (1994); Richard E. Morgan, "Coming Clean About *Brown*," City Journal, Summer 1996, at 42.

41. Robert H. Bork, "Our Judicial Oligarchy," First Things, November 1996, at 21; reprinted in The End of Democracy? The Judicial Usurpation of Politics 10, 10–11 (Mitchell S. Muncy ed. 1997).

42. 518 U.S. 515, 116 S. Ct. at 2276.

43. Id. at 2276.

44. Bork, "Our Judicial Oligarchy," n. 41, at 21–23. (The quoted passages appear in The End of Democracy, n. 41, at 16.)

45. Bork, "Our Judicial Oligarchy," n. 41, at 21 (in The End of Democracy, n. 41, at 10).

46. 518 U.S. 515, 116 S. Ct. at 2292 (Scalia, J., dissenting).

47. Id. at 2293.

48. Id. at 2292–93.

49. Id. at 2293.

50. 347 U.S. 483 (1954).

51. Graglia, n. 40, at 637.

52. It's not as if a skeptical rejection of the practice, the institution, of judicial review is animating Justice Scalia's approach to adjudication under the Fourteenth Amendment. From time to time, Scalia is willing, if not eager, to strike down governmental action, even when the action is in the form of legislation duly enacted by a coordinate branch of the federal government (the Congress) and signed into law by the head of the third coordinate branch, the President of the United States. See, e.g., United States v. Lopez, 514 U.S. 549 (1995); City of Boerne v. Flores, 117 S. Ct. 2157 (1997).

53. 517 U.S. 620, 116 S. Ct. 1620 (1996).

54. See ch. 3, n. 98 & accompanying text.

55. Although in *Washington v. Davis*, 426 U.S. 229 (1976), the Supreme Court rejected the constitutional challenge to the police department's hiring test, the Court made it clear that it would not have rejected a challenge had it been shown that the hiring test was used for the purpose of minimizing the number of black employees in the police department.

56. Although in *Personnel Administrator of Massachusetts v. Feeney*, 442 U.S. 256 (1979), the Supreme Court rejected the constitutional challenge to Massachusetts' veterans' preference program, the Court made it clear that it would not have rejected a challenge had it been shown that the program was used for the purpose of minimizing the number of women in certain civil service positions.

57. Imagine a law that outlaws not all sexual activity outside of marriage, but all oral and anal sex outside of marriage. (Assume that out of respect for marital privacy, the law stops short of outlawing oral and anal sex inside of marriage.) Does this law discriminate against homosexuals? The crucial question is whether the law would have been enacted even in the absence of a purpose of preventing homosexuals from living lives in fulfillment of their homosexual desire.

58. Richard Posner, Sex and Reason 346 (1992) (emphasis added).

59. 478 U.S. 186, 188 n. 2 (1986).

60. Id. at 192.

61. See, e.g., n. 17 & accompanying text.

62. 388 U.S. 1 (1967).

63. 842 S.W.2d 487 (Ky. 1993). See Case Comment, 106 Harvard L. Rev. 1370, 1373 (1993): "With *Wasson*, the Kentucky Supreme Court became the highest state court to extend privacy protection to homosexual sodomy since *Bowers v. Hardwick*. More importantly, *Wasson* broke from the trend of other courts and recognized homosexuals as a 'separate and identifiable class' for equal protection purposes."

64. 842 S.W.2d at 499, 501.

65. Id. at 501.

66. 478 U.S. at 219.

67. Andrew Koppelman, Antidiscrimination Law & Social Equality 165 (1996). On gay bashing, see Andrew Koppelman, "Three Arguments for Gay Rights," 95 Michigan L. Rev. 1636, 1658 n. 94 (1997).

68. Id. at 149.

69. See Thomas C. Grey, *"Bowers v. Hardwick* Diminished," 68 U. Colorado L. Rev. 373 (1997). See also Ronald Dworkin, "Sex, Death, and the Courts," New York Review, Aug. 8, 1996, at 50.

70. Albeit on the basis of a rationale different from that given by the Colorado Supreme Court. See Romer v. Evans, 116 Sup. Ct. 1620, 1624 (1996).

71. Id. at 1628.

72. Id. at 1629, 1631.

73. Id. at 1633. In his dissent, Scalia allowed for the possibility that Amendment 2 might be unconstitutional as applied "to individuals who do not engage in homosexual acts, but are merely of homosexual 'orientation'." Id. at 1632. See id. at 1632–33. The majority's position, however, was that Amendment 2 would be unconstitutional even if by its terms Amendment 2 applied only to persons who engage in homosexual acts, and not to homosexuals who do not engage in such acts. My discussion of the constitutionality of Amendment 2 proceeds as if Amendment 2 applied only to "practicing" homosexuals.

74. Dworkin, n. 69, at 50.

75. For a defense of the traditional Roman Catholic position, see John M. Finnis, "Law, Morality, and Sexual Orientation," 9 Notre Dame J. L., Ethics & Public Policy 11 (1995). For my critique of Finnis' argument, see Michael J. Perry, "The Morality of Homosexual Conduct: A Response to John Finnis," 11 Notre Dame J. L., Ethics & Public Policy 41 (1995).

On the constitutionality of laws regulating the use and distribution of contraceptives designed solely to prevent conception (not contraceptives designed partly to prevent the spread of disease), see Griswold v. Connecticut, 381 U.S. 479 (1965) (ban on use of contraceptives by a married couple unconstitutional); Eisenstadt v. Baird, 405 U.S. 438 (1972) (ban on distribution of contraceptives to unmarried persons, but not to married persons, unconstitutional). Of course, the Court's decision in *Roe v. Wade*, 410 U.S. 113 (1973), striking down antiabortion legislation, makes the issues involved in *Griswold* and *Eisenstadt* seem quaint by comparison. If a state may not outlaw abortion, surely it may not—surely it would not want to— outlaw the use or distribution of contraceptives.

76. Robert F. Nagel, "Playing Defense in Colorado," First Things, May 1998, at 34, 35.

77. Rosemary Ruether, "The Personalization of Sexuality," in From Machismo to Mutuality: Essays on Sexism and Woman-Man Liberation 70, 83 (Eugene Bianchi & Rosemary Ruether eds., 1976) (emphasis added).

78. Margaret A. Farley, "An Ethic for Same-Sex Relations," in A Challenge to Love: Gay and Lesbian Catholics in the Church 93, 105 (Robert Nugent ed., 1983). Cf. Gustav Niebuhr, "Laws Aside, Some in Clergy Quietly Bless Gay 'Marriage'," New York Times, Apr. 17, 1998, at A1.

79. 517 U.S. 620, 116 S. Ct. at 1628.

80. [1998] 1 S.C.R. 493.

81. Laws against polygamy, by contrast, are based not on any fear and loathing of polygamists more for who they are than for what they do, but on moral disapproval of polygamy itself. Cf. 517 U.S. 620, 116 S. Ct. at 1635–36 (Scalia, J., dissenting).

82. Id. at 1637.

83. See, e.g., Hadley Arkes, "A Culture Corrupted," First Things, November 1996, at 30, reprinted in The End of Democracy? n. 41, at 30; Charles W. Colson, "Kingdoms in Conflict," First Things, November 1996, at 34, reprinted in The End of Democracy? n. 41, at 41; Lino A. Graglia, *"Romer v. Evans*: The People Foiled Again by the Constitution," 68 U. Colorado L. Rev. 409 (1997).

84. Bork, Slouching Towards Gommorah, n. 39, at 114.

85. See James Davidson Hunter, Culture Wars (1991).

86. For a sampling, see John Corvino, ed., Same-Sex: Debating the Ethics, Science and Culture of Homosexuality (1998); Jeffrey S. Siker, ed., Homosexuality in the Church: Both Sides of the Debate (1994); Andrew Sullivan, ed., Same-Sex Marriage: Pro and Con (1997).

87. For a book-length discussion of the constitutional dimension of the issue, see William N. Eskridge, Jr., The Case for Same-Sex Marriage: From Sexual Liberty to Civilized Commitment (1996). See also Richard A. Posner, "Should There Be Homosexual Marriage? And If So, Who Should Decide?" 95 Michigan L. Rev. 1578 (1997) (reviewing Eskridge's book).

88. For a state to refuse to extend legal recognition to same-sex unions is for it to deny certain legal benefits to persons as partners in a same-sex union— namely, the benefits granted to persons as partners in a traditional marriage; at least, it is for the state to make it significantly more difficult for the partners in a same-sex union to qualify for the relevant benefits.

89. See nn. 77–78 & accompanying text.

90. For an argument that might serve as such an explanation in a society, unlike our own, whose citizens generally accept the traditional Roman Catholic position that *all* deliberately nonprocreative genital acts, *including such acts between a man and a woman no less than between two persons of the same sex*, are immoral, see Finnis, n. 75. For my critique of Finnis' argument, see Perry, "The Morality of Homosexual Conduct," n. 75.

91. See Michael J. Perry, Religion in Politics: Constitutional and Moral Perspectives 33–37 (1997).

92. Roderick M. Hills, Jr., "You Say You Want a Revolution? The Case Against the Transformation of Culture Through Antidiscrimination Laws," 95 Michigan L. Rev. 1588, 1610–11 (1997) (citing Roger Scruton, Sexual Desire: A Moral Philosophy of the Erotic 305–11 (1986)).

93. See Martha C. Nussbaum, "Platonic Love and Colorado Law: The Relevance of Ancient Greek Norms to Modern Sexual Controversies," 80 Virginia L. Rev. 1515, 1601 (1994):

> Scruton's argument was always a peculiar one: for why should one believe that all individuals of one sex are more like each other in quality than any of them is like any member of the opposite sex? And would Scruton really wish to generalize his argument, as consistency seems to demand, preferring relationships between partners different in age, and race, and nationality, and religion? Even if he were to do so, Plato's dialogues offer good argument against him. Along with Aristotle's ethical thought, they argue that people who are alike in the goals they share and the aspirations they cherish may be more likely to promote genuine social goods than people who are unlike in character and who do not share any aspirations. In addition, the dialogues show that the kind of "otherness" that is valuable in love re-

lationships—that one's partner is another separate and, to some extent, hidden world; that the body shows only traces of the soul within; and that lovers never can be completely welded together into a single person—is quite different from the "qualitative" otherness of physiology and character. Indeed, the "otherness" of mystery and separateness is actually defended in Scruton's argument, as it is in Plato's, as an erotic good.

94. See Andrew Sullivan, "Three's a Crowd," *New Republic*, June 17, 1996, at 10, 12:

> [M]arriage acts both as an incentive for virtuous behavior—and as a social blessing for the effort. In the past, we have wisely not made nitpicking assessments as to who deserves the right to marry and who does not. We have provided it to anyone prepared to embrace it and hoped for the best. . . . For some, it comes easily. For others, its responsibilities and commitments are crippling. But we do not premise the right to marry upon the ability to perform its demands flawlessly. We accept that human beings are variably virtuous, but that, as citizens, they should be given the same rights and responsibilities—period.

Andrew Koppelman has argued that "even in the present regime in which they are not permitted to marry, same-sex couples do not seem to be much less stable than heterosexual couples. [The] data suggests that same-sex couples are not all that different in terms of their capacity to function or to remain stable from heterosexual couples." Koppelman, "Three Arguments for Gay Rights," n. 67, at 1666. See id. at 1664–66.

95. Posner, "Should There Be Homosexual Marriage?" n. 87, at 1584.

96. Id. at 1584–85. For a similar position, see Cass R. Sunstein, "Homosexuality and the Constitution," 70 Indiana L. J. 1, 23–28 (1994). For a critical response, see Marc A. Fajer, "With All Deliberate Speed? A Reply to Professor Sunstein," 70 Indiana L. J. 39 (1994).

97. Posner, "Should There Be Homosexual Marriage?" n. 87, at 1585–86.

98. Id. at 1586.

99. 410 U.S. 113 (1973).

100. Posner, "Should There Be Homosexual Marriage?" n. 87, at 1586.

101. Id. at 1586–87.

102. Cf. Nagel, n. 76, at 38:

> It seems quite possible that in the years ahead the pace of social change will only accelerate and that many Americans, caught up in large and uncontrollable forces, will feel increasingly frightened, isolated, and unable to control their lives. Moreover, lawyers and judges seem likely to continue to play a major role in producing this destabilization and alienation. Among other questions the legal establishment might ponder is what people in such a condition will do if their naive faith in legalistic defenses is destroyed.

This is an ominous warning—but one more suited, in my view, to the southeastern part of the United States in the period after the Court's decision, in 1954, in *Brown v. Board of Education*. Next to the Court's methodical attack on racially segregated public schools and the other institutions of apartheid in the Old South, extending legal recognition to same-sex unions seems to me like small change. Cf.

Gustav Niebuhr, "Laws Aside, Some in Clergy Quietly Bless Gay 'Marriage'," New York Times, Apr. 17, 1998, at A1.

103. Notice the way in which discrimination against homosexuals is, whatever else it is, a species of discrimination based on sex. "If a business fires Ricky, or if the state prosecutes him, because of his sexual activities with Fred, while these actions would not be taken against Lucy if she did exactly the same things with Fred, then Ricky is being disadvantaged solely because of his sex. If Lucy is permitted to marry Fred, but Ricky may not marry Fred, then Ricky is being disadvantaged because of his sex. It is sex discrimination when an option is expressly made available only to one sex but not to the other." Koppelman, Antidiscrimination Law & Social Equality, n. 67, at 154. For a discussion of this interesting and important point, see id. at 154 et seq.; Koppelman, "Three Arguments for Gay Rights," n. 67, at 1661–66.

The International Covenant on Civil and Political Rights explicitly bans some discrimination based on "sex", but it does not explicitly ban any discrimination based on "sexual orientation". The Human Rights Committee is the organ charged with interpreting the International Covenant. In a case arising out of Tasmania (one of Australia's six constitutive states), the Human Rights Committee has ruled that in outlawing "various forms of sexual contacts between men, including all forms of sexual contacts between consenting adult homosexual men in private", the Tasmanian Criminal Code discriminates on the basis of "sex" in violation of the International Covenant. See Toonen v. Australia, Communication No. 488/1992, U.N. Doc. CCPR/C/50/D/488/1992 (1994).

104. 347 U.S. 483 (1954).

105. 347 U.S. 475 (1954) (systematic exclusion of persons of Mexican descent from service as jury commissioners, grand jurors, and petit jurors deprived petitioner, a person of Mexican descent convicted of murder, of the equal protection of the laws). In the *United States Reports*, the Court's opinion in *Hernandez* immediately precedes its opinion in *Brown*.

106. 347 U.S. at 478.

Chapter 6

1. 410 U.S. 113, 163.

2. Sheryl Gay Stolberg, "Shifting Certainties in the Abortion War," New York Times, Jan. 11, 1998, § 4, p. 3.

3. 410 U.S. at 164.

4. Even as I draft this chapter (Winter 1997/98), the fury continues. See Editorial, "*Roe*: Twenty-five Years Later," First Things, January 1998, at 9; Editorial, "Dead Reckoning," National Review, Jan. 26, 1998. Cf. Carey Goldberg with Janet Elder, "Public Still Backs Abortion, But Wants Limits, Poll Says," New York Times, Jan. 16, 1998, at A1: "[T]he country remains irreconcilably riven over what many consider to be the most divisive American issue since slavery, with half the population considering abortion murder, the poll found. Despite a quarter-century of lobbying, debating and protesting by the camps that call themselves 'pro-choice' and 'pro-life,' that schism has remained virtually unaltered."

5. 347 U.S. 483 (1954).

6. Cf. Gregory Bassham, Original Intent and the Constitution: A Philosophical Study 105 (1992): "The acid test of originalism, as indeed of any theory of constitutional adjudication, is its capacity to justify what is now almost universally regarded as the Supreme Court's finest hour: its decision in *Brown v. Board of Education*."

7. John Hart Ely, "The Wages of Crying Wolf: A Comment on *Roe v. Wade*," 82 Yale L. J. 920, 926 (1973).

8. Id. at 947.

9. By liberal constitutional scholar, I mean a constitutional scholar who is generally supportive of the major constitutional decisions handed down by the Supreme Court during the tenure of Chief Justice Earl Warren, especially the major decisions of the 1960s.

10. Archibald Cox, The Role of the Supreme Court in American Government 113 (1976).

11. Gerald Gunther, "Some Reflections on the Judicial Role: Distinctions, Roots, and Prospects," 1979 Washington U. L. Q. 817, 819.

12. See ch. 1, section II.

13. Ch. 3, pp. 75–77.

14. Anti-abortion legislation does not violate the requirement—applicable to the national government under the First Amendment and to state government under the Fourteenth Amendment—that government not establish religion; at least, anti-abortion legislation does not violate the nonestablishment requirement on any plausible understanding of the requirement. For a discussion of the point, see Michael J. Perry, Religion in Politics: Constitutional and Moral Perspectives 33–37, 70–72 (1997).

15. See ch. 3, n. 96 & accompanying text.

16. See ch. 3, pp. 77–78.

17. 410 U.S. at 162.

18. Id. at 153.

19. Richard A. Posner, Sex and Reason 337 (1992).

20. Ely, n. 7, at 923.

21. 410 U.S. at 155.

22. See ch. 5, pp. 101–2.

23. As I explained in chapter 4, this is also the function of strict scrutiny in the context of race-based affirmative action—a fact also noticed by Jed Rubenfeld and emphasized in his essay on affirmative action. See Jed Rubenfeld, "Affirmative Action," 107 Yale L. J. 427, 428 (1997). (I quote Robenfeld's passage in chapter 4. See ch. 4, n. 70.)

24. 117 S. Ct. 2258, 2281, 2283 (1997) (Souter, J., concurring in the judgment).

25. See Ely, n. 7, at 924–25. For Ely's critique of the Court's point that fetuses are not "persons" within the meaning of the Fourteenth Amendment, see id. at 925–26.

26. Robert F. George, Book Review, 88 American Political Science Rev. 445, 445–46 (1994) (reviewing Ronald Dworkin, Life's Dominion: An Argument About Abortion, Euthanasia, and Individual Freedom (1993)). "In any event, Dworkin here fails to make much progress toward meeting it." Id. at 446. Cf. Mary Warnock, "The Limits of Toleration," in On Toleration 123, 125 (Susan Mendus & David Edwards eds., 1987) (commenting on John Stuart Mill's failure to address, inter alia, the question "Who is to count as a possible object of harm?").

27. Cf. Amy Gutman & Dennis Thompson, Democracy and Disagreement: Why Moral Conflict Cannot Be Avoided in Politics, and What Should Be Done About It 75 (1996): "Although pro-life advocates sometimes invoke a religious conception of human life, the belief that the fetus is a human being with constitutional rights does not depend on a distinctively religious conception of personhood."

28. 410 U.S. at 159.

29. Ely, n. 7, at 943.

30. 410 U.S. at 162.

31. Richard Epstein, "Substantive Due Process by Any Other Name: The Abortion Cases," 1973 Sup. Ct. Rev. 159, 182.

32. Ely, n. 7, at 942. See id. at 924–25 (explaining why, if the Court wanted to "second-guess legislative balances . . . when the Constitution has designated neither of the values in conflict as entitled to special protection[,] . . . *Roe* seems a curious place to have begun").

33. In 1992, in *Planned Parenthood of Southeastern Pennsylvania v. Casey*, Justice Scalia explained: "The whole argument of abortion opponents is that what the Court calls the fetus and what others call the unborn child *is a human life*. Thus, whatever answer Roe came up with after 'balancing' is bound to be wrong, unless it is correct that the human fetus is in some critical sense merely potentially human. There is of course no way to determine that as a legal matter; it is in fact a value judgment. Some societies have considered newborn children not yet human, or the incompetent elderly no longer so." 505 U.S. 833, 982 (1992) (Scalia, J., joined by Rehnquist, C.J., & White & Thomas, JJ., concurring in the judgment in part and dissenting in part).

34. There is a sense in which legislation that violates the central component of the antidiscrimination norm necessarily violates the reasonableness component: Legislation that violates the central component is not a "reasonable" regulation for the public good. But legislation that violates the central component and therefore violates the reasonableness component does not violate the reasonableness component on the ground that it fails to achieve the proportionality that is an essential ingredient of "reasonable" regulation. Rather, it violates the reasonableness component on a different ground, namely, because it treats some persons as less than truly, fully human in violation of the central component of the antidiscrimination norm.

35. See, e.g., Ruth Bader Ginsburg, "Some Thoughts on Autonomy and Equality in Relation to Roe v. Wade," 63 North Carolina L. Rev. 375 (1985); Laurence H. Tribe, American Constitutional Law 1353–59 (2d ed. 1988); Guido Calabresi, "Foreword: Antidiscrimination and Constitutional Accountability (What the Bork-Brennan Debate Ignores)," 105 Harvard L. Rev. 80, 146–48 (1991); Cass Sunstein, "Neutrality in Constitutional Law (With Special Reference to Pornography, Abortion, and Surrogacy)," 92 Columbia L. Rev. 1, 29–44 (1992). (Some other articles in this vein were cited by Justice Blackmun in *Planned Parenthood of Southeastern Pennsylvania v. Casey*. See 505 U.S. 833, 928 n. 4 (Blackmun, J., concurring in part, concurring in the judgment in part, and dissenting in part).) But see Ely, n. 7, at 934–35: "Compared with men, women may constitute [a discrete and insular minority]; compared with the unborn, they do not. I'm not sure I'd know a discrete and insular minority if I saw one, but confronted with a multiple choice question requiring me to designate (a) women or (b) fetuses as one, I'd expect no credit for the former answer."

36. See Michael J. Perry, Morality, Politics, and Law 172–78 (1988); Michael J. Perry, The Constitution in the Courts: Law or Politics? 184–89 (1994).

37. The following material is drawn from my book *The Constitution in the Courts*, id., at 184–89.

38. See Paul Brest, "Foreword: In Defense of the Antidiscrimination Principle," 90 Harvard L. Rev. 1 (1976).

39. 442 U.S. 256, 279 (1979).

40. Michael W. McConnell, "The Selective Funding Problem: Abortion and Religious Schools," 104 Harvard L. Rev. 989, 1042 (1991).

41. According to Richard Posner, "For many opponents of abortion, opposition to abortion is part and parcel of opposition to a broader set of practices and values—call it feminism. . . . Should the Supreme Court take sides between feminism and antifeminism?" Posner, Sex and Reason, n. 19, at 340. If by "antifeminism" we mean a constellation of beliefs, attitudes, etc., rooted in and representing the conviction or sensibility that a person's sex is relevant to her status as a human being, then yes, the Court *should* take sides—against antifeminism, i.e., against it *as a predicate for state action*—because, unless the Court accepts that a person's sex is relevant to her status as a human being, enforcement of the central component of the antidiscrimination norm requires that it do so.

42. Id. at 443 (emphasis added).

43. John Hart Ely, Democracy and Distrust: A Theory of Judicial Review 138 (1980).

44. 417 U.S. 484 (1974).

45. See McConnell, n. 40, at 1041–42.

46. That a state may not, consistently with the antidiscrimination norm, disallow *all* abortions in a particular category does not entail that it may not disallow *any* abortions in the category; nor am I suggesting that a state may not regulate abortions it may not disallow. Even if disallowing all abortions in a particular category (e.g., rape or incest) is an expression of sex-selective sympathy and indifference, it does not necessarily follow that disallowing some abortions in that category (e.g., abortions late in a pregnancy) or regulating abortions it may not disallow (e.g., by insisting that a woman seeking an abortion be provided with information about available alternatives before the abortion may be performed) is an expression of sex-selective sympathy and indifference. The Court's decision in *Planned Parenthood of Southeastern Pennsylvania v. Casey*, 505 U.S. 833 (1992)—which sustained several regulations of abortions that, under "the essential holding of *Roe v. Wade*" (reaffirmed by the Court in *Casey*, id. at 846), no state may disallow—is consistent with the antidiscrimination argument I have offered here.

47. 410 U.S. 179 (1973).

48. Roe v. Wade, 410 U.S. at 116.

49. Id. at 118.

50. Doe v. Bolton, 410 U.S. at 182.

51. Id. at 183.

52. Id. at 183 n. 5.

53. For a different perspective, see Editorial, n. 4, at 10.

54. Id. at 140 n. 37.

55. Roe v. Wade, 410 U.S. at 175–78.

56. M. Hirsley, "Presbyterians Shift to Middle on Abortion," Chicago Tribune, June 9, 1992, § 1, p. 4.

57. Goldberg, n. 4, at A1.

58. Ginsburg, n. 35, at 385–86.

59. 505 U.S. 833.

60. See id. at 912 (Stevens, J., concurring in part and dissenting in part) ("Roe is an integral part of a correct understanding of both the concept of liberty and the basic equality of men and women"); id. at 923 (Blackmun, J., concurring in part, concurring in the judgment in part, and dissenting in part) ("I remain steadfast in

my belief that the right to reproductive choice is entitled to the full protection afforded by this Court [in *Roe*]").

61. Id. at 846.

62. See ch. 2, section I.C.

63. See id. at 855–56. This was not the only argument offered by Justices O'Connor, Kennedy, and Souter, but their other principal argument is difficult to take seriously: that for the Court to overrule *Roe v. Wade* would make it seem that the Court had caved in to political pressure to overrule *Roe*, thereby diminishing the Court's legitimacy. See id. at 866–69. But what if that political pressure is rooted in a conviction that *Roe* was wrongly—very wrongly—decided? What is the principle here—that the more outrageous a decision, and the more political pressure there is, therefore, to overrule the decision, the more important it is for the Court to stand by the decision, even though the decision is a great mistake? Consider Justice Scalia's searing response:

> I am appalled by[] the Court's suggestion that the decision whether to stand by an erroneous constitutional decision must be strongly influenced—*against* overruling, no less—by the substantial and continuing public opposition the decision has generated. . . . [T]he notion that we would decide a case differently from the way we otherwise would have in order to show that we can stand firm against public disapproval is frightening. . . . [T]he notion that the Court must adhere to a decision for as long as the decision faces "great opposition" and the Court is "under fire" [has] a character of almost czarist arrogance. We are offended by these marchers who descend upon us, every year on the anniversary of Roe, to protest our saying that the Constitution requires what our society never thought the Constitution requires. These people . . . must be taught a lesson. We have no Cossacks, but at least we can stubbornly refuse to abandon an erroneous opinion that we might otherwise change—to show how little they intimidate us.

Id. at 998–99 (Scalia, J., joined by Rehnquist, C.J., & White & Thomas, JJ., concurring in the judgment in part and dissenting in part). According to Robert Nagel, the plurality opinion in *Casey*—the opinion of Justices O'Connor, Kennedy, and Souter—was "an extravagant expression of hubris." Robert F. Nagel, Judicial Power and American Character 138 (1994). Mary Ann Glendon has predicted that the plurality opinion will be "remembered less for its result than for its grandiose portrayal of the role of the Supreme Court in American society." Mary Ann Glendon, A Nation Under Lawyers 113 (1994). Steve Smith has observed that "whether one finds the justices' self-important declarations exasperating or merely comical, the statements surely exude a presumption that would be remarkable coming from *any* source, and that is all the more remarkable given the character of these authors." Steven D. Smith, The Constitution and the Pride of Reason 146 (1998). Richard Posner, in his Holmes Lectures, called the plurality opinion both "patronizing and self-important". Richard A. Posner, "The Problematics of Moral and Legal Theory," 111 Harvard L. Rev. 1637, 1812 (1998).

64. See id. at 944 (Rehnquist, C.J., joined by White, Scalia, & Thomas, JJ., concurring in the judgment in part and dissenting on part); id. at 979 (Scalia, J., joined by Rehnquist, C.J., & White & Thomas, JJ., concurring in the judgment in part and dissenting in part); id. at 979 (Scalia, J., joined by Rehnquist, C.J., &

White & Thomas, JJ., concurring in the judgment in part and dissenting in part).

65. See Washington v. Glucksberg, 117 S. Ct. 2258, 2266 n. 16 (1997).

66. See, e.g., "Symposium on the Right to Die," 9 Notre Dame J. L., Ethics & Public Policy 345–564 (1995); "A Symposium on Physician-Assisted Suicide," 35 Duquesne L. Rev. 1–531 (1996); "Physician-Assisted Suicide Symposium," 1 DePaul J. Health Care Law 445–653 (1997); "Symposium: Physician-Assisted Suicide," 19 Western New England L. Rev. 313–420 (1997).

67. 117 S. Ct. 2258 (1997).

68. 117 S. Ct. 2293 (1997). In *Washington v. Glucksberg*, the Court wrote it was the constitutionality of "Washington's physician-assisted suicide statute . . . as applied to the 'class of terminally ill, mentally competent patients' . . . that is before us today." 117 S. Ct. at 2262 n. 6.

69. See ch. 1, section I.

70. Editors of First Things, "Introduction," First Things, November 1996, at 18; reprinted in The End of Democracy? The Judicial Usurpation of Politics 3 (Mitchell S. Muncy ed., 1997).

71. For an appropriately skeptical discussion of the position that the Court's decision in the physician-assisted suicide cases is less conclusive than my statement of the Court's ruling suggests, see Note, "Leading Cases," 111 Harvard L. Rev. 237, 244–48 (1997).

72. See p. 154.

73. See Compassion in Dying v. Washington, 850 F. Supp. 1454, 1456–57 (W.D. Wash. 1994); Quill v. Vacco, 80 F.2d 716, 720 (2d Cir. 1996).

74. Roe v. Wade, 410 U.S. at 155.

75. 117 S. Ct. at 2271.

76. Id. at 2282 (Souter, J., concurring in the judgment). See also Vacco v. Quill, 117 S. Ct. 2293, 2302 (1997) (Souter, J., concurring in the judgment): "I accord the claims raised by the patients and physicians in this case and in *Washington v. Gluckberg* a high degree of importance, requiring a commensurate justification."

77. See 117 S. Ct. at 2290 (Souter, J., concurring in the judgment): "In my judgment, the importance of the individual interest here, as within that class of 'certain interests' demanding careful scrutiny of the State's contrary claim, cannot be gainsaid."

78. Id. at 2272.

79. Id. at 2273.

80. Id.

81. Id.

82. Id. See George P. Fletcher, Letter to the Editor, New York Review, May 29, 1997, at 45:

> Admittedly, not all physicians care whether assisting death violates the Hippocratic oath to further life. The question, then, is whether the state has a legitimate interest in regulating the medical profession by prescribing that physicians willing to facilitate death should not be able to do so—at least not consciously and intentionally. It is difficult for me to see a constitutional violation in this effort to preserve the integrity of the medical profession. Those in great pain may commit suicide. They may terminate life-sustaining therapy. But they may not convert the medical profession into killers for hire.

83. 117 S. Ct. at 2274.

84. Id. at 2274–75.

85. Id. at 2283.

86. Id. at 2261.

87. Id. at 2261 n. 2.

88. 117 S. Ct. at 2296.

89. Id. at 2298.

90. Id. at 2301.

91. See id. at 2300 n. 9.

92. Id. at 2298 n. 6.

93. Consider, in that regard, the amici curiae brief submitted to the Supreme Court in the physician-assisted suicide cases by the United States Catholic Conference, the Evangelical Lutheran Church in America, the Lutheran Church–Missouri Synod, the National Association of Evangelicals, the Christian Legal Society, and the Christian Medical and Dental Society. The brief is reprinted in *Origins*, Feb. 8, 1996, at 553–62. Cf. M. Kathleen Kaveny, "Assisted Suicide, Euthanasia, and the Law," 58 Theological Studies 124 (1997).

94. For a recent, clear discussion and defense of the distinction, see Richard A. McCormick, SJ, *"Vive la Difference!* Killing and Allowing to Die," America, Dec. 6, 1997, at 6. Other recent defenses of the distinction include: Yale Kamisar, "The 'Right to Die': On Drawing (and Erasing) Lines," 35 Duquesne L. Rev. 481 (1996); Susan R. Martyn & Henry J. Bourguignon, "Physician-Assisted Suicide: The Lethal Flaws of the Ninth and Second Circuit Decisions," 85 California L. Rev. 371 (1997); Stephen R. Latham, "Aquinas and Morphine: Notes on the Double Effect at the End of Life," 1 DePaul J. Health Care Law 625 (1997). One of the arguments McCormick criticizes in his article is the argument presented in "The Philosophers' Brief". See Ronald Dworkin, Thomas Nagel, Robert Nozick, John Rawls, Thomas Scanlon, & Judith Jarvis Thomson, "Assisted Suicide: The Philosophers' Brief," New York Review, Mar. 27, 1997, at 41.

95. I argued in the preceding chapter that it is difficult to the point of impossible to avoid the conclusion that, in a society, like ours, in which the traditional Roman Catholic position that all deliberately nonprocreative genital acts are immoral is widely rejected, the refusal to extend legal recognition to same-sex unions presupposes the lesser humanity of homosexuals. It would not be arrogant, much less "incredibly arrogant", for the Court to reach a conclusion that is unavoidable.

96. 117 S. Ct. at 2275.

97. As the Court reported, other countries too—Australia, Canada, Great Britain, and New Zealand among them—"are embroiled in similar debates." Id. at 2266 n. 16.

98. Id. at 2265–66.

99. Id. at 2266.

100. Id. at 2267.

101. Timothy Egan, "The 1997 Elections: Right to Die," New York Times, Nov. 6, 1997, at A26.

102. Id. The *Times* article referred to "court challenges". In 1995, a federal trial court ruled that the law violated the Fourteenth Amendment. Lee v. Oregon, 891 F. Supp. 1429 (D. Ore. 1995). In 1997, a federal appeals court vacated the judgment of the trial court and remanded "with instructions to dismiss Plaintiff's complaint for lack of jurisdiction." Lee v. Oregon, 107 F.3d 1382, 1392 (9th Cir. 1997). On October 14, 1997, three weeks before the referendum in Oregon, the Supreme Court of the United States refused to review the case. Lee v. Har-

cleroad, 118 S. Ct. 328 (1997). Thus, the decision of the federal appeals court is final.

103. See Ronald Dworkin et al., "Assisted Suicide: The Philosophers' Brief," n. 94. See also Ronald Dworkin, "Assisted Suicide: What the Court Really Said," New York Rev., Sept. 25, 1997, at 40; Ronald Dworkin's comments in "The Fifth Annual Fritz B. Burns Lecture: Euthanasia, Morality, and the Law," 30 Loyola L.A. L. Rev. 1465, 1488–1500 & 1503–5 (1997). For some critical responses to the philosophers' brief, see J. Bottum, "Debriefing the Philosophers," First Things, June/July 1997, at 26; McCormick, n. 94; Michael J. Sandel, "The Hard Questions: Last Rights," New Republic, Apr. 14, 1997, at 27; Michael Walzer, "The Hard Questions: Feed the Face," New Republic, June 9, 1997, at 29. For a strong critique of Dworkin's position in particular, see John Finnis' comments in "The Fifth Annual Fritz B. Burns Lecture: Euthanasia, Morality, and the Law," 30 Loyola L.A. L. Rev. 1465, 1473–88 & 1501–3 (1997).

104. Washington v. Glucksberg, 117 S. Ct. at 2267.

105. Anthony T. Kronman, "The Value of Moral Philosophy," 111 Harvard L. Rev. 1739, 1764 (1998). See also Posner, "The Problematics of Moral and Legal Theory," n. 63, at 1810 (agreeing with Kronman about Dworkin).

106. See Finnis, n. 103, at 1482, 1484:

> In his evidence before the Walton Committee, the British Parliamentary Committee on Euthanasia in 1993, Ronald Dworkin was asked again and again about these problems, and his answer I think can be fairly summarized in one quotation. "This sort of bad consequence of legalization," he said, and I quote,
>
>> is not an argument for caution, because it would be wrong to harm a lot of people by keeping the present law against euthanasia, just because we feel that in some instance a decision might be made on the wrong basis. Those in charge of these decisions and the doctors would be in the front line, would simply have to be very careful to observe the kinds of conditions that the model uniform statute on living wills directs doctors to attend to.
>
> But, of course, doctors would simply not have to, and the committee unanimously rejected [Dworkin's] reassurances. . . .
>
> The twenty-four members of the [New York] task force set up in 1984 by Governor Cuomo were even more representative of secular liberals than the Walton Committee. Some of them think suicide and euthanasia morally acceptable in conscience. After considering a mass of evidence, *including Ronald Dworkin's work to which they carefully reply,* with the aid of consultants, some of whom are strongly pro-euthanasia, they unanimously concluded that legalizing assisted suicide and euthanasia would pose profound risks to many patients, especially those who are poor, elderly, members of a minority group, or without access to good medical care.
>
> The bottom line—the secular highly experienced and sophisticated members of the Walton Committee and the New York State Task Force judged—is that if euthanasia were legalized at all, the right not to be killed would be catastrophically nullified for very many more people than the few whose supposed right to die is compromised by present law.

107. 117 S. Ct. at 2303. See also Cass R. Sunstein, "The Right to Die," 106 Yale L. J. 1123, 1123 (1996): "In this Essay, I argue that the Supreme Court should not invalidate laws forbidding physician-assisted suicide. My basic claim is institutional: The Court should be wary of recognizing rights of this kind amid complex issues of fact and value, at least if reasonable people can decide those issues either way, and if the Court cannot identify malfunctions in the system of deliberative democracy that might justify a more aggressive judicial role."

108. Richard Posner too makes the point: Posner, "The Problematics of Moral and Legal Theory," n. 63, at 1703.

109. 117 S. Ct. at 2275.

110. Roe v. Wade, 410 U.S. at 140 n. 37.

111. Ginsburg, n. 35, at 385–86.

Chapter 7

1. Robert G. McCloskey, The Modern Supreme Court 290–91 (1972). See also J. Segall, "A Century Lost: The End of the Originalism Debate," 15 Constitutional Commentary 411 (1998).

2. Except in passing (see, e.g., ch. 2, n. 99), I have not commented in this book on a recent, dramatic instance of judicial usurpation—an instance that concerns the Supreme Court's interpretation of the Fourteenth Amendment. The reason for this omission is that the relevant point has been made recently and persuasively by Michael McConnell. See Michael W. McConnell, "Institutions and Interpretations: A Critique of *City of Boerne v. Flores*," 111 Harvard L. Rev. 153 (1997). In 1997, in *City of Boerne v. Flores*, 117 S. Ct. 2157, the Court struck down congressional legislation—the Religious Freedom Restoration Act (RFRA)—on the ground that in enacting RFRA, Congress acted *ultra vires*: Congress exceeded its power under section five of the Fourteenth Amendment to enforce section one of the Amendment. Specifically, the Court ruled that in enacting RFRA, Congress exceeded its power to protect the free exercise of religion against the states. (The First Amendment protects the free exercise of religion against the national government; section one of the Fourteenth Amendment is deemed to protect the free exercise of religion against state government.) The Court claimed that it, and it alone, has the power to say what section one of the Fourteenth Amendment, by protecting the free exercise of religion against the states, requires the states to do or to refrain from doing; because Congress, in RFRA, said that the states are required to do something that in the Court's view they are not required to do, the Court struck down RFRA. The Court's position was mistaken. The correct position is that Congress has power—albeit, a limited power—to say what section one, by protecting free exercise, requires the states to do: If the congressional judgment about what the states are required to do is more demanding of the states than the Court's own judgment, and if, in the Court's view, the congressional judgment is a reasonable one, the Court should defer to the judgment. (Thus, the correct position is Thayerian. See ch. 2, n. 78.) For the Court to impose on Congress its own judgment about what the states (in the name of free exercise) are required to do, *if Congress' more demanding judgment, though different from the Court's own, is nonetheless reasonable,* is a judicial usurpation of politics. In particular, it is a judicial usurpation of Congress' power under section five of the Fourteenth Amendment to enforce section one of the Amendment. (In *City of Boerne*, the Court never even inquired whether the congressional judgment, though different from its own, was

reasonable. That the congressional judgment was different from its own was, for the Court, dispositive.) The reader interested in a careful elaboration and powerful defense of the point can read McConnell's essay. See also David Cole, "The Value of Seeing Things Differently: Boerne v. Flores and Congressional Enforcement of the Bill of Rights," 1997 Sup. Ct. Rev. 31 (1998); Douglas Laycock, "Conceptual Gulfs in *City of Boerne v. Flores*," 39 William & Mary L. Rev. 743 (1998). It bears mention that the organizer of the *First Things* symposium, Richard John Neuhaus, is sympathetic to the point. See Richard John Neuhaus, "The Anatomy of a Controversy," in The End of Democracy? The Judicial Usurpation of Politics 173, 257–58 (Mitchell S. Muncy ed., 1997) (supporting a large congressional authority under section five of the Fourteenth Amendment to interpret the Amendment). For a collection of essays on the Supreme Court's decision in *City of Boerne*, see "Symposium: Reflections on *City f Boerne v. Flores*," 39 William & Mary L. Rev. 601–960 (1998).

3. If, like the *First Things* symposiasts, one is convinced that the judicial usurpation of politics is a serious problem, what might one want to do about it? Among other things, one might want to reflect on the Canadian experience. In Canada, both the national Parliament and the provincial legislatures are given a larger role in the process of shaping constitutional values than is given either to Congress or to the state legislatures in the United States. See Peter W. Hogg & Allison A. Bushell, "The *Charter* Dialogue Between Courts and Legislatures," 35 Osgoode Hall L. J. 75 (1997). For a brief discussion of a Canadian-style arrangement as a possibility for the United States, see Michael J. Perry, The Constitution in the Courts: Law or Politics? 197–201 (1994).

In the United States, the Supreme Court has done what it can—wrongly, in my judgment—to prevent the emergence of a larger congressional role in shaping constitutional values. See n. 2.

4. See Richard A. Posner, "Against Constitutional Theory," 73 New York U. L. Rev. 1 (1997). See also Richard A. Posner, Overcoming Law, ch. 6 (1995) ("Have We Constitutional Theory?").

5. Gerald Graff, Beyond the Culture Wars: How Teaching the Conflicts Can Revitalize American Education 52–53 (1992).

6. If I were addressing constitutional issues different in kind from those I have addressed in this book—if I were addressing, for example, "separation of powers" issues (i.e., issues concerning the constitutionally proper allocation of power among the three branches of the national government) or "federalism" issues (issues concerning the constitutionally proper division of power between the national government and the governments of the states)—I might require one or more premises beyond those I defended in chapter 2. But for purposes of the constitutional issues I have addressed here, the premises defended in chapter 2 are sufficient.

7. Cf. J. M. Balkin, "Does the Constitution Deserve Our Fidelity?" 65 Fordham L. Rev. 1703 (1997).

8. See ch. 2, section I.B.

9. I once made such an argument myself. See Michael J. Perry, The Constitution, the Courts, and Human Rights (1982); Michael J. Perry, Morality, Politics, and Law, ch. 6 (1988). But see Michael J. Perry, The Constitution in the Courts: Law or Politics? (1994). For a superb discussion of the evolution of my constitutional-theoretical views, see Richard B. Saphire, "Originalism and the Importance of Constitutional Aspirations," 24 Hastings Constitutional L. Q. 599 (1997).

10. Learned Hand, The Bill of Rights 73 (1958). Hand continued:

> If they [the Platonic Guardians] were in charge, I should miss the stimulus of living in a society where I have, at least theoretically, some part in the direction of public affairs. Of course I know how illusory would be the belief that my vote determined anything; but nevertheless when I go to the polls I have a satisfaction in the sense that we are all engaged in a common venture. If you retort that a sheep in the flock may feel something like it, I reply, following St. Francis, "My brother, the sheep."

Id. at 73–74.

11. See Posner, "Against Constitutional Theory," n. 4.

One of the most prominent constitutional theorists of our time is Ronald Dworkin. In my view, Michael McConnell's critique of Dworkin's constitutional jurisprudence is persuasive and devastating. See Michael W. McConnell, "The Importance of Humility in Judicial Review: A Comment on Ronald Dworkin's 'Moral Reading' of the Constitution," 65 Fordham L. Rev. 1269 (1997). See also Gregory Bassham, "Freedom's Politics: A Review Essay of Ronald Dworkin's *Freedom's Law: The Moral Reading of the American Constitution*," 72 Notre Dame L. Rev. 1235 (1997).

12. See ch. 5, nn. 95–97 & accompanying text.

13. Consider two other liberal democracies. In Japan for most of the period since World War II, the judges generally played only a negligible role in protecting the Japanese Constitution. In England, where there is no written constitution, the judges play no role in protecting the unwritten constitution that is anything like the role played by the U.S. Supreme Court in protecting the U.S. Constitution.

INDEX

McGraw-Hill Series in Electrical and Computer Engineering

Senior Consulting Editor

Stephen W. Director, Carnegie Mellon University

Circuits and Systems
Communications and Signal Processing
Computer Engineering
Control Theory
Electromagnetics
Electronics and VLSI Circuits
Introductory
Power and Energy
Radar and Antennas

Previous Consulting Editors

PROBABILITY, RANDOM VARIABLES
AND RANDOM SIGNAL PRINCIPLES

Communications and Signal Processing

Senior Consulting Editor

Stephen W. Director, Carnegie Mellon University

Also Available from McGraw-Hill

Schaum's Outline Series in Electronics & Electrical Engineering

Most outlines include basic theory, definitions, and hundreds of solved problems and supplementary problems with answers.

Titles on the Current List Include:

Acoustics
Basic Circuit Analysis, 2d edition
Basic Electrical Engineering
Basic Electricity
Basic Equations of Engineering
Basic Mathematics for Electricity and
   Electronics
Digital Principles, 2d edition
Electric Circuits, 2d edition
Electric Machines and Electromechanics

Electric Power Systems
Electronic Circuits
Electronic Communication
Electronic Devices and Circuits
Electronics Technology
Feedback and Control Systems, 2d edition
Microprocessor Fundamentals, 2d edition
State Space and Linear Systems
Transmission Lines

Schaum's Solved Problems Books

Each title in this series is a complete and expert source of solved problems containing thousands of problems with worked out solutions.

Related Titles on the Current List Include:

3000 Solved Problems in Calculus
2500 Solved Problems in Differential Equations
3000 Solved Problems in Electric Circuits
2000 Solved Problems in Electromagnetics
2000 Solved Problems in Electronics
3000 Solved Problems in Linear Algebra
2000 Solved Problems in Numerical Analysis
3000 Solved Problems in Physics

Available at your College Bookstore. A complete list of Schaum titles may be obtained by writing to: Schaum Division
             McGraw-Hill, Inc.
             Princeton Road, S-1
             Hightstown, NJ 08520

PROBABILITY, RANDOM VARIABLES, AND RANDOM SIGNAL PRINCIPLES

Third Edition

Peyton Z. Peebles, Jr., Ph.D.

Professor of Electrical Engineering
University of Florida

McGraw-Hill, Inc.

New York St. Louis San Francisco Auckland Bogotá Caracas
Lisbon London Madrid Mexico Milan Montreal New Delhi
Paris San Juan Singapore Sydney Tokyo Toronto

This book was set in Times Roman.
The editors were Anne T. Brown and John M. Morriss;
the production supervisor was Denise L. Puryear.
The cover was designed by Rafael Hernandez.
Project supervision was done by Keyword Publishing Services.
R. R. Donnelley & Sons Company was printer and binder.

**PROBABILITY, RANDOM VARIABLES,
AND RANDOM SIGNAL PRINCIPLES**

2 3 4 5 6 7 8 9 0 DOC DOC 9 0 9 8 7 6 5 4 3

ISBN 0-07-049273-5

Library of Congress Cataloging-in-Publication Data

Peebles, Peyton Z.
  Probability, random variables, and random signal principles /
Peyton Z. Peebles, Jr. — 3rd ed.
    p.   cm. — (McGraw-Hill series in electrical and computer
engineering. Communications and signal processing)
  Includes bibliographical references and index.
  ISBN 0-07-049273-5
  1. Probabilities.   2. Random variables.   3. Signal theory
(Telecommunication)   I. Series.
TA340.P43   1993
519.2—dc20   92-30122

ABOUT THE AUTHOR

Peyton Z. Peebles, Jr., is Professor and formerly Associate Chairman of the Department of Electrical Engineering at the University of Florida. His twenty-three years of teaching experience include time spent at the University of Tennessee and the University of Hawaii, as well as the University of Florida. He earned his Ph.D. degree in 1967 from the University of Pennsylvania where he held a David Sarnoff Fellowship from RCA for 2 years.

Professor Peebles has authored or coauthored over 50 journal articles and conference papers as well as three other textbooks: *Principles of Electrical Engineering* (McGraw-Hill, 1991); *Digital Communication Systems* (Prentice-Hall, 1987); and *Communication System Principles* (Addison-Wesley, 1976).

Dr. Peebles is a member of Tau Beta Pi, Eta Kappa Nu, Sigma Xi, Sigma Pi Sigma, Phi Beta Chi, and is a Fellow of the IEEE.

CONTENTS

★ Star indicates more advanced material.

PREFACE TO THE THIRD EDITION

This third edition differs from the second mainly by four significant and two minor changes. Probably the most important is the addition of 180 new problems at the ends of the chapters. The book now contains 811 problems (a 28.5% increase over the second edition). As with earlier editions, the added problems are separately listed so that instructors using the book can easily identify the new exercises. The book's solutions manual, available from the publisher to instructors that use the book, has also been updated to include all problems.

The three remaining significant changes are: two new sections were added on the computer generation of random variables with prescribed probability density functions; a new section was added on the Poisson random process; a new section was added on the measurement of the power density spectrums of random processes.

The two minor, although very useful, additions were: an approximation for the binomial coefficient, and the introduction of the Q-function that is useful in calculating probabilities from the gaussian density. An excellent closed-form approximation is also given for the Q-function.

The new additions have not significantly lengthened the book, and it should continue to serve its principal purpose as a text for a 1-quarter or 1-semester course at the level of junior, senior, or first-year graduate students that have had no prior exposure to the book's topics.

Although special efforts have been made to prevent errors, it seems impossible to create an error-free book. Therefore, I invite anyone who uses the book to advise me of any errors they find, and I thank all in advance for their assistance.

McGraw-Hill and I would like to thank the following reviewers for their many helpful comments and suggestions: Hari Krishna, Syracuse University; J. K. Tugnait, Auburn University; and William J. Williams, University of Michigan.

Peyton Z. Peebles, Jr.

PREFACE TO THE
SECOND EDITION

Because the first edition of this book was well received by the academic and engineering community, a special attempt was made in the second edition to include only those changes that seemed to clearly improve the book's use in the classroom. Most of the modifications were included only after obtaining input from several users of the book.

Except for a few minor corrections and additions, just six significant changes were made. Only two, a new section on the central limit theorem and one on gaussian random processes, represent modification of the original text. A third change, a new chapter (10) added at the end of the book, serves to illustrate a number of the book's theoretical principles by applying them to problems encountered in practice. A fourth change is the addition of Appendix F, which is a convenient list of some useful probability densities that are often encountered.

The remaining two changes are probably the most significant, especially for instructors using the book. First, the number of examples that illustrate the topics discussed has been increased by about 30 percent (over 85 examples are now included). These examples were carefully scattered throughout the text in an effort to include at least one in each section where practical to do so. Second, over 220 new student exercises (problems) have been added at the ends of the chapters (a 54 percent increase).

The book now contains 631 problems and a complete solutions manual is available to instructors from the publisher. This addition was in response to instructors that had used most of the exercises in the first edition. For these instructors' convenience in identifying the new problems, they are listed in each chapter as "Additional Problems."

All other aspects of the book, such as its purpose (a textbook), intended audience (juniors, seniors, first-year graduate students), level, and style of presentation, remain as before.

I would like to thank D. I. Starry for her excellent work in typing the manuscript and the University of Florida for making her services available. Finally,

I am again indebted to my wife, Barbara, for her selfless efforts in helping me proofread the book. If the number of in-print errors is small, it is greatly due to her work.

Peyton Z. Peebles, Jr.

PREFACE TO THE FIRST EDITION

This book has been written specifically as a textbook with the purpose of introducing the principles of probability, random variables, and random signals to either junior or senior engineering students.

The *level* of material included in the book has been selected to apply to a typical undergraduate program. However, a small amount of more advanced material is scattered throughout to serve as stimulation for the more advanced student, or to fill out course content in schools where students are at a more advanced level. (Such topics are keyed by a star ★.) The *amount* of material included has been determined by my desire to fit the text to courses of up to one semester in length. (More is said below about course structure.)

The *need* for the book is easily established. The engineering applications of probability concepts have historically been taught at the graduate level, and many excellent texts exist at that level. In recent times, however, many colleges and universities are introducing these concepts into the undergraduate curricula, especially in electrical engineering. This fact is made possible, in part, by refinements and simplifications in the theory such that it can now be grasped by junior or senior engineering students. Thus, there is a definite need for a text that is clearly written in a manner appealing to such students. I have tried to respond to this need by paying careful attention to the organization of the contents, the development of discussions in simple language, and the inclusion of text examples and many problems at the end of each chapter. The book contains over 400 problems and a solutions manual for all problems is available to instructors from the publisher.

Many of the examples and problems have purposely been made very simple in an effort to instill a sense of accomplishment in the student, which, hopefully, will provide the encouragement to go on to the more challenging problems. Although emphasis is placed on examples and problems of electrical engineering, the concepts and theory are applicable to all areas of engineering.

The International System of Units (SI) has been used primarily throughout

xxi

the text. However, because technology is presently in a transitional stage with regard to measurements, some of the more established customary units (gallons, °F, etc.) are also utilized; in such instances, values in SI units follow in parentheses.

The *student background* required to study the book is only that typical of junior or senior engineering students. Specifically, it is assumed the student has been introduced to multivariable calculus, Fourier series, Fourier transforms, impulse functions, and some linear system theory (transfer function concepts, especially). I recognize, however, that students tend to forget a fair amount of what is initially taught in many of these areas, primarily through lack of opportunity to apply the material in later courses. Therefore, I have inserted short reviews of some of these required topics. These reviews are occasionally included in the text, but, for the most part, exist in appendixes at the end of the book.

The *order of the material* is dictated by the main topic. Chapter 1 introduces probability from the axiomatic definition using set theory. In my opinion this approach is more modern and mathematically correct than other definitions. It also has the advantage of creating a better base for students desiring to go on to graduate work. Chapter 2 introduces the theory of a single random variable. Chapter 3 introduces operations on one random variable that are based on statistical expectation. Chapter 4 extends the theory to several random variables, while Chapter 5 defines operations with several variables. Chapters 6 and 7 introduce random processes. Definitions based on temporal characterizations are developed in Chapter 6. Spectral characterizations are included in Chapter 7.

The remainder of the text is concerned with the response of linear systems with random inputs. Chapter 8 contains the general theory, mainly for linear time-invariant systems; while Chapter 9 considers specific optimum systems that either maximize system output signal-to-noise ratio or minimize a suitably defined average error.

Finally, the book closes with a number of appendixes that contain material helpful to the student in working problems, in reviewing background topics, and in the interpretation of the text.

The book can profitably be used in curricula based on either the quarter or the semester system. At the University of Tennessee, a *one-quarter undergraduate course* at the junior level has been successfully taught that covers Chapters 1 through 8, except for omitting Sections 2.6, 3.4, 4.4, 8.7 through 8.9, and all starred material. The class met three hours per week.

A *one-semester undergraduate course* (three hours per week) can readily be structured to cover Chapters 1 through 9, omitting all starred material except that in Sections 3.3, 5.3, 7.4, and 8.6.

Although the text is mainly developed for the undergraduate, I have also successfully used it in a *one-quarter graduate course* (first-year, three hours per week) that covers Chapters 1 through 7, including all starred material.

It should be possible to cover the entire book, including all starred material, in a *one-semester graduate course* (first-year, three hours per week).

I am indebted to many people who have helped make the book possible. Drs. R. C. Gonzalez and M. O. Pace read portions of the manuscript and suggested a number of improvements. Dr. T. V. Blalock taught from an early version of the manuscript, independently worked a number of the problems, and provided various improvements. I also extend my appreciation to the Advanced Book Program of Addison-Wesley Publishing Company for allowing me to adapt and use several of the figures from my earlier book *Communication System Principles* (1976), and to Dr. J. M. Googe, head of the electrical engineering department of the University of Tennessee, for his support and encouragement of this project. Typing of the bulk of the manuscript was ably done by Ms. Belinda Hudgens; other portions and various corrections were typed by Kymberly Scott, Sandra Wilson, and Denise Smiddy. Finally, I thank my wife, Barbara, for her aid in proofreading the entire book.

Peyton Z. Peebles, Jr.

CHAPTER

1

PROBABILITY

1.0 INTRODUCTION TO BOOK AND CHAPTER

The primary goals of this book are to introduce the reader to the principles of random signals and to provide tools whereby one can deal with systems involving such signals. Toward these goals, perhaps the first thing that should be done is define what is meant by random signal. A *random signal* is a time waveform† that can be characterized only in some probablistic manner. In general, it can be either a desired or undesired waveform.

The reader has no doubt heard background hiss while listening to an ordinary broadcast radio receiver. The waveform causing the hiss, when observed on an oscilloscope, would appear as a randomly fluctuating voltage with time. It is undesirable, since it interferes with our ability to hear the radio program, and is called *noise*.

Undesired random waveforms (noise) also appear in the outputs of other types of systems. In a radio astronomer's receiver, noise interferes with the desired signal from outer space (which itself is a random, but desirable, signal). In a television system, noise shows up in the form of picture interference often called "snow." In a sonar system, randomly generated sea sounds give rise to a noise that interferes with the desired echoes.

---

† We shall usually assume random signals to be voltage-time waveforms. However, the theory to be developed throughout the book will apply, in most cases, to random functions other than voltage, of arguments other than time.

The number of desirable random signals is almost limitless. For example, the bits in a computer bit stream appear to fluctuate randomly with time between the zero and one states, thereby creating a random signal. In another example, the output voltage of a wind-powered generator would be random because wind speed fluctuates randomly. Similarly, the voltage from a solar detector varies randomly due to the randomness of cloud and weather conditions. Still other examples are: the signal from an instrument designed to measure instantaneous ocean wave height; the space-originated signal at the output of the radio astronomer's antenna (the relative intensity of this signal from space allows the astronomer to form radio maps of the heavens); and the voltage from a vibration analyzer attached to an automobile driving over rough terrain.

In Chapters 8 and 9 we shall study methods of characterizing systems having random input signals. However, from the above examples, it is obvious that random signals only represent the behavior of more fundamental underlying random phenomena. Phenomena associated with the desired signals of the last paragraph are: information source for computer bit stream; wind speed; various weather conditions such as cloud density and size, cloud speed, etc.; ocean wave height; sources of outer space signals; and terrain roughness. All these phenomena must be described in some probabilistic way.

Thus, there are actually two things to be considered in characterizing random signals. One is how to describe any one of a variety of random phenomena; another is how to bring time into the problem so as to create the random signal of interest. To accomplish the first item, we shall introduce mathematical concepts in Chapters 2, 3, 4, and 5 (random variables) that are sufficiently general they can apply to any suitably defined random phenomena. To accomplish the second item, we shall introduce another mathematical concept, called a random process, in Chapters 6 and 7. All these concepts are based on probability theory.

The purpose of this chapter is to introduce the elementary aspects of probability theory on which all of our later work is based. Several approaches exist for the definition and discussion of probability. Only two of these are worthy of modern-day consideration, while all others are mainly of historical interest and are not commented on further here. Of the more modern approaches, one uses the relative frequency definition of probability. It gives a degree of physical insight which is popular with engineers, and is often used in texts having principal topics other than probability theory itself (for example, see Peebles, 1976).†

The second approach to probability uses the axiomatic definition. It is the most mathematically sound of all approaches and is most appropriate for a text having its topics based principally on probability theory. The axiomatic approach also serves as the best basis for readers wishing to proceed beyond the scope of this book to more advanced theory. Because of these facts, we adopt the axiomatic approach in this book.

---

† References are quoted by name and date of publication. They are listed at the end of the book.

Prior to the introduction of the axioms of probability, it is necessary that we first develop certain elements of set theory.†

1.1 SET DEFINITIONS

A *set* is a collection of objects. The objects are called *elements* of the set and may be anything whatsoever. We may have a set of voltages, a set of airplanes, a set of chairs, or even a set of sets, sometimes called a *class* of sets. A set is usually denoted by a capital letter while an element is represented by a lower-case letter. Thus, if a is an element of set A, then we write

$$a \in A \qquad (1.1\text{-}1)$$

If a is not an element of A, we write

$$a \notin A \qquad (1.1\text{-}2)$$

A set is specified by the content of two braces: $\{\cdot\}$. Two methods exist for specifying content, the tabular method and the rule method. In the tabular method the elements are enumerated explicitly. For example, the set of all integers between 5 and 10 would be $\{6, 7, 8, 9\}$. In the rule method, a set's content is determined by some rule, such as: {integers between 5 and 10}.‡ The rule method is usually more convenient to use when the set is large. For example, {integers from 1 to 1000 inclusive} would be cumbersome to write explicitly using the tabular method.

A set is said to be *countable* if its elements can be put in one-to-one correspondence with the natural numbers, which are the integers 1, 2, 3, etc. If a set is not countable it is called *uncountable*. A set is said to be *empty* if it has no elements. The empty set is given the symbol $\varnothing$ and is often called the *null set*.

A *finite set* is one that is either empty or has elements that can be counted, with the counting process terminating. In other words, it has a finite number of elements. If a set is not finite it is called *infinite*. An infinite set having countable elements is called *countably infinite*.

If every element of a set A is also an element in another set B, A is said to be contained in B. A is known as a *subset* of B and we write

$$A \subseteq B \qquad (1.1\text{-}3)$$

If at least one element exists in B which is not in A, then A is a *proper subset* of B, denoted by (Thomas, 1969)

$$A \subset B \qquad (1.1\text{-}4)$$

The null set is clearly a subset of all other sets.

---

† Our treatment is limited to the level required to introduce the desired probability concepts. For additional details the reader is referred to McFadden (1963), or Milton and Tsokos (1976).

‡ Sometimes notations such as $\{I \,|\, 5 < I < 10, I \text{ an integer}\}$ or $\{I: 5 < I < 10, I \text{ an integer}\}$ are seen in the literature.

Two sets, A and B, are called *disjoint* or *mutually exclusive* if they have no common elements.

Example 1.1-1 To illustrate the topics discussed above, we identify the sets listed below.

$$A = \{1, 3, 5, 7\} \qquad D = \{0.0\}$$
$$B = \{1, 2, 3, \ldots\} \qquad E = \{2, 4, 6, 8, 10, 12, 14\}$$
$$C = \{0.5 < c \leq 8.5\} \qquad F = \{-5.0 < f \leq 12.0\}$$

The set A is tabularly specified, countable, and finite. B is also tabularly specified and countable, but is infinite. Set C is rule-specified, uncountable, and infinite, since it contains *all* numbers greater than 0.5 but not exceeding 8.5. Similarly, sets D and E are countably finite, while set F is uncountably infinite. It should be noted that D is *not* the null set; it has one element, the number zero.

Set A is contained in sets B, C, and F. Similarly, $C \subset F$, $D \subset F$, and $E \subset B$. Sets B and F are not subsets of any of the other sets or of each other. Sets A, D, and E are mutually exclusive of each other. The reader may wish to identify which of the remaining sets are also mutually exclusive.

The largest or all-encompassing set of objects under discussion in a given situation is called the *universal set*, denoted S. All sets (of the situation considered) are subsets of the universal set. An example will help clarify the concept of a universal set.

Example 1.1-2 Suppose we consider the problem of rolling a die. We are interested in the numbers that show on the upper face. Here the universal set is $S = \{1, 2, 3, 4, 5, 6\}$. In a gambling game, suppose a person wins if the number comes up odd. This person wins for any number in the set $A = \{1, 3, 5\}$. Another person might win if the number shows four or less; that is, for any number in the set $B = \{1, 2, 3, 4\}$.

Observe that both A and B are subsets of S. For any universal set with N elements, there are 2^N possible subsets of S. (The reader should check this for a few values of N.) For the present example, $N = 6$ and $2^N = 64$, so that there are 64 ways one can define "winning" with one die.

It should be noted that winning or losing in the above gambling game is related to a set. The game itself is partially specified by its universal set (other games typically have a different universal set). These facts are not just coincidence, and we shall shortly find that sets form the basis on which our study of probability is constructed.

1.2 SET OPERATIONS

In working with sets, it is helpful to introduce a geometrical representation that enables us to associate a physical picture with sets.

Venn Diagram

Such a representation is the Venn diagram.† Here sets are represented by closed-plane figures. Elements of the sets are represented by the enclosed points (area). The universal set S is represented by a rectangle as illustrated in Figure 1.2-1*a*. Three sets A, B, and C are shown. Set C is disjoint from both A and B, while set B is a subset of A.

---

† After John Venn (1834–1923), an Englishman.

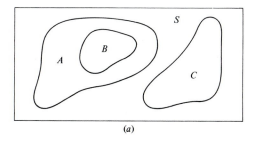

(*a*)

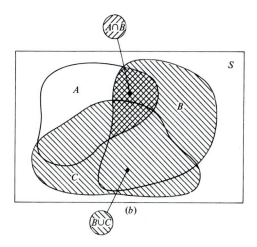

(*b*)

FIGURE 1.2-1
Venn diagrams. (*a*) Illustration of subsets and mutually exclusive sets, and (*b*) illustration of intersection and union of sets. [*Adapted from Peebles, (1976) with permission of publishers Addison–Wesley, Advanced Book Program.*]

Equality and Difference

Two sets A and B are *equal* if all elements in A are present in B and all elements in B are present in A; that is, if $A \subseteq B$ and $B \subseteq A$. For equal sets we write $A = B$.

The *difference* of two sets A and B, denoted $A - B$, is the set containing all elements of A that are not present in B. For example, with $A = \{0.6 < a \leq 1.6\}$ and $B = \{1.0 \leq b \leq 2.5\}$, then $A - B = \{0.6 < c < 1.0\}$ or $B - A = \{1.6 < d \leq 2.5\}$. Note that $A - B \neq B - A$.

Union and Intersection

The *union* (call it C) of two sets A and B is written

$$C = A \cup B \tag{1.2-1}$$

It is the set of all elements of A or B or both. The union is sometimes called the *sum* of two sets.

The *intersection* (call it D) of two sets A and B is written

$$D = A \cap B \tag{1.2-2}$$

It is the set of all elements common to both A and B. Intersection is sometimes called the *product* of two sets. For mutually exclusive sets A and B, $A \cap B = \varnothing$. Figure 1.2-1b illustrates the Venn diagram area to be associated with the intersection and union of sets.

By repeated application of (1.2-1) or (1.2-2), the union and intersection of N sets $A_n, n = 1, 2, \ldots, N$, become

$$C = A_1 \cup A_2 \cup \cdots \cup A_N = \bigcup_{n=1}^{N} A_n \tag{1.2-3}$$

$$D = A_1 \cap A_2 \cap \cdots \cap A_N = \bigcap_{n=1}^{N} A_n \tag{1.2-4}$$

Complement

The *complement* of a set A, denoted by $\bar{A}$, is the set of all elements not in A. Thus,

$$\bar{A} = S - A \tag{1.2-5}$$

It is also easy to see that $\overline{\varnothing} = S$, $\bar{S} = \varnothing$, $A \cup \bar{A} = S$, and $A \cap \bar{A} = \varnothing$.

Example 1.2-1 We illustrate intersection, union, and complement by taking an example with the four sets

$$S = \{1 \leq \text{integers} \leq 12\} \qquad B = \{2, 6, 7, 8, 9, 10, 11\}$$
$$A = \{1, 3, 5, 12\} \qquad C = \{1, 3, 4, 6, 7, 8\}$$

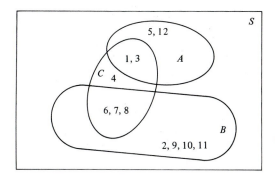

FIGURE 1.2-2
Venn diagram applicable to Example 1.2-1.

Applicable unions and intersections here are:

$A \cup B = \{1, 2, 3, 5, 6, 7, 8, 9, 10, 11, 12\}$ $A \cap B = \varnothing$

$A \cup C = \{1, 3, 4, 5, 6, 7, 8, 12\}$ $A \cap C = \{1, 3\}$

$B \cup C = \{1, 2, 3, 4, 6, 7, 8, 9, 10, 11\}$ $B \cap C = \{6, 7, 8\}$

Complements are:

$$\bar{A} = \{2, 4, 6, 7, 8, 9, 10, 11\}$$

$$\bar{B} = \{1, 3, 4, 5, 12\}$$

$$\bar{C} = \{2, 5, 9, 10, 11, 12\}$$

The various sets are illustrated in Figure 1.2-2.

Algebra of Sets

All subsets of the universal set form an algebraic system for which a number of theorems may be stated (Thomas, 1969). Three of the most important of these relate to laws involving unions and intersections. The *commutative law* states that

$$A \cap B = B \cap A \tag{1.2-6}$$

$$A \cup B = B \cup A \tag{1.2-7}$$

The *distributive law* is written as

$$A \cap (B \cup C) = (A \cap B) \cup (A \cap C) \tag{1.2-8}$$

$$A \cup (B \cap C) = (A \cup B) \cap (A \cup C) \tag{1.2-9}$$

The *associative law* is written as

$$(A \cup B) \cup C = A \cup (B \cup C) = A \cup B \cup C \tag{1.2-10}$$

$$(A \cap B) \cap C = A \cap (B \cap C) = A \cap B \cap C \tag{1.2-11}$$

These are just restatements of (1.2-3) and (1.2-4).

De Morgan's Laws

By use of a Venn diagram we may readily prove *De Morgan's laws*†, which state that the complement of a union (intersection) of two sets A and B equals the intersection (union) of the complements $\bar{A}$ and $\bar{B}$. Thus,

$$\overline{(A \cup B)} = \bar{A} \cap \bar{B} \tag{1.2-12}$$

$$\overline{(A \cap B)} = \bar{A} \cup \bar{B} \tag{1.2-13}$$

From the last two expressions one can show that if in an identity we replace unions by intersections, intersections by unions, and sets by their complements, then the identity is preserved (Papoulis, 1965, p. 23).

Example 1.2-2 We verify De Morgan's law (1.2-13) by using the example sets $A = \{2 < a \leq 16\}$ and $B = \{5 < b \leq 22\}$ when $S = \{2 < s \leq 24\}$. First, if we define $C = A \cap B$, the reader can readily see from Venn diagrams that $C = A \cap B = \{5 < c \leq 16\}$ so $\bar{C} = \overline{A \cap B} = \{2 < c \leq 5, 16 < c \leq 24\}$. This result is the left side of (1.2-13).

Second, we compute $\bar{A} = S - A = \{16 < a \leq 24\}$ and $\bar{B} = S - B = \{2 < b \leq 5, 22 < b \leq 24\}$. Thus, $C = \bar{A} \cup \bar{B} = \{2 < c \leq 5, 16 < c \leq 24\}$. This result is the right side of (1.2-13) and De Morgan's law is verified.

Duality Principle

This principle (see Papoulis, 1965, for additional reading) states: if in an identity we replace unions by intersections, intersections by unions, S by $\varnothing$, and $\varnothing$ by S, then the identity is preserved. For example, since

$$A \cap (B \cup C) = (A \cap B) \cup (A \cap C) \tag{1.2-14}$$

is a valid identity from (1.2-8), it follows that

$$A \cup (B \cap C) = (A \cup B) \cap (A \cup C) \tag{1.2-15}$$

is also valid, which is just (1.2-9).

1.3 PROBABILITY INTRODUCED THROUGH SETS

Basic to our study of probability is the idea of a physical *experiment*. In this section we develop a mathematical model of an experiment. Of course, we are interested only in experiments that are regulated in some probabilistic

---

† After Augustus De Morgan (1806–1871), an English mathematician.

way. A single performance of the experiment is called a *trial* for which there is an *outcome*.

Experiments and Sample Spaces

Although there exists a precise mathematical procedure for defining an experiment, we shall rely on reason and examples. This simplified approach will ultimately lead us to a valid mathematical model for any real experiment.† To illustrate, one experiment might consist of rolling a single die and observing the number that shows up. There are six such numbers and they form all the possible outcomes in the experiment. If the die is "unbiased" our intuition tells us that each outcome is equally likely to occur and the *likelihood* of any one occurring is $\frac{1}{6}$ (later we call this number the *probability* of the outcome). This experiment is seen to be governed, in part, by two *sets*. One is the set of all possible outcomes, and the other is the set of the likelihoods of the outcomes. Each set has six elements. For the present, we consider only the set of outcomes.

The set of all possible outcomes in any given experiment is called the *sample space* and it is given the symbol *S*. In effect, the sample space is a universal set for the given experiment. *S* may be different for different experiments, but all experiments are governed by some sample space. The definition of sample space forms the first of three elements in our mathematical model of experiments. The remaining elements are *events* and *probability*, as discussed below.

Discrete and Continuous Sample Spaces

In the earler die-tossing experiment, *S* was a finite set with six elements. Such sample spaces are said to be *discrete* and finite. The sample space can also be discrete and *infinite* for some experiments. For example, *S* in the experiment "choose randomly a positive integer" is the countably infinite set $\{1, 2, 3, \ldots\}$.

Some experiments have an uncountably infinite sample space. An illustration would be the experiment "obtain a number by spinning the pointer on a wheel of chance numbered from 0 to 12." Here any number *s* from 0 to 12 can result and $S = \{0 < s \leq 12\}$. Such a sample space is called *continuous*.

Events

In most situations, we are interested in some *characteristic* of the outcomes of our experiment as opposed to the outcomes themselves. In the experiment "draw a card from a deck of 52 cards," we might be more interested in whether we draw a spade as opposed to having any interest in individual cards. To handle such situations we define the concept of an event.

---

† Most of our early definitions involving probability are rigorously established only through concepts beyond our scope. Although we adopt a simplified development of the theory, our final results are no less valid or useful than if we had used the advanced concepts.

An *event* is defined as a subset of the sample space. Because an event is a set, all the earlier definitions and operations applicable to sets will apply to events. For example, if two events have no common outcomes they are *mutually exclusive*.

In the above card experiment, 13 of the 52 possible outcomes are spades. Since any one of the spade outcomes satisfies the event "draw a spade," this event is a set with 13 elements. We have earlier stated that a set with N elements can have as many as 2^N subsets (events defined on a sample space having N possible outcomes). In the present example, $2^N = 2^{52} \approx 4.5(10^{15})$ events.

As with the sample space, events may be either discrete or continuous. The card event "draw a spade" is a discrete, finite event. An example of a discrete, countably infinite event would be "select an odd integer" in the experiment "randomly select a positive integer." The event has a countably infinite number of elements: $\{1, 3, 5, 7, \dots\}$. However, events defined on a countably infinite sample space do not *have* to be countably infinite. The event $\{1, 3, 5, 7\}$ is clearly not infinite but applies to the integer selection experiment.

Events defined on continuous sample spaces are usually continuous. In the experiment "choose randomly a number a from 6 to 13," the sample space is $S = \{6 \leq s \leq 13\}$. An event of interest might correspond to the chosen number falling between 7.4 and 7.6; that is, the event (call it A) is $A = \{7.4 < a < 7.6\}$.

Discrete events may also be defined on continuous sample spaces. An example of such an event is $A = \{6.13692\}$ for the sample space $S = \{6 \leq s \leq 13\}$ of the previous paragraph. We comment later on this type of event.

The above definition of an event as a subset of the sample space forms the second of three elements in our mathematical model of experiments. The third element involves defining probability.

Probability Definition and Axioms

To each event defined on a sample space S, we shall assign a nonnegative number called *probability*. Probability is therefore a function; it is a function of the events defined. We adopt the notation $P(A)$† for "the probability of event A." When an event is stated explicitly as a set by using braces, we employ the notation $P\{\cdot\}$ instead of $P(\{\cdot\})$.

The assigned probabilities are chosen so as to satisfy three *axioms*. Let A be any event defined on a sample space S. Then the first two axioms are

axiom 1: $$p(A) \geq 0 \qquad (1.3\text{-}1a)$$

axiom 2: $$P(S) = 1 \qquad (1.3\text{-}1b)$$

The first only represents our desire to work with nonnegative numbers. The second axiom recognizes that the sample space itself is an event, and, since it is the all

---

† Occasionally it will be convenient to use brackets, such as $P[A]$ when A is itself an event such as $C - (B \cap D)$.

encompassing event, it should have the highest possible probability, which is selected as unity. For this reason, S is known as the *certain event*. Alternatively, the null set $\varnothing$ is an event with no elements; it is known as the *impossible event* and its probability is 0.

The third axiom applies to N events $A_n, n = 1, 2, \ldots, N$, where N may possibly be infinite, defined on a sample space S, and having the property $A_m \cap A_n = \varnothing$ for all $m \neq n$. It is

axiom 3: $\qquad P\left(\bigcup_{n=1}^{N} A_n \right) = \sum_{n=1}^{N} P(A_n) \qquad$ if $\qquad A_m \cap A_n = \varnothing \qquad$ (1.3-1c)

for all $m \neq n = 1, 2, \ldots, N$, with N possibly infinite. The axiom states that the probability of the event equal to the union of any number of mutually exclusive events is equal to the sum of the individual event probabilities.

An example should help give a physical picture of the meaning of the above axioms.

Example 1.3-1 Let an experiment consist of obtaining a number x by spinning the pointer on a "fair" wheel of chance that is labeled from 0 to 100 points. The sample space is $S = \{0 < x \leq 100\}$. We reason that probability of the pointer falling between any two numbers $x_2 \geq x_1$ should be $(x_2 - x_1)/100$ since the wheel is fair. As a check on this assignment, we see that the event $A = \{x_1 < x \leq x_2\}$ satisfies axiom 1 for all x_1 and x_2, and axiom 2 when $x_2 = 100$ and $x_1 = 0$.

Now suppose we break the wheel's periphery into N contiguous segments $A_n = \{x_{n-1} < x \leq x_n\}$, $x_n = (n)100/N$, $n = 1, 2, \ldots, N$, with $x_0 = 0$. Then $P(A_n) = 1/N$, and, for any N,

$$ P\left(\bigcup_{n=1}^{N} A_n \right) = \sum_{n=1}^{N} P(A_n) = \sum_{n=1}^{N} \frac{1}{N} = 1 = P(S) $$

from axiom 3.

Example 1.3-1 allows us to return to our earlier discussion of discrete events defined on continuous sample spaces. If the interval $x_n - x_{n-1}$ is allowed to approach zero $(\rightarrow 0)$, the probability $P(A_n) \rightarrow P(x_n)$; that is, $P(A_n)$ becomes the probability of the pointer falling exactly on the point x_n. Since $N \rightarrow \infty$ in this situation, $P(A_n) \rightarrow 0$. Thus, the probability of a discrete event defined on a continuous sample space is 0. This fact is true in general.

A consequence of the above statement is that events can occur even if their probability is 0. Intuitively, any number can be obtained from the wheel of chance, but that precise number may never occur again. The infinite sample space has only one outcome satisfying such a discrete event, so its probability is 0. Such events are *not* the same as the impossible event which has *no* elements and *cannot* occur. The converse situation can also happen where events with probability 1 may *not* occur. An example for the wheel of chance experiment would be the event $A = \{$all numbers except the number $x_n\}$. Events with probability 1 (that may not occur) are not the same as the certain event which *must* occur.

Mathematical Model of Experiments

The axioms of probability, introduced above, complete our mathematical model of an experiment. We pause to summarize. Given some real physical experiment having a set of particular outcomes possible, we first defined a *sample space* to mathematically represent the physical outcomes. Second, it was recognized that certain characteristics of the outcomes in the real experiment were of interest, as opposed to the outcomes themselves; *events* were defined to mathematically represent these characteristics. Finally, *probabilities* were assigned to the defined events to mathematically account for the random nature of the experiment.

Thus, a real experiment is defined mathematically by three things: (1) assignment of a sample space; (2) definition of events of interest; and (3) making probability assignments to the events such that the axioms are satisfied. Establishing the correct model for an experiment is probably the single most difficult step in solving probability problems.

Example 1.3-2 An experiment consists of observing the sum of the numbers showing up when two dice are thrown. We develop a model for this experiment.

The sample space consists of $6^2 = 36$ points as shown in Figure 1.3-1. Each possible outcome corresponds to a sum having values from 2 to 12.

Suppose we are mainly interested in three events defined by $A = \{\text{sum} = 7\}$, $B = \{8 < \text{sum} \le 11\}$, and $C = \{10 < \text{sum}\}$. In assigning probabilities to these events, it is first convenient to define 36 *elementary events*

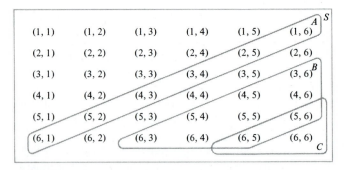

FIGURE 1.3-1
Sample space applicable to Example 1.3-2.

$A_{ij} = \{$sum for outcome $(i, j) = i + j\}$, where i represents the row and j represents the column locating a particular possible outcome in Figure 1.3-1. An elementary event has only one element.

For probability assignments, intuition indicates that each possible outcome has the same likelihood of occurrence if the dice are fair, so $P(A_{ij}) = \frac{1}{36}$. Now because the events A_{ij}, i and $j = 1, 2, \ldots, N = 6$, are mutually exclusive, they must satisfy axiom 3. But since the events, A, B, and C are simply the unions of appropriate elementary events, their probabilities are derived from axiom 3. From Figure 1.3-1 we easily find

$$P(A) = P\left(\bigcup_{i=1}^{6} A_{i, 7-i}\right) = \sum_{i=1}^{6} P(A_{i, 7-i}) = 6\left(\frac{1}{36}\right) = \frac{1}{6}$$

$$P(B) = 9\left(\frac{1}{36}\right) = \frac{1}{4}$$

$$P(C) = 3\left(\frac{1}{36}\right) = \frac{1}{12}$$

As a matter of interest, we also observe the probabilities of the events $B \cap C$ and $B \cup C$ to be $P(B \cap C) = 2(\frac{1}{36}) = \frac{1}{18}$ and $P(B \cup C) = 10(\frac{1}{36}) = \frac{5}{18}$.

1.4 JOINT AND CONDITIONAL PROBABILITY

In some experiments, such as in Example 1.3-2 above, it may be that some events are not mutually exclusive because of common elements in the sample space. These elements correspond to the simultaneous or *joint* occurrence of the non-exclusive events. For two events A and B, the common elements form the event $A \cap B$.

Joint Probability

The probability $P(A \cap B)$ is called the *joint probability* for two events A and B which intersect in the sample space. A study of a Venn diagram will readily show that

$$P(A \cap B) = P(A) + P(B) - P(A \cup B) \tag{1.4-1}$$

Equivalently,

$$P(A \cup B) = P(A) + P(B) - P(A \cap B) \le P(A) + P(B) \tag{1.4-2}$$

In other words, the probability of the union of two events never exceeds the sum of the event probabilities. The equality holds only for mutually exclusive events because $A \cap B = \emptyset$, and therefore, $P(A \cap B) = P(\emptyset) = 0$.

Conditional Probability

Given some event B with nonzero probability

$$P(B) > 0 \qquad (1.4\text{-}3)$$

we define the *conditional probability* of an event A, given B, by

$$P(A|B) = \frac{P(A \cap B)}{P(B)} \qquad (1.4\text{-}4)$$

The probability $P(A|B)$ simply reflects the fact that the probability of an event A may depend on a second event B. If A and B are mutually exclusive, $A \cap B = \varnothing$, and $P(A|B) = 0$.

Conditional probability is a defined quantity and cannot be proven. However, as a probability it must satisfy the three axioms given in (1.3-1). $P(A|B)$ obviously satisfies axiom 1 by its definition because $P(A \cap B)$ and $P(B)$ are nonnegative numbers. The second axiom is shown to be satisfied by letting $S = A$:

$$P(S|B) = \frac{P(S \cap B)}{P(B)} = \frac{P(B)}{P(B)} = 1 \qquad (1.4\text{-}5)$$

The third axiom may be shown to hold by considering the union of A with an event C, where A and C are mutually exclusive. If $P(A \cup C|B) = P(A|B) + P(C|B)$ is true, then axiom 3 holds. Since $A \cap C = \varnothing$ then events $A \cap B$ and $B \cap C$ are mutually exclusive (use a Venn diagram to verify this fact) and

$$P[(A \cup C) \cap B] = P[(A \cap B) \cup (C \cap B)] = P(A \cap B) + P(C \cap B) \quad (1.4\text{-}6)$$

Thus, on substitution into (1.4-4)

$$P[(A \cup C)|B] = \frac{P[(A \cup C) \cap B]}{P(B)} = \frac{P(A \cap B)}{P(B)} + \frac{P(C \cap B)}{P(B)}$$

$$= P(A|B) + P(C|B) \qquad (1.4\text{-}7)$$

and axiom 3 holds.

TABLE 1.4-1
Numbers of resistors in a box having given resistance and tolerance.

Resistance (Ω)	Tolerance		Total
	5%	10%	
22	10	14	24
47	28	16	44
100	24	8	32
Total	62	38	100

Example 1.4-1 In a box there are 100 resistors having resistance and tolerance as shown in Table 1.4-1. Let a resistor be selected from the box and assume each resistor has the same likelihood of being chosen. Define three events: A as "draw a 47-Ω resistor," B as "draw a resistor with 5% tolerance," and C as "draw a 100-Ω resistor." From the table, the applicable probabilities are†

$$P(A) = P(47\ \Omega) = \frac{44}{100}$$

$$P(B) = P(5\%) = \frac{62}{100}$$

$$P(C) = P(100\ \Omega) = \frac{32}{100}$$

The joint probabilities are

$$P(A \cap B) = P(47\ \Omega \cap 5\%) = \frac{28}{100}$$

$$P(A \cap C) = P(47\ \Omega \cap 100\ \Omega) = 0$$

$$P(B \cap C) = P(5\% \cap 100\ \Omega) = \frac{24}{100}$$

By using (1.4-4) the conditional probabilities become

$$P(A|B) = \frac{P(A \cap B)}{P(B)} = \frac{28}{62}$$

$$P(A|C) = \frac{P(A \cap C)}{P(C)} = 0$$

$$P(B|C) = \frac{P(B \cap C)}{P(C)} = \frac{24}{32}$$

$P(A|B) = P(47\ \Omega|5\%)$ is the probability of drawing a 47-Ω resistor given that the resistor drawn is 5%. $P(A|C) = P(47\ \Omega|100\ \Omega)$ is the probability of drawing a 47-Ω resistor given that the resistor drawn is 100 Ω; this is clearly an impossible event so the probability of it is 0. Finally, $P(B|C) = P(5\%|100\ \Omega)$ is the probability of drawing a resistor of 5% tolerance given that the resistor is 100 Ω.

---

† It is reasonable that probabilities are related to the *number* of resistors in the box that satisfy an event, since each resistor is equally likely to be selected. An alternative approach would be based on elementary events similar to that used in Example 1.3-2. The reader may view the latter approach as more rigorous but less readily applied.

Total Probability

The probability $P(A)$ of any event A defined on a sample space S can be expressed in terms of conditional probabilities. Suppose we are given N mutually exclusive events $B_n, n = 1, 2, \ldots, N$, whose union equals S as illustrated in Figure 1.4-1. These events satisfy

$$B_m \cap B_n = \emptyset \qquad m \neq n = 1, 2, \ldots, N \tag{1.4-8}$$

$$\bigcup_{n=1}^{N} B_n = S \tag{1.4-9}$$

We shall prove that

$$P(A) = \sum_{n=1}^{N} P(A|B_n)P(B_n) \tag{1.4-10}$$

which is known as the *total probability* of event A.

Since $A \cap S = A$, we may start the proof using (1.4-9) and (1.2-8):

$$A \cap S = A \cap \left(\bigcup_{n=1}^{N} B_n \right) = \bigcup_{n=1}^{N} (A \cap B_n) \tag{1.4-11}$$

Now the events $A \cap B_n$ are mutually exclusive as seen from the Venn diagram (Fig. 1.4-1). By applying axiom 3 to these events, we have

$$P(A) = P(A \cap S) = P\left[\bigcup_{n=1}^{N} (A \cap B_n) \right] = \sum_{n=1}^{N} P(A \cap B_n) \tag{1.4-12}$$

where (1.4-11) has been used. Finally, (1.4-4) is substituted into (1.4-12) to obtain (1.4-10).

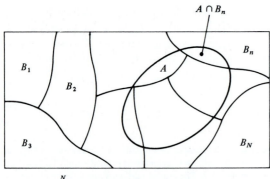

$$\bigcup_{n=1}^{N} B_n = S, \; B_m \cap B_n = \emptyset \quad \text{for all } m \neq n$$

FIGURE 1.4-1
Venn diagram of N mutually exclusive events B_n and another event A.

Bayes' Theorem†

The definition of conditional probability, as given by (1.4-4), applies to any two events. In particular, let B_n be one of the events defined above in the subsection on total probability. Equation (1.4-4) can be written

$$P(B_n|A) = \frac{P(B_n \cap A)}{P(A)} \qquad (1.4\text{-}13)$$

if $P(A) \neq 0$, or, alternatively,

$$P(A|B_n) = \frac{P(A \cap B_n)}{P(B_n)} \qquad (1.4\text{-}14)$$

if $P(B_n) \neq 0$. One form of Bayes' theorem is obtained by equating these two expressions:

$$P(B_n|A) = \frac{P(A|B_n)P(B_n)}{P(A)} \qquad (1.4\text{-}15)$$

Another form derives from a substitution of $P(A)$ as given by (1.4-10),

$$P(B_n|A) = \frac{P(A|B_n)P(B_n)}{P(A|B_1)P(B_1) + \cdots + P(A|B_N)P(B_N)} \qquad (1.4\text{-}16)$$

for $n = 1, 2, \ldots, N$.

An example will serve to illustrate Bayes' theorem and conditional probability.

Example 1.4-2 An elementary binary communication system consists of a transmitter that sends one of two possible symbols (a 1 or a 0) over a channel to a receiver. The channel occasionally causes errors to occur so that a 1 shows up at the receiver as a 0, and vice versa.

The sample space has two elements (0 or 1). We denote by B_i, $i = 1, 2$, the events "the symbol before the channel is 1," and "the symbol before the channel is 0," respectively. Furthermore, define A_i, $i = 1, 2$, as the events "the symbol after the channel is 1," and "the symbol after the channel is 0," respectively. The probabilities that the symbols 1 and 0 are selected for transmission are assumed to be

$$P(B_1) = 0.6 \quad \text{and} \quad P(B_2) = 0.4$$

Conditional probabilities describe the effect the channel has on the transmitted symbols. The reception probabilities given a 1 was transmitted

---

† The theorem is named for Thomas Bayes (1702–1761), an English theologian and mathematician.

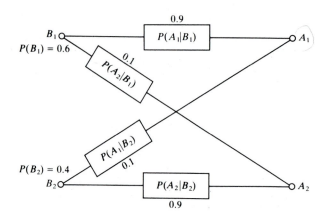

FIGURE 1.4-2
Binary symmetric communication system diagrammatical model applicable to Example 1.4-2.

are assumed to be

$$P(A_1|B_1) = 0.9$$

$$P(A_2|B_1) = 0.1$$

The channel is presumed to affect 0s in the same manner so

$$P(A_1|B_2) = 0.1$$

$$P(A_2|B_2) = 0.9$$

In either case, $P(A_1|B_i) + P(A_2|B_i) = 1$ because A_1 and A_2 are mutually exclusive and are the only "receiver" events (other than the uninteresting events $\varnothing$ and S) possible. The channel is often shown diagrammatically as illustrated in Figure 1.4-2. Because of its form it is usually called a *binary symmetric channel*.

From (1.4-10) we obtain the "received" symbol probabilities

$$P(A_1) = P(A_1|B_1)P(B_1) + P(A_1|B_2)P(B_2)$$
$$= 0.9(0.6) + 0.1(0.4) = 0.58$$
$$P(A_2) = P(A_2|B_1)P(B_1) + P(A_2|B_2)P(B_2)$$
$$= 0.1(0.6) + 0.9(0.4) = 0.42$$

From either (1.4-15) or (1.4-16) we have

$$P(B_1|A_1) = \frac{P(A_1|B_1)P(B_1)}{P(A_1)} = \frac{0.9(0.6)}{0.58} = \frac{0.54}{0.58} \approx 0.931$$

$$P(B_2|A_2) = \frac{P(A_2|B_2)P(B_2)}{P(A_2)} = \frac{0.9(0.4)}{0.42} = \frac{0.36}{0.42} \approx 0.857$$

$$P(B_1|A_2) = \frac{P(A_2|B_1)P(B_1)}{P(A_2)} = \frac{0.1(0.6)}{0.42} = \frac{0.06}{0.42} \approx 0.143$$

$$P(B_2|A_1) = \frac{P(A_1|B_2)P(B_2)}{P(A_1)} = \frac{0.1(0.4)}{0.58} = \frac{0.04}{0.58} \approx 0.069$$

These last two numbers are probabilities of system error while $P(B_1|A_1)$ and $P(B_2|A_2)$ are probabilities of correct system transmission of symbols.

In Bayes' theorem (1.4-16), the probabilities $P(B_n)$ are usually referred to as *a priori probabilities*, since they apply to the events B_n before the performance of the experiment. Similarly, the probabilities $P(A|B_n)$ are numbers typically known prior to conducting the experiment. Example 1.4-2 described such a case. The conditional probabilities are sometimes called *transition probabilities* in a communications context. On the other hand, the probabilities $P(B_n|A)$ are called *a posteriori probabilities*, since they apply after the experiment's performance when some event A is obtained.

1.5 INDEPENDENT EVENTS

In this section we introduce the concept of statistically independent events. Although a given problem may involve any number of events in general, it is most instructive to consider first the simplest possible case of two events.

Two Events

Let two events A and B have nonzero probabilities of occurrence; that is, assume $P(A) \neq 0$ and $P(B) \neq 0$. We call the events *statistically independent* if the probability of occurrence of one event is not affected by the occurrence of the other event. Mathematically, this statement is equivalent to requiring

$$P(A|B) = P(A) \qquad (1.5\text{-}1)$$

for statistically independent events. We also have

$$P(B|A) = P(B) \qquad (1.5\text{-}2)$$

for statistically independent events. By substitution of (1.5-1) into (1.4-4), in-dependence† also means that the probability of the joint occurrence (intersection) of two events must equal the product of the two event probabilities:

$$P(A \cap B) = P(A)P(B) \qquad (1.5\text{-}3)$$

Not only is (1.5-3) [or (1.5-1)] necessary for two events to be independent but it is sufficient. As a consequence, (1.5-3) can, and often does, serve as a test of independence.

Statistical independence is fundamental to much of our later work. When events are independent it will often be found that probability problems are greatly simplified.

---

† We shall often use only the word independence to mean statistical independence.

It has already been stated that the joint probability of two mutually exclusive events is 0:

$$P(A \cap B) = 0 \tag{1.5-4}$$

If the two events have nonzero probabilities of occurrence, then, by comparison of (1.5-4) with (1.5-3), we easily establish that two events cannot be both mutually exclusive and statistically independent. Hence, in order for two events to be independent they *must* have an intersection $A \cap B \neq \emptyset$.

If a problem involves more than two events, those events satisfying either (1.5-3) or (1.5-1) are said to be *independent by pairs*.

Example 1.5-1 In an experiment, one card is selected from an ordinary 52-card deck. Define events A as "select a king," B as "select a jack or queen," and C as "select a heart." From intuition, these events have probabilities $P(A) = {}^4/_{52}$, $P(B) = {}^8/_{52}$, and $P(C) = {}^{13}/_{52}$.

It is also easy to state joint probabilities. $P(A \cap B) = 0$ (it is not possible to simultaneously select a king and a jack or queen), $P(A \cap C) = {}^1/_{52}$, and $P(B \cap C) = {}^2/_{52}$.

We determine whether A, B, and C are independent by pairs by applying (1.5-3):

$$P(A \cap B) = 0 \neq P(A)P(B) = \frac{32}{52^2}$$

$$P(A \cap C) = \frac{1}{52} = P(A)P(C) = \frac{1}{52}$$

$$P(B \cap C) = \frac{2}{52} = P(B)P(C) = \frac{2}{52}$$

Thus, A and C are independent as a pair, as are B and C. However, A and B are not independent, as we might have guessed from the fact that A and B are mutually exclusive.

In many practical problems, statistical independence of events is often *assumed*. The justification hinges on there being no apparent physical connection between the mechanisms leading to the events. In other cases, probabilities assumed for elementary events may lead to independence of other events defined from them (Cooper and McGillem, 1971, p. 24).

Multiple Events

When more than two events are involved, independence by pairs is not sufficient to establish the events as statistically independent, even if *every* pair satisfies (1.5-3).

In the case of three events A_1, A_2, and A_3, they are said to be independent if, and only if, they are independent by all pairs and are also independent as a triple; that is, they must satisfy the *four* equations:

$$P(A_1 \cap A_2) = P(A_1)P(A_2) \qquad (1.5\text{-}5a)$$

$$P(A_1 \cap A_3) = P(A_1)P(A_3) \qquad (1.5\text{-}5b)$$

$$P(A_2 \cap A_3) = P(A_2)P(A_3) \qquad (1.5\text{-}5c)$$

$$P(A_1 \cap A_2 \cap A_3) = P(A_1)P(A_2)P(A_3) \qquad (1.5\text{-}5d)$$

The reader may wonder if satisfaction of (1.5-5d) might be sufficient to guarantee independence by pairs, and therefore, satisfaction of all four conditions? The answer is no, and supporting examples are relatively easy to construct. The reader might try this exercise.

More generally, for N events $A_1, A_2, \ldots, A_N$ to be called statistically independent, we require that all the conditions

$$P(A_i \cap A_j) = P(A_i)P(A_j)$$

$$P(A_i \cap A_j \cap A_k) = P(A_i)P(A_j)P(A_k)$$

$$\vdots \qquad\qquad (1.5\text{-}6)$$

$$P(A_1 \cap A_2 \cap \cdots \cap A_N) = P(A_1)P(A_2) \cdots P(A_N)$$

be satisfied for all $1 \le i < j < k < \cdots \le N$. There are $2^N - N - 1$ of these conditions (Davenport, 1970, p. 83).

Example 1.5-2 Consider drawing four cards from an ordinary 52-card deck. Let events A_1, A_2, A_3, A_4 define drawing an ace on the first, second, third, and fourth cards, respectively. Consider two cases. First, draw the cards assuming each is replaced after the draw. Intuition tells us that these events are independent so $P(A_1 \cap A_2 \cap A_3 \cap A_4) = P(A_1)P(A_2)P(A_3)P(A_4) = (4/52)^4 \approx 3.50(10^{-5})$.

On the other hand, suppose we keep each card after it is drawn. We now expect these are not indpendent events. In the general case we may write

$$P(A_1 \cap A_2 \cap A_3 \cap A_4)$$

$$= P(A_1)P(A_2 \cap A_3 \cap A_4 | A_1)$$

$$= P(A_1)P(A_2|A_1)P(A_3 \cap A_4|A_1 \cap A_2)$$

$$= P(A_1)P(A_2|A_1)P(A_3|A_1 \cap A_2)P(A_4|A_1 \cap A_2 \cap A_3)$$

$$= \frac{4}{52} \cdot \frac{3}{51} \cdot \frac{2}{50} \cdot \frac{1}{49} \approx 3.69(10^{-6})$$

Thus, we have approximately 9.5-times better chance of drawing four aces when cards are replaced than when kept. This is an intuitively satisfying result since replacing the ace drawn raises chances for an ace on the succeeding draw.

Properties of Independent Events

Many properties of independent events may be summarized by the statement: If N events $A_1, A_2, \ldots, A_N$ are independent, then any one of them is independent of any event formed by unions, intersections, and complements of the others (Papoulis, 1965, p. 42). Several examples of the application of this statement are worth listing for illustration.

For two independent events A_1 and A_2 it results that A_1 is independent of $\bar{A}_2$, $\bar{A}_1$ is independent of A_2, and $\bar{A}_1$ is independent of $\bar{A}_2$. These statements are proved as a problem at the end of this chapter.

For three independent events A_1, A_2, and A_3 any one is independent of the joint occurrence of the other two. For example

$$P[A_1 \cap (A_2 \cap A_3)] = P(A_1)P(A_2)P(A_3) = P(A_1)P(A_2 \cap A_3) \qquad (1.5\text{-}7)$$

with similar statements possible for the other cases $A_2 \cap (A_1 \cap A_3)$ and $A_3 \cap (A_1 \cap A_2)$. Any one event is also independent of the union of the other two. For example

$$P[A_1 \cap (A_2 \cup A_3)] = P(A_1)P(A_2 \cup A_3) \qquad (1.5\text{-}8)$$

This result and (1.5-7) do not necessarily hold if the events are only independent by pairs.

*1.6 COMBINED EXPERIMENTS

All of our work up to this point is related to outcomes from a single experiment. Many practical problems arise where such a constrained approach does not apply. One example would be the simultaneous measurement of wind speed and barometric pressure at some location and instant in time. *Two* experiments are actually being conducted; one has the outcome "speed"; the other outcome is "pressure." Still another type of problem involves conducting the *same* experiment several times, such as flipping a coin N times. In this case there are N performances of the same experiment. To handle these situations we introduce the concept of a combined experiment.

A *combined experiment* consists of forming a *single* experiment by suitably combining individual experiments, which we now call *subexperiments*. Recall that an experiment is defined by specifying three quantities. They are: (1) the applicable sample space, (2) the events defined on the sample space, and (3) the probabilities of the events. We specify these three quantities below, beginning with the sample space, for a combined experiment.

*Combined Sample Space

Consider only two subexperiments first. Let S_1 and S_2 be the sample spaces of the two subexperiments and let s_1 and s_2 represent the elements of S_1 and S_2 respectively. We form a new space S, called the *combined sample space*,† whose elements are all the ordered pairs (s_1, s_2). Thus, if S_1 has M elements and S_2 has N elements, then S will have MN elements. The combined sample space is denoted

$$S = S_1 \times S_2 \qquad (1.6\text{-}1)$$

Example 1.6-1 If S_1 corresponds to flipping a coin, then $S_1 = \{H, T\}$, where H is the element "heads" and T represents "tails." Let $S_2 = \{1, 2, 3, 4, 5, 6\}$ corresponding to rolling a single die. The combined sample space $S = S_1 \times S_2$ becomes

$$S = \{(H, 1), (H, 2), (H, 3), (H, 4), (H, 5), (H, 6), (T, 1), (T, 2),$$
$$(T, 3), (T, 4), (T, 5), (T, 6)\}$$

In the new space, elements are considered to be single objects, each object being a pair of items.

Example 1.6-2 We flip a coin twice, each flip being taken as one subexperiment. The applicable sample spaces are now

$$S_1 = \{H, T\}$$
$$S_2 = \{H, T\}$$
$$S = \{(H, H), (H, T), (T, H), (T, T)\}$$

In this last example, observe that the element (H, T) is considered different from the element (T, H); this fact emphasizes the elements of S are *ordered* pairs of objects.

The more general situation of N subexperiments is a direct extension of the above concepts. For N sample spaces $S_n, n = 1, 2, \ldots, N$, having elements s_n, the combined sample space S is denoted

$$S = S_1 \times S_2 \times \cdots \times S_N \qquad (1.6\text{-}2)$$

and it is the set of all ordered N-tuples

$$(s_1, s_2, \ldots, s_N) \qquad (1.6\text{-}3)$$

---

† Also called the *cartesian product space* in some texts.

★Events on the Combined Space

Events may be defined on the combined sample space through their relationship with events defined on the subexperiment sample spaces. Consider two subexperiments with sample spaces S_1 and S_2. Let A be any event defined on S_1 and B be any event defined on S_2, then

$$C = A \times B \qquad (1.6\text{-}4)$$

is an event defined on S consisting of all pairs (s_1, s_2) such that

$$s_1 \in A \quad \text{and} \quad s_2 \in B \qquad (1.6\text{-}5)$$

Since elements of A correspond to elements of the event $A \times S_2$ defined on S, and elements of B correspond to the event $S_1 \times B$ defined on S, we easily find that

$$A \times B = (A \times S_2) \cap (S_1 \times B) \qquad (1.6\text{-}6)$$

Thus, the event defined by the subset of S given by $A \times B$ is the intersection of the subsets $A \times S_2$ and $S_1 \times B$. We consider all subsets of S of the form $A \times B$ as events. All intersections and unions of such events are also events (Papoulis, 1965, p. 50).

Example 1.6-3 Let $S_1 = \{0 \le x \le 100\}$ and $S_2 = \{0 \le y \le 50\}$. The combined sample space is the set of all pairs of numbers (x, y) with $0 \le x \le 100$ and $0 \le y \le 50$ as illustrated in Figure 1.6-1. For events

$$A = \{x_1 < x < x_2\}$$
$$B = \{y_1 < y < y_2\}$$

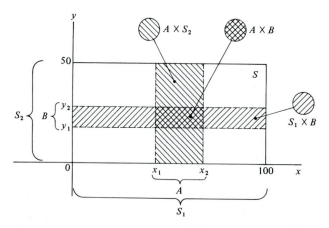

FIGURE 1.6-1
A combined sample space for two subexperiments.

where $0 \le x_1 < x_2 \le 100$ and $0 \le y_1 < y_2 \le 50$, the events $S_1 \times B$ and $A \times S_2$ are horizontal and vertical strips as shown. The event

$$A \times B = \{x_1 < x < x_2\} \times \{y_1 < y < y_2\}$$

is the rectangle shown. An event $S_1 \times \{y = y_1\}$ would be a horizontal line.

In the more general case of N subexperiments with sample spaces S_n on which events A_n are defined, the events on the combined sample space S will all be sets of the form

$$A_1 \times A_2 \times \cdots \times A_N \tag{1.6-7}$$

and unions and intersections of such sets (Papoulis, 1965, pp. 53–54).

*Probabilities

To complete the definition of a combined experiment we must assign probabilities to the events defined on the combined sample space S. Consider only two subexperiments first. Since all events defined on S will be unions and intersections of events of the form $A \times B$, where $A \subset S_1$ and $B \subset S_2$, we only need to determine $P(A \times B)$ for any A and B. We shall only consider the case where

$$P(A \times B) = P(A)P(B) \tag{1.6-8}$$

Subexperiments for which (1.6-8) is valid are called *independent experiments*.

To see what elements of S correspond to elements of A and B, we only need substitute S_2 for B or S_1 for A in (1.6-8):

$$P(A \times S_2) = P(A)P(S_2) = P(A) \tag{1.6-9}$$

$$P(S_1 \times B) = P(S_1)P(B) = P(B) \tag{1.6-10}$$

Thus, elements in the set $A \times S_2$ correspond to elements of A, and those of $S_1 \times B$ correspond to those of B.

For N independent experiments, the generalization of (1.6-8) becomes

$$P(A_1 \times A_2 \times \cdots \times A_N) = P(A_1)P(A_2) \cdots P(A_N) \tag{1.6-11}$$

where $A_n \subset S_n$, $n = 1, 2, \ldots, N$.

With independent experiments, the above results show that probabilities for events defined on S are completely determined from probabilities of events defined in the subexperiments.

1.7 BERNOULLI TRIALS

We shall close this chapter on probability by considering a very practical problem. It involves any experiment for which there are only two possible outcomes on any trial. Examples of such an experiment are numerous: flipping a coin, hitting or missing the target in artillery, passing or failing an exam, receiving a 0 or a 1 in a computer bit stream, or winning or losing in a game of chance, are just a few.

For this type of experiment, we let A be the elementary event having one of the two possible outcomes as its element. $\bar{A}$ is the only other possible elementary event. Specifically, we shall repeat the basic experiment N times and determine the probability that A is observed exactly k times out of the N trials. Such repeated experiments are called *Bernoulli trials.*† Those readers familiar with combined experiments will recognize this experiment as the combination of N identical subexperiments. For readers who omitted the section on combined experiments, we shall develop the problem so that the omission will not impair their understanding of the material.

Assume that elementary events are statistically independent for every trial. Let event A occur on any given trial with probability

$$P(A) = p \tag{1.7-1}$$

The event $\bar{A}$ then has probability

$$P(\bar{A}) = 1 - p \tag{1.7-2}$$

After N trials of the basic experiment, one *particular* sequence of outcomes has A occurring k times, followed by $\bar{A}$ occurring $N - k$ times.‡ Because of assumed statistical independence of trials, the probability of this one sequence is

$$\underbrace{P(A)P(A) \cdots P(A)}_{k \text{ terms}} \underbrace{P(\bar{A})P(\bar{A}) \cdots P(\bar{A})}_{N - k \text{ terms}} = p^k(1 - p)^{N-k} \tag{1.7-3}$$

Now there are clearly other particular sequences that will yield k events A and $N - k$ events $\bar{A}$.§ The probability of each of these sequences is given by (1.7-3). Since the sum of all such probabilities will be the desired probability of A occurring exactly k times in N trials, we only need find the number of such sequences. Some thought will reveal that this is the number of ways of taking k objects at a time from N objects. From combinatorial analysis, the number is known to be

$$\binom{N}{k} = \frac{N!}{k!(N - k)!} \tag{1.7-4}$$

The quantity $\binom{N}{k}$ is called the *binomial coefficient*. It is sometimes given the symbol C_k^N.

---

† After the Swiss mathematician Jacob Bernoulli (1654–1705).

‡ This particular sequence corresponds to one N-dimensional element in the combined sample space S.

§ All such sequences define all the elements of S that satisfy the event {A occurs exactly k times in N trials} defined on the combined sample space.

From the product of (1.7-4) and (1.7-3) we finally obtain

$$P\{A \text{ occurs exactly } k \text{ times}\} = \binom{N}{k} p^k (1-p)^{N-k} \qquad (1.7\text{-}5)$$

Example 1.7-1 A submarine attempts to sink an aircraft carrier. It will be successful only if two or more torpedoes hit the carrier. If the sub fires three torpedoes and the probability of a hit is 0.4 for each torpedo, what is the probability that the carrier will be sunk?

Define the event $A = \{$torpedo hits$\}$. Then $P(A) = 0.4$, and $N = 3$. Probabilities are found from (1.7-5):

$$P\{\text{exactly no hits}\} = \binom{3}{0}(0.4)^0(1 - 0.4)^3 = 0.216$$

$$P\{\text{exactly one hit}\} = \binom{3}{1}(0.4)^1(1 - 0.4)^2 = 0.432$$

$$P\{\text{exactly two hits}\} = \binom{3}{2}(0.4)^2(1 - 0.4)^1 = 0.288$$

$$P\{\text{exactly three hits}\} = \binom{3}{3}(0.4)^3(1 - 0.4)^0 = 0.064$$

The answer we desire is

$$P\{\text{carrier sunk}\} = P\{\text{two or more hits}\}$$
$$= P\{\text{exactly two hits}\} + P\{\text{exactly three hits}\}$$
$$= 0.352$$

Example 1.7-2 In a culture used for biological research the growth of unavoidable bacteria occasionally spoils results of an experiment that requires at least three out of four cultures to be unspoiled to obtain a single datum point. Experience has shown that about 6 of every 100 cultures are randomly spoiled by the bacteria. If the experiment requires three simultaneously derived, unspoiled data points for success, we find the probability of success for any given set of 12 cultures (three data points of four cultures each).

We treat individual datum points first as a Bernoulli trial problem with $N = 4$ and $p = P\{\text{good culture}\} = {}^{94}/_{100} = 0.94$. Here

$$P\{\text{valid datum point}\} = P\{3 \text{ good cultures}\} + P\{4 \text{ good cultures}\}$$

$$= \binom{4}{3}(0.94)^3(1 - 0.94)^1 + \binom{4}{4}(0.94)^4(1 - 0.94)^0 \approx 0.98$$

Finally, we treat the required three data points as a Bernoulli trial problem with $N = 3$ and $p = P\{\text{valid datum point}\} = 0.98$. Now

$$P\{\text{successful experiment}\} = P\{3 \text{ valid data points}\}$$

$$= \binom{3}{3}(0.98)^3(1 - 0.98)^0 \approx 0.941$$

Thus, the given experiment will be successful about 94.1 percent of the time.

When N, k, and $(N - k)$ are large, the factorials in (1.7-5) are difficult to evaluate, so approximations become useful. One approximation, called *Stirling's formula*, is

$$m! \approx (2\pi m)^{1/2} m^m e^{-m}, \qquad m \text{ large} \tag{1.7-6}$$

It is exact for $m \to \infty$ in the sense that the ratio of $m!$ to the right side of (1.7-6) tends to unity. For other values of m its fractional error is on the order of $1/(12m)$, which is quite good (better than 1 percent) even for m as small as 10.

By applying Stirling's formula to the factorials in (1.7-5), and then approximating some resulting factors by the first two terms in their series expansions, it can be shown (see Davenport, 1970, pp. 276–278) that

$$P\{A \text{ occurs exactly } k \text{ times}\} = \binom{N}{k}p^k(1 - p)^{N-k}$$

$$\approx \frac{1}{\sqrt{2\pi N p(1 - p)}} \exp\left[-\frac{(k - Np)^2}{2Np(1 - p)}\right] \tag{1.7-7}$$

This equation, called the *De Moivre–Laplace*† *approximation*, holds for N, k, and $(N - k)$ large, k near Np such that its deviations from Np (higher or lower) are small in magnitude relative to both Np and $N(1 - p)$. We illustrate these restrictions by example.

Example 1.7-3 Suppose a certain machine gun fires rounds (cartridges) for 3 seconds at a rate of 2400 per minute, and the probability of any bullet hitting a large target is 0.4. We find the probability that exactly 50 of the bullets hit the target.

---

† Abraham De Moivre (1667–1754) was a French-born scientist who lived most of his life in England and contributed to the mathematics of probability. Marquis Pierre Simon De Laplace (1749–1827) was an outstanding French mathematician.

Here $N = 3(2400/60) = 120$, $k = 50$, $p = 0.4$, $Np = 120(0.4) = 48$, and $N(1 - p) = 120(0.6) = 72$. Thus, since N, k, and $(N - k) = 70$ are all large, while k is near Np and the deviation of k from Np, which is $50 - 48 = 2$, is much smaller than both $Np = 48$ and $N(1 - p) = 72$, we can use (1.7-7):

$$P\{\text{exactly 50 bullets hit the target}\} = \binom{N}{k} p^k (1 - p)^{N - k}$$

$$\approx \frac{1}{\sqrt{2\pi(48)0.6}} \exp\left[-\frac{(50 - 48)^2}{2(48)0.6} \right] = 0.0693$$

The approximation of (1.7-7) fails to be accurate when N becomes very large while p is very small. For these conditions another approximation is helpful. It is called the *Poisson†* approximation:

$$\binom{N}{k} p^k (1 - p)^{N - k} \approx \frac{(Np)^k e^{-Np}}{k!}, \qquad N \text{ large and } p \text{ small} \qquad (1.7-8)$$

PROBLEMS

1-1 Specify the following sets by the rule method.

$$A = \{1, 2, 3\}, B = \{8, 10, 12, 14\}, C = \{1, 3, 5, 7, \ldots\}$$

1-2 Use the tabular method to specify a class of sets for the sets of Problem 1-1.

1-3 State whether the following sets are countable or uncountable, or, finite or infinite. $A = \{1\}$, $B = \{x = 1\}$, $C = \{0 < \text{integers}\}$, $D = \{\text{children in public school No. 5}\}$, $E = \{\text{girls in public school No. 5}\}$, $F = \{\text{girls in class in public school No. 5 at 3:00 A.M.}\}$, $G = \{\text{all lengths not exceeding one meter}\}$, $H = \{-25 \le x \le -3\}$, $I = \{-2, -1, 1 \le x \le 2\}$.

1-4 For each set of Problem 1-3, determine if it is equal to, or a subset of, any of the other sets.

1-5 State every possible subset of the set of letters $\{a, b, c, d\}$.

1-6 A thermometer measures temperatures from -40 to $130°F$ (-40 to $54.4°C$).
   (a) State a universal set to describe temperature measurements. Specify subsets for:
   (b) Temperature measurements not exceeding water's freezing point, and
   (c) Measurements exceeding the freezing point but not exceeding $100°F$ ($37.8°C$).

---

† After the French mathematician Siméon Denis Poisson (1781–1840).

$\star$**1-7** Prove that a set with N elements has 2^N subsets.

1-8 A random noise voltage at a given time may have any value from -10 to 10 V.

    (a) What is the universal set describing noise voltage?

    (b) Find a set to describe the voltages available from a half-wave rectifier for positive voltages that has a linear output-input voltage characteristic.

    (c) Repeat parts (a) and (b) if a dc voltage of -3 V is added to the random noise.

1-9 Show that $C \subset A$ if $C \subset B$ and $B \subset A$.

1-10 Two sets are given by $A = \{-6, -4, -0.5, 0, 1.6, 8\}$ and $B = \{-0.5, 0, 1, 2, 4\}$. Find:

    (a) $A - B$ (b) $B - A$ (c) $A \cup B$ (d) $A \cap B$

1-11 A universal set is given as $S = \{2, 4, 6, 8, 10, 12\}$. Define two subsets as $A = \{2, 4, 10\}$ and $B = \{4, 6, 8, 10\}$. Determine the following:

    (a) $\bar{A} = S - A$ (b) $A - B$ and $B - A$ (c) $A \cup B$ (d) $A \cap B$ (e) $\bar{A} \cap B$

1-12 Using Venn diagrams for three sets A, B, C, shade the areas corresponding to the sets:

    (a) $(A \cup B) - C$ (b) $\bar{B} \cap A$ (c) $A \cap B \cap C$ (d) $\overline{(A \cup B)} \cap C$

1-13 Sketch a Venn diagram for three events where $A \cap B \neq \emptyset$, $B \cap C \neq \emptyset$, $C \cap A \neq \emptyset$, but $A \cap B \cap C = \emptyset$.

1-14 Use Venn diagrams to show that the following identities are true:

    (a) $(\overline{A \cup B}) \cap C = C - [(A \cap C) \cup (B \cap C)]$

    (b) $(A \cup B \cup C) - (A \cap B \cap C) = (\bar{A} \cap B) \cup (\bar{B} \cap C) \cup (\bar{C} \cap A)$

    (c) $(\overline{A \cap B \cap C}) = \bar{A} \cup \bar{B} \cup \bar{C}$

1-15 Use Venn diagrams to prove De Morgan's laws $(\overline{A \cup B}) = \bar{A} \cap \bar{B}$ and $(\overline{A \cap B}) = \bar{A} \cup \bar{B}$.

1-16 A universal set is $S = \{-20 < s \leq -4\}$. If $A = \{-10 \leq s \leq -5\}$ and $B = \{-7 < s < -4\}$, find:

    (a) $A \cup B$

    (b) $A \cap B$

    (c) A third set C such that the sets $A \cap C$ and $B \cap C$ are as large as possible while the smallest element in C is -9.

    (d) What is the set $A \cap B \cap C$?

1-17 Use De Morgan's laws to show that:

    (a) $\overline{A \cap (B \cup C)} = (\bar{A} \cup \bar{B}) \cap (\bar{A} \cup \bar{C})$

    (b) $(\overline{A \cap B \cap C}) = \bar{A} \cup \bar{B} \cup \bar{C}$

    In each case check your results using a Venn diagram.

1-18 A die is tossed. Find the probabilities of the events $A = \{$odd number shows up$\}$, $B = \{$number larger than 3 shows up$\}$, $A \cup B$, and $A \cap B$.

1-19 In a game of dice, a "shooter" can win outright if the sum of the two numbers showing up is either 7 or 11 when two dice are thrown. What is his probability of winning outright?

1-20 A pointer is spun on a fair wheel of chance having its periphery labeled from 0 to 100.
   (*a*) What is the sample space for this experiment?
   (*b*) What is the probability that the pointer will stop between 20 and 35?
   (*c*) What is the probability that the wheel will stop on 58?

1-21 An experiment has a sample space with 10 equally likely elements $S = \{a_1, a_2, \ldots, a_{10}\}$. Three events are defined as $A = \{a_1, a_5, a_9\}$, $B = \{a_1, a_2, a_6, a_9\}$, and $C = \{a_6, a_9\}$. Find the probabilities of:
   (*a*) $A \cup C$
   (*b*) $B \cup \bar{C}$
   (*c*) $A \cap (B \cup C)$
   (*d*) $\overline{A \cup B}$
   (*e*) $(A \cup B) \cap C$

1-22 Let A be an arbitrary event. Show that $P(\bar{A}) = 1 - P(A)$.

1-23 An experiment consists of rolling a single die. Two events are defined as: $A = \{$a 6 shows up$\}$ and $B = \{$a 2 or a 5 shows up$\}$.
   (*a*) Find $P(A)$ and $P(B)$.
   (*b*) Define a third event C so that $P(C) = 1 - P(A) - P(B)$.

1-24 In a box there are 500 colored balls: 75 black, 150 green, 175 red, 70 white, and 30 blue. What are the probabilities of selecting a ball of each color?

1-25 A single card is drawn from a 52-card deck.
   (*a*) What is the probability that the card is a jack?
   (*b*) What is the probability the card will be a 5 or smaller?
   (*c*) What is the probability that the card is a red 10?

1-26 Two cards are drawn from a 52-card deck (the first is not replaced).
   (*a*) Given the first card is a queen, what is the probability that the second is also a queen?
   (*b*) Repeat part (*a*) for the first card a queen and the second card a 7.
   (*c*) What is the probability that both cards will be a queen?

1-27 An ordinary 52-card deck is thoroughly shuffled. You are dealt four cards up. What is the probability that all four cards are sevens?

1-28 For the resistor selection experiment of Example 1.4-1, define event D as "draw a 22-Ω resistor," and E as "draw a resistor with 10% tolerance." Find $P(D)$, $P(E)$, $P(D \cap E)$, $P(D|E)$, and $P(E|D)$.

1-29 For the resistor selection experiment of Example 1.4-1, define two mutually exclusive events B_1 and B_2 such that $B_1 \cup B_2 = S$.
   (*a*) Use the total probability theorem to find the probability of the event "select a 22-Ω resistor," denoted D.
   (*b*) Use Bayes' theorem to find the probability that the resistor selected had 5% tolerance, given it was 22 Ω.

1-30 In three boxes there are capacitors as shown in Table P1-30. An experiment consists of first randomly selecting a box, assuming each has the same likelihood of selection, and then selecting a capacitor from the chosen box.

TABLE P1-30
Capacitors

Value (μF)	Number in box			Totals
	1	2	3	
0.01	20	95	25	140
0.1	55	35	75	165
1.0	70	80	145	295
Totals	145	210	245	600

(a) What is the probability of selecting a 0.01-μF capacitor, given that box 2 is selected?

(b) If a 0.01-μF capacitor is selected, what is the probability it came from box 3? (*Hint:* Use Bayes' and total probability theorems.)

1-31 For Problem 1-30, list the nine conditional probabilities of capacitor selection, given certain box selections.

1-32 Rework Example 1.4-2 if $P(B_1) = 0.6$, $P(B_2) = 0.4$, $P(A_1|B_1) = P(A_2|B_2) = 0.95$, and $P(A_2|B_1) = P(A_1|B_2) = 0.05$.

1-33 Rework Example 1.4-2 if $P(B_1) = 0.7$, $P(B_2) = 0.3$, $P(A_1|B_1) = P(A_2|B_2) = 1.0$, and $P(A_2|B_1) = P(A_1|B_2) = 0$. What type of channel does this system have?

1-34 A company sells high fidelity amplifiers capable of generating 10, 25, and 50 W of audio power. It has on hand 100 of the 10-W units, of which 15% are defective, 70 of the 25-W units with 10% defective, and 30 of the 50-W units with 10% defective.

(a) What is the probability that an amplifier sold from the 10-W units is defective?

(b) If each wattage amplifier sells with equal likelihood, what is the probability of a randomly selected unit being 50 W and defective?

(c) What is the probability that a unit randomly selected for sale is defective?

1-35 A missile can be accidentially launched if two relays A and B both have failed. The probabilities of A and B failing are know to be 0.01 and 0.03 respectively. It is also known that B is more likely to fail (probability 0.06) if A has failed.

(a) What is the probability of an accidental missile launch?

(b) What is the probability that A will fail if B has failed?

(c) Are the events "A fails" and "B fails" statistically independent?

1-36 Determine whether the three events A, B, and C of Example 1.4-1 are statistically independent.

1-37 List the various equations that four events A_1, A_2, A_3, and A_4 must satisfy if they are to be statistically independent.

★**1-38** Given that two events A_1 and A_2 are statistically independent, show that:

(a) A_1 is independent of $\bar{A}_2$

(b) $\bar{A}_1$ is independent of A_2

(c) $\bar{A}_1$ is independent of $\bar{A}_2$

★1-39 An experiment consists of randomly selecting one of five cities on Florida's west coast for a vacation. Another experiment consists of selecting at random one of four acceptable motels in which to stay. Define sample spaces S_1 and S_2 for the two experiments and a combined space $S = S_1 \times S_2$ for the combined experiment having the two subexperiments.

★1-40 Sketch the area in the combined sample space of Example 1.6-3 corresponding to the event $A \times B$ where:

(a) $A = \{10 < x \leq 15\}$ and $B = \{20 < y \leq 50\}$

(b) $A = \{x = 40\}$ and $B = \{5 < y \leq 40\}$

1-41 A production line manufactures 5-gal (18.93-liter) gasoline cans to a volume tolerance of 5%. The probability of any one can being out of tolerance is 0.03. If four cans are selected at random:

(a) What is the probability they are all out of tolerance?

(b) What is the probability of exactly two being out?

(c) What is the probability that all are in tolerance?

1-42 Spacecraft are expected to land in a prescribed recovery zone 80% of the time. Over a period of time, six spacecraft land.

(a) Find the probability that none lands in the prescribed zone.

(b) Find the probability that at least one will land in the prescribed zone.

(c) The landing program is called successful if the probability is 0.9 or more that three or more out of six spacecraft will land in the prescribed zone. Is the program successful?

1-43 In the submarine problem of Example 1.7-1, find the probabilities of sinking the carrier when fewer ($N = 2$) or more ($N = 4$) torpedoes are fired.

ADDITIONAL PROBLEMS, SECOND EDITION

1-44 Use the tabular method to define a set A that contains all integers with magnitudes not exceeding 7. Define a second set B having odd integers larger than -2 and not larger than 5. Determine if $A \subset B$ and $B \subset A$.

1-45 A set A has three elements a_1, a_2, and a_3. Determine all possible subsets of A.

1-46 Shade Venn diagrams to illustrate each of the following sets: (a) $(A \cup \bar{B}) \cap \bar{C}$, (b) $\overline{(A \cap B)} \cup \bar{C}$, (c) $(A \cup \bar{B}) \cup (C \cap D)$, (d) $(A \cap B \cap \bar{C}) \cup (\bar{B} \cap C \cap D)$.

1-47 A universal set S is comprised of all points in a rectangular area defined by $0 \leq x \leq 3$ and $0 \leq y \leq 4$. Define three sets by $A = \{y \leq 3(x - 1)/2\}$, $B = \{y \geq 1\}$, and $C = \{y \geq 3 - x\}$. Shade in Venn diagrams corresponding to the sets (a) $A \cap B \cap C$, and (b) $C \cap B \cap \bar{A}$.

1-48 The take-off roll distance for aircraft at a certain airport can be any number from 80 m to 1750 m. Propeller aircraft require from 80 m to 1050 m while jets use from 950 m to 1750 m. The overall runway is 2000 m.

(a) Determine sets A, B, and C defined as "propeller aircraft take-off distances," "jet aircraft take-off distances," and "runway length safety margin," respectively.

(b) Determine the set $A \cap B$ and give its physical significance.

(c) What is the meaning of the set $\overline{A \cup B}$?

(d) What are the meanings of the sets $\overline{A \cup B \cup C}$ and $A \cup B$?

1-49 Prove that De Morgan's law (1.2-13) can be extended to N events A_i, $i = 1, 2, \ldots, N$ as follows:

$$\overline{(A_1 \cap A_2 \cap \cdots \cap A_N)} = (\bar{A}_1 \cup \bar{A}_2 \cup \cdots \cup \bar{A}_N)$$

1-50 Work Problem 1-49 for (1.2-12) to prove

$$\overline{(A_1 \cup A_2 \cup \cdots \cup A_N)} = (\bar{A}_1 \cap \bar{A}_2 \cap \cdots \cap \bar{A}_N)$$

1-51 A pair of fair dice are thrown in a gambling problem. Person A wins if the sum of numbers showing up is six or less *and* one of the dice shows four. Person B wins if the sum is five or more *and* one of the dice shows a four. Find: (a) The probability that A wins, (b) the probability of B winning, and (c) the probability that both A and B win.

1-52 You (person A) and two others (B and C) each toss a fair coin in a two-step gambling game. In step 1 the person whose toss is not a match to either of the other two is "odd man out." Only the remaining two whose coins match go on to step 2 to resolve the ultimate winner.

(a) What is the probability you will advance to step 2 after the first toss?

(b) What is the probability you will be out after the first toss?

(c) What is the probability that no one will be out after the first toss?

★1-53 The communication system of Example 1.4-2 is to be extended to the case of three transmitted symbols 0, 1, and 2. Define appropriate events A_i and B_i, $i = 1, 2, 3$, to represent symbols after and before the channel, respectively. Assume channel transition probabilities are all equal at $P(A_i|B_j) = 0.1$, $i \neq j$, and are $P(A_i|B_j) = 0.8$ for $i = j = 1, 2, 3$, while symbol transmission probabilities are $P(B_1) = 0.5$, $P(B_2) = 0.3$, and $P(B_3) = 0.2$.

(a) Sketch the diagram analogous to Fig. 1.4-2.

(b) Compute received symbol probabilities $P(A_1)$, $P(A_2)$, and $P(A_3)$.

(c) Compute the a posteriori probabilities for this system.

(d) Repeat parts (b) and (c) for all transmission symbol probabilities equal. Note the effect.

1-54 Show that there are $2^N - N - 1$ equations required in (1.5-6). (*Hint:* Recall that the binomial coefficent is the number of combinations of N things taken n at a time.)

1-55 A student is known to arrive late for a class 40% of the time. If the class meets five times each week find: (a) the probability the student is late for at least three classes in a given week, and (b) the probability the student will not be late at all during a given week.

1-56 An airline in a small city has five departures each day. It is known that any given flight has a probability of 0.3 of departing late. For any given day find the probabilities that: (a) no flights depart late, (b) all flights depart late, and (c) three or more depart on time.

1-57 The local manager of the airline of Problem 1-56 desires to make sure that the probability that all flights leave on time is 0.9. What is the largest probability of being late that the individual flights can have if the goal is to be achieved? Will the operation have to be improved significantly?

1-58 A man wins in a gambling game if he gets two heads in five flips of a biased coin. The probability of getting a head with the coin is 0.7.
(a) Find the probability the man will win. Should he play this game?
(b) What is his probability of winning if he wins by getting at least four heads in five flips? Should he play this new game?

★1-59 A rifleman can achieve a "marksman" award if he passes a test. He is allowed to fire six shots at a target's bull's eye. If he hits the bull's eye with at least five of his six shots he wins a set. He becomes a marksman only if he can repeat the feat three times straight, that is, if he can win three straight sets. If his probability is 0.8 of hitting a bull's eye on any one shot, find the probabilities of his: (a) winning a set, and (b) becoming a marksman.

ADDITIONAL PROBLEMS, THIRD EDITION

1-60 Specify, by both the tabular and rule methods, each of the following sets: (a) all integers between 1 and 9, (b) all integers from 1 to 9, (c) the five values of equivalent resistance for n identical 10-Ω resistors in parallel where $n = 1, 2, \ldots, 5$, and (d) the six values of equivalent resistance for n identical 2.2-Ω resistors in series where $n = 1, 2, \ldots, 6$.

1-61 A box contains 100 capacitors (universal set) of which 40 are 0.01 μF with a 100-V voltage rating, 35 are 0.1 μF at a rating of 50 V, and 25 are 1.0 μF and have a 10-V rating. Determine the number of elements in the following sets:
(a) $A = \{$capacitors with capacitance $\geq 0.1 \, \mu$F$\}$
(b) $B = \{$capacitors with voltage rating $> 5 \, V\}$
(c) $C = \{$capacitors with both capacitance $\geq 0.1 \, \mu$F *and* voltage rating $\geq 50 \, V\}$.

1-62 Sets $A = \{1 \leq s \leq 14\}$, $B = \{3, 6, 14\}$, and $C = \{2 < s \leq 9\}$ are defined on a sample space S. State if each of the following conditions is true or false. (a) $C \subset B$, (b) $C \subset A$, (c) $B \cap C = \varnothing$, (d) $C \cup B = S$, (e) $\bar{S} = \varnothing$, (f) $A \cap \bar{S} = \varnothing$, and (g) $C \subset A \subset B$.

1-63 Draw Venn diagrams and shade the areas corresponding to the sets (a) $(A \cup B \cup C) \cap (\bar{A} \cup \bar{B} \cup \bar{C})$, and (b) $[(A \cup \bar{B}) \cap C] \cup (\overline{A \cup C})$.

1-64 Work Problem 1-63 except assume sets (a) $(A \cap B \cap C) \cup (\overline{A \cup B \cup C})$, (b) $B - (A \cap B)$, and (c) $(A \cap B) \cup (A \cap C) \cup (B \cap C) - (A \cap B \cap C)$.

1-65 A particular electronic device is known to contain only 10-, 22-, and 48-Ω resistors, but these resistors may have 0.25-, 0.5-, or 1-W ratings, depending on how purchases are made to minimize cost. Historically, it is found that the probabilities of the 10-Ω resistors being 0.25, 0.5, or 1 W are 0.08, 0.10, and 0.01, respectively. For the 22-Ω resistors the similar probabilities are 0.20, 0.26, and 0.05. It is also historically found that the probabilities are 0.40, 0.51, and 0.09 that any resistors are 0.25, 0.50, and 1 W, respectively. What are the probabilities that the 48-Ω resistors are (a) 0.25, (b) 0.50, and (c) 1 W?

1-66 For the sample space defined in Example 1.3-2 find the probabilities that: (a) one die will show a 2 and the other will show a 3 or larger, and (b) the sum of the two numbers showing up will be 4 or less or will be 10 or more.

1-67 In a game two dice are thrown. Let one die be "weighted" so that a 4 shows up with probability $\frac{2}{7}$, while its other numbers all have probabilities of $\frac{1}{7}$. The same probabilities apply to the other die except the number 3 is "weighted." Determine the probability the shooter will win outright by having the sum of the numbers showing up be 7. What would be the probability for fair dice?

1-68 A pharmaceutical product consists of 100 pills in a bottle. Two production lines used to produce the product are selected with probabilities 0.45 (line one) and 0.55 (line two). Each line can overfill or underfill bottles by at most 2 pills. Given that line one is observed, the probabilities are 0.02, 0.06, 0.88, 0.03, and 0.01 that the numbers of pills in a bottle will be 102, 101, 100, 99, and 98, respectively. For line two, the similar respective probabilities are 0.03, 0.08, 0.83, 0.04, and 0.02.

(a) Find the probability that a bottle of the product will contain 102 pills. Repeat for 101, 100, 99, and 98 pills.

(b) Given that a bottle contains the correct number of pills, what is the probability it came from line one?

(c) What is the probability that a purchaser of the product will receive less than 100 pills?

1-69 A manufacturing plant makes radios that each contains an integrated circuit (IC) supplied by three sources A, B, and C. The probability that the IC in a radio came from one of the sources is $\frac{1}{3}$, the same for all sources. ICs are known to be defective with probabilities 0.001, 0.003, and 0.002 for sources A, B, and C, respectively.

(a) What is the probability any given radio will contain a defective IC?

(b) If a radio contains a defective IC, find the probability it came from source A. Repeat for sources B and C.

1-70 There are three special decks of cards. The first, deck D_1, has all 52 cards of a regular deck. The second, D_2 has only the 16 face cards of a regular deck (only 4 each of jacks, queens, kings, and aces). The third, D_3, has only the 36 numbered cards of a regular deck (4 twos through 4 tens). A random experiment consists of first randomly choosing one of the three decks, then second, randomly choosing a card from the chosen deck. If $P(D_1) = \frac{1}{2}$, $P(D_2) = \frac{1}{3}$, and $P(D_3) = \frac{1}{6}$, find the probabilities: (a) of drawing an ace, (b) of drawing a three, and (c) of drawing a red card.

1-71 In a communication system the signal sent from point a to point b arrives by two paths in parallel. Over each path the signal passes through two repeaters (in series). Each repeater in one path has a probability of failing (becoming an open circuit) of 0.005. This probability is 0.008 for each repeater on the other path. All repeaters fail independently of each other. Find the probability that the signal will not arrive at point b.

1-72 Work Problem 1-71, except assume the paths and repeaters of Figure P1-72, where the probabilities of the repeaters failing (independently) are $p_1 = P(R_1) = 0.005$, $p_2 = P(R_2) = P(R_3) = P(R_4) = 0.01$, and $p_3 = P(R_5) = P(R_6) = 0.05$.

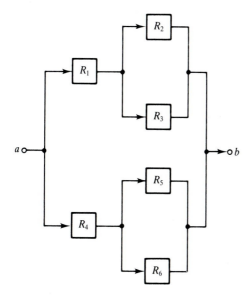

FIGURE P1-72

1-73 A ship can successfully arrive at its destination if its engine and its satellite navigation system do not fail in route. If the engine and navigation system are known to fail independently with respective probabilities of 0.05 and 0.001, what is the probability of a successful arrival?

1-74 At a certain military installation six similar radars are placed in operation. It is known that a radar's probability of failing to operate before 500 hours of "on" time have accumulated is 0.06. What are the probabilities that, before 500 hours have elapsed, (a) all will operate, (b) all will fail, and (c) only one will fail?

1-75 A particular model of automobile is recalled to fix a mechanical problem. The probability that a car will be properly repaired is 0.9. During the week a dealer has eight cars to repair.

(*a*) What is the probability that two or more of the eight cars will have to be repaired more than once?

(*b*) What is the probability all eight cars will be properly repaired?

1-76 In a large hotel it is known that 99% of all guests return room keys when checking out. If 250 engineers check out after a large conference, what is the probability that not more than three will fail to return their keys? [*Hint:* Use the approximation of (1.7-8).]

CHAPTER
2

THE RANDOM VARIABLE

2.0 INTRODUCTION

In the previous chapter we introduced the concept of an event to describe characteristics of outcomes of an experiment. Events allowed us more flexibility in determining properties of an experiment than could be obtained by considering only the outcomes themselves. An event could be almost anything from "descriptive," such as "draw a spade," to numerical, such as "the outcome is 3."

In this chapter, we introduce a new concept that will allow events to be defined in a more consistent manner; they will always be numerical. The new concept is that of a *random variable*, and it will constitute a powerful tool in the solution of practical probabilistic problems.

2.1 THE RANDOM VARIABLE CONCEPT

Definition of a Random Variable

We define a real *random variable*† as a real *function* of the elements of a sample space *S*. We shall represent a random variable by a capital letter (such as *W*, *X*, or *Y*) and any particular value of the random variable by a lowercase letter (such

---

† Complex random variables are considered in Chapter 5.

as w, x, or y). Thus, given an experiment defined by a sample space S with elements s, we assign to every s a real number

$$X(s) \qquad\qquad (2.1\text{-}1)$$

according to some rule and call $X(s)$ a random variable.

A random variable X can be considered to be a function that maps all elements of the sample space into points on the real line or some parts thereof. We illustrate, by two examples, the mapping of a random variable.

Example 2.1-1 An experiment consists of rolling a die and flipping a coin. The applicable sample space is illustrated in Figure 2.1-1. Let the random variable be a function X chosen such that (1) a coin head (H) outcome corresponds to positive values of X that are equal to the numbers that show up on the die, and (2) a coin tail (T) outcome corresponds to negative values of X that are equal in magnitude to *twice* the number that shows on the die. Here X maps the sample space of 12 elements into 12 values of X from -12 to 6 as shown in Figure 2.1-1.

Example 2.1-2 Figure 2.1-2 illustrates an experiment where the pointer on a wheel of chance is spun. The possible outcomes are the numbers from 0 to 12 marked on the wheel. The sample space consists of the numbers in the set $\{0 < s \le 12\}$. We define a random variable by the function

$$X = X(s) = s^2$$

Points in S now map onto the real line as the set $\{0 < x \le 144\}$.

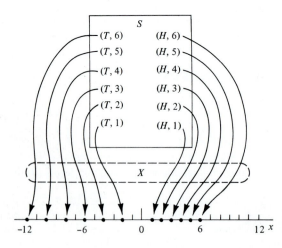

FIGURE 2.1-1
A random variable mapping of a sample space.

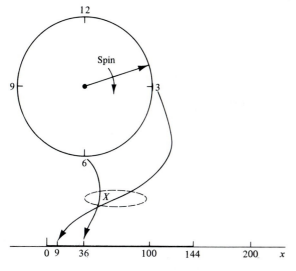

FIGURE 2.1-2
Mapping applicable to Example 2.1-2.

As seen in these two examples, a random variable is a function that maps each point in S into some point on the real line. It is not necessary that the sample-space points map uniquely, however. More than one point in S may map into a single value of X. For example, in the extreme case, we might map all six points in the sample space for the experiment "throw a die and observe the number that shows up" into the one point $X = 2$.

Conditions for a Function to be a Random Variable

Thus, a random variable may be almost any function we wish. We shall, however, require that it not be multivalued. That is, every point in S must correspond to only one value of the random variable.

Moreover, we shall require that two additional conditions be satisfied in order that a function X be a random variable (Papoulis, 1965, p. 88). First, the set $\{X \leq x\}$ shall be an event for any real number x. The satisfaction of this condition will be no trouble in practical problems. This set corresponds to those points s in the sample space for which the random variable $X(s)$ does not exceed the number x. The probability of this event, denoted by $P\{X \leq x\}$, is equal to the sum of the probabilities of all the elementary events corresponding to $\{X \leq x\}$.

The second condition we require is that the probabilities of the events $\{X = \infty\}$ and $\{X = -\infty\}$ be 0:

$$P\{X = -\infty\} = 0 \qquad P\{X = \infty\} = 0 \qquad (2.1\text{-}2)$$

This condition does not prevent X from being either $-\infty$ or ∞ for some values of s; it only requires that the probability of the set of those s be zero.

Discrete and Continuous Random Variables

A *discrete random variable* is one having only discrete values. Example 2.1-1 illustrated a discrete random variable. The sample space for a discrete random variable can be discrete, continuous, or even a mixture of discrete and continuous points. For example, the "wheel of chance" of Example 2.1-2 has a continuous sample space, but we could define a discrete random variable as having the value 1 for the set of outcomes $\{0 < s \leq 6\}$ and -1 for $\{6 < s \leq 12\}$. The result is a discrete random variable defined on a continuous sample space.

A *continuous random variable* is one having a continuous range of values. It cannot be produced from a discrete sample space because of our requirement that all random variables be single-valued functions of all sample-space points. Similarly, a purely continuous random variable cannot result from a mixed sample space because of the presence of the discrete portion of the sample space. The random variable of Example 2.1-2 is continuous.

Mixed Random Variable

A *mixed random variable* is one for which some of its values are discrete and some are continuous. The mixed case is usually the least important type of random variable, but it occurs in some problems of practical significance.

2.2 DISTRIBUTION FUNCTION

The probability $P\{X \leq x\}$ is the probability of the event $\{X \leq x\}$. It is a number that depends on x; that is, it is a function of x. We call this function, denoted $F_X(x)$, the *cumulative probability distribution function* of the random variable X. Thus,

$$F_X(x) = P\{X \leq x\} \tag{2.2-1}$$

We shall often call $F_X(x)$ just the *distribution function* of X. The argument x is any real number ranging from $-\infty$ to ∞.

The distribution function has some specific properties derived from the fact that $F_X(x)$ is a probability. These are:†

$$(1) \quad F_X(-\infty) = 0 \tag{2.2-2a}$$

$$(2) \quad F_X(\infty) = 1 \tag{2.2-2b}$$

$$(3) \quad 0 \leq F_X(x) \leq 1 \tag{2.2-2c}$$

$$(4) \quad F_X(x_1) \leq F_X(x_2) \quad \text{if} \quad x_1 < x_2 \tag{2.2-2d}$$

$$(5) \quad P\{x_1 < X \leq x_2\} = F_X(x_2) - F_X(x_1) \tag{2.2-2e}$$

$$(6) \quad F_X(x^+) = F_X(x) \tag{2.2-2f}$$

---

† We use the notation x^+ to imply $x + \varepsilon$ where $\varepsilon > 0$ is infinitesimally small; that is, $\varepsilon \to 0$.

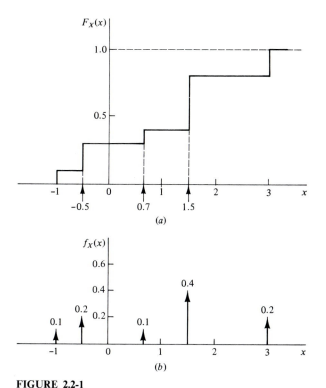

FIGURE 2.2-1
Distribution function (*a*) and density function (*b*) applicable to the discrete random variable of Example 2.2-1. [*Adapted from Peebles (1976) with permission of publishers Addison–Wesley, Advanced Book Program.*]

The first three of these properties are easy to justify, and the reader should justify them as an exercise. The fourth states that $F_X(x)$ is a nondecreasing function of x. The fifth property states that the probability that X will have values larger than some number x_1 but not exceeding another number x_2 is equal to the difference in $F_X(x)$ evaluated at the two points. It is justified from the fact that the events $\{X \leq x_1\}$ and $\{x_1 < X \leq x_2\}$ are mutually exclusive, so the probability of the event $\{X \leq x_2\} = \{X \leq x_1\} \cup \{x_1 < X \leq x_2\}$ is the sum of the probabilities $P\{X \leq x_1\}$ and $P\{x_1 < X \leq x_2\}$. The sixth property states that $F_X(x)$ is a function continuous from the right.

Properties 1, 2, 4, and 6 may be used as tests to determine if some function, say $G_X(x)$, could be a valid distribution function. If so, all four tests must be passed.

If X is a discrete random variable, consideration of its distribution function defined by (2.2-1) shows that $F_X(x)$ must have a stairstep form, such as shown in Figure 2.2-1*a*. The amplitude of a step will equal the probability of occurrence of the value of X where the step occurs. If the values of X are denoted x_i, we may write $F_X(x)$ as

$$F_X(x) = \sum_{i=1}^{N} P\{X = x_i\}u(x - x_i) \tag{2.2-3}$$

where $u(\cdot)$ is the unit-step function defined by†

$$u(x) = \begin{cases} 1 & x \geq 0 \\ 0 & x < 0 \end{cases} \tag{2.2-4}$$

and N may be infinite for some random variables. By introducing the shortened notation

$$P(x_i) = P\{X = x_i\} \tag{2.2-5}$$

(2.2-3) can be written as

$$F_X(x) = \sum_{i=1}^{N} P(x_i)u(x - x_i) \tag{2.2-6}$$

We next consider an example that illustrates the distribution function of a discrete random variable.

Example 2.2-1 Let X have the discrete values in the set $\{-1, -0.5, 0.7, 1.5, 3\}$. The corresponding probabilities are assumed to be $\{0.1, 0.2, 0.1, 0.4, 0.2\}$. Now $P\{X < -1\} = 0$ because there are no sample space points in the set $\{X < -1\}$. Only when $X = -1$ do we obtain one outcome. Thus, there is an immediate jump in probability of 0.1 in the function $F_X(x)$ at the point $x = -1$. For $-1 < x < -0.5$, there are no additional sample space points so $F_X(x)$ remains constant at the value 0.1. At $x = -0.5$ there is another jump of 0.2 in $F_X(x)$. This process continues until all points are included. $F_X(x)$ then equals 1.0 for all x above the last point. Figure 2.2-1a illustrates $F_X(x)$ for this discrete random variable.

A continuous random variable will have a continuous distribution function. We consider an example for which $F_X(x)$ is the continuous function shown in Figure 2.2-2a.

Example 2.2-2. We return to the fair wheel-of-chance experiment. Let the wheel be numbered from 0 to 12 as shown in Figure 2.1-2. Clearly the probability of the event $\{X \leq 0\}$ is 0 because there are no sample space points in this set. For $0 < x \leq 12$ the probability of $\{0 < X \leq x\}$ will increase linearly with x for a fair wheel. Thus, $F_X(x)$ will behave as shown in Figure 2.2-2a.

---

† This definition differs slightly from (A-5) by including the equality so that $u(x)$ satisfies (2.2-2f).

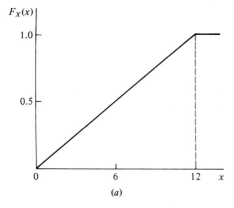

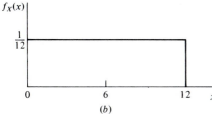

FIGURE 2.2-2
Distribution function (*a*) and density function (*b*) applicable to the continuous random variable of Example 2.2-2. [*Adapted from Peebles (1976) with permission of publishers Addison–Wesley, Advanced Book Program.*]

   The distribution function of a mixed random variable will be a sum of two parts, one of stairstep form, the other continuous.

2.3   DENSITY FUNCTION

The *probability density function*, denoted by $f_X(x)$, is defined as the derivative of the distribution function:

$$f_X(x) = \frac{dF_X(x)}{dx} \tag{2.3-1}$$

We often call $f_X(x)$ just the *density function* of the random variable X.

Existence

If the derivative of $F_X(x)$ exists then $f_X(x)$ exists and is given by (2.3-1). There may, however, be places where $dF_X(x)/dx$ is not defined. For example, a continuous random variable will have a continuous distribution $F_X(x)$, but $F_X(x)$ may have corners (points of abrupt change in slope). The distribution shown in Figure 2.2-2*a* is such a function. For such cases, we plot $f_X(x)$ as a function with step-type discontinuities (such as in Figure 2.2-2*b*).

   For discrete random variables having a stairstep form of distribution function, we introduce the concept of the *unit-impulse function* $\delta(x)$ to describe the derivative of $F_X(x)$ at its stairstep points. The unit-impulse function and its properties are reviewed in Appendix A. It is shown there that $\delta(x)$ may be defined by its integral property

$$\phi(x_0) = \int_{-\infty}^{\infty} \phi(x)\delta(x - x_0)\, dx \tag{2.3-2}$$

where $\phi(x)$ is any function continuous at the point $x = x_0$; $\delta(x)$ can be interpreted as a "function" with infinite amplitude, area of unity, and zero duration. The unit-impulse and the unit-step functions are related by

$$\delta(x) = \frac{du(x)}{dx} \tag{2.3-3}$$

or

$$\int_{-\infty}^{x} \delta(\xi)\, d\xi = u(x) \tag{2.3-4}$$

The more general impulse function is shown symbolically as a vertical arrow occurring at the point $x = x_0$ and having an amplitude equal to the amplitude of the step function for which it is the derivative.

We return to the case of a discrete random variable and differentiate $F_X(x)$, as given by (2.2-6), to obtain

$$f_X(x) = \sum_{i=1}^{N} P(x_i)\delta(x - x_i) \tag{2.3-5}$$

Thus, the density function for a discrete random variable exists in the sense that we use impulse functions to describe the derivative of $F_X(x)$ at its stairstep points. Figure 2.2-1b is an example of the density function for the random variable having the function of Figure 2.2-1a as its distribution.

A physical interpretation of (2.3-5) is readily achieved. Clearly, the probability of X having one of its particular values, say x_i, is a number $P(x_i)$. If this probability is assigned to the *point* x_i, then the *density* of probability is infinite because a point has no "width" on the x axis. The infinite "amplitude" of the impulse function describes this infinite density. The "size" of the density of probability at $x = x_i$ is accounted for by the scale factor $P(x_i)$ giving $P(x_i)\delta(x - x_i)$ for the density at the point $x = x_i$.

Properties of Density Functions

Several properties that $f_X(x)$ satisfies may be stated:

$$(1) \quad 0 \le f_X(x) \qquad \text{all } x \tag{2.3-6a}$$

$$(2) \quad \int_{-\infty}^{\infty} f_X(x)\, dx = 1 \tag{2.3-6b}$$

$$(3) \quad F_X(x) = \int_{-\infty}^{x} f_X(\xi)\, d\xi \tag{2.3-6c}$$

$$(4) \quad P\{x_1 < X \le x_2\} = \int_{x_1}^{x_2} f_X(x)\, dx \tag{2.3-6d}$$

Proofs of these properties are left to the reader as exercises. Properties 1 and 2 require that the density function be nonnegative and have an area of unity. These two properties may also be used as tests to see if some function, say $g_X(x)$, can be a valid probability density function. Both tests must be satisfied for validity. Property 3 is just another way of writing (2.3-1) and serves as the link between $F_X(x)$ and $f_X(x)$. Property 4 relates the probability that X will have values from x_1 to, and including, x_2 to the density function.

Example 2.3-1 Let us test the function $g_X(x)$ shown in Figure 2.3-1a to see if it can be a valid density function. It obviously satisfies property 1 since it is nonnegative. Its area is $a\alpha$ which must equal unity to satisfy property 2. Therefore $a = 1/\alpha$ is necessary if $g_X(x)$ is to be a density.

Suppose $a = 1/\alpha$. To find the applicable distribution function we first write

$$g_X(x) = \begin{cases} 0 & x_0 - \alpha > x \geq x_0 + \alpha \\[2mm] \dfrac{1}{\alpha^2}(x - x_0 + \alpha) & x_0 - \alpha \leq x < x_0 \\[2mm] \dfrac{1}{\alpha} - \dfrac{1}{\alpha^2}(x - x_0) & x_0 \leq x < x_0 + \alpha \end{cases}$$

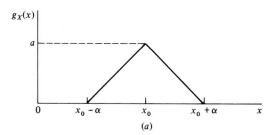

(a)

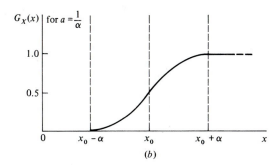

(b)

FIGURE 2.3-1
A possible probability density function (a) and a distribution function (b) applicable to Example 2.3-1.

Next, by using (2.3-6c), we obtain

$$G_X(x) =$$

$$
\begin{cases}
0 & x_0 - \alpha > x \\[2mm]
\displaystyle\int_{x_0-\alpha}^{x} g_X(\xi)\,d\xi = \frac{1}{2\alpha^2}(x - x_0 + \alpha)^2 & x_0 - \alpha \leq x < x_0 \\[2mm]
\displaystyle\frac{1}{2} + \int_{x_0}^{x} g_X(\xi)\,d\xi = \frac{1}{2} + \frac{1}{\alpha}(x - x_0) - \frac{1}{2\alpha^2}(x - x_0)^2 & x_0 \leq x < x_0 + \alpha \\[2mm]
1 & x_0 + \alpha \leq x
\end{cases}
$$

This function is plotted in Figure 2.3-1b.

Example 2.3-2 Suppose a random variable is known to have the triangular probability density of the preceding example with $x_0 = 8$, $\alpha = 5$ and $a = 1/\alpha = {}^1/_5$. From the earlier work

$$
f_X(x) = \begin{cases}
0 & 3 > x \geq 13 \\
(x - 3)/25 & 3 \leq x < 8 \\
0.2 - (x - 8)/25 & 8 \leq x < 13
\end{cases}
$$

We shall use this probability density in (2.3-6d) to find the probability that X has values greater than 4.5 but not greater than 6.7. The probability is

$$
P\{4.5 < X \leq 6.7\} = \int_{4.5}^{6.7} [(x - 3)/25]\,dx
$$

$$
= \frac{1}{25}\left[\frac{x^2}{2} - 3x\right]\Bigg|_{4.5}^{6.7} = 0.2288
$$

Thus, the event $\{4.5 < X \leq 6.7\}$ has a probability of 0.2288 or 22.88%.

2.4 THE GAUSSIAN RANDOM VARIABLE

A random variable X is called *gaussian*† if its density function has the form

$$
f_X(x) = \frac{1}{\sqrt{2\pi\sigma_X^2}}\, e^{-(x - a_X)^2/2\sigma_X^2} \tag{2.4-1}
$$

---

† After the German mathematician Johann Friedrich Carl Gauss (1777-1855). The gaussian density is often called the *normal density*.

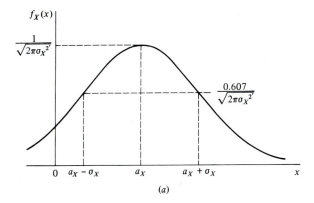

(a)

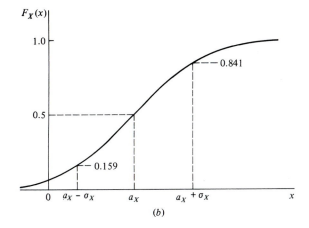

(b)

FIGURE 2.4-1
Density (a) and distribution (b)
functions of a gaussian random
variable.

where $\sigma_X > 0$ and $-\infty < a_X < \infty$ are real constants. This function is sketched in
Figure 2.4-1a. Its maximum value $(2\pi\sigma_X^2)^{-1/2}$ occurs at $x = a_X$. Its "spread" about
the point $x = a_X$ is related to σ_X. The function decreases to 0.607 times its
maximum at $x = a_X + \sigma_X$ and $x = a_X - \sigma_X$. It was first derived by De Moivre
some 200 years ago and later independently derived by both Gauss and Laplace
(Kennedy and Neville, 1986, p. 175).

The gaussian density is the most important of all densities and it enters
into nearly all areas of science and engineering. This importance stems from
its accurate description of many practical and significant real-world quantities, especially when such quantities are the result of many small independent
random effects acting to create the quantity of interest. For example, the voltage
across a resistor at the output of an amplifier can be random (a noise voltage)
due to a random current that is the result of many contributions from other
random currents at various places within the amplifier. Random thermal agitation
of electrons causes the randomness of the various currents. This type of noise is
called *gaussian* because the random variable representing the noise voltage has
the gaussian density.

The distribution function is found from (2.3-6c) using (2.4-1). The integral is

$$F_X(x) = \frac{1}{\sqrt{2\pi\sigma_X^2}} \int_{-\infty}^{x} e^{-(\xi-a_X)^2/2\sigma_X^2}\, d\xi \tag{2.4-2}$$

This integral has no known closed-form solution and must be evaluated by numerical or approximation methods. To make the results generally available, we could develop a set of tables of $F_X(x)$ for various x with a_X and σ_X as parameters. However, this approach has limited value because there is an infinite number of possible combinations of a_X and σ_X, which requires an infinite number of tables. A better approach is possible where only one table of $F_X(x)$ is developed that corresponds to normalized (specific) values of a_X and σ_X. We then show that the one table can be used in the general case where a_X and σ_X can be arbitrary.

We start by first selecting the normalized case where $a_X = 0$ and $\sigma_X = 1$. Denote the corresponding distribution function by $F(x)$. From (2.4-2), $F(x)$ is

$$F(x) = \frac{1}{\sqrt{2\pi}} \int_{-\infty}^{x} e^{-\xi^2/2}\, d\xi \tag{2.4-3}$$

which is a function of x only. This function is tabularized in Appendix B for $x \geq 0$. For a negative value of x we use the relationship

$$F(-x) = 1 - F(x) \tag{2.4-4}$$

To show that the general distribution function $F_X(x)$ of (2.4-2) can be found in terms of $F(x)$ of (2.4-3), we make the variable change

$$u = (\xi - a_X)/\sigma_X \tag{2.4-5}$$

in (2.4-2) to obtain

$$F_X(x) = \frac{1}{\sqrt{2\pi}} \int_{-\infty}^{(x-a_X)/\sigma_X} e^{-u^2/2}\, du \tag{2.4-6}$$

From (2.4-3), this expression is clearly equivalent to

$$F_X(x) = F\left(\frac{x - a_X}{\sigma_X}\right) \tag{2.4-7}$$

Figure 2.4-1b depicts the behavior of $F_X(x)$.

We consider two examples to illustrate the application of (2.4-7).

Example 2.4-1 We find the probability of the event $\{X \leq 5.5\}$ for a gaussian random variable having $a_X = 3$ and $\sigma_X = 2$.

Here $(x - a_X)/\sigma_X = (5.5-3)/2 = 1.25$. From (2.4-7) and the definition of $F_X(x)$

$$P\{X \leq 5.5\} = F_X(5.5) = F(1.25)$$

By using the table in Appendix B

$$P\{X \le 5.5\} = F(1.25) = 0.8944$$

Example 2.4-2 Assume that the height of clouds above the ground at some location is a gaussian random variable X with $a_X = 1830$ m and $\sigma_X = 460$ m. We find the probability that clouds will be higher than 2750 m (about 9000 ft). From (2.4-7) and Appendix B:

$$P\{X > 2750\} = 1 - P\{X \le 2750\} = 1 - F_X(2750)$$

$$= 1 - F\left(\frac{2750 - 1830}{460}\right) = 1 - F(2.0)$$

$$= 1 - 0.9772 = 0.0228$$

The probability that clouds are higher than 2750 m is therefore about 2.28 percent if their behavior is as assumed.

The function $F(x)$ can also be evaluated by approximation. First, we write $F(x)$ of (2.4-3) as

$$F(x) = 1 - Q(x), \tag{2.4-8}$$

where

$$Q(x) = \frac{1}{\sqrt{2\pi}} \int_x^\infty e^{-\xi^2/2} \, d\xi \tag{2.4-9}$$

is known as the *Q-function*. As with $F(x)$, $Q(x)$ has no known closed-form solution, but does have an excellent approximation given by

$$Q(x) \approx \left[\frac{1}{(1-a)x + a\sqrt{x^2 + b}}\right]\frac{e^{-x^2/2}}{\sqrt{2\pi}}, \qquad x \ge 0 \tag{2.4-10}$$

where a and b are constants. This approximation has been found to give minimum absolute relative error, for any $x \ge 0$, when $a = 0.339$ and $b = 5.510$ (see Börjesson and Sundberg, 1979). With these values of a and b, the approximation of (2.4-10) is said to equal the true value of $Q(x)$ within a maximum absolute error of 0.27% of $Q(x)$ for any $x \ge 0$. We consider a simple example.

Example 2.4-3 We assume a gaussian random variable for which $a_X = 7$ and $\sigma_X = 0.5$ and find the probability of the event $\{X \le 7.3\}$. From (2.4-7) and (2.4-8)

$$P\{X \le 7.3\} = F_X(7.3) = F\left(\frac{7.3 - 7}{0.5}\right) = F(0.6) = 1 - Q(0.6)$$

$$\approx 1 - \left(\frac{1}{0.661(0.6) + 0.339\sqrt{(0.6)^2 + 5.51}}\right)\frac{e^{-(0.6)^2/2}}{\sqrt{2\pi}} \approx 0.7264$$

From Table B-1 the answer is $F(0.6) = 0.7257$ so an absolute error of about $|0.7264 - 0.7257|/0.7257 = 0.00096$ (or 0.096%) exists.

2.5 OTHER DISTRIBUTION AND DENSITY EXAMPLES

Many distribution functions are important enough to have been given names. We give five examples. The first two are for discrete random variables; the remaining three are for continuous random variables. Other distributions are listed in Appendix F.

Binomial

Let $0 < p < 1$, and $N = 1, 2, \ldots$, then the function

$$f_X(x) = \sum_{k=0}^{N} \binom{N}{k} p^k (1-p)^{N-k} \delta(x-k) \tag{2.5-1}$$

is called the *binomial density function*. The quantity $\binom{N}{k}$ is the binomial coefficient defined in (1.7-4) as

$$\binom{N}{k} = \frac{N!}{k!(N-k)!} \tag{2.5-2}$$

The binomial density can be applied to the Bernoulli trial experiment of Chapter 1. It applies to many games of chance, detection problems in radar and sonar, and many experiments having only two possible outcomes on any given trial.

By integration of (2.5-1), the *binomial distribution function* is found:

$$F_X(x) = \sum_{k=0}^{N} \binom{N}{k} p^k (1-p)^{N-k} u(x-k) \tag{2.5-3}$$

Figure 2.5-1 illustrates the binomial density and distribution functions for $N = 6$ and $p = 0.25$.

Poisson

The *Poisson* random variable X has a density and distribution given by

$$f_X(x) = e^{-b} \sum_{k=0}^{\infty} \frac{b^k}{k!} \delta(x-k) \tag{2.5-4}$$

$$F_X(x) = e^{-b} \sum_{k=0}^{\infty} \frac{b^k}{k!} u(x-k) \tag{2.5-5}$$

where $b > 0$ is a real constant. When plotted, these functions appear quite similar to those for the binomial random variable (Figure 2.5-1). In fact, if $N \to \infty$ and

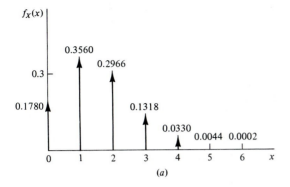

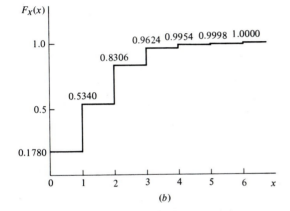

FIGURE 2.5-1
Binomial density (*a*) and distribution (*b*) functions for the case $N = 6$ and $p = 0.25$.

$p \to 0$ for the binomial case in such a way that $Np = b$, a constant, the Poisson case results.

The Poisson random variable applies to a wide variety of counting-type applications. It describes the number of defective units in a sample taken from a production line, the number of telephone calls made during a period of time, the number of electrons emitted from a small section of a cathode in a given time interval, etc. If the time interval of interest has duration T, and the events being counted are known to occur at an average rate λ and have a Poisson distribution, then b in (2.5-4) is given by

$$b = \lambda T \tag{2.5-6}$$

We illustrate these points by means of an example.

Example 2.5-1 Assume automobile arrivals at a gasoline station are Poisson and occur at an average rate of 50/h. The station has only one gasoline pump. If all cars are assumed to require one minute to obtain fuel, what is the probability that a waiting line will occur at the pump?

A waiting line will occur if two or more cars arrive in any one-minute interval. The probability of this event is one minus the probability that either none or one car arrives. From (2.5-6), with $\lambda = {}^{50}/_{60}$ cars/minute and $T = 1$ minute, we have $b = {}^{5}/_{6}$. On using (2.5-5)

Probability of a waiting line $= 1 - F_X(1)$

$$= 1 - e^{-5/6}\left[1 + \frac{5}{6}\right] = 0.2032$$

We therefore expect a line at the pump about 20.32% of the time.

Uniform

The *uniform* probability density and distribution functions are defined by:

$$f_X(x) = \begin{cases} 1/(b-a) & a \le x \le b \\ 0 & \text{elsewhere} \end{cases} \tag{2.5-7}$$

$$F_X(x) = \begin{cases} 0 & x < a \\ (x-a)/(b-a) & a \le x < b \\ 1 & b \le x \end{cases} \tag{2.5-8}$$

for real constants $-\infty < a < \infty$ and $b > a$. Figure 2.5-2 illustrates the behavior of the above two functions.

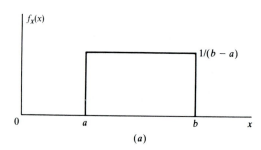

(a)

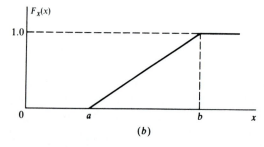

(b)

FIGURE 2.5-2
Uniform probability density function (a) and its distribution function (b).

The uniform density finds a number of practical uses. A particularly important application is in the quantization of signal samples prior to encoding in digital communication systems. Quantization amounts to "rounding off" the actual sample to the nearest of a large number of discrete "quantum levels." The errors introduced in the round-off process are uniformly distributed.

Exponential

The *exponential* density and distribution functions are:

$$f_X(x) = \begin{cases} \dfrac{1}{b} e^{-(x-a)/b} & x > a \\ 0 & x < a \end{cases} \qquad (2.5\text{-}9)$$

$$F_X(x) = \begin{cases} 1 - e^{-(x-a)/b} & x > a \\ 0 & x < a \end{cases} \qquad (2.5\text{-}10)$$

for real numbers $-\infty < a < \infty$ and $b > 0$. These functions are plotted in Figure 2.5-3.

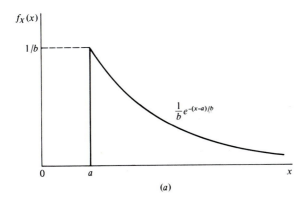

(a)

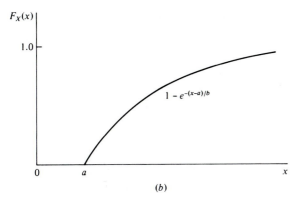

(b)

FIGURE 2.5-3
Exponential density (*a*) and distribution (*b*) functions.

The exponential density is useful in describing raindrop sizes when a large number of rainstorm measurements are made. It is also known to approximately describe the fluctuations in signal strength received by radar from certain types of aircraft as illustrated by the following example.

Example 2.5-2 The power reflected from an aircraft of complicated shape that is received by a radar can be described by an exponential random variable P. The density of P is therefore

$$f_P(p) = \begin{cases} \dfrac{1}{P_0} e^{-p/P_0} & p > 0 \\ 0 & p < 0 \end{cases}$$

where P_0 is the average amount of received power. At some given time P may have a value different from its average value and we ask: what is the probability that the received power is larger than the power received on the average?

We must find $P\{P > P_0\} = 1 - P\{P \leq P_0\} = 1 - F_P(P_0)$. From (2.5-10)

$$P\{P > P_0\} = 1 - (1 - e^{-P_0/P_0}) = e^{-1} \approx 0.368$$

In other words, the received power is larger than its average value about 36.8 percent of the time.

Rayleigh

The *Rayleigh*† density and distribution functions are:

$$f_X(x) = \begin{cases} \dfrac{2}{b}(x - a)e^{-(x-a)^2/b} & x \geq a \\ 0 & x < a \end{cases} \tag{2.5-11}$$

$$F_X(x) = \begin{cases} 1 - e^{-(x-a)^2/b} & x \geq a \\ 0 & x < a \end{cases} \tag{2.5-12}$$

for real constants $-\infty < a < \infty$ and $b > 0$. These functions are plotted in Figure 2.5-4.

The Rayleigh density describes the envelope of one type of noise when passed through a bandpass filter. It also is important in analysis of errors in various measurement systems.

---

† Named for the English physicist John William Strutt, Lord Rayleigh (1842–1919).

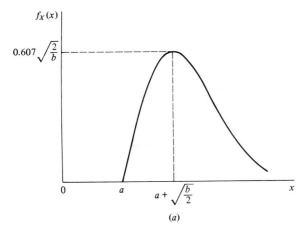

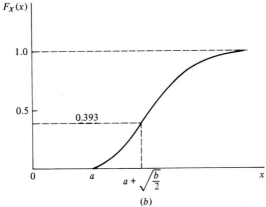

FIGURE 2.5-4
Rayleigh density (*a*) and distribution (*b*) functions.

2.6 CONDITIONAL DISTRIBUTION AND DENSITY FUNCTIONS

The concept of conditional probability was introduced in Chapter 1. Recall that, for two events A and B where $P(B) \neq 0$, the conditional probability of A given B had occurred was

$$P(A|B) = \frac{P(A \cap B)}{P(B)} \tag{2.6-1}$$

In this section we extend the conditional probabilitty concept to include random variables.

Conditional Distribution

Let A in (2.6-1) be identified as the event $\{X \leq x\}$ for the random variable X. The resulting probability $P\{X \leq x | B\}$ is defined as the *conditional distribution function* of X, which we denote $F_X(x|B)$. Thus

$$F_X(x|B) = P\{X \le x|B\} = \frac{P\{X \le x \cap B\}}{P(B)} \tag{2.6-2}$$

where we use the notation $\{X \le x \cap B\}$ to imply the joint event $\{X \le x\} \cap B$. This joint event consists of all outcomes s such that

$$X(s) \le x \qquad \text{and} \qquad s \in B \tag{2.6-3}$$

The conditional distribution (2.6-2) applies to discrete, continuous, or mixed random variables.

Properties of Conditional Distribution

All the properties of ordinary distributions apply to $F_X(x|B)$. In other words, it has the following characteristics:

$$\text{(1)} \quad F_X(-\infty|B) = 0 \tag{2.6-4a}$$

$$\text{(2)} \quad F_X(\infty|B) = 1 \tag{2.6-4b}$$

$$\text{(3)} \quad 0 \le F_X(x|B) \le 1 \tag{2.6-4c}$$

$$\text{(4)} \quad F_X(x_1|B) \le F_X(x_2|B) \qquad \text{if} \qquad x_1 < x_2 \tag{2.6-4d}$$

$$\text{(5)} \quad P\{x_1 < X \le x_2|B\} = F_X(x_2|B) - F_X(x_1|B) \tag{2.6-4e}$$

$$\text{(6)} \quad F_X(x^+|B) = F_X(x|B) \tag{2.6-4f}$$

These characteristics have the same general meanings as described earlier following (2.2-2).

Conditional Density

In a manner similar to the ordinary density function, we define *conditional density function* of the random variable X as the derivative of the conditional distribution function. If we denote this density by $f_X(x|B)$, then

$$f_X(x|B) = \frac{dF_X(x|B)}{dx} \tag{2.6-5}$$

If $F_X(x|B)$ contains step discontinuities, as when X is a discrete or mixed random variable, we assume that impulse functions are present in $f_X(x|B)$ to account for the derivatives at the discontinuities.

Properties of Conditional Density

Because conditional density is related to conditional distribution through the derivative, it satisfies the same properties as the ordinary density function. They are:

$$(1) \quad f_X(x|B) \geq 0 \tag{2.6-6a}$$

$$(2) \quad \int_{-\infty}^{\infty} f_X(x|B)\,dx = 1 \tag{2.6-6b}$$

$$(3) \quad F_X(x|B) = \int_{-\infty}^{x} f_X(\xi|B)\,d\xi \tag{2.6-6c}$$

$$(4) \quad P\{x_1 < X \leq x_2|B\} = \int_{x_1}^{x_2} f_X(x|B)\,dx \tag{2.6-6d}$$

We take an example to illustrate conditional density and distribution.

Example 2.6-1 Two boxes have red, green, and blue balls in them; the number of balls of each color is given in Table 2.6-1. Our experiment will be to select a box and then a ball from the selected box. One box (number 2) is slightly larger than the other, causing it to be selected more frequently. Let B_2 be the event "select the larger box" while B_1 is the event "select the smaller box." Assume $P(B_1) = {}^2/_{10}$ and $P(B_2) = {}^8/_{10}$. (B_1 and B_2 are mutually exclusive and $B_1 \cup B_2$ is the certain event, since some box must be selected; therefore, $P(B_1) + P(B_2)$ must equal unity.)

Now define a discrete random variable X to have values $x_1 = 1, x_2 = 2$, and $x_3 = 3$ when a red, green, or blue ball is selected, and let B be an event equal to either B_1 or B_2. From Table 2.6-1:

$$P(X = 1|B = B_1) = \frac{5}{100} \qquad P(X = 1|B = B_2) = \frac{80}{150}$$

$$P(X = 2|B = B_1) = \frac{35}{100} \qquad P(X = 2|B = B_2) = \frac{60}{150}$$

$$P(X = 3|B = B_1) = \frac{60}{100} \qquad P(X = 3|B = B_2) = \frac{10}{150}$$

TABLE 2.6-1
Numbers of colored balls in two boxes

		Box		
x_i	Ball color	1	2	Totals
1	Red	5	80	85
2	Green	35	60	95
3	Blue	60	10	70
Totals		100	150	250

The conditional probability density $f_X(x|B_1)$ becomes

$$f_X(x|B_1) = \frac{5}{100} \delta(x-1) + \frac{35}{100} \delta(x-2) + \frac{60}{100} \delta(x-3)$$

By direct integration of $f_X(x|B_1)$:

$$F_X(x|B_1) = \frac{5}{100} u(x-1) + \frac{35}{100} u(x-2) + \frac{60}{100} u(x-3)$$

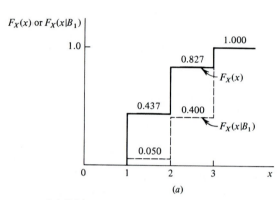

(a)

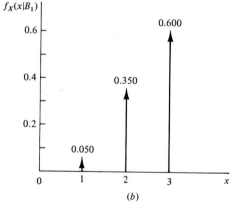

(b)

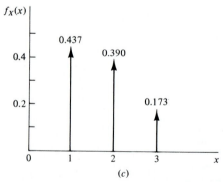

(c)

FIGURE 2.6-1
Distributions (a) and densities (b) and (c) applicable to Example 2.6-1.

For comparison, we may find the density and distribution of X by determining the probabilities $P(X = 1)$, $P(X = 2)$, and $P(X = 3)$. These are found from the total probability theorem embodied in (1.4-10):

$$P(X = 1) = P(X = 1|B_1)P(B_1) + P(X = 1|B_2)P(B_2)$$

$$= \frac{5}{100}\left(\frac{2}{10}\right) + \frac{80}{150}\left(\frac{8}{10}\right) = 0.437$$

$$P(X = 2) = \frac{35}{100}\left(\frac{2}{10}\right) + \frac{60}{150}\left(\frac{8}{10}\right) = 0.390$$

$$P(X = 3) = \frac{60}{100}\left(\frac{2}{10}\right) + \frac{10}{150}\left(\frac{8}{10}\right) = 0.173$$

Thus

$$f_X(x) = 0.437\,\delta(x - 1) + 0.390\,\delta(x - 2) + 0.173\,\delta(x - 3)$$

and

$$F_X(x) = 0.437u(x - 1) + 0.390u(x - 2) + 0.173u(x - 3)$$

These distributions and densities are plotted in Figure 2.6-1.

★Methods of Defining Conditioning Event

The preceding example illustrates how the conditioning event B can be defined from some characteristic of the physical experiment. There are several other ways of defining B (Cooper and McGillem, 1971, p. 61). We shall consider two of these in detail.

In one method, event B is defined in terms of the random variable X. We discuss this case further in the next paragraph. In another method, event B may depend on some random variable other than X. We discuss this case further in Chapter 4.

One way to define event B in terms of X is to let

$$B = \{X \le b\} \tag{2.6-7}$$

where b is some real number $-\infty < b < \infty$. After substituting (2.6-7) in (2.6-2), we get†

$$F_X(x|X \le b) = P\{X \le x|X \le b\} = \frac{P\{X \le x \cap X \le b\}}{P\{X \le b\}} \tag{2.6-8}$$

---

† Notation used has allowed for deletion of some braces for convenience. Thus, $F_X(x|\{X \le b\})$ is written $F_X(x|X \le b)$ and $P(\{X \le x\} \cap \{X \le b\})$ becomes $P\{X \le x \cap X \le b\}$.

for all events $\{X \le b\}$ for which $P\{X \le b\} \neq 0$. Two cases must be considered; one is where $b \le x$; the second is where $x < b$. If $b \le x$, the event $\{X \le b\}$ is a subset of the event $\{X \le x\}$, so $\{X \le x\} \cap \{X \le b\} = \{X \le b\}$. Equation (2.6-8) becomes

$$F_X(x|X \le b) = \frac{P\{X \le x \cap X \le b\}}{P\{X \le b\}} = \frac{P\{X \le b\}}{P\{X \le b\}} = 1 \qquad b \le x \qquad (2.6\text{-}9)$$

When $x < b$ the event $\{X \le x\}$ is a subset of the event $\{X \le b\}$, so $\{X \le x\} \cap \{X \le b\} = \{X \le x\}$ and (2.6-8) becomes

$$F_X(x|X \le b) = \frac{P\{X \le x \cap X \le b\}}{P\{X \le b\}} = \frac{P\{X \le x\}}{P\{X \le b\}} = \frac{F_X(x)}{F_X(b)} \qquad x < b \qquad (2.6\text{-}10)$$

By combining the last two expressions, we obtain

$$F_X(x|X \le b) = \begin{cases} \dfrac{F_X(x)}{F_X(b)} & x < b \\ 1 & b \le x \end{cases} \qquad (2.6\text{-}11)$$

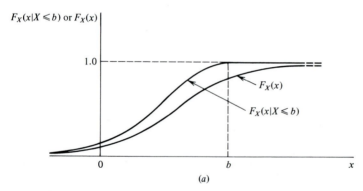

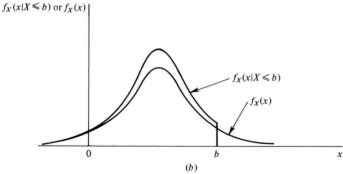

FIGURE 2.6-2
Possible distribution functions (*a*) and density functions (*b*) applicable to a conditioning event $B = \{X \le b\}$.

The conditional density function derives from the derivative of (2.6-11):

$$f_X(x|X \leq b) = \begin{cases} \dfrac{f_X(x)}{F_X(b)} = \dfrac{f_X(x)}{\int_{-\infty}^{b} f_X(x)\, dx} & x < b \\ 0 & x \geq b \end{cases} \tag{2.6-12}$$

Figure 2.6-2 sketches possible functions representing (2.6-11) and (2.6-12).

From our assumptions that the conditioning event has nonzero probability, we have $0 < F_X(b) \leq 1$, so the expression of (2.6-11) shows that the conditional distribution function is never smaller than the ordinary distribution function:

$$F_X(x|X \leq b) \geq F_X(x) \tag{2.6-13}$$

A similar statement holds for the conditional density function of (2.6-12) wherever it is nonzero:

$$f_X(x|X \leq b) \geq f_X(x) \qquad x < b \tag{2.6-14}$$

The principal results (2.6-11) and (2.6-12) can readily be extended to the more general event $B = \{a < X \leq b\}$ (see Problem 2-39).

Example 2.6-2 The radial "miss-distance" of landings from parachuting sky divers, as measured from a target's center, is a Rayleigh random variable with $b = 800 \text{ m}^2$ and $a = 0$. From (2.5-12) we have

$$F_X(x) = [1 - e^{-x^2/800}]u(x)$$

The target is a circle of 50-m radius with a bull's eye of 10-m radius. We find the probability of a parachuter hitting the bull's eye given that the landing is on the target.

The required probability is given by (2.6-11) with $x = 10$ and $b = 50$:

$$P(\text{bull's eye}|\text{landing on target}) = F_X(10)/F_X(50)$$

$$= (1 - e^{-100/800})/(1 - e^{-2500/800}) = 0.1229$$

Parachuter accuracy is such that about 12.29% of landings falling on the target will actually hit the bull's eye.

PROBLEMS

2-1 The sample space for an experiment is $S = \{0, 1, 2.5, 6\}$. List all possible values of the following random variables:

(a) $X = 2s$

(b) $X = 5s^2 - 1$

(c) $X = \cos(\pi s)$

(d) $X = (1 - 3s)^{-1}$

2-2   Work Problem 2-1 for $S = \{-2 < s \le 5\}$.

2-3   Given that a random variable X has the following possible values, state if X is discrete, continuous, or mixed.
  (a) $\{-20 < x < -5\}$
  (b) $\{10, 12 < x \le 14, 15, 17\}$
  (c) $\{-10 \text{ for } s > 2 \text{ and } 5 \text{ for } s \le 2, \text{ where } 1 < s \le 6\}$
  (d) $\{4, 3.1, 1, -2\}$

2-4   A random variable X is a function. So is probability P. Recall that the *domain* of a function is the set of values its argument may take on while its *range* is the set of corresponding values of the function. In terms of sets, events, and sample spaces, state the domain and range for X and P.

2-5   A man matches coin flips with a friend. He wins \$2 if coins match and loses \$2 if they do not match. Sketch a sample space showing possible outcomes for this experiment and illustrate how the points map onto the real line x that defines the values of the random variable X = "dollars won on a trial." Show a second mapping for a random variable Y = "dollars won by the friend on a trial."

2-6   Temperature in a given city varies randomly during any year from -21 to $49°C$. A house in the city has a thermostat that assumes only three positions: 1 represents "call for heat below $18.3°C$," 2 represents "dead or idle zone," and 3 represents "call for air conditioning above $21.7°C$." Draw a sample space for this problem showing the mapping necessary to define a random variable X = "thermostat setting."

2-7   A random voltage can have any value defined by the set $S = \{a \le s \le b\}$. A quantizer divides S into 6 equal-sized contiguous subsets and generates a voltage random variable X having values $\{-4, -2, 0, 2, 4, 6\}$. Each value of X is equal to the midpoint of the subset of S from which it is mapped.
  (a) Sketch the sample space and the mapping to the line x that defines the values of X.
  (b) Find a and b.

★2-8   A random signal can have any voltage value (at a given time) defined by the set $S = \{a_0 < s \le a_N\}$, where a_0 and a_N are real numbers and N is any integer $N \ge 1$. A voltage quantizer divides S into N equal-sized contiguous subsets and converts the signal level into one of a set of discrete levels a_n, $n = 1, 2, \ldots, N$, that correspond to the "input" subsets $\{a_{n-1} < s \le a_n\}$. The set $\{a_1, a_2, \ldots, a_N\}$ can be taken as the discrete values of an "output" random variable X of the quantizer. If the smallest "input" subset is defined by $\Delta = a_1 - a_0$ and other subsets by $a_n - a_{n-1} = 2^{n-1}\Delta$, determine Δ and the quantizer levels a_n in terms of a_0, a_N, and N.

2-9   An honest coin is tossed three times.
  (a) Sketch the applicable sample space S showing all possible elements. Let X be a random variable that has values representing the number of heads obtained on any triple toss. Sketch the mapping of S onto the real line defining X.
  (b) Find the probabilities of the values of X.

2-10 Work Problem 2-9 for a biased coin for which $P\{\text{head}\} = 0.6$.

2-11 Resistor R_2 in Figure P2-11 is randomly selected from a box of resistors containing 180-Ω, 470-Ω, 1000-Ω, and 2200-Ω resistors. All resistor values have the same likelihood of being selected. The voltage E_2 is a discrete random variable. Find the set of values E_2 can have and give their probabilities.

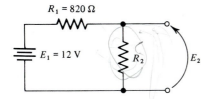

$R_1 = 820\ \Omega$

$E_1 = 12\ \text{V}$

R_2

E_2

FIGURE P2-11

2-12 Bolts made on a production line are nominally designed to have a 760-mm length. A go-no-go testing device eliminates all bolts less than 650 mm and over 920 mm in length. The surviving bolts are then made available for sale and their lengths are known to be described by a uniform probability density function. A certain buyer orders all bolts that can be produced with a $\pm 5\%$ tolerance about the nominal length. What fraction of the production line's output is he purchasing?

2-13 Find and sketch the density and distribution functions for the random variables of parts (a), (b), and (c) in Problem 2-1 if the sample space elements have equal likelihoods of occurrence.

2-14 If temperature in Problem 2-6 is uniformly distributed, sketch the density and distribution functions of the random variable X.

2-15 For the uniform random variable defined by (2.5-7) find:
(a) $P\{0.9a + 0.1b < X \leq 0.7a + 0.3b\}$
(b) $P\{(a + b)/2 < X \leq b\}$

2-16 Determine which of the following are valid distribution functions:

(a) $G_X(x) = \begin{cases} 1 - e^{-x/2} & x \geq 0 \\ 0 & x < 0 \end{cases}$

(b) $G_X(x) = \begin{cases} 0 & x < 0 \\ 0.5 + 0.5\sin\left[\pi(x-1)/2\right] & 0 \leq x < 2 \\ 1 & x \geq 2 \end{cases}$

(c) $G_X(x) = \dfrac{x}{a}\left[u(x-a) - u(x-2a)\right]$

2-17 Determine the real constant a, for arbitrary real constants m and $0 < b$, such that

$$f_X(x) = ae^{-|x-m|/b}$$

is a valid density function (called the *Laplace density*).

2-18 An intercom system master station provides music to six hospital rooms. The probability that any one room will be switched on and draw power at any time is 0.4. When on, a room draws 0.5 W.
(a) Find and plot the density and distribution functions for the random variable "power delivered by the master station."
(b) If the master-station amplifier is overloaded when more than 2 W is demanded, what is its probability of overload?

★2-19 The amplifier in the master station of Problem 2-18 is replaced by a 4-W unit that must now supply 12 rooms. Is the probability of overload better than if two independent 2-W units supplied six rooms each?

2-20 Justify that a distribution function $F_X(x)$ satisfies (2.2-2a, b, c).

2-21 Use the definition of the impulse function to evaluate the following integrals. (*Hint:* Refer to Appendix A.)

(a) $\displaystyle\int_3^4 (3x^2 + 2x - 4)\delta(x - 3.2)\, dx$

(b) $\displaystyle\int_{-\infty}^{\infty} \cos(6\pi x)\delta(x - 1)\, dx$

(c) $\displaystyle\int_{-\infty}^{\infty} \frac{24\delta(x - 2)\, dx}{x^4 + 3x^2 + 2}$

(d)† $\displaystyle\int_{-\infty}^{\infty} \delta(x - x_0)e^{-j\omega x}\, dx$

(e) $\displaystyle\int_{-3}^3 u(x - 2)\delta(x - 3)\, dx$

2-22 Show that the properties of a density function $f_X(x)$, as given by (2.3-6), are valid.

2-23 For the random variable defined in Example 2.3-1, find:
(a) $P\{x_0 - 0.6\alpha < X \le x_0 + 0.3\alpha\}$
(b) $P\{X = x_0\}$

2-24 A random variable X is gaussian with $a_X = 0$ and $\sigma_X = 1$.
(a) What is the probability that $|X| > 2$?
(b) What is the probability that $X > 2$?

2-25 Work Problem 2-24 if $a_X = 4$ and $\sigma_X = 2$.

2-26 For the gaussian density function of (2.4-1), show that

$$\int_{-\infty}^{\infty} x f_X(x)\, dx = a_X$$

---

† The quantity j is the unit-imaginary; that is, $j = \sqrt{-1}$.

2-27 For the gaussian density function of (2.4-1), show that

$$\int_{-\infty}^{\infty} (x - a_X)^2 f_X(x)\, dx = \sigma_X^2$$

2-28 A production line manufactures 1000-Ω resistors that must satisfy a 10% tolerance.

(a) If resistance is adequately described by a gaussian random variable X for which $a_X = 1000\ \Omega$ and $\sigma_X = 40\ \Omega$, what fraction of the resistors is expected to be rejected?

(b) If a machine is not properly adjusted, the product resistances change to the case where $a_X = 1050\ \Omega$ (5% shift). What fraction is now rejected?

2-29 Cannon shell impact position, as measured along the line of fire from the target point, can be described by a guassian random variable X. It is found that 15.15% of shells fall 11.2 m or farther from the target in a direction toward the cannon, while 5.05% fall farther than 95.6 m beyond the target. What are a_X and σ_X for X?

2-30 (a) Use the exponential density of (2.5-9) and solve for I_2 defined by

$$I_2 = \int_{-\infty}^{\infty} x^2 f_X(x)\, dx$$

(b) Solve for I_1 defined by

$$I_1 = \int_{-\infty}^{\infty} x f_X(x)\, dx$$

(c) Verify that I_1 and I_2 satisfy the equation $I_2 - I_1^2 = b^2$.

2-31 Verify that the maximum value of $f_X(x)$ for the Rayleigh density function of (2.5-11) occurs at $x = a + \sqrt{b/2}$ and is equal to $\sqrt{2/b}\exp(-1/2) \approx 0.607\sqrt{2/b}$. This value of x is called the *mode* of the random variable. (In general, a random variable may have more than one such value—explain.)

2-32 Find the value $x = x_0$ of a Rayleigh random variable for which $P\{X \le x_0\} = P\{x_0 < X\}$. This value of x is called the *median* of the random variable.

2-33 The lifetime of a system expressed in weeks is a Rayleigh random variable X for which

$$f_X(x) = \begin{cases} (x/200)e^{-x^2/400} & 0 \le x \\ 0 & x < 0 \end{cases}$$

(a) What is the probability that the system will not last a full week?

(b) What is the probability the system lifetime will exceed one year?

2-34 The *Cauchy*† random variable has the probability density function

$$f_X(x) = \frac{b/\pi}{b^2 + (x - a)^2}$$

† After the French mathematician Augustin Louis Cauchy (1789–1857).

for real numbers $0 < b$ and $-\infty < a < \infty$. Show that the distribution function of X is

$$F_X(x) = \frac{1}{2} + \frac{1}{\pi} \tan^{-1}\left(\frac{x-a}{b}\right)$$

2-35 The *Log-Normal density* function is given by

$$f_X(x) = \begin{cases} \dfrac{\exp\{-[\ln(x-b) - a_X]^2/2\sigma_X^2\}}{\sqrt{2\pi}\sigma_X(x-b)} & x \geq b \\ 0 & x < b \end{cases}$$

for real constants $0 < \sigma_X$, $-\infty < a_X < \infty$, and $-\infty < b < \infty$, where $\ln(x)$ denotes the natural logarithm of x. Show that the corresponding distribution function is

$$F_X(x) = \begin{cases} F\left[\dfrac{\ln(x-b) - a_X}{\sigma_X}\right] & x \geq b \\ 0 & x < b \end{cases}$$

where $F(\cdot)$ is given by (2.4-3).

2-36 A random variable X is known to be Poisson with $b = 4$.
(a) Plot the density and distribution functions for this random variable.
(b) What is the probability of the event $\{0 \leq X \leq 5\}$?

2-37 The number of cars arriving at a certain bank drive-in window during any 10-min period is a Poisson random variable X with $b = 2$. Find:
(a) The probability that more than 3 cars will arrive during any 10-min period.
(b) The probability that no cars will arrive.

2-38 Rework Example 2.6-1 to find $f_X(x|B_2)$ and $F_X(x|B_2)$. Sketch the two functions.

★ **2-39** Extend the analysis of the text, that leads to (2.6-11) and (2.6-12), to the more general event $B = \{a < X \leq b\}$. Specifically, show that now

$$F_X(x|a < X \leq b) = \begin{cases} 0 & x < a \\ \dfrac{F_X(x) - F_X(a)}{F_X(b) - F_X(a)} & a \leq x < b \\ 1 & b \leq x \end{cases}$$

and

$$f_X(x|a < X \leq b) = \begin{cases} 0 & x < a \\ \dfrac{f_X(x)}{F_X(b) - F_X(a)} = \dfrac{f_X(x)}{\int_a^b f_X(x)\,dx} & a \leq x < b \\ 0 & b \leq x \end{cases}$$

★2-40 Consider the system having a lifetime defined by the random variable X in Problem 2-33. Given that the system will survive beyond 20 weeks, find the probability that it will survive beyond 26 weeks.

ADDITIONAL PROBLEMS, SECOND EDITION

2-41 A sample space is defined by $S = \{1, 2 \le s \le 3, 4, 5\}$. A random variable is defined by: $X = 2$ for $0 \le s \le 2.5$, $X = 3$ for $2.5 < s < 3.5$, and $X = 5$ for $3.5 \le s \le 6$.
(a) Is X discrete, continuous, or mixed?
(b) Give a set that defines the values X can have.

2-42 A gambler flips a fair coin three times.
(a) Draw a sample space S for this experiment. A random variable X representing his winnings is defined as follows: He loses \$1 if he gets no heads in three flips; he wins \$1, \$2, and \$3 if he obtains 1, 2, or 3 heads, respectively. Show how elements of S map to values of X.
(b) What are the probabilities of the various values of X?

2-43 A function $G_X(x) = a[1 + (2/\pi) \sin^{-1}(x/c)]$ rect $(x/2c) + (a + b)u(x - c)$ is defined for all $-\infty < x < \infty$, where $c > 0$, b, and a are real constants and rect $(\cdot)$ is defined by (E-2). Find any conditions on a, b, and c that will make $G_X(x)$ a valid probability distribution function. Discuss what choices of constants correspond to a continuous, discrete, or mixed random variable.

2-44 (a) Generalize Problem 2-16(a) by finding values of real constants a and b such that

$$G_X(x) = [1 - a \exp(-x/b)]u(x)$$

is a valid distribution function.
(b) Are there any values of a and b such that $G_X(x)$ corresponds to a mixed random variable X?

2-45 Find a constant $b > 0$ so that the function

$$f_X(x) = \begin{cases} e^{3x}/4 & 0 \le x \le b \\ 0 & \text{elsewhere} \end{cases}$$

is a valid probability density.

2-46 Given the function

$$g_X(x) = 4 \cos(\pi x/2b) \text{ rect } (x/2b)$$

find a value of b so that $g_X(x)$ is a valid probability density.

2-47 A random variable X has the density function.

$$f_X(x) = (1/2)u(x) \exp(-x/2)$$

Define events $A = \{1 < X \le 3\}$, $B = \{X \le 2.5\}$, and $C = A \cap B$. Find the probabilities of events (a) A, (b) B, and (c) C.

★**2-48** Let $\phi(x)$ be a continuous, but otherwise arbitrary real function, and let a and b be real constants. Find $G(a, b)$ defined by

$$G(a, b) = \int_{-\infty}^{\infty} \phi(x)\, \delta(ax + b)\, dx$$

(*Hint:* Use the definition of the impulse function.)

2-49 For real constants $b > 0$, $c > 0$, and any a, find a condition on constant a and a relationship between c and a (for given b) such that the function

$$f_X(x) = \begin{cases} a[1 - (x/b)] & 0 \le x \le c \\ 0 & \text{elsewhere} \end{cases}$$

is a valid probability density.

2-50 A gaussian random variable X has $a_X = 2$, and $\sigma_X = 2$.
(*a*) Find $P\{X > 1.0\}$.
(*b*) Find $P\{X \le -1.0\}$.

2-51 In a certain "junior" olympics, javelin throw distances are well approximated by a gaussian distribution for which $a_X = 30$ m and $\sigma_X = 5$ m. In a qualifying round, contestants must throw farther than 26 m to qualify. In the main event the record throw is 42 m.
(*a*) What is the probability of being disqualified in the qualifying round?
(*b*) In the main event what is the probability the record will be broken?

2-52 Suppose height to the bottom of clouds is a gaussian random variable X for which $a_X = 4000$ m, and $\sigma_X = 1000$ m. A person bets that cloud height tomorrow will fall in the set $A = \{1000 \text{ m} < X \le 3300 \text{ m}\}$ while a second person bets that height will be satisfied by $B = \{2000 \text{ m} < X \le 4200 \text{ m}\}$. A third person bets they are both correct. Find the probabilities that each person will win the bet.

2-53 Let X be a Rayleigh random variable with $a = 0$. Find the probability that X will have values larger than its mode (see Problem 2-31).

2-54 A certain large city averages three murders per week and their occurrences follow a Poisson distribution.
(*a*) What is the probability that there will be five or more murders in a given week?
(*b*) On the average, how many weeks a year can this city expect to have no murders?
(*c*) How many weeks per year (average) can the city expect the number of murders per week to equal or exceed the average number per week?

2-55 A certain military radar is set up at a remote site with no repair facilities. If the radar is known to have a *mean-time-between-failures* (MTBF) of 200 h find the probability that the radar is still in operation one week later when picked up for maintenance and repairs.

2-56 If the radar of Problem 2-55 is permanently located at the remote site, find the probability that it will be operational as a function of time since its set up.

2-57 A computer undergoes down-time if a certain critical component fails. This component is known to fail at an average rate of once per four weeks. No significant down-time occurs if replacement components are on hand because repair can be made rapidly. There are three components on hand and ordered replacements are not due for six weeks.

(*a*) What is the probability of significant down-time occurring before the ordered components arrive?

(*b*) If the shipment is delayed two weeks what is the probability of significant down-time occurring before the shipment arrives?

★**2-58** Assume the lifetime of a laboratory research animal is defined by a Rayleigh density with $a = 0$ and $b = 30$ weeks in (2.5-11) and (2.5-12). If for some clinical reasons it is known that the animal will live *at most* 20 weeks, what is the probability it will live 10 weeks or less?

★**2-59** Suppose the depth of water, measured in meters, behind a dam is described by an exponential random variable having a density

$$f_X(x) = (1/13.5)u(x)\exp(-x/13.5)$$

There is an emergency overflow at the top of the dam that prevents the depth from exceeding 40.6 m. There is a pipe placed 32.0 m below the overflow (ignore the pipe's finite diameter) that feeds water to a hydroelectric generator.

(*a*) What is the probability that water is wasted through emergency overflow?

(*b*) Given that water is not wasted in overflow, what is the probability the generator will have water to drive it?

(*c*) What is the probability that water will be too low to produce power?

★**2-60** In Problem 2-59 find and sketch the distribution and density functions of water depth given that water will be deep enough to generate power but no water is wasted by emergency overflow. Also sketch for comparisons the distribution and density of water depth without any conditions.

★**2-61** In Example 2.6-2 a parachuter is an "expert" if he hits the bull's eye. If he falls outside the bull's eye but within a circle of 25-m radius he is called "qualified" for competition. Given that a parachuter is not an expert but hits the target what is the probability of being "qualified?"

ADDITIONAL PROBLEMS, THIRD EDITION

2-62 A random current is described by the sample space $S = \{-4 \le i \le 12\}$. A random variable X is defined by

$$X(i) = \begin{cases} -2 & i \le -2 \\ i & -2 < i \le 1 \\ 1 & 1 < i \le 4 \\ 6 & 4 < i \end{cases}$$

(a) Show, by a sketch, the values x into which the values of i are mapped by X.

(b) What type of random variable is X?

2-63 (a) Find the probabilities associated with all values of the random variable X of Problem 2-62.

(b) Sketch the probability distribution function of the random variable X.

2-64 A random variable X has the distribution function

$$F_X(x) = \sum_{n=1}^{12} \frac{n^2}{650} u(x - n).$$

Find the probabilities: (a) $P\{-\infty < X \le 6.5\}$, (b) $P\{X > 4\}$, and (c) $P\{6 < X \le 9\}$.

2-65 If the function

$$G_X(x) = K \sum_{n=1}^{N} n^3 u(x - n)$$

must be a valid probability distribution function, determine K to make it valid. (*Hint:* Use a series from Appendix C.)

2-66 Use the properties or definition of the impulse function (Appendix A) to evaluate the following integrals:

(a) $\displaystyle\int_{-\infty}^{\infty} \delta(x + 5) \frac{x^2}{1 + x^2} \, dx$

(b) $\displaystyle\int_{-\infty}^{\infty} \delta(x - 3) \cos(\pi x/6) \, dx$

(c) $\displaystyle\int_{-\infty}^{\infty} e^{-4(x+1)} \delta(x + 1) \, dx$

2-67 Work Problem 2-66 except for the following integrals:

(a) $\displaystyle\int_{-2}^{6} [\delta(x - 1) + \delta(x + 3) + \delta(x - 5)] \, dx$

(b) $\displaystyle\int_{-\infty}^{6} \delta(x - 7) u(x + 3) \, dx$

(c) $\displaystyle\int_{-3}^{2} [\delta(x - 1) - \delta(x + 2)] \frac{e^{-2x^2}}{1 + x^2 + x^4} \, dx$

2-68 Find a value for constant A such that

$$f_X(x) = \begin{cases} 0 & x < -1 \\ A(1 - x^2) \cos(\pi x/2) & -1 \le x \le 1 \\ 0 & 1 < x \end{cases}$$

is a valid probability density function.

2-69 The output voltage X from the receiver in a particular binary digital communication system, when a binary zero is being received, is gaussian (noise only) as defined by $a_X = 0$ and $\sigma_X = 0.3$. When a binary one is being received it is also gaussian (signal-plus-noise now), but as defined by $a_X = 0.9$ and $\sigma_X = 0.3$. The receiver's decision logic specifies that, at the end of a binary (bit) interval, if $X > 0.45$ a binary one is being received. If $X \leq 0.45$ a binary zero is decided. If it is given that a binary zero is truly being received, find the probabilities that (a) a binary one (mistake) will be decided, and (b) a binary zero is decided (correct decision).

2-70 A gaussian random voltage X for which $a_X = 0$ and $\sigma_X = 4.2$ V, appears across a 100-Ω resistor with a power rating of 0.25 W. What is the probability that the voltage will cause an instantaneous power that exceeds the resistor's rating?

2-71 Work Problem 2-70 except assume a 0.5-W resistor.

2-72 For the gaussian random variable, show that the curve's points of inflection (where the first derivative of the probability density function with respect to x has a zero slope) occur at $a_X \pm \sigma_X$.

2-73 A random variable X is known to be gaussian with $a_X = 1.6$ and $\sigma_X = 0.4$. Find: (a) $P\{1.4 < X \leq 2.0\}$, and (b) $P\{-0.6 < (X - 1.6) \leq 0.6\}$.

2-74 The radial distance to the impact points for shells fired over land by a cannon is well-approximated as a gaussian random variable with $a_X = 2000$ m and $\sigma_X = 40$ m when the cannon is aimed at a target located at 1980 m distance.
(a) Find the probability that shells will fall within ± 68 m of the target.
(b) Find the probability that shells will fall at distances of 2050 m or more.

2-75 Assume that the time of arrival of birds at a particular place on a migratory route, as measured in days from the first of the year (January 1 is the first day), is approximated as a gaussian random variable X with $a_X = 200$ and $\sigma_X = 20$ days.
(a) What is the probability the birds arrive after 160 days but on or before the 210th day?
(b) What is the probability the birds will arrive after the 231st day?

2-76 Assume fluorescent lamps made by a manufacturer have a probability of 0.05 of being inoperable when new. A person purchases eight of the lamps for home use.
(a) Plot the probability distribution function for a random variable "the number of inoperable lamps."
(b) What is the probability that exactly one lamp is inoperable of the eight?
(c) What is the probability that all eight lamps are functional?
(d) Determine the probability that one or more lamps are not operable.

2-77 The envelope (amplitude) of the output signal of a radar system that is receiving only noise (no signal) is a Rayleigh random voltage X for which $a = 0$ and $b = 2$ V. The system gets a false target detection if X exceeds a threshold level V volts. How large must V be to make the probability of false detection 0.001?

2-78 In a game show contestants choose one of three doors to determine what prize they win. History shows that the three doors, 1, 2, and 3, are chosen with probabilities 0.30, 0.45, and 0.25, respectively. It is also known that, given door 1 is chosen, the probabilities of winning prizes of $0, $100, and $1000 are 0.10, 0.20, and 0.70. For door 2 the respective probabilities are 0.50, 0.35, and 0.15, and for door 3 they are 0.80, 0.15, and 0.05. If X is a random variable describing dollars won, and D describes the door selected (values of D are $D_1 = 1$, $D_2 = 2$, and $D_3 = 3$), find: (a) $F_X(x|D = D_1)$ and $f_X(x|D = D_1)$, (b) $f_X(x|D = D_2)$, (c) $f_X(x|D = D_3)$, and (d) $f_X(x)$.

2-79 Again consider the game show of Problem 2-78 and find the probabilities of winning (a) $0, (b) $100, and (c) $1000.

★2-80 Divers return each day to the site of a sunken treasure ship. Due to random navigational errors, they arrive with a radial positional error (from the true site) described by a random variable X (in kilometers) defined by

$$F_X(x) = [1 - e^{-x^{3/2}}]u(x)$$

(this is the *Weibull*† distribution, see Appendix F). If they must arrive with an error of not more than 1.2 km to prevent having to move to a new position, and within 0.6 km for optimum use of air tanks, what is the probability of optimum use of tanks given they arrive on site on the first effort?

★2-81 For the navigational errors of Problem 2-80 find and plot the conditional density $f_X(x|X \leq 1.2 \text{ km})$.

---

† After Ernst Hjalmar Waloddi Weibull (1887–), as Swedish applied physicist.

CHAPTER
3

OPERATIONS ON ONE RANDOM VARIABLE— EXPECTATION

3.0 INTRODUCTION

The random variable was introduced in Chapter 2 as a means of providing a systematic definition of events defined on a sample space. Specifically, it formed a mathematical model for describing characteristics of some real, physical world random phenomenon. In this chapter we extend our work to include some important *operations* that may be performed on a random variable. Most of these operations are based on a single concept—expectation.

3.1 EXPECTATION

Expectation is the name given to the process of averaging when a random variable is involved. For a random variable X, we use the notation $E[X]$, which may be read "the mathematical *expectation* of X," "the *expected* value of X," "the *mean* value of X," or "the *statistical average* of X." Occasionally we also use the notation $\bar{X}$ which is read the same way as $E[X]$; that is, $\bar{X} = E[X]$.†

---

† Up to this point in this book an overbar represented the complement of a set or event. Henceforth, unless specifically stated otherwise, the overbar will always represent a mean value.

Nearly everyone is familiar with averaging procedures. An example that serves to tie a familiar problem to the new concept of expectation may be the easiest way to proceed.

Example 3.1-1 Ninety people are randomly selected and the fractional dollar value of coins in their pockets is counted. If the count goes above a dollar, the dollar value is discarded and only the portion from 0¢ to 99¢ is accepted. It is found that 8, 12, 28, 22, 15, and 5 people had 18¢, 45¢, 64¢, 72¢, 77¢, and 95¢ in their pockets, respectively.

Our everyday experiences indicate that the average of these values is

$$\text{Average } \$ = 0.18\left(\frac{8}{90}\right) + 0.45\left(\frac{12}{90}\right) + 0.64\left(\frac{28}{90}\right) + 0.72\left(\frac{22}{90}\right)$$

$$+ 0.77\left(\frac{15}{90}\right) + 0.95\left(\frac{5}{90}\right)$$

$$\approx \$0.632$$

Expected Value of a Random Variable

The everyday averaging procedure used in the above example carries over directly to random variables. In fact, if X is the discrete random variable "fractional dollar value of pocket coins," it has 100 discrete values x_i that occur with probabilities $P(x_i)$, and its expected value $E[X]$ is found in the same way as in the example:

$$E[X] = \sum_{i=1}^{100} x_i P(x_i) \tag{3.1-1}$$

The values x_i identify with the fractional dollar values in the example, while $P(x_i)$ is identified with the ratio of the number of people for the given dollar value to the total number of people. If a large number of people had been used in the "sample" of the example, all fractional dollar values would have shown up and the ratios would have approached $P(x_i)$. Thus, the average in the example would have become more like (3.1-1) for many more than 90 people.

In general, the expected value of any random variable X is defined by

$$E[X] = \bar{X} = \int_{-\infty}^{\infty} x f_X(x) \, dx \tag{3.1-2}$$

If X happens to be discrete with N possible values x_i having probabilities $P(x_i)$ of occurrence, then

$$f_X(x) = \sum_{i=1}^{N} P(x_i)\delta(x - x_i) \tag{3.1-3}$$

from (2.3-5). Upon substitution of (3.1-3) into (3.1-2), we have

$$E[X] = \sum_{i=1}^{N} x_i P(x_i) \qquad \text{discrete random variable} \qquad (3.1\text{-}4)$$

Hence, (3.1-1) is a special case of (3.1-4) when $N = 100$. For some discrete random variables, N may be infinite in (3.1-3) and (3.1-4).

Example 3.1-2 We determine the mean value of the continuous, exponentially distributed random variable for which (2.5-9) applies:

$$f_X(x) = \begin{cases} \dfrac{1}{b} e^{-(x-a)/b} & x > a \\ 0 & x < a \end{cases}$$

From (3.1-2) and an integral from Appendix C:

$$E[X] = \int_a^\infty \frac{x}{b} e^{-(x-a)/b} \, dx = \frac{e^{a/b}}{b} \int_a^\infty x e^{-x/b} \, dx = a + b$$

If a random variable's density is symmetrical about a line $x = a$, then $E[X] = a$; that is,

$$E[X] = a \qquad \text{if} \qquad f_X(x + a) = f_X(-x + a) \qquad (3.1\text{-}5)$$

Expected Value of a Function of a Random Variable

As will be evident in the next section, many useful parameters relating to a random variable X can be derived by finding the expected value of a real function $g(\cdot)$ of X. It can be shown (see Papoulis, 1965, p. 142) that this expected value is given by

$$E[g(X)] = \int_{-\infty}^{\infty} g(x) f_X(x) \, dx \qquad (3.1\text{-}6)$$

If X is a discrete random variable, (3.1-3) applies and (3.1-6) reduces to

$$E[g(X)] = \sum_{i=1}^{N} g(x_i) P(x_i) \qquad \text{discrete random variable} \qquad (3.1\text{-}7)$$

where N may be infinite for some random variables.

Example 3.1-3 It is known that a particular random voltage can be represented as a Rayleigh random variable V having a density function given by (2.5-11) with $a = 0$ and $b = 5$. The voltage is applied to a device that generates a voltage $Y = g(V) = V^2$ that is equal, numerically, to the power in V (in a 1-Ω resistor). We find the average power in V by means of (3.1-6):

$$\text{Power in } V = E[g(V)] = E[V^2] = \int_0^\infty \frac{2v^3}{5} e^{-v^2/5} \, dv$$

By letting $\xi = v^2/5$, $d\xi = 2v \, dv/5$, we obtain

$$\text{Power in } V = 5 \int_0^\infty \xi e^{-\xi} \, d\xi = 5 \text{ W}$$

after using (C-46).

Note that if $g(X)$ in (3.1-6) is a sum of N functions $g_n(X)$, $n = 1, 2, \ldots, N$, then the expected value of the sum of N functions of a random variable X is the sum of the N expected values of the individual functions of the random variable.

★Conditional Expected Value

If, in (3.1-2), $f_X(x)$ is replaced by the conditional density $f_X(x|B)$, where B is any event defined on the sample space, we have the *conditional expected value* of X, denoted $E[X|B]$:

$$E[X|B] = \int_{-\infty}^\infty x f_X(x|B) \, dx \tag{3.1-8}$$

One way to define event B, as shown in Chapter 2, is to let it depend on the random variable X by defining

$$B = \{X \le b\} \qquad -\infty < b < \infty \tag{3.1-9}$$

We showed there that

$$f_X(x|X \le b) = \begin{cases} \dfrac{f_X(x)}{\int_{-\infty}^b f_X(x) \, dx} & x < b \\ 0 & x \ge b \end{cases} \tag{3.1-10}$$

Thus, by substituting (3.1-10) into (3.1-8):

$$E[X|X \le b] = \frac{\int_{-\infty}^b x f_X(x) \, dx}{\int_{-\infty}^b f_X(x) \, dx} \tag{3.1-11}$$

which is the mean value of X when X is constrained to the set $\{X \le b\}$.

3.2 MOMENTS

An immediate application of the expected value of a function $g(\cdot)$ of a random variable X is in calculating moments. Two types of moments are of interest, those about the origin and those about the mean.

Moments About the Origin

The function

$$g(X) = X^n \qquad n = 0, 1, 2, \ldots \tag{3.2-1}$$

when used in (3.1-6) gives the moments about the origin of the random variable X. Denote the nth moment by m_n. Then,

$$m_n = E[X^n] = \int_{-\infty}^{\infty} x^n f_X(x)\, dx \tag{3.2-2}$$

Clearly $m_0 = 1$, the area of the function $f_X(x)$, while $m_1 = \bar{X}$, the expected value of X.

Central Moments

Moments about the mean value of X are called *central moments* and are given the symbol μ_n. They are defined as the expected value of the function

$$g(X) = (X - \bar{X})^n \qquad n = 0, 1, 2, \ldots \tag{3.2-3}$$

which is

$$\mu_n = E[(X - \bar{X})^n] = \int_{-\infty}^{\infty} (x - \bar{X})^n f_X(x)\, dx \tag{3.2-4}$$

The moment $\mu_0 = 1$, the area of $f_X(x)$, while $\mu_1 = 0$. (Why?)

Variance and Skew

The second central moment μ_2 is so important we shall give it the name *variance* and the special notation σ_X^2. Thus, variance is given by†

$$\sigma_X^2 = \mu_2 = E[(X - \bar{X})^2] = \int_{-\infty}^{\infty} (x - \bar{X})^2 f_X(x)\, dx \tag{3.2-5}$$

The positive square root σ_X of variance is called the *standard deviation* of X; it is a measure of the spread in the function $f_X(x)$ about the mean.

Variance can be found from a knowledge of first and second moments. By expanding (3.2-5), we have‡

$$\sigma_X^2 = E[X^2 - 2\bar{X}X + \bar{X}^2] = E[X^2] - 2\bar{X}E[X] + \bar{X}^2$$
$$= E[X^2] - \bar{X}^2 = m_2 - m_1^2 \tag{3.2-6}$$

---

† The subscript indicates that σ_X^2 is the variance of a random variable X. For a random variable Y its variance would be σ_Y^2.

‡ We use the fact that the expected value of a sum of functions of X equals the sum of expected values of individual functions, as previously noted.

Example 3.2-1 Let X have the exponential density function given in Example 3.1-2. By substitution into (3.2-5), the variance of X is

$$\sigma_X^2 = \int_a^\infty (x - \bar{X})^2 \frac{1}{b} e^{-(x-a)/b} \, dx$$

By making the change of variable $\xi = x - \bar{X}$ we obtain

$$\sigma_X^2 = \frac{e^{-(\bar{X}-a)/b}}{b} \int_{a-\bar{X}}^\infty \xi^2 e^{-\xi/b} \, d\xi = (a + b - \bar{X})^2 + b^2$$

after using an integral from Appendix C. However, from Example 3.1-2, $\bar{X} = E[X] = (a + b)$, so

$$\sigma_X^2 = b^2$$

The reader may wish to verify this result by finding the second moment $E[X^2]$ and using (3.2-6).

The third central moment $\mu_3 = E[(X - \bar{X})^3]$ is a measure of the asymmetry of $f_X(x)$ about $x = \bar{X} = m_1$. It will be called the *skew* of the density function. If a density is symmetric about $x = \bar{X}$, it has zero skew. In fact, for this case $\mu_n = 0$ for all odd values of n. (Why?) The normalized third central moment μ_3/σ_X^3 is known as the *skewness* of the density function, or, alternatively, as the *coefficient of skewness*.

Example 3.2-2 We continue Example 3.2-1 and compute the skew and coefficient of skewness for the exponential density. From (3.2-4) with $n = 3$ we have

$$\mu_3 = E[(X - \bar{X})^3] = E[X^3 - 3\bar{X}X^2 + 3\bar{X}^2 X - \bar{X}^3]$$
$$= \overline{X^3} - 3\bar{X}\overline{X^2} + 2\bar{X}^3 = \overline{X^3} - 3\bar{X}(\sigma_X^2 + \bar{X}^2) + 2\bar{X}^3$$
$$= \overline{X^3} - 3\bar{X}\sigma_X^2 - \bar{X}^3$$

Next, we have

$$\overline{X^3} = \int_a^\infty \frac{x^3}{b} e^{-(x-a)/b} \, dx = a^3 + 3a^2 b + 6ab^2 + 6b^3$$

after using (C-48). On substituting $\bar{X} = a + b$ and $\sigma_X^2 = b^2$ from the earlier example, and reducing the algebra we find

$$\mu_3 = 2b^3$$

$$\frac{\mu_3}{\sigma_X^3} = 2$$

This density has a relatively large coefficient of skewness, as can be seen intuitively from Figure 2.5-3.

⋆3.3 FUNCTIONS THAT GIVE MOMENTS

Two functions can be defined that allow moments to be calculated for a random variable X. They are the characteristic function and the moment generating function.

⋆Characteristic Function

The *characteristic function* of a random variable X is defined by

$$\Phi_X(\omega) = E[e^{j\omega X}] \tag{3.3-1}$$

where $j = \sqrt{-1}$. It is a function of the real number $-\infty < \omega < \infty$. If (3.3-1) is written in terms of the density function, $\Phi_X(\omega)$ is seen to be the *Fourier transform*† (with the sign of ω reversed) of $f_X(x)$:

$$\Phi_X(\omega) = \int_{-\infty}^{\infty} f_X(x)e^{j\omega x}\,dx \tag{3.3-2}$$

Because of this fact, if $\Phi_X(\omega)$ is known, $f_X(x)$ can be found from the *inverse Fourier transform* (with sign of x reversed)

$$f_X(x) = \frac{1}{2\pi}\int_{-\infty}^{\infty} \Phi_X(\omega)e^{-j\omega x}\,d\omega \tag{3.3-3}$$

By formal differentiation of (3.3-2) n times with respect to ω and setting $\omega = 0$ in the derivative, we may show that the nth moment of X is given by

$$m_n = (-j)^n \left.\frac{d^n\Phi_X(\omega)}{d\omega^n}\right|_{\omega=0} \tag{3.3-4}$$

A major advantage of using $\Phi_X(\omega)$ to find moments is that $\Phi_X(\omega)$ always exists (Davenport, 1970, p. 426), so the moments can always be found if $\Phi_X(\omega)$ is known, provided, of course, both the moments and the derivatives of $\Phi_X(\omega)$ exist.

It can be shown that the maximum magnitude of a characteristic function is unity and occurs at $\omega = 0$; that is,

$$|\Phi_X(\omega)| \le \Phi_X(0) = 1 \tag{3.3-5}$$

(See Problem 3-24.)

---

† Readers unfamiliar with Fourier transforms should interpret $\Phi_X(\omega)$ as simply the expected value of the function $g(X) = \exp(j\omega X)$. Appendix D is included as a review for others wishing to refresh their background in Fourier transform theory.

Example 3.3-1 Again we consider the random variable with the exponential density of Example 3.1-2 and find its characteristic function and first moment. By substituting the density function into (3.3-2), we get

$$\Phi_X(\omega) = \int_a^\infty \frac{1}{b} e^{-(x-a)/b} e^{j\omega x} \, dx = \frac{e^{a/b}}{b} \int_a^\infty e^{-(1/b - j\omega)x} \, dx$$

Evaluation of the integral follows the use of an integral from Appendix C:

$$\Phi_X(\omega) = \frac{e^{a/b}}{b} \left[\frac{e^{-(1/b - j\omega)x}}{-(1/b - j\omega)} \Big|_a^\infty \right]$$

$$= \frac{e^{j\omega a}}{1 - j\omega b}$$

The derivative of $\Phi_X(\omega)$ is

$$\frac{d\Phi_X(\omega)}{d\omega} = e^{j\omega a} \left[\frac{ja}{1 - j\omega b} + \frac{jb}{(1 - j\omega b)^2} \right]$$

so the first moment becomes

$$m_1 = (-j) \frac{d\Phi_X(\omega)}{d\omega} \Big|_{\omega = 0} = a + b,$$

in agreement with m_1 found in Example 3.1-2.

★Moment Generating Function

Another statistical average closely related to the characteristic function is the *moment generating function*, defined by

$$M_X(v) = E[e^{vX}] \tag{3.3-6}$$

where v is a real number $-\infty < v < \infty$. Thus, $M_X(v)$ is given by

$$M_X(v) = \int_{-\infty}^\infty f_X(x) e^{vx} \, dx \tag{3.3-7}$$

The main advantage of the moment generating function derives from its ability to give the moments. Moments are related to $M_X(v)$ by the expression:

$$m_n = \frac{d^n M_X(v)}{dv^n} \Big|_{v = 0} \tag{3.3-8}$$

The main disadvantage of the moment generating function, as opposed to the characteristic function, is that it may not exist for all random variables and all values of v. However, if $M_X(v)$ exists for all values of v in the neighborhood of $v = 0$ the moments are given by (3.3-8) (Wilks, 1962, p. 114).

Example 3.3-2 To illustrate the calculation and use of the moment generating function, let us reconsider the exponential density of the earlier examples. On use of (3.3-7) we have

$$M_X(v) = \int_a^\infty \frac{1}{b} e^{-(x-a)/b} e^{vx} \, dx$$

$$= \frac{e^{a/b}}{b} \int_a^\infty e^{[v-(1/b)]x} \, dx$$

$$= \frac{e^{av}}{1 - bv}$$

In evaluating $M_X(v)$ we have used an integral from Appendix C.
By differentiation we have the first moment

$$m_1 = \frac{dM_X(v)}{dv}\bigg|_{v=0}$$

$$= \frac{e^{av}[a(1 - bv) + b]}{(1 - bv)^2}\bigg|_{v=0} = a + b$$

which, of course, is the same as previously found.

3.4 TRANSFORMATIONS OF A RANDOM VARIABLE

Quite often one may wish to transform (change) one random variable X into a new random variable Y by means of a transformation

$$Y = T(X) \tag{3.4-1}$$

Typically, the density function $f_X(x)$ or distribution function $F_X(x)$ of X is known, and the problem is to determine either the density function $f_Y(y)$ or distribution function $F_Y(y)$ of Y. The problem can be viewed as a "black box" with input X, output Y, and "transfer characteristic" $Y = T(X)$, as illustrated in Figure 3.4-1.

In general, X can be a discrete, continuous, or a mixed random variable. In turn, the transformation T can be linear, nonlinear, segmented, staircase, etc. Clearly, there are many cases to consider in a general study, depending on the form of X and T. In this section we shall consider only three cases: (1) X continuous and T continuous and either monotonically increasing or decreasing with X; (2)

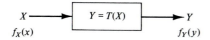

FIGURE 3.4-1
Transformation of a random variable X to a new random variable Y.

X continuous and T continuous but nonmonotonic; (3) X discrete and T continuous. Note that the transformation in all three cases is assumed continuous. The
concepts introduced in these three situations are broad enough that the reader
should have no difficulty in extending them to other cases (see Problem 3-32).

Monotonic Transformations of a Continuous Random Variable

A transformation T is called *monotonically increasing* if $T(x_1) < T(x_2)$ for any
$x_1 < x_2$. It is *monotonically decreasing* if $T(x_1) > T(x_2)$ for any $x_1 < x_2$.

Consider first the increasing transformation. We assume that T is continuous
and differentiable at all values of x for which $f_X(x) \neq 0$. Let Y have a particular
value y_0 corresponding to the particular value x_0 of X as shown in Figure 3.4-2a.
The two numbers are related by

$$y_0 = T(x_0) \quad \text{or} \quad x_0 = T^{-1}(y_0) \tag{3.4-2}$$

where T^{-1} represents the inverse of the transformation T. Now the probability of
the event $\{Y \leq y_0\}$ must equal the probability of the event $\{X \leq x_0\}$ because of

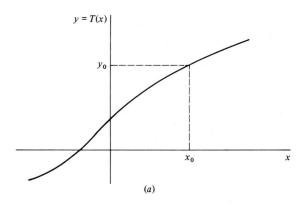

(a)

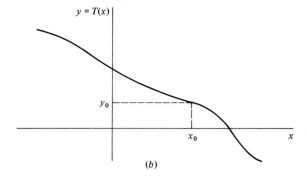

(b)

FIGURE 3.4-2
Monotonic transformations: (a) increasing, and (b) decreasing. [*Adapted from Peebles (1976) with permission of publishers Addison–
Wesley, Advanced Book Program.*]

the one-to-one correspondence between X and Y. Thus,

$$F_Y(y_0) = P\{Y \le y_0\} = P\{X \le x_0\} = F_X(x_0) \qquad (3.4\text{-}3)$$

or

$$\int_{-\infty}^{y_0} f_Y(y)\,dy = \int_{-\infty}^{x_0 = T^{-1}(y_0)} f_X(x)\,dx \qquad (3.4\text{-}4)$$

Next, we differentiate both sides of (3.4-4) with respect to y_0 using Leibniz's rule†
to get

$$f_Y(y_0) = f_X[T^{-1}(y_0)]\frac{dT^{-1}(y_0)}{dy_0} \qquad (3.4\text{-}5)$$

Since this result applies for any y_0, we may now drop the subscript and write

$$f_Y(y) = f_X[T^{-1}(y)]\frac{dT^{-1}(y)}{dy} \qquad (3.4\text{-}6)$$

or, more compactly,

$$f_Y(y) = f_X(x)\frac{dx}{dy} \qquad (3.4\text{-}7)$$

In (3.4-7) it is understood that x is a function of y through (3.4-2).

A consideration of Figure 3.4-2b for the decreasing transformation verifies
that

$$F_Y(y_0) = P\{Y \le y_0\} = P\{X \ge x_0\} = 1 - F_X(x_0) \qquad (3.4\text{-}8)$$

A repetition of the steps leading to (3.4-6) will again produce (3.4-6) except that
the right side is negative. However, since the slope of $T^{-1}(y)$ is also negative, we
conclude that for either type of monotonic transformation

$$f_Y(y) = f_X[T^{-1}(y)]\left|\frac{dT^{-1}(y)}{dy}\right| \qquad (3.4\text{-}9)$$

or simply

$$f_Y(y) = f_X(x)\left|\frac{dx}{dy}\right| \qquad (3.4\text{-}10)$$

---

† Leibniz's rule, after the great German mathematician Gottfried Wilhelm von Leibniz (1646–1716),
states that, if $H(x, u)$ is continuous in x and u and

$$G(u) = \int_{\alpha(u)}^{\beta(u)} H(x, u)\,dx$$

then the derivative of the integral with respect to the parameter u is

$$\frac{dG(u)}{du} = H[\beta(u), u]\frac{d\beta(u)}{du} - H[\alpha(u), u]\frac{d\alpha(u)}{du} + \int_{\alpha(u)}^{\beta(u)} \frac{\partial H(x, u)}{\partial u}\,dx$$

Example 3.4-1 If we take T to be the linear transformation $Y = T(X) = aX + b$, where a and b are any real constants, then $X = T^{-1}(Y) = (Y - b)/a$ and $dx/dy = 1/a$. From (3.4-9)

$$f_Y(y) = f_X\left(\frac{y - b}{a}\right)\left|\frac{1}{a}\right|$$

If X is assumed to be gaussian with the density function given by (2.4-1), we get

$$f_Y(y) = \frac{1}{\sqrt{2\pi\sigma_X^2}} e^{-[(y-b)/a-a_X]^2/2\sigma_X^2}\left|\frac{1}{a}\right|$$

$$= \frac{1}{\sqrt{2\pi a^2\sigma_X^2}} e^{-[y-(aa_X+b)]^2/2a^2\sigma_X^2}$$

which is the density function of another gaussian random variable having

$$a_Y = aa_X + b \qquad \text{and} \qquad \sigma_Y^2 = a^2\sigma_X^2$$

Thus, *a linear transformation of a gaussian random variable produces another gaussian random variable.* A linear amplifier having a random voltage X as its input is one example of a linear transformation.

Nonmonotonic Transformations of a Continuous Random Variable

A transformation may not be monotonic in the more general case. Figure 3.4-3 illustrates one such transformation. There may now be more than one interval of values of X that correspond to the event $\{Y \leq y_0\}$. For the value of y_0 shown in the figure, the event $\{Y \leq y_0\}$ corresponds to the event $\{X \leq x_1 \text{ and } x_2 \leq X \leq x_3\}$.

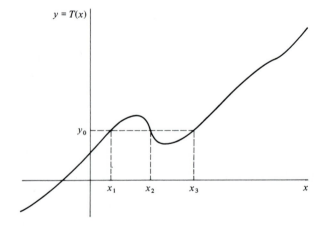

FIGURE 3.4-3
A nonmonotonic transformation. [*Adapted from Peebles (1976) with permission of publishers Addison–Wesley, Advanced Book Program.*]

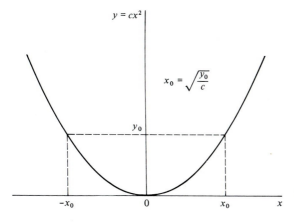

FIGURE 3.4-4
A square-law transformation. [*Adapted from Peebles (1976) with permission of publishers Addison–Wesley, Advanced Book Program.*]

Thus, the probability of the event $\{Y \leq y_0\}$ now equals the probability of the event $\{x$ values yielding $Y \leq y_0\}$, which we shall write as $\{x \mid Y \leq y_0\}$. In other words

$$F_Y(y_0) = P\{Y \leq y_0\} = P\{x \mid Y \leq y_0\} = \int_{\{x \mid Y \leq y_0\}} f_X(x)\, dx \qquad (3.4\text{-}11)$$

Formally, one may differentiate to obtain the density function of Y:

$$f_Y(y_0) = \frac{d}{dy_0} \int_{\{x \mid Y \leq y_0\}} f_X(x)\, dx \qquad (3.4\text{-}12)$$

Although we shall not give a proof, the density function is also given by (Papoulis, 1965, p. 126)

$$f_Y(y) = \sum_n \frac{f_X(x_n)}{\left| \dfrac{dT(x)}{dx} \right|_{x=x_n}} \qquad (3.4\text{-}13)$$

where the sum is taken so as to include all the roots x_n, $n = 1, 2, \ldots$, which are the real solutions of the equation†

$$y = T(x) \qquad (3.4\text{-}14)$$

We illustrate the above concepts by an example.

Example 3.4-2 We find $f_Y(y)$ for the square-law transformation

$$Y = T(X) = cX^2$$

shown in Figure 3.4-4, where c is a real constant $c > 0$. We shall use both the procedure leading to (3.4-12) and that leading to (3.4-13).

---

† If $y = T(x)$ has no real roots for a given value of y, then $f_Y(y) = 0$.

In the former case, the event $\{Y \le y\}$ occurs when $\{-\sqrt{y/c} \le x \le \sqrt{y/c}\} = \{x \mid Y \le y\}$, so (3.4-12) becomes

$$f_Y(y) = \frac{d}{dy} \int_{-\sqrt{y/c}}^{\sqrt{y/c}} f_X(x) \, dx \qquad y \ge 0$$

Upon use of Leibniz's rule we obtain

$$f_Y(y) = f_X(\sqrt{y/c}) \frac{d(\sqrt{y/c})}{dy} - f_X(-\sqrt{y/c}) \frac{d(-\sqrt{y/c})}{dy}$$

$$= \frac{f_X(\sqrt{y/c}) + f_X(-\sqrt{y/c})}{2\sqrt{cy}} \qquad y \ge 0$$

In the latter case where we use (3.4-13), we have $X = \pm\sqrt{Y/c}$, $Y \ge 0$, so $x_1 = -\sqrt{y/c}$ and $x_2 = \sqrt{y/c}$. Furthermore, $dT(x)/dx = 2cx$ so

$$\left. \frac{dT(x)}{dx} \right|_{x=x_1} = 2cx_1 = -2c\sqrt{\frac{y}{c}} = -2\sqrt{cy}$$

$$\left. \frac{dT(x)}{dx} \right|_{x=x_2} = 2\sqrt{cy}$$

From (3.4-13) we again have

$$f_Y(y) = \frac{f_X(\sqrt{y/c}) + f_X(-\sqrt{y/c})}{2\sqrt{cy}} \qquad y \ge 0$$

Transformation of a Discrete Random Variable

If X is a discrete random variable while $Y = T(X)$ is a continuous transformation, the problem is especially simple. Here

$$f_X(x) = \sum_n P(x_n)\delta(x - x_n) \qquad (3.4\text{-}15)$$

$$F_X(x) = \sum_n P(x_n)u(x - x_n) \qquad (3.4\text{-}16)$$

where the sum is taken to include all the possible values x_n, $n = 1, 2, \ldots$, of X.

If the transformation is monotonic, there is a one-to-one correspondence between X and Y so that a set $\{y_n\}$ corresponds to the set $\{x_n\}$ through the equation

$y_n = T(x_n)$. The probability $P(y_n)$ equals $P(x_n)$. Thus,

$$f_Y(y) = \sum_n P(y_n)\delta(y - y_n) \qquad (3.4\text{-}17)$$

$$F_Y(y) = \sum_n P(y_n)u(y - y_n) \qquad (3.4\text{-}18)$$

where

$$y_n = T(x_n) \qquad (3.4\text{-}19)$$

$$P(y_n) = P(x_n) \qquad (3.4\text{-}20)$$

If T is not monotonic, the above procedure remains valid except there now exists the possibility that more than one value x_n corresponds to a value y_n. In such a case $P(y_n)$ will equal the sum of the probabilities of the various x_n for which $y_n = T(x_n)$.

3.5 COMPUTER GENERATION OF ONE RANDOM VARIABLE

A digital computer is often used to simulate systems in order to estimate their performance with noise prior to the actual construction of the system. These simulations usually require that random numbers be generated that are values of random variables having prescribed distributions. If software (a computer program, or subroutine, that can be called up on demand) exists for the specified distribution, there is no problem. However, if the computer "library" does not contain the desired program, it is necessary for the simulation to generate its own random numbers. In this section we briefly describe how to generate a random variable with specified probability distribution, given mainly that the computer is able to generate random numbers that are values of a random variable with uniform distribution on (0,1), a commonly satisfied condition in most cases.

The problem, then, is to find the transformation $T(X)$ in Figure 3.4-1 that will create a random variable Y of prescribed distribution function when X has a uniform distribution on (0,1). We assume initially that $T(X)$ is a monotonically nondecreasing function so that (3.4-3) applies. Our work will show that this condition is automatically satisfied. From (3.4-3) we have (for any x and y)

$$F_Y[y = T(x)] = F_X(x) \qquad (3.5\text{-}1)$$

But for uniform X, $F_X(x) = x$ when $0 < x < 1$, from (2.5-8). Thus, we solve for the inverse in (3.5-1) to get

$$y = T(x) = F_Y^{-1}(x) \qquad 0 < x < 1 \qquad (3.5\text{-}2)$$

Since any distribution function $F_Y(y)$ is nondecreasing, its inverse is nondecreasing, and the initial assumption is always satisfied.

Equation (3.5-2) is our principal result. It states that, given a specified distribution $F_Y(y)$ for Y, we find the inverse function by solving $F_Y(y) = x$ for y.

The result is $T(x)$. An example will illustrate this simple procedure to create a Rayleigh random variable.

Example 3.5-1 We find the transformation required to generate the Rayleigh random variable of (2.5-12) with $a = 0$. On setting

$$F_Y(y) = 1 - e^{-y^2/b} = x \qquad \text{for } 0 < x < 1$$

we solve for y and find

$$y = T(x) = \sqrt{-b \ln(1 - x)} \qquad 0 < x < 1$$

Equation (3.5-2) can be readily applied to any distribution for which its inverse can by analytically determined (see Problems 3-75 through 3-78 for other examples). For other distributions the required inverse can be stored in the computer for a number of points (y, x), and the simulation can then use interpolation between computed points to obtain values of y for any value of x.

The gaussian random variable is an important example of a distribution for which the inverse cannot be found analytically. Because computer simulations often require gaussian random numbers to be generated, we show in Section 5.6 how this important problem can be solved by extension of the methods of this section.

PROBLEMS

3-1 A discrete random variable X has possible values $x_i = i^2$, $i = 1, 2, 3, 4, 5$, which occur with probabilities 0.4, 0.25, 0.15, 0.1, and 0.1, respectively. Find the mean value $\bar{X} = E[X]$ of X.

3-2 The natural numbers are the possible values of a random variable X; that is, $x_n = n, n = 1, 2, \ldots$. These numbers occur with probabilities $P(x_n) = (^1/_2)^n$. Find the expected value of X.

3-3 If the probabilities in Problem 3-2 are $P(x_n) = p^n$, $0 < p < 1$, show that $p = {}^1/_2$ is the only value of p that is allowed for the problem as formulated. (*Hint:* Use the fact that $\int_{-\infty}^{\infty} f_X(x)\, dx = 1$ is necessary.)

3-4 Give an example of a random variable where its mean value might not equal any of its possible values.

3-5 Find:
(a) the expected value, and
(b) the variance of the random variable with the triangular density of Figure 2.3-1a if $a = 1/\alpha$.

3-6 Show that the mean value and variance of the random variable having the uniform density function of (2.5-7) are:

$$\bar{X} = E[X] = (a + b)/2$$

and

$$\sigma_X^2 = (b - a)^2/12$$

3-7 A pointer is spun on a fair wheel of chance numbered from 0 to 100 around its circumference.

(a) What is the average value of all possible pointer positions?

(b) What deviation from its average value will pointer position take on the average; that is, what is the pointer's root-mean-squared deviation from its mean? (*Hint:* Use results of Problem 3-6.)

3-8 Find:

(a) the mean value, and

(b) the variance of the random variable X defined by Problems 2-6 and 2-14 of Chapter 2.

⋆3-9 For the *binomial density* of (2.5-1), show that

$$E[X] = \bar{X} = Np$$

and

$$\sigma_X^2 = Np(1 - p)$$

3-10 (a) Let resistance be a random variable in Problem 2-11 of Chapter 2. Find the mean value of resistance.

(b) What is the output voltage E_2 if an *average* resistor were used in the circuit?

(c) For the resistors specified, what is the mean value of E_2? Does the voltage of part (b) equal this value? Explain your results.

3-11 (a) Use the symmetry of the density function given by (2.4-1) to justify that the parameter a_X in the *gaussian density* is the mean value of the random variable: $\bar{X} = a_X$.

(b) Prove that the parameter σ_X^2 is the variance. (*Hint:* Use an equation from Appendix C.)

3-12 Show that the mean value $E[X]$ and variance σ_X^2 of the Rayleigh random variable, with density given by (2.5-11), are

$$E[X] = a + \sqrt{\pi b/4}$$

and

$$\sigma_X^2 = b(4 - \pi)/4$$

3-13 What is the expected lifetime of the system defined in Problem 2-33 of Chapter 2?

3-14 Find:

(a) the mean value, and

(b) the variance for a random variable with the *Laplace* density

$$f_X(x) = \frac{1}{2b} e^{-|x-m|/b}$$

where b and m are real constants, $b > 0$ and $-\infty < m < \infty$.

3-15 Determine the mean value of the *Cauchy* random variable in Problem 2-34 of Chapter 2. What can you say about the variance of this random variable?

★3-16 For the *Poisson* random variable defined in (2.5-4) show that:

(a) the mean value is b and

(b) the variance also equals b.

3-17 (a) Use (3.2-2) to find the first three moments m_1, m_2, and m_3 for the exponential density of Example 3.1-2.

(b) Find m_1, m_2, and m_3 from the characteristic function found in Example 3.3-1. Verify that they agree with those of part (a).

3-18 Find the expressions for all the moments about the origin and central moments for the uniform density of (2.5-7).

3-19 Define a function $g(\cdot)$ of a random variable X by

$$g(X) = \begin{cases} 1 & x \geq x_0 \\ 0 & x < \dot{x}_0 \end{cases}$$

where x_0 is a real number $-\infty < x_0 < \infty$. Show that

$$E[g(X)] = 1 - F_X(x_0)$$

3-20 Show that the second moment of any random variable X about an arbitrary point a is minimum when $a = \bar{X}$; that is, show that $E[(X-a)^2]$ is minimum for $a = \bar{X}$.

3-21 For any discrete random variable X with values x_i having probabilities of occurrence $P(x_i)$, show that the moments of X are

$$m_n = \sum_{i=1}^{N} x_i^n P(x_i)$$

$$\mu_n = \sum_{i=1}^{N} (x_i - \bar{X})^n P(x_i)$$

where N may be infinite for some X.

3-22 Prove that central moments μ_n are related to moments m_k about the origin by

$$\mu_n = \sum_{k=0}^{n} \binom{n}{k} (-\bar{X})^{n-k} m_k$$

3-23 A random variable X has a density function $f_X(x)$ and moments m_n. If the density is shifted higher in x by an amount $\alpha > 0$ to a new origin, show that the moments of the shifted density, denoted m'_n, are related to the moments m_n by

$$m'_n = \sum_{k=0}^{n} \binom{n}{k} \alpha^{n-k} m_k$$

⋆3-24 Show that any characteristic function $\Phi_X(\omega)$ satisfies

$$|\Phi_X(\omega)| \le \Phi_X(0) = 1$$

3-25 A random variable X is uniformly distributed on the interval $(-5, 15)$. Another random variable $Y = e^{-X/5}$ is formed. Find $E[Y]$.

3-26 A gaussian voltage random variable X [see (2.4-1)] has a mean value $\bar{X} = a_X = 0$ and variance $\sigma_X^2 = 9$. The voltage X is applied to a square-law, full-wave diode detector with a transfer characteristic $Y = 5X^2$. Find the mean value of the output voltage Y.

⋆3-27 For the system having a lifetime specified in Problem 2-33 of Chapter 2, determine the expected lifetime of the system given that the system has survived 20 weeks.

⋆3-28 The characteristic function for a gaussian random variable X, having a mean value of 0, is

$$\Phi_X(\omega) = \exp\left(-\sigma_X^2 \omega^2/2\right)$$

Find all the moments of X using $\Phi_X(\omega)$.

⋆3-29 Work Problem 3-28 using the moment generating function

$$M_X(v) = \exp\left(\sigma_X^2 v^2/2\right)$$

for the zero-mean gaussian random variable.

⋆3-30 A discrete random variable X can have $N+1$ values $x_k = k\Delta$, $k = 0, 1, \ldots, N$, where $\Delta > 0$ is a real number. Its values occur with equal probability. Show that the characteristic function of X is

$$\Phi_X(\omega) = \frac{1}{N+1} \frac{\sin\left[(N+1)\omega\Delta/2\right]}{\sin\left(\omega\Delta/2\right)} e^{jN\omega\Delta/2}$$

3-31 A random variable X is uniformly distributed on the interval $(-\pi/2, \pi/2)$. X is transformed to the new random variable $Y = T(X) = a \tan(X)$, where $a > 0$. Find the probability density function of Y.

3-32 Work Problem 3-31 if X is uniform on the interval $(-\pi, \pi)$.

3-33 A random variable X undergoes the transformation $Y = a/X$, where a is a real number. Find the density function of Y.

3-34 A random variable X is uniformly distributed on the interval $(-a, a)$. It is transformed to a new variable Y by the transformation $Y = cX^2$ defined in Example 3.4-2. Find and sketch the density function of Y.

3-35 A zero-mean gaussian random variable X is transformed to the random variable Y determined by

$$Y = \begin{cases} cX & X > 0 \\ 0 & X \le 0 \end{cases}$$

where c is a real constant, $c > 0$. Find and sketch the density function of Y.

3-36 If the transformation of Problem 3-35 is applied to a Rayleigh random variable with $a \ge 0$, what is its effect?

★3-37 A random variable Θ is uniformly distributed on the interval (θ_1, θ_2) where θ_1 and θ_2 are real and satisfy

$$0 \le \theta_1 < \theta_2 < \pi$$

Find and sketch the probability density function of the transformed random variable $Y = \cos(\Theta)$.

3-38 A random variable X can have values -4, $-1, 2, 3$, and 4, each with probability $^1/_5$. Find:
(a) the density function,
(b) the mean, and
(c) the variance of the random $Y = 3X^3$.

ADDITIONAL PROBLEMS, SECOND EDITION

3-39 (a) Find the average amount the gambler in Problem 2-42 can expect to win.
(b) What is his probability of winning on any given playing of the game?

3-40 The *arcsine* probability density is defined by

$$f_X(x) = \frac{\text{rect}(x/2a)}{\pi\sqrt{a^2 - x^2}}$$

for any real constant $a > 0$. Show that $\bar{X} = 0$ and $\overline{X^2} = a^2/2$ for this density.

★3-41 For the animal described in Problem 2-58 find its expected lifetime given that it will not live beyond 20 weeks.

3-42 Find the expected value of the function $g(X) = X^3$ where X is a random variable defined by the density

$$f_X(x) = (^1/_2)u(x)\exp(-x/2)$$

3-43 Continue Problem 3-25 by finding all moments of Y. (*Hint:* Treat Y^n as a function of Y, not as a transformation.)

3-44 Reconsider the production line that manufactures bolts in Problem 2-12.
(a) What is the average length of bolts that are placed up for sale?
(b) What is the standard deviation of length of bolts sold?
(c) What percentage of all bolts sold are expected to have a length within one standard deviation of the average length?

(d) By what tolerance (as a percentage) does the average length of bolts sold match the nominally desired length of 760 mm?

3-45 A random variable X has a probability density

$$f_X(x) = \begin{cases} (\pi/16) \cos (\pi x/8) & -4 \le x \le 4 \\ 0 & \text{elsewhere} \end{cases}$$

Find: (a) its mean value $\bar{X}$, (b) its second moment $\overline{X^2}$, and (c) its variance.

3-46 A certain meter is designed to measure small dc voltages but makes errors because of noise. The errors are accurately represented as a gaussian random variable with a mean of zero and a standard deviation of 10^{-3} V. When the dc voltage is disconnected it is found that the probability is 0.5 that the meter reading is positive due to noise. With the dc voltage present this probability becomes 0.2514. What is the dc voltage?

3-47 Find the skew and coefficient of skewness for a Rayleigh random variable for which $a = 0$ in (2.5-11).

3-48 A random variable X has the density

$$f_X(x) = \begin{cases} (^3/_{32})(-x^2 + 8x - 12) & 2 \le x \le 6 \\ 0 & \text{elsewhere} \end{cases}$$

Find the following moments: (a) m_0, (b) m_1, (c) m_2, and (d) μ_2.

3-49 The *chi-square density* with N degrees of freedom is defined by

$$f_X(x) = \frac{x^{(N/2)-1}}{2^{N/2}\Gamma(N/2)} u(x) e^{-x/2}$$

where $\Gamma(\cdot)$ is the gamma function

$$\Gamma(z) = \int_0^\infty \xi^{z-1} e^{-\xi} \, d\xi \qquad \text{real part of } z > 0$$

and $N = 1, 2, \ldots$. Show that (a) $\bar{X} = N$, (b) $\overline{X^2} = N(N + 2)$, and (c) $\sigma_X^2 = 2N$ for this density.

3-50 For the density of Problem 3-49 find its arbitrary moment $\overline{X^n}, n = 0, 1, 2, \ldots$.

3-51 A random variable X is called *Weibull* if its density has the form

$$f_X(x) = abx^{b-1} \exp(-ax^b) u(x)$$

where $a > 0$ and $b > 0$ are real constants. Use the definition of the gamma function of Problem 3-49 to find (a) the mean value, (b) the second moment, and (c) the variance of X.

★3-52 Show that the characteristic function of a random variable having the binomial density of (2.5-1) is

$$\Phi_X(\omega) = [1 - p + pe^{j\omega}]^N$$

★3-53 Show that the characteristic function of a Poisson random variable defined by (2.5-4) is

$$\Phi_X(\omega) = \exp[-b(1 - e^{j\omega})]$$

★**3-54** The *Erlang*† *random variable* X has a characteristic function

$$\Phi_X(\omega) = \left[\frac{a}{a - j\omega} \right]^N$$

for $a > 0$ and $N = 1, 2, \ldots$. Show that $\bar{X} = N/a$, $\overline{X^2} = N(N+1)/a^2$, and $\sigma_X^2 = N/a^2$.

3-55 A random variable X has $\bar{X} = -3$, $\overline{X^2} = 11$, and $\sigma_X^2 = 2$. For a new random variable $Y = 2X - 3$, find (a) $\bar{Y}$, (b) $\overline{Y^2}$, and (c) σ_Y^2.

★**3-56** For any real random variable X with mean $\bar{X}$ and variance σ_X^2, *Chebychev's inequality*‡ is

$$P\{|X - \bar{X}| \geq \lambda \sigma_X\} \leq 1/\lambda^2$$

where $\lambda > 0$ is a real constant. Prove the inequality. (*Hint:* Define a new random variable $Y = 0$ for $|X - \bar{X}| < \lambda \sigma_X$ and $Y = \lambda^2 \sigma_X^2$ for $|X - \bar{X}| > \lambda \sigma_X$, observe that $Y \leq (X - \bar{X})^2$ and find $E[Y]$.)

3-57 A gaussian random variable, for which

$$f_X(x) = (2/\sqrt{\pi}) \exp(-4x^2)$$

is applied to a square-law device to produce a new (output) random variable $Y = X^2/2$. (a) Find the density of Y. (b) Find the moments $m_n = E[Y^n]$, $n = 0, 1, \ldots$. (*Hint:* Put your answer in terms of the gamma function defined in Problem 3-49).

3-58 A gaussian random variable, for which $\bar{X} = 0.6$ and $\sigma_X = 0.8$, is transformed to a new random variable by the transformation

$$Y = T(X) = \begin{cases} 4 & 1.0 \leq X < \infty \\ 2 & 0 \leq X < 1.0 \\ -2 & -1.0 \leq X < 0 \\ -4 & -\infty < X < -1.0 \end{cases}$$

(a) Find the density function of Y.
(b) Find the mean and variance of Y.

3-59 Work Problem 3-31 except assume a transformation $Y = T(X) = a \sin(X)$ with $a > 0$.

3-60 Let X be a gaussian random variable with density given by (2.4-1). If X is transformed to a new random variable $Y = b + e^X$, where b is a real constant, show that the density of Y is log-normal as defined in Problem 2-35. This transformation allows log-normal random numbers to be generated from gaussian random numbers by a digital computer.

---

† A. K. Erlang (1878–1929) was a Danish engineer.
‡ After the Russian mathematician Pafnuty Lvovich Chebychev (1821–1894).

3-61 A random variable X is uniformly distributed on $(0, 6)$. If X is transformed to a new random variable $Y = 2(X - 3)^2 - 4$, find: (a) the density of Y, (b) $\bar{Y}$, (c) σ_Y^2.

ADDITIONAL PROBLEMS, THIRD EDITION

3-62 A random variable X represents the value of coins (in cents) given in change when purchases are made at a particular store. Suppose the probabilities of 1¢, 5¢, 10¢, 25¢, and 50¢ being present in change are 0.35, 0.25, 0.20, 0.15, and 0.05, respectively.
(a) Write an expression for the probability density function of X.
(b) Find the mean of X.

3-63 In the circuit of Figure P2-11 of Chapter 2 let the resistance of R_1 be a random variable uniformly distributed on $(R_0 - \Delta R, R_0 + \Delta R)$ where R_0 and ΔR are constants.
(a) Find an expression for the power dissipated in R_2 for any constant voltage E_1.
(b) Find the mean value of power when R_1 is random.
(c) Evaluate the mean power for $E_1 = 12$ V, $R_2 = 1000$ Ω, $R_0 = 1500$ Ω, and $\Delta R = 100$ Ω.

★3-64 The power (in milliwatts) returned to a radar from a certain class of aircraft has the probability density function

$$f_P(p) = \frac{1}{10} e^{-p/10} u(p).$$

Suppose a given aircraft belongs to this class but is known to not produce a power larger than 15 mW.
(a) Find the probability density function of X conditional on $P \leq 15$ mW.
(b) Find the conditional mean value of P.

3-65 A random variable X has a probability density

$$f_X(x) = \begin{cases} (1/2) \cos (x) & -\pi/2 < x < \pi/2 \\ 0 & \text{elsewhere in } x \end{cases}$$

Find the mean value of the function $g(X) = 4X^2$.

3-66 Work Problem 3-65, except assume a function $g(X) = 4X^4$.

3-67 A random variable has a probability density

$$f_X(x) = \begin{cases} (5/4)(1 - x^4) & 0 < x \leq 1 \\ 0 & \text{elsewhere in } x \end{cases}$$

Find: (a) $E[X]$, (b) $E[4X + 2]$, and (c) $E[X^2]$.

3-68 Use the definition of the gamma function as given by (F-1f) in Appendix F to obtain an expression for the moments $E[X^n]$, $n = 0, 1, 2, \ldots$, for the gamma density defined by (F-50). Use the expression to prove that (F-52) and (F-53) are true.

3-69 Suppose it is found that the function

$$f_X(x) = \frac{16/\pi}{(4 + x^2)^2}$$

is a good empirical fit to the probability density function of some random experimental data represented by a random variable X. Find the mean, second moment, and variance of X.

★3-70 The characteristic function of the Laplace density of Problem 3-14 is known to be

$$\Phi_X(\omega) = \frac{e^{jm\omega}}{1 + (b\omega)^2}$$

Use this result to find the mean, second moment, and variance of the random variable X.

★3-71 The Chi-square density of Problem 3-49 has a characteristic function

$$\Phi_X(\omega) = \frac{1}{(1 - j2\omega)^{N/2}}$$

Use this function with (3.3-4) to verify the mean and second moment found in Problem 3-49.

3-72 It is known that the envelope of the bandpass noise that emerges from a communication or radar receiver can be modeled as a Rayleigh random variable X with the probability density of (2.5-11) when $a = 0$, $b = 2\sigma_X^2$ and σ_X^2 is the power in the bandpass noise. If the envelope is transformed to a new variable $Y = cX^2$, where c is a constant, find the density of Y. This transformation is equivalent to a diode envelope detector where the noise level is small and the diode behaves approximately as a square-law device.

3-73 A certain "soft" limiter accepts a random input voltage X and limits the amplitudes of an output random variable Y according to

$$Y = \begin{cases} V(1 - e^{-X/a}) & 0 \le X \\ -V(1 - e^{X/a}) & X \le 0 \end{cases}$$

where $V > 0$ and $a > 0$ are constants. Show that the probability density of Y is

$$f_Y(y) = \frac{a}{(V - y)} f_X\left[a \ln\left(\frac{V}{(V - y)}\right)\right] u(y)$$

$$+ \frac{a}{(V + y)} f_X\left[-a \ln\left(\frac{V}{(V + y)}\right)\right] u(-y)$$

where $f_X(x)$ is the probability density of X.

3-74 If X in Problem 3-73 has the Laplace density of Problem 3-14 with $m = 0$, find the density of the output Y. If $a = b$, how is Y distributed?

3-75 In a computer simulation it is desired to transform numbers, that are values of a random variable uniformly distributed on $(0, 1)$, to numbers that are values of an exponentially-distributed random variable, as defined by (2.5-10) with $a = 0$. Find the required transformation.

3-76 Work Problem 3-75, except to generate a random variable with a *Weibull* distribution as defined by (F-91) in Appendix F.

3-77 Work Problem 3-75, except to generate a *Cauchy* random variable as defined by (F-31) of Appendix F with $a = 0$.

3-78 Work Problem 3-75, except to generate a random variable with the *arcsine* distribution of (F-23) of Appendix F.

CHAPTER

4

MULTIPLE
RANDOM
VARIABLES

4.0 INTRODUCTION

In Chapters 2 and 3, various aspects of the theory of a single random variable were studied. The random variable was found to be a powerful concept. It enabled many realistic problems to be described in a probabilistic way such that practical measures could be applied to the problem even though it was random. For example, we have seen that shell impact position along the line of fire from a cannon to a target can be described by a random variable (Problem 2-29). From knowledge of the probability distribution or density function of impact position, we can solve for such practical measures as the mean value of impact position, its variance, and skew. These measures are not, however, a complete enough description of the problem in most cases.

Naturally, we may also be interested in how much the impact positions deviate *from* the line of fire in, say, the perpendicular (cross-fire) direction. In other words, we prefer to describe impact position as a point in a plane as opposed to being a point along a line. To handle such situations it is necessary that we extend our theory to include *two* random variables, one for each coordinate axis of the plane in our example. In other problems it may be necessary to extend the theory to include *several* random variables. We accomplish these extensions in this and the next chapter.

Fortunately, many situations of interest in engineering can be handled by the theory of two random variables.† Because of this fact, we emphasize the two-variable case, although the more general theory is also stated in most discussions to follow.

4.1 VECTOR RANDOM VARIABLES

Suppose two random variables X and Y are defined on a sample space S, where specific values of X and Y are denoted by x and y, respectively. Then any ordered pair of numbers (x, y) may be conveniently considered to be a *random point* in the xy plane. The point may be taken as a specific value of a *vector random variable* or a *random vector*.‡ Figure 4.1-1 illustrates the mapping involved in going from S to the xy plane.

The plane of all points (x, y) in the ranges of X and Y may be considered a new sample space. It is in reality a vector space where the components of any vector are the values of the random variables X and Y. The new space is sometimes called the *range sample space* (Davenport, 1970) or the *two-dimensional product space*. In this section and all following work we shall just call it a *joint sample space* and give it the symbol S_J.

---

† In particular, it will be found in Chapter 6 that such important concepts as autocorrelation, cross-correlation, and covariance functions, which apply to random processes, are based on two random variables.

‡ There are some specific conditions that must be satisfied in a complete definition of a random vector (Davenport, 1970, Chapter 5). They are somewhat advanced for our scope and we shall simply assume the validity of our random vectors.

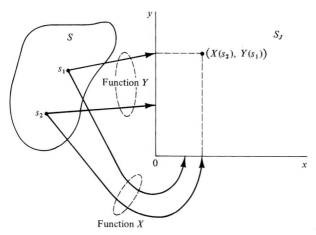

FIGURE 4.1-1
Mapping from the sample space S to the joint sample space S_J (xy plane).

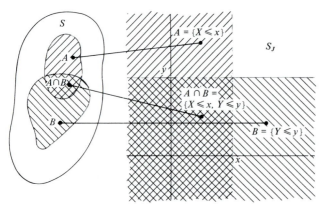

FIGURE 4.1-2
Comparisons of events in S with those in S_J.

As in the case of one random variable, let us define an event A by

$$A = \{X \le x\} \tag{4.1-1}$$

A similar event B can be defined for Y:

$$B = \{Y \le y\} \tag{4.1-2}$$

Events A and B refer to the sample space S, while events $\{X \le x\}$ and $\{Y \le y\}$ refer to the joint sample space S_J.† Figure 4.1-2 illustrates the correspondences between events in the two spaces. Event A corresponds to all points in S_J for which the X coordinate values are not greater than x. Similarly, event B corresponds to the Y coordinate values in S_J not exceeding y. Of special interest is to observe that the event $A \cap B$ defined on S corresponds to the *joint event* $\{X \le x$ and $Y \le y\}$ defined on S_J, which we write $\{X \le x, Y \le y\}$. This joint event is shown crosshatched in Figure 4.1-2.

In the more general case where N random variables $X_1, X_2, \ldots, X_N$ are defined on a sample space S, we consider them to be components of an *N-dimensional random vector* or *N-dimensional random variable*. The joint sample space S_J is now N-dimensional.

4.2 JOINT DISTRIBUTION AND ITS PROPERTIES

The probabilities of the two events $A = \{X \le x\}$ and $B = \{Y \le y\}$ have already been defined as functions of x and y, respectively, called probability distribution

---

† Do not forget that elements s of S form the link between the two events since by writing $\{X \le x\}$ we really refer to the set of those s such that $X(s) \le x$ for some real number x. A similar statement holds for the event $\{Y \le y\}$.

functions:

$$F_X(x) = P\{X \le x\} \qquad (4.2\text{-}1)$$

$$F_Y(y) = P\{Y \le y\} \qquad (4.2\text{-}2)$$

We must introduce a new concept to include the probability of the joint event $\{X \le x, Y \le y\}$.

Joint Distribution Function

We define the probability of the joint event $\{X \le x, Y \le y\}$, which is a function of the numbers x and y, by a *joint probability distribution function* and denote it by the symbol $F_{X,Y}(x, y)$. Hence,

$$F_{X,Y}(x, y) = P\{X \le x, Y \le y\} \qquad (4.2\text{-}3)$$

It should be clear that $P\{X \le x, Y \le y\} = P(A \cap B)$, where the joint event $A \cap B$ is defined on S.

To illustrate joint distribution, we take an example where both random variables X and Y are discrete.

Example 4.2-1 Assume that the joint sample space S_J has only three possible elements: $(1, 1)$, $(2, 1)$, and $(3, 3)$. The probabilities of these elements are assumed to be $P(1, 1) = 0.2$, $P(2, 1) = 0.3$, and $P(3, 3) = 0.5$. We find $F_{X,Y}(x, y)$.

In constructing the joint distribution function, we observe that the event $\{X \le x, Y \le y\}$ has no elements for any $x < 1$ and/or $y < 1$. Only at the point $(1, 1)$ does the function assume a step value. So long as $x \ge 1$ and $y \ge 1$, this probability is maintained so that $F_{X,Y}(x, y)$ has a stair step holding in the region $x \ge 1$ and $y \ge 1$ as shown in Figure 4.2-1a. For larger x and y, the point $(2, 1)$ produces a second stair step of amplitude 0.3 which holds in the region $x \ge 2$ and $y \ge 1$. The second step adds to the first. Finally, a third stair step of amplitude 0.5 is added to the first two when x and y are in the region $x \ge 3$ and $y \ge 3$. the final function is shown in Figure 4.2-1a.

The preceding example can be used to identify the form of the joint distribution function for two general discrete random variables. Let X have N possible values x_n and Y have M possible values y_m, then

$$F_{X,Y}(x, y) = \sum_{n=1}^{N} \sum_{m=1}^{M} P(x_n, y_m) u(x - x_n) u(y - y_m) \qquad (4.2\text{-}4)$$

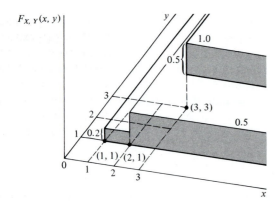

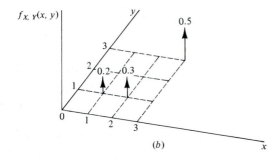

FIGURE 4.2-1
A joint distribution function (a), and its corresponding joint density function (b), that apply to Examples 4.2-1 and 4.2-2.

where $P(x_n, y_m)$ is the probability of the joint event $\{X = x_n, Y = y_m\}$ and $u(\cdot)$ is the unit-step function. As seen in Example 4.2-1, some couples (x_n, y_m) may have zero probability. In some cases N or M, or both, may be infinite.

If $F_{X,Y}(x, y)$ is plotted for continuous random variables X and Y, the same general behavior as shown in Figure 4.2-1a is obtained except the surface becomes smooth and has no stairstep discontinuities.

For N random variables $X_n, n = 1, 2, \ldots, N$, the generalization of (4.2-3) is direct. The joint distribution function, denoted by $F_{X_1, X_2, \ldots, X_N}(x_1, x_2, \ldots, x_N)$, is defined as the probability of the joint event $\{X_1 \le x_1, X_2 \le x_2, \ldots, X_N \le x_N\}$:

$$F_{X_1, X_2, \ldots, X_N}(x_1, x_2, \ldots, x_N) = P\{X_1 \le x_1, X_2 \le x_2, \ldots, X_N \le x_N\} \quad (4.2\text{-}5)$$

For a single random variable X, we found in Chapter 2 that $F_X(x)$ could be expressed in general as the sum of a function of stairstep form (due to the discrete portion of a mixed random variable X) and a function that was continuous (due to the continuous portion of X). Such a simple decomposition of the joint distribution when $N > 1$ is not generally true [Cramér, 1946, Section 8.4]. However, it is true that joint density functions in practice often correspond to all random variables being either discrete or continuous. Therefore, we shall limit our consideration in this book almost entirely to these two cases when $N > 1$.

Properties of the Joint Distribution

A joint distribution function for two random variables X and Y has several properties that follow readily from its definition. We list them:

(1) $F_{X,Y}(-\infty, -\infty) = 0$ $\quad F_{X,Y}(-\infty, y) = 0$ $\quad F_{X,Y}(x, -\infty) = 0$ (4.2-6a)

(2) $F_{X,Y}(\infty, \infty) = 1$ $\qquad\qquad\qquad\qquad\qquad\qquad\qquad\qquad$ (4.2-6b)

(3) $0 \le F_{X,Y}(x, y) \le 1$ $\qquad\qquad\qquad\qquad\qquad\qquad\qquad\quad$ (4.2-6c)

(4) $F_{X,Y}(x, y)$ is a nondecreasing function of both x and y $\qquad$ (4.2-6d)

(5) $F_{X,Y}(x_2, y_2) + F_{X,Y}(x_1, y_1) - F_{X,Y}(x_1, y_2) - F_{X,Y}(x_2, y_1)$

$\qquad = P\{x_1 < X \le x_2, y_1 < Y \le y_2\} \ge 0$ $\qquad\qquad\qquad$ (4.2-6e)

(6) $F_{X,Y}(x, \infty) = F_X(x)$ $\quad F_{X,Y}(\infty, y) = F_Y(y)$ $\qquad\qquad$ (4.2-6f)

The first five of these properties are just the two-dimensional extensions of the properties of one random variable given in (2.2-2). Properties 1, 2, and 5 may be used as tests to determine whether some function can be a valid distribution function for two random variables X and Y (Papoulis, 1965, p. 169). Property 6 deserves a few special comments.

Marginal Distribution Functions

Property 6 above states that the distribution function of one random variable can be obtained by setting the value of the other variable to infinity in $F_{X,Y}(x, y)$. The functions $F_X(x)$ or $F_Y(y)$ obtained in this manner are called *marginal distribution functions*.

To justify property 6, it is easiest to return to the basic events A and B, defined by $A = \{X \le x\}$ and $B = \{Y \le y\}$, and observe that $F_{X,Y}(x, y) = P\{X \le x, Y \le y\} = P(A \cap B)$. Now if we set y to ∞, this is equivalent to making B the certain event; that is, $B = \{Y \le \infty\} = S$. Furthermore, since $A \cap B = A \cap S = A$, then we have $F_{X,Y}(x, \infty) = P(A \cap S) = P(A) = P\{X \le x\} = F_X(x)$. A similar proof can be stated for obtaining $F_Y(y)$.

Example 4.2-2 We find explicit expressions for $F_{X,Y}(x, y)$, and the marginal distributions $F_X(x)$ and $F_Y(y)$ for the joint sample space of Example 4.2-1.

The joint distribution derives from (4.2-4) if we recognize that only three probabilities are nonzero:

$$F_{X,Y}(x, y) = P(1, 1)u(x - 1)u(y - 1)$$
$$+ P(2, 1)u(x - 2)u(y - 1)$$
$$+ P(3, 3)u(x - 3)u(y - 3)$$

where $P(1, 1) = 0.2$, $P(2, 1) = 0.3$, and $P(3, 3) = 0.5$. If we set $y = \infty$:

$$F_X(x) = F_{X,Y}(x, \infty)$$
$$= P(1, 1)u(x - 1) + P(2, 1)u(x - 2) + P(3, 3)u(x - 3)$$
$$= 0.2u(x - 1) + 0.3u(x - 2) + 0.5u(x - 3)$$

If we set $x = \infty$:

$$F_Y(y) = F_{X,Y}(\infty, y)$$
$$= 0.2u(y - 1) + 0.3u(y - 1) + 0.5u(y - 3)$$
$$= 0.5u(y - 1) + 0.5u(y - 3)$$

Plots of these marginal distributions are shown in Figure 4.2-2.

From an N-dimensional joint distribution function we may obtain a k-dimensional *marginal distribution function*, for any selected group of k of the N

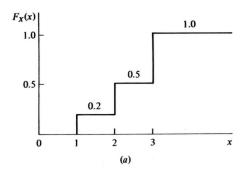

(a)

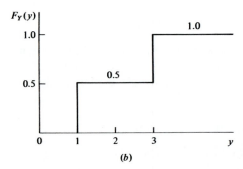

(b)

FIGURE 4.2-2
Marginal distributions applicable to Figure 4.2-1 and Example 4.2-2: (a) $F_X(x)$ and (b) $F_Y(y)$.

random variables, by setting the values of the other $N - k$ random variables to infinity. Here k can be any integer $1, 2, 3, \ldots, N - 1$.

4.3 JOINT DENSITY AND ITS PROPERTIES

In this section the concept of a probability density function is extended to include multiple random variables.

Joint Density Function

For two random variables X and Y, the *joint probability density function*, denoted $f_{X,Y}(x, y)$, is defined by the second derivative of the joint distribution function wherever it exists:

$$f_{X,Y}(x, y) = \frac{\partial^2 F_{X,Y}(x, y)}{\partial x \, \partial y} \tag{4.3-1}$$

We shall refer often to $f_{X,Y}(x, y)$ as the *joint density function.*

If X and Y are discrete random variables, $F_{X,Y}(x, y)$ will possess step discontinuities (see Example 4.2-1 and Figure 4.2-1). Derivatives at these discontinuities are normally undefined. However, by admitting impulse functions (see Appendix A), we are able to define $f_{X,Y}(x, y)$ at these points. Therefore, the joint density function may be found for any two discrete random variables by substitution of (4.2-4) into (4.3-1):

$$f_{X,Y}(x, y) = \sum_{n=1}^{N} \sum_{m=1}^{M} P(x_n, y_m) \, \delta(x - x_n) \, \delta(y - y_m) \tag{4.3-2}$$

An example of the joint density function of two discrete random variables is shown in Figure 4.2-1b.

When N random variables $X_1, X_2, \ldots, X_N$ are involved, the joint density function becomes the N-fold partial derivative of the N-dimensional distribution function:

$$f_{X_1, X_2, \ldots, X_N}(x_1, x_2, \ldots, x_N) = \frac{\partial^N F_{X_1, X_2, \ldots, X_N}(x_1, x_2, \ldots, x_N)}{\partial x_1 \, \partial x_2 \cdots \partial x_N} \tag{4.3-3}$$

By direct integration this result is equivalent to

$$
\begin{aligned}
F_{X_1, X_2, \ldots, X_N}&(x_1, x_2, \ldots, x_N) \\
&= \int_{-\infty}^{x_N} \cdots \int_{-\infty}^{x_2} \int_{-\infty}^{x_1} f_{X_1, X_2, \ldots, X_N}(\xi_1, \xi_2, \ldots, \xi_N) \, d\xi_1 \, d\xi_2 \cdots d\xi_N
\end{aligned}
\tag{4.3-4}
$$

Properties of the Joint Density

Several properties of a joint density function may be listed that derive from its definition (4.3-1) and the properties (4.2-6) of the joint distribution function:

(1) $f_{X,Y}(x, y) \geq 0$ (4.3-5a)

(2) $\displaystyle\int_{-\infty}^{\infty} \int_{-\infty}^{\infty} f_{X,Y}(x, y) \, dx \, dy = 1$ (4.3-5b)

(3) $\displaystyle F_{X,Y}(x, y) = \int_{-\infty}^{y} \int_{-\infty}^{x} f_{X,Y}(\xi_1, \xi_2) \, d\xi_1 \, d\xi_2$ (4.3-5c)

(4) $\displaystyle F_X(x) = \int_{-\infty}^{x} \int_{-\infty}^{\infty} f_{X,Y}(\xi_1, \xi_2) \, d\xi_2 \, d\xi_1$ (4.3-5d)

$\displaystyle F_Y(y) = \int_{-\infty}^{y} \int_{-\infty}^{\infty} f_{X,Y}(\xi_1, \xi_2) \, d\xi_1 \, d\xi_2$ (4.3-5e)

(5) $\displaystyle P\{x_1 < X \leq x_2, y_1 < Y \leq y_2\} = \int_{y_1}^{y_2} \int_{x_1}^{x_2} f_{X,Y}(x, y) \, dx \, dy$ (4.3-5f)

(6) $\displaystyle f_X(x) = \int_{-\infty}^{\infty} f_{X,Y}(x, y) \, dy$ (4.3-5g)

$\displaystyle f_Y(y) = \int_{-\infty}^{\infty} f_{X,Y}(x, y) \, dx$ (4.3-5h)

Properties 1 and 2 may be used as sufficient tests to determine if some function can be a valid density function. Both tests must be satisfied (Papoulis, 1965, p. 169).

The first five of these properties are readily verified from earlier work and the reader should go through the necessary logic as an exercise. Property 6 introduces a new concept.

Marginal Density Functions

The functions $f_X(x)$ and $f_Y(y)$ of property 6 are called *marginal probability density functions* or just *marginal density functions*. They are the density functions of the single variables X and Y and are defined as the derivatives of the marginal distribution functions:

$$f_X(x) = \frac{dF_X(x)}{dx}$$ (4.3-6)

$$f_Y(y) = \frac{dF_Y(y)}{dy}$$ (4.3-7)

By substituting (4.3-5d) and (4.3-5e) into (4.3-6) and (4.3-7), respectively, we are able to verify the equations of property 6.

We shall illustrate the calculation of marginal density functions from a given joint density function with an example.

Example 4.3-1 We find $f_X(x)$ and $f_Y(y)$ when the joint density function is given by (Clarke and Disney, 1970, p. 108):

$$f_{X,Y}(x, y) = u(x)u(y)xe^{-x(y+1)}$$

From (4.3-5g) and the above equation:

$$f_X(x) = \int_0^\infty u(x)xe^{-x(y+1)}\,dy = u(x)xe^{-x}\int_0^\infty e^{-xy}\,dy$$

$$= u(x)xe^{-x}(1/x) = u(x)e^{-x}$$

after using an integral from Appendix C.
From (4.3-5h):

$$f_Y(y) = \int_0^\infty u(y)xe^{-x(y+1)}\,dx = \frac{u(y)}{(y+1)^2}$$

after using another integral from Appendix C.

For N random variables $X_1, X_2, \ldots, X_N$, the *k-dimensional marginal density function* is defined as the k-fold partial derivative of the k-dimensional marginal distribution function. It can also be found from the joint density function by integrating out all variables except the k variables of interest $X_1, X_2, \ldots, X_k$:

$$f_{X_1, X_2, \ldots, X_k}(x_1, x_2, \ldots, x_k)$$

$$= \int_{-\infty}^\infty \cdots \int_{-\infty}^\infty f_{X_1, X_2, \ldots, X_N}(x_1, x_2, \ldots, x_N)\,dx_{k+1}\,dx_{k+2}\cdots dx_N \quad (4.3\text{-}8)$$

4.4 CONDITIONAL DISTRIBUTION AND DENSITY

In Section 2.6, the conditional distribution function of a random variable X, given some event B, was defined as

$$F_X(x|B) = P\{X \le x|B\} = \frac{P\{X \le x \cap B\}}{P(B)} \quad (4.4\text{-}1)$$

for any event B with nonzero probability. The corresponding conditional density function was defined through the derivative

$$f_X(x|B) = \frac{dF_X(x|B)}{dx} \quad (4.4\text{-}2)$$

In this section these two functions are extended to include a second random variable through suitable definitions of event B.

Conditional Distribution and Density— Point Conditioning

Often in practical problems we are interested in the distribution function of one random variable X conditioned by the fact that a second random variable Y has some specific value y. This is called *point conditioning* and we can handle such problems by defining event B by

$$B = \{y - \Delta y < Y \leq y + \Delta y\} \tag{4.4-3}$$

where Δy is a small quantity that we eventually let approach 0. For this event, (4.4-1) can be written

$$F_X(x | y - \Delta y < Y \leq y + \Delta y) = \frac{\int_{y-\Delta y}^{y+\Delta y} \int_{-\infty}^{x} f_{X,Y}(\xi_1, \xi_2) \, d\xi_1 \, d\xi_2}{\int_{y-\Delta y}^{y+\Delta y} f_Y(\xi) \, d\xi} \tag{4.4-4}$$

where we have used (4.3-5f) and (2.3-6d).

Consider two cases of (4.4-4). In the first case, assume X and Y are both discrete random variables with values x_i, $i = 1, 2, \ldots, N$, and $y_j = 1, 2, \ldots, M$, respectively, while the probabilities of these values are denoted $P(x_i)$ and $P(y_j)$, respectively. The probability of the joint occurrence of x_i and y_j is denoted $P(x_i, y_j)$. Thus,

$$f_Y(y) = \sum_{j=1}^{M} P(y_j) \, \delta(y - y_j) \tag{4.4-5}$$

$$f_{X,Y}(x, y) = \sum_{i=1}^{N} \sum_{j=1}^{M} P(x_i, y_j) \, \delta(x - x_i) \, \delta(y - y_j) \tag{4.4-6}$$

Now suppose that the specific value of y of interest is y_k. With substitution of (4.4-5) and (4.4-6) into (4.4-4) and allowing $\Delta y \to 0$, we obtain

$$F_X(x | Y = y_k) = \sum_{i=1}^{N} \frac{P(x_i, y_k)}{P(y_k)} u(x - x_i) \tag{4.4-7}$$

After differentiation we have

$$f_X(x | Y = y_k) = \sum_{i=1}^{N} \frac{P(x_i, y_k)}{P(y_k)} \delta(x - x_i) \tag{4.4-8}$$

Example 4.4-1 To illustrate the use of (4.4-8) assume a joint density function as given in Figure 4.4-1a. Here $P(x_1, y_1) = {}^2/_{15}$, $P(x_2, y_1) = {}^3/_{15}$, etc. Since $P(y_3) = ({}^4/_{15}) + ({}^5/_{15}) = {}^9/_{15}$, use of (4.4-8) will give $f_X(x | Y = y_3)$ as shown in Figure 4.4-1b.

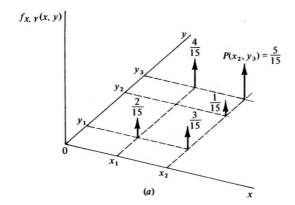

(a)

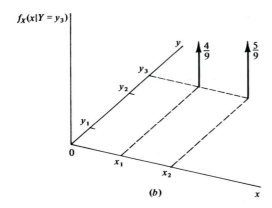

(b)

FIGURE 4.4-1
A joint density function (*a*) and a conditional density function (*b*) applicable to Example 4.4.1.

The second case of (4.4-4) that is of interest corresponds to X and Y both continuous random variables. As $\Delta y \to 0$ the denominator in (4.4-4) becomes 0. However, we can still show that the conditional density $f_X(x|Y=y)$ may exist. If Δy is very small, (4.4-4) can be written as

$$F_X(x|y - \Delta y < Y \le y + \Delta y) = \frac{\int_{-\infty}^{x} f_{X,Y}(\xi_1, y)\, d\xi_1\, 2\Delta y}{f_Y(y) 2\Delta y} \qquad (4.4-9)$$

and, in the limit as $\Delta y \to 0$

$$F_X(x|Y=y) = \frac{\int_{-\infty}^{x} f_{X,Y}(\xi, y)\, d\xi}{f_Y(y)} \qquad (4.4-10)$$

for every y such that $f_Y(y) \neq 0$. After differentiation of both sides of (4.4-10) with respect to x:

$$f_X(x|Y=y) = \frac{f_{X,Y}(x, y)}{f_Y(y)} \qquad (4.4-11)$$

When there is no confusion as to meaning, we shall often write (4.4-11) as

$$f_X(x|y) = \frac{f_{X,Y}(x,y)}{f_Y(y)} \tag{4.4-12}$$

It can also be shown that

$$f_Y(y|x) = \frac{f_{X,Y}(x, y)}{f_X(x)} \tag{4.4-13}$$

Example 4.4-2 We find $f_Y(y|x)$ for the density functions defined in Example 4.3-1. Since

$$f_{X,Y}(x, y) = u(x)u(y)xe^{-x(y+1)}$$

and

$$f_X(x) = u(x)e^{-x}$$

are nonzero only for $0 < y$ and $0 < x$, $f_Y(y|x)$ is nonzero only for $0 < y$ and $0 < x$. It is

$$f_Y(y|x) = u(x)u(y)xe^{-xy}$$

from (4.4-13).

---

*Conditional Distribution and Density— Interval Conditioning

It is sometimes convenient to define event B in (4.4-1) and (4.4-2) in terms of a random variable Y by

$$B = \{y_a < Y \le y_b\} \tag{4.4-14}$$

where y_a and y_b are real numbers and we assume $P(B) = P\{y_a < Y \le y_b\} \ne 0$. With this definition it is readily shown that (4.4-1) and (4.4-2) become

$$F_X(x|y_a < Y \le y_b) = \frac{F_{X,Y}(x, y_b) - F_{X,Y}(x, y_a)}{F_Y(y_b) - F_Y(y_a)}$$

$$= \frac{\int_{y_a}^{y_b} \int_{-\infty}^{x} f_{X,Y}(\xi, y) \, d\xi \, dy}{\int_{y_a}^{y_b} \int_{-\infty}^{\infty} f_{X,Y}(x, y) \, dx \, dy} \tag{4.4-15}$$

and

$$f_X(x|y_a < Y \le y_b) = \frac{\int_{y_a}^{y_b} f_{X,Y}(x, y) \, dy}{\int_{y_a}^{y_b} \int_{-\infty}^{\infty} f_{X,Y}(x, y) \, dx \, dy} \tag{4.4-16}$$

These last two expressions hold for X and Y either continuous or discrete random variables. In the discrete case, the joint density is given by (4.3-2). The resulting distribution and density will be defined, however, only for y_a and y_b such that the denominators of (4.4-15) and (4.4-16) are nonzero. This requirement is satisfied so long as the interval $y_a < y \leq y_b$ spans at least one possible value of Y having a nonzero probability of occurrence.

An example will serve to illustrate the application of (4.4-16) when X and Y are continuous random variables.

Example 4.4-3 We use (4.4-16) to find $f_X(x \mid Y \leq y)$ for the joint density function of Example 4.3-1. Since we have here defined $B = \{Y \leq y\}$, then $y_a = -\infty$ and $y_b = y$. Furthermore, since $f_{X,Y}(x, y)$ is nonzero only for $0 < x$ and $0 < y$, we need only consider this region of x and y in finding the conditional density function. The denominator of (4.4-16) can be written as $\int_{-\infty}^{y} f_Y(\xi) \, d\xi$. By using results from Example 4.3-1:

$$\int_{-\infty}^{y} f_Y(\xi) \, d\xi = \int_{-\infty}^{y} \frac{u(\xi) \, d\xi}{(\xi + 1)^2} = \int_{0}^{y} \frac{d\xi}{(\xi + 1)^2} = \frac{y}{y + 1} \qquad y > 0$$

and zero for $y < 0$, after using an integral from Appendix C. The numerator of (4.4-16) becomes

$$\int_{-\infty}^{y} f_{X,Y}(x, \xi) \, d\xi = \int_{0}^{y} u(x) x e^{-x(\xi + 1)} \, d\xi$$

$$= u(x) x e^{-x} \int_{0}^{y} e^{-x\xi} \, d\xi$$

$$= u(x) e^{-x}(1 - e^{-xy}) \qquad y > 0$$

and zero for $y < 0$, after using another integral from Appendix C. Thus

$$f_X(x \mid Y \leq y) = u(x) u(y) \left(\frac{y + 1}{y} \right) e^{-x}(1 - e^{-xy})$$

This function is plotted in Figure 4.4-2 for several values of y.

4.5 STATISTICAL INDEPENDENCE

It will be recalled from (1.5-3) that two events A and B are statistically independent if (and only if)

$$P(A \cap B) = P(A)P(B) \tag{4.5-1}$$

This condition can be used to apply to two random variables X and Y by defining the events $A = \{X \leq x\}$ and $B = \{Y \leq y\}$ for two real numbers x and y. Thus, X

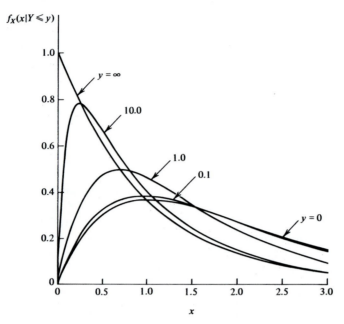

FIGURE 4.4-2
Conditional probability density functions applicable to Example 4.4-3.

and Y are said to be *statistically independent random variables* if (and only if)

$$P\{X \leq x, Y \leq y\} = P\{X \leq x\}P\{Y \leq y\} \tag{4.5-2}$$

From this expression and the definitions of distribution functions, it follows that

$$F_{X,Y}(x, y) = F_X(x)F_Y(y) \tag{4.5-3}$$

if X and Y are independent. From the definitions of density functions, (4.5-3) gives

$$f_{X,Y}(x, y) = f_X(x)f_Y(y) \tag{4.5-4}$$

by differentiation, if X and Y are independent. Either (4.5-3) or (4.5-4) may serve as a sufficient definition of, or test for, independence of two random variables.

The form of the conditional distribution function for independent events is found by use of (4.4-1) with $B = \{Y \leq y\}$:

$$F_X(x|Y \leq y) = \frac{P\{X \leq x, Y \leq y\}}{P\{Y \leq y\}} = \frac{F_{X,Y}(x, y)}{F_Y(y)} \tag{4.5-5}$$

By substituting (4.5-3) into (4.5-5), we have

$$F_X(x|Y \leq y) = F_X(x) \tag{4.5-6}$$

In other words, the conditional distribution ceases to be conditional and simply equals the marginal distribution for independent random variables. It can also be shown that

$$F_Y(y|X \le x) = F_Y(y) \tag{4.5-7}$$

Conditional density function forms, for independent X and Y, are found by differentiation of (4.5-6) and (4.5-7):

$$f_X(x|Y \le y) = f_X(x) \tag{4.5-8}$$

$$f_Y(y|X \le x) = f_Y(y) \tag{4.5-9}$$

Example 4.5-1 For the densities of Example 4.3-1:

$$f_{X,Y}(x, y) = u(x)u(y)xe^{-x(y+1)}$$

$$f_X(x)f_Y(y) = u(x)u(y)\frac{e^{-x}}{(y+1)^2} \ne f_{X,Y}(x, y)$$

Therefore the random variables X and Y are not independent.

In the more general study of the statistical independence of N random variables $X_1, X_2, \ldots, X_N$, we define events A_i by

$$A_i = \{X_i \le x_i\} \qquad i = 1, 2, \ldots, N \tag{4.5-10}$$

where the x_i are real numbers. With these definitions, the random variables X_i are said to be statistically indpendent if (1.5-6) is satisfied.

It can be shown that if $X_1, X_2, \ldots, X_N$ are statistically independent then any group of these random variables is independent of any other group. Furthermore, a function of any group is independent of any function of any other group of the random variables. For example, with $N = 4$ random variables: X_4 is independent of $X_3 + X_2 + X_1$; X_3 is independent of $X_2 + X_1$, etc. (see Papoulis, 1965, p. 238).

4.6 DISTRIBUTION AND DENSITY OF A SUM OF RANDOM VARIABLES

The problem of finding the distribution and density functions for a sum of *statistically independent* random variables is considered in this section.

Sum of Two Random Variables

Let W be a random variable equal to the sum of two independent random variables X and Y:

$$W = X + Y \tag{4.6-1}$$

This is a very practical problem because X might represent a random signal voltage and Y could represent random noise at some instant in time. The sum W would represent a signal-plus-noise voltage available to some receiver.

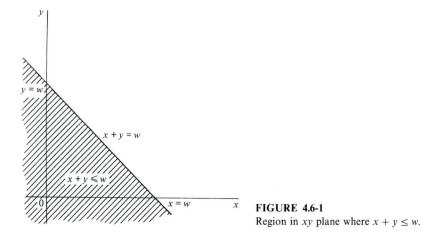

FIGURE 4.6-1
Region in xy plane where $x + y \le w$.

The probability distribution function we seek is defined by

$$F_W(w) = P\{W \le w\} = P\{X + Y \le w\} \tag{4.6-2}$$

Figure 4.6-1 illustrates the region in the xy plane where $x + y \le w$. Now from (4.3-5f), the probability corresponding to an elemental area $dx\,dy$ in the xy plane located at the point (x, y) is $f_{X,Y}(x, y)\,dx\,dy$. If we sum all such probabilities over the region where $x + y \le w$ we will obtain $F_W(w)$. Thus

$$F_W(w) = \int_{-\infty}^{\infty} \int_{x=-\infty}^{w-y} f_{X,Y}(x, y)\,dx\,dy \tag{4.6-3}$$

and, after using (4.5-4):

$$F_W(w) = \int_{-\infty}^{\infty} f_Y(y) \int_{x=-\infty}^{w-y} f_X(x)\,dx\,dy \tag{4.6-4}$$

By differentiating (4.6-4), using Leibniz's rule, we get the desired density function

$$f_W(w) = \int_{-\infty}^{\infty} f_Y(y)f_X(w - y)\,dy \tag{4.6-5}$$

This expression is recognized as a convolution integral. Consequently, we have shown that *the density function of the sum of two statistically independent random variables is the convolution of their individual density functions.*

Example 4.6-1 We use (4.6-5) to find the density of $W = X + Y$ where the densities of X and Y are assumed to be

$$f_X(x) = \frac{1}{a}\,[u(x) - u(x - a)]$$

$$f_Y(y) = \frac{1}{b}\,[u(y) - u(y - b)]$$

with $0 < a < b$, as shown in Figure 4.6-2a and b. Now because $0 < X$ and $0 < Y$, we only need examine the case $W = X + Y > 0$. From (4.6-5) we write

$$f_W(w) = \int_{-\infty}^{\infty} \frac{1}{ab} [u(y) - u(y-b)][u(w-y) - u(w-y-a)] \, dy$$

$$= \frac{1}{ab} \int_{0}^{\infty} [1 - u(y-b)][u(w-y) - u(w-y-a)] \, dy$$

$$= \frac{1}{ab} \left[\int_{0}^{\infty} u(w-y) \, dy - \int_{0}^{\infty} u(w-y-a) \, dy \right.$$

$$\left. - \int_{0}^{\infty} u(y-b)u(w-y) \, dy + \int_{0}^{\infty} u(y-b)u(w-y-a) \, dy \right]$$

All these integrands are unity; the values of the integrals are determined by the unit-step functions through their control over limits of integration. After

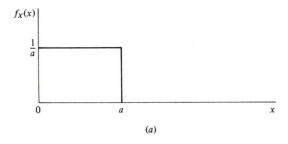

(a)

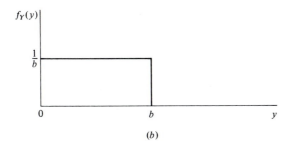

(b)

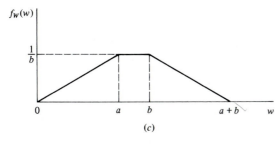

(c)

FIGURE 4.6-2
Two density functions (a) and (b) and their convolution (c).

straightforward evaluation we get

$$
f_W(w) = \begin{cases} w/ab & 0 \le w < a \\ 1/b & a \le w < b \\ (a + b - w)/ab & b \le w < a + b \\ 0 & w \ge a + b \end{cases}
$$

which is sketched in Figure 4.6-2c.

*Sum of Several Random Variables

When the sum of Y of N independent random variables $X_1, X_2, \ldots, X_N$ is to be considered, we may extend the above analysis for two random variables. Let $Y_1 = X_1 + X_2$. Then we know from the preceding work that $f_{Y_1}(y_1) = f_{X_2}(x_2) * f_{X_1}(x_1)$.† Next, we know that X_3 will be independent of $Y_1 = X_1 + X_2$ because X_3 is independent of both X_1 and X_2. Thus, by applying (4.6-5) to the two variables X_3 and Y_1 to find the density function of $Y_2 = X_3 + Y_1$, we get

$$
\begin{aligned}
f_{Y_2 = X_1 + X_2 + X_3}(y_2) &= f_{X_3}(x_3) * f_{Y_1 = X_1 + X_2}(y_1) \\
&= f_{X_3}(x_3) * f_{X_2}(x_2) * f_{X_1}(x_1)
\end{aligned}
\tag{4.6-6}
$$

By continuing the process we find that the density function of $Y = X_1 + X_2 + \cdots + X_N$ is the $(N - 1)$-fold convolution of the N individual density functions:

$$
f_Y(y) = f_{X_N}(x_N) * f_{X_{N-1}}(x_{N-1}) * \cdots * f_{X_1}(x_1)
\tag{4.6-7}
$$

The distribution function of Y is found from the integral of $f_Y(y)$ using (2.3-6c).

*4.7 CENTRAL LIMIT THEOREM

Broadly defined, the *central limit theorem* says that the probability distribution function of the sum of a large number of random variables approaches a gaussian distribution. Although the theorem is known to apply to some cases of statistically *dependent* random variables (Cramér, 1946, p. 219), most applications, and the largest body of knowledge, are directed toward statistically independent random variables. Thus, in all succeeding discussions we assume statistically independent random variables.

---

† The asterisk denotes convolution.

*Unequal Distributions

Let $\bar{X}_i$ and $\sigma^2_{X_i}$ be the means and variances, respectively, of N random variables X_i, $i = 1, 2, \ldots, N$, which may have arbitrary probability densities. The central limit theorem states that the sum $Y_N = X_1 + X_2 + \cdots + X_N$, which has mean $\bar{Y}_N = \bar{X}_1 + \bar{X}_2 + \cdots + \bar{X}_N$ and variance $\sigma^2_{Y_N} = \sigma^2_{X_1} + \sigma^2_{X_2} + \cdots + \sigma^2_{X_N}$, has a probability distribution that asymptotically approaches gaussian as $N \to \infty$. Necessary conditions for the theorem's validity are difficult to state, but sufficient conditions are known to be (Cramér, 1946; Thomas, 1969)

$$\sigma^2_{X_i} > B_1 > 0 \qquad i = 1, 2, \ldots, N \qquad (4.7\text{-}1a)$$

$$E[|X_i - \bar{X}_i|^3] < B_2 \qquad i = 1, 2, \ldots, N \qquad (4.7\text{-}1b)$$

where B_1 and B_2 are positive numbers. These conditions guarantee that no one random variable in the sum dominates.

The reader should observe that the central limit theorem guarantees only that the *distribution* of the sum of random variables becomes gaussian. It does not follow that the probability *density* is always gaussian. For continuous random variables there is usually no problem, but certain conditions imposed on the individual random variables (Cramér, 1946; Papoulis, 1965 and 1984) will guarantee that the density is gaussian.

For discrete random variables X_i the sum Y_N will also be discrete so its density will contain impulses and is, therefore, not gaussian, even though the distribution approaches gaussian. When the possible discrete values of each random variable are kb, $k = 0, \pm 1, \pm 2, \ldots$, with b a constant,† the envelope of the impulses in the density of the sum will be gaussian (with mean $\bar{Y}_N$ and variance $\sigma^2_{Y_N}$). This case is discussed in some detail by Papoulis (1965).

The practical usefulness of the central limit theorem does not reside so much in the exactness of the gaussian distribution for $N \to \infty$ because the variance of Y_N becomes infinite from (4.7-1a). Usefulness derives more from the fact that Y_N for *finite* N may have a distribution that is closely approximated as gaussian. The approximation can be quite accurate, even for relatively small values of N, in the central region of the gaussian curve near the mean. However, the approximation can be very inaccurate in the tail regions away from the mean, even for large values of N (Davenport, 1970; Melsa and Sage, 1973). Of course, the approximation is made more accurate by increasing N.

*Equal Distributions

If all of the statistically independent random variables being summed are continuous and have the same distribution function, and therefore the same density, the proof of the central limit theorem is relatively straightforward and is next developed.

---

† These are called *lattice-type* discrete random variables (Papoulis, 1965).

Because the sum $Y_N = X_1 + X_2 + \cdots + X_N$ has an infinite variance as $N \to \infty$, we shall work with the zero-mean, unit-variance random variable

$$W_N = (Y_N - \bar{Y}_N)/\sigma_{Y_N} = \sum_{i=1}^{N} (X_i - \bar{X}_i) \bigg/ \left[\sum_{i=1}^{N} \sigma_{X_i}^2 \right]^{1/2}$$

$$= \frac{1}{\sqrt{N}\,\sigma_X} \sum_{i=1}^{N} (X_i - \bar{X}) \tag{4.7-2}$$

instead. Here we define $\bar{X}$ and σ_X^2 by

$$\bar{X}_i = \bar{X} \qquad \text{all } i \tag{4.7-3}$$

$$\sigma_{X_i}^2 = \sigma_X^2 \qquad \text{all } i \tag{4.7-4}$$

since all the X_i have the same distribution.

The theorem's proof consists of showing that the characteristic function of W_N is that of a zero-mean, unit-variance gaussian random variable, which is

$$\Phi_{W_N}(\omega) = \exp(-\omega^2/2) \tag{4.7-5}$$

from Problem 3-28. If this is proved the density of W_N must be gaussian from (3.3-3) and the fact that Fourier transforms are unique. The characteristic function of W_N is

$$\Phi_{W_N}(\omega) = E[e^{j\omega W_N}] = E\left[\exp\left\{ \frac{j\omega}{\sqrt{N}\,\sigma_X} \sum_{i=1}^{N} (X_i - \bar{X}) \right\} \right]$$

$$= \left\langle E\left\{ \exp\left[\frac{j\omega}{\sqrt{N}\,\sigma_X} (X_i - \bar{X}) \right] \right\} \right\rangle^N \tag{4.7-6}$$

The last step in (4.7-6) follows from the independence and equal distribution of the X_i. Next, the exponential in (4.7-6) is expanded in a Taylor polynomial with a remainder term R_N/N:

$$E\left\{ \exp\left[\frac{j\omega}{\sqrt{N}\,\sigma_X} (X_i - \bar{X}) \right] \right\}$$

$$= E\left\{ 1 + \left(\frac{j\omega}{\sqrt{N}\,\sigma_X} \right)(X_i - \bar{X}) + \left(\frac{j\omega}{\sqrt{N}\,\sigma_X} \right)^2 \frac{(X_i - \bar{X})^2}{2} + \frac{R_N}{N} \right\}$$

$$= 1 - (\omega^2/2N) + E[R_N]/N \tag{4.7-7}$$

where $E[R_N]$ approaches zero as $N \to \infty$ (Davenport, 1970, p. 442). On substitution of (4.7-7) into (4.7-6) and forming the natural logarithm, we have

$$\ln[\Phi_{W_N}(\omega)] = N \ln\{1 - (\omega^2/2N) + E[R_N]/N\} \tag{4.7-8}$$

Since

$$\ln (1 - z) = -\left[z + \frac{z^2}{2} + \frac{z^3}{3} + \cdots \right] \qquad |z| < 1 \qquad (4.7\text{-}9)$$

we identify z with $(\omega^2/2N) - E[R_N]/N$ and write (4.7-8) as

$$\ln [\Phi_{W_N}(\omega)] = -(\omega^2/2) + E[R_N] - \frac{N}{2}\left[\frac{\omega^2}{2N} - \frac{E[R_N]}{N} \right]^2 + \cdots \qquad (4.7\text{-}10)$$

so

$$\lim_{N \to \infty} \{\ln [\Phi_{W_N}(\omega)]\} = \ln \left\{ \lim_{N \to \infty} \Phi_{W_N}(\omega) \right\} = -\omega^2/2 \qquad (4.7\text{-}11)$$

Finally, we have

$$\lim_{N \to \infty} \Phi_{W_N}(\omega) = e^{-\omega^2/2} \qquad (4.7\text{-}12)$$

which was to be shown.

We illustrate the use of the central limit theorem through an example.

Example 4.7-1 Consider the sum of just two independent uniformly distributed random variables X_1 and X_2 having the same density

$$f_X(x) = \frac{1}{a} [u(x) - u(x - a)]$$

where $a > 0$ is a constant. The means and variances of X_1 and X_2 are $\bar{X} = a/2$ and $\sigma_X^2 = a^2/12$, respectively. The density of the sum $W = X_1 + X_2$ is available from Example 4.6-1 (with $b = a$):

$$f_W(w) = \frac{1}{a} \text{tri}\left(\frac{w}{a} \right)$$

where the function tri $(\cdot)$ is defined in (E-4). The gaussian approximation to W has variance $\sigma_W^2 = 2\sigma_X^2 = a^2/6$ and mean $\bar{W} = 2(a/2) = a$:

$$\text{Approximation to } f_W(w) = \frac{e^{-(w-a)^2/(a^2/3)}}{\sqrt{\pi(a^2/3)}}$$

Figure 4.7-1 illustrates $f_W(w)$ and its gaussian approximation. Even for the case of only two random variables being summed the gaussian approximation is a fairly good one. For other densities the approximation may be very poor (see Problem 4-63).

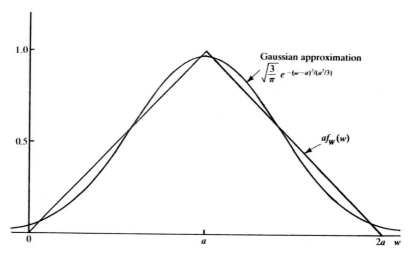

FIGURE 4.7-1
The triangular density function of Example 4.7-1 and its gaussian approximation.

PROBLEMS

4-1 Two events A and B defined on a sample space S are related to a joint sample space through random variables X and Y and are defined by $A = \{X \le x\}$ and $B = \{y_1 < Y \le y_2\}$. Make a sketch of the two sample spaces showing areas corresponding to both events and the event $A \cap B = \{X \le x, y_1 < Y \le y_2\}$.

4-2 Work Problem 4-1 for the two events $A = \{x_1 < X \le x_2\}$ and $B = \{y_1 < Y \le y_2\}$.

4-3 Work Problem 4-1 for the two events $A = \{x_1 < X \le x_2 \text{ or } x_3 < X \le x_4\}$ and $B = \{y_1 < Y \le y_2\}$.

4-4 Three events A, B, and C satisfy $C \subset B \subset A$ and are defined by $A = \{X \le x_a, Y \le y_a\}$, $B = \{X \le x_b, Y \le y_b\}$, and $C = \{X \le x_c, Y \le y_c\}$ for two random variables X and Y.

(a) Sketch the two sample spaces S and S_J and show the regions corresponding to the three events.

(b) What region corresponds to the event $A \cap B \cap C$?

4-5 A joint sample space for two random variables X and Y has four elements (1, 1), (2, 2), (3, 3), and (4, 4). Probabilities of these elements are 0.1, 0.35, 0.05, and 0.5 respectively.

(a) Determine through logic and sketch the distribution function $F_{X,Y}(x, y)$.

(b) Find the probability of the event $\{X \le 2.5, Y \le 6\}$.

(c) Find the probability of the event $\{X \le 3\}$.

4-6 Write a mathematical equation for $F_{X,Y}(x, y)$ of Problem 4-5.

4-7 The joint distribution function for two random variables X and Y is

$$F_{X,Y}(x, y) = u(x)u(y)[1 - e^{-ax} - e^{-ay} + e^{-a(x+y)}]$$

where $u(\cdot)$ is the unit-step function and $a > 0$. Sketch $F_{X,Y}(x, y)$.

4-8 By use of the joint distribution function in Problem 4-7, and assuming $a = 0.5$ in each case, find the probabilities:
(a) $P\{X \leq 1, Y \leq 2\}$
(b) $P\{0.5 < X < 1.5\}$
(c) $P\{-1.5 < X \leq 2, 1 < Y \leq 3\}$.

4-9 Find and sketch the marginal distribution functions for the joint distribution function of Problem 4-5.

4-10 Find and sketch the marginal distribution functions for the joint distribution function of Problem 4-7.

4-11 Given the function

$$G_{X,Y}(x, y) = u(x)u(y)[1 - e^{-(x+y)}]$$

Show that this function satisfies the first four properties of (4.2-6) but fails the fifth one. The function is therefore not a valid joint probability distribution function.

4-12 Random variables X and Y are components of a two-dimensional random vector and have a joint distribution

$$F_{X,Y}(x, y) = \begin{cases} 0 & x < 0 \quad \text{or} \quad y < 0 \\ xy & 0 \leq x < 1 \quad \text{and} \quad 0 \leq y < 1 \\ x & 0 \leq x < 1 \quad \text{and} \quad 1 \leq y \\ y & 1 \leq x \quad \text{and} \quad 0 \leq y < 1 \\ 1 & 1 \leq x \quad \text{and} \quad 1 \leq y \end{cases}$$

(a) Sketch $F_{X,Y}(x, y)$.
(b) Find and sketch the marginal distribution functions $F_X(x)$ and $F_Y(y)$.

4-13 Show the function

$$G_{X,Y}(x, y) = \begin{cases} 0 & x < y \\ 1 & x \geq y \end{cases}$$

cannot be a valid joint distribution function. [*Hint:* Use (4.2-6e).]

4-14 A fair coin is tossed twice. Define random variables by: $X =$ "number of heads on the first toss" and $Y =$ "number of heads on the second toss" (note that X and Y can have only the values 0 or 1).
(a) Find and sketch the joint density function of X and Y.
(b) Find and sketch the joint distribution function.

4-15 A joint probability density function is

$$f_{X,Y}(x, y) = \begin{cases} 1/ab & 0 < x < a \quad \text{and} \quad 0 < y < b \\ 0 & \text{elsewhere} \end{cases}$$

Find and sketch $F_{X,Y}(x, y)$.

4-16 If $a < b$ in Problem 4-15, find:
   (a) $P\{X + Y \leq 3a/4\}$ (b) $P\{Y \leq 2bX/a\}$.

4-17 Find the joint distribution function applicable to Example 4.3-1.

4-18 Sketch the joint density function $f_{X,Y}(x, y)$ applicable to Problem 4-5. Write an equation for $f_{X,Y}(x, y)$.

4-19 Determine the joint density and both marginal density functions for Problem 4-7.

4-20 Find and sketch the joint density function for the distribution function in Problem 4-12.

4-21 (a) Find a constant b (in terms of a) so that the function

$$f_{X,Y}(x, y) = \begin{cases} be^{-(x+y)} & 0 < x < a \quad \text{and} \quad 0 < y < \infty \\ 0 & \text{elsewhere} \end{cases}$$

is a valid joint density function.
   (b) Find an expression for the joint distribution function.

4-22 (a) By use of the joint density function of Problem 4-21, find the marginal density functions.
   (b) What is $P\{0.5a < X \leq 0.75a\}$ in terms of a and b?

4-23 Determine a constant b such that each of the following are valid joint density functions:

(a) $f_{X,Y}(x, y) = \begin{cases} 3xy & 0 < x < 1 \quad \text{and} \quad 0 < y < b \\ 0 & \text{elsewhere} \end{cases}$

(b) $f_{X,Y}(x, y) = \begin{cases} bx(1 - y) & 0 < x < 0.5 \quad \text{and} \quad 0 < y < 1 \\ 0 & \text{elsewhere} \end{cases}$

(c) $f_{X,Y}(x, y) = \begin{cases} b(x^2 + 4y^2) & 0 \leq |x| < 1 \quad \text{and} \quad 0 \leq y < 2 \\ 0 & \text{elsewhere} \end{cases}$

★**4-24** Given the function

$$f_{X,Y}(x, y) = \begin{cases} (x^2 + y^2)/8\pi & x^2 + y^2 < b \\ 0 & \text{elsewhere} \end{cases}$$

(a) Find a constant b so that this is a valid joint density function.
   (b) Find $P\{0.5b < X^2 + Y^2 \leq 0.8b\}$. (*Hint:* Use polar coordinates in both parts.)

★**4-25** On a firing range the coordinates of bullet strikes relative to the target bull's-eye are random variables X and Y having a joint density given by

$$f_{X,Y}(x, y) = \frac{e^{-(x^2+y^2)/2\sigma^2}}{2\pi\sigma^2}$$

Here σ^2 is a constant related to the accuracy of manufacturing a gun's barrel. What value of σ^2 will allow 80% of all bullets to fall inside a circle of diameter 6 cm? (*Hint:* Use polar coordinates.)

4-26 Given the function

$$f_{X,Y}(x, y) = \begin{cases} b(x + y)^2 & -2 < x < 2 \quad \text{and} \quad -3 < y < 3 \\ 0 & \text{elsewhere} \end{cases}$$

(a) Find the constant b such that this is a valid joint density function.
(b) Determine the marginal density functions $f_X(x)$ and $f_Y(y)$.

4-27 Find the conditional density functions $f_X(x|y_1)$, $f_X(x|y_2)$, $f_Y(y|x_1)$, and $f_Y(y|x_2)$ for the joint density defined in Example 4.4-1.

4-28 Find the conditional density function $f_X(x|y)$ applicable to Example 4.4-2.

4-29 By using the results of Example 4.4-2, calculate the probability of the event $\{Y \leq 2 | X = 1\}$.

4-30 Random variables X and Y are *jointly gaussian and normalized* if

$$f_{X,Y}(x, y) = \frac{1}{2\pi\sqrt{1 - \rho^2}} \exp\left[-\frac{x^2 - 2\rho xy + y^2}{2(1 - \rho^2)}\right] \quad \text{where} \quad -1 \leq \rho \leq 1$$

(a) Show that the marginal density functions are

$$f_X(x) = \frac{1}{\sqrt{2\pi}} \exp(-x^2/2) \qquad f_Y(y) = \frac{1}{\sqrt{2\pi}} \exp(-y^2/2)$$

(*Hint:* Complete the square and use the fact that the area under a gaussian density is unity.)
(b) Are X and Y statistically independent?

4-31 By use of the joint density of Problem 4-30, show that

$$f_X(x|Y = y) = \frac{1}{\sqrt{2\pi(1 - \rho^2)}} \exp\left[-\frac{(x - \rho y)^2}{2(1 - \rho^2)}\right]$$

4-32 Given the joint distribution function

$$F_{X,Y}(x, y) = u(x)u(y)[1 - e^{-ax} - e^{-ay} + e^{-a(x+y)}]$$

find:
(a) The conditional density functions $f_X(x|Y = y)$ and $f_Y(y|X = x)$.
(b) Are the random variables X and Y statistically independent?

4-33 For two independent random variables X and Y show that

$$P\{Y \leq X\} = \int_{-\infty}^{\infty} F_Y(x)f_X(x) \, dx$$

or

$$P\{Y \leq X\} = 1 - \int_{-\infty}^{\infty} F_X(y)f_Y(y) \, dy$$

4-34 Two random variables X and Y have a joint probability density function

$$f_{X,Y}(x, y) = \begin{cases} \dfrac{5}{16} x^2 y & 0 < y < x < 2 \\ 0 & \text{elsewhere} \end{cases}$$

(a) Find the marginal density functions of X and Y.
(b) Are X and Y statistically independent?

4-35 Show, by use of (4.4-13), that the area under $f_Y(y|x)$ is unity.

★**4-36** Two random variables R and Θ have the joint density function

$$f_{R,\Theta}(r, \theta) = \frac{u(r)[u(\theta) - u(\theta - 2\pi)]r}{2\pi} e^{-r^2/2}$$

(a) Find $P\{0 < R \le 1, 0 < \Theta \le \pi/2\}$.
(b) Find $f_R(r|\Theta = \pi)$.
(c) Find $f_R(r|\Theta \le \pi)$ and compare to the result found in part (b), and explain the comparison.

4-37 Random variables X and Y have respective density functions

$$f_X(x) = \frac{1}{a}[u(x) - u(x - a)]$$

$$f_Y(y) = bu(y)e^{-by}$$

where $a > 0$ and $b > 0$. Find and sketch the density function of $W = X + Y$ if X and Y are statistically independent.

4-38 Random variables X and Y have respective density functions

$$f_X(x) = 0.1\delta(x - 1) + 0.2\delta(x - 2) + 0.4\delta(x - 3) + 0.3\delta(x - 4)$$

$$f_Y(y) = 0.4\delta(y - 5) + 0.5\delta(y - 6) + 0.1\delta(y - 7)$$

Find and sketch the density function of $W = X + Y$ if X and Y are independent.

4-39 Find and sketch the density function of $W = X + Y$, where the random variable X is that of Problem 4-37 with $a = 5$ and Y is that of Problem 4-38. Assume X and Y are independent.

4-40 Find the density function of $W = X + Y$, where the random variable X is that of Problem 4-38 and Y is that of Problem 4-37. Assume X and Y are independent. Sketch the density function for $b = 1$ and $b = 4$.

★**4-41** Three statistically independent random variables X_1, X_2, and X_3 all have the same density function

$$f_{X_i}(x_i) = \frac{1}{a}[u(x_i) - u(x_i - a)] \qquad i = 1, 2, 3$$

Find and sketch the density function of $Y = X_1 + X_2 + X_3$ if $a > 0$ is constant.

ADDITIONAL PROBLEMS,
SECOND EDITION

4-42 In a gambling game two fair dice are tossed and the sum of the numbers that show up determines who wins among two players. Random variables X and Y represent the winnings of the first and second numbered players, respectively. The first wins \$3 if the sum is 4, 5, or 6, and loses \$2 if the sum is 11 or 12; he neither wins nor loses for all other sums. The second player wins \$2 for a sum of 8 or more, loses \$3 for a sum of 5 or less, and neither wins nor loses for other sums.

(a) Draw sample spaces S and S_J and show how elements of S map to elements of S_J.

(b) Find the probabilities of all joint outcomes possible in S_J.

4-43 Discrete random variables X and Y have a joint distribution function

$$F_{X,Y}(x, y) = 0.10u(x + 4)u(y - 1) + 0.15u(x + 3)u(y + 5)$$

$$+ 0.17u(x + 1)u(y - 3) + 0.05u(x)u(y - 1)$$

$$+ 0.18u(x - 2)u(y + 2) + 0.23u(x - 3)u(y - 4)$$

$$+ 0.12u(x - 4)u(y + 3)$$

Find: (a) the marginal distributions $F_X(x)$ and $F_Y(y)$ and sketch the two functions, (b) $\bar{X}$ and $\bar{Y}$, and (c) the probability $P\{-1 < X \leq 4, -3 < Y \leq 3\}$.

4-44 Random variables X and Y have the joint distribution

$$F_{X,Y}(x, y) = \begin{cases} \dfrac{5}{4}\left(\dfrac{x + e^{-(x+1)y^2}}{x + 1} - e^{-y^2} \right)u(y) & 0 \leq x < 4 \\ 0 & x < 0 \text{ or } y < 0 \\ 1 + \dfrac{1}{4}e^{-5y^2} - \dfrac{5}{4}e^{-y^2} & 4 \leq x \text{ and any } y \geq 0 \end{cases}$$

Find: (a) The marginal distribution functions of X and Y, and (b) the probability $P\{3 < X \leq 5, 1 < Y \leq 2\}$.

4-45 Find the joint distribution function of the random variables having the joint density of Problem 4-48.

4-46 Find a value of the constant b so that the function

$$f_{X,Y}(x, y) = bxy^2 \exp(-2xy)u(x - 2)u(y - 1)$$

is a valid joint probability density.

4-47 The locations of hits of darts thrown at a round dartboard of radius r are determined by a vector random variable with components X and Y. The joint density of X and Y is uniform, that is,

$$f_{X,Y}(x, y) = \begin{cases} 1/\pi r^2 & x^2 + y^2 < r^2 \\ 0 & \text{elsewhere} \end{cases}$$

Find the densities of X and Y.

4-48 Two random variables X and Y have a joint density

$$f_{X,Y}(x, y) = {}^{10}/_4[u(x) - u(x - 4)]u(y)y^3 \exp\left[-(x + 1)y^2\right]$$

Find the marginal densities and distributions of X and Y.

4-49 Find the marginal densities of X and Y using the joint density

$$f_{X,Y}(x, y) = 2u(x)u(y) \exp\left[-\left(4y + \frac{x}{2}\right)\right]$$

4-50 Random variables X and Y have the joint density of Problem 4-49. Find the probability that the values of Y are not greater than twice the values of X for $x \leq 3$.

4-51 Find the conditional densities $f_X(x|Y = y)$ and $f_Y(y|X = x)$ applicable to the joint density of Problem 4-47.

4-52 For the joint density of Problem 4-48 determine the conditional densities $f_X(x|Y = y)$ and $f_Y(y|X = x)$.

⋆4-53 The time it takes a person to drive to work is a random variable Y. Because of traffic driving time depends on the (random) time of departure, denoted X, which occurs in an interval of duration T_0 that begins at 7:30 A.M. each day. There is a minimum driving time T_1 required, regardless of the time of departure. The joint density of X and Y is known to be

$$f_{X,Y}(x, y) = c(y - T_1)^3 u(y - T_1)[u(x) - u(x - T_0)] \exp\left[-(y - T_1)(x + 1)\right]$$

where

$$c = (1 + T_0)^3/2[(1 + T_0)^3 - 1]$$

(a) Find the average driving time that results when it is given that departure occurs at 7:30 A.M. Evaluate your results for $T_0 = 1$ h.

(b) Repeat part (a) given that departure time is 7:30 A.M. plus T_0.

(c) What is the average time of departure if $T_0 = 1$ h? (*Hint:* Note that point conditioning applies.)

⋆4-54 Start with the expressions

$$F_Y(y|B) = P\{Y \leq y|B\} = \frac{P\{Y \leq y \cap B\}}{P(B)}$$

$$f_Y(y|B) = \frac{dF_Y(y|B)}{dy}$$

which are analogous to (4.4-1) and (4.4-2), and derive $F_Y(y|x_a < X \leq x_b)$ and $f_Y(y|x_a < X \leq x_b)$ which are analogous to (4.4-15) and (4.4-16).

⋆4-55 Extend the procedures of the text that lead to (4.4-16) to show that the joint distribution and density of random variables X and Y, conditional on the event $B = \{y_a < Y \leq y_b\}$, are

$$F_{X,Y}(x, y | y_a < Y \leq y_b) = \begin{cases} 0 & y \leq y_a \\ \dfrac{F_{X,Y}(x, y) - F_{X,Y}(x, y_a)}{F_Y(y_b) - F_Y(y_a)} & y_a < y \leq y_b \\ \dfrac{F_{X,Y}(x, y_b) - F_{X,Y}(x, y_a)}{F_Y(y_b) - F_Y(y_a)} & y_b < y \end{cases}$$

and

$$f_{X,Y}(x, y | y_a < Y \leq y_b) = \begin{cases} 0 & y \leq y_a \quad \text{and} \quad y > y_b \\ \dfrac{f_{X,Y}(x, y)}{F_Y(y_b) - F_Y(y_a)} & y_a < y \leq y_b \end{cases}$$

4-56 Determine if random variables X and Y of Problem 4-53 are statistically independent.

4-57 Determine if X and Y of Problem 4-49 are statistically independent.

4-58 The joint density of four random variables X_i, $i = 1, 2, 3$, and 4, is

$$f_{X_1, X_2, X_3, X_4}(x_1, x_2, x_3, x_4) = \prod_{i=1}^{4} \exp(-2|x_i|)$$

Find densities
(a) $f_{X_1, X_2, X_3}(x_1, x_2, x_3 | x_4)$
(b) $f_{X_1, X_2}(x_1, x_2 | x_3, x_4)$, and
(c) $f_{X_1}(x_1 | x_2, x_3, x_4)$.

4-59 If the difference $W = X - Y$ is formed instead of the sum in (4.6-1), develop the probability density of W. Compare the result with (4.6-5). Is the density still a convolution of the densities of X and Y? Discuss.

4-60 Statistically independent random variables X and Y have respective densities

$$f_X(x) = [u(x + 12) - u(x - 12)][1 - |x/12|]/12$$
$$f_Y(y) = (1/4)u(y) \exp(-y/4)$$

Find the probabilities of the events:
(a) $\{Y \leq 8 - (2|X|/3)\}$, and (b) $\{Y \leq 8 + (2|X|/3)\}$.
Compare the two results.

4-61 Statistically independent random variables X and Y have respective densities

$$f_X(x) = 5u(x) \exp(-5x)$$
$$f_Y(y) = 2u(y) \exp(-2y)$$

Find the density of the sum $W = X + Y$.

★4-62 N statistically independent random variables X_i, $i = 1, 2, \ldots, N$, all have the same density

$$f_{X_i}(x_i) = au(x_i) \exp(-ax_i)$$

where $a > 0$ is a constant. Find an expression for the density of the sum $W = X_1 + X_2 + \cdots + X_N$ for any N.

★**4-63** Find the exact probability density for the sum of two statistically independent random variables each having the density

$$f_X(x) = 3[u(x + a) - u(x - a)]x^2/2a^3$$

where $a > 0$ is a constant. Plot the density along with the gaussian approximation (to the density of the sum) that has variance $2\sigma_X^2$ and mean $2\bar{X}$. Is the approximation a good one?

★**4-64** Work Problem 4-63 except assume

$$f_X(x) = (1/2) \cos (x) \, \text{rect} \, (x/\pi)$$

ADDITIONAL PROBLEMS, THIRD EDITION

4-65 Sketch the joint sample space for two random variables X and Y and define the regions that correspond to the events $A = \{Y \le 2X\}$, $B = \{X \le 4\}$, and $C = \{Y > -2\}$. Indicate the region defined by $A \cap B \cap C$.

4-66 The function

$$F_{X,Y}(x, y) = a\left[\frac{\pi}{2} + \tan^{-1}\left(\frac{x}{2}\right)\right]\left[\frac{\pi}{2} + \tan^{-1}\left(\frac{y}{3}\right)\right]$$

is a valid joint distribution function for random variables X and Y if the constant a is chosen properly. What should be the value of a?

4-67 Work Problem 4-66, except assume the function

$$F_{X,Y}(x, y) = a\left[\frac{\pi}{2} + \frac{\sqrt{3}\,x}{3 + x^2} + \tan^{-1}\left(\frac{x}{\sqrt{3}}\right)\right]$$

$$\cdot \left[\frac{\pi}{2} + \frac{\sqrt{5}\,y}{5 + y^2} + \tan^{-1}\left(\frac{y}{\sqrt{5}}\right)\right]$$

4-68 Suppose that a pair of random numbers generated by a computer are represented as values of random variables X and Y having the joint distribution function

$$F_{X,Y}(x, y) = \begin{cases} 0 & x < 0 \text{ or } y < 0 \\ \dfrac{27}{26}x\left(1 - \dfrac{x^2}{27}\right) & 0 \le x < 1 \text{ and } 1 \le y \\ \dfrac{27}{26}y\left(1 - \dfrac{y^2}{27}\right) & 1 \le x \text{ and } 0 \le y < 1 \\ \dfrac{27}{26}xy\left(1 - \dfrac{x^2y^2}{27}\right) & 0 \le x < 1 \text{ and } 0 \le y < 1 \\ 1 & 1 \le x \text{ and } 1 \le y \end{cases}$$

(a) Determine the marginal distribution functions of X and Y.

(b) Find the probability of the event $\{0 < X \le 0.5, 0 < Y \le 0.25\}$.

4-69 The joint density of two random variables X and Y is

$$f_{X,Y}(x, y) = 0.1\delta(x)\delta(y) + 0.12\delta(x - 4)\delta(y)$$

$$+ 0.05\delta(x)\delta(y - 1) + 0.25\delta(x - 2)\delta(y - 1)$$

$$+ 0.3\delta(x - 2)\delta(y - 3) + 0.18\delta(x - 4)\delta(y - 3)$$

Find and plot the marginal distributions of X and Y.

4-70 Assume a has the proper value in Problem 4-66 and determine the joint density of X and Y. Find the marginal densities of X and Y.

4-71 Work Problem 4-70 but assume the distribution of Problem 4-67.

4-72 (a) Find the joint probability density function for the computer-generated numbers of Problem 4-68.

(b) Find the marginal densities of X and Y.

(c) Find the probability of the event $\{Y > 1 - X\}$.

4-73 The joint density function of random variables X and Y is

$$f_{X,Y}(x, y) = \begin{cases} \dfrac{25}{23ab}\left(\dfrac{y}{a}\right)\left[1 - \left(\dfrac{x}{b}\right)^4\left(\dfrac{y}{a}\right)^3\right] & \begin{array}{l} -b < x < b \text{ and} \\ 0 < y < a \end{array} \\ 0 & \text{elsewhere} \end{cases}$$

where $a > 0$ and $b > 0$ are constants. Find the marginal densities of X and Y.

★4-74 Assume that transoceanic aircraft arrive at a random point x (value of random variable X) within a strip of coastal region of width 10 km centered on a small city. Aircraft altitude at the time of arrival is not more than 25 km and is a random variable Y. If X and Y have the joint density of Problem 4-73, find the probability density of arrival altitude, given that aircraft arrive on one side of the city. Repeat for arrivals on the other side of the city.

★4-75 Work Problem 4-74 except find the probability density of arrival point X, given that arrival altitude is above 10 km.

4-76 Assume that random variables X and Y have the joint density

$$f_{X,Y}(x, y) = \begin{cases} k \cos^2\left(\dfrac{\pi}{2}xy\right) & -1 < x < 1 \text{ and } -1 < y < 1 \\ 0 & \text{elsewhere} \end{cases}$$

where

$$k = \frac{\pi/2}{\pi + \text{Si}(\pi)} \approx 0.315$$

and the *sine integral* is defined by

$$\text{Si}(x) = \int_0^x \frac{\sin(\xi)}{\xi}\, d\xi$$

(see Abramowitz and Stegun, 1964). By use of (4.5-4), determine whether X and Y are statistically independent.

4-77 Random variables X and Y have the joint density

$$f_{X,Y}(x, y) = \tfrac{1}{12}u(x)u(y)e^{-(x/4)-(y/3)}.$$

Find:

(a) $P\{2 < X \le 4, -1 < Y \le 5\}$ and

(b) $P\{0 < X < \infty, -\infty < Y \le -2\}$.

(c) Are X and Y statistically independent?

★4-78 Statistically independent random variables X and Y have probability densities

$$f_X(x) = \frac{3}{2a^3}\left[u(x + a) - u(x - a)\right]x^2 \qquad a > \pi/2$$

$$f_Y(y) = \frac{1}{2}\,\mathrm{rect}\left(\frac{y}{\pi}\right)\cos{(y)}$$

Find the exact probability density of the sum $W = X + Y$.

4-79 The probability density functions of two statistically independent random variables X and Y are

$$f_X(x) = \tfrac{1}{2}u(x - 1)e^{-(x-1)/2}$$

$$f_Y(y) = \tfrac{1}{4}u(y - 3)e^{-(y-3)/4}$$

Find the probability density of the sum $W = X + Y$.

4-80 Statistically independent random variables X and Y have probability densities

$$f_X(x) = \begin{cases} \dfrac{3}{32}(4 - x^2) & -2 \le x \le 2 \\ 0 & \text{elsewhere in } x \end{cases}$$

$$f_Y(y) = \tfrac{1}{2}[u(y + 1) - u(y - 1)]$$

Find the exact probability density of the sum $W = X + Y$.

★4-81 Three statistically independent random variables X_1, X_2, and X_3 are defined by

$$\bar{X}_1 = -1 \qquad \sigma_{X_1}^2 = 2.0$$

$$\bar{X}_2 = 0.6 \qquad \sigma_{X_2}^2 = 1.5$$

$$\bar{X}_3 = 1.8 \qquad \sigma_{X_3}^2 = 0.8$$

Write the equation describing the gaussian approximation for the density function of the sum $X = X_1 + X_2 + X_3$. (*Hint:* Refer to the text on the central limit theorem.)

★**4-82** Two statistically independent random variables X_1 and X_2 have the same probability density given by

$$f_{X_i}(x_i) = \begin{cases} 2x_i/a^2 & 0 \le x_i < a \\ 0 & \text{elsewhere in } x_i \end{cases}$$

for $i = 1$ and 2, where $a > 0$ is a constant.

(a) Find the exact density of the sum $W = X_1 + X_2$.

(b) Compute the mean and variance of W and find a gaussian approximation for the density of W having the computed mean and variance.

(c) Plot the density of W and the gaussian approximation to see the accuracy of the approximation.

★**4-83** The probability density functions of statistically independent random variables X and Y are

$$f_X(x) = \begin{cases} \dfrac{2x}{a^2} & 0 \le x < a \\ 0 & \text{elsewhere in } x \end{cases}$$

$$f_Y(y) = bu(y)e^{-by}$$

where $a > 0$ and $b > 0$ are constants.

(a) Find the probability density function of the sum $W = X + Y$.

(b) Find a gaussian approximation for W that has the same mean and variance as W.

(c) Plot the approximation and the density of W for products $ab = 1/2$, 1, and 2.

CHAPTER
5

OPERATIONS
ON MULTIPLE
RANDOM
VARIABLES

5.0 INTRODUCTION

After establishing some of the basic theory of several random variables in the previous chapter, it is appropriate to now extend the operations described in Chapter 3 to include multiple random variables. This chapter is dedicated to these extensions. Mainly, the concept of expectation is enlarged to include two or more random variables. Other operations involving moments, characteristic functions, and transformations are all special applications of expectation.

5.1 EXPECTED VALUE OF A
FUNCTION OF RANDOM VARIABLES

When more than a single random variable is involved, expectation must be taken with respect to all the variables involved. For example, if $g(X, Y)$ is some function of two random variables X and Y the expected value of $g(\cdot, \cdot)$ is given by

$$\bar{g} = E[g(X, Y)] = \int_{-\infty}^{\infty} \int_{-\infty}^{\infty} g(x, y) f_{X,Y}(x, y)\, dx\, dy \qquad (5.1\text{-}1)$$

This expression is the two-variable extension of (3.1-6).

For N random variables $X_1, X_2, \ldots, X_N$ and some function of these variables, denoted $g(X_1, \ldots, X_N)$, the expected value of the function becomes

$$\bar{g} = E[g(X_1, \ldots, X_N)]$$

$$= \int_{-\infty}^{\infty} \cdots \int_{-\infty}^{\infty} g(x_1, \ldots, x_N) f_{X_1, \ldots, X_N}(x_1, \ldots, x_N) \, dx_1 \cdots dx_N \quad (5.1\text{-}2)$$

Thus, expectation in general involves an N-fold integration when N random variables are involved.

We illustrate the application of (5.1-2) with an example that will develop an important point.

Example 5.1-1 We shall find the mean (expected) value of a sum of N weighted random variables. If we let

$$g(X_1, \ldots, X_N) = \sum_{i=1}^{N} \alpha_i X_i$$

where the "weights" are the constants α_i, the mean value of the weighted sum becomes

$$E[g(X_1, \ldots, X_N)] = E\left[\sum_{i=1}^{N} \alpha_i X_i \right]$$

$$= \sum_{i=1}^{N} \int_{-\infty}^{\infty} \cdots \int_{-\infty}^{\infty} \alpha_i x_i f_{X_1, \ldots, X_N}(x_1, \ldots, x_N) \, dx_1 \cdots dx_N$$

from (5.1-2). After using (4.3-8), the terms in the sum all reduce to the form

$$\int_{-\infty}^{\infty} \alpha_i x_i f_{X_i}(x_i) \, dx_i = E[\alpha_i X_i] = \alpha_i E[X_i]$$

so

$$E\left[\sum_{i=1}^{N} \alpha_i X_i \right] = \sum_{i=1}^{N} \alpha_i E[X_i]$$

which says that *the mean value of a weighted sum of random variables equals the weighted sum of mean values.*

The above extensions (5.1-1) and (5.1-2) of expectation do not invalidate any of our single random variable results. For example, let

$$g(X_1, \ldots, X_N) = g(X_1) \quad (5.1\text{-}3)$$

and substitute into (5.1-2). After integrating with respect to all random variables except X_1, (5.1-2) becomes

$$\bar{g} = E[g(X_1)] = \int_{-\infty}^{\infty} g(x_1) f_{X_1}(x_1)\, dx_1 \tag{5.1-4}$$

which is the same as previously given in (3.1-6) for one random variable. Some reflection on the reader's part will verify that (5.1-4) also validates such earlier topics as moments, central moments, characteristic function, etc., for a single random variable.

Joint Moments About the Origin

One important application of (5.1-1) is in defining *joint moments* about the origin. They are denoted by m_{nk} and are defined by

$$m_{nk} = E[X^n Y^k] = \int_{-\infty}^{\infty} \int_{-\infty}^{\infty} x^n y^k f_{X,Y}(x, y)\, dx\, dy \tag{5.1-5}$$

for the case of two random variables X and Y. Clearly $m_{n0} = E[X^n]$ are the moments m_n of X, while $m_{0k} = E[Y^k]$ are the moments of Y. The sum $n + k$ is called the *order* of the moments. Thus m_{02}, m_{20}, and m_{11} are all second-order moments of X and Y. The first-order moments $m_{01} = E[Y] = \bar{Y}$ and $m_{10} = E[X] = \bar{X}$ are the expected values of Y and X, respectively, and are the coordinates of the "center of gravity" of the function $f_{X,Y}(x, y)$.

The second-order moment $m_{11} = E[XY]$ is called the *correlation* of X and Y. It is so important to later work that we give it the symbol R_{XY}. Hence,

$$R_{XY} = m_{11} = E[XY] = \int_{-\infty}^{\infty} \int_{-\infty}^{\infty} xy f_{X,Y}(x, y)\, dx\, dy \tag{5.1-6}$$

If correlation can be written in the form

$$R_{XY} = E[X]E[Y] \tag{5.1-7}$$

then X and Y are said to be *uncorrelated*. Statistical independence of X and Y is sufficient to guarantee they are uncorrelated, as is readily proven by (5.1-6) using (4.5-4). The converse of this statement, that is, that X and Y are independent if X and Y are uncorrelated, is *not* necessarily true in general.†

If

$$R_{XY} = 0 \tag{5.1-8}$$

for two random variables X and Y, they are called *orthogonal*.

A simple example is next developed that illustrates the important new topic of correlation.

---

† Uncorrelated *gaussian* random variables are, however, known to also be independent (see Section 5.3).

Example 5.1-2 Let X be a random variable that has a mean value $\bar{X} = E[X] = 3$ and variance $\sigma_X^2 = 2$. From (3.2-6) we easily determine the second moment of X about the origin: $E[X^2] = m_{20} = \sigma_X^2 + \bar{X}^2 = 11$.

Next, let another random variable Y be defined by

$$Y = -6X + 22$$

The mean value of Y is $\bar{Y} = E[Y] = E[-6X + 22] = -6\bar{X} + 22 = 4$. The correlation of X and Y is found from (5.1-6)

$$R_{XY} = m_{11} = E[XY] = E[-6X^2 + 22X] = -6E[X^2] + 22\bar{X}$$

$$= -6(11) + 22(3) = 0$$

Since $R_{XY} = 0$, X and Y are orthogonal from (5.1-8). On the other hand, $R_{XY} \neq E[X]E[Y] = 12$, so X and Y are *not* uncorrelated [see (5.1-7)].

We note that two random variables can be orthogonal even though correlated when one, Y, is related to the other, X, by the linear function $Y = aX + b$. It can be shown that X and Y are always correlated if $|a| \neq 0$, regardless of the value of b (see Problem 5-9). They are uncorrelated if $a = 0$, but this is not a case of much practical interest. Orthogonality can likewise be shown to occur when a and b are related by $b = -aE[X^2]/E[X]$ whenever $E[X] \neq 0$. If $E[X] = 0$, X and Y cannot be orthogonal for any value of a except $a = 0$, a noninteresting problem. The reader may wish to verify these statements as an exercise.

For N random variables $X_1, X_2, \ldots, X_N$, the $(n_1 + n_2 + \cdots + n_N)$-order joint moments are defined by

$$m_{n_1 n_2 \cdots n_N} = E[X_1^{n_1} X_2^{n_2} \cdots X_N^{n_N}]$$

$$= \int_{-\infty}^{\infty} \cdots \int_{-\infty}^{\infty} X_1^{n_1} \cdots X_N^{n_N} f_{X_1, \ldots, X_N}(x_1, \ldots, x_N) \, dx_1 \cdots dx_N \quad (5.1\text{-}9)$$

where $n_1, n_2, \ldots, n_N$ are all integers $= 0, 1, 2, \ldots$.

Joint Central Moments

Another important application of (5.1-1) is in defining *joint central moments*. For two random variables X and Y, these moments, denoted by μ_{nk}, are given by

$$\mu_{nk} = E[(X - \bar{X})^n (Y - \bar{Y})^k]$$

$$= \int_{-\infty}^{\infty} \int_{-\infty}^{\infty} (x - \bar{X})^n (y - \bar{Y})^k f_{X,Y}(x, y) \, dx \, dy \quad (5.1\text{-}10)$$

The second-order central moments

$$\mu_{20} = E[(X - \bar{X})^2] = \sigma_X^2 \tag{5.1-11}$$

$$\mu_{02} = E[(Y - \bar{Y})^2] = \sigma_Y^2 \tag{5.1-12}$$

are just the variances of X and Y.

The second-order joint moment μ_{11} is very important. It is called the *covariance* of X and Y and is given the symbol C_{XY}. Hence

$$C_{XY} = \mu_{11} = E[(X - \bar{X})(Y - \bar{Y})]$$

$$= \int_{-\infty}^{\infty} \int_{-\infty}^{\infty} (x - \bar{X})(y - \bar{Y}) f_{X,Y}(x, y) \, dx \, dy \tag{5.1-13}$$

By direct expansion of the product $(x - \bar{X})(y - \bar{Y})$, this integral reduces to the form

$$C_{XY} = R_{XY} - \bar{X}\bar{Y} = R_{XY} - E[X]E[Y] \tag{5.1-14}$$

when (5.1-6) is used. If X and Y are either independent or uncorrelated, then (5.1-7) applies and (5.1-14) shows their covariance is zero:

$$C_{XY} = 0 \qquad X \text{ and } Y \text{ independent or uncorrelated} \tag{5.1-15}$$

If X and Y are orthogonal random variables, then

$$C_{XY} = -E[X]E[Y] \qquad X \text{ and } Y \text{ orthogonal} \tag{5.1-16}$$

from use of (5.1-8) with (5.1-14). Clearly, $C_{XY} = 0$ if either X or Y also has zero mean value.

The normalized second-order moment

$$\rho = \mu_{11}/\sqrt{\mu_{20}\mu_{02}} = C_{XY}/\sigma_X\sigma_Y \tag{5.1-17a}$$

given by

$$\rho = E\left[\frac{(X - \bar{X})}{\sigma_X} \frac{(Y - \bar{Y})}{\sigma_Y}\right] \tag{5.1-17b}$$

is known as the *correlation coefficient* of X and Y. It can be shown (see Problem 5-10) that

$$-1 \leq \rho \leq 1 \tag{5.1-18}$$

For N random variables $X_1, X_2, \ldots, X_N$ the $(n_1 + n_2 + \cdots + n_N)$-order joint central moment is defined by

$$\mu_{n_1 n_2 \cdots n_N} = E[(X_1 - \bar{X}_1)^{n_1}(X_2 - \bar{X}_2)^{n_2} \cdots (X_N - \bar{X}_N)^{n_N}]$$

$$= \int_{-\infty}^{\infty} \cdots \int_{-\infty}^{\infty} (x_1 - \bar{X}_1)^{n_1} \cdots$$

$$(x_N - \bar{X}_N)^{n_N} f_{X_1, \ldots, X_N}(x_1, \ldots, x_N) \, dx_1 \cdots dx_N \tag{5.1-19}$$

An example is next developed that involves the use of covariances.

Example 5.1-3 Again let X be a weighted sum of N random variables X_i; that is, let

$$X = \sum_{i=1}^{N} \alpha_i X_i$$

where the α_i are real weighting constants. The variance of X will be found. From Example 5.1-1,

$$E[X] = \sum_{i=1}^{N} \alpha_i E[X_i] = \sum_{i=1}^{N} \alpha_i \bar{X}_i = \bar{X}$$

so we have

$$X - \bar{X} = \sum_{i=1}^{N} \alpha_i (X_i - \bar{X}_i)$$

and

$$\sigma_X^2 = E[(X - \bar{X})^2] = E\left[\sum_{i=1}^{N} \alpha_i (X_i - \bar{X}_i) \sum_{j=1}^{N} \alpha_j (X_j - \bar{X}_j) \right]$$

$$= \sum_{i=1}^{N} \sum_{j=1}^{N} \alpha_i \alpha_j E[(X_i - \bar{X}_i)(X_j - \bar{X}_j)] = \sum_{i=1}^{N} \sum_{j=1}^{N} \alpha_i \alpha_j C_{X_i X_j}$$

Thus, the variance of a weighted sum of N random variables X_i (weights α_i) equals the weighted sum of all their covariances $C_{X_i X_j}$ (weights $\alpha_i \alpha_j$). For the special case of uncorrelated random variables, where

$$C_{X_i X_j} = \begin{cases} 0 & i \neq j \\ \sigma_{X_i}^2 & i = j \end{cases}$$

is true, we get

$$\sigma_X^2 = \sum_{i=1}^{N} \alpha_i^2 \sigma_{X_i}^2$$

In words: *the variance of a weighted sum of uncorrelated random variables (weights α_i) equals the weighted sum of the variances of the random variables (weights α_i^2).*

⋆5.2 JOINT CHARACTERISTIC FUNCTIONS

The *joint characteristic function* of two random variables X and Y is defined by

$$\Phi_{X,Y}(\omega_1, \omega_2) = E[e^{j\omega_1 X + j\omega_2 Y}] \tag{5.2-1}$$

where ω_1 and ω_2 are real numbers. An equivalent form is

$$\Phi_{X,Y}(\omega_1, \omega_2) = \int_{-\infty}^{\infty} \int_{-\infty}^{\infty} f_{X,Y}(x, y) e^{j\omega_1 x + j\omega_2 y} \, dx \, dy \qquad (5.2\text{-}2)$$

This expression is recognized as the two-dimensional Fourier transform (with signs of ω_1 and ω_2 reversed) of the joint density function. From the inverse Fourier transform we also have

$$f_{X,Y}(x, y) = \frac{1}{(2\pi)^2} \int_{-\infty}^{\infty} \int_{-\infty}^{\infty} \Phi_{X,Y}(\omega_1, \omega_2) e^{-j\omega_1 x - j\omega_2 y} \, d\omega_1 \, d\omega_2 \qquad (5.2\text{-}3)$$

By setting either $\omega_2 = 0$ or $\omega_1 = 0$ in (5.2-2), the characteristic functions of X or Y are obtained. They are called *marginal characteristic functions*:

$$\Phi_X(\omega_1) = \Phi_{X,Y}(\omega_1, 0) \qquad (5.2\text{-}4)$$

$$\Phi_Y(\omega_2) = \Phi_{X,Y}(0, \omega_2) \qquad (5.2\text{-}5)$$

Joint moments m_{nk} can be found from the joint characteristic function as follows:

$$m_{nk} = (-j)^{n+k} \frac{\partial^{n+k} \Phi_{X,Y}(\omega_1, \omega_2)}{\partial \omega_1^n \, \partial \omega_2^k} \bigg|_{\omega_1 = 0, \, \omega_2 = 0} \qquad (5.2\text{-}6)$$

This expression is the two-dimensional extension of (3.3-4).

Example 5.2-1 Two random variables X and Y have the joint characteristic function

$$\Phi_{X,Y}(\omega_1, \omega_2) = \exp(-2\omega_1^2 - 8\omega_2^2)$$

We show that X and Y are both zero-mean random variables and that they are uncorrelated.

The means derive from (5.2-6):

$$\bar{X} = E[X] = m_{10} = -j \frac{\partial \Phi_{X,Y}(\omega_1, \omega_2)}{\partial \omega_1} \bigg|_{\omega_1 = 0, \, \omega_2 = 0}$$

$$= -j(-4\omega_1) \exp(-2\omega_1^2 - 8\omega_2^2) \bigg|_{\omega_1 = 0, \, \omega_2 = 0} = 0$$

$$\bar{Y} = E[Y] = m_{01} = -j(-16\omega_2) \exp(-2\omega_1^2 - 8\omega_2^2) \bigg|_{\omega_1 = 0, \, \omega_2 = 0} = 0$$

Also from (5.2-6):

$$R_{XY} = E[XY] = m_{11} = (-j)^2 \frac{\partial^2}{\partial \omega_1 \, \partial \omega_2} [\exp(-2\omega_1^2 - 8\omega_2^2)] \bigg|_{\omega_1 = 0, \, \omega_2 = 0}$$

$$= -(-4\omega_1)(-16\omega_2) \exp(-2\omega_1^2 - 8\omega_2^2) \bigg|_{\omega_1 = 0, \, \omega_2 = 0} = 0$$

Since means are zero, $C_{XY} = R_{XY}$ from (5.1-14). Therefore, $C_{XY} = 0$ and X and Y are uncorrelated.

The joint characteristic function for N random variables $X_1, X_2, \ldots, X_N$ is defined by

$$\Phi_{X_1, \ldots, X_N}(\omega_1, \ldots, \omega_N) = E[e^{j\omega_1 X_1 + \cdots + j\omega_N X_N}] \tag{5.2-7}$$

Joint moments are obtained from

$$m_{n_1 n_2 \cdots n_N} = (-j)^R \frac{\partial^R \Phi_{X_1, \ldots, X_N}(\omega_1, \ldots, \omega_N)}{\partial \omega_1^{n_1} \partial \omega_2^{n_2} \cdots \partial \omega_N^{n_N}} \bigg|_{\text{all } \omega_i = 0} \tag{5.2-8}$$

where

$$R = n_1 + n_2 + \cdots + n_N \tag{5.2-9}$$

5.3 JOINTLY GAUSSIAN RANDOM VARIABLES

Gaussian random variables are very important because they show up in nearly every area of science and engineering. In this section, the case of two gaussian random variables is first examined. The more advanced case of N random variables is then introduced.

Two Random Variables

Two random variables X and Y are said to be *jointly gaussian* if their joint density function is of the form

$$f_{X,Y}(x, y) = \frac{1}{2\pi\sigma_X\sigma_Y\sqrt{1 - \rho^2}}$$

$$\cdot \exp\left\{\frac{-1}{2(1 - \rho^2)}\left[\frac{(x - \bar{X})^2}{\sigma_X^2} - \frac{2\rho(x - \bar{X})(y - \bar{Y})}{\sigma_X\sigma_Y} + \frac{(y - \bar{Y})^2}{\sigma_Y^2}\right]\right\} \tag{5.3-1}$$

which is sometimes called the *bivariate gaussian density*. Here

$$\bar{X} = E[X] \tag{5.3-2}$$

$$\bar{Y} = E[Y] \tag{5.3-3}$$

$$\sigma_X^2 = E[(X - \bar{X})^2] \tag{5.3-4}$$

$$\sigma_Y^2 = E[(Y - \bar{Y})^2] \tag{5.3-5}$$

$$\rho = E[(X - \bar{X})(Y - \bar{Y})]/\sigma_X\sigma_Y \tag{5.3-6}$$

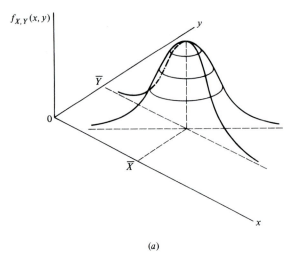

(a)

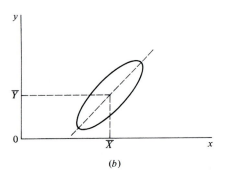

(b)

FIGURE 5.3-1
Sketch of the joint density function of two gaussian random variables.

Figure 5.3-1*a* illustrates the appearance of the joint gaussian density function (5.3-1). Its maximum is located at the point $(\bar{X}, \bar{Y})$. The maximum value is obtained from

$$f_{X,Y}(x, y) \leq f_{X,Y}(\bar{X}, \bar{Y}) = \frac{1}{2\pi\sigma_X\sigma_Y\sqrt{1 - \rho^2}} \tag{5.3-7}$$

The locus of constant values of $f_{X,Y}(x, y)$ will be an ellipse† as shown in Figure 5.3-1*b*. This is equivalent to saying that the line of intersection formed by slicing the function $f_{X,Y}(x, y)$ with a plane parallel to the xy plane is an ellipse.

Observe that if $\rho = 0$, corresponding to uncorrelated X and Y, (5.3-1) can be written as

$$f_{X,Y}(x, y) = f_X(x)f_Y(y) \tag{5.3-8}$$

---

† When $\sigma_X = \sigma_Y$ and $\rho = 0$ the ellipse degenerates into a circle; when $\rho = +1$ or -1 the ellipses degenerate into axes rotated by angles $\pi/4$ and $-\pi/4$ respectively that pass through the point $(\bar{X}, \bar{Y})$.

where $f_X(x)$ and $f_Y(y)$ are the marginal density functions of X and Y given by

$$f_X(x) = \frac{1}{\sqrt{2\pi\sigma_X^2}} \exp\left[-\frac{(x - \bar{X})^2}{2\sigma_X^2}\right] \tag{5.3-9}$$

$$f_Y(y) = \frac{1}{\sqrt{2\pi\sigma_Y^2}} \exp\left[-\frac{(y - \bar{Y})^2}{2\sigma_Y^2}\right] \tag{5.3-10}$$

Now the form of (5.3-8) is sufficient to guarantee that X and Y are statistically independent. Therefore we conclude that *any uncorrelated gaussian random variables are also statistically independent*. It results that a coordinate rotation (linear transformation of X and Y) through an angle

$$\theta = \frac{1}{2}\tan^{-1}\left[\frac{2\rho\sigma_X\sigma_Y}{\sigma_X^2 - \sigma_Y^2}\right] \tag{5.3-11}$$

is sufficient to convert correlated random variables X and Y, having variances σ_X^2 and σ_Y^2, respectively, correlation coefficient ρ, and the joint density of (5.3-1), into two statistically independent gaussian random variables.†

By direct application of (4.4-12) and (4.4-13), the conditional density functions $f_X(x|Y = y)$ and $f_Y(y|X = x)$ can be found from the above expressions (see Problem 5-29).

Example 5.3-1 We show by example that (5.3-11) applies to arbitrary as well as gaussian random variables. Consider random variables Y_1 and Y_2 related to arbitrary random variables X and Y by the coordinate rotation

$$Y_1 = X\cos(\theta) + Y\sin(\theta)$$

$$Y_2 = -X\sin(\theta) + Y\cos(\theta)$$

If $\bar{X}$ and $\bar{Y}$ are the means of X and Y, respectively, the means of Y_1 and Y_2 are clearly $\bar{Y}_1 = \bar{X}\cos(\theta) + \bar{Y}\sin(\theta)$ and $\bar{Y}_2 = -\bar{X}\sin(\theta) + \bar{Y}\cos(\theta)$, respectively. The covariance of Y_1 and Y_2 is

$$\begin{aligned} C_{Y_1Y_2} &= E[(Y_1 - \bar{Y}_1)(Y_2 - \bar{Y}_2)] \\ &= E[\{(X - \bar{X})\cos(\theta) + (Y - \bar{Y})\sin(\theta)\} \\ &\quad \cdot \{-(X - \bar{X})\sin(\theta) + (Y - \bar{Y})\cos(\theta)\}] \\ &= (\sigma_Y^2 - \sigma_X^2)\sin(\theta)\cos(\theta) + C_{XY}[\cos^2(\theta) - \sin^2(\theta)] \\ &= (\sigma_Y^2 - \sigma_X^2)(^1/_2)\sin(2\theta) + C_{XY}\cos(2\theta) \end{aligned}$$

---

† Wozencraft and Jacobs (1965), p. 155.

Here $C_{XY} = E[(X - \bar{X})(Y - \bar{Y})] = \rho\sigma_X\sigma_Y$. If we require Y_1 and Y_2 to be uncorrelated, we must have $C_{Y_1Y_2} = 0$. By equating the above equation to zero we obtain (5.3-11). Thus, (5.3-11) applies to arbitrary as well as gaussian random variables.

⋆N Random Variables

N random variables $X_1, X_2, \ldots, X_N$ are called *jointly gaussian* if their joint density function can be written as†

$$f_{X_1,\ldots,X_N}(x_1,\ldots,x_N) = \frac{|[C_X]^{-1}|^{1/2}}{(2\pi)^{N/2}} \exp\left\{ -\frac{[x - \bar{X}]'[C_X]^{-1}[x - \bar{X}]}{2} \right\} \quad (5.3\text{-}12)$$

where we define matrices

$$[x - \bar{X}] = \begin{bmatrix} x_1 - \bar{X}_1 \\ x_2 - \bar{X}_2 \\ \vdots \\ x_N - \bar{X}_N \end{bmatrix} \quad (5.3\text{-}13)$$

and

$$[C_X] = \begin{bmatrix} C_{11} & C_{12} & \cdots & C_{1N} \\ C_{21} & C_{22} & \cdots & C_{2N} \\ \vdots & \vdots & & \vdots \\ C_{N1} & C_{N2} & \cdots & C_{NN} \end{bmatrix} \quad (5.3\text{-}14)$$

We use the notation $[\cdot]'$ for the matrix transpose, $[\cdot]^{-1}$ for the matrix inverse, and $|[\cdot]|$ for the determinant. Elements of $[C_X]$, called the *covariance matrix* of the N random variables, are given by

$$C_{ij} = E[(X_i - \bar{X}_i)(X_j - \bar{X}_j)] = \begin{cases} \sigma_{X_i}^2 & i = j \\ C_{X_iX_j} & i \neq j \end{cases} \quad (5.3\text{-}15)$$

The density (5.3-12) is often called the *N-variate gaussian density* function.

For the special case where $N = 2$, the covariance matrix becomes

$$[C_X] = \begin{bmatrix} \sigma_{X_1}^2 & \rho\sigma_{X_1}\sigma_{X_2} \\ \rho\sigma_{X_1}\sigma_{X_2} & \sigma_{X_2}^2 \end{bmatrix} \quad (5.3\text{-}16)$$

so

$$[C_X]^{-1} = \frac{1}{(1 - \rho^2)} \begin{bmatrix} 1/\sigma_{X_1}^2 & -\rho/\sigma_{X_1}\sigma_{X_2} \\ -\rho/\sigma_{X_1}\sigma_{X_2} & 1/\sigma_{X_2}^2 \end{bmatrix} \quad (5.3\text{-}17)$$

$$|[C_X]^{-1}| = 1/\sigma_{X_1}^2\sigma_{X_2}^2(1 - \rho^2) \quad (5.3\text{-}18)$$

---

† We denote a matrix symbolically by use of heavy brackets $[\cdot]$.

On substitution of (5.3-17) and (5.3-18) into (5.3-12), and letting $X_1 = X$ and $X_2 = Y$, it is easy to verify that the bivariate density of (5.3-1) results.

*Some Properties of Gaussian Random Variables

We state without proof some of the properties exhibited by N jointly gaussian random variables $X_1, \ldots, X_N$.

1. Gaussian random variables are completely defined through only their first- and second-order moments; that is, by their means, variances, and covariances. This fact is readily apparent since only these quantities are needed to completely determine (5.3-12).
2. If the random variables are uncorrelated, they are also statistically independent. This property was given earlier for two variables.
3. Random variables produced by a linear transformation of $X_1, \ldots, X_N$ will also be gaussian, as will be proven in Section 5.5.
4. Any k-dimensional (k-variate) marginal density function obtained from the N-dimensional density function (5.3-12) by integrating out $N - k$ random variables will be gaussian. If the variables are ordered so that $X_1, \ldots, X_k$ occur in the marginal density and $X_{k+1}, \ldots, X_N$ are integrated out, then the covariance matrix of $X_1, \ldots, X_k$ is equal to the leading $k \times k$ submatrix of the covariance matrix of $X_1, \ldots, X_N$ (Wilks, 1962, p. 168).
5. The conditional density $f_{X_1, \ldots, X_k}(x_1, \ldots, x_k | X_{k+1} = x_{k+1}, \ldots, X_N = x_N)$ is gaussian (Papoulis, 1965, p. 257). This holds for any $k < N$.

*5.4 TRANSFORMATIONS OF MULTIPLE RANDOM VARIABLES

The function g in either (5.1-1) or (5.1-2) can be considered a transformation involving more than one random variable. By defining a new variable $Y = g(X_1, X_2, \ldots, X_N)$, we see that (5.1-2) is the expected value of Y. In calculating expected values it was not necessary to determine the density function of the new random variable Y. It may be, however, that the density function Y is required in some practical problems, and its determination is briefly considered in this section.

In fact, one may be more generally interested in finding the joint density function for a set of new random variables

$$Y_i = T_i(X_1, X_2, \ldots, X_N) \qquad i = 1, 2, \ldots, N \qquad (5.4\text{-}1)$$

defined by functional transformations T_i. Now all the possible cases described in Chapter 3 for one random variable carry over to the N-dimensional problem. That is, the X_i can be continuous, discrete, or mixed, while the functions T_i can be linear, nonlinear, continuous, segmented, etc. Because so many cases are possible, many of them being beyond our scope, we shall discuss only one representative problem.

We shall assume that the new random variables Y_i, given by (5.4-1), are produced by single-valued continuous functions T_i having continuous partial derivatives everywhere. It is further assumed that a set of inverse continuous functions T_j^{-1} exists such that the old variables may be expressed as single-valued continuous functions of the new variables:

$$X_j = T_j^{-1}(Y_1, Y_2, \ldots, Y_N) \qquad j = 1, 2, \ldots, N \qquad (5.4\text{-}2)$$

These assumptions mean that a point in the joint sample space of the X_i maps into only one point in the space of the new variables Y_j.

Let R_X be a closed region of points in the space of the X_i and R_Y be the corresponding region of mapped points in the space of the Y_j, then the probability that a point falls in R_X will equal the probability that its mapped point falls in R_Y. These probabilities, in terms of joint densities, are given by

$$\int_{R_X} \cdots \int f_{X_1,\ldots,X_N}(x_1, \ldots, x_N)\, dx_1 \cdots dx_N = \int_{R_Y} \cdots \int f_{Y_1,\ldots,Y_N}(y_1, \ldots, y_N)\, dy_1 \cdots dy_N$$

$$(5.4\text{-}3)$$

This equation may be solved for $f_{Y_1,\ldots,Y_N}(y_1, \ldots, y_N)$ by treating it as simply a multiple integral involving a change of variables.

By working on the left side of (5.4-3) we change the variables x_i to new variables y_j by means of the variable changes (5.4-2). The integrand is changed by direct functional substitution. The limits change from the region R_X to the region R_Y. Finally, the differential hypervolume $dx_1 \cdots dx_N$ will change to the value $|J|\, dy_1 \cdots dy_N$ (Speigel, 1963, p. 182), where $|J|$ is the magnitude of the jacobian† J of the transformations. The jacobian is the determinant of a matrix of derivatives defined by

$$J = \begin{vmatrix} \dfrac{\partial T_1^{-1}}{\partial Y_1} & \cdots & \dfrac{\partial T_1^{-1}}{\partial Y_N} \\ \vdots & & \vdots \\ \dfrac{\partial T_N^{-1}}{\partial Y_1} & \cdots & \dfrac{\partial T_N^{-1}}{\partial Y_N} \end{vmatrix} \qquad (5.4\text{-}4)$$

Thus, the left side of (5.4-3) becomes

$$\int_{R_X} \cdots \int f_{X_1,\ldots,X_N}(x_1, \ldots, x_N)\, dx_1 \cdots dx_N$$

$$= \int_{R_Y} \cdots \int f_{X_1,\ldots,X_N}(x_1 = T_1^{-1}, \ldots, x_N = T_N^{-1})|J|\, dy_1 \cdots dy_N \quad (5.4\text{-}5)$$

---

† After the German mathematician Karl Gustav Jakob Jacobi (1804–1851).

Since this result must equal the right side of (5.4-3), we conclude that

$$f_{Y_1,\ldots,Y_N}(y_1,\ldots,y_N) = f_{X_1,\ldots,X_N}(x_1 = T_1^{-1},\ldots,x_N = T_N^{-1})|J| \qquad (5.4\text{-}6)$$

When $N = 1$, (5.4-6) reduces to (3.4-9) previously derived for a single random variable.

The solution (5.4-6) for the joint density of the new variables Y_j is illustrated here with an example.

Example 5.4-1 Let the transformations be linear and given by

$$Y_1 = T_1(X_1, X_2) = aX_1 + bX_2$$

$$Y_2 = T_2(X_1, X_2) = cX_1 + dX_2$$

where $a, b, c,$ and d are real constants. The inverse functions are easy to obtain by solving these two equations for the two variables X_1 and X_2:

$$X_1 = T_1^{-1}(Y_1, Y_2) = (dY_1 - bY_2)/(ad - bc)$$

$$X_2 = T_2^{-1}(Y_1, Y_2) = (-cY_1 + aY_2)/(ad - bc)$$

where we shall assume $(ad - bc) \neq 0$. From (5.4-4):

$$J = \begin{vmatrix} d/(ad-bc) & -b/(ad-bc) \\ -c/(ad-bc) & a/(ad-bc) \end{vmatrix} = \frac{1}{(ad-bc)}$$

Finally, from (5.4-6),

$$f_{Y_1,Y_2}(y_1, y_2) = \frac{f_{X_1,X_2}\left(\dfrac{dy_1 - by_2}{ad - bc}, \dfrac{-cy_1 + ay_2}{ad - bc}\right)}{|ad - bc|}$$

★5.5 LINEAR TRANSFORMATION OF GAUSSIAN RANDOM VARIABLES

Equation (5.4-6) can be readily applied to the problem of linearly transforming a set of gaussian random variables $X_1, X_2, \ldots, X_N$ for which the joint density of (5.3-12) applies. The new variables $Y_1, Y_2, \ldots, Y_N$ are

$$Y_1 = a_{11}X_1 + a_{12}X_2 + \cdots + a_{1N}X_N$$

$$Y_2 = a_{21}X_1 + a_{22}X_2 + \cdots + a_{2N}X_N \qquad (5.5\text{-}1)$$

$$\vdots$$

$$Y_N = a_{N1}X_1 + a_{N2}X_2 + \cdots + a_{NN}X_N$$

where the coefficients a_{ij}, i and $j = 1, 2, \ldots, N$, are real numbers. Now if we define the following matrices:

$$[T] = \begin{bmatrix} a_{11} & a_{12} & \cdots & a_{1N} \\ a_{21} & a_{22} & \cdots & a_{2N} \\ \vdots & \vdots & & \vdots \\ a_{N1} & a_{N2} & \cdots & a_{NN} \end{bmatrix} \tag{5.5-2}$$

$$[Y] = \begin{bmatrix} Y_1 \\ \vdots \\ Y_N \end{bmatrix} \quad [\bar{Y}] = \begin{bmatrix} \bar{Y}_1 \\ \vdots \\ \bar{Y}_N \end{bmatrix} \quad [X] = \begin{bmatrix} X_1 \\ \vdots \\ X_N \end{bmatrix} \quad [\bar{X}] = \begin{bmatrix} \bar{X}_1 \\ \vdots \\ \bar{X}_N \end{bmatrix} \tag{5.5-3}$$

then it is clear from (5.5-1) that

$$[Y] = [T][X] \qquad [Y - \bar{Y}] = [T][X - \bar{X}] \tag{5.5-4}$$

$$[X] = [T]^{-1}[Y] \qquad [X - \bar{X}] = [T]^{-1}[Y - \bar{Y}] \tag{5.5-5}$$

so long as $[T]$ is nonsingular. Thus,

$$X_i = T_i^{-1}(Y_1, \ldots, Y_N) = a^{i1}Y_1 + a^{i2}Y_2 + \cdots + a^{iN}Y_N \tag{5.5-6}$$

$$\frac{\partial X_i}{\partial Y_j} = \frac{\partial T_i^{-1}}{\partial Y_j} = a^{ij} \tag{5.5-7}$$

$$X_i - \bar{X}_i = a^{i1}(Y_1 - \bar{Y}_1) + \cdots + a^{iN}(Y_N - \bar{Y}_N) \tag{5.5-8}$$

from (5.5-5). Here a^{ij} represents the ijth element of $[T]^{-1}$.

The density function of the new variables $Y_1, \ldots, Y_N$ is found by solving the right side of (5.4-6) in two steps. The first step is to determine $|J|$. By using (5.5-7) with (5.4-4) we find that J equals the determinant of the matrix $[T]^{-1}$. Hence,†

$$|J| = ||[T]^{-1}|| = \frac{1}{||[T]||} \tag{5.5-9}$$

The second step in solving (5.4-6) proceeds by using (5.5-8) to obtain

$$C_{X_iX_j} = E[(X_i - \bar{X}_i)(X_j - \bar{X}_j)] = \sum_{k=1}^{N} a^{ik} \sum_{m=1}^{N} a^{jm} E[(Y_k - \bar{Y}_k)(Y_m - \bar{Y}_m)]$$

$$= \sum_{k=1}^{N} a^{ik} \sum_{m=1}^{N} a^{jm} C_{Y_kY_m} \tag{5.5-10}$$

Since $C_{X_iX_j}$ is the ijth element in the covariance matrix $[C_X]$ of (5.3-12) and $C_{Y_kY_m}$ is the kmth element in the covariance matrix of the new variables Y_i, which we denote $[C_Y]$, (5.5-10) can be written in the form

$$[C_X] = [T]^{-1}[C_Y]([T]^t)^{-1} \tag{5.5-11}$$

---

† We represent the magnitude of the determinant of a matrix by $||[\cdot]||$.

Here $[T]'$ represents the transpose of $[T]$. The inverse of (5.5-11) is

$$[C_X]^{-1} = [T]'[C_Y]^{-1}[T] \qquad (5.5\text{-}12)$$

which has a determinant

$$|[C_X]^{-1}| = |[C_Y]^{-1}||[T]|^2 \qquad (5.5\text{-}13)$$

On substitution of (5.5-13) and (5.5-12) into (5.3-12):

$$f_{X_1,\dots,X_N}(x_1 = T_1^{-1}, \dots, x_N = T_N^{-1})$$
$$= \frac{||[T]||[C_Y]^{-1}|^{1/2}}{(2\pi)^{N/2}} \exp\left\{ -\frac{[x - \bar{X}]'[T]'[C_Y]^{-1}[T][x - \bar{X}]}{2} \right\} \qquad (5.5\text{-}14)$$

Finally, (5.5-14) and (5.5-9) are substituted into (5.4-6), and (5.5-4) is used to obtain

$$f_{Y_1,\dots,Y_N}(y_1, \dots, y_N) = \frac{|[C_Y]^{-1}|^{1/2}}{(2\pi)^{N/2}} \exp\left\{ -\frac{[y - \bar{Y}]'[C_Y]^{-1}[y - \bar{Y}]}{2} \right\} \qquad (5.5\text{-}15)$$

This result shows that the new random variables $Y_1, Y_2, \dots, Y_N$ are jointly gaussian because (5.5-15) is of the required form.

In summary, (5.5-15) shows that a linear transformation of gaussian random variables produces gaussian random variables. The new variables have mean values

$$\bar{Y}_j = \sum_{k=1}^{N} a_{jk}\bar{X}_k \qquad (5.5\text{-}16)$$

from (5.5-1) and covariances given by the elements of the covariance matrix

$$[C_Y] = [T][C_X][T]' \qquad (5.5\text{-}17)$$

as found from (5.5-11).

Example 5.5-1 Two gaussian random variables X_1 and X_2 have zero means and variances $\sigma_{X_1}^2 = 4$ and $\sigma_{X_2}^2 = 9$. Their covariance $C_{X_1 X_2}$ equals 3. If X_1 and X_2 are linearly transformed to new variables Y_1 and Y_2 according to

$$Y_1 = X_1 - 2X_2$$
$$Y_2 = 3X_1 + 4X_2$$

we use the above results to find the means, variances, and covariance of Y_1 and Y_2.

Here

$$[T] = \begin{bmatrix} 1 & -2 \\ 3 & 4 \end{bmatrix} \quad \text{and} \quad [C_X] = \begin{bmatrix} 4 & 3 \\ 3 & 9 \end{bmatrix}$$

Since X_1 and X_2 are zero-mean and gaussian, Y_1 and Y_2 will also be zero-mean and gaussian, thus $\bar{Y}_1 = 0$ and $\bar{Y}_2 = 0$. From (5.5-17):

$$[C_Y] = [T][C_X][T]^t = \begin{bmatrix} 1 & -2 \\ 3 & 4 \end{bmatrix} \begin{bmatrix} 4 & 3 \\ 3 & 9 \end{bmatrix} \begin{bmatrix} 1 & 3 \\ -2 & 4 \end{bmatrix} = \begin{bmatrix} 28 & -66 \\ -66 & 252 \end{bmatrix}$$

Thus $\sigma_{Y_1}^2 = 28$, $\sigma_{Y_2}^2 = 252$, and $C_{Y_1 Y_2} = -66$.

★5.6 COMPUTER GENERATION OF MULTIPLE RANDOM VARIABLES

In Section 3.5 we discussed the generation of a single random variable of prescribed probability density by transformation of a random variable that was uniformly distributed on (0, 1). Here, we shall utilize results of the preceding two sections to show how some usefully-distributed random variables can be generated by computer when the generation initially requires either two uniformly distributed random variables or two gaussian variables. We describe several examples, the first based on transformation of two statistically independent random variables X_1 and X_2, both uniformly distributed on (0, 1).

One common problem in the simulation of systems by a digital computer is the generation of gaussian random variables. As a first example, we note that two statistically independent gaussian random variables Y_1 and Y_2, each with zero mean and unit variance, can be generated by the transformations (see Dillard, 1967)

$$Y_1 = T_1(X_1, X_2) = \sqrt{-2\ln(X_1)} \cos(2\pi X_2) \tag{5.6-1a}$$

$$Y_2 = T_2(X_1, X_2) = \sqrt{-2\ln(X_1)} \sin(2\pi X_2) \tag{5.6-1b}$$

It can be shown (Problem 5-65) that the joint density of Y_1 and Y_2 is

$$f_{Y_1,Y_2}(y_1, y_2) = \frac{e^{-y_1^2/2}}{\sqrt{2\pi}} \frac{e^{-y_2^2/2}}{\sqrt{2\pi}} \tag{5.6-2}$$

as it should be for statistically independent Y_1 and Y_2. Our example can be generalized to include arbitrary means and variances (Problem 5-66).

As another example, assume we start with two zero-mean, unit-variance, statistically independent gaussian random variables Y_1 and Y_2 (perhaps generated as in our first example above), and seek to transform them to two zero-mean gaussian variates W_1 and W_2 that have arbitrary variances, $\sigma_{W_1}^2$ and $\sigma_{W_2}^2$, and arbitrary correlation coefficient ρ_W. From (5.3-16) applied to W_1 and W_2, and from (5.5-17) for a linear transformation, we have

$$[C_W] = \begin{bmatrix} \sigma_{W_1}^2 & \rho_W \sigma_{W_1}\sigma_{W_2} \\ \rho_W \sigma_{W_1}\sigma_{W_2} & \sigma_{W_2}^2 \end{bmatrix} = [T][T]^t \tag{5.6-3}$$

The covariance matrix of Y_1 and Y_1 does not explicitly appear in (5.5-17) because it is a unit matrix due to the unit-variance assumption about Y_1 and Y_2. Our goal is obtained if we solve for $[T]$ that makes (5.6-3) true for arbitrarily specified $\sigma_{W_1}^2$, $\sigma_{W_2}^2$ and ρ_W. As long as $[C_W]$ is nonsingular (the usual case), $[T]$ can be expressed as a lower triangular matrix of the form

$$[T] = \begin{bmatrix} T_{11} & 0 \\ T_{21} & T_{22} \end{bmatrix} \tag{5.6-4}$$

On using (5.6-4) in (5.6-3), and solving for the elements, we have

$$T_{11} = \sigma_{W_1} \tag{5.6-5a}$$

$$T_{21} = \rho_W \sigma_{W_2} \tag{5.6-5b}$$

$$T_{22} = \sigma_{W_2}\sqrt{1 - \rho_W^2} \tag{5.6-5c}$$

The final transformations yielding W_1 and W_2 become

$$W_1 = T_{11}Y_1 = \sigma_{W_1}Y_1 \tag{5.6-6a}$$

$$W_2 = T_{21}Y_1 + T_{22}Y_2 = \rho_W \sigma_{W_2}Y_1 + \sigma_{W_2}\sqrt{1 - \rho_W^2}\, Y_2 \tag{5.6-6b}$$

from the *form* of (5.5-4). Thus, if zero-mean, unit-variance, statistically independent gaussian random variables Y_1 and Y_2 are transformed according to (5.6-6), then W_1 and W_2 are correlated gaussian random variables having zero means, respective variances of $\sigma_{W_1}^2$ and $\sigma_{W_2}^2$, and correlation coefficient ρ_W.

If arbitrary means $\bar{W}_1$ and $\bar{W}_2$ are desired for W_1 and W_2 in the preceding example, we only need to add these to the right sides of (5.6-6):

$$W_1 = \bar{W}_1 + \sigma_{W_1}Y_1 \tag{5.6-7a}$$

$$W_2 = \bar{W}_2 + \rho_W \sigma_{W_2}Y_1 + \sigma_{W_2}\sqrt{1 - \rho_W^2}\, Y_2 \tag{5.6-7b}$$

The foregoing transformations can be extended to generate any number of zero-mean correlated gaussian random variables by tranforming the same number of zero-mean, unit-variance, independent gaussian random variables. For N random variables, $[C_W]$ becomes an $N \times N$ specified (arbitrary) symmetric matrix and the form of (5.6-3) again applies. The elements of $[T]$ can be found from the Cholesky method of factoring matrices, as described in Ralston and Wilf (1967).

As a final example, suppose two statistically independent gaussian random variables W_1 and W_2, with respective means $\bar{W}_1$ and $\bar{W}_2$ and variances both equal to σ^2, are subjected to the transformations

$$R = T_1(W_1, W_2) = \sqrt{W_1^2 + W_2^2} \tag{5.6-8}$$

$$\Theta = T_2(W_1, W_2) = \tan^{-1}(W_2/W_1) \tag{5.6-9}$$

From the inverse transformations

$$W_1 = T_1^{-1}(R, \Theta) = R \cos(\Theta) \tag{5.6-10}$$

$$W_2 = T_2^{-1}(R, \Theta) = R \sin(\Theta) \tag{5.6-11}$$

and the use of (5.4-4), we find the Jacobian equals R. Since

$$f_{W_1, W_2}(w_1, w_2) = \frac{1}{2\pi\sigma^2} e^{-[(w_1 - \bar{W}_1)^2 + (w_2 - \bar{W}_2)^2]/(2\sigma^2)} \tag{5.6-12}$$

(5.4-6) yields

$$f_{R, \Theta}(r, \theta) = \frac{ru(r)}{2\pi\sigma^2} \exp\left\{-\left[[r\cos(\theta) - \bar{W}_1]^2 + [r\sin(\theta) - \bar{W}_2]^2\right]/(2\sigma^2)\right\}$$

$$= \frac{ru(r)}{2\pi\sigma^2} \exp\left\{-\frac{1}{2\sigma^2}[r^2 + (\bar{W}_1^2 + \bar{W}_2^2) - 2r\bar{W}_1\cos(\theta) - 2r\bar{W}_2\sin(\theta)]\right\} \tag{5.6-13}$$

where $u(r)$ is the unit-step function. If we now define

$$A_0 = \sqrt{\bar{W}_1^2 + \bar{W}_2^2} \tag{5.6-14}$$

$$\theta_0 = \tan^{-1}(\bar{W}_2/\bar{W}_1) \tag{5.6-15}$$

(5.6-13) can be written as

$$f_{R, \Theta}(r, \theta) = \frac{ru(r)}{2\pi\sigma^2} \exp\left\{-\frac{1}{2\sigma^2}[r^2 + A_0^2 - 2rA_0\cos(\theta - \theta_0)]\right\} \tag{5.6-16}$$

Equation (5.6-16) is our principal result. It is important in system simulations because it is the joint density of the envelope (R) and phase (θ) of the sum of a sinusoidal signal (with peak amplitude A_0 and phase θ_0) and a zero-mean gaussian *bandpass* noise of power σ^2. This density is developed further in Section 10.6.

*5.7 COMPLEX RANDOM VARIABLES

A *complex random variable* Z can be defined in terms of real random variables X and Y by

$$Z = X + jY \tag{5.7-1}$$

where $j = \sqrt{-1}$. In considering expected values involving Z, the joint density of X and Y must be used. For instance, if $g(\cdot)$ is some function (real or complex) of Z, the expected value of $g(Z)$ is obtained from

$$E[g(Z)] = \int_{-\infty}^{\infty} \int_{-\infty}^{\infty} g(z)f_{X,Y}(x, y)\, dx\, dy \tag{5.7-2}$$

Various important quantities such as the mean value and variance are obtained through application of (5.7-2). The mean value of Z is

$$\bar{Z} = E[Z] = E[X] + jE[Y] = \bar{X} + j\bar{Y} \tag{5.7-3}$$

The variance σ_Z^2 of Z is defined as the mean value of the function $g(Z) = |Z - E[Z]|^2$; that is,

$$\sigma_Z^2 = E[|Z - E[Z]|^2] \tag{5.7-4}$$

Equation (5.7-2) can be extended to include functions of two random variables

$$Z_m = X_m + jY_m \tag{5.7-5}$$

and

$$Z_n = X_n + jY_n \tag{5.7-6}$$

$n \neq m$, if expectation is taken with respect to four random variables X_m, Y_m, X_n, Y_n through their joint density function $f_{X_m, Y_m, X_n, Y_n}(x_m, y_m, x_n, y_n)$. If this density satisfies

$$f_{X_m, Y_m, X_n, Y_n}(x_m, y_m, x_n, y_n) = f_{X_m, Y_m}(x_m, y_m) f_{X_n, Y_n}(x_n, y_n) \tag{5.7-7}$$

then Z_m and Z_n are called *statistically independent*. The extension to N random variables is straightforward.

The *correlation* and *covariance* of Z_m and Z_n are defined by

$$R_{Z_m Z_n} = E[Z_m^* Z_n] \qquad n \neq m \tag{5.7-8}$$

and

$$C_{Z_m Z_n} = E[\{Z_m - E[Z_m]\}^* \{Z_n - E[Z_n]\}] \qquad n \neq m \tag{5.7-9}$$

respectively, where the superscripted asterisk* represents the complex conjugate. If the covariance is 0, Z_m and Z_n are said to be *uncorrelated random variables*. By setting (5.7-9) to 0, we find that

$$R_{Z_m Z_n} = E[Z_m^*]E[Z_n] \qquad m \neq n \tag{5.7-10}$$

for uncorrelated random variables. Statistical independence is sufficient to guarantee that Z_m and Z_n are uncorrelated.

Finally, we note that two complex random variables are called *orthogonal* if their correlation, given by (5.7-8), equals 0.

PROBLEMS

5-1 Random variables X and Y have the joint density

$$f_{X,Y}(x, y) = \begin{cases} \dfrac{1}{24} & 0 < x < 6 \quad \text{and} \quad 0 < y < 4 \\ 0 & \text{elsewhere} \end{cases}$$

What is the expected value of the function $g(X, Y) = (XY)^2$?

5-2 Extend Problem 5-1 by finding the expected value of $g(X_1, X_2, X_3, X_4) = X_1^{n_1} X_2^{n_2} X_3^{n_3} X_4^{n_4}$, where n_1, n_2, n_3, and n_4 are integers ≥ 0 and

$$f_{X_1, X_2, X_3, X_4}(x_1, x_2, x_3, x_4) = \begin{cases} \dfrac{1}{abcd} & 0 < x_1 < a \text{ and } 0 < x_2 < b \text{ and } 0 < x_3 < c \\ & \text{and } 0 < x_4 < d \\ 0 & \text{elsewhere} \end{cases}$$

5-3 The density function of two random variables X and Y is

$$f_{X,Y}(x, y) = u(x)u(y)16e^{-4(x+y)}$$

Find the mean value of the function

$$g(X, Y) = \begin{cases} 5 & 0 < X \leq \dfrac{1}{2} \quad \text{and} \quad 0 < Y \leq \dfrac{1}{2} \\ -1 & \dfrac{1}{2} < X \quad \text{and/or} \quad \dfrac{1}{2} < Y \\ 0 & \text{all other } X \text{ and } Y \end{cases}$$

5-4 For the random variables in Problem 5-3, find the mean value of the function

$$g(X, Y) = e^{-2(X^2 + Y^2)}$$

5-5 Three statistically independent random variables X_1, X_2, and X_3 have mean values $\bar{X}_1 = 3$, $\bar{X}_2 = 6$, and $\bar{X}_3 = -2$. Find the mean values of the following functions:
(a) $g(X_1, X_2, X_3) = X_1 + 3X_2 + 4X_3$
(b) $g(X_1, X_2, X_3) = X_1 X_2 X_3$
(c) $g(X_1, X_2, X_3) = -2X_1 X_2 - 3X_1 X_3 + 4X_2 X_3$
(d) $g(X_1, X_2, X_3) = X_1 + X_2 + X_3$

5-6 Find the mean value of the function

$$g(X, Y) = X^2 + Y^2$$

where X and Y are random variables defined by the density function

$$f_{X,Y}(x, y) = \frac{e^{-(x^2 + y^2)/2\sigma^2}}{2\pi\sigma^2}$$

with σ^2 a constant.

5-7 Two statistically independent random variables X and Y have mean values $\bar{X} = E[X] = 2$ and $\bar{Y} = E[Y] = 4$. They have second moments $\overline{X^2} = E[X^2] = 8$ and $\overline{Y^2} = E[Y^2] = 25$. Find:
(a) the mean value   (b) the second moment and
(c) the variance of the random variable $W = 3X - Y$.

5-8 Two random variables X and Y have means $\bar{X} = 1$ and $\bar{Y} = 2$, variances $\sigma_X^2 = 4$ and $\sigma_Y^2 = 1$, and a correlation coefficient $\rho_{XY} = 0.4$. New random variables W and V are defined by

$$V = -X + 2Y \qquad W = X + 3Y$$

Find:
(a) the means   (b) the variances   (c) the correlation and
(d) the correlation coefficient ρ_{VW} of V and W.

5-9 Two random variables X and Y are related by the expression

$$Y = aX + b$$

where a and b are any real numbers.

(a) Show that their correlation coefficient is

$$\rho = \begin{cases} 1 & \text{if } a > 0 \text{ for any } b \\ -1 & \text{if } a < 0 \text{ for any } b \end{cases}$$

(b) Show that their covariance is

$$C_{XY} = a\sigma_X^2$$

where σ_X^2 is the variance of X.

★5-10 Show that the correlation coefficient satisfies the expression

$$|\rho| = \frac{|\mu_{11}|}{\sqrt{\mu_{02}\mu_{20}}} \le 1$$

5-11 Find all the second-order moments and central moments for the density function given in Problem 5-3.

5-12 Random variables X and Y have the joint density function

$$f_{X,Y}(x, y) = \begin{cases} (x + y)^2/40 & -1 < x < 1 \quad \text{and} \quad -3 < y < 3 \\ 0 & \text{elsewhere} \end{cases}$$

(a) Find all the second-order moments of X and Y.

(b) What are the variances of X and Y?

(c) What is the correlation coefficient?

5-13 Find all the third-order moments by using (5.1-5) for X and Y defined in Problem 5-12.

5-14 For discrete random variables X and Y, show that:

(a) Joint moments are

$$m_{nk} = \sum_{i=1}^{N} \sum_{j=1}^{M} P(x_i, y_j)x_i^n y_j^k$$

(b) Joint central moments are

$$\mu_{nk} = \sum_{i=1}^{N} \sum_{j=1}^{M} P(x_i, y_j)(x_i - \bar{X})^n(y_j - \bar{Y})^k$$

where $P(x_i, y_j) = P\{X = x_i, Y = y_j\}$, X has N possible values x_i, and Y has M possible values y_j.

5-15 For two random variables X and Y:

$$f_{X,Y}(x, y) = 0.15\delta(x + 1)\delta(y) + 0.1\delta(x)\delta(y) + 0.1\delta(x)\delta(y - 2)$$
$$+ 0.4\delta(x - 1)\delta(y + 2) + 0.2\delta(x - 1)\delta(y - 1) + 0.05\delta(x - 1)\delta(y - 3)$$

Find: (a) the correlation, (b) the covariance, and (c) the correlation coefficient of X and Y.

(d) Are X and Y either uncorrelated or orthogonal?

5-16 Discrete random variables X and Y have the joint density

$$f_{X,Y}(x, y) = 0.4\delta(x + \alpha)\delta(y - 2) + 0.3\delta(x - \alpha)\delta(y - 2)$$
$$+ 0.1\delta(x - \alpha)\delta(y - \alpha) + 0.2\delta(x - 1)\delta(y - 1)$$

Determine the value of α, if any, that minimizes the correlation between X and Y and find the minimum correlation. Are X and Y orthogonal?

5-17 For two discrete random variables X and Y:

$$f_{X,Y}(x, y) = 0.3\delta(x - \alpha)\delta(y - \alpha) + 0.5\delta(x + \alpha)\delta(y - 4) + 0.2\delta(x + 2)\delta(y + 2)$$

Determine the value of α, if any, that minimizes the covariance of X and Y. Find the minimum covariance. Are X and Y uncorrelated?

5-18 The density function

$$f_{X,Y}(x, y) = \begin{cases} \dfrac{xy}{9} & 0 < x < 2 \quad \text{and} \quad 0 < y < 3 \\ 0 & \text{elsewhere} \end{cases}$$

applies to two random variables X and Y.

(a) Show, by use of (5.1-6) and (5.1-7), that X and Y are uncorrelated.

(b) Show that X and Y are also statistically independent.

5-19 Two random variables X and Y have the density function

$$f_{X,Y}(x, y) = \begin{cases} \dfrac{2}{43}(x + 0.5y)^2 & 0 < x < 2 \quad \text{and} \quad 0 < y < 3 \\ 0 & \text{elsewhere} \end{cases}$$

(a) Find all the first- and second-order moments.

(b) Find the covariance.

(c) Are X and Y uncorrelated?

5-20 Define random variables V and W by

$$V = X + aY$$
$$W = X - aY$$

where a is a real number and X and Y are random variables. Determine a in terms of moments of X and Y such that V and W are orthogonal.

★5-21 If X and Y in Problems 5-20 are gaussian, show that W and V are statistically independent if $a^2 = \sigma_X^2/\sigma_Y^2$, where σ_X^2 and σ_Y^2 are the variances of X and Y, respectively.

5-22 Three uncorrelated random variables X_1, X_2, and X_3 have means $\bar{X}_1 = 1$, $\bar{X}_2 = -3$, and $\bar{X}_3 = 1.5$ and second moments $E[X_1^2] = 2.5$, $E[X_2^2] = 11$, and $E[X_3^2] = 3.5$. Let $Y = X_1 - 2X_2 + 3X_3$ be a new random variable and find:

(a) the mean value,   (b) the variance of Y.

5-23 Given $W = (aX + 3Y)^2$ where X and Y are zero-mean random variables with variances $\sigma_X^2 = 4$ and $\sigma_Y^2 = 16$. Their correlation coefficient is $\rho = -0.5$.
(a) Find a value for the parameter a that minimizes the mean value of W.
(b) Find the minimum mean value.

★5-24 Find the joint characteristic function for X and Y defined in Problem 5-3.

★5-25 Show that the joint characteristic function of N independent random variables X_i, having characteristic functions $\Phi_{X_i}(\omega_i)$ is

$$\Phi_{X_1,\ldots,X_N}(\omega_1,\ldots,\omega_N) = \prod_{i=1}^{N} \Phi_{X_i}(\omega_i)$$

★5-26 For N random variables, show that

$$|\Phi_{X_1,\ldots,X_N}(\omega_1,\ldots,\omega_N)| \le \Phi_{X_1,\ldots,X_N}(0,\ldots,0) = 1$$

★5-27 For two zero-mean gaussian random variables X and Y, show that their joint characteristic function is

$$\Phi_{X,Y}(\omega_1,\omega_2) = \exp\{-\tfrac{1}{2}[\sigma_X^2\omega_1^2 + 2\rho\sigma_X\sigma_Y\omega_1\omega_2 + \sigma_Y^2\omega_2^2]\}$$

★5-28 Zero-mean gaussian random variables X and Y have variances $\sigma_X^2 = 3$ and $\sigma_Y^2 = 4$, respectively, and a correlation coefficient $\rho = -\tfrac{1}{4}$.
(a) Write an expression for the joint density function.
(b) Show that a rotation of coordinates through the angle given by (5.3-11) will produce new statistically independent random variables.

★5-29 Find the conditional density functions $f_X(x\,|\,Y = y)$ and $f_Y(y\,|\,X = x)$ applicable to two gaussian random variables X and Y defined by (5.3-1) and show that they are also gaussian.

★5-30 Zero-mean gaussian random variables X_1, X_2, and X_3 having a covariance matrix

$$[C_X] = \begin{bmatrix} 4 & 2.05 & 1.05 \\ 2.05 & 4 & 2.05 \\ 1.05 & 2.05 & 4 \end{bmatrix}$$

are transformed to new variables

$$Y_1 = 5X_1 + 2X_2 - X_3$$
$$Y_2 = -X_1 + 3X_2 + X_3$$
$$Y_3 = 2X_1 - X_2 + 2X_3$$

(a) Find the covariance matrix of Y_1, Y_2, and Y_3.
(b) Write an expression for the joint density function of Y_1, Y_2, and Y_3.

★5-31 A complex random variable Z is defined by

$$Z = \cos(X) + j\sin(Y)$$

where X and Y are independent real random variables uniformly distributed from $-\pi$ to π.
(a) Find the mean value of Z.
(b) Find the variance of Z.

ADDITIONAL PROBLEMS, SECOND EDITION

5-32 Two random variables have a uniform density on a circular region defined by

$$f_{X,Y}(x, y) = \begin{cases} 1/\pi r^2 & x^2 + y^2 \le r^2 \\ 0 & \text{elsewhere} \end{cases}$$

Find the mean value of the function $g(X, Y) = X^2 + Y^2$.

$\star$**5-33** Define the conditional expected value of a function $g(X, Y)$ of random variables X and Y as

$$E[g(X, Y)|B] = \int_{-\infty}^{\infty} \int_{-\infty}^{\infty} g(x, y) f_{X,Y}(x, y|B) \, dx \, dy$$

(a) If event B is defined as $B = \{y_a < Y \le y_b\}$, where $y_a < y_b$ are constants, evaluate $E[g(X, Y)|B]$. (*Hint:* Use results of Problem 4-55.)

(b) If B is defined by $B = \{Y = y\}$ what does the conditional expected value of part (a) become?

5-34 For random variables X and Y having $\bar{X} = 1$, $\bar{Y} = 2$, $\sigma_X^2 = 6$, $\sigma_Y^2 = 9$ and $\rho = -2/3$, find (a) the covariance of X and Y, (b) the correlation of X and Y, and (c) the moments m_{20} and m_{02}.

5-35 $\bar{X} = 1/2$, $\overline{X^2} = 5/2$, $\bar{Y} = 2$, $\overline{Y^2} = 19/2$, and $C_{XY} = -1/(2\sqrt{3})$ for random variables X and Y.

(a) Find σ_X^2, σ_Y^2, R_{XY}, and ρ.

(b) What is the mean value of the random variable $W = (X + 3Y)^2 + 2X + 3$?

5-36 Let X and Y be statistically independent random variables with $\bar{X} = 3/4$, $\overline{X^2} = 4$, $\bar{Y} = 1$, and $\overline{Y^2} = 5$. For a random variable $W = X - 2Y + 1$ find (a) R_{XY}, (b) R_{XW}, (c) R_{YW}, and (d) C_{XY}. (e) Are X and Y uncorrelated?

5-37 Statistically independent random variables X and Y have moments $m_{10} = 2$, $m_{20} = 14$, $m_{02} = 12$, and $m_{11} = -6$. Find the moment μ_{22}.

5-38 A joint density is given as

$$f_{X,Y}(x, y) = \begin{cases} x(y + 1.5) & 0 < x < 1 \quad \text{and} \quad 0 < y < 1 \\ 0 & \text{elsewhere} \end{cases}$$

Find all the joint moments m_{nk}, n and $k = 0, 1, \ldots$.

5-39 Find all the joint central moments μ_{nk}, n and $k = 0, 1, \ldots$, for the density of Problem 5-38.

$\star$**5-40** Find the joint characteristic function for random variables X and Y defined by

$$f_{X,Y}(x, y) = (1/2\pi) \text{ rect } (x/\pi) \text{ rect } [(x + y)/\pi] \cos (x + y)$$

Use the result to find the marginal characteristic functions of X and Y.

★5-41 Random variables X_1 and X_2 have the joint characteristic function

$$\Phi_{X_1, X_2}(\omega_1, \omega_2) = [(1 - j2\omega_1)(1 - j2\omega_2)]^{-N/2}$$

where $N > 0$ is an integer.
(a) Find the correlation and moments m_{20} and m_{02}.
(b) Determine the means of X_1 and X_2.
(c) What is the correlation coefficient?

★5-42 The joint probability density of two discrete random variables X and Y consists of impulses located at all lattice points (mb, nd), where $m = 0, 1, \ldots, M$ and $n = 1, 2, \ldots, N$ with $b > 0$ and $d > 0$ being constants. All possible points are equally probable. Determine the joint characteristic function.

★5-43 Let $X_k, k = 1, 2, \ldots, K$, be statistically independent Poisson random variables, each with its own variance b_k (Problem 3-16). Show that the sum $X = X_1 + X_2 + \cdots + X_K$ is a Poisson random variable. (*Hint:* Use results of Problems 5-25 and 3-53.)

5-44 Assume $\sigma_X = \sigma_Y = \sigma$ in (5.3-1) and show that the locus of the maximum of the joint density is a line passing through the point $(\bar{X}, \bar{Y})$ with slope $\pi/4$ (or $-\pi/4$) when $\rho = 1$ (or -1).

5-45 Two gaussian random variables X and Y have variances $\sigma_X^2 = 9$ and $\sigma_Y^2 = 4$, respectively, and correlation coefficient ρ. It is known that a coordinate rotation by an angle $-\pi/8$ results in new random variables Y_1 and Y_2 that are uncorrelated. What is ρ?

★5-46 Let X and Y be jointly gaussian random variables where $\sigma_X^2 = \sigma_Y^2$ and $\rho = -1$. Find a transformation matrix such that new random variables Y_1 and Y_2 are statistically independent.

★5-47 Random variables X and Y having the joint density

$$f_{X,Y}(x, y) = (^8/_3)u(x - 2)u(y - 1)xy^2 \exp(4 - 2xy)$$

undergo a transformation

$$[T] = \begin{bmatrix} 1 & 1 \\ 1 & -1 \end{bmatrix}$$

to generate new random variables Y_1 and Y_2.
(a) Find the joint density of Y_1 and Y_2.
(b) Show what points in the $y_1 y_2$ plane correspond to a nonzero value of the new density.

★5-48 Equation (5.4-5) can sometimes be used to find the density of a single function of several random variables if *auxiliary random variables* are used. Apply the idea to finding the density function of $Z = aXY$, where a is a constant and X and Y are random variables, by defining the auxiliary variable $W = X$.

★5-49 Apply the method of Problem 5-48 to finding the density function of $Z = bY/X$, with b a constant, when using the auxiliary variable $W = X$.

★5-50 Two gaussian random variables X_1 and X_2 are defined by the mean and covariance matrices

$$[\bar{X}] = \begin{bmatrix} 2 \\ -1 \end{bmatrix} \quad [C_X] = \begin{bmatrix} 5 & -2/\sqrt{5} \\ -2/\sqrt{5} & 4 \end{bmatrix}$$

Two new random variables Y_1 and Y_2 are formed using the transformation

$$[T] = \begin{bmatrix} 1 & {}^1\!/_2 \\ {}^1\!/_2 & 1 \end{bmatrix}$$

Find matrices (a) $[\bar{Y}]$ and (b) $[C_Y]$. (c) Also find the correlation coefficient of Y_1 and Y_2.

★5-51 Complex random variables Z_1 and Z_2 have zero means. The correlation of the real parts of Z_1 and Z_2 is 4, while the correlation of the imaginary parts is 6. The real part of Z_1 and the imaginary part of Z_2 are statistically independent as a pair, as are the imaginary part of Z_1 and the real part of Z_2.
(a) What is the correlation of Z_1 and Z_2?
(b) Are Z_1 and Z_2 statistically independent?

ADDITIONAL PROBLEMS, THIRD EDITION

5-52 Random variables X and Y are defined by the joint density of Problem 4-69. Find all first- and second-order joint moments for these random variables. Are X and Y orthogonal? Are they uncorrelated?

5-53 In a control system, a random voltage X is known to have a mean value $\bar{X} = m_1 = -2$ V and a second moment $\overline{X^2} = m_2 = 9$ V^2. If the voltage X is amplified by an amplifier that gives an output $Y = -1.5X + 2$, find σ_X^2, $\bar{Y}$, $\overline{Y^2}$, σ_Y^2, and R_{XY}.

5-54 Two random variables X and Y are defined by $\bar{X} = 0$, $\bar{Y} = -1$, $\overline{X^2} = 2$, $\overline{Y^2} = 4$, and $R_{XY} = -2$. Two new random variables W and U are:

$$W = 2X + Y$$
$$U = -X - 3Y.$$

Find $\bar{W}$, $\bar{U}$, $\overline{W^2}$, $\overline{U^2}$, R_{WU}, σ_X^2, and σ_Y^2.

5-55 Statistically independent random variables X and Y have respective means $\bar{X} = 1$ and $\bar{Y} = -1/2$. Their second moments are $\overline{X^2} = 4$ and $\overline{Y^2} = 11/4$. Another random variable is defined as $W = 3X^2 + 2Y + 1$. Find σ_X^2, σ_Y^2, R_{XY}, C_{XY}, $\bar{W}$, and R_{WY}.

5-56 Determine the correlation R_{XY} and correlation coefficient for the random variables defined in Problem 4-76.

★ **5-57** Show that the sum X of N statistically independent Poisson random variables X_i, with different means b_i, is also a Poisson random variable but its mean is $b = b_1 + b_2 + \cdots + b_N$. [*Hint:* Use (5.2-7) and the result of Problem 5-25.]

★ **5-58** Show that the sum of N identically distributed statistically independent exponential random variables X_i, as given by (2.5-9) with $a = 0$ and b replaced by $1/a$, is an Erlang random variable, as defined in Problem 3-54 and in Appendix F. [*Hint:* Use (5.2-7) and the result of Problem 5-25.]

★ **5-59** The chi-square random variable with one degree of freedom is defined by the density

$$f_X(x) = \frac{u(x)e^{-x/2}}{\Gamma(1/2)\sqrt{2x}}$$

where $\Gamma(1/2)$ is a constant approximately equal to 1.772. Show that the sum X of N identically distributed statistcally independent chi-square random variables, each with one degree of freedom, is a chi-square random variable with N degrees of freedom as defined in Problem 3-49 and Appendix F [see (F-35) through (F-39)]. [*Hint:* Use (5.2-7) and the result of Problem 5-25].

5-60 Gaussian random variables X and Y have first- and second-order moments $\bar{X} = -1.0$, $\overline{X^2} = 1.16$, $\bar{Y} = 1.5$, $\overline{Y^2} = 2.89$, and $R_{XY} = -1.724$. Find: (a) C_{XY} and (b) ρ. Also find the angle θ of a coordinate rotation that will generate new random variables that are statistically independent.

5-61 Suppose the annual snowfalls (accumulated depths in meters) for two nearby alpine ski resorts are adequately represented by jointly gaussian random variables X and Y, for which $\rho = 0.82$, $\sigma_X = 1.5 \, \text{m}$, $\sigma_Y = 1.2 \, \text{m}$, and $R_{XY} = 81.476 \, \text{m}^2$. If the average snowfall at one resort is 10 m what is the average at the other resort?

5-62 Two gaussian random variables X and Y have a correlation coefficient $\rho = 0.25$. The standard deviation of X is 1.9. A linear transformation (coordinate rotation of $\pi/6$) is known to transform X and Y to new random variables that are statistically independent. What is σ_Y^2?

★ **5-63** Gaussian random variables X_1 and X_2, for which $\bar{X}_1 = 2$, $\sigma_{X_1}^2 = 9$, $\bar{X}_2 = -1$, $\sigma_{X_2}^2 = 4$, and $C_{X_1X_2} = -3$, are transformed to new random variables Y_1 and Y_2 according to

$$Y_1 = -X_1 + X_2$$
$$Y_2 = -2X_1 - 3X_2.$$

Find: (a) $\overline{X_1^2}$, (b) $\overline{X_2^2}$, (c) $\rho_{X_1X_2}$, (d) $\sigma_{Y_1}^2$, (e) $\sigma_{Y_2}^2$, and (f) $C_{Y_1Y_2}$.

★ **5-64** Three random variables X_1, X_2, and X_3 represent samples of a random noise voltage taken at three times. Their covariance matrix is defined by

$$[C_X] = \begin{bmatrix} 3.0 & 1.8 & 1.1 \\ 1.8 & 3.0 & 1.8 \\ 1.1 & 1.8 & 3.0 \end{bmatrix}.$$

A transformation matrix

$$[T] = \begin{bmatrix} 4 & -1 & -2 \\ 2 & 2 & 1 \\ -3 & -1 & 3 \end{bmatrix}$$

converts the variables to new random variables Y_1, Y_2, and Y_3. Find the covariance matrix of the new random variables.

★**5-65** Show that (5.6-2) results from the transformations of (5.6-1).

★**5-66** Extend the text and show that (5.6-1) can be replaced by

$$Y_1 = T_1(X_1, X_2) = \bar{Y}_1 + \sqrt{-2\sigma_{Y_1}^2 \ln(X_1)} \cos(2\pi X_2)$$

$$Y_2 = T_2(X_1, X_2) = \bar{Y}_2 + \sqrt{-2\sigma_{Y_2}^2 \ln(X_1)} \sin(2\pi X_2)$$

to generate statistically independent gaussian random variables Y_1 and Y_2, with respective means $\bar{Y}_1$ and $\bar{Y}_2$, and respective variances $\sigma_{Y_1}^2$ and $\sigma_{Y_2}^2$.

★**5-67** Extend the text that leads to (5.6-7) and find transformations of two statistically independent random variables X_1 and X_2, both uniform on (0, 1), that will directly create two correlated gaussian random variables W_1 and W_2 having correlation coefficient ρ_W, means $\bar{W}_1$ and $\bar{W}_2$, and variances $\sigma_{W_1}^2$ and $\sigma_{W_2}^2$.

★**5-68** Work Problem 5-67, except generate the random variables R and Θ for which (5.6-16) applies.

CHAPTER

6

RANDOM PROCESSES

6.0 INTRODUCTION

In the real world of engineering and science, it is necessary that we be able to deal with time waveforms. Indeed, we frequently encounter *random* time waveforms in practical systems. More often than not, a *desired* signal in some system is random. For example, the bit stream in a binary communication system is a random message because each bit in the stream occurs randomly. On the other hand, a desired signal is often accompanied by an *undesired* random waveform, noise. The noise interferes with the message and ultimately limits the performance of the system. Thus, any hope we have of determining the performance of systems with random waveforms hinges on our ability to describe and deal with such waveforms. In this chapter we introduce concepts that allow the description of random waveforms in a probabilistic sense.

6.1 THE RANDOM PROCESS CONCEPT

The concept of a random process is based on enlarging the random variable concept to include time. Since a random variable X is, by its definition, a function of the possible outcomes s of an experiment, it now becomes a function of both s and time. In other words, we assign, according to some rule, a time function

$$x(t, s) \tag{6.1-1}$$

to every outcome s. The family of all such functions, denoted $X(t, s)$, is called a *random process*. As with random variables where x was denoted as a specific value of the random variable X, we shall often use the convenient short-form notation $x(t)$ to represent a specific waveform of a random process denoted by $X(t)$.

Clearly, a random process $X(t, s)$ represents a family or *esemble* of time functions when t and s are variables. Figure 6.1-1 illustrates a few members of an ensemble. Each member time function is called a *sample function, ensemble member*, or sometimes a *realization* of the process. Thus, a random process also represents a *single* time function when t is a variable and s is fixed at a specific value (outcome).

A random process also represents a random variable when t is fixed and s is a variable. For example, the random variable $X(t_1, s) = X(t_1)$ is obtained from the process when time is "frozen" at the value t_1. We often use the notation X_1 to denote the random variable associated with the process $X(t)$ at time t_1. X_1 corresponds to a vertical "slice" through the ensemble at time t_1, as illustrated in Figure 6.1-1. The statistical properties of $X_1 = X(t_1)$ describe the statistical properties of the random process at time t_1. The expected value of X_1 is called the *ensemble average* as well as the expected or mean value of the random process

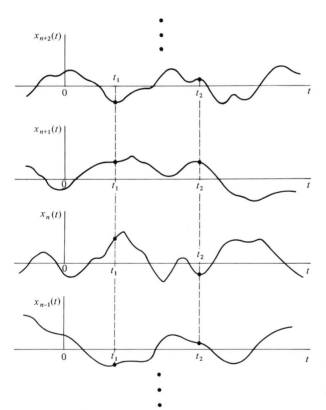

FIGURE 6.1-1
A continuous random process. [*Reproduced from Peebles (1976) with permission of publishers Addison–Wesley, Advanced Book Program.*]

(at time t_1). Since t_1 may have various values, the mean value of a process may not be constant; in general, it may be a function of time. We easily visualize any number of random variables X_i derived from a random process $X(t)$ at times t_i, $i = 1, 2, \ldots$:

$$X_i = X(t_i, s) = X(t_i) \qquad (6.1\text{-}2)$$

A random process can also represent a mere number when t and s are both fixed.

Classification of Processes

It is convenient to classify random processes according to the characteristics of t and the random variable $X = X(t)$ at time t. We shall consider only four cases based on t and X having values in the ranges $-\infty < t < \infty$ and $-\infty < x < \infty$.†

If X is continuous and t can have any of a continuum of values, then $X(t)$ is called a *continuous random process*. Figure 6.1-1 is an illustration of this class of process. Thermal noise generated by any realizable network is a practical example of a waveform that is modeled as a sample function of a continuous random process. In this example, the network is the outcome in the underlying random experiment of selecting a network. (The presumption is that many networks are available from which to choose; this may not be the case in the real world, but it should not prevent us from imagining a production line producing any number of similar networks.) Each network establishes a sample function, and all sample functions form the process.‡

A second class of random process, called a *discrete random process*, corresponds to the random variable X having only discrete values while t is continuous. Figure 6.1-2 illustrates such a process derived by heavily limiting the sample functions shown in Figure 6.1-1. The sample functions have only two discrete values: the positive level is generated whenever a sample function in Figure 6.1-1 is positive and the negative level occurs for other times.

A random process for which X is continuous but time has only discrete values is called a *continuous random sequence* (Thomas, 1969, p. 80). Such a sequence can be formed by periodically sampling the ensemble members of Figure 6.1-1. The result is illustrated in Figure 6.1-3.

A fourth class of random process, called a *discrete random sequence*, corresponds to both time and the random variable being discrete. Figure 6.1-4 illustrates a discrete random sequence developed by sampling the sample functions of Figure 6.1-2.

---

† Other cases can be defined based on a definition of random processes on a finite time interval (see for example: Rosenblatt (1974), p. 91; Prabhu (1965), p. 1; Miller (1974), p. 31; Parzen (1962), p. 7; Dubes (1968), p. 320; Ross (1972), p. 56). Other recent texts on random processes are Helstrom (1984), and Gray and Davisson (1986).

‡ Note that finding the mean value of the process at any time t is equivalent to finding the average voltage that would be produced by all the various networks at time t.

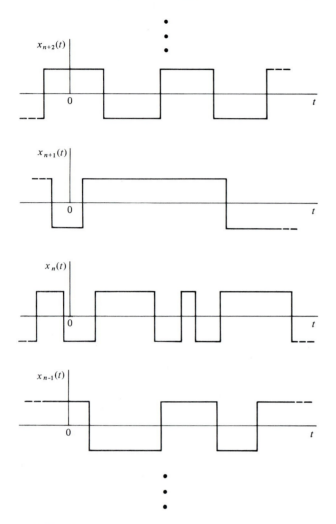

FIGURE 6.1-2

A discrete random process formed by heavily limiting the waveforms of figure 6.1-1. [*Reproduced from Peebles (1976) with permission of publishers Addison–Wesley, Advanced Book Program.*]

In this text we are concerned almost entirely with discrete and continuous random processes.

Deterministic and Nondeterministic Processes

In addition to the classes described above, a random process can be described by the form of its sample functions. If future values of any sample function cannot

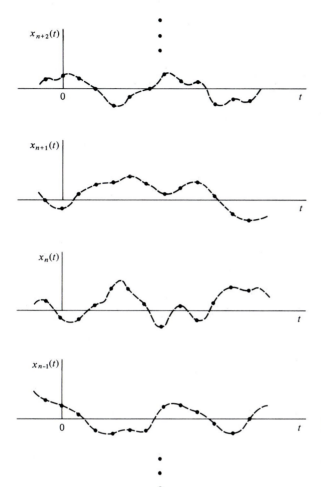

FIGURE 6.1-3
A continuous random sequence formed by sampling the waveforms of Figure 6.1-1. [*Reproduced from Peebles (1976), with permission of publishers Addison–Wesley, Advanced Book Program.*]

be predicted exactly from observed past values, the process is called *nondeterministic*. The process of Figure 6.1-1 is one example.

A process is called *deterministic* if future values of any sample function can be predicted from past values. An example is the random process defined by

$$X(t) = A \cos (\omega_0 t + \Theta) \qquad (6.1\text{-}3)$$

Here A, Θ, or ω_0 (or all) may be random variables. Any one sample function corresponds to (6.1-3) with particular values of these random variables. Therefore, knowledge of the sample function prior to any time instant automatically allows prediction of the sample function's future values because its form is known.

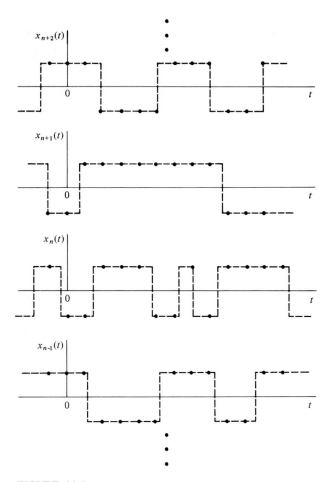

FIGURE 6.1-4

A discrete random sequence formed by sampling the waveforms of Figure 6.1-2. [*Adapted from Peebles* (1976) *with permission of publishers Addison–Wesley, Advanced Book Program.*]

6.2 STATIONARITY AND INDEPENDENCE

As previously stated, a random process becomes a random variable when time is fixed at some particular value. The random variable will possess statistical properties, such as a mean value, moments, variance, etc., that are related to its density function. If *two* random variables are obtained from the process for two time instants, they will have statistical properties (means, variances, joint moments, etc.) related to their joint density function. More generally, N random variables will possess statistical properties related to their N-dimensional joint density function.

Broadly speaking, a random process is said to be *stationary* if all its statistical properties do not change with time. Other processes are called *nonstationary*. These statements are not intended as definitions of stationarity but are meant to convey only a general meaning. More concrete definitions follow. Indeed, there are several "levels" of stationarity, all of which depend on the density functions of the random variables of the process.

Distribution and Density Functions

To define stationarity, we must first define distribution and density functions as they apply to a random process $X(t)$. For a particular time t_1, the distribution function associated with the random variable $X_1 = X(t_1)$ will be denoted $F_X(X_1; t_1)$. It is defined as†

$$F_X(x_1; t_1) = P\{X(t_1) \leq x_1\} \tag{6.2-1}$$

for any real number x_1. This is the same definition used all along for the distribution function of one random variable. Only the notation has been altered to reflect the fact that it is possibly now a function of time choice t_1.

For two random variables $X_1 = X(t_1)$ and $X_2 = X(t_2)$, the *second-order joint distribution function* is the two-dimensional extension of (6.2-1):

$$F_X(x_1, x_2; t_1, t_2) = P\{X(t_1) \leq x_1, X(t_2) \leq x_2\} \tag{6.2-2}$$

In a similar manner, for N random variables $X_i = X(t_i)$, $i = 1, 2, \ldots, N$, the *Nth-order joint distribution function* is

$$F_X(x_1, \ldots, x_N; t_1, \ldots, t_N) = P\{X(t_1) \leq x_1, \ldots, X(t_N) \leq x_N\} \tag{6.2-3}$$

Joint density functions of interest are found from appropriate derivatives of the above three relationships:‡

$$f_X(x_1; t_1) = dF_X(x_1; t_1)/dx_1 \tag{6.2-4}$$

$$f_X(x_1, x_2; t_1, t_2) = \partial^2 F_X(x_1, x_2; t_1, t_2)/(\partial x_1 \, \partial x_2) \tag{6.2-5}$$

$$f_X(x_1, \ldots, x_N; t_1, \ldots, t_N) = \partial^N F_X(x_1, \ldots, x_N; t_1, \ldots, t_N)/(\partial x_1 \cdots \partial x_N) \tag{6.2-6}$$

Statistical Independence

Two processes $X(t)$ and $Y(t)$ are *statistically independent* if the random variable group $X(t_1)$, $X(t_2)$, $\ldots$, $X(t_N)$ is independent of the group $Y(t'_1)$, $Y(t'_2)$, $\ldots$, $Y(t'_M)$ for any choice of times $t_1, t_2, \ldots, t_N, t'_1, t'_2, \ldots, t'_M$. Independence requires that the joint density be factorable by groups:

$$f_{X,Y}(x_1, \ldots, x_N, y_1, \ldots, y_M; t_1, \ldots, t_N, t'_1, \ldots, t'_M)$$
$$= f_X(x_1, \ldots, x_N; t_1, \ldots, t_N) f_Y(y_1, \ldots, y_M; t'_1, \ldots, t'_M) \tag{6.2-7}$$

---

† $F_X(x_1; t_1)$ is known as the *first-order distribution function* of the process $X(t)$.

‡ Analogous to distribution functions, these are called *first-, second-, and Nth-order density functions*, respectively.

First-Order Stationary Processes

A random process is called *stationary to order one* if its first-order density function does not change with a shift in time origin. In other words

$$f_X(x_1; t_1) = f_X(x_1; t_1 + \Delta) \tag{6.2-8}$$

must be true for any t_1 and any real number Δ if $X(t)$ is to be a first-order stationary process.

Consequences of (6.2-8) are that $f_X(x_1; t_1)$ is independent of t_1 and the process mean value $E[X(t)]$ is a constant:

$$E[X(t)] = \bar{X} = \text{constant} \tag{6.2-9}$$

To prove (6.2-9), we find mean values of the random variables $X_1 = X(t_1)$ and $X_2 = X(t_2)$. For X_1:

$$E[X_1] = E[X(t_1)] = \int_{-\infty}^{\infty} x_1 f_X(x_1; t_1) \, dx_1 \tag{6.2-10}$$

For X_2:

$$E[X_2] = E[X(t_2)] = \int_{-\infty}^{\infty} x_1 f_X(x_1; t_2) \, dx_1 \dagger \tag{6.2-11}$$

Now by letting $t_2 = t_1 + \Delta$ in (6.2-11), substituting (6.2-8), and using (6.2-10), we get

$$E[X(t_1 + \Delta)] = E[X(t_1)] \tag{6.2-12}$$

which must be a constant because t_1 and Δ are arbitrary.

Second-Order and Wide-Sense Stationarity

A process is called *stationary to order two* if its second-order density function satisfies

$$f_X(x_1, x_2; t_1, t_2) = f_X(x_1, x_2; t_1 + \Delta, t_2 + \Delta) \tag{6.2-13}$$

for all t_1, t_2, and Δ. After some thought, the reader will conclude that (6.2-13) is a function of time differences $t_2 - t_1$ and not absolute time (let arbitrary $\Delta = -t_1$). A second-order stationary process is also first-order stationary because the second-order density function determines the lower, first-order, density.

Now the correlation $E[X_1 X_2] = E[X(t_1)X(t_2)]$ of a random process will, in general, be a function of t_1 and t_2. Let us denote this function by $R_{XX}(t_1, t_2)$ and call it the *autocorrelation function* of the random process $X(t)$:

$$R_{XX}(t_1, t_2) = E[X(t_1)X(t_2)]. \tag{6.2-14}$$

---

† Note that the variable x_2 of integration has been replaced by the alternative variable x_1 for convenience.

A consequence of (6.2-13), however, is that the autocorrelation function of a second-order stationary process is a function only of time differences and not absolute time; that is, if

$$\tau = t_2 - t_1 \tag{6.2-15}$$

then (6.2-14) becomes

$$R_{XX}(t_1, t_1 + \tau) = E[X(t_1)X(t_1 + \tau)] = R_{XX}(\tau) \tag{6.2-16}$$

Proof of (6.2-16) uses (6.2-13); it is left as a reader exercise (see Problem 6-6).

Many practical problems require that we deal with the autocorrelation function and mean value of a random process. Problem solutions are greatly simplified if these quantities are not dependent on absolute time. Of course, second-order stationarity is sufficient to guarantee these characteristics. However, it is often more restrictive than necessary, and a more relaxed form of stationarity is desirable. The most useful form is the *wide-sense stationary process*, defined as that for which two conditions are true:

$$E[X(t)] = \bar{X} = \text{constant} \tag{6.2-17a}$$

$$E[X(t)X(t + \tau)] = R_{XX}(\tau) \tag{6.2-17b}$$

A process stationary to order 2 is clearly wide-sense stationary. However, the converse is not necessarily true.

Example 6.2-1 We show that the random process

$$X(t) = A \cos(\omega_0 t + \Theta)$$

is wide-sense stationary if it is assumed that A and ω_0 are constants and Θ is a uniformly distributed random variable on the interval $(0, 2\pi)$. The mean value is

$$E[X(t)] = \int_0^{2\pi} A \cos(\omega_0 t + \theta) \frac{1}{2\pi} d\theta = 0$$

The autocorrelation function, from (6.2-14) with $t_1 = t$ and $t_2 = t + \tau$, becomes

$$R_{XX}(t, t + \tau) = E[A \cos(\omega_0 t + \Theta)A \cos(\omega_0 t + \omega_0 \tau + \Theta)]$$

$$= \frac{A^2}{2} E[\cos(\omega_0 \tau) + \cos(2\omega_0 t + \omega_0 \tau + 2\Theta)]$$

$$= \frac{A^2}{2} \cos(\omega_0 \tau) + \frac{A^2}{2} E[\cos(2\omega_0 t + \omega_0 \tau + 2\Theta)]$$

The second term easily evaluates to 0. Thus, the autocorrelation function depends only on τ and the mean value is a constant, so $X(t)$ is wide-sense stationary.

When we are concerned with two random processes $X(t)$ and $Y(t)$, we say they are *jointly* wide-sense stationary if each satisfies (6.2-17) and their *cross-correlation function*, defined in general by

$$R_{XY}(t_1, t_2) = E[X(t_1)Y(t_2)] \qquad (6.2\text{-}18)$$

is a function only of time difference $\tau = t_2 - t_1$ and not absolute time; that is, if

$$R_{XY}(t, t + \tau) = E[X(t)Y(t + \tau)] = R_{XY}(\tau) \qquad (6.2\text{-}19)$$

N-Order and Strict-Sense Stationarity

By extending the above reasoning to N random variables $X_i = X(t_i), i = 1, 2, \ldots, N$, we say a random process is *stationary to order N* if its Nth-order density function is invariant to a time origin shift; that is, if

$$f_X(x_1, \ldots, x_N; t_1, \ldots, t_N) = f_X(x_1, \ldots, x_N; t_1 + \Delta, \ldots, t_N + \Delta) \qquad (6.2\text{-}20)$$

for all $t_1, \ldots, t_N$ and Δ. Stationarity of order N implies stationarity to all orders $k \leq N$. A process stationary to *all* orders $N = 1, 2, \ldots$, is called *strict-sense stationary*.

Time Averages and Ergodicity

The time average of a quantity is defined as

$$A[\cdot] = \lim_{T \to \infty} \frac{1}{2T} \int_{-T}^{T} [\cdot] \, dt \qquad (6.2\text{-}21)$$

Here A is used to denote time average in a manner analogous to E for the statistical average. Time average is taken over all time because, as applied to random processes, sample functions of processes are presumed to exist for all time.

Specific averages of interest are the mean value $\bar{x} = A[x(t)]$ of a sample function (a lower case letter is used to imply a sample function), and the *time autocorrelation function*, denoted $\mathscr{R}_{xx}(\tau) = A[x(t)x(t + \tau)]$. These functions are defined by

$$\bar{x} = A[x(t)] = \lim_{T \to \infty} \frac{1}{2T} \int_{-T}^{T} x(t) \, dt \qquad (6.2\text{-}22)$$

$$\mathscr{R}_{xx}(\tau) = A[x(t)x(t + \tau)]$$

$$= \lim_{T \to \infty} \frac{1}{2T} \int_{-T}^{T} x(t)x(t + \tau) \, dt \qquad (6.2\text{-}23)$$

For any *one* sample function of the process $X(t)$, these last two integrals simply produce two numbers (for a fixed value of τ). However, when all sample functions are considered, we see that $\bar{x}$ and $\mathscr{R}_{xx}(\tau)$ are actually *random variables*. By taking the expected value on both sides of (6.2-22) and (6.2-23), and assuming the expectation can be brought inside the integrals, we obtain†

$$E[\bar{x}] = \bar{X} \tag{6.2-24}$$

$$E[\mathscr{R}_{xx}(\tau)] = R_{XX}(\tau) \tag{6.2-25}$$

Now suppose by some theorem the random variables $\bar{x}$ and $\mathscr{R}_{xx}(\tau)$ could be made to have zero variances; that is, $\bar{x}$ and $\mathscr{R}_{xx}(\tau)$ actually become constants. Then we could write

$$\bar{x} = \bar{X} \tag{6.2-26}$$

$$\mathscr{R}_{xx}(\tau) = R_{XX}(\tau) \tag{6.2-27}$$

In other words, the time averages $\bar{x}$ and $\mathscr{R}_{xx}(\tau)$ equal the statistical averages $\bar{X}$ and $R_{XX}(\tau)$ respectively. The *ergodic theorem* allows the validity of (6.2-26) and (6.2-27). Stated in loose terms, it more generally allows all time averages to equal the corresponding statistical averages. Processes that satisfy the ergodic theorem are called *ergodic processes*.

Ergodicity is a very restrictive form of stationarity and it may be difficult to prove that it constitutes a reasonable assumption in any physical situation. Nevertheless, we shall often assume a process is ergodic to simplify problems. In the real world, we are usually forced to work with only one sample function of a process and therefore must, like it or not, derive mean value, correlation functions, etc. from the time waveform. By assuming ergodicity, we may infer the similar statistical characteristics of the process. The reader may feel that our theory is on shaky ground based on these comments. However, it must be remembered that all our theory only serves to model real-world conditions. Therefore, what difference do our assumptions really make provided the assumed model does truly reflect real conditions?

Two random processes are called *jointly ergodic* if they are individually ergodic and also have a *time cross-correlation function* that equals the statistical cross-correlation function:‡

$$\mathscr{R}_{xy}(\tau) = \lim_{T \to \infty} \frac{1}{2T} \int_{-T}^{T} x(t)y(t + \tau)\, dt = R_{XY}(\tau) \tag{6.2-28}$$

6.3 CORRELATION FUNCTIONS

The autocorrelation and cross-correlation functions were introduced in the previous section. These functions are examined further in this section, along with their

---

† We assume also that $X(t)$ is a stationary process so that the mean and the autocorrelation function are not time-dependent.

‡ As in ordinary stationarity, there are various *orders* of ergodic stationarity. For more details on ergodic processes, the reader is referred to Papoulis (1965), pp. 323-332, and Gray and Davisson (1986), pp. 170–178.

properties. In addition, other correlation-type functions are introduced that are important to the study of random processes.

Autocorrelation Function and Its Properties

Recall that the autocorrelation function of a random process $X(t)$ is the correlation $E[X_1 X_2]$ of two random variables $X_1 = X(t_1)$ and $X_2 = X(t_2)$ defined by the process at times t_1 and t_2. Mathematically,

$$R_{XX}(t_1, t_2) = E[X(t_1)X(t_2)] \tag{6.3-1}$$

For time assignments, $t_1 = t$ and $t_2 = t_1 + \tau$, with τ a real number, (6.3-1) assumes the convenient form

$$R_{XX}(t, t + \tau) = E[X(t)X(t + \tau)] \tag{6.3-2}$$

If $X(t)$ is at least wide-sense stationary, it was noted in Section 6.2 that $R_{XX}(t, t + \tau)$ must be a function only of time difference $\tau = t_2 - t_1$. Thus, for wide-sense stationary processes

$$R_{XX}(\tau) = E[X(t)X(t + \tau)] \tag{6.3-3}$$

For such processes the autocorrelation function exhibits the following properties:

$$(1) \quad |R_{XX}(\tau)| \leq R_{XX}(0) \tag{6.3-4}$$

$$(2) \quad R_{XX}(-\tau) = R_{XX}(\tau) \tag{6.3-5}$$

$$(3) \quad R_{XX}(0) = E[X^2(t)] \tag{6.3-6}$$

The first property shows that $R_{XX}(\tau)$ is bounded by its value at the origin, while the third property states that this bound is equal to the mean-squared value called the *power* in the process. The second property indicates that an autocorrelation function has even symmetry.

Other properties of stationary processes may also be stated [see Cooper and McGillem (1971), pp. 112–114, and (1986), pp. 196–199, Melsa and Sage (1973), pp. 207–208, and Leon-Garcia (1989), pp. 357–358]:

(4) If $E[X(t)] = \bar{X} \neq 0$ and $X(t)$ is ergodic with no periodic components then

$$\lim_{|\tau| \to \infty} R_{XX}(\tau) = \bar{X}^2 \tag{6.3-7}$$

(5) If $X(t)$ has a periodic component, then $R_{XX}(\tau)$ will have a periodic component with the same period. (6.3-8)

(6) If $X(t)$ is ergodic, zero-mean, and has no periodic component, then

$$\lim_{|\tau| \to \infty} R_{XX}(\tau) = 0 \tag{6.3-9}$$

(7) $R_{XX}(\tau)$ cannot have an arbitrary shape. (6.3-10)

Properties 4 through 6 are more or less self-explanatory. Property 7 simply says that any arbitrary function cannot be an autocorrelation function. This fact will be more apparent when the *power density spectrum* is introduced in Chapter 7. It will be shown there that $R_{XX}(\tau)$ is related to the power density spectrum through the Fourier transform and the form of the spectrum is not arbitrary.

Example 6.3-1 Given the autocorrelation function, for a stationary ergodic process with no periodic components, is

$$R_{XX}(\tau) = 25 + \frac{4}{1 + 6\tau^2}$$

we shall find the mean value and variance of the process $X(t)$. From property 4, the mean value is $E[X(t)] = \bar{X} = \sqrt{25} = \pm 5$. Note that property 4 yields only the magnitude of $\bar{X}$, it cannot reveal its sign. The variance is given by (3.2-6), so

$$\sigma_X^2 = E[X^2(t)] - (E[X(t)])^2$$

But $E[X^2(t)] = R_{XX}(0) = 25 + 4 = 29$ from property 3, so

$$\sigma_X^2 = 29 - 25 = 4$$

Cross-Correlation Function and Its Properties

The cross-correlation function of two random processes $X(t)$ and $Y(t)$ was defined in (6.2-18). Setting $t_1 = t$ and $\tau = t_2 - t_1$, we may write (6.2-18) as

$$R_{XY}(t, t + \tau) = E[X(t)Y(t + \tau)] \tag{6.3-11}$$

If $X(t)$ and $Y(t)$ are at least jointly wide-sense stationary, $R_{XY}(t, t + \tau)$ is independent of absolute time and we can write

$$R_{XY}(\tau) = E[X(t)Y(t + \tau)] \tag{6.3-12}$$

If

$$R_{XY}(t, t + \tau) = 0 \tag{6.3-13}$$

then $X(t)$ and $Y(t)$ are called *orthogonal processes*. If the two processes are statistically independent, the cross-correlation function becomes

$$R_{XY}(t, t + \tau) = E[X(t)]E[Y(t + \tau)] \tag{6.3-14}$$

If, in addition to being independent, $X(t)$ and $Y(t)$ are at least wide-sense stationary, (6.3-14) becomes

$$R_{XY}(\tau) = \bar{X}\bar{Y} \tag{6.3-15}$$

which is a constant.

We may list some properties of the cross-correlation function applicable to processes that are at least wide-sense stationary:

(1) $\quad R_{XY}(-\tau) = R_{YX}(\tau)$ $\hspace{4cm}$ (6.3-16)

(2) $\quad |R_{XY}(\tau)| \leq \sqrt{R_{XX}(0)R_{YY}(0)}$ $\hspace{2.5cm}$ (6.3-17)

(3) $\quad |R_{XY}(\tau)| \leq {}^1\!/_2[R_{XX}(0) + R_{YY}(0)]$ $\hspace{2cm}$ (6.3-18)

Property 1 follows from the definition (6.3-12). It describes the symmetry of $R_{XY}(\tau)$. Property 2 can be proven by expanding the inequality

$$E[\{Y(t+\tau) + \alpha X(t)\}^2] \geq 0 \qquad (6.3\text{-}19)$$

where α is a real number (see Problem 6-27). Properties 2 and 3 both constitute bounds on the magnitude of $R_{XY}(\tau)$. Equation (6.3-17) represents a tighter bound than that of (6.3-18), because the geometric mean of two positive numbers cannot exceed their arithmetic mean; that is

$$\sqrt{R_{XX}(0)R_{YY}(0)} \leq {}^1\!/_2[R_{XX}(0) + R_{YY}(0)] \qquad (6.3\text{-}20)$$

Example 6.3-2 Let two random processes $X(t)$ and $Y(t)$ be defined by

$$X(t) = A \cos(\omega_0 t) + B \sin(\omega_0 t)$$
$$Y(t) = B \cos(\omega_0 t) - A \sin(\omega_0 t)$$

where A and B are random variables and ω_0 is a constant. It can be shown (Problem 6-12) that $X(t)$ is wide-sense stationary if A and B are uncorrelated, zero-mean random variables with the same variance (they may have different density functions, however). With these same constraints on A and B, $Y(t)$ is also wide-sense stationary. We shall now find the cross-correlation function $R_{XY}(t, t+\tau)$ and show that $X(t)$ and $Y(t)$ are *jointly* wide-sense stationary. By use of (6.3-11) we have

$$\begin{aligned}
R_{XY}(t, t+\tau) &= E[X(t)Y(t+\tau)] \\
&= E[AB \cos(\omega_0 t) \cos(\omega_0 t + \omega_0 \tau) \\
&\quad + B^2 \sin(\omega_0 t) \cos(\omega_0 t + \omega_0 \tau) \\
&\quad - A^2 \cos(\omega_0 t) \sin(\omega_0 t + \omega_0 \tau) \\
&\quad - AB \sin(\omega_0 t) \sin(\omega_0 t + \omega_0 \tau)] \\
&= E[AB] \cos(2\omega_0 t + \omega_0 \tau) \\
&\quad + E[B^2] \sin(\omega_0 t) \cos(\omega_0 t + \omega_0 \tau) \\
&\quad - E[A^2] \cos(\omega_0 t) \sin(\omega_0 t + \omega_0 \tau)
\end{aligned}$$

Since A and B are assumed to be zero-mean, uncorrelated random variables, $E[AB] = 0$. Also, since A and B are assumed to have equal variances, $E[A^2] = E[B^2] = \sigma^2$ and we obtain

$$R_{XY}(t, t + \tau) = -\sigma^2 \sin(\omega_0 \tau)$$

Thus, $X(t)$ and $Y(t)$ are jointly wide-sense stationary because $R_{XY}(t, t + \tau)$ depends only on τ.

Note from the above results that cross-correlation functions are not necessarily even functions of τ with the maximum at $\tau = 0$, as is the case with autocorrelation functions.

Covariance Functions

The concept of the covariance of two random variables, as defined by (5.1-13), can be extended to random processes. The *autocovariance function* is defined by

$$C_{XX}(t, t + \tau) = E[\{X(t) - E[X(t)]\}\{X(t + \tau) - E[X(t + \tau)]\}] \quad (6.3\text{-}21)$$

which can also be put in the form

$$C_{XX}(t, t + \tau) = R_{XX}(t, t + \tau) - E[X(t)]E[X(t + \tau)] \quad (6.3\text{-}22)$$

The *cross-covariance function* for two processes $X(t)$ and $Y(t)$ is defined by

$$C_{XY}(t, t + \tau) = E[\{X(t) - E[X(t)]\}\{Y(t + \tau) - E[Y(t + \tau)]\}] \quad (6.3\text{-}23)$$

or, alternatively,

$$C_{XY}(t, t + \tau) = R_{XY}(t, t + \tau) - E[X(t)]E[Y(t + \tau)] \quad (6.3\text{-}24)$$

For processes that are at least jointly wide-sense stationary, (6.3-22) and (6.3-24) reduce to

$$C_{XX}(\tau) = R_{XX}(\tau) - \bar{X}^2 \quad (6.3\text{-}25)$$

and

$$C_{XY}(\tau) = R_{XY}(\tau) - \bar{X}\,\bar{Y} \quad (6.3\text{-}26)$$

The *variance* of a random process is given in general by (6.3-21) with $\tau = 0$. For a wide-sense stationary process, variance does not depend on time and is given by (6.3-25) with $\tau = 0$:

$$\sigma_X^2 = E[\{X(t) - E[X(t)]\}^2] = R_{XX}(0) - \bar{X}^2 \quad (6.3\text{-}27)$$

For two random processes, if

$$C_{XY}(t, t + \tau) = 0 \quad (6.3\text{-}28)$$

they are called *uncorrelated*. From (6.3-24) this means that

$$R_{XY}(t, t + \tau) = E[X(t)]E[Y(t + \tau)] \quad (6.3\text{-}29)$$

Since this result is the same as (6.3-14), which applies to independent processes, we conclude that independent processes are uncorrelated. The converse case is not necessarily true, although it is true for *jointly gaussian processes*, which we consider in Section 6.5.

6.4 MEASUREMENT OF CORRELATION FUNCTIONS

In the real world, we can never measure the true correlation functions of two random processes $X(t)$ and $Y(t)$ because we never have *all* sample functions of the ensemble at our disposal. Indeed, we may typically have available for measurements only a portion of one sample function from each process. Thus, our only recourse is to determine time averages based on finite time portions of single sample functions, taken large enough to approximate true results for ergodic processes. Because we are able to work only with time functions, we are forced, like it or not, to presume that given processes are ergodic. This fact should not prove too disconcerting, however, if we remember that assumptions only reflect the details of our mathematical model of a real-world situation. Provided that the model gives consistent agreement with the real situation, it is of little importance whether ergodicity is assumed or not.

Figure 6.4-1 illustrates the block diagram of a possible system for measuring the approximate time cross-correlation function of two jointly ergodic random processes $X(t)$ and $Y(t)$. Sample functions $x(t)$ and $y(t)$ are delayed by amounts T and $T - \tau$, respectively, and the product of the delayed waveforms is formed. This product is then integrated to form the output which equals the integral at time $t_1 + 2T$, where t_1 is arbitrary and $2T$ is the integration period. The integrator can be of the integrate-and-dump variety described by Peebles (1976, p. 361).

If we assume $x(t)$ and $y(t)$ exist at least during the interval $-T < t$ and t_1 is an arbitrary time except $0 \le t_1$, then the output is easily found to be

$$R_o(t_1 + 2T) = \frac{1}{2T} \int_{t_1 - T}^{t_1 + T} x(t)y(t + \tau)\, dt \qquad (6.4\text{-}1)$$

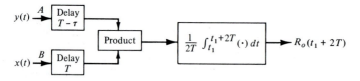

FIGURE 6.4-1
A time cross-correlation function measurement system. Autocorrelation function measurement is possible by connecting points A and B and applying either $x(t)$ or $y(t)$.

Now if we choose $t_1 = 0$† and assume T is large, then we have

$$R_o(2T) = \frac{1}{2T} \int_{-T}^{T} x(t) y(t + \tau) \, dt \approx \mathcal{R}_{xy}(\tau) = R_{XY}(\tau) \tag{6.4-2}$$

Thus, for jointly ergodic processes, the system of Figure 6.4-1 can approximately measure their cross-correlation function (τ is varied to obtain the complete function).

Clearly, by connecting points A and B and applying either $x(t)$ or $y(t)$ to the system, we can also measure the autocorrelation functions $R_{XX}(\tau)$ and $R_{YY}(\tau)$.

Example 6.4-1 We connect points A and B together in Figure 6.4-1 and use the system to measure the autocorrelation function of the process $X(t)$ of Example 6.2-1. From (6.4-2)

$$R_o(2T) = \frac{1}{2T} \int_{-T}^{T} A^2 \cos(\omega_0 t + \theta) \cos(\omega_0 t + \theta + \omega_0 \tau) \, dt$$

$$= \frac{A^2}{4T} \int_{-T}^{T} [\cos(\omega_0 \tau) + \cos(2\omega_0 t + 2\theta + \omega_0 \tau)] \, dt$$

In writing this result θ represents a specific value of the random variable Θ; the value that corresponds to the specific ensemble member being used in (6.4-2). On straightforward reduction of the above integral we obtain

$$R_o(2T) = R_{XX}(\tau) + \varepsilon(T)$$

where

$$R_{XX}(\tau) = (A^2/2) \cos(\omega_0 \tau)$$

is the true autocorrelation function of $X(t)$, and

$$\varepsilon(T) = (A^2/2) \cos(\omega_0 \tau + 2\theta) \frac{\sin(2\omega_0 T)}{2\omega_0 T}$$

is an error term. If we require the error term's magnitude to be at least 20 times smaller than the largest value of the true autocorrelation function then $|\varepsilon(T)| < 0.05 R_{XX}(0)$ is necessary. Thus, we must have $1/2\omega_0 T \leq 0.05$ or

$$T \geq 10/\omega_0$$

In other words, if $T \geq 10/\omega_0$ the error in using Figure 6.4-1 to measure the autocorrelation function of the process $X(t) = A \cos(\omega_0 t + \Theta)$ will be 5% or less of the largest value of the true autocorrelation function.

---

† Since the processes are assumed jointly ergodic and therefore jointly stationary, the integral (6.4-1) will tend to be independent of t_1 if T is large enough.

6.5 GAUSSIAN RANDOM PROCESSES

A number of random processes are important enough to have been given names. In this section we shall discuss the most important of these, the *gaussian random process*.

Consider a continuous random process such as illustrated in Figure 6.1-1 and define N random variables $X_1 = X(t_1), \ldots, X_i = X(t_i), \ldots, X_N = X(t_N)$ corresponding to N time instants $t_1, \ldots, t_i, \ldots, t_N$. If, for any $N = 1, 2, \ldots$ and any times $t_1, \ldots, t_N$, these random variables are jointly gaussian, that is, they have a joint density as given by (5.3-12), the process is called gaussian. Equation (5.3-12) can be written in the form

$$f_X(x_1, \ldots, x_N; t_1, \ldots, t_N) = \frac{\exp\left\{-(1/2)[x - \bar{X}]'[C_X]^{-1}[x - \bar{X}]\right\}}{\sqrt{(2\pi)^N |[C_X]|}} \quad (6.5\text{-}1)$$

where matrices $[x - \bar{X}]$ and $[C_X]$ are defined in (5.3-13) and (5.3-14) and (5.3-15), respectively. The mean values $\bar{X}_i$ of $X(t_i)$ are

$$\bar{X}_i = E[X_i] = E[X(t_i)] \quad (6.5\text{-}2)$$

The elements of the covariance matrix $[C_X]$ are

$$
\begin{aligned}
C_{ik} = C_{X_i X_k} &= E[(X_i - \bar{X}_i)(X_k - \bar{X}_k)] \\
&= E[\{X(t_i) - E[X(t_i)]\}\{X(t_k) - E[X(t_k)]\}] \\
&= C_{XX}(t_i, t_k)
\end{aligned}
\quad (6.5\text{-}3)
$$

which is the autocovariance of $X(t_i)$ and $X(t_k)$ from (6.3-21).

From (6.5-2) and (6.5-3), when used in (6.5-1), we see that the mean and autocovariance functions are all that are needed to completely specify a gaussian random process. By expanding (6.5-3) to get

$$C_{XX}(t_i, t_k) = R_{XX}(t_i, t_k) - E[X(t_i)]E[X(t_k)] \quad (6.5\text{-}4)$$

we see that an alternative specification using only the mean and autocorrelation function $R_{XX}(t_i, t_k)$ is possible.

If the gaussian process is not stationary the mean and autocovariance functions will, in general, depend on absolute time. However, for the important case where the process is wide-sense stationary, the mean will be constant,

$$\bar{X}_i = E[X(t_i)] = \bar{X} \quad \text{(constant)} \quad (6.5\text{-}5)$$

while the autocovariance and autocorrelation functions will depend only on time differences and not absolute time,

$$C_{XX}(t_i, t_k) = C_{XX}(t_k - t_i) \quad (6.5\text{-}6)$$

$$R_{XX}(t_i, t_k) = R_{XX}(t_k - t_i) \quad (6.5\text{-}7)$$

It follows from the preceding discussions that a wide-sense stationary gaussian process is also strictly stationary.

We illustrate some of the above remarks with an example.

Example 6.5-1 A gaussian random process is known to be wide-sense stationary with a mean of $\bar{X} = 4$ and autocorrelation function

$$R_{XX}(\tau) = 25e^{-3|\tau|}$$

We seek to specify the joint density function for three random variables $X(t_i)$, $i = 1, 2, 3$, defined at times $t_i = t_0 + [(i-1)/2)]$, with t_0 a constant.

Here $t_k - t_i = (k-i)/2$, i and $k = 1, 2, 3$, so

$$R_{XX}(t_k - t_i) = 25e^{-3|k-i|/2}$$

and

$$C_{XX}(t_k - t_i) = 25e^{-3|k-i|/2} - 16$$

from (6.5-4) through (6.5-7). Elements of the covariance matrix are found from (6.5-3). Thus

$$[C_X] = \begin{bmatrix} (25-16) & (25e^{-3/2}-16) & (25e^{-6/2}-16) \\ (25e^{-3/2}-16) & (25-16) & (25e^{-3/2}-16) \\ (25e^{-6/2}-16) & (25e^{-3/2}-16) & (25-16) \end{bmatrix}$$

and $\bar{X}_i = 4$ completely determine (6.5-1) for this case where $N = 3$.

Two random processes $X(t)$ and $Y(t)$ are said to be *jointly gaussian* if the random variables $X(t_1), \ldots, X(t_N)$, $Y(t'_1), \ldots, Y(t'_M)$ defined at times $t_1, \ldots, t_N$ for $X(t)$ and times $t'_1, \ldots, t'_M$ for $Y(t)$, are jointly gaussian for any N, $t_1, \ldots, t_N$, M, $t'_1, \ldots, t'_M$.

6.6 POISSON RANDOM PROCESS

In this section we consider an important example of a discrete random process known as the *Poisson process*.† It describes the number of times that some event has occurred as a function of time, where the events occur at random times. The event might be the arrival of a customer at a bank or supermarket check-out register, the occurrence of a lightning strike within some prescribed area, the failure of some component in a system, or the emission of an electron from the surface of a light-sensitive material (photodetector). In each of these examples a single event occurs at a random time and the process amounts to counting the number

---

† For additional reading, some recent books that also cover this topic are Shanmugan and Briepohl (1988) and Gardner (1990).

of such occurrences with time. For this reason, the process is also known as the *Poisson counting process*.

To visualize the Poisson process, let $X(t)$ represent the number of event occurrences with time (the process); then $X(t)$ has integer-valued, nondecreasing sample functions, as illustrated in Figure 6.6-1a for the random occurrence times of Figure 6.6-1b. For convenience, we take $X(t) = 0$ at $t = 0$; for $t > 0$, $X(t)$ is the number of occurrences in the interval $(0, t)$; for $t < 0$, $X(t)$ is the *negative* of the number of occurrences in the interval $(t, 0)$. (See Shanmugan and Briepohl, 1988, p. 296.) In many situations only the process' behavior for $t > 0$ is of interest, and in the remainder of this section we shall assume the process is defined only for $t > 0$ (and is zero for $t < 0$).

To define the Poisson process we shall require two conditions. First, we require that the event occur only once in any vanishingly small interval of time. In essence, we require that only one event can occur at a time. This condition does not prevent the times of occurrence of events from being very close together, only that they do not coincide. Second, we require that occurrence times be statistically independent so that the number that occurs in any given time interval is independent of the number in any other nonoverlaping time interval; this independence is required to apply regardless of the number of time intervals of interest. A consequence of the two conditions is that the number of event

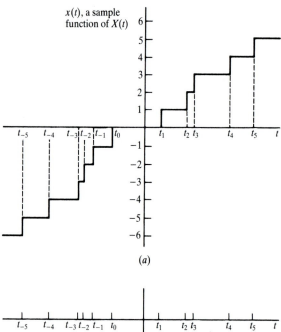

(a)

(b)

FIGURE 6.6-1
(a) a sample function of a Poisson discrete random process, and (b) the random times of occurrence of events being counted to form the process.

occurrences in any finite interval of time is described by the Poisson distribution where the average rate of occurrences is denoted by λ [See Section 2.5, equations (2.5-4)–(2.5-6)]. [For more detail, see Gray and Davisson (1986), pp. 282-284.]

Probability Density Function

Thus, from (2.5-4) with $b = \lambda t$, the probability of exactly k occurrences over a time interval $(0, t)$ is

$$P[X(t) = k] = \frac{(\lambda t)^k e^{-\lambda t}}{k!} \qquad k = 0, 1, 2, \ldots \qquad (6.6\text{-}1)$$

and the probability density of the number of occurrences is

$$f_X(x) = \sum_{k=0}^{\infty} \frac{(\lambda t)^k e^{-\lambda t}}{k!} \delta(x - k) \qquad (6.6\text{-}2)$$

From Problem 3-16 we know that the mean and variance of a Poisson random variable are each equal to λt. Thus, from (3.2-6) we also know the second moment, which is $E[X^2(t)] = \sigma_X^2 + \{E[X(t)]\}^2 = \lambda t + \lambda^2 t^2$. These facts are used to establish useful equations by formally computing the mean and second moment:

$$E[X(t)] = \int_{-\infty}^{\infty} x f_X(x)\, dx = \int_{-\infty}^{\infty} x \sum_{k=0}^{\infty} \frac{(\lambda t)^k e^{-\lambda t}}{k!} \delta(x - k)\, dx$$

$$= \sum_{k=0}^{\infty} \frac{k(\lambda t)^k e^{-\lambda t}}{k!} = \lambda t \qquad (6.6\text{-}3)$$

$$E[X^2(t)] = \int_{-\infty}^{\infty} x^2 f_X(x)\, dx = \sum_{k=0}^{\infty} \frac{k^2 (\lambda t)^k e^{-\lambda t}}{k!} = \lambda t[1 + \lambda t] \qquad (6.6\text{-}4)$$

Joint Probability Density

To determine the joint probability density function for the Poisson process at times $0 < t_1 < t_2$, first observe that the probability of k_1 event occurrences over $(0, t_1)$ is

$$P[X(t_1) = k_1] = \frac{(\lambda t_1)^{k_1} e^{-\lambda t_1}}{k_1!} \qquad k_1 = 0, 1, 2, \ldots \qquad (6.6\text{-}5)$$

from (6.6-1). Next, the conditional probability of k_2 occurrences over $(0, t_2)$, given that k_1 events occurred over $(0, t_1)$, is just the probability that $k_2 - k_1$ events occurred over (t_1, t_2), which is

$$P[X(t_2) = k_2 | X(t_1) = k_1] = \frac{[\lambda(t_2 - t_1)]^{k_2 - k_1} e^{-\lambda(t_2 - t_1)}}{(k_2 - k_1)!} \qquad (6.6\text{-}6)$$

for $k_2 \geq k_1$. The joint probability of k_2 occurrences at time t_2 and k_1 occurrences at time t_1 is the product of (6.6-5) and (6.6-6):

$$P(k_1, k_2) = P[X(t_2) = k_2 | X(t_1) = k_1] \cdot P[X(t_1) = k_1]$$

$$= \frac{(\lambda t_1)^{k_1} [\lambda(t_2 - t_1)]^{k_2 - k_1} e^{-\lambda t_2}}{k_1! (k_2 - k_1)!} \qquad k_2 \geq k_1 \qquad (6.6\text{-}7)$$

The joint density now becomes

$$f_X(x_1, x_2) = \sum_{k_1 = 0}^{\infty} \sum_{k_2 = k_1}^{\infty} P(k_1, k_2) \delta(x_1 - k_1) \delta(x_2 - k_2) \qquad (6.6\text{-}8)$$

for the process' random variables $X(t_1) = X_1$, and $X(t_2) = X_2$.

A principal reason for developing (6.6-8) is that the autocorrelation function of the process can be determined. This is left as an exercise for the reader (see Problem 6-75).

Example 6.6-1 By example, we illustrate how the higher-dimensional probability density of the Poisson process can be derived. We take only the case of three random variables defined at times $0 < t_1 < t_2 < t_3$. For $k_1 \leq k_2 \leq k_3$ occurrences at the respective times, we have

$$P(k_1, k_2, k_3) = P[X(t_3) = k_3 | X(t_2) = k_2, X(t_1) = k_1]$$

$$\cdot P[X(t_2) = k_2 | X(t_1) = k_1] P[X(t_1) = k_1]$$

$$= \frac{[\lambda(t_3 - t_2)]^{k_3 - k_2} e^{-\lambda(t_3 - t_2)}}{(k_3 - k_2)!} \cdot \frac{[\lambda(t_2 - t_1)]^{k_2 - k_1} e^{-\lambda(t_2 - t_1)}}{(k_2 - k_1)!}$$

$$\cdot \frac{(\lambda t_1)^{k_1} e^{-\lambda t_1}}{k_1!} = \frac{(\lambda t_1)^{k_1} [\lambda(t_2 - t_1)]^{k_2 - k_1} [\lambda(t_3 - t_2)]^{k_3 - k_2} e^{-\lambda t_3}}{k_1! (k_2 - k_1)! (k_3 - k_2)!}$$

and

$$f_X(x_1, x_2, x_3) = \sum_{k_1 = 0}^{\infty} \sum_{k_2 = k_1}^{\infty} \sum_{k_3 = k_2}^{\infty} P(k_1, k_2, k_3) \delta(x_1 - k_1) \delta(x_2 - k_2) \delta(x_3 - k_3)$$

★6.7 COMPLEX RANDOM PROCESSES

If the complex random variable of Section 5.7 is generalized to include time, the result is a *complex random process* $Z(t)$ given by

$$Z(t) = X(t) + jY(t) \qquad (6.7\text{-}1)$$

where $X(t)$ and $Y(t)$ are real processes. $Z(t)$ is called stationary if $X(t)$ and $Y(t)$ are jointly stationary. If $X(t)$ and $Y(t)$ are jointly wide-sense stationary, then $Z(t)$ is said to be wide-sense stationary.

Two complex processes $Z_i(t)$ and $Z_j(t)$ are jointly wide-sense stationary if each is wide-sense stationary and their cross-correlation function (defined below) is a function of time differences only and not absolute time.

We may extend the operations involving process mean value, autocorrelation function, and autocovariance function to include complex processes. The *mean value* of $Z(t)$ is

$$E[Z(t)] = E[X(t)] + jE[Y(t)] \tag{6.7-2}$$

Autocorrelation function is defined by

$$R_{ZZ}(t, t + \tau) = E[Z^*(t)Z(t + \tau)] \tag{6.7-3}$$

where the asterisk * denotes the complex conjugate. *Autocovariance function* is defined by

$$C_{ZZ}(t, t + \tau) = E[\{Z(t) - E[Z(t)]\}^*\{Z(t + \tau) - E[Z(t + \tau)]\}] \tag{6.7-4}$$

If $Z(t)$ is at least wide-sense stationary, the mean value becomes a constant

$$\bar{Z} = \bar{X} + j\bar{Y} \tag{6.7-5}$$

and the correlation functions are independent of absolute time:

$$R_{ZZ}(t, t + \tau) = R_{ZZ}(\tau) \tag{6.7-6}$$

$$C_{ZZ}(t, t + \tau) = C_{ZZ}(\tau) \tag{6.7-7}$$

For two complex processes $Z_i(t)$ and $Z_j(t)$, *cross-correlation* and *cross-covariance functions* are defined by

$$R_{Z_iZ_j}(t, t + \tau) = E[Z_i^*(t)Z_j(t + \tau)] \qquad i \neq j \tag{6.7-8}$$

and

$$C_{Z_iZ_j}(t, t + \tau) = E[\{Z_i(t) - E[Z_i(t)]\}^*\{Z_j(t + \tau) - E[Z_j(t + \tau)]\}] \qquad i \neq j \tag{6.7-9}$$

respectively. If the two processes are at least jointly wide-sense stationary, we obtain

$$R_{Z_iZ_j}(t, t + \tau) = R_{Z_iZ_j}(\tau) \qquad i \neq j \tag{6.7-10}$$

$$C_{Z_iZ_j}(t, t + \tau) = C_{Z_iZ_j}(\tau) \qquad i \neq j \tag{6.7-11}$$

$Z_i(t)$ and $Z_j(t)$ are said to be *uncorrelated processes* if $C_{Z_iZ_j}(t, t + \tau) = 0, i \neq j$. They are called *orthogonal processes* if $R_{Z_iZ_j}(t, t + \tau) = 0, i \neq j$.

Example 6.7-1 A complex random process $V(t)$ is comprised of a sum of N complex signals:

$$V(t) = \sum_{n=1}^{N} A_n e^{j\omega_0 t + j\Theta_n}$$

Here $\omega_0/2\pi$ is the (constant) frequency of each signal. A_n is a random variable representing the random amplitude of the nth signal. Similarly, Θ_n is a random variable representing a random phase angle. We assume all the variables A_n and Θ_n, for $n = 1, 2, \ldots, N$, are statistically independent and the Θ_n are uniformly distributed on $(0, 2\pi)$. We find the autocorrelation function of $V(t)$.

From (6.7-3):

$$R_{VV}(t, t + \tau) = E[V^*(t)V(t + \tau)]$$

$$= E\left[\sum_{n=1}^{N} A_n e^{-j\omega_0 t - j\Theta_n} \sum_{m=1}^{N} A_m e^{j\omega_0 t + j\omega_0 \tau + j\Theta_m} \right]$$

$$= \sum_{n=1}^{N} \sum_{m=1}^{N} e^{j\omega_0 \tau} E[A_n A_m e^{j(\Theta_m - \Theta_n)}] = R_{VV}(\tau)$$

From statistical independence:

$$R_{VV}(\tau) = e^{j\omega_0 \tau} \sum_{n=1}^{N} \sum_{m=1}^{N} E[A_n A_m] E[\exp\{j(\Theta_m - \Theta_n)\}]$$

However,

$$E[\exp\{j(\Theta_m - \Theta_n)\}] = E[\cos(\Theta_m - \Theta_n)] + jE[\sin(\Theta_m - \Theta_n)]$$

$$= \int_0^{2\pi} \int_0^{2\pi} \frac{1}{(2\pi)^2} [\cos(\theta_m - \theta_n) + j\sin(\theta_m - \theta_n)] \, d\theta_n \, d\theta_m$$

$$= \begin{cases} 0 & m \neq n \\ 1 & m = n \end{cases}$$

so

$$R_{VV}(\tau) = e^{j\omega_0 \tau} \sum_{n=1}^{N} \overline{A_n^2}$$

PROBLEMS

6-1 A random experiment consists of selecting a point on some city street that has two-way automobile traffic. Define and classify a random process for this experiment that is related to traffic flow.

6-2 A 10-meter section of a busy downtown sidewalk is actually the platform of a scale that produces a voltage proportional to the total weight of people on the scale at any time.
(a) Sketch a typical sample function for this process.
(b) What is the underlying random experiment for the process?
(c) Classify the process.

*6-3 An experiment consists of measuring the weight W of some person each 10 minutes. The person is randomly male or female (which is not known though) with equal probability. A two-level discrete process $X(t)$ is generated where

$$X(t) = \pm 10$$

The level -10 is generated in the period following a measurement if the measured weight does not exceed W_0 (some constant). Level $+10$ is generated if weight exceeds W_0. Let the weight of men in kg be a random variable having the gaussian density

$$f_W(w|\text{male}) = \frac{1}{\sqrt{2\pi}11.3} \exp\left[-(w - 77.1)^2/2(11.3)^2\right]$$

Similarly, for women

$$f_W(w|\text{female}) = \frac{1}{\sqrt{2\pi}6.8} \exp\left[-(w - 54.4)^2/2(6.8)^2\right]$$

(a) Find W_0 so that $P\{W > W_0|\text{male}\}$ is equal to $P\{W \le W_0|\text{female}\}$
(b) If the levels ± 10 are interpreted as "decisions" about whether the weight measurement of a person corresponds to a male or female, give a physical significance to their generation.
(c) Sketch a possible sample function.

6-4 The two-level *semirandom binary process* is defined by

$$X(t) = A \text{ or } -A \qquad (n - 1)T < t < nT$$

where the levels A and $-A$ occur with equal probability, T is a positive constant, and $n = 0, \pm 1, \pm 2, \ldots$.
(a) Sketch a typical sample function.
(b) Classify the process.
(c) Is the process deterministic?

6-5 Sample functions in a discrete random process are constants; that is

$$X(t) = C = \text{constant}$$

where C is a discrete random variable having possible values $c_1 = 1$, $c_2 = 2$, and $c_3 = 3$ occurring with probabilities 0.6, 0.3, and 0.1 respectively.
(a) Is $X(t)$ deterministic?
(b) Find the first-order density function of $X(t)$ at any time t.

6-6 Utilize (6.2-13) to prove (6.2-16).

*6-7 A random process $X(t)$ has periodic sample functions as shown in Figure P6-7 where B, T, and $4t_0 \le T$ are constants but ε is a random variable uniformly distributed on the interval $(0, T)$.

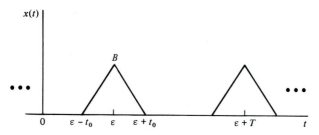

FIGURE P6-7

(a) Find the first-order distribution function of $X(t)$.
(b) Find the first-order density function.
(c) Find $E[X(t)]$, $E[X^2(t)]$, and σ_X^2.

6-8 Work Problem 6-7 for the waveform of Figure P6-8. Assume $2t_0 < T$.

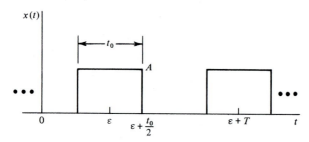

FIGURE P6-8

★6-9 Work Problem 6-7 for the waveform of Figure P6-9. Assume $4t_0 \leq T$.

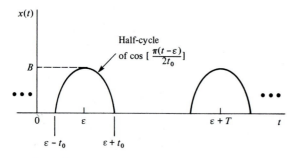

FIGURE P6-9

6-10 Given the random process

$$X(t) = A \sin (\omega_0 t + \Theta)$$

where A and ω_0 are constants and Θ is a random variable uniformly distributed on the interval $(-\pi, \pi)$. Define a new random process $Y(t) = X^2(t)$.
(a) Find the autocorrelation function of $Y(t)$.
(b) Find the cross-correlation function of $X(t)$ and $Y(t)$.
(c) Are $X(t)$ and $Y(t)$ wide-sense stationary?
(d) Are $X(t)$ and $Y(t)$ jointly wide-sense stationary?

6-11 A random process is defined by

$$Y(t) = X(t) \cos (\omega_0 t + \Theta)$$

where $X(t)$ is a wide-sense stationary random process that amplitude-modulates a carrier of constant angular frequency ω_0 with a random phase Θ independent of $X(t)$ and uniformly distributed on $(-\pi, \pi)$.
(a) Find $E[Y(t)]$.
(b) Find the autocorrelation function of $Y(t)$.
(c) Is $Y(t)$ wide-sense stationary?

6-12 Given the random process

$$X(t) = A \cos (\omega_0 t) + B \sin (\omega_0 t)$$

where ω_0 is a constant, and A and B are uncorrelated zero-mean random variables having different density functions but the same variances σ^2. Show that $X(t)$ is wide-sense stationary but not strictly stationary.

6-13 If $X(t)$ is a stationary random process having a mean value $E[X(t)] = 3$ and autocorrelation function $R_{XX}(\tau) = 9 + 2e^{-|\tau|}$, find:
(a) the mean value and
(b) the variance of the random variable

$$Y = \int_0^2 X(t)\, dt$$

(*Hint:* Assume expectation and integration operations are interchangeable.)

6-14 Define a random process by

$$X(t) = A \cos (\pi t)$$

where A is a gaussian random variable with zero mean and variance σ_A^2.
(a) Find the density functions of $X(0)$ and $X(1)$.
(b) Is $X(t)$ stationary in any sense?

6-15 For the random process of Problem 6-4, calculate:
(a) the mean value $E[X(t)]$ (b) $R_{XX}(t_1 = 0.5T, t_2 = 0.7T)$
(c) $R_{XX}(t_1 = 0.2T, t_2 = 1.2T)$.

6-16 A random process consists of three sample functions $X(t, s_1) = 2$, $X(t, s_2) = 2 \cos (t)$, and $X(t, s_3) = 3 \sin (t)$, each occurring with equal probabilitty. Is the process stationary in any sense?

6-17 Statistically independent, zero-mean random process $X(t)$ and $Y(t)$ have autocorrelation functions

$$R_{XX}(\tau) = e^{-|\tau|}$$

and

$$R_{YY}(\tau) = \cos(2\pi\tau)$$

respectively.
(a) Find the autocorrelation function of the sum $W_1(t) = X(t) + Y(t)$.
(b) Find the autocorrelation function of the difference $W_2(t) = X(t) - Y(t)$.
(c) Find the cross-correlation function of $W_1(t)$ and $W_2(t)$.

6-18 Define a random process as $X(t) = p(t + \varepsilon)$, where $p(t)$ is any periodic waveform with period T and ε is a random variable uniformly distributed on the interval $(0, T)$. Show that

$$E[X(t)X(t + \tau)] = \frac{1}{T} \int_0^T p(\xi)p(\xi + \tau)\, d\xi = R_{XX}(\tau)$$

★6-19 Use the result of Problem 6-18 to find the autocorrelation function of random processes having periodic sample function waveforms $p(t)$ defined
(a) by Figure P6-7 with $\varepsilon = 0$ and $4t_0 \le T$, and
(b) by Figure P6-8 with $\varepsilon = 0$ and $2t_0 \le T$.

6-20 Define two random processes by $X(t) = p_1(t + \varepsilon)$ and $Y(t) = p_2(t + \varepsilon)$ when $p_1(t)$ and $p_2(t)$ are both periodic waveforms with period T and ε is a random variable uniformly distributed on the interval $(0, T)$. Find an expression for the cross-correlation function $E[X(t)Y(t + \tau)]$.

6-21 Prove:
(a) (6.3-4)   and   (b) (6.3-5).

6-22 Give arguments to justify (6.3-9).

6-23 For a stationary ergodic random process having the autocorrelation function shown in Figure P6-23, find:
(a) $E[X(t)]$ (b) $E[X^2(t)]$ and   (c) σ_X^2.

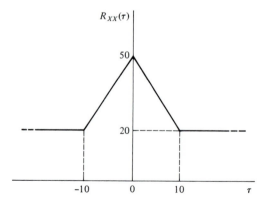

FIGURE P6-23

6-24 A random process $Y(t) = X(t) - X(t + \tau)$ is defined in terms of a process $X(t)$ that is at least wide-sense stationary.

(a) Show that mean value of $Y(t)$ is 0 even if $X(t)$ has a nonzero mean value.

(b) Show that

$$\sigma_Y^2 = 2[R_{XX}(0) - R_{XX}(\tau)]$$

(c) If $Y(t) = X(t) + X(t + \tau)$, find $E[Y(t)]$ and σ_Y^2. How do these results compare to those of parts (a) and (b)?

6-25 For two zero-mean, jointly wide-sense stationary random processes $X(t)$ and $Y(t)$, it is known that $\sigma_X^2 = 5$ and $\sigma_Y^2 = 10$. Explain why each of the following functions cannot apply to the processes if they have no periodic components.

(a) $R_{XX}(\tau) = 6u(\tau)\exp(-3\tau)$ (b) $R_{XX}(\tau) = 5\sin(5\tau)$

(c) $R_{XY}(\tau) = 9(1 + 2\tau^2)^{-1}$ (d) $R_{YY}(\tau) = -\cos(6\tau)\exp(-|\tau|)$

(e) $R_{YY}(\tau) = 5\left[\dfrac{\sin(3\tau)}{3\tau}\right]^2$ (f) $R_{YY}(\tau) = 6 + 4\left[\dfrac{\sin(10\tau)}{10\tau}\right]$

6-26 Given two random processes $X(t)$ and $Y(t)$. Find expressions for autocorrelation function of $W(t) = X(t) + Y(t)$ if:

(a) $X(t)$ and $Y(t)$ are correlated.

(b) They are uncorrelated.

(c) They are uncorrelated with zero means.

6-27 Use (6.3-19) to prove (6.3-17).

6-28 Let $X(t)$ be a stationary continuous random process that is differentiable. Denote its time-derivative by $\dot{X}(t)$.

(a) Show that $E[\dot{X}(t)] = 0$.

(b) Find $R_{X\dot{X}}(\tau)$ in terms of $R_{XX}(\tau)$.

(c) Find $R_{\dot{X}\dot{X}}(\tau)$ in terms of $R_{XX}(\tau)$. (*Hint:* Use the definition of the derivative

$$\dot{X}(t) = \lim_{\varepsilon \to 0} \frac{X(t + \varepsilon) - X(t)}{\varepsilon}$$

and assume the order of the limit and expectation operations can be interchanged.)

6-29 A gaussian random process has an autocorrelation function

$$R_{XX}(\tau) = 6\exp(-|\tau|/2)$$

Determine a covariance matrix for the random variables $X(t)$, $X(t + 1)$, $X(t + 2)$, and $X(t + 3)$.

6-30 Work Problem 6-29 if

$$R_{XX}(\tau) = 6\frac{\sin(\pi\tau)}{\pi\tau}$$

6-31 An ensemble member of a stationary random process $X(t)$ is sampled at N times t_i, $i = 1, 2, \ldots, N$. By treating the samples as random variables $X_i = X(t_i)$, an *estimate* or *measurement* $\hat{\bar{X}}$ of the mean value $\bar{X} = E[X(t)]$ of the process is sometimes formed by averaging the samples:

$$\hat{\bar{X}} = \frac{1}{N} \sum_{i=1}^{N} X_i$$

(a) Show that $E[\hat{\bar{X}}] = \bar{X}$.

(b) If the samples are separated far enough in time so that the random variables X_i can be considered statistically independent, show that the variance of the estimate of the process mean is

$$(\sigma_{\hat{\bar{X}}})^2 = \sigma_X^2 / N$$

6-32 For the random process and samples defined in Problem 6-31, let an estimate of the variance of the process be defined by

$$\widehat{\sigma_X^2} = \frac{1}{N} \sum_{i=1}^{N} (X_i - \hat{\bar{X}})^2$$

Show that the mean value of this estimate is

$$E[\widehat{\sigma_X^2}] = \frac{N-1}{N} \sigma_X^2$$

6-33 Assume that $X(t)$ of Problem 6-31 is a zero-mean stationary gaussian process and let

$$\widehat{\sigma_X^2} = \frac{1}{N} \sum_{i=1}^{N} X_i^2$$

be an estimate of the variance σ_X^2 of $X(t)$ formed from the samples. Show that the variance of the estimate is

$$\text{variance of } \widehat{\sigma_X^2} = \frac{2\sigma_X^4}{N}$$

(*Hint:* Use the facts that $E[X^2] = \sigma_X^2$, $E[X^3] = 0$, and $E[X^4] = 3\sigma_X^4$ for a gaussian random variable having mean zero.)

6-34 How many samples must be taken in Problem 6-33 if the standard deviation of the estimate of the variance of $X(t)$ is to not exceed 5% of σ_X^2?

★6-35 A complex random process $Z(t) = X(t) + jY(t)$ is defined by jointly stationary real processes $X(t)$ and $Y(t)$. Show that

$$E[|Z(t)|^2] = R_{XX}(0) + R_{YY}(0)$$

★6-36 Let $X_1(t)$, $X_2(t)$, $Y_1(t)$ and $Y_2(t)$ be real random processes and define

$$Z_1(t) = X_1(t) + jY_1(t) \qquad Z_2(t) = X_2(t) - jY_2(t)$$

Find expressions for the cross-correlation function of $Z_1(t)$ and $Z_2(t)$ if:

(a) All the real processes are correlated.

(b) They are uncorrelated.

(c) They are uncorrelated with zero means.

★**6-37** Let $Z(t)$ be a stationary complex random process with an autocorrelation function $R_{ZZ}(\tau)$. Define the random variable

$$W = \int_a^{a+T} Z(t)\, dt$$

where $T > 0$ and a are real numbers. Show that

$$E[|W|^2] = \int_{-T}^T (T - |\tau|)R_{ZZ}(\tau)\, d\tau$$

ADDITIONAL PROBLEMS, SECOND EDITION

6-38 For a random process $X(t)$ it is known that $f_X(x_1, x_2, x_3; t_1, t_2, t_3) = f_X(x_1, x_2, x_3; t_1 + \Delta, t_2 + \Delta, t_3 + \Delta)$ for any t_1, t_2, t_3 and Δ. Indicate which of the following statements are unequivocally true: $X(t)$ is (a) stationary to order 1, (b) stationary to order 2, (c) stationary to order 3, (d) strictly stationary, (e) wide-sense stationary, (f) not stationary in any sense, and (g) ergodic.

6-39 A random process is defined by $X(t) = X_0 + Vt$ where X_0 and V are statistically independent random variables uniformly distributed on intervals $[X_{01}, X_{02}]$ and $[V_1, V_2]$, respectively. Find (a) the mean, (b) the autocorrelation, and (c) the autocovariance functions of $X(t)$. (d) Is $X(t)$ stationary in any sense? If so, state the type.

★**6-40** (a) Find the first-order density of the random process of Problem 6-39.

(b) Plot the density for $t = k(X_{02} - X_{01})/(V_2 - V_1)$ with $k = 0, \frac{1}{2}, 1$, and 2. Assume $V_2 = 3V_1$ in all plots.

6-41 Assume a wide-sense stationary process $X(t)$ has a known mean $\bar{X}$ and a known autocorrelation function $R_{XX}(\tau)$. Now suppose the process is observed at time t_1 and we wish to *estimate*, that is, *predict*, what the process will be at time $t_1 + \tau$ with $\tau > 0$. We assume the estimate has the form

$$\hat{X}(t_1 + \tau) = \alpha X(t_1) + \beta$$

where α and β are constants.

(a) Find α and β so that the mean-squared prediction error

$$\overline{\varepsilon^2} = E[\{X(t_1 + \tau) - \hat{X}(t_1 + \tau)\}^2]$$

is minimum.

(b) Find the minimum mean-squared error in terms of $R_{XX}(\tau)$. Develop an alternative form in terms of the autocovariance function.

6-42 Find the time average and time autocorrelation function of the random process of Example 6.2-1. Compare these results with the statistical mean and autocorrelation found in the example.

6-43 Assume that an ergodic random process $X(t)$ has an autocorrelation function

$$R_{XX}(\tau) = 18 + \frac{2}{6 + \tau^2}[1 + 4\cos{(12\tau)}]$$

(a) Find $|\bar{X}|$.

(b) Does this process have a periodic component?

(c) What is the average power in $X(t)$?

6-44 Define a random process $X(t)$ as follows: (1) $X(t)$ assumes only one of two possible levels 1 or -1 at any time, (2) $X(t)$ switches back and forth between its two levels randomly with time, (3) the number of level transitions in any time interval τ is a Poisson random variable, that is, the probability of exactly k transitions, when the average rate of transitions is λ, is given by $[(\lambda\tau)^k/k!]\exp{(-\lambda\tau)}$, (4) transitions occurring in any time interval are statistically independent of transitions in any other interval, and (5) the levels at the start of any interval are equally probable. $X(t)$ is usually called the *random telegraph process*. It is an example of a discrete random process.

(a) Find the autocorrelation function of the process.

(b) Find probabilities $P\{X(t) = 1\}$ and $P\{X(t) = -1\}$ for any t.

(c) What is $E[X(t)]$?

(d) Discuss the stationarity of $X(t)$.

6-45 Work Problem 6-44 assuming the random telegraph signal has levels 0 and 1.

6-46 $\bar{X} = 6$ and $R_{XX}(t, t + \tau) = 36 + 25\exp{(-|\tau|)}$ for a random process $X(t)$. Indicate which of the following statements are true based on what is known with certainty. $X(t)$ (a) is first-order stationary, (b) has total average power of 61 W, (c) is ergodic, (d) is wide-sense stationary, (e) has a periodic component, and (f) has an ac power of 36 W.

6-47 A stationary zero-mean random process $X(t)$ is ergodic, has average power of 24 W, and has no periodic components. Which of the following can be a valid autocorrelation function? If one cannot, state at least one reason why. (a) $16 + 18\cos{(3\tau)}$, (b) $24\text{Sa}^2(2\tau)$, (c) $[1 + 3\tau^2]^{-1}\exp{(-6\tau)}$, and (d) $24\delta(t - \tau)$.

6-48 Use the result of Problem 6-18 to find the autocorrelation function of a random process with periodic sample function waveform $p(t)$ defined by

$$p(t) = A\cos^2{(2\pi t/T)}$$

where A and $T > 0$ are constants.

6-49 An engineer wants to measure the mean value of a noise signal that can be well-modeled as a sample function of a gaussian process. He uses the sampling estimator of Problem 6-31. After 100 samples he wishes his estimate to be within ± 0.1 V of the true mean with probability 0.9606. What is the largest variance the process can have such that his wishes will be true?

6-50 Let $X(t)$ be the sum of a deterministic signal $s(t)$ and a wide-sense stationary noise process $N(t)$. Find the mean value, and autocorrelation and auto-covariance functions of $X(t)$. Discuss the stationarity of $X(t)$.

6-51 Random processes $X(t)$ and $Y(t)$ are defined by

$$X(t) = A \cos (\omega_0 t + \Theta)$$

$$Y(t) = B \sin (\omega_0 t + \Theta)$$

where A, B, and ω_0 are constants while Θ is a random variable uniform on $(0, 2\pi)$. By the procedures of Example 6.2-1 it is easy to find that $X(t)$ and $Y(t)$ are zero-mean, wide-sense stationary with autocorrelation functions

$$R_{XX}(\tau) = (A^2/2) \cos (\omega_0 \tau)$$

$$R_{YY}(\tau) = (B^2/2) \cos (\omega_0 \tau)$$

(a) Find the cross-correlation function $R_{XY}(t, t + \tau)$ and show that $X(t)$ and $Y(t)$ are jointly wide-sense stationary.

(b) Solve (6.4-2) and show that the response of the system of Figure 6.4-1 equals the true cross-correlation function plus an error term $\varepsilon(T)$ that decreases as T increases.

(c) Sketch $|\varepsilon(T)|$ versus T to show its behavior. How large must T be to make $|\varepsilon(T)|$ less than 1% of the largest value the correct cross-correlation function can have?

6-52 Consider random processes

$$X(t) = A \cos (\omega_0 t + \Theta)$$

$$Y(t) = B \cos (\omega_1 t + \Phi)$$

where A, B, ω_1, and ω_0 are constants, while Θ and Φ are statistically independent random variables each uniform on $(0, 2\pi)$.

(a) Show that $X(t)$ and $Y(t)$ are not jointly wide-sense stationary.

(b) If $\Theta = \Phi$ show that $X(t)$ and $Y(t)$ are not jointly wide-sense stationary unless $\omega_1 = \omega_0$.

6-53 A zero-mean gaussian random process has an autocorrelation function

$$R_{XX}(\tau) = \begin{cases} 13[1 - (|\tau|/6)] & |\tau| \leq 6 \\ 0 & \text{elsewhere} \end{cases}$$

Find the covariance function necessary to specify the joint density of random variables defined at times $t_i = 2(i - 1)$, $i = 1, 2, \ldots, 5$. Give the covariance matrix for the $X_i = X(t_i)$.

6-54 If the gaussian process of Problem 6-53 is shifted to have a constant mean $\bar{X} = -2$ but all else is unchanged, discuss how the autocorrelation function and covariance matrix change. What is the effect on the joint density of the five random variables?

★6-55 Extend Example 6.7-1 to allow the sum of complex-amplitude unequal-frequency phasors. Let $Z_i, i = 1, 2, \ldots, N$ be N complex zero-mean, uncorrelated random variables with variances $\sigma_{Z_i}^2$. Form a random process

$$Z(t) = \sum_{i=1}^{N} Z_i e^{j\omega_i t}$$

where ω_i are the angular frequencies of the phasors.
(a) Show that $E[Z(t)] = 0$.
(b) Derive the autocorrelation function and show that $Z(t)$ is wide-sense stationary.

★6-56 A complex random process is defined by

$$Z(t) = \exp(j\Omega t)$$

where Ω is a zero-mean random variable uniformly distributed on the interval from $\omega_0 - \Delta\omega$ to $\omega_0 + \Delta\omega$, where ω_0 and $\Delta\omega$ are positive constants. Find:
(a) The mean value, and (b) the autocorrelation function of $Z(t)$.
(c) Is $Z(t)$ wide-sense stationary?

★6-57 Work Problem 6-56 except assume the process

$$Z(t) = e^{j\Omega t} + e^{-j\Omega t} = 2\cos(\Omega t)$$

★6-58 Let $X(t)$ and $Y(t)$ be statistically independent wide-sense stationary real processes having the same autocorrelation function $R(\tau)$. Define the complex process

$$Z(t) = X(t)\cos(\omega_0 t) + jY(t)\sin(\omega_0 t)$$

where ω_0 is a positive constant. Find the autocorrelation function of $Z(t)$. Is $Z(t)$ wide-sense stationary?

ADDITIONAL PROBLEMS, THIRD EDITION

6-59 A random process is defined by $X(t) = A$, where A is a continuous random variable uniformly distributed on $(0, 1)$,
(a) Determine the form of the sample functions.
(b) Classify the process.
(c) Is it deterministic?

6-60 Work Problem 6-59 except assume $X(t) = At$ (t represents time).

6-61 (a) Determine whether the process of Problem 6-59 is first-order stationary.
(b) Also determine whether it is wide-sense stationary.
(c) How would the results of (a) and (b) change if the random variable A had a nonuniform density?

6-62 Find the first- and second-order density functions for the process of Problem 6-59.

6-63 Find the antocorrelation function and mean of the process of Problem 6-59.

6-64 For the random process of Problem 6-60, find
(a) $E[X(t)]$.
(b) $R_{XX}(t, t + \tau)$.
(c) Is the process stationary in any sense?

6-65 A number of practical systems have "square-law" detectors that produce an output $W(t)$ that is the square of its input $Y(t)$. Let the detector's output be defined by

$$W(t) = Y^2(t) = X^2(t) \cos^2 (\omega_0 t + \Theta)$$

where ω_0 is a constant, $X(t)$ is second-order stationary, and Θ is a random variable independent of $X(t)$ and uniform on $(0, 2\pi)$. Find (a) $E[W(t)]$, (b) $R_{WW}(t, t + \tau)$, and (c) whether or not $W(t)$ is wide-sense stationary.

6-66 A random process $X(t)$ is known to be wide-sense stationary with $E[X^2(t)] = 11$. Give one or more reasons why each of the following expressions cannot be the autocorrelation function of the process.

(a) $R_{XX}(t, t + \tau) = \cos (8t) e^{-(t + \tau)^2}$

(b) $R_{XX}(t, t + \tau) = \dfrac{\sin (2\tau)}{1 + \tau^2}$

(c) $R_{XX}(t, t + \tau) = \dfrac{11 \sin [5(\tau - 2)]}{5(\tau - 2)}$

(d) $R_{XX}(t, t + \tau) = -11 e^{-|\tau|}$

(e) $R_{XX}(t, t + \tau) = \dfrac{11\tau}{1 + 3\tau^2 + 4\tau^4}$

6-67 A wide-sense stationary random process $Y(t)$ has a power of $E[Y^2(t)] = 4$. Give at least one reason why each of the following expressions cannot be its autocorrelation function.

(a) $R_{YY}(t, t + \tau) = 4 \tan^{-1} (\tau)$

(b) $R_{YY}(t, t + \tau) = 6 \exp [-2\tau^2 - |\tau|]$

(c) $R_{YY}(t, t + \tau) = \dfrac{1}{2} u(\tau)$

(d) $R_{YY}(t, t + \tau) = \dfrac{-0.5 + u(\tau)}{1 + 8\tau^4}$

(e) $R_{YY}(t, t + \tau) = \dfrac{\cos^2 (6\tau)}{2 + \cos^2 (4t)}$

6-68 Two random processes are defined by

$$Y_1(t) = X(t) \cos (\omega_0 t)$$

$$Y_2(t) = Y(t) \cos (\omega_0 t + \Theta)$$

where $X(t)$ and $Y(t)$ are jointly wide-sense stationary processes.

(a) If Θ is a constant (nonrandom), is there any value of Θ that will make $Y_1(t)$ and $Y_2(t)$ orthogonal?

(b) If Θ is a uniform random variable, statistically independent of $X(t)$ and $Y(t)$, are there any conditions on Θ that will make $Y_1(t)$ and $Y_2(t)$ orthogonal?

6-69 Determine the largest constant K such that the function

$$R_{XY}(\tau) = Ke^{-\tau^2} \sin (\pi\tau)$$

can possibly be a valid cross-correlation function of two jointly wide-sense stationary processes $X(t)$ and $Y(t)$ for which $E[X^2(t)] = 6$ and $E[Y^2(t)] = 4$.

6-70 A random process, as defined by $Y(t) = X(t) \cos (\omega_0 t + \Theta)$ in Problem 6-65, is applied to both inputs of the measurement system of Figure 6.4-1. Determine $R_0(2T)$ if ω_0 is large enough so that $\cos (\omega_0 t + \Theta)$ cycles rapidly compared to $X(t)$.

6-71 Aircraft arrive at an airport according to a Poisson process at a rate of 12 per hour. All aircraft are handled by one air-traffic controller. If the controller takes a 2-minute coffee break, what is the probability that he will miss one or more arriving aircraft?

6-72 Telephone calls are initiated through an exchange at the average rate of 75 per minute and are described by a Poisson process. Find the probability that more than 3 calls are initiated in any 5-second period.

6-73 A small store has two check-out lanes that develop waiting lines if more than two customers arrive in any one-minute interval. Assume that a Poisson process describes the number of customers that arrives for check-out. Find the proability of a waiting line if the average rate of customer arrivals is (a) 2 per minute, (b) 1 per minute, and (c) $^1/_2$ per minute.

6-74 A particular commercial system for controlling a petroleum distillation plant has failures (resulting in plant down time) that occur at the average rate of two per 30 days. Assume that the number of failures is a Poisson process and find the probability that one failure will occur during the first 30 days and no other failures will occur for the next 30 days.

6-75 Show that the autocorrelation function of the Poisson process is

$$R_{XX}(t_1, t_2) = \begin{cases} \lambda t_1[1 + \lambda t_2] & t_1 < t_2 \\ \lambda t_2[1 + \lambda t_1] & t_1 > t_2 \end{cases}$$

(*Hint:* Make use of the sums in (6.6-3) and (6.6-4).]

6-76 Determine the autocovariance function of the Poisson process. (*Hint:* Make use of the result of Problem 6-75).

CHAPTER
7

SPECTRAL
CHARACTERISTICS
OF RANDOM
PROCESSES

7.0 INTRODUCTION

All of the foregoing discussions concerning random processes have involved the time domain. That is, we have characterized processes by means of autocorrelation, cross-correlation, and covariance functions without any consideration of spectral properties. As is well known, both time domain *and* frequency domain analysis methods exist for analyzing linear systems and deterministic waveforms. But what about random waveforms? Is there some way to describe random processes in the frequency domain? The answer is yes, and it is the purpose of this chapter to introduce the most important concepts that apply to characterizing random processes in the frequency domain.

The spectral description of a deterministic waveform is obtained by Fourier transforming the waveform, and the reader would be correct in concluding that Fourier transforms play an important role in the spectral characterization of random waveforms. However, the direct transformation approach is not attractive for random waveforms because the transform may not exist. Thus, spectral analysis of random processes requires a bit more subtlety than do deterministic signals.

An appropriate spectrum to be associated with a random process is introduced in the following section. The concepts rely heavily on theory of Fourier transforms. Readers wishing to refresh their background on Fourier theory are referred to Appendix D where a short review is given.

7.1 POWER DENSITY SPECTRUM AND ITS PROPERTIES

The spectral properties of a *deterministic* signal $x(t)$ are contained in its *Fourier transform $X(\omega)$* given by

$$X(\omega) = \int_{-\infty}^{\infty} x(t)e^{-j\omega t} \, dt \qquad (7.1\text{-}1)$$

The function $X(\omega)$, sometimes called simply the *spectrum* of $x(t)$, has the unit of volts per hertz when $x(t)$ is a voltage and describes the way in which relative signal voltage is distributed with frequency. The Fourier transform can, therefore, be considered to be a *voltage density spectrum* applicable to $x(t)$. Both the amplitudes and phases of the frequencies present in $x(t)$ are described by $X(\omega)$. For this reason, if $X(\omega)$ is known then $x(t)$ can be recovered by means of the *inverse Fourier transform*

$$x(t) = \frac{1}{2\pi} \int_{-\infty}^{\infty} X(\omega)e^{j\omega t} \, d\omega \qquad (7.1\text{-}2)$$

In other words, $X(\omega)$ forms a complete description of $x(t)$ and vice versa.

In attempting to apply (7.1-1) to a random process, we immediately encounter problems. The principal problem is the fact that $X(\omega)$ may not exist for most sample functions of the process. Thus, we conclude that a spectral description of a random process utilizing a voltage density spectrum (Fourier transform) is not feasible because such a spectrum may not exist. Other problems arise if Laplace transforms are considered (Cooper and McGillem, 1971, p. 132).

On the other hand, if we turn our attention to the description of the *power* in the random process as a function of frequency, instead of voltage, it results that such a function does exist. We next proceed to develop this function, called the *power density spectrum†* of the random process.

The Power Density Spectrum

For a random process $X(t)$, let $x_T(t)$ be defined as that portion of a sample function $x(t)$ that exists between $-T$ and T; that is

$$x_T(t) = \begin{cases} x(t) & -T < t < T \\ 0 & \text{elsewhere} \end{cases} \qquad (7.1\text{-}3)$$

Now so long as T is finite, we presume that $x_T(t)$ will satisfy

$$\int_{-T}^{T} |x_T(t)| \, dt < \infty \qquad (7.1\text{-}4)$$

---

† Many books call this function a *power spectral density*. We shall occasionally use also the names *power density* or *power spectrum*.

and will have a Fourier transform (see Appendix D for conditions sufficient for the existence of Fourier transforms), which we denote $X_T(\omega)$, given by

$$X_T(\omega) = \int_{-T}^{T} x_T(t)e^{-j\omega t}\, dt = \int_{-T}^{T} x(t)e^{-j\omega t}\, dt \tag{7.1-5}$$

The energy contained in $x(t)$ in the interval $(-T, T)$ is†

$$E(T) = \int_{-T}^{T} x_T^2(t)\, dt = \int_{-T}^{T} x^2(t)\, dt \tag{7.1-6}$$

Since $x_T(t)$ is Fourier transformable, its energy must also be related to $X_T(\omega)$ by Parseval's theorem. Thus, from (7.1-6) and (D-21) of Appendix D

$$E(T) = \int_{-T}^{T} x^2(t)\, dt = \frac{1}{2\pi} \int_{-\infty}^{\infty} |X_T(\omega)|^2\, d\omega \tag{7.1-7}$$

By dividing the expressions in (7.1-7) by $2T$, we obtain the average power $P(T)$ in $x(t)$ over the interval $(-T, T)$:

$$P(T) = \frac{1}{2T} \int_{-T}^{T} x^2(t)\, dt = \frac{1}{2\pi} \int_{-\infty}^{\infty} \frac{|X_T(\omega)|^2}{2T}\, d\omega \tag{7.1-8}$$

At this point we observe that $|X_T(\omega)|^2/2T$ is a power density spectrum because power results through its integration. However, it is not the function that we seek for two reasons. One is the fact that (7.1-8) does not represent the power in an entire sample function. There remains the step of letting T become arbitrarily large so as to include all power in the ensemble member. The second reason is that (7.1-8) is only the power in one sample function and does not represent the process. In other words, $P(T)$ is actually a random variable with respect to the random process. By taking the expected value in (7.1-8), we can obtain an average power P_{XX} for the random process.‡

From the above discussion it is clear that we must still form the limit as $T \to \infty$ and take the expected value of (7.1-8) to obtain a suitable power density spectrum for the random process. It is important that the limiting operation be done last (Thomas, 1969, p. 98, or Cooper and McGillem, 1971, p. 134). After these operations are performed, (7.1-8) can be written

$$P_{XX} = \lim_{T \to \infty} \frac{1}{2T} \int_{-T}^{T} E[X^2(t)]\, dt = \frac{1}{2\pi} \int_{-\infty}^{\infty} \lim_{T \to \infty} \frac{E[|X_T(\omega)|^2]}{2T}\, d\omega \tag{7.1-9}$$

---

† We assume a real process $X(t)$ and interpret $x(t)$ as either the voltage across a 1-Ω impedance or the current through 1 Ω. In other words, we shall assume a 1-Ω real impedance whenever we discuss energy or power in subsequent work, unless specifically stated otherwise.

‡ In taking the expected value we replace $x(t)$ by $X(t)$ in (7.1-8) since the integral of $x^2(t)$ is an operation performed on all sample functions of $X(t)$.

Equation (7.1-9) establishes two important facts. First, average power P_{XX} in a random process $X(t)$ is given by the time average of its second moment:

$$P_{XX} = \lim_{T \to \infty} \frac{1}{2T} \int_{-T}^{T} E[X^2(t)] \, dt = A\{E[X^2(t)]\} \qquad (7.1\text{-}10)$$

For a process that is at least wide-sense stationary, $E[X^2(t)] = \overline{X^2}$, a constant, and $P_{XX} = \overline{X^2}$. Second, P_{XX} can be obtained by a frequency domain integration. If we define the *power density spectrum* for the random process by

$$\mathcal{S}_{XX}(\omega) = \lim_{T \to \infty} \frac{E[|X_T(\omega)|^2]}{2T} \qquad (7.1\text{-}11)$$

the applicable integral is

$$P_{XX} = \frac{1}{2\pi} \int_{-\infty}^{\infty} \mathcal{S}_{XX}(\omega) \, d\omega \qquad (7.1\text{-}12)$$

from (7.1-9). Two examples will illustrate the above concepts.

Example 7.1-1 Consider the random process

$$X(t) = A \cos (\omega_0 t + \Theta)$$

where A and ω_0 are real constants and Θ is a random variable uniformly distributed on the interval $(0, \pi/2)$. We shall find the average power P_{XX} in $X(t)$ by use of (7.1-10). Mean-squared value is

$$E[X^2(t)] = E[A^2 \cos^2 (\omega_0 t + \Theta)] = E\left[\frac{A^2}{2} + \frac{A^2}{2} \cos (2\omega_0 t + 2\Theta)\right]$$

$$= \frac{A^2}{2} + \frac{A^2}{2} \int_{0}^{\pi/2} \frac{2}{\pi} \cos (2\omega_0 t + 2\theta) \, d\theta$$

$$= \frac{A^2}{2} - \frac{A^2}{\pi} \sin (2\omega_0 t)$$

This process is not even wide-sense stationary, since the above function is time-dependent. The time average of the above expression is

$$A\{E[X^2(t)]\} = \lim_{T \to \infty} \frac{1}{2T} \int_{-T}^{T} \left[\frac{A^2}{2} - \frac{A^2}{\pi} \sin (2\omega_0 t)\right] dt$$

which easily evaluates to

$$P_{XX} = A\{E[X^2(t)]\} = A^2/2$$

Example 7.1-2 We reconsider the process of the above example to find $\mathcal{S}_{XX}(\omega)$ and average power P_{XX} by use of (7.1-11) and (7.1-12), respectively.

First we find $X_T(\omega)$:

$$
X_T(\omega) = \int_{-T}^{T} A \cos(\omega_0 t + \Theta) \exp(-j\omega t)\, dt
$$

$$
= \frac{A}{2} \exp(j\Theta) \int_{-T}^{T} \exp[j(\omega_0 - \omega)t]\, dt
$$

$$
+ \frac{A}{2} \exp(-j\Theta) \int_{-T}^{T} \exp[-j(\omega_0 + \omega)t]\, dt
$$

$$
= AT \exp(j\Theta) \frac{\sin[(\omega - \omega_0)T]}{(\omega - \omega_0)T}
$$

$$
+ AT \exp(-j\Theta) \frac{\sin[(\omega + \omega_0)T]}{(\omega + \omega_0)T}
$$

Next we determine $|X_T(\omega)|^2 = X_T(\omega)X_T^*(\omega)$ and find its expected value. After some simple algebraic reduction we obtain

$$
\frac{E[|X_T(\omega)|^2]}{2T} = \frac{A^2\pi}{2} \left\{ \frac{T}{\pi} \frac{\sin^2[(\omega - \omega_0)T]}{[(\omega - \omega_0)T]^2} + \frac{T}{\pi} \frac{\sin^2[(\omega + \omega_0)T]}{[(\omega + \omega_0)T]^2} \right\}
$$

Now it is known that

$$
\lim_{T \to \infty} \frac{T}{\pi} \left[\frac{\sin(\alpha T)}{\alpha T} \right]^2 = \delta(\alpha)
$$

(Lathi, 1968, p. 24), so (7.1-11) and the above result give

$$
\mathcal{S}_{XX}(\omega) = \frac{A^2\pi}{2} [\delta(\omega - \omega_0) + \delta(\omega + \omega_0)]
$$

Finally, we use this result to obtain average power from (7.1-12):

$$
P_{XX} = \frac{1}{2\pi} \int_{-\infty}^{\infty} \frac{A^2\pi}{2} [\delta(\omega - \omega_0) + \delta(\omega + \omega_0)]\, d\omega = \frac{A^2}{2}
$$

Thus, P_{XX} found here agrees with that of the earlier Example 7.1-1.

Properties of the Power Density Spectrum

The power density spectrum possesses a number of important properties:

$$
(1) \quad \mathcal{S}_{XX}(\omega) \geq 0 \tag{7.1-13}
$$

$$
(2) \quad \mathcal{S}_{XX}(-\omega) = \mathcal{S}_{XX}(\omega) \qquad X(t) \text{ real} \tag{7.1-14}
$$

$$
(3) \quad \mathcal{S}_{XX}(\omega) \text{ is real} \tag{7.1-15}
$$

$$
(4) \quad \frac{1}{2\pi} \int_{-\infty}^{\infty} \mathcal{S}_{XX}(\omega)\, d\omega = A\{E[X^2(t)]\} \tag{7.1-16}
$$

Property 1 follows from the definition (7.1-11) and the fact that the expected value of a nonnegative function is nonnegative. Similarly, property 3 is true from (7.1-11) since $|X_T(\omega)|^2$ is real. Some reflection on the properties of Fourier transforms of real functions will verify property 2 (see Problem 7-9). Property 4 is just another statement of (7.1-9).

Sometimes another property is included in a list of properties:

$$(5) \quad \mathscr{S}_{\dot{X}\dot{X}}(\omega) = \omega^2 \mathscr{S}_{XX}(\omega) \tag{7.1-17}$$

It says that the power density spectrum of the derivative $\dot{X}(t) = dX(t)/dt$ is ω^2 times the power spectrum of $X(t)$. Proof of this property is left as a reader exercise (Problem 7-10).

A final property we list is

$$(6) \quad \frac{1}{2\pi} \int_{-\infty}^{\infty} \mathscr{S}_{XX}(\omega)e^{j\omega\tau}\,d\omega = A[R_{XX}(t, t+\tau)] \tag{7.1-18}$$

$$\mathscr{S}_{XX}(\omega) = \int_{-\infty}^{\infty} A[R_{XX}(t, t+\tau)]e^{-j\omega t}\,d\tau \tag{7.1-19}$$

It states that the power density spectrum and the time average of the autocorrelation function form a Fourier transform pair. We prove this very important property in Section 7.2. Of course, if $X(t)$ is at least wide-sense stationary, $A[R_{XX}(t, t+\tau)] = R_{XX}(\tau)$, and property 6 indicates that the power spectrum and the autocorrelation function form a Fourier transform pair. Thus

$$\mathscr{S}_{XX}(\omega) = \int_{-\infty}^{\infty} R_{XX}(\tau)e^{-j\omega\tau}\,d\tau \tag{7.1-20}$$

$$R_{XX}(\tau) = \frac{1}{2\pi} \int_{-\infty}^{\infty} \mathscr{S}_{XX}(\omega)e^{j\omega\tau}\,d\omega \tag{7.1-21}$$

for a wide-sense stationary process.

Bandwidth of the Power Density Spectrum

Assume that $X(t)$ is a lowpass process; that is, its spectral components are clustered near $\omega = 0$ and have decreasing magnitudes at higher frequencies. Except for the fact that the area of $\mathscr{S}_{XX}(\omega)$ is not necessarily unity, $\mathscr{S}_{XX}(\omega)$ has characteristics similar to a probability density function (it is nonnegative and real). Indeed, by dividing $\mathscr{S}_{XX}(\omega)$ by its area, a new function is formed with area of unity that is analogous to a density function.

Recall that standard deviation is a measure of the spread in a density function. The analogous quantity for the normalized power spectrum is a measure of its spread that we call *rms bandwidth*,† which we denote $W_{\text{rms}}(\text{rad/s})$. Now since

---

† The notation rms bandwidth stands for *root-mean-squared* bandwidth.

$\mathcal{S}_{XX}(\omega)$ is an even function for a real process, its "mean value" is zero and its "standard deviation" is the square root of its second moment. Thus, upon normalization, the rms bandwidth is given by

$$W_{\text{rms}}^2 = \frac{\int_{-\infty}^{\infty} \omega^2 \mathcal{S}_{XX}(\omega)\, d\omega}{\int_{-\infty}^{\infty} \mathcal{S}_{XX}(\omega)\, d\omega} \qquad , \tag{7.1-22}$$

Example 7.1-3 Given the power spectrum

$$\mathcal{S}_{XX}(\omega) = \frac{10}{[1 + (\omega/10)^2]^2}$$

where the 6-dB bandwidth is 10 radians per second, we find W_{rms}. First, using (C-28) from Appendix C,

$$\int_{-\infty}^{\infty} \frac{10\, d\omega}{[1 + (\omega/10)^2]^2} = 10^5 \int_{-\infty}^{\infty} \frac{d\omega}{(100 + \omega^2)^2}$$

$$= 10^5 \left\{ \frac{\omega}{200(100 + \omega^2)} \bigg|_{-\infty}^{\infty} + \frac{1}{2000} \tan^{-1}\left(\frac{\omega}{10}\right) \bigg|_{-\infty}^{\infty} \right\}$$

$$= 50\pi$$

Next, from (C-30) of Appendix C:

$$\int_{-\infty}^{\infty} \frac{10\omega^2\, d\omega}{[1 + (\omega/10)^2]^2} = 10^5 \int_{-\infty}^{\infty} \frac{\omega^2\, d\omega}{(100 + \omega^2)^2}$$

$$= 10^5 \left\{ \frac{-\omega}{2(100 + \omega^2)} \bigg|_{-\infty}^{\infty} + \frac{1}{20} \tan^{-1}\left(\frac{\omega}{10}\right) \bigg|_{-\infty}^{\infty} \right\}$$

$$= 5000\pi$$

Thus

$$W_{\text{rms}} = \sqrt{\frac{5000\pi}{50\pi}} = 10 \text{ rad/s}$$

Although W_{rms} and the 6-dB bandwidth of $\mathcal{S}_{XX}(\omega)$ are equal in this case, they are not equal in general.

The above concept is readily extended to a process that has a bandpass form of power spectrum; that is, its significant spectral components cluster near some frequencies $\bar{\omega}_0$ and $-\bar{\omega}_0$. If we assume that the process $X(t)$ is real, $\mathcal{S}_{XX}(\omega)$ will be real and have even symmetry about $\omega = 0$. With this assumption we define a *mean* frequency $\bar{\omega}_0$ by

$$\bar{\omega}_0 = \frac{\int_0^{\infty} \omega \mathcal{S}_{XX}(\omega)\, d\omega}{\int_0^{\infty} \mathcal{S}_{XX}(\omega)\, d\omega} \tag{7.1-23}$$

and rms bandwidth by

$$W_{rms}^2 = \frac{4 \int_0^\infty (\omega - \bar{\omega}_0)^2 \mathcal{S}_{XX}(\omega) \, d\omega}{\int_0^\infty \mathcal{S}_{XX}(\omega) \, d\omega} \tag{7.1-24}$$

The reader is encouraged to sketch a few lowpass and bandpass power spectrums and justify for himself why the factor of 4 appears in (7.1-24).

7.2 RELATIONSHIP BETWEEN POWER SPECTRUM AND AUTOCORRELATION FUNCTION

In Section 7.1 it was stated that the inverse Fourier transform of the power density spectrum is the time average of the autocorrelation function; that is

$$\frac{1}{2\pi} \int_{-\infty}^{\infty} \mathcal{S}_{XX}(\omega) e^{j\omega\tau} \, d\omega = A[R_{XX}(t, t + \tau)] \tag{7.2-1}$$

This expression will now be proved.

If we use (7.1-5), which is the definition of $X_T(\omega)$, in the defining equation (7.1-11) for the power spectrum we have†

$$\mathcal{S}_{XX}(\omega) = \lim_{T \to \infty} E\left[\frac{1}{2T} \int_{-T}^{T} X(t_1) e^{j\omega t_1} \, dt_1 \int_{-T}^{T} X(t_2) e^{-j\omega t_2} \, dt_2 \right]$$

$$= \lim_{T \to \infty} \frac{1}{2T} \int_{-T}^{T} \int_{-T}^{T} E[X(t_1)X(t_2)] e^{-j\omega(t_2 - t_1)} \, dt_2 \, dt_1 \tag{7.2-2}$$

The expectation in the integrand of (7.2-2) is identified as the autocorrelation function of $X(t)$:

$$E[X(t_1)X(t_2)] = R_{XX}(t_1, t_2) \qquad -T < (t_1 \text{ and } t_2) < T \tag{7.2-3}$$

Thus, (7.2-2) becomes

$$\mathcal{S}_{XX}(\omega) = \lim_{T \to \infty} \frac{1}{2T} \int_{-T}^{T} \int_{-T}^{T} R_{XX}(t_1, t_2) e^{-j\omega(t_2 - t_1)} \, dt_1 \, dt_2 \tag{7.2-4}$$

Suppose we next make the variable changes

$$t = t_1 \qquad\qquad dt = dt_1 \tag{7.2-5a}$$

$$\tau = t_2 - t_1 = t_2 - t \qquad d\tau = dt_2 \tag{7.2-5b}$$

in (7.2-4); we obtain

$$\mathcal{S}_{XX}(\omega) = \lim_{T \to \infty} \frac{1}{2T} \int_{-T-t}^{T-t} \int_{-T}^{T} R_{XX}(t, t + \tau) \, dt \, e^{-j\omega\tau} \, d\tau \tag{7.2-6}$$

---

† We use $X(t)$ in (7.1-5), rather than $x(t)$, to imply that the operations performed take place on the process as opposed to one sample function.

Next, taking the limit with respect to the τ integral first will allow us to interchange the limit and τ integral operations to get

$$\mathscr{S}_{XX}(\omega) = \int_{-\infty}^{\infty} \left\{ \lim_{T \to \infty} \frac{1}{2T} \int_{-T}^{T} R_{XX}(t, t + \tau)\, dt \right\} e^{-j\omega\tau}\, d\tau \qquad (7.2\text{-}7)$$

The quantity within braces is recognized as the time average of the process autocorrelation function

$$A[R_{XX}(t, t + \tau)] = \lim_{T \to \infty} \frac{1}{2T} \int_{-T}^{T} R_{XX}(t, t + \tau)\, dt \qquad (7.2\text{-}8)$$

Thus, (7.2-7) becomes

$$\mathscr{S}_{XX}(\omega) = \int_{-\infty}^{\infty} A[R_{XX}(t, t + \tau)] e^{-j\omega\tau}\, d\tau \qquad (7.2\text{-}9)$$

which shows that $\mathscr{S}_{XX}(\omega)$ and $A[R_{XX}(t, t + \tau)]$ form a Fourier transform pair:

$$A[R_{XX}(t, t + \tau)] \leftrightarrow \mathscr{S}_{XX}(\omega) \qquad (7.2\text{-}10)$$

This expression implies (7.2-1), which we started out to prove.

For the important case where $X(t)$ is at least wide-sense stationary, $A[R_{XX}(t, t + \tau)] = R_{XX}(\tau)$ and we get

$$\mathscr{S}_{XX}(\omega) = \int_{-\infty}^{\infty} R_{XX}(\tau) e^{-j\omega\tau}\, d\tau \qquad (7.2\text{-}11)$$

$$R_{XX}(\tau) = \frac{1}{2\pi} \int_{-\infty}^{\infty} \mathscr{S}_{XX}(\omega) e^{j\omega\tau}\, d\omega \qquad (7.2\text{-}12)$$

or

$$R_{XX}(\tau) \leftrightarrow \mathscr{S}_{XX}(\omega) \qquad (7.2\text{-}13)$$

The expressions (7.2-11) and (7.2-12) are usually called the *Wiener-Khinchin relations* after the great American mathematician Norbert Wiener (1894–1964) and the German mathematician A. I. Khinchin (1894–1959). They form the basic link between the time domain description (correlation functions) of processes and their description in the frequency domain (power spectrum).

From (7.2-13), it is clear that knowledge of the power spectrum of a process allows complete recovery of the autocorrelation function when $X(t)$ is at least wide-sense stationary; for a nonstationary process, only the time average of the autocorrelation function is recoverable from (7.2-10).

Example 7.2-1 The power spectrum will be found for the random process of Example 6.2-1 that has the autocorrelation function

$$R_{XX}(\tau) = (A^2/2) \cos(\omega_0 \tau)$$

where A and ω_0 are constants. This equation can be written in the form

$$R_{XX}(\tau) = \frac{A^2}{4} \left(e^{j\omega_0\tau} + e^{-j\omega_0\tau} \right)$$

Now we note that the inverse transform of a frequency domain impulse function is

$$\frac{1}{2\pi} \int_{-\infty}^{\infty} \delta(\omega) e^{j\omega\tau} \, d\omega = \frac{1}{2\pi}$$

from (A-2) of Appendix A. Thus

$$1 \leftrightarrow 2\pi\delta(\omega)$$

and, from the frequency-shifting property of Fourier transforms given by (D-7) of Appendix D, we get

$$e^{j\omega_0\tau} \leftrightarrow 2\pi\delta(\omega - \omega_0)$$

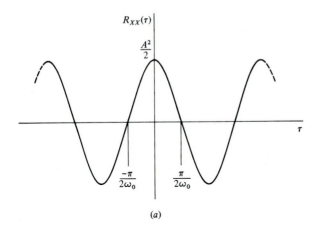

(a)

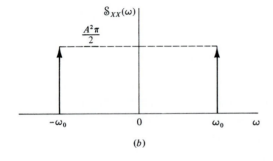

(b)

FIGURE 7.2-1
The autocorrelation function (a) and power density spectrum (b) of the wide-sense stationary random process of Example 7.2-1.

By using this last result, the Fourier transform of $R_{XX}(\tau)$ becomes

$$\mathscr{S}_{XX}(\omega) = \frac{A^2\pi}{2}[\delta(\omega - \omega_0) + \delta(\omega + \omega_0)]$$

This function and $R_{XX}(\tau)$ are illustrated in Figure 7.2-1.

7.3 CROSS-POWER DENSITY SPECTRUM AND ITS PROPERTIES

Consider a real random process $W(t)$ given by the sum of two other real processes $X(t)$ and $Y(t)$:

$$W(t) = X(t) + Y(t) \tag{7.3-1}$$

The autocorrelation function of $W(t)$ is

$$
\begin{aligned}
R_{WW}(t, t + \tau) &= E[W(t)W(t + \tau)] \\
&= E\{[X(t) + Y(t)][X(t + \tau) + Y(t + \tau)]\} \\
&= R_{XX}(t, t + \tau) + R_{YY}(t, t + \tau) \\
&\quad + R_{XY}(t, t + \tau) + R_{YX}(t, t + \tau)
\end{aligned}
\tag{7.3-2}
$$

Now if we take the time average of both sides of (7.3-2) and Fourier transform the resulting expression by applying (7.2-9), we have

$$\mathscr{S}_{WW}(\omega) = \mathscr{S}_{XX}(\omega) + \mathscr{S}_{YY}(\omega) + \mathscr{F}\{A[R_{XY}(t, t + \tau)]\} + \mathscr{F}\{A[R_{YX}(t, t + \tau)]\} \tag{7.3-3}$$

where $\mathscr{F}\{\cdot\}$ represents the Fourier transform. It is clear that the left side of (7.3-3) is just the power spectrum of $W(t)$. Similarly, the first two right-side terms are the power spectrums of $X(t)$ and $Y(t)$, respectively. The second two right-side terms are new quantities that are the subjects of this section. It will be shown that they are *cross-power density spectrums* defined by (7.3-12) and (7.3-14) below.

The Cross-Power Density Spectrum

For two real random processes $X(t)$ and $Y(t)$, we define $x_T(t)$ and $y_T(t)$ as truncated ensemble members; that is

$$x_T(t) = \begin{cases} x(t) & -T < t < T \\ 0 & \text{elsewhere} \end{cases} \tag{7.3-4}$$

and

$$y_T(t) = \begin{cases} y(t) & -T < t < T \\ 0 & \text{elsewhere} \end{cases} \tag{7.3-5}$$

Both $x_T(t)$ and $y_T(t)$ are assumed to be magnitude integrable over the interval $(-T, T)$ as indicated by (7.1-4). As a consequence, they will possess Fourier transforms that we denote by $X_T(\omega)$ and $Y_T(\omega)$, respectively:

$$x_T(t) \leftrightarrow X_T(\omega) \tag{7.3-6}$$

$$y_T(t) \leftrightarrow Y_T(\omega) \tag{7.3-7}$$

We next define the *cross power* $P_{XY}(T)$ in the two processes within the interval $(-T, T)$ by

$$P_{XY}(T) = \frac{1}{2T} \int_{-T}^{T} x_T(t) y_T(t) \, dt = \frac{1}{2T} \int_{-T}^{T} x(t) y(t) \, dt \tag{7.3-8}$$

Since $x_T(t)$ and $y_T(t)$ are Fourier transformable, Parseval's theorem (D-20) applies; its left side is the same as (7.3-8). Thus, we may write

$$P_{XY}(T) = \frac{1}{2T} \int_{-T}^{T} x(t) y(t) \, dt = \frac{1}{2\pi} \int_{-\infty}^{\infty} \frac{X_T^*(\omega) Y_T(\omega)}{2T} \, d\omega \tag{7.3-9}$$

This cross power is a random quantity since its value will vary depending on which ensemble member is considered. We form the average cross power, denoted $\bar{P}_{XY}(T)$, by taking the expected value in (7.3-9). The result is

$$\bar{P}_{XY}(T) = \frac{1}{2T} \int_{-T}^{T} R_{XY}(t, t) \, dt = \frac{1}{2\pi} \int_{-\infty}^{\infty} \frac{E[X_T^*(\omega) Y_T(\omega)]}{2T} \, d\omega \tag{7.3-10}$$

Finally, we form the total average cross power P_{XY} by letting $T \to \infty$:

$$P_{XY} = \lim_{T \to \infty} \frac{1}{2T} \int_{-T}^{T} R_{XY}(t, t) \, dt = \frac{1}{2\pi} \int_{-\infty}^{\infty} \lim_{T \to \infty} \frac{E[X_T^*(\omega) Y_T(\omega)]}{2T} \, d\omega \tag{7.3-11}$$

It is clear that the integrand involving ω can be defined as a *cross-power density spectrum*; it is a function of ω which we denote

$$\mathscr{S}_{XY}(\omega) = \lim_{T \to \infty} \frac{E[X_T^*(\omega) Y_T(\omega)]}{2T} \tag{7.3-12}$$

Thus

$$P_{XY} = \frac{1}{2\pi} \int_{-\infty}^{\infty} \mathscr{S}_{XY}(\omega) \, d\omega \tag{7.3-13}$$

By repeating the above procedure, we can also define another cross-power density spectrum by

$$\mathscr{S}_{YX}(\omega) = \lim_{T \to \infty} \frac{E[Y_T^*(\omega) X_T(\omega)]}{2T} \tag{7.3-14}$$

Cross power is given by

$$P_{YX} = \frac{1}{2\pi} \int_{-\infty}^{\infty} \mathscr{S}_{YX}(\omega) \, d\omega = P_{XY} \tag{7.3-15}$$

Total cross power $P_{XY} + P_{YX}$ can be interpreted as the additional power two processes are capable of generating, over and above their individual powers, due to the fact that they are correlated.

Properties of the Cross-Power Density Spectrum

Some properties of the cross-power spectrum of real random processes $X(t)$ and $Y(t)$ are listed below without formal proofs.

(1) $\mathcal{S}_{XY}(\omega) = \mathcal{S}_{YX}(-\omega) = \mathcal{S}^*_{YX}(\omega)$ $\qquad$ (7.3-16)

(2) $\text{Re}\,[\mathcal{S}_{XY}(\omega)]$ and $\text{Re}\,[\mathcal{S}_{YX}(\omega)]$ are even functions of ω (see Problem 7-40).

$\qquad$ (7.3-17)

(3) $\text{Im}\,[\mathcal{S}_{XY}(\omega)]$ and $\text{Im}\,[\mathcal{S}_{YX}(\omega)]$ are odd functions of ω (see Problem 7-40).

$\qquad$ (7.3-18)

(4) $\mathcal{S}_{XY}(\omega) = 0$ and $\mathcal{S}_{YX}(\omega) = 0$ if $X(t)$ and $Y(t)$ are orthogonal. $\qquad$ (7.3-19)

(5) If $X(t)$ and $Y(t)$ are uncorrelated and have constant means $\bar{X}$ and $\bar{Y}$

$$\mathcal{S}_{XY}(\omega) = \mathcal{S}_{YX}(\omega) = 2\pi \bar{X}\,\bar{Y}\,\delta(\omega) \qquad (7.3\text{-}20)$$

(6) $\qquad A[R_{XY}(t, t + \tau)] \leftrightarrow \mathcal{S}_{XY}(\omega) \qquad (7.3\text{-}21)$

$$A[R_{YX}(t, t + \tau)] \leftrightarrow \mathcal{S}_{YX}(\omega) \qquad (7.3\text{-}22)$$

In the above properties, $\text{Re}\,[\cdot]$ and $\text{Im}\,[\cdot]$ represent the real and imaginary parts, respectively, and $A[\cdot]$ represents the time average, as usual, defined by (6.2-21).

$\qquad$ Property 1 follows from (7.3-12) and (7.3-14). Properties 2 and 3 are proved by considering the symmetry that $X_T(\omega)$ and $Y_T(\omega)$ must possess for real processes. Properties 4 and 5 may be proved by substituting the integral (Fourier transform) forms for $X_T(\omega)$ and $Y_T(\omega)$ into $E[X_T^*(\omega)Y_T(\omega)]$ and showing that the function has the necessary behavior under the stated assumptions.

$\qquad$ Property 6 states that the cross-power density spectrum and the time average of the cross-correlation function are a Fourier transform pair; its development is given in Section 7.4. For the case of jointly wide-sense stationary processes, (7.3-21) and (7.3-22) reduce to the especially useful forms

$$\mathcal{S}_{XY}(\omega) = \int_{-\infty}^{\infty} R_{XY}(\tau)e^{-j\omega\tau}\,d\tau \qquad (7.3\text{-}23)$$

$$\mathcal{S}_{YX}(\omega) = \int_{-\infty}^{\infty} R_{YX}(\tau)e^{-j\omega\tau}\,d\tau \qquad (7.3\text{-}24)$$

$$R_{XY}(\tau) = \frac{1}{2\pi}\int_{-\infty}^{\infty} \mathcal{S}_{XY}(\omega)e^{j\omega\tau}\,d\omega \qquad (7.3\text{-}25)$$

$$R_{YX}(\tau) = \frac{1}{2\pi}\int_{-\infty}^{\infty} \mathcal{S}_{YX}(\omega)e^{j\omega\tau}\,d\omega \qquad (7.3\text{-}26)$$

Example 7.3-1 Suppose we are given a cross-power spectrum defined by

$$
\mathcal{S}_{XY}(\omega) = \begin{cases} a + jb\omega/W & -W < \omega < W \\ 0 & \text{elsewhere} \end{cases}
$$

where $W > 0$, a and b are real constants. We use (7.3-25) to find the cross-correlation function. It is

$$
R_{XY}(\tau) = \frac{1}{2\pi} \int_{-W}^{W} \left(a + j\frac{b\omega}{W} \right) e^{j\omega\tau} \, d\omega
$$

$$
= \frac{a}{2\pi} \int_{-W}^{W} e^{j\omega\tau} \, d\omega + j\frac{b}{2\pi W} \int_{-W}^{W} \omega e^{j\omega\tau} \, d\omega
$$

On using (C-45) and (C-46) this expression will readily reduce to

$$
R_{XY}(\tau) = \frac{a}{2\pi} \left[\frac{e^{j\omega\tau}}{j\tau} \Big|_{-W}^{W} \right] + j\frac{b}{2\pi W} \left\{ e^{j\omega\tau} \left[\frac{\omega}{j\tau} - \frac{1}{(j\tau)^2} \right] \Big|_{-W}^{W} \right\}
$$

$$
= \frac{1}{\pi W\tau^2} \left[(aW\tau - b)\sin(W\tau) + bW\tau\cos(W\tau) \right]
$$

★7.4 RELATIONSHIP BETWEEN CROSS-POWER SPECTRUM AND CROSS-CORRELATION FUNCTION

In the following discussion we show that

$$
\mathcal{S}_{XY}(\omega) = \int_{-\infty}^{\infty} \left\{ \lim_{T \to \infty} \frac{1}{2T} \int_{-T}^{T} R_{XY}(t, t + \tau) \, dt \right\} e^{-j\omega\tau} \, d\tau \qquad (7.4\text{-}1)
$$

as indicated in (7.3-21).

The development consists of using the transforms of the truncated ensemble members, given by

$$
X_T(\omega) = \int_{-T}^{T} x(t)e^{-j\omega t} \, dt \qquad (7.4\text{-}2)
$$

$$
Y_T(\omega) = \int_{-T}^{T} y(t)e^{-j\omega t} \, dt \qquad (7.4\text{-}3)
$$

in (7.3-12) and then taking the expected value and limit as indicated to obtain $\mathcal{S}_{XY}(\omega)$. From (7.4-2) and (7.4-3):

$$
X_T^*(\omega)Y_T(\omega) = \int_{-T}^{T} x(t_1)e^{j\omega t_1} \, dt_1 \int_{-T}^{T} y(t_2)e^{-j\omega t_2} \, dt_2
$$

$$
= \int_{-T}^{T} \int_{-T}^{T} x(t_1)y(t_2)e^{-j\omega(t_2 - t_1)} \, dt_1 \, dt_2 \qquad (7.4\text{-}4)
$$

Now by changing variables according to (7.2-5), dividing by $2T$, and taking the expected value, (7.4-4) becomes

$$\frac{E[X_T^*(\omega)Y_T(\omega)]}{2T} = E\left[\int_{-T-t}^{T-t} \left\{\frac{1}{2T}\int_{-T}^{T} x(t)y(t+\tau)\,dt\right\}e^{-j\omega\tau}\,d\tau\right]$$

$$= \int_{-T-t}^{T-t} \left\{\frac{1}{2T}\int_{-T}^{T} R_{XY}(t, t+\tau)\,dt\right\}e^{-j\omega\tau}\,d\tau \qquad (7.4\text{-}5)$$

After the limit is taken:

$$\mathscr{S}_{XY}(\omega) = \lim_{T\to\infty} \frac{E[X_T^*(\omega)Y_T(\omega)]}{2T}$$

$$= \lim_{T\to\infty} \int_{-T-t}^{T-t} \left\{\frac{1}{2T}\int_{-T}^{T} R_{XY}(t, t+\tau)\,dt\right\}e^{-j\omega\tau}\,d\tau$$

$$= \int_{-\infty}^{\infty} \left\{\lim_{T\to\infty}\frac{1}{2T}\int_{-T}^{T} R_{XY}(t, t+\tau)\,dt\right\}e^{-j\omega\tau}\,d\tau \qquad (7.4\text{-}6)$$

which is the same as (7.4-1). Since (7.4-6) is a Fourier transform, and such transforms are unique, the inverse transform applies:

$$\lim_{T\to\infty}\frac{1}{2T}\int_{-T}^{T} R_{XY}(t, t+\tau)\,dt = \frac{1}{2\pi}\int_{-\infty}^{\infty} \mathscr{S}_{XY}(\omega)e^{j\omega\tau}\,d\omega \qquad (7.4\text{-}7)$$

It should be noted from (7.4-7) that, given the cross-power spectrum, the cross-correlation function cannot in general be recovered, only its time average can. For jointly wide-sense stationary processes, however, the cross-correlation function $R_{XY}(\tau)$ *can* be found from $\mathscr{S}_{XY}(\omega)$ since its time average is just $R_{XY}(\tau)$.

Although we shall not give the proof, a development similar to the above shows that (7.3-22) is true.

Example 7.4-1 Let the cross-correlation function of two processes $X(t)$ and $Y(t)$ be

$$R_{XY}(t, t+\tau) = \frac{AB}{2}\{\sin(\omega_0\tau) + \cos[\omega_0(2t+\tau)]\}$$

where A, B, and ω_0 are constants. We find the cross-power spectrum by use of (7.4-1). First, the time average is formed

$$\lim_{T\to\infty}\frac{1}{2T}\int_{-T}^{T} R_{XY}(t, t+\tau)\,dt$$

$$= \frac{AB}{2}\sin(\omega_0\tau) + \frac{AB}{2}\lim_{T\to\infty}\frac{1}{2T}\int_{-T}^{T} \cos[\omega_0(2t+\tau)]\,dt$$

The integral is readily evaluated and is found to be zero. Finally we Fourier transform the time-averaged cross-correlation function with the aid of pair 12 of Appendix E:

$$\mathcal{S}_{XY}(\omega) = \mathcal{F}\left\{\frac{AB}{2}\sin(\omega_0 \tau)\right\}$$

$$= \frac{-j\pi AB}{2}[\delta(\omega - \omega_0) - \delta(\omega + \omega_0)]$$

7.5   SOME NOISE DEFINITIONS AND OTHER TOPICS

In many practical problems it is helpful to sometimes characterize noise through its power density spectrum. Indeed, in the following discussions we *define* two forms of noise on the basis of their power spectrums. We also consider the response of a product device when one of its input waveforms is a random signal or noise.

White and Colored Noise

A sample function $n(t)$ of a wide-sense stationary noise random process $N(t)$ is called *white noise* if the power density spectrum of $N(t)$ is a constant at all frequencies. Thus, we define

$$\mathcal{S}_{NN}(\omega) = \mathcal{N}_0/2 \tag{7.5-1}$$

for white noise, where $\mathcal{N}_0$ is a real positive constant. By inverse Fourier transformation of (7.5-1), the autocorrelation function of $N(t)$ is found to be

$$R_{NN}(\tau) = (\mathcal{N}_0/2)\,\delta(\tau) \tag{7.5-2}$$

The above two functions are illustrated in Figure 7.5-1. White noise derives its name by analogy with "white" light, which contains all visible light frequencies in its spectrum.

White noise is unrealizable as can be seen by the fact that it possesses infinite average power:

$$\frac{1}{2\pi}\int_{-\infty}^{\infty} \mathcal{S}_{NN}(\omega)\,d\omega = \infty \tag{7.5-3}$$

However, one type of real-world noise closely approximates white noise. *Thermal noise* generated by thermal agitation of electrons in any electrical conductor has a power spectrum that is constant up to very high frequencies and then decreases.

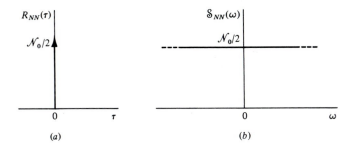

FIGURE 7.5-1
(a) The autocorrelation function and (b) the power density spectrum of white noise. [*Adapted from Peebles (1976) with permission of publishers Addison-Wesley, Advanced Book Program.*]

For example, a resistor at temperature T in kelvin produces a noise voltage across its open-circuited terminals having the power spectrum† (Carlson, 1975, p. 118)

$$\mathscr{S}_{NN}(\omega) = \frac{(\mathscr{N}_0/2)(\alpha|\omega|/T)}{e^{\alpha|\omega|/T} - 1} \qquad (7.5\text{-}4)$$

where $\alpha = 7.64(10^{-12})$ kelvin-seconds is a constant. At a temperature of $T = 290$ K (usually called *room temperature* although it corresponds to a rather cool room at $63°$F), this function remains above 0.9 $(\mathscr{N}_0/2)$ for frequencies up to 10^{12} Hz or 1000 GHz. Thus, thermal noise has a nearly flat spectrum at all frequencies that are likely to ever be used in radio, microwave, or millimeter-wave systems.‡

Noise having a nonzero and constant power spectrum over a *finite* frequency band and zero everywhere else is called *band-limited white noise*. Figure 7.5-2a depicts such a power spectrum that is lowpass. Here

$$\mathscr{S}_{NN}(\omega) = \begin{cases} \dfrac{P\pi}{W} & -W < \omega < W \\ 0 & \text{elsewhere} \end{cases} \qquad (7.5\text{-}5)$$

Inverse transformation of (7.5-5) gives the autocorrelation function shown in Figure 7.5-2b:

$$R_{NN}(\tau) = P\,\frac{\sin(W\tau)}{W\tau} \qquad (7.5\text{-}6)$$

The constant P equals the power in the noise.

---

† The unit of $\mathscr{S}_{NN}(\omega)$ is actually volts squared per hertz. According to our convention, we obtain watts per hertz by presuming the voltage exists across a 1-Ω resistor.

‡ This statement must be reexamined for $T < 290$ K, such as in some superconducting systems or other low-temperature devices (masers).

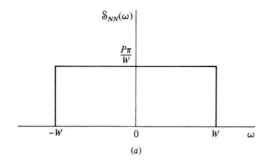

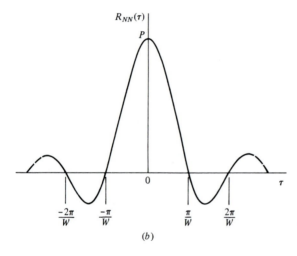

FIGURE 7.5-2
Power density spectrum (*a*) and auto-correlation function (*b*) of lowpass band-limited white noise.

Band-limited white noise can also be bandpass as illustrated in Figure 7.5-3. The applicable power spectrum and autocorrelation function are:

$$\mathcal{S}_{NN}(\omega) = \begin{cases} P\pi/W & \omega_0 - (W/2) < |\omega| < \omega_0 + (W/2) \\ 0 & \text{elsewhere} \end{cases} \tag{7.5-7}$$

and

$$R_{NN}(\tau) = P\,\frac{\sin\,(W\tau/2)}{(W\tau/2)}\,\cos\,(\omega_0\,\tau) \tag{7.5-8}$$

where ω_0 and W are constants and P is the power in the noise.

Again, by analogy with colored light that has only a portion of the visible light frequencies in its spectrum, we define *colored noise* as any noise that is not white. An example serves to illustrate colored noise.

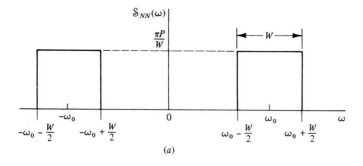

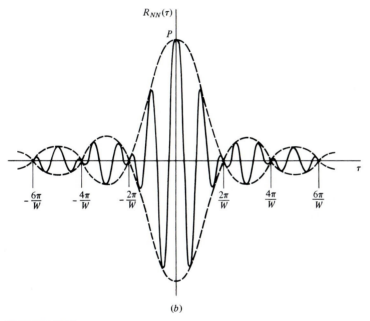

(b)

FIGURE 7.5-3
Power density spectrum (a) and autocorrelation function (b) for bandpass band-limited white noise.
[*Adapted from Peebles (1976) with permission of publishers Addison-Wesley, Advanced Book Program.*]

Example 7.5-1 A wide-sense stationary noise process $N(t)$ has an auto-correlation function

$$R_{NN}(\tau) = Pe^{-3|\tau|}$$

where P is a constant. We find its power spectrum. It is

$$\mathcal{S}_{NN}(\omega) = \int_{-\infty}^{\infty} Pe^{-3|\tau|}e^{-j\omega\tau}\, d\tau$$

$$= P\int_{0}^{\infty} e^{-(3+j\omega)\tau}\, d\tau + P\int_{-\infty}^{0} e^{(3-j\omega)\tau}\, d\tau$$

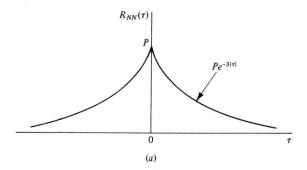

(a)

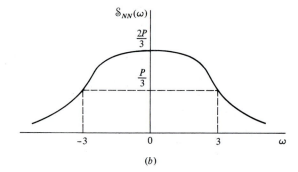

(b)

FIGURE 7.5-4
The autocorrelation function (a) and power spectrum (b) of the colored noise of Example 7.5-1 [*Adapted from Peebles (1976) with permission of publishers Addison-Wesley, Advanced Book Program.*]

These integrals easily evaluate using (C-45) to give

$$\mathcal{S}_{NN}(\omega) = \frac{P}{3 + j\omega} + \frac{P}{3 - j\omega} = \frac{6P}{9 + \omega^2}$$

This power spectrum is sketched in Figure 7.5-4 along with the preceding autocorrelation function.

Product Device Response to a Random Signal

Product devices are frequently encountered in electrical systems. Often they involve the product of a random waveform $X(t)$ (either signal or noise or the sum of signal and noise) with a cosine (or sine) "carrier" wave as illustrated in Figure 7.5-5. The response is the new process

$$Y(t) = X(t)A_0 \cos(\omega_0 t) \tag{7.5-9}$$

where A_0 and ω_0 are constants. We seek to find the power spectrum $\mathcal{S}_{YY}(\omega)$ of $Y(t)$ in terms of the power spectrum $\mathcal{S}_{XX}(\omega)$ of $X(t)$.

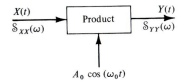

FIGURE 7.5-5
A product of interest in electrical systems. [*Adapted from Peebles (1976) with permission of publishers Addison-Wesley, Advanced Book Program.*]

The autocorrelation function of $Y(t)$ is

$$R_{YY}(t, t + \tau) = E[Y(t)Y(t + \tau)]$$

$$= E[A_0^2 X(t)X(t + \tau) \cos(\omega_0 t) \cos(\omega_0 t + \omega_0 \tau)]$$

$$= \frac{A_0^2}{2} R_{XX}(t, t + \tau)[\cos(\omega_0 \tau) + \cos(2\omega_0 t + \omega_0 \tau)] \quad (7.5\text{-}10)$$

Even if $X(t)$ is wide-sense stationary $Y(t)$ is not since $R_{YY}(t, t + \tau)$ depends on t. Thus, we apply (7.1-19) to obtain $\mathscr{S}_{YY}(\omega)$ after we take the time average of $R_{YY}(t, t + \tau)$. Let $X(t)$ be assumed wide-sense stationary. Then (7.5-10) becomes

$$A[R_{YY}(t, t + \tau)] = \frac{A_0^2}{2} R_{XX}(\tau) \cos(\omega_0 \tau) \quad (7.5\text{-}11)$$

On Fourier transforming (7.5-11) we have

$$\mathscr{S}_{YY}(\omega) = \frac{A_0^2}{4} [\mathscr{S}_{XX}(\omega - \omega_0) + \mathscr{S}_{XX}(\omega + \omega_0)] \quad (7.5\text{-}12)$$

A possible power density spectrum of $X(t)$ and that given by (7.5-12) are illustrated in Figure 7.5-6. It presumes that $X(t)$ is a lowpass process, although this is not a constraint in applying (7.5-12).

Example 7.5-2 One important use of the product device is in recovery (demodulation) of the information signal (music, speech, etc.) conveyed in the wave transmitted from a conventional broadcast radio station that uses AM (*amplitude modulation*). The wave received by a receiver tuned to a station with frequency $\omega_0/2\pi$ is one input to the product device. The other is a "local oscillator" signal $A_0 \cos(\omega_0 t)$ generated within the receiver. The product device output passes through a lowpass filter which has as its output the desired information signal. Unfortunately, this signal also contains noise because noise is also present at the input to the product device; the input noise is added to the received radio wave. We shall calculate the power in the output noise of the product demodulator.

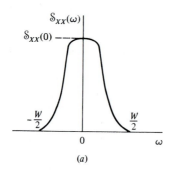

(a)

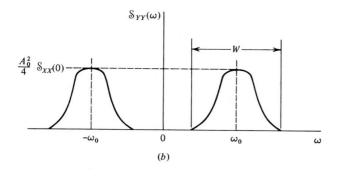

(b)

FIGURE 7.5-6
Power density spectrums applicable to Figure 7.5-5; (a) at the input and (b) at the output. [*Adapted from Peebles (1976) with permission of publishers Addison-Wesley, Advanced Book Program.*]

Let the power spectrum of the input noise, denoted $X(t)$, be approximated by an idealized (rectangular) function with bandwidth W_{RF} centered at $\pm\omega_0$. Thus,

$$\mathcal{S}_{XX}(\omega) = \begin{cases} \mathcal{N}_0/2 & -\omega_0 - (W_{RF}/2) < \omega < -\omega_0 + (W_{RF}/2) \\ \mathcal{N}_0/2 & \omega_0 - (W_{RF}/2) < \omega < \omega_0 + (W_{RF}/2) \\ 0 & \text{elsewhere} \end{cases}$$

where $\mathcal{N}_0/2$ is the power density within the noise band. By applying (7.5-12) the power density spectrum of the output noise $Y(t)$ of the product device is readily found (by sketch) to be

$$\mathcal{S}_{YY}(\omega) = \begin{cases} \mathcal{N}_0 A_0^2/8 & -2\omega_0 - (W_{RF}/2) < \omega < -2\omega_0 + (W_{RF}/2) \\ \mathcal{N}_0 A_0^2/4 & -W_{RF}/2 < \omega < W_{RF}/2 \\ \mathcal{N}_0 A_0^2/8 & 2\omega_0 - (W_{RF}/2) < \omega < 2\omega_0 + (W_{RF}/2) \\ 0 & \text{elsewhere} \end{cases}$$

Now only the noise in the band $-W_{RF}/2 < \omega < W_{RF}/2$ cannot be removed by a lowpass filter (which usually follows the product device to remove unwanted noise and other undesired outputs) because the desired signal is in the same band. This remaining component of $\mathscr{S}_{YY}(\omega)$ gives rise to the final output noise power, denoted N_o,

$$N_o = \frac{1}{2\pi} \int_{-W_{RF}/2}^{W_{RF}/2} \frac{\mathscr{N}_0 A_0^2}{4} \, d\omega = \frac{\mathscr{N}_0 A_0^2 W_{RF}}{8\pi}$$

⋆7.6 POWER SPECTRUMS OF COMPLEX PROCESSES

Power spectrums may readily be defined for complex processes. We consider only those processes that are at least wide-sense stationary. In terms of the autocorrelation function $R_{ZZ}(\tau)$ of a complex random process $Z(t)$, the power density spectrum is defined as its Fourier transform

$$\mathscr{S}_{ZZ}(\omega) = \int_{-\infty}^{\infty} R_{ZZ}(\tau)e^{-j\omega\tau} \, d\tau \tag{7.6-1}$$

The inverse transform applies, so

$$R_{ZZ}(\tau) = \frac{1}{2\pi} \int_{-\infty}^{\infty} \mathscr{S}_{ZZ}(\omega)e^{j\omega\tau} \, d\omega \tag{7.6-2}$$

For two jointly wide-sense stationary complex processes $Z_m(t)$ and $Z_n(t)$, their cross-power density spectrum and cross-correlation function are a Fourier transform pair:

$$\mathscr{S}_{Z_m Z_n}(\omega) = \int_{-\infty}^{\infty} R_{Z_m Z_n}(\tau)e^{-j\omega\tau} \, d\tau \tag{7.6-3}$$

$$R_{Z_m Z_n}(\tau) = \frac{1}{2\pi} \int_{-\infty}^{\infty} \mathscr{S}_{Z_m Z_n}(\omega)e^{j\omega\tau} \, d\omega \tag{7.6-4}$$

An equivalent statement is:

$$R_{Z_m Z_n}(\tau) \leftrightarrow \mathscr{S}_{Z_m Z_n}(\omega) \tag{7.6-5}$$

Example 7.6-1 We reconsider the complex process $V(t)$ of Example 6.7-1 and find its power spectrum. From the previous example

$$R_{VV}(\tau) = e^{j\omega_0\tau} \sum_{n=1}^{N} \overline{A_n^2}$$

On Fourier transforming this autocorrelation function we obtain

$$
\mathscr{S}_{VV}(\omega) = \mathscr{F}\left\{ e^{j\omega_0 \tau} \sum_{n=1}^{N} \overline{A_n^2} \right\}
$$

$$
= \sum_{n=1}^{N} \overline{A_n^2} \mathscr{F}\{e^{j\omega_0 \tau}\}
$$

$$
= 2\pi\delta(\omega - \omega_0) \sum_{n=1}^{N} \overline{A_n^2}
$$

after using pair 9 of Appendix E.

PROBLEMS

7-1 We are given the random process

$$
X(t) = A \cos(\omega_0 t + \Theta)
$$

where A and ω_0 are constants and Θ is a random variable uniformly distributed on the interval $(0, \pi)$.
(a) Is $X(t)$ wide-sense stationary?
(b) Find the power in $X(t)$ by using (7.1-10).
(c) Find the power spectrum of $X(t)$ by using (7.1-11) and calculate power from (7.1-12). Do your two powers agree?

7-2 Work Problem 7-1 if the process is defined by

$$
X(t) = u(t)A \cos(\omega_0 t + \Theta)
$$

where $u(t)$ is the unit-step function.

★7-3 Work Problem 7-2 assuming Θ is uniform on the interval $(0, \pi/2)$.

7-4 Work Problem 7-1 if the random process is given by $X(t) = A \sin(\omega_0 t + \Theta)$.

★7-5 Work Problem 7-1 if the random process is

$$
X(t) = A^2 \cos^2(\omega_0 t + \Theta)
$$

7-6 Let A and B be random variables. We form the random process

$$
X(t) = A \cos(\omega_0 t) + B \sin(\omega_0 t)
$$

where ω_0 is a real constant.
(a) Show that if A and B are uncorrelated with zero means and equal variances, then $X(t)$ is wide-sense stationary.
(b) Find the autocorrelation function of $X(t)$.
(c) Find the power density spectrum.

7-7 A limiting form for the impulse function was given in Example 7.1-2. Give arguments to show that the following are also true:

(a) $\lim_{T \to \infty} T \exp\left[-\pi \alpha^2 T^2\right] = \delta(\alpha)$

(b) $\lim_{T \to \infty} \dfrac{T}{2} \exp\left[-|\alpha|T\right] = \delta(\alpha)$

7-8 Work Problem 7-7 for the following cases:

(a) $\lim_{T \to \infty} \dfrac{T}{\pi} \dfrac{\sin(\alpha T)}{\alpha T} = \delta(\alpha)$

(b) $\lim_{\substack{T \to \infty \\ |\alpha| < 1/T}} T[1 - |\alpha|T] = \delta(\alpha)$

7-9 Show that (7.1-14) is true.

7-10 Prove (7.1-17). [*Hint:* Use (D-6) of Appendix D and the definition of the derivative.]

7-11 A random process is defined by

$$Y(t) = X(t) \cos(\omega_0 t + \Theta)$$

where $X(t)$ is a lowpass wide-sense stationary process, ω_0 is a real constant, and Θ is a random variable uniformly distributed on the interval $(0, 2\pi)$. Find and sketch the power density spectrum of $Y(t)$ in terms of that of $X(t)$. Assume Θ is independent of $X(t)$.

7-12 Determine which of the following functions can and cannot be valid power density spectrums. For those that are not, explain why.

(a) $\dfrac{\omega^2}{\omega^6 + 3\omega^2 + 3}$

(b) $\exp\left[-(\omega - 1)^2\right]$

(c) $\dfrac{\omega^2}{\omega^4 + 1} - \delta(\omega)$

(d) $\dfrac{\omega^4}{1 + \omega^2 + j\omega^6}$

7-13 Work Problem 7-12 for the following functions.

(a) $\dfrac{\cos(3\omega)}{1 + \omega^2}$

(b) $\dfrac{1}{(1 + \omega^2)^2}$

(c) $\dfrac{|\omega|}{1 + 2\omega + \omega^2}$

(d) $\dfrac{1}{\sqrt{1 - 3\omega^2}}$

7-14 Given that $X(t) = \sum_{i=1}^{N} \alpha_i X_i(t)$ where $\{\alpha_i\}$ is a set of real constants and the processes $X_i(t)$ are stationary and orthogonal, show that

$$\mathscr{S}_{XX}(\omega) = \sum_{i=1}^{N} \alpha_i^2 \mathscr{S}_{X_i X_i}(\omega)$$

7-15 A random process is given by

$$X(t) = A \cos (\Omega t + \Theta)$$

where A is a real constant, Ω is a random variable with density function $f_\Omega(\cdot)$, and Θ is a random variable uniformly distributed on the interval $(0, 2\pi)$ independent of Ω. Show that the power spectrum of $X(t)$ is

$$\mathcal{S}_{XX}(\omega) = \frac{\pi A^2}{2} [f_\Omega(\omega) + f_\Omega(-\omega)]$$

7-16 If $X(t)$ is a stationary process, find the power spectrum of

$$Y(t) = A + BX(t)$$

in terms of the power spectrum of $X(t)$ if A and B are real constants.

7-17 Find the power density spectrum of the random process for which

$$R_{XX}(\tau) = P \cos^4 (\omega_0 \tau)$$

if P and ω_0 are constants. Determine the power in the process by use of (7.1-12).

7-18 A random process has the power density spectrum

$$\mathcal{S}_{XX}(\omega) = \frac{6\omega^2}{1 + \omega^4}$$

Find the average power in the process.

7-19 Work Problem 7-18 for the power spectrum

$$\mathcal{S}_{XX}(\omega) = \frac{6\omega^2}{[1 + \omega^2]^3}$$

7-20 Work Problem 7-18 for the power spectrum

$$\mathcal{S}_{XX}(\omega) = \frac{6\omega^2}{(1 + \omega^2)^4}$$

7-21 Assume $X(t)$ is a wide-sense stationary process with nonzero mean value $\bar{X} \neq 0$. Show that

$$\mathcal{S}_{XX}(\omega) = 2\pi \bar{X}^2 \delta(\omega) + \int_{-\infty}^{\infty} C_{XX}(\tau) e^{-j\omega\tau} \, d\tau$$

where $C_{XX}(\tau)$ is the autocovariance function of $X(t)$.

7-22 For a random process $X(t)$, assume that

$$R_{XX}(\tau) = Pe^{-\tau^2/2a^2}$$

where $P > 0$ and $a > 0$ are constants. Find the power density spectrum of $X(t)$. [*Hint:* Use Appendix E to evaluate the Fourier transform of $R_{XX}(\tau)$.]

7-23 A random process has an autocorrelation function

$$R_{XX}(\tau) = \begin{cases} P[1 - (2\tau/T)] & 0 < \tau \le T/2 \\ P[1 + (2\tau/T)] & -T/2 \le \tau \le 0 \\ 0 & \tau < -T/2 \quad \text{and} \quad \tau > T/2 \end{cases}$$

Find and sketch its power density spectrum. (*Hint:* Use Appendix E.)

⋆7-24 A random process $X(t)$ has a periodic autocorrelation function where the function of Problem 7-23 forms the central period of duration T. Find and sketch the power spectrum.

7-25 If the random processes of Problem 7-14 are stationary, zero-mean, statistically independent processes, show that the power spectrum of the sum is the same as for orthogonal processes. For stationary independent processes with nonzero means, what is $\mathscr{S}_{XX}(\omega)$?

7-26 Given that a process $X(t)$ has the autocorrelation function

$$R_{XX}(\tau) = Ae^{-\alpha|\tau|} \cos(\omega_0 \tau)$$

where $A > 0$, $\alpha > 0$, and ω_0 are real constants, find the power spectrum of $X(t)$.

7-27 A random process $X(t)$ having the power spectrum of Problem 7-19 is applied to an ideal differentiator.
(a) Find the power spectrum of the differentiator's output.
(b) What is the power in the derivative?

7-28 Work Problem 7-27 for the power spectrum of Problem 7-20.

7-29 A wide-sense stationary random process $X(t)$ is used to define another process by

$$Y(t) = \int_{-\infty}^{\infty} h(\xi)X(t - \xi) \, d\xi$$

where $h(t)$ is some real function having a Fourier transform $H(\omega)$. Show that the power spectrum of $Y(t)$ is given by

$$\mathscr{S}_{YY}(\omega) = \mathscr{S}_{XX}(\omega)|H(\omega)|^2$$

7-30 A deterministic signal $A \cos(\omega_0 t)$, where A and ω_0 are real constants, is added to a noise process $N(t)$ for which

$$\mathscr{S}_{NN}(\omega) = \frac{W^2}{W^2 + \omega^2}$$

and $W > 0$ is a constant.
(a) Find the ratio of average signal power to average noise power.
(b) What value of W maximizes the signal-to-noise ratio? What is the consequence of choosing this value of W?

7-31 Find the rms bandwidth of the power spectrum

$$\mathcal{S}_{XX}(\omega) = \begin{cases} \dfrac{P}{1 + (\omega/W)^2} & |\omega| < KW \\ 0 & |\omega| > KW \end{cases}$$

where P, W, and K are real positive constants. If $K \to \infty$, what happens?

7-32 Find the rms bandwidth of the power spectrum

$$\mathcal{S}_{XX}(\omega) = \begin{cases} P \cos{(\pi\omega/2W)} & |\omega| \le W \\ 0 & |\omega| > W \end{cases}$$

where $W > 0$ and $P > 0$ are constants.

7-33 Determine the rms bandwidths of the power spectrums given by:

(a) $\mathcal{S}_{XX}(\omega) = \begin{cases} P & |\omega| < W \\ 0 & |\omega| > W \end{cases}$

(b) $\mathcal{S}_{XX}(\omega) = \begin{cases} P[1 - |\omega/W|] & |\omega| \le W \\ 0 & |\omega| > W \end{cases}$

where P and W are real positive constants.

$\star$**7-34** Given the power spectrum

$$\mathcal{S}_{XX}(\omega) = \dfrac{P}{\left[1 + \left(\dfrac{\omega - \alpha}{W}\right)^2\right]^2} + \dfrac{P}{\left[1 + \left(\dfrac{\omega + \alpha}{W}\right)^2\right]^2}$$

where P, α, and W are real positive constants, find the mean frequency and rms bandwidth.

7-35 Show that the rms bandwidth of the power spectrum of a real bandpass process $X(t)$ is given by

$$W_{\text{rms}}^2 = 4[\overline{W^2} - \bar{\omega}_0^2]$$

where $\bar{\omega}_0$ is given by (7.1-23) and $\overline{W^2}$ is given by the right side of (7.1-22).

$\star$**7-36** Jointly wide-sense stationary random processes $X(t)$ and $Y(t)$ define a process $W(t)$ by

$$W(t) = X(t) \cos{(\omega_0 t)} + Y(t) \sin{(\omega_0 t)}$$

where ω_0 is a real positive constant.

(a) Develop some conditions on the mean values and correlation functions of $X(t)$ and $Y(t)$ such that $W(t)$ is wide-sense stationary.

(b) With the conditions of part (a) applied to $W(t)$, find its power spectrum in terms of power spectrums of $X(t)$ and $Y(t)$.

(c) If $X(t)$ and $Y(t)$ are also uncorrelated, what is the power spectrum of $W(t)$?

7-37 A random process is given by

$$W(t) = AX(t) + BY(t)$$

where A and B are real constants and $X(t)$ and $Y(t)$ are jointly wide-sense stationary processes.

(a) Find the power spectrum $\mathscr{S}_{WW}(\omega)$ of $W(t)$.

(b) Find $\mathscr{S}_{WW}(\omega)$ if $X(t)$ and $Y(t)$ are uncorrelated.

(c) Find the cross-power spectrums $\mathscr{S}_{XW}(\omega)$ and $\mathscr{S}_{YW}(\omega)$.

★**7-38** Define two random processes by

$$X(t) = A \cos(\omega_0 t + \Theta)$$

$$Y(t) = W(t) \cos(\omega_0 t + \Theta)$$

where A and ω_0 are real positive constants, Θ is a random variable independent of $W(t)$, and $W(t)$ is a random process with a constant mean value $\bar{W}$. By using (7.3-12), show that

$$\mathscr{S}_{XY}(\omega) = \frac{A\bar{W}\pi}{2} [\delta(\omega - \omega_0) + \delta(\omega + \omega_0)]$$

regardless of the form of the probability density function of Θ.

★**7-39** Again consider the random processes of Problem 7-38.

(a) Use (6.3-11) to show that the cross-correlation function is given by

$$R_{XY}(t, t+\tau) = \frac{A\bar{W}}{2} \{\cos(\omega_0 \tau) + E[\cos(2\Theta)] \cos(2\omega_0 t + \omega_0 \tau)$$

$$- E[\sin(2\Theta)] \sin(2\omega_0 t + \omega_0 \tau)\}$$

where the expectation is with respect to Θ only.

(b) Find the time average of $R_{XY}(t, t+\tau)$ and determine the cross-power density spectrum $\mathscr{S}_{XY}(\omega)$.

7-40 Decompose the cross-power spectrums into real and imaginary parts according to

$$\mathscr{S}_{XY}(\omega) = R_{XY}(\omega) + jI_{XY}(\omega)$$

$$\mathscr{S}_{YX}(\omega) = R_{YX}(\omega) + jI_{YX}(\omega)$$

and prove that

$$R_{XY}(\omega) = R_{YX}(-\omega) = R_{YX}(\omega)$$

$$I_{XY}(\omega) = I_{YX}(-\omega) = -I_{YX}(\omega)$$

7-41 From the results of Problem 7-40, prove (7.3-16).

7-42 Show that (7.3-19) and (7.3-20) are true.

7-43 (a) Sketch the power spectrum of (7.5-4) as a function of $\alpha\omega/T$.

(b) For what values of ω will $\mathscr{S}_{NN}(\omega)$ remain above $0.5(\mathcal{N}_0/2)$ when $T = 4.2$ K (the value of liquid helium at one atmosphere of pressure)? These values form the region where thermal noise is approximately white in some amplifiers operated at very low temperatures, such as a *maser*.

7-44 For the power spectrum given in Figure 7.5-2a, show that (7.5-6) defines the corresponding band-limited noise autocorrelation function.

7-45 Show that (7.5-8) gives the autocorrelation function of the bandpass band-limited noise defined by Figure 7.5-3a.

7-46 A lowpass random process $X(t)$ has a continuous power spectrum $\mathscr{S}_{XX}(\omega)$ and $\mathscr{S}_{XX}(0) \neq 0$. Find the bandwidth W of a lowpass band-limited white-noise power spectrum having a density $\mathscr{S}_{XX}(0)$ and the same total power as in $X(t)$.

7-47 Work Problem 7-46 for a bandpass process assuming $\mathscr{S}_{XX}(\omega_0) \neq 0$, where ω_0 is some convenient frequency about which the spectral components of $X(t)$ cluster.

★7-48 A complex random process is given by

$$Z(t) = Ae^{j\Omega t}$$

where Ω is a random variable with probability density function $f_\Omega(\cdot)$ and A is a complex constant. Show that the power spectrum of $Z(t)$ is

$$\mathscr{S}_{ZZ}(\omega) = 2\pi |A|^2 f_\Omega(\omega)$$

ADDITIONAL PROBLEMS, SECOND EDITION

7-49 The autocorrelation function of a random process $X(t)$ is

$$R_{XX}(\tau) = 3 + 2 \exp(-4\tau^2)$$

(a) Find the power spectrum of $X(t)$.
(b) What is the average power in $X(t)$?
(c) What fraction of the power lies in the frequency band $-1/\sqrt{2} \leq \omega \leq 1/\sqrt{2}$?

7-50 State whether or not each of the following functions can be a valid power density spectrum. For those that cannot, explain why.

(a) $\dfrac{|\omega| \exp(-4\omega^2)}{1 + j\omega}$ 　　　(b) $\cos(3\omega) \exp(-\omega^2 + j2\omega)$

(c) $\dfrac{\omega^6}{(12 + \omega^2)^6}$ 　　　(d) $6 \tan[12\omega/(1 + \omega^2)]$

(e) $\cos^2(\omega) \exp(-8\omega^2)$ 　　　(f) $(-j\omega)(j\omega)/(3 - j\omega)^2(3 + j\omega)^2$

7-51 If $\mathscr{S}_{XX}(\omega)$ is a valid power spectrum of a random process $X(t)$, discuss whether the functions $d\mathscr{S}_{XX}(\omega)/d\omega$ and $d^2\mathscr{S}_{XX}(\omega)/d\omega^2$ can be valid power spectrums.

7-52 (a) Rework Problem 7-15 and show that even if Θ is a constant (not random) the power spectrum is still given by

$$\mathscr{S}_{XX}(\omega) = (\pi A^2/2)[f_\Omega(\omega) + f_\Omega(-\omega)]$$

[*Hint:* Time-average the autocorrelation function before Fourier transforming to obtain $\mathscr{S}_{XX}(\omega)$.]

(b) Find the total power in $X(t)$ and show that it is independent of the form
of the density function $f_\Omega(\omega)$.

7-53 Find the rms bandwidth of the power spectrum

$$\mathscr{S}_{XX}(\omega) = 1/[1 + (\omega/W)^2]^3$$

where $W > 0$ is a constant.

7-54 Work Problem 7-53 for the power spectrum

$$\mathscr{S}_{XX}(\omega) = \omega^2/[1 + (\omega/W)^2]^3$$

7-55 Work Problem 7-53 for the power spectrum

$$\mathscr{S}_{XX}(\omega) = 1/[1 + (\omega/W)^2]^4$$

7-56 Work Problem 7-53 for the power spectrum

$$\mathscr{S}_{XX}(\omega) = \omega^2/[1 + (\omega/W)^2]^4$$

★7-57 Generalize Problems 7-53 and 7-55 by finding the rms bandwidth of the
power spectrum

$$\mathscr{S}_{XX}(\omega) = 1/[1 + (\omega/W)^2]^N$$

where $N \geq 2$ is an integer.

★7-58 Generalize Problems 7-54 and 7-56 by finding the rms bandwidth of the
power spectrum

$$\mathscr{S}_{XX}(\omega) = \omega^2/[1 + (\omega/W)^2]^N$$

where $N \geq 3$ is an integer.

7-59 Assume a random process has a power spectrum

$$\mathscr{S}_{XX}(\omega) = \begin{cases} 4 - (\omega^2/9) & |\omega| \leq 6 \\ 0 & \text{elsewhere} \end{cases}$$

Find (a) the average power, (b) the rms bandwidth, and (c) the autocorrelation
function of the process.

7-60 Show that rms bandwidth of a lowpass random process $X(t)$, as given by
(7.1-22), can also be obtained from

$$W^2_{\text{rms}} = \frac{-1}{R_{XX}(0)} \frac{d^2 R_{XX}(\tau)}{d\tau^2}\bigg|_{\tau=0}$$

where $R_{XX}(\tau)$ is the autocorrelation function of $X(t)$.

7-61 A random process has the autocorrelation function

$$R_{XX}(\tau) = B \cos^2(\omega_0 \tau) \exp(-W|\tau|)$$

where B, ω_0, and W are positive constants.

(a) Find and sketch the power spectrum of $X(t)$ when ω_0 is at least several
times larger than W.

(b) Compute the average power in the lowpass part of the power spectrum. Repeat for the bandpass part. In each case assume $\omega_0 \gg W$.

★**7-62** Generalize Problem 7-61 by replacing $\cos^2(\omega_0 \tau)$ with $\cos^N(\omega_0 \tau)$ where $N \geq 0$ is an integer. What is the resulting power spectrum when N is (a) odd, and (b) even?

★**7-63** The product of a wide-sense stationary gaussian random process $X(t)$ with itself delayed by T seconds forms a new process $Y(t) = X(t)X(t - T)$. Determine (a) the autocorrelation function, and (b) the power spectrum of $Y(t)$. {*Hint:* Use the fact that $E[X_1 X_2 X_3 X_4] = E[X_1 X_2]E[X_3 X_4] + E[X_1 X_3]E[X_2 X_4] + E[X_1 X_4]E[X_2 X_3] - 2E[X_1]E[X_2]E[X_3]E[X_4]$ for gaussian random variables X_1, X_2, X_3, and X_4. (Thomas, 1969, p. 64.)}

7-64 Find the cross-correlation function $R_{XY}(t, t + \tau)$ and cross-power spectrum $\mathcal{S}_{XY}(\omega)$ for the delay-and-multiply device of Problem 7-63. {*Hint:* Use the fact that $E[X_1 X_2 X_3] = E[X_1]E[X_2 X_3] + E[X_2]E[X_3 X_1] + E[X_3]E[X_1 X_2] - 2E[X_1]E[X_2]E[X_3]$ for three gaussian random variables X_1, X_2, and X_3. (Thomas, 1969, p. 64.)}

7-65 If $X(t)$ and $Y(t)$ are real random processes determine which of the following functions can be valid. For those that are not, state at least one reason why.

(a) $R_{XX}(\tau) = \exp(-|\tau|)$ (b) $|R_{XY}(\tau)| \leq j\sqrt{R_{XX}(0)R_{YY}(0)}$

(c) $R_{XX}(\tau) = 2\sin(3\tau)$ (d) $\mathcal{S}_{XX}(\omega) = 6/(6 + 7\omega^3)$

(e) $\mathcal{S}_{XX}(\omega) = \dfrac{4\exp(-3|\tau|)}{1 + \omega^2}$ (f) $\mathcal{S}_{XY}(\omega) = 3 + j\omega^2$

(g) $\mathcal{S}_{XY}(\omega) = 18\delta(\omega)$

7-66 Form the product of two statistically independent jointly wide-sense stationary random processes $X(t)$ and $Y(t)$ as

$$W(t) = X(t)Y(t)$$

Find general expressions for the following correlation functions and power spectrums in terms of those of $X(t)$ and $Y(t)$: (a) $R_{WW}(t, t + \tau)$ and $\mathcal{S}_{WW}(\omega)$, (b) $R_{XW}(t, t + \tau)$ and $\mathcal{S}_{XW}(\omega)$, and (c) $R_{WX}(t, t + \tau)$ and $\mathcal{S}_{WX}(\omega)$. (d) If

$$R_{XX}(\tau) = (W_1/\pi)\text{Sa}(W_1 \tau)$$

and

$$R_{YY}(\tau) = (W_2/\pi)\text{Sa}(W_2 \tau)$$

with constants $W_2 > W_1$, find explicit functions for $R_{WW}(t, t + \tau)$ and $\mathcal{S}_{WW}(\omega)$.

7-67 An engineer is working with the function

$$R_{XY}(\tau) = P(1 + \tau)\exp(-W^2\tau^2)$$

where $P > 0$ and $W > 0$ are constants. He suspects that the function may not be a valid cross-correlation for two jointly stationary processes $X(t)$ and $Y(t)$, as he has been told. Determine if his suspicions are true. [*Hint:* Find the cross-power spectrum and see if it satisfies properties (7.3-16) through (7.3-18).]

7-68 A wide-sense stationary process $X(t)$ is applied to an ideal differentiator having the response $Y(t) = dX(t)/dt$. The cross-correlation of the input-output processes is known to be

$$R_{XY}(\tau) = dR_{XX}(\tau)/d\tau$$

(a) Determine $\mathscr{S}_{XY}(\omega)$ and $\mathscr{S}_{YX}(\omega)$ in terms of the power spectrum $\mathscr{S}_{XX}(\omega)$ of $X(t)$.

(b) Since $\mathscr{S}_{XX}(\omega)$ must be real, nonnegative, and have even symmetry, what are the properties of $\mathscr{S}_{XY}(\omega)$?

7-69 The cross-correlation of jointly wide-sense stationary processes $X(t)$ and $Y(t)$ is assumed to be

$$R_{XY}(\tau) = Bu(\tau)\exp(-W\tau)$$

where $B > 0$ and $W > 0$ are constants.

(a) Find $R_{YX}(\tau)$.

(b) Find $\mathscr{S}_{XY}(\omega)$ and $\mathscr{S}_{YX}(\omega)$.

7-70 Work Problem 7-69 for the function

$$R_{XY}(\tau) = Bu(\tau)\tau\exp(-W\tau)$$

7-71 The cross-power spectrum for random processes $X(t)$ and $Y(t)$ can be written as

$$\mathscr{S}_{XY}(\omega) = \mathscr{S}_{XX}(\omega)H(\omega)$$

where $\mathscr{S}_{XX}(\omega)$ is the power spectrum of $X(t)$ and $H(\omega)$ is a function with an inverse Fourier transform $h(\tau)$. Derive expressions for $R_{XY}(\tau)$ and $R_{YX}(\tau)$ in terms of $R_{XX}(\tau)$ and $h(\tau)$.

7-72 The power spectrum of a bandpass process $X(t)$ is shown in Figure P7-72. $X(t)$ is applied to a product device where the second multiplying input is $3\cos(\omega_0 t)$. Plot the power spectrum of the device's output $3X(t)\cos(\omega_0 t)$.

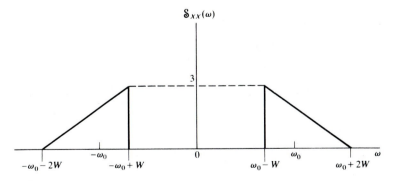

FIGURE P7-72

7-73 Let the "carrier" $A_0 \cos(\omega_0 t)$ in Figure 7.5-5 be modified to add a phase random variable Θ so that $Y(t) = A_0 X(t) \cos(\omega_0 t + \Theta)$. If Θ is uniformly distributed on $(0, 2\pi)$ and is independent of $X(t)$, find $R_{YY}(t, t + \tau)$ and $\mathscr{S}_{YY}(\omega)$ when $X(t)$ is wide-sense stationary.

7-74 Assume a stationary bandpass process $X(t)$ is adequately approximated by the power spectrum

$$\mathscr{S}_{XX}(\omega) = Pu(\omega - \omega_0)(\omega - \omega_0) \exp\left[-(\omega - \omega_0)^2/b\right]$$
$$+ Pu(-\omega - \omega_0)(-\omega - \omega_0) \exp\left[-(\omega + \omega_0)^2/b\right]$$

where ω_0, $P > 0$, and $b > 0$ are constants. The product $Y(t) = X(t) \cos(\omega_0 t)$ is formed.
(a) Find and sketch the power spectrum of $Y(t)$.
(b) Determine the average power in $X(t)$ and $Y(t)$.

★7-75 Compute the power spectrum of the complex process of Problem 6-55.

★7-76 Let $X(t)$ and $Y(t)$ be statistically independent processes with power spectrums

$$\mathscr{S}_{XX}(\omega) = 2\delta(\omega) + 1/[1 + (\omega/10)^2]$$

and

$$\mathscr{S}_{YY}(\omega) = 4/[1 + (\omega/2)^2]$$

A complex process

$$Z(t) = [X(t) + jY(t)] \exp(j\omega_0 t)$$

is formed where ω_0 is a constant much larger than 10.
(a) Determine the autocorrelation function of $Z(t)$.
(b) Find and sketch the power spectrum of $Z(t)$.

ADDITIONAL PROBLEMS, THIRD EDITION

7-77 Assume a random process $X(t)$ has a power spectrum

$$\mathscr{S}_{XX}(\omega) = \frac{6|\omega|}{(W^2 + \omega^2)^2}$$

where $W > 0$ is a constant.
(a) Sketch $\mathscr{S}_{XX}(\omega)$.
(b) At what positive value of ω, denoted by ω_{max}, does $\mathscr{S}_{XX}(\omega)$ reach a maximum value?

7-78 Treat the power spectrum of Problem 7-77 as bandpass and find its mean frequency $\bar{\omega}_0$ and rms bandwidth W_{rms}.

7-79 Work Problem 7-78, except assume the power spectrum

$$\mathscr{S}_{XX}(\omega) = \frac{6|\omega|}{(W^2 + \omega^2)^3}$$

7-80 Determine which of the following functions can be a valid power density of some random process. For those that cannot, give at least one reason why.

(a) $\sum_{n=-3}^{3} (-2)^n \delta(\omega - 3n)$

(b) $\exp[-4 \sin(6\omega)]$

(c) $\delta(\omega - 4) + \delta(\omega + 4) + e^{-|\omega|} \cos^2(10\omega)$

(d) $\dfrac{-5\omega}{(10 + \omega^4)^2}$

7-81 Find $\bar{\omega}_0$ and W_{rms} for the power spectrum shown in Figure P7-72.

7-82 For a random process $X(t)$, assume its autocorrelation function is

$$R_{XX}(t, t + \tau) = 12e^{-4\tau^2} \cos^2(24t).$$

(a) Is $X(t)$ wide-sense stationary?
(b) Find $R_{XX}(\tau)$.
(c) Find the power spectrum of $X(t)$.

7-83 A random process is defined by $Y(t) = X(t) - X(t - a)$, where $X(t)$ is a wide-sense stationary process and $a > 0$ is a constant. Find the autocorrelation function and power density spectrum of $Y(t)$ in terms of the corresponding quantities for $X(t)$.

7-84 Find the autocorrelation function corresponding to the power density spectrum

$$\mathscr{S}_{XX}(\omega) = \frac{157 + 12\omega^2}{(16 + \omega^2)(9 + \omega^2)}$$

[*Hint:* Use a partial fraction expansion (Peebles and Giuma, 1991, pp. 149–156) and Table E-1.]

7-85 Find the autocorrelation function corresponding to the power spectrum

$$\mathscr{S}_{XX}(\omega) = \frac{8}{(9 + \omega^2)^2}$$

[*Hint:* Use the convolution property of Fourier transforms given by (D-16).]

★7-86 Find the power spectrum corresponding to the autocorrelation function

$$R_{XX}(\tau) = [\cos(\alpha\tau) + \sin(\alpha|\tau|)]e^{-\alpha|\tau|}$$

where $\alpha > 0$ is a constant.

7-87 Determine the cross-power density spectrum corresponding to the cross-correlation function

$$R_{XY}(\tau) = u(-\tau)\frac{e^{b\tau}}{a + b} + \frac{u(\tau)e^{-b\tau}}{a^2 - b^2}[a + b - 2be^{-(a-b)\tau}]$$

where $a > 0$ and $b > 0$ are constants.

7-88 Determine the cross-correlation function corresponding to the cross-power density spectrum

$$\mathcal{S}_{XY}(\omega) = \frac{8}{(\alpha + j\omega)^3}$$

where $\alpha > 0$ is a constant.

★7-89 Work Problem 7-88 except assume the cross-power spectrum is

$$\mathcal{S}_{XY}(\omega) = \frac{6}{(9 + \omega^2)(3 + j\omega)^2}$$

7-90 Approximate (7.5-4) as a rectangular lowpass power spectrum with a constant amplitude $\mathcal{N}_0/2$ for $|\omega| < W$ where W is the angular frequency at which (7.5-4) drops to $\mathcal{N}_0/4$ when $T = 2$ K. What average noise power exists in the approximate power spectrum if $\mathcal{N}_0/2 = 5.5(10^{-19})$? (*Hint:* Assume the exponential is adquately approximated by the first three terms in its series representation.)

7-91 A signal $s_i(t) = 2.3 \cos(1000t)$ plus an input noise process $N_i(t)$ having the power spectrum shown in Figure P7-91(*a*) are applied to the product device shown in (*b*). The ideal lowpass filter (LPF) acts only to remove all spectral components (signal and noise) that are outside the band $|\omega| < 500$ rad/s and does not affect components inside the band.
(*a*) Find the output dc level V_0.
(*b*) Sketch the power density spectrum of $N_0(t)$.
(*c*) What signal power to average noise power ratio, $V_0^2/E[N_0^2(t)]$, occurs at the output? Note that this circuit acts as a detector of the signal's amplitude in the presence of noise.

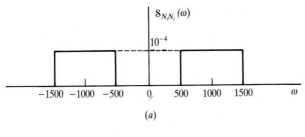

(*a*)

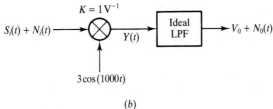

(*b*)

FIGURE P7-91

CHAPTER
8

LINEAR SYSTEMS WITH RANDOM INPUTS

8.0 INTRODUCTION

A large part of our preceding work has been aimed at describing a random signal by modeling it as a sample function of a random process. We have found that time domain methods based on correlation functions, and frequency domain techniques based on power spectrums, constitute powerful ways of defining the behavior of random signals. Our work must not stop here, however, because one of the most important aspects of random signals is how they interact with linear systems. The knowledge of how to describe a random waveform would be of little value to a communication or control system engineer, for example, unless he was also able to determine how such a waveform will alter the desired output of his system.

In this chapter, we explore methods of describing the response of a linear system when the applied waveform is random. We begin by discussing some basic aspects of linear systems in the following section. Those readers well-versed in linear system theory can proceed directly to Section 8.2 without loss. For others, the topics of Section 8.1 should serve as a brief review and summary.

8.1 LINEAR SYSTEM FUNDAMENTALS

In this section, a brief summary of the basic aspects of linear systems is given. Attention will be limited to a system having only one input and one output, or response, as illustrated in Figure 8.1-1. It is assumed that the input signal $x(t)$ and the response $y(t)$ are deterministic signals, even though some of the topics discussed apply to random waveforms. Which topics are applicable to random signals will be made clear when they are used in later sections.

The General Linear System

Clearly, the linear system (Figure 8.1-1*a*) will, in general, cause the response $y(t)$ to be different from the input signal $x(t)$. We think of the system as *operating* on $x(t)$ to cause $y(t)$ and write

$$y(t) = L[x(t)] \tag{8.1-1}$$

Here L is an *operator* representing the action of the system on $x(t)$.

A system is said to be linear if its response to a sum of inputs $x_n(t)$, $n = 1, 2, \ldots, N$, is equal to the sum of responses taken separately. Thus, if $x_n(t)$ causes a response $y_n(t)$, $n = 1, 2, \ldots, N$, then for a linear system

$$y(t) = L\left[\sum_{n=1}^{N} \alpha_n x_n(t)\right] = \sum_{n=1}^{N} \alpha_n L[x_n(t)] = \sum_{n=1}^{N} \alpha_n y_n(t) \tag{8.1-2}$$

must hold, where the α_n are arbitrary constants and N may be infinite.

From the definition (2.3-2) and properties of the impulse function we may write

$$x(t) = \int_{-\infty}^{\infty} x(\xi)\delta(t - \xi)\, d\xi \tag{8.1-3}$$

By substituting (8.1-3) into (8.1-1) and observing that the operator operates on the time function, we obtain

$$y(t) = L[x(t)] = L\left[\int_{-\infty}^{\infty} x(\xi)\delta(t - \xi)\, d\xi\right] = \int_{-\infty}^{\infty} x(\xi)L[\delta(t - \xi)]\, d\xi \tag{8.1-4}$$

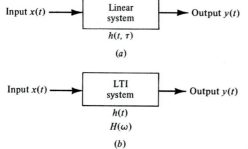

(a)

(b)

FIGURE 8.1-1
(a) A general single-input single-output linear system, and (b) a similar linear, time-invariant (LTI) system.

We now *define* a new function $h(t, \xi)$ as the *impulse response* of the linear system; that is,

$$L[\delta(t - \xi)] = h(t, \xi) \tag{8.1-5}$$

Equation (8.1-4) becomes

$$y(t) = \int_{-\infty}^{\infty} x(\xi)h(t, \xi) \, d\xi \tag{8.1-6}$$

which shows that the response of a general linear system is completely determined by its impulse response through (8.1-6).

Linear Time-Invariant Systems

A general linear system is said to be also time-invariant if the *form* of its impulse response $h(t, \xi)$ does not depend on the time that the impulse is applied. Thus, if an impulse $\delta(t)$, occurring at $t = 0$, causes the response $h(t)$, then an impulse $\delta(t - \xi)$, occurring at $t = \xi$, must cause the response $h(t - \xi)$ if the system is time-invariant. This fact means that

$$h(t, \xi) = h(t - \xi) \tag{8.1-7}$$

for a linear-time-invariant system, so (8.1-6) becomes

$$y(t) = \int_{-\infty}^{\infty} x(\xi)h(t - \xi) \, d\xi \tag{8.1-8}$$

Equation (8.1-8) is known as the *convolution integral* of $x(t)$ and $h(t)$; it is sometimes written in the short form

$$y(t) = x(t) * h(t) \tag{8.1-9}$$

By a suitable change of variables, (8.1-8) can be put in the alternative form

$$y(t) = \int_{-\infty}^{\infty} h(\xi)x(t - \xi) \, d\xi \tag{8.1-10}$$

Time-Invariant System Transfer Function

Either (8.1-8) or (8.1-10) shows that a linear time-invariant system is completely characterized by its impulse response, which is a temporal characterization. By Fourier transformation of $y(t)$, we may derive an equivalent characterization in the frequency domain. Hence, if $X(\omega)$, $Y(\omega)$ and $H(\omega)$ are the respective Fourier transforms of $x(t)$, $y(t)$, and $h(t)$, then

$$
Y(\omega) = \int_{-\infty}^{\infty} y(t)e^{-j\omega t}\, dt = \int_{-\infty}^{\infty} \left[\int_{-\infty}^{\infty} x(\xi)h(t-\xi)\, d\xi \right] e^{-j\omega t}\, dt
$$

$$
= \int_{-\infty}^{\infty} x(\xi) \left[\int_{-\infty}^{\infty} h(t-\xi)e^{-j\omega(t-\xi)}\, dt \right] e^{-j\omega\xi}\, d\xi
$$

$$
= \int_{-\infty}^{\infty} x(\xi)H(\omega)e^{-j\omega\xi}\, d\xi = X(\omega)H(\omega) \tag{8.1-11}
$$

The function $H(\omega)$ is called the *transfer function* of the system. Equation (8.1-11) shows that the Fourier transform of the response of any linear time-invariant system is equal to the product of the transform of the input signal and the transform of the network impulse response.

In the actual calculation of a transfer function for a given network, an alternative definition based on the response of the system to an exponential signal

$$
x(t) = e^{j\omega t} \tag{8.1-12}
$$

may be more convenient. It can be shown (Thomas, 1969, p. 142, or Papoulis, 1962, p. 83) that†

$$
H(\omega) = \frac{L[e^{j\omega t}]}{e^{j\omega t}} = \frac{y(t)}{x(t)} \tag{8.1-13}
$$

where

$$
y(t) = L[e^{j\omega t}] \tag{8.1-14}
$$

An example serves to illustrate the determination of $H(\omega)$ by means of (8.1-13).

Example 8.1-1   We find $H(\omega)$ for the network shown in Figure 8.1-2. By assuming a clockwise current i (and no loading in the output circuit), we have‡

$$
x(t) = L\frac{di}{dt} + y(t)
$$

But $y(t) = iR$ so

$$
\frac{di}{dt} = \frac{1}{R}\frac{dy(t)}{dt}
$$

---

† It should be carefully observed that (8.1-13) holds *only* for $x(t)$ given by (8.1-12); that is, for an exponential waveform.

‡ L in the network is an inductance and should not be confused with L above, which stands for a linear system operator.

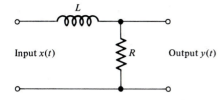

Input $x(t)$ R Output $y(t)$

FIGURE 8.1-2
A linear time-invariant network. [*Reproduced from Peebles (1976) with permission of publishers Addison-Wesley, Advanced Book Program.*]

and

$$x(t) = \frac{L}{R}\frac{dy(t)}{dt} + y(t)$$

With $x(t) = \exp(j\omega t)$ as the input we must have an output $y(t) = H(\omega)x(t)$ from (8.1-13). Hence, $dy(t)/dt = H(\omega)j\omega x(t)$ and

$$x(t) = \frac{L}{R} H(\omega)j\omega x(t) + H(\omega)x(t)$$

Finally, we solve for $H(\omega)$:

$$H(\omega) = \frac{1}{1 + (j\omega L/R)}$$

Idealized Systems

To simplify the analysis of many complex systems, it is often convenient to *approximate* the system's transfer function $H(\omega)$ by an idealized one. Idealized transfer functions are illustrated in Figure 8.1-3a for a lowpass system; (b) applies to a highpass system and (c) applies to a bandpass system. In every case the *idealized system* has a transfer function magnitude that is flat within its passband and zero outside this band; its midband gain is unity and its phase $\theta(\omega)$ is defined to be a linear function of frequency.

In replacing an actual system with an idealized one, the latter would be assigned a midband gain and phase slope that approximate the actual values. The bandwidth W (in lowpass and bandpass cases) is chosen according to some convenient basis. For example, W could be made equal to the 3-dB bandwidth of the actual system, or alternatively, it could be chosen to satisfy a specific requirement. An example of the latter case is considered in Section 8.5 where W, called *noise bandwidth*, is selected to cause the actual and ideal systems to produce the same output noise power when each is excited by the same noise source.

Causal and Stable Systems

To complete our summary of basic topics in linear system theory, we consider two final items.

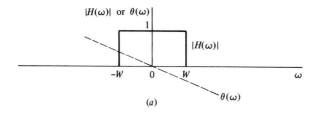

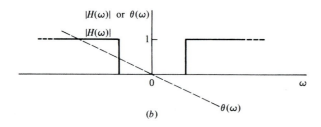

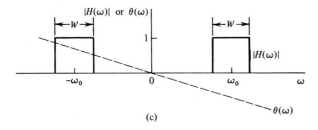

FIGURE 8.1-3
Ideal system transfer functions. (*a*) Lowpass, (*b*) highpass, and (*c*) bandpass systems. [*Reproduced from Peebles (1976) with permission of publishers Addison-Wesley, Advanced Book Program.*]

A linear time-invariant system is said to be *causal* if it does not respond prior to the application of an input signal. Mathematically, this implies $y(t) = 0$ for $t < t_0$ if $x(t) = 0$ for $t < t_0$, where t_0 is any real constant. From (8.1-10), this condition requires that

$$h(t) = 0 \quad \text{for} \quad t < 0 \quad \quad (8.1\text{-}15)$$

All passive, linear time-invariant networks that can be constructed will satisfy (8.1-15). As a consequence, a system satisfying (8.1-15) is often called *physically realizable*.

A linear time-invariant system is said to be *stable* if its response to any bounded input is bounded; that is, if $|x(t)| < M$, where M is some constant, then $|y(t)| < MI$ for a stable system where I is another constant independent of the input. By considering (8.1-10), it is readily shown that

$$I = \int_{-\infty}^{\infty} |h(t)| \, dt < \infty \qquad (8.1\text{-}16)$$

will ensure that a system having the impulse response $h(t)$ will be stable.

8.2 RANDOM SIGNAL RESPONSE OF LINEAR SYSTEMS

With the preceding summary of linear system theory in mind, we proceed now to determine characteristics of the response of a stable, linear, time-invariant system as illustrated in Figure 8.1-1b when the applied waveform is an ensemble member $x(t)$ of a random process $X(t)$. We assume in all work that the system's impulse response $h(t)$ is a real function.† In this section we restrict our attention to temporal characteristics such as mean value and mean-squared value of the response, its autocorrelation function, and applicable cross-correlation functions. Spectral characteristics are developed in Section 8.4.

System Response—Convolution

Even when $x(t)$ is a random signal, the network's response $y(t)$ is given by the convolution integral:

$$y(t) = \int_{-\infty}^{\infty} x(\xi)h(t - \xi) \, d\xi \qquad (8.2\text{-}1)$$

or

$$y(t) = \int_{-\infty}^{\infty} h(\xi)x(t - \xi) \, d\xi \qquad (8.2\text{-}2)$$

where $h(t)$ is the network's impulse response.

We may view (8.2-2) as an operation on an ensemble member $x(t)$ of the random process $X(t)$ that produces an ensemble member of a new process $Y(t)$. With this viewpoint, we may think of (8.2-2) as defining the process $Y(t)$ in terms of the process $X(t)$:

$$Y(t) = \int_{-\infty}^{\infty} h(\xi)X(t - \xi) \, d\xi \qquad (8.2\text{-}3)$$

Thus, we may envision the system as accepting the random process $X(t)$ as its input and responding with the new process $Y(t)$ according to (8.2-3).

---

† All real-world networks have real impulse responses.

Mean and Mean-Squared Value of System Response

We may readily apply (8.2-3) to find the mean value of the system's response. By assuming $X(t)$ is wide-sense stationary, we have†

$$
E[Y(t)] = E\left[\int_{-\infty}^{\infty} h(\xi)X(t - \xi)\, d\xi\right]
$$

$$
= \int_{-\infty}^{\infty} h(\xi)E[X(t - \xi)]\, d\xi
$$

$$
= \bar{X} \int_{-\infty}^{\infty} h(\xi)\, d\xi = \bar{Y} \qquad \text{(constant)} \qquad (8.2\text{-}4)
$$

This expression indicates that the mean value of $Y(t)$ equals the mean value of $X(t)$ times the area under the impulse response if $X(t)$ is wide-sense stationary.

For the mean-squared value of $Y(t)$, we calculate

$$
E[Y^2(t)] = E\left[\int_{-\infty}^{\infty} h(\xi_1)X(t - \xi_1)\, d\xi_1 \int_{-\infty}^{\infty} h(\xi_2)X(t - \xi_2)\, d\xi_2\right]
$$

$$
= \int_{-\infty}^{\infty}\int_{-\infty}^{\infty} E[X(t - \xi_1)X(t - \xi_2)]h(\xi_1)h(\xi_2)\, d\xi_1\, d\xi_2 \qquad (8.2\text{-}5)
$$

If we assume the input is wide-sense stationary then

$$
E[X(t - \xi_1)X(t - \xi_2)] = R_{XX}(\xi_1 - \xi_2) \qquad (8.2\text{-}6)
$$

and (8.2-5) becomes independent of t:

$$
\overline{Y^2} = E[Y^2(t)] = \int_{-\infty}^{\infty}\int_{-\infty}^{\infty} R_{XX}(\xi_1 - \xi_2)h(\xi_1)h(\xi_2)\, d\xi_1\, d\xi_2 \qquad (8.2\text{-}7)
$$

Although this expression gives the power in $Y(t)$, it may be tedious to calculate in most cases. We develop an example of its solution for a simple case.

---

† We shall assume that expectation and integration operations are interchangeable whenever needed. Some justification can be found in Cooper and McGillem (1986), p. 288, who state that the operation

$$
E\left[\int_{t_1}^{t_2} W(t)h(t)\, dt\right] = \int_{t_1}^{t_2} E[W(t)]h(t)\, dt
$$

is valid, where $W(t)$ is some bounded function of a random process [on the interval (t_1, t_2)] and $h(t)$ is a nonrandom time function, if

$$
\int_{t_1}^{t_2} E[|W(t)|]|h(t)|\, dt < \infty
$$

where t_1 and t_2 are real constants that may be infinite. This condition is satisfied in all *physical* cases if $W(t)$ is wide-sense stationary because $W(t)$ will be bounded and the systems are stable [see (8.1-16)].

Example 8.2-1 We find $\overline{Y^2}$ for a system having white noise at its input. Here

$$R_{XX}(\xi_1 - \xi_2) = (\mathcal{N}_0/2)\delta(\xi_1 - \xi_2)$$

where $\mathcal{N}_0$ is a positive real constant. From (8.2-7):

$$\overline{Y^2} = \int_{-\infty}^{\infty} \int_{-\infty}^{\infty} (\mathcal{N}_0/2)\delta(\xi_1 - \xi_2)h(\xi_1)\,d\xi_1\,h(\xi_2)\,d\xi_2$$

$$= (\mathcal{N}_0/2) \int_{-\infty}^{\infty} h^2(\xi_2)\,d\xi_2$$

Output power becomes proportional to the area under the square of $h(t)$ in this case.

Autocorrelation Function of Response

Let $X(t)$ be wide-sense stationary. The autocorrelation function of $Y(t)$ is

$$R_{YY}(t, t + \tau) = E[Y(t)Y(t + \tau)]$$

$$= E\left[\int_{-\infty}^{\infty} h(\xi_1)X(t - \xi_1)\,d\xi_1 \int_{-\infty}^{\infty} h(\xi_2)X(t + \tau - \xi_2)\,d\xi_2 \right]$$

$$= \int_{-\infty}^{\infty} \int_{-\infty}^{\infty} E[X(t - \xi_1)X(t + \tau - \xi_2)]h(\xi_1)h(\xi_2)\,d\xi_1\,d\xi_2 \quad (8.2\text{-}8)$$

which reduces to

$$R_{YY}(\tau) = \int_{-\infty}^{\infty} \int_{-\infty}^{\infty} R_{XX}(\tau + \xi_1 - \xi_2)h(\xi_1)h(\xi_2)\,d\xi_1\,d\xi_2 \quad (8.2\text{-}9)$$

because $X(t)$ is assumed wide-sense stationary.

Two facts result from (8.2-9). First, $Y(t)$ is wide-sense stationary if $X(t)$ is wide-sense stationary because $R_{YY}(\tau)$ does not depend on t and $E[Y(t)]$ is a constant from (8.2-4). Second, the form of (8.2-9) shows that $R_{YY}(\tau)$ is the two-fold convolution of the input autocorrelation function with the network's impulse response; that is

$$R_{YY}(\tau) = R_{XX}(\tau) * h(-\tau) * h(\tau) \quad (8.2\text{-}10)$$

Cross-Correlation Functions of Input and Output

The cross-correlation function of $X(t)$ and $Y(t)$ is

$$R_{XY}(t, t + \tau) = E[X(t)Y(t + \tau)] = E\left[X(t) \int_{-\infty}^{\infty} h(\xi)X(t + \tau - \xi)\,d\xi \right]$$

$$= \int_{-\infty}^{\infty} E[X(t)X(t + \tau - \xi)]h(\xi)\,d\xi \quad (8.2\text{-}11)$$

If $X(t)$ is wide-sense stationary, (8.2-11) reduces to

$$R_{XY}(\tau) = \int_{-\infty}^{\infty} R_{XX}(\tau - \xi)h(\xi)\,d\xi \qquad (8.2\text{-}12)$$

which is the convolution $R_{XX}(\tau)$ with $h(\tau)$:

$$R_{XY}(\tau) = R_{XX}(\tau) * h(\tau) \qquad (8.2\text{-}13)$$

A similar development shows that

$$R_{YX}(\tau) = \int_{-\infty}^{\infty} R_{XX}(\tau - \xi)h(-\xi)\,d\xi \qquad (8.2\text{-}14)$$

or

$$R_{YX}(\tau) = R_{XX}(\tau) * h(-\tau) \qquad (8.2\text{-}15)$$

From (8.2-12) and (8.2-14), it is clear that the cross-correlation functions depend on τ and not on absolute time t. As a consequence of this fact $X(t)$ and $Y(t)$ are *jointly* wide-sense stationary if $X(t)$ is wide-sense stationary, because we have already shown $Y(t)$ to be wide-sense stationary.

By substituting (8.2-12) into (8.2-9), autocorrelation function and cross-correlation functions are seen to be related by

$$R_{YY}(\tau) = \int_{-\infty}^{\infty} R_{XY}(\tau + \xi_1)h(\xi_1)\,d\xi_1 \qquad (8.2\text{-}16)$$

or

$$R_{YY}(\tau) = R_{XY}(\tau) * h(-\tau) \qquad (8.2\text{-}17)$$

A similar substitute of (8.2-14) into (8.2-9) gives

$$R_{YY}(\tau) = \int_{-\infty}^{\infty} R_{YX}(\tau - \xi_2)h(\xi_2)\,d\xi_2 \qquad (8.2\text{-}18)$$

or

$$R_{YY}(\tau) = R_{YX}(\tau) * h(\tau) \qquad (8.2\text{-}19)$$

Example 8.2-2 We shall continue Example 8.2-1 by finding the cross-correlation functions $R_{XY}(\tau)$ and $R_{YX}(\tau)$. From (8.2-12)

$$R_{XY}(\tau) = \int_{-\infty}^{\infty} (\mathcal{N}_0/2)\delta(\tau - \xi)h(\xi)\,d\xi$$

$$= (\mathcal{N}_0/2)h(\tau)$$

From (8.2-14)

$$R_{YX}(\tau) = \int_{-\infty}^{\infty} (\mathcal{N}_0/2)\delta(\tau - \xi)h(-\xi)\,d\xi$$

$$= (\mathcal{N}_0/2)h(-\tau) = R_{XY}(-\tau)$$

These two results are seen to satisfy (6.3-16), as they should.

8.3 SYSTEM EVALUATION USING RANDOM NOISE

A practical application of the foregoing theory can be immediately developed; it is based on the cross-correlation function of (8.2-12). Suppose we desire to find the impulse response of some linear time-invariant system. If we have available a broadband (relative to the system) noise source having a flat power spectrum, and a cross-correlation measurement device, such as shown in Figure 6.4-1, $h(t)$ can easily be determined.

For the approximately white noise source

$$R_{XX}(\tau) \approx \left(\frac{\mathcal{N}_0}{2}\right)\delta(\tau) \tag{8.3-1}$$

With this noise applied to the system, the cross-correlation function from (8.2-12) or Example 8.2-2 becomes

$$R_{XY}(\tau) \approx \int_{-\infty}^{\infty} \left(\frac{\mathcal{N}_0}{2}\right)\delta(\tau - \xi)h(\xi)\,d\xi$$

$$= \left(\frac{\mathcal{N}_0}{2}\right)h(\tau) \tag{8.3-2}$$

or

$$h(\tau) \approx \left(\frac{2}{\mathcal{N}_0}\right)R_{XY}(\tau) \tag{8.3-3}$$

Since a measurement $\hat{R}_{XY}(\tau)$ of $R_{XY}(\tau)$ can be obtained from the cross-correlation measurement device, (8.3-3) gives us a measurement $\hat{h}(\tau)$ of $h(\tau)$

$$\hat{h}(\tau) = \left(\frac{2}{\mathcal{N}_0}\right)\hat{R}_{XY}(\tau) \approx h(\tau) \tag{8.3-4}$$

Figure 8.3-1 illustrates the concepts described here.

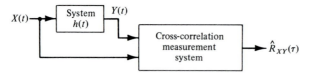

FIGURE 8.3-1
A method for finding a system's impulse response. [*Reproduced from Peebles (1976) with permission of publishers Addison-Wesley, Advanced Book Program.*]

8.4 SPECTRAL CHARACTERISTICS OF SYSTEM RESPONSE

Because the Fourier transform of a correlation function (autocorrelation or cross-correlation) is a power spectrum for wide-sense stationary processes, it would seem that if $R_{XX}(\tau)$ is known for the input process one can find $R_{YY}(\tau)$, $R_{XY}(\tau)$, and $R_{YX}(\tau)$ as described in Section 8.2 and therefore obtain power spectrums by transformation. Indeed, this approach is conceptually valid. However, from a practical standpoint the integrals involved may be difficult to evaluate.

In this section an alternative approach is taken where the desired power spectrum involving the system's response is related to the power spectrum of the input. In every case, the input process $X(t)$ is assumed to be wide-sense stationary, which, as previously proved, means that $Y(t)$ and $X(t)$ are jointly wide-sense stationary.

Power Density Spectrum of Response

We show now that the power density spectrum $\mathscr{S}_{YY}(\omega)$ of the response of a linear time-invariant system having a transfer function $H(\omega)$ is given by

$$\mathscr{S}_{YY}(\omega) = \mathscr{S}_{XX}(\omega)|H(\omega)|^2 \tag{8.4-1}$$

where $\mathscr{S}_{XX}(\omega)$ is the power spectrum of the input process $X(t)$. We call $|H(\omega)|^2$ the *power transfer function* of the system.

The proof of (8.4-1) begins by writing $\mathscr{S}_{YY}(\omega)$ as the Fourier transform of the output autocorrelation function

$$\mathscr{S}_{YY}(\omega) = \int_{-\infty}^{\infty} R_{YY}(\tau)e^{-j\omega\tau} \, d\tau \tag{8.4-2}$$

On substitution of (8.2-9), (8.4-2) becomes

$$\mathscr{S}_{YY}(\omega) = \int_{-\infty}^{\infty} h(\xi_1) \int_{-\infty}^{\infty} h(\xi_2) \int_{-\infty}^{\infty} R_{XX}(\tau + \xi_1 - \xi_2)e^{-j\omega\tau} \, d\tau \, d\xi_2 \, d\xi_1 \tag{8.4-3}$$

The change of variable $\xi = \tau + \xi_1 - \xi_2$, $d\xi = d\tau$, produces

$$\mathscr{S}_{YY}(\omega) = \int_{-\infty}^{\infty} h(\xi_1)e^{j\omega\xi_1}\,d\xi_1 \int_{-\infty}^{\infty} h(\xi_2)e^{-j\omega\xi_2}\,d\xi_2 \int_{-\infty}^{\infty} R_{XX}(\xi)e^{-j\omega\xi}\,d\xi \quad (8.4\text{-}4)$$

These three integrals are recognized as $H^*(\omega)$, $H(\omega)$, and $\mathscr{S}_{XX}(\omega)$ respectively. Hence

$$\mathscr{S}_{YY}(\omega) = H^*(\omega)H(\omega)\mathscr{S}_{XX}(\omega) = \mathscr{S}_{XX}(\omega)|H(\omega)|^2 \quad (8.4\text{-}5)$$

and (8.4-1) is proved.

The average power, denoted P_{YY}, in the system's response is readily found by using (8.4-5):

$$P_{YY} = \frac{1}{2\pi}\int_{-\infty}^{\infty} \mathscr{S}_{XX}(\omega)|H(\omega)|^2\,d\omega \quad (8.4\text{-}6)$$

Example 8.4-1 The power spectrum and average power of the response of the network of Example 8.1-1 will be found when $X(t)$ is white noise for which

$$\mathscr{S}_{XX}(\omega) = \frac{\mathcal{N}_0}{2}$$

Here $H(\omega) = [1 + (j\omega L/R)]^{-1}$ so

$$|H(\omega)|^2 = \frac{1}{1 + (\omega L/R)^2}$$

and

$$\mathscr{S}_{YY}(\omega) = \mathscr{S}_{XX}(\omega)|H(\omega)|^2 = \frac{\mathcal{N}_0/2}{1 + (\omega L/R)^2}$$

Average power in $Y(t)$, from (8.4-6), is

$$P_{YY} = \frac{1}{2\pi}\int_{-\infty}^{\infty} \mathscr{S}_{YY}(\omega)\,d\omega = \frac{\mathcal{N}_0}{4\pi}\int_{-\infty}^{\infty} \frac{d\omega}{1 + (\omega L/R)^2} = \frac{\mathcal{N}_0 R}{4L}$$

after an integral from Appendix C is used.

As a check on the calculation of P_{YY}, we note that (pair 15, Appendix E)

$$h(t) = (R/L)u(t)e^{-Rt/L} \leftrightarrow H(\omega) = \frac{1}{1 + (j\omega L/R)}$$

for this network, and, using the result of Example 8.2-1, we get

$$P_{YY} = \overline{Y^2} = \left(\frac{\mathcal{N}_0}{2}\right)\int_{0}^{\infty} \left(\frac{R}{L}\right)^2 e^{-2Rt/L}\,dt = \frac{\mathcal{N}_0 R}{4L}$$

The two powers are in agreement.

Cross-Power Density Spectrums of Input and Output

It is easily shown (see Problem 8-42) that the Fourier transforms of the cross-correlation functions of (8.2-12) and (8.2-14) may be written as

$$\mathcal{S}_{XY}(\omega) = \mathcal{S}_{XX}(\omega)H(\omega) \qquad (8.4\text{-}7)$$

$$\mathcal{S}_{YX}(\omega) = \mathcal{S}_{XX}(\omega)H(-\omega) \qquad (8.4\text{-}8)$$

respectively.

Measurement of Power Density Spectrums

The practical measurement of a power density spectrum is usually discussed in books as an "estimation" of the power spectrum. Although the theory behind spectral estimation is extensive and detailed,† a simple discussion can be given that provides insight and a plausible basis for measuring power spectrums.

To measure the power spectrum of a lowpass process $X(t)$, consider the system of Figure 8.4-1a. $X(t)$, having the power spectrum of (b), is applied to a real linear filter with a very narrowband, bandpass transfer function as illustrated in (c). The center frequency, ω_f, of the filter's transfer function is presumed adjustable from near $\omega = 0$ out to angular frequency W, the spectral extent of $X(t)$. The filter's output, $Y(t)$, is applied to a power meter that measures the average power in $Y(t)$. Both $X(t)$ and $Y(t)$ are assumed stationary, ergodic processes. We also assume that the power meter averages $Y^2(t)$ over a very long time such that any fluctuations in its reading are small relative to the measured power.

By assuming the spectral extent, W_f, of the filter is very small relative to W, and using the facts that $|H(\omega)|^2$ and $\mathcal{S}_{XX}(\omega)$ are even functions of ω for real filters and real $X(t)$, we can expand the power, $P_{YY}(\omega_f)$, in $Y(t)$ as

$$
\begin{aligned}
P_{YY}(\omega_f) &= \frac{1}{2\pi} \int_{-\infty}^{\infty} \mathcal{S}_{XX}(\omega)|H(\omega)|^2 \, d\omega \\[6pt]
&= \frac{1}{\pi} \int_{0}^{\infty} \mathcal{S}_{XX}(\omega)|H(\omega)|^2 \, d\omega \\[6pt]
&\approx \frac{1}{\pi} \mathcal{S}_{XX}(\omega_f) \int_{0}^{\infty} |H(\omega)|^2 \, d\omega \\[6pt]
&= \frac{\mathcal{S}_{XX}(\omega_f)|H(\omega_f)|^2 \, W_N}{\pi} \qquad (8.4\text{-}9)
\end{aligned}
$$

---

† For additional detail the reader is referred to some of the literature, such as Bendat and Piersol (1986), Kay (1986), and Blackman and Tukey (1958).

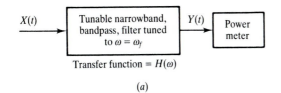

(a)

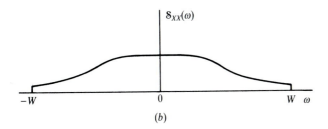

(b)

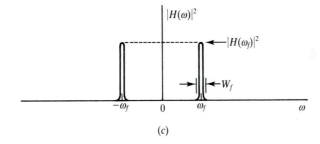

(c)

FIGURE 8.4-1
(a) A system for the measurement of a lowpass power density spectrum as in (b), and (c) the squared magnitude of the filter's transfer function.

The last form in (8.4-9) uses a quantity called *noise bandwidth*, defined in the next section, as given by

$$W_N = \frac{\int_0^\infty |H(\omega)|^2 \, d\omega}{|H(\omega_f)|^2} \qquad (8.4\text{-}10)$$

Finally, we write (8.4-9) as

$$\mathscr{S}_{XX}(\omega_f) \approx \frac{\pi P_{YY}(\omega_f)}{W_N |H(\omega_f)|^2} \qquad (8.4\text{-}11)$$

In words, the power $P_{YY}(\omega_f)$, measured when the filter is tuned to $\omega = \omega_f$, is multiplied by the known constant $\pi/[W_N|H(\omega_f)|^2]$, and the result is an approximation to $\mathscr{S}_{XX}(\omega)$ at $\omega = \omega_f$. By varying ω_f, the system can measure the power spectrum for various ω.

When $X(t)$ is a bandpass process, the system of Figure 8.4-2a is more convenient to use. Here $X(t)$ has a power spectrum centered at some high angular frequency ω_0, as sketched in (b). From (7.5-12), the effect of the product device is

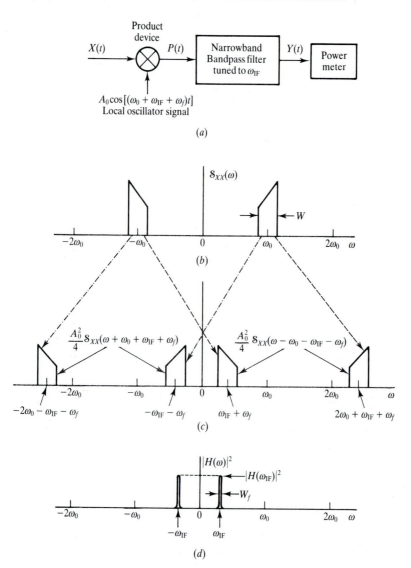

FIGURE 8.4-2
(a) System for the measurement of a bandpass power spectrum as in (b). (c) The power density spectrum of P(t). (d) The squared magnitude of the filter's transfer function.

to scale the power spectrum of $X(t)$ by $A_0^2/4$ and shift it both higher and lower in angular frequency by an amount $\omega_0 + \omega_{IF} + \omega_f$, the frequency of the local oscillator. Four spectral components are created, as shown in (c), for the product signal $P(t)$. The narrowband filter has a transfer function centered at a fixed angular frequency ω_{IF}, as sketched in (d). Its spectral extent W_f is assumed to be much smaller than the spectral extent W of the process $X(t)$.

For the system of Figure 8.4-2, the power in $Y(t)$ becomes

$$P_{YY}(\omega_0 + \omega_f) = \frac{1}{2\pi} \int_{-\infty}^{\infty} \frac{A_0^2}{4} [\mathscr{S}_{XX}(\omega - \omega_0 - \omega_{IF} - \omega_f)$$

$$+ \mathscr{S}_{XX}(\omega + \omega_0 + \omega_{IF} + \omega_f)] |H(\omega)|^2 \, d\omega$$

$$= 2 \frac{1}{2\pi} \int_{-\infty}^{\infty} \frac{A_0^2}{4} \mathscr{S}_{XX}(\omega - \omega_0 - \omega_{IF} - \omega_f) |H(\omega)|^2 \, d\omega$$

$$= \frac{A_0^2}{2} \frac{1}{2\pi} \int_{0}^{\infty} \mathscr{S}_{XX}(\omega - \omega_0 - \omega_{IF} - \omega_f) |H(\omega)|^2 \, d\omega$$

$$\approx \frac{A_0^2}{4\pi} \mathscr{S}_{XX}(-\omega_0 - \omega_f) \int_{0}^{\infty} |H(\omega)|^2 \, d\omega$$

$$= \frac{A_0^2}{4\pi} \mathscr{S}_{XX}(\omega_0 + \omega_f) W_N |H(\omega_{IF})|^2 \qquad (8.4\text{-}12)$$

where W_N is the filter's noise bandwidth according to (8.4-10). Thus,

$$\mathscr{S}_{XX}(\omega_0 + \omega_f) \approx \frac{4\pi P_{YY}(\omega_0 + \omega_f)}{A_0^2 W_N |H(\omega_{IF})|^2} \qquad (8.4\text{-}13)$$

In words, an approximation (measurement) of $\mathscr{S}_{XX}(\omega)$ at angular frequency $\omega_0 + \omega_f$ is equal to the known constant $4\pi/[A_0^2 W_N |H(\omega_{IF})|^2]$ multiplied by the average power $P_{YY}(\omega_0 + \omega_f)$, measured in $Y(t)$ when the local oscillator is tuned to an angular frequency *larger* than the center frequency ω_{IF} of the filter by an amount $\omega_0 + \omega_f$. By varying the frequency of the local oscillator (changing ω_f), $\mathscr{S}_{XX}(\omega)$ can be measured for all frequencies around ω_0.

For proper performance of the system of Figure 8.4-2, $W_f \ll W$ is required so that $\mathscr{S}_{PP}(\omega) \approx \mathscr{S}_{PP}(\omega_{IF})$ for all frequencies near ω_{IF} that are in the passband of the filter. Furthermore ω_{IF} must not be chosen too small; it should satisfy $\omega_{IF} > W + (W_f/2)$ if the spectral terms in Figure 8.4-2c are not to overlap when changes take place in ω_f. We next discuss an upper bound for ω_{IF} by means of an example.

Example 8.4-2 When a real, practical device is used to form the product in Figure 8.4-2, the output $P(t)$ always contains a term proportional to the input $X(t)$ because of practical "leakage," sometimes called "feedthrough." This leakage causes two additional terms in the spectrum of (c) centered at ω_0 and $-\omega_0$. As the other spectral terms change their positions in frequency in response to the oscillator's frequency adjustments, the leakage terms do not move. When ω_f has its largest value of $(W + W_f)/2$, the highest frequency in the spectral component being measured is at $\omega_{IF} + (W + W_f)/2 + (W/2) = \omega_{IF} + W + (W_f/2)$. If this frequency is to be lower than the lowest frequency in the leakage spectrum, which is $\omega_0 - (W/2)$, then we require

$$\omega_{IF} < \omega_0 - [(3W + W_f)/2]$$

This expression provides an upper bound on the choice of ω_{IF} in design.

8.5 NOISE BANDWIDTH

Consider a system having a lowpass transfer function $H(\omega)$. Assume white noise is applied at the input. The power density of this white noise is $\mathcal{N}_0/2$ where $\mathcal{N}_0$ is a real positive constant. The total average power emerging from the network is [from (8.4-6)]

$$P_{YY} = \frac{1}{2\pi} \int_{-\infty}^{\infty} \left(\frac{\mathcal{N}_0}{2}\right) |H(\omega)|^2 \, d\omega \tag{8.5-1}$$

By assuming the system impulse response is real,† $|H(\omega)|^2$ will be an even function of ω and (8.5-1) can be written

$$P_{YY} = \frac{\mathcal{N}_0}{2\pi} \int_0^{\infty} |H(\omega)|^2 \, d\omega \tag{8.5-2}$$

Now consider an idealized system that is equivalent to the actual system in the sense that both produce the same output average power when they both are excited by the same white noise source, and both have the same value of power transfer function at midband; that is, $|H(0)|^2$ is the same in both systems. The principal difference between the two systems is that the idealized one has a rectangularly shaped power transfer function $|H_I(\omega)|^2$ defined by

$$|H_I(\omega)|^2 = \begin{cases} |H(0)|^2 & |\omega| < W_N \\ 0 & |\omega| > W_N \end{cases} \tag{8.5-3}$$

where W_N is a positive constant selected to make output powers in the two systems equal. The output power in the idealized system is

$$\frac{1}{2\pi} \int_{-\infty}^{\infty} \left(\frac{\mathcal{N}_0}{2}\right) |H_I(\omega)|^2 \, d\omega = \frac{\mathcal{N}_0}{2\pi} \int_0^{W_N} |H(0)|^2 \, d\omega = \frac{\mathcal{N}_0 |H(0)|^2 W_N}{2\pi} \tag{8.5-4}$$

By equating (8.5-2) and (8.5-4), we require that W_N be given by

$$W_N = \frac{\int_0^{\infty} |H(\omega)|^2 \, d\omega}{|H(0)|^2} \tag{8.5-5}$$

W_N is called the *noise bandwidth* of the system.

---

† The impulse response of any physical system is always real.

Example 8.5-1 The noise bandwidth is found for a system having the power transfer function

$$|H(\omega)|^2 = \frac{1}{1 + (\omega/W)^2}$$

where W is the 3-dB bandwidth in radians per second. Here $|H(0)|^2 = 1$, so

$$W_N = \int_0^\infty \frac{W^2 \, d\omega}{W^2 + \omega^2} = W \tan^{-1}\left(\frac{\omega}{W}\right)\Big|_0^\infty = \frac{W\pi}{2}$$

This expression shows that W_N is larger than the system 3-dB bandwidth by a factor of about 1.57.

If we repeat the above development for a bandpass transfer function with a centerband frequency ω_0 it will be found that

$$W_N = \frac{\int_0^\infty |H(\omega)|^2 \, d\omega}{|H(\omega_0)|^2} \tag{8.5-6}$$

Proof of this result is left as a reader exercise (see Problem 8-45). The development also provides a simple expression for output noise power in terms of noise bandwidth:

$$P_{YY} = \frac{\mathcal{N}_0}{2\pi} |H(\omega_0)|^2 W_N \tag{8.5-7}$$

For a lowpass filter, (8.5-7) applies by letting $\omega_0 = 0$.

*8.6 BANDPASS, BAND-LIMITED, AND NARROWBAND PROCESSES

A random process $N(t)$ will be called *bandpass* if its power density spectrum $\mathcal{S}_{NN}(\omega)$ has its significant components clustered in a band of width W (rad/s) that does not include $\omega = 0$. Such a power spectrum is illustrated in Figure 8.6-1a.† Our definition does not prevent the power spectrum from being nonzero at $\omega = 0$; it only requires that $\mathcal{S}_{NN}(0)$ be small in relation to more significant values, so as to distinguish the bandpass case from a lowpass power spectrum with significant peaking at higher frequencies.

All subsequent discussions in this section will relate to special forms of bandpass processes.

---

† Power spectrums arising in physical systems will always decrease as frequency becomes sufficiently large, so a suitable value of W can always be found. For example, W could be chosen to include all frequencies for which $\mathcal{S}_{NN}(\omega) \geq 0.1\mathcal{S}_{NN}(\omega_0)$ where ω_0 is some convenient frequency near where $\mathcal{S}_{NN}(\omega)$ has its largest magnitude (see Figure 8.6-1).

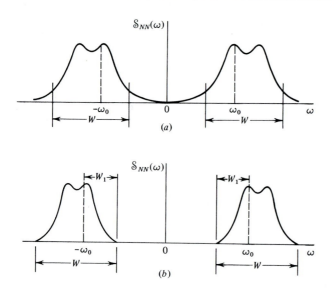

FIGURE 8.6-1
Power density spectrums (a) for a bandpass random process and (b) for a band-limited bandpass process.

⋆Band-Limited Processes

If the power spectrum of a bandpass random process is *zero* outside some frequency band of width W (rad/s) that does not include $\omega = 0$, the process is called *band-limited*. The concept of a band-limited process forms a convenient approximation for physical processes that often allows analytical problem solutions that otherwise might not be possible. A band-limited bandpass process power spectrum is illustrated in Figure 8.6-1b.

⋆Narrowband Processes

A band-limited random process is said to be *narrowband* if $W \ll \omega_0$, where ω_0 is some conveniently chosen frequency near band-center or near where the power spectrum is at its maximum. A power spectrum of a narrowband process is sketched in Figure 8.6-2a. A typical sample function, if viewed on an oscilloscope, might look as shown in (b). The appearance of $n(t)$ suggests that the process might be represented by a cosine function with angular frequency ω_0 and slowly varying amplitude and phase; that is, by

$$N(t) = A(t) \cos [\omega_0 t + \Theta(t)] \qquad (8.6\text{-}1)$$

where $A(t)$ is a random process representing the slowly varying amplitude and $\Theta(t)$ is a process representing the slowly varying phase. Indeed this is the case, and, for the important practical case where $N(t)$ is gaussian noise, it is known that $A(t)$ and $\Theta(t)$ have Rayleigh and uniform (over 2π) first-order probability density

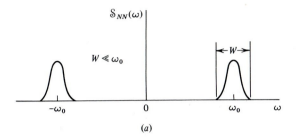

(a)

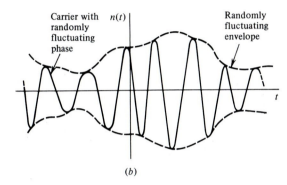

Carrier with randomly fluctuating phase $n(t)$ Randomly fluctuating envelope

(b)

FIGURE 8.6-2
(a) A power spectrum of a narrow-band random process $N(t)$ and (b) a typical ensemble member $n(t)$. [*Reproduced from Peebles (1976) with permission of publishers Addison-Wesley, Advanced Book Program.*]

functions respectively. The processes $A(t)$ and $\Theta(t)$ are not statistically independent when $N(t)$ is gaussian (Davenport, 1970, p. 522, or Davenport and Root, 1958, pp. 161–165), but for any one instant in time the process *random variables* are independent.

In some problems, (8.6-1) is a preferred representation for $N(t)$. For others, it is convenient to use the equivalent form

$$N(t) = X(t) \cos(\omega_0 t) - Y(t) \sin(\omega_0 t) \qquad (8.6\text{-}2)$$

where the processes $X(t)$ and $Y(t)$ are given by

$$X(t) = A(t) \cos[\Theta(t)] \qquad (8.6\text{-}3)$$

$$Y(t) = A(t) \sin[\Theta(t)] \qquad (8.6\text{-}4)$$

Expressions relating $A(t)$ and $\Theta(t)$ to $X(t)$ and $Y(t)$ are

$$A(t) = \sqrt{X^2(t) + Y^2(t)} \qquad (8.6\text{-}5)$$

$$\Theta(t) = \tan^{-1}[Y(t)/X(t)] \qquad (8.6\text{-}6)$$

⋆Properties of Band-Limited Processes

The representations (8.6-1) and (8.6-2) are actually more general than implied above; they can also be applied to any band-limited random process. For the remainder of this section we concern ourselves only with (8.6-2).

Let $N(t)$ be any band-limited wide-sense stationary real random process with a mean value of zero and a power density spectrum that satisfies

$$\mathcal{S}_{NN}(\omega) \neq 0 \qquad 0 < \omega_0 - W_1 < |\omega| < \omega_0 - W_1 + W$$

$$\mathcal{S}_{NN}(\omega) = 0 \qquad \text{elsewhere} \tag{8.6-7}$$

where W_1 and W are real positive constants. Then $N(t)$ can be represented by the right side of (8.6-2),† where the random processes $X(t)$ and $Y(t)$ have the following properties:

(1) $X(t)$ and $Y(t)$ are jointly wide-sense stationary   (8.6-8)

(2) $E[X(t)] = 0 \qquad E[Y(t)] = 0$ (8.6-9)

(3) $E[X^2(t)] = E[Y^2(t)] = E[N^2(t)]$ (8.6-10)

(4) $R_{XX}(\tau) = \dfrac{1}{\pi} \displaystyle\int_0^\infty \mathcal{S}_{NN}(\omega) \cos\left[(\omega - \omega_0)\tau\right] d\omega$ (8.6-11)

(5) $R_{YY}(\tau) = R_{XX}(\tau)$ (8.6-12)

(6) $R_{XY}(\tau) = \dfrac{1}{\pi} \displaystyle\int_0^\infty \mathcal{S}_{NN}(\omega) \sin\left[(\omega - \omega_0)\tau\right] d\omega$ (8.6-13)

(7) $R_{YX}(\tau) = -R_{XY}(\tau) \qquad R_{XY}(\tau) = -R_{XY}(-\tau)$ (8.6-14)

(8) $R_{XY}(0) = E[X(t)Y(t)] = 0 \qquad R_{YX}(0) = 0$ (8.6-15)

(9) $\mathcal{S}_{XX}(\omega) = L_p[\mathcal{S}_{NN}(\omega - \omega_0) + \mathcal{S}_{NN}(\omega + \omega_0)]$ (8.6-16)

(10) $\mathcal{S}_{YY}(\omega) = \mathcal{S}_{XX}(\omega)$ (8.6-17)

(11) $\mathcal{S}_{XY}(\omega) = jL_p[\mathcal{S}_{NN}(\omega - \omega_0) - \mathcal{S}_{NN}(\omega + \omega_0)]$ (8.6-18)

(12) $\mathcal{S}_{YX}(\omega) = -\mathcal{S}_{XY}(\omega)$ (8.6-19)

In the preceding 12 results, ω_0 is any convenient frequency within the band of $\mathcal{S}_{NN}(\omega)$; $R_{XX}(\tau)$, $R_{YY}(\tau)$, $R_{XY}(\tau)$, and $R_{YX}(\tau)$ are autocorrelation and cross-correlation functions of $X(t)$ and $Y(t)$ while $\mathcal{S}_{XX}(\omega)$, $\mathcal{S}_{YY}(\omega)$, $\mathcal{S}_{XY}(\omega)$, and $\mathcal{S}_{YX}(\omega)$ are the corresponding power spectrums; and $L_p[\cdot]$ denotes taking the lowpass part of the quantity within the brackets.

We outline the proofs of the above properties in the next subsection. Here we discuss their meaning and develop an example. We see that in addition to being zero-mean (property 2) wide-sense stationary (property 1) processes, $X(t)$ and $Y(t)$ also have equal powers (property 3), the same autocorrelation function

---

† If we denote the right side of (8.6-2) by $\hat{N}(t)$ the equality in (8.6-2) must be interpreted in the sense of zero mean-squared error; that is $N(t)$ equals $\hat{N}(t)$ in the sense that

$$E[\{N(t) - \hat{N}(t)\}^2] = 0$$

(Ziemer and Tranter, 1976, p. 241).

(property 5), and therefore the same power spectrum (property 10). Random variables defined for the processes $X(t)$ and $Y(t)$ at any one time are orthogonal (property 8). If $N(t)$ has a power spectrum with components having even symmetry about $\omega = \pm\omega_0$, then $X(t)$ and $Y(t)$ will be orthogonal processes (property 6). A consequence of this last point is that the cross-power spectrums of $X(t)$ and $Y(t)$ are zero (properties 11 and 12).

Example 8.6-1 Consider the bandpass process having the power density spectrum shown in Figure 8.6-3a. We shall find $\mathscr{S}_{XX}(\omega)$, $\mathscr{S}_{XY}(\omega)$, and $R_{XY}(\tau)$. By shifting $\mathscr{S}_{NN}(\omega)$ by $+\omega_0$ and $-\omega_0$, as shown in (b), we may construct $\mathscr{S}_{XX}(\omega)$ according to (8.6-16) as the lowpass portion of $\mathscr{S}_{NN}(\omega - \omega_0) + \mathscr{S}_{NN}(\omega + \omega_0)$, as illustrated in (c). This function also equals $\mathscr{S}_{YY}(\omega)$ by (8.6-17).

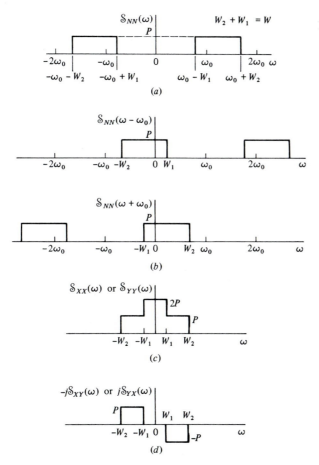

FIGURE 8.6-3
Power spectrums applicable to Example 8.6-1.

Similarly, we form the difference of the spectrums in (b) to obtain $\mathscr{S}_{XY}(\omega)$ according to (8.6-18) as shown in (d). This function also gives $\mathscr{S}_{YX}(\omega)$ from (8.6-19) as shown.

To find $R_{XY}(\tau)$ we apply (8.6-13):

$$R_{XY}(\tau) = \frac{1}{\pi} \int_{\omega_0 - W_1}^{\omega_0 + W_2} P \sin\left[(\omega - \omega_0)\tau\right] d\omega = \frac{P}{\pi\tau} \int_{-W_1\tau}^{W_2\tau} \sin(x)\, dx$$

$$= \frac{P}{\pi\tau} \left[\cos(W_1\tau) - \cos(W_2\tau)\right]$$

$$= \frac{P}{\pi\tau} \left\{\cos\left[\frac{(W_2 + W_1)\tau}{2} - \frac{(W_2 - W_1)\tau}{2}\right]\right.$$

$$\left. - \cos\left[\frac{(W_2 + W_1)\tau}{2} + \frac{(W_2 - W_1)\tau}{2}\right]\right\}$$

$$= \frac{2P}{\pi\tau} \sin\left[\frac{(W_2 + W_1)\tau}{2}\right] \sin\left[\frac{(W_2 - W_1)\tau}{2}\right]$$

Now since $W_1 + W_2 = W$, we may write this result as

$$R_{XY}(\tau) = \frac{WP}{\pi} \frac{\sin(W\tau/2)}{(W\tau/2)} \sin\left[(W - 2W_1)\tau/2\right]$$

which is an odd function of τ as (8.6-14) indicates it should be. Figure 8.6-4 illustrates a plot of $R_{XY}(\tau)$ for the special case $W_1 = W/6$.

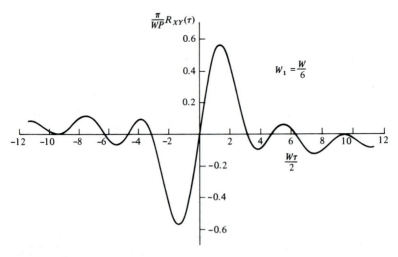

FIGURE 8.6-4
Cross-correlation function of Example 8.6-1.

It should be noted that if $W_1 = W/2$, corresponding to $\mathscr{S}_{NN}(\omega)$ having even components about $\omega = \pm\omega_0$, we get $R_{XY}(\tau) = 0$ for all τ. In this case, $X(t)$ and $Y(t)$ are orthogonal processes; they are also independent if $N(t)$ is gaussian.

★Proof of Properties of Band-Limited Processes

It is a quite long and involved task to prove all 12 properties of band-limited processes in detail. Therefore, we shall outline most of the proofs and give the details on only a few.

Property 2 is proved by taking the expected value on both sides of (8.6-2). Since $N(t)$ is assumed wide-sense stationary with a mean value of zero, then $E[X(t)] = 0$ and $E[Y(t)] = 0$ are necessary and property 2 follows.

The sequence of developments leading to the proofs of properties 9 and 4 will now be given. We begin by assuming the usual case $W_1 = W/2$ (see Figure 8.6-1b) and observing that the network of Figure 8.6-5a gives $X(t)$ at its output if the ideal lowpass filter has a bandwidth $W/2$ and if $\omega_0 > W/2$.† We shall assume these conditions true. Thus

$$
\begin{aligned}
V_1(t) &= 2N(t)\cos{(\omega_0\,t)} \\
&= 2[X(t)\cos^2{(\omega_0\,t)} - Y(t)\sin{(\omega_0\,t)}\cos{(\omega_0\,t)}] \\
&= X(t) + [X(t)\cos{(2\omega_0\,t)} - Y(t)\sin{(2\omega_0\,t)}] \quad\quad (8.6\text{-}20)
\end{aligned}
$$

---

† These are idealized values based on an ideal product device. Practical values of bandwidth and ω_0 may be considerably different. The assumption $W_1 = W/2$ is for simple definition of filter bandwidth and is not a constraint in properties 9 or 4.

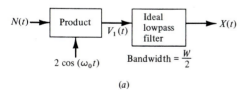

(a)

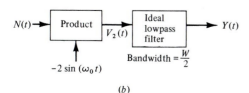

(b)

FIGURE 8.6-5

Block diagrams of networks that realize (a) $X(t)$ and (b) $Y(t)$ from a random process $N(t) = X(t)\cos{(\omega_0\,t)} - Y(t)\sin{(\omega_0\,t)}$. [Reproduced from Peebles (1976) with permission of publishers Addison-Wesley, Advanced Book Program.]

The filter will remove the bandpass process contained within the brackets so that only $X(t)$ appears in the output. Next, we develop an expression for $R_{XX}(t, t + \tau)$:

$$R_{XX}(t, t + \tau) = E[X(t)X(t + \tau)]$$

$$= E\left[\int_{-\infty}^{\infty} h(u)V_1(t - u)\, du \int_{-\infty}^{\infty} h(v)V_1(t + \tau - v)\, dv \right]$$

$$= \int_{-\infty}^{\infty} \int_{-\infty}^{\infty} h(u)h(v)R_{NN}(\tau + u - v)4 \cos\left[\omega_0(t - u) \right]$$

$$\cdot \cos\left[\omega_0(t + \tau - v) \right] du\, dv \qquad (8.6\text{-}21)$$

In developing (8.6-21), we have written $X(t)$ and $X(t + \tau)$ in terms of the convolution integral involving $h(t)$, the impulse response of the lowpass filter, substituted $V_1(t)$ from (8.6-20), and used the fact that $N(t)$ is assumed wide-sense stationary. The further reduction of (8.6-21) is lengthy (Peebles, 1976, p. 157) and will only be outlined. If the cosine factors are replaced by their exponential forms and if $R_{NN}(\tau + u - v)$ is replaced by its equivalent, the inverse transform of the power spectrum $\mathscr{S}_{NN}(\omega)$, (8.6-21) becomes the sum of four integrals. It can be shown that two of these integrals, the only two involving t, are zero. Thus, $R_{XX}(t, t + \tau)$ becomes a function of τ only and $X(t)$ is therefore wide-sense stationary, proving part of property 1. The two remaining integrals are used to prove properties 9 and 4.

A procedure exactly the same as discussed in the last paragraph can be used to prove first that $Y(t)$ is wide-sense stationary, thereby providing the proof of another part of property 1. The development also proves properties 10 and 5; it is based on the fact that $Y(t)$ is produced by the operations shown in Figure 8.6-5b.

Property 3 next results from use of property 5 with $\tau = 0$ and the integration of $\mathscr{S}_{XX}(\omega)$ using property 9.

Properties 11, 6, 8, and the balance of property 1 are proved by considering the cross-correlation function

$$R_{XY}(t, t + \tau) = E[X(t)Y(t + \tau)]$$

$$= E\left[\int_{-\infty}^{\infty} h(u)V_1(t - u)\, du \int_{-\infty}^{\infty} h(v)V_2(t + \tau - v)\, dv \right]$$

$$= -\int_{-\infty}^{\infty} \int_{-\infty}^{\infty} h(u)h(v)R_{NN}(\tau + u - v)4 \cos\left[\omega_0(t - u) \right]$$

$$\cdot \sin\left[\omega_0(t + \tau - v) \right] dv\, du \qquad (8.6\text{-}22)$$

which is developed in a manner analogous to (8.6-21). Reduction of (8.6-22) as discussed earlier shows that $R_{XY}(t, t + \tau)$ depends only on τ, so that $X(t)$ and $Y(t)$ are jointly wide-sense stationary (proving property 1); it also proves properties 11 and 6. Property 8 results from property 6 with $\tau = 0$.

Proofs of the remaining properties, 7 and 12, follow from consideration of the autocorrelation function of $N(t)$. It is readily found by using (8.6-2) that

$$R_{NN}(t, t + \tau) = E[N(t)N(t + \tau)]$$

$$= [R_{XX}(\tau) + R_{YY}(\tau)]^{1}/_{2} \cos{(\omega_0 \tau)}$$

$$+ [R_{XX}(\tau) - R_{YY}(\tau)]^{1}/_{2} \cos{(2\omega_0 t + \omega_0 \tau)}$$

$$- [R_{XY}(\tau) - R_{YX}(\tau)]^{1}/_{2} \sin{(\omega_0 \tau)}$$

$$- [R_{XY}(\tau) + R_{YX}(\tau)]^{1}/_{2} \sin{(2\omega_0 t + \omega_0 \tau)} \qquad (8.6\text{-}23)$$

Since $N(t)$ is wide-sense stationary by original assumption, its autocorrelation function cannot be a function of t. Thus, we require

$$R_{XX}(\tau) = R_{YY}(\tau) \qquad (8.6\text{-}24)$$

and

$$R_{XY}(\tau) = -R_{YX}(\tau) \qquad (8.6\text{-}25)$$

in (8.6-23); these results prove property 12 and the first part of property 7. Finally, recognizing that $R_{XY}(\tau) = R_{YX}(-\tau)$ for a cross-correlation function, we obtain the second part of property 7, which says that $R_{XY}(\tau)$ is an odd function of τ.

8.7 MODELING OF NOISE SOURCES

All our work in this chapter so far has related to finding the response of a linear system when a random waveform (desired signal or undesired noise) was applied at its input. In every case, the system was assumed to not contain any internal sources. In particular, the system was assumed to be free of any internally generated *noise*. In the real world, such an assumption is never justified because all networks (systems) generate one or more types of noise internally. For example, all conductors or semiconductors in a circuit are known to generate *thermal noise* (see Section 7.5) because of thermal agitation of free electrons.† The question naturally arises: How can we handle practical networks that produce internally generated noise? The remainder of this chapter is concerned with answering this question.

We shall find that, by suitable modeling techniques for both the network and for the external source that drives the network, all the internally generated network noise can be thought of as having been caused *by the external source*. In effect, we shall replace the noisy practical network with a noise-free identical network that is driven by a "more noisy" source.

Our work begins by developing models for noise sources.

---

† There are many other types of internally generated noise such as *shot noise, partition noise, induced grid noise, flicker noise, secondary emission noise*, etc. The reader is referred to the literature for more detail (Mumford and Scheibe, 1968; van der Ziel, 1970).

Resistive (Thermal) Noise Source

Suppose we have an ideal (noise-free, infinite input impedance) voltmeter that responds to voltages that fall in a small ideal (rectangular) frequency band $d\omega/2\pi$ centered at angular frequency ω. If such a voltmeter is used to measure the voltage across a resistor of resistance R (ohms), it is found, both in practice and theoretically, that a noise voltage $e_n(t)$ would exist having a mean-squared value given by

$$\overline{e_n^2(t)} = \frac{2kTR\, d\omega}{\pi} \tag{8.7-1}$$

Here $k = 1.38(10^{-23})$ joule per Kelvin is *Boltzmann's constant*,† and T is temperature in Kelvin. This result is independent of the value of ω up to extremely high frequencies. (See Section 7.5 where $\mathcal{N}_0/2$ equals $2kTR$ here. The reader should justify this fact as an exercise.)

Now because the voltmeter does not load the resistor, $\overline{e_n^2(t)}$ is the mean-squared open-circuit voltage of the resistor which can be treated as a voltage source with internal impedance R. In other words, the noisy resistor can be modeled as a Thevenin‡ voltage source as shown in Figure 8.7-1a. An equivalent

---

† Ludwig Boltzmann (1844–1906) was an Austrian physicist.
‡ Named for the French physicist Léon Thevenin (1857–1926).

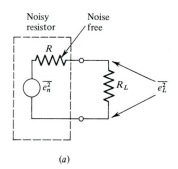

(a)

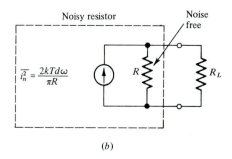

(b)

FIGURE 8.7-1
Equivalent circuit models of a noisy resistor: (a) voltage model and (b) current model. [*Adapted from Peebles (1976) with permission of publishers Addison-Wesley, Advanced Book Program.*]

current source is shown in (b) where

$$\overline{i_n^2(t)} = \overline{e_n^2(t)}/R^2 = \frac{2kT\,d\omega}{\pi R} \tag{8.7-2}$$

is the short-circuit mean-squared current.

From Figure 8.7-1a it is found that the *incremental noise power* dN_L delivered to the load in the incremental band $d\omega$ by the noisy resistor as a source is

$$dN_L = \frac{\overline{e_n^2(t)}R_L}{(R + R_L)^2} = \frac{2kTRR_L\,d\omega}{\pi(R + R_L)^2} \tag{8.7-3}$$

The maximum delivered power occurs when $R_L = R$. We call this maximum power the *incremental available power* of the source and denote it by dN_{as}; it is given by

$$dN_{as} = \overline{e_n^2(t)}/4R = \frac{kT\,d\omega}{2\pi} \tag{8.7-4}$$

We see from (8.7-4) that the incremental power *available* from a resistor source is *independent of the resistance of the source* and depends only on its physical temperature T. These facts may be used as a basis for modeling arbitrary sources.

Arbitrary Noise Sources, Effective Noise Temperature

Suppose an actual noise source has an incremental available noise power dN_{as}, open-circuit output mean-squared voltage $\overline{e_n^2(t)}$, and impedance as measured between its output terminals of $Z_o(\omega) = R_o(\omega) + jX_o(\omega)$. The available noise power is easily found to be

$$dN_{as} = \frac{\overline{e_n^2(t)}}{4R_o(\omega)} \tag{8.7-5}$$

If we now ascribe all the source's noise to the resistive part $R_o(\omega)$ of its output impedance by *defining* an *effective noise temperature* T_s such that (8.7-1) applies, then

$$\overline{e_n^2(t)} = 2kT_sR_o(\omega)\frac{d\omega}{\pi} \tag{8.7-6}$$

As with a purely resistive source, available power is still independent of the source impedance but depends on the source's temperature

$$dN_{as} = kT_s\frac{d\omega}{2\pi} \tag{8.7-7}$$

We consider two examples that illustrate effective noise temperature.

Example 8.7-1 Two different resistors at different physical temperatures are placed in series. The effective noise temperature of the series combination as a noise source is to be found.

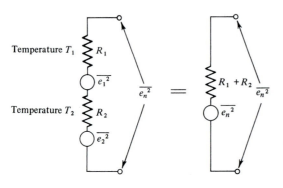

FIGURE 8.7-2
Equivalent circuits for two resistors at different temperatures in series.

Figure 8.7-2 illustrates Thevenin equivalent circuits for the combination. Since the individual resistors as sources may be considered independent, their mean-squared voltages add. Hence,

$$\overline{e_1^2(t)} + \overline{e_2^2(t)} = \overline{e_n^2(t)}$$

By applying (8.7-1) to both sides of the preceding expression, we obtain

$$2k[T_1 R_1 + T_2 R_2]\frac{d\omega}{\pi} = 2k[T_s(R_1 + R_2)]\frac{d\omega}{\pi}$$

or

$$T_s = \frac{T_1 R_1 + T_2 R_2}{R_1 + R_2}$$

Example 8.7-1 clearly shows that effective noise temperature of a source is not necessarily equal to its physical temperature. In the special case where $T_1 = T_2 = T$, then $T_s = T$. More generally, it is true that any passive, two-terminal source that contains only resistors, capacitors, and inductors, all at the same physical temperature T, will have an effective noise temperature $T_s = T$. (Ziemer and Tranter, 1976, p. 471). The next example can be used to illustrate this last point.

Example 8.7-2 We reconsider Example 8.7-1, except we now allow a capacitor to be placed across one resistor as shown in Figure 8.7-3.

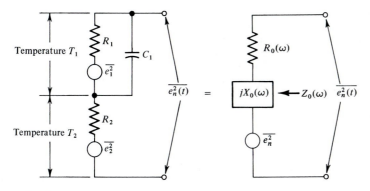

FIGURE 8.7-3
Equivalent circuits for a linear, passive, two-terminal network of two resistors and one capacitor.

By superposition, $\overline{e_n^2(t)}$ is the sum of contributions from each resistor as a noise source. The mean-squared voltage, denoted $\overline{e_{n1}^2(t)}$, due to the first resistor is readily seen to be

$$\overline{e_{n1}^2(t)} = \overline{e_1^2(t)} \left| \frac{1}{1 + j\omega R_1 C_1} \right|^2 = \frac{\overline{e_1^2(t)}}{1 + \omega^2 R_1^2 C_1^2}$$

That due to the second resistor is

$$\overline{e_{n2}^2(t)} = \overline{e_2^2(t)}$$

Thus, by applying (8.7-1) to the two individual resistor mean-squared voltages, we have

$$\overline{e_n^2(t)} = \overline{e_{n1}^2(t)} + \overline{e_{n2}^2(t)} = 2k \left[\frac{T_1 R_1}{1 + \omega^2 R_1^2 C_1^2} + T_2 R_2 \right] \frac{d\omega}{\pi}$$

Next, we find the output impedance of the network as an overall source by imagining the noise sources set to 0. We get

$$Z_o(\omega) = R_2 + \frac{R_1 (1/j\omega C_1)}{R_1 + (1/j\omega C_1)} = R_2 + \frac{R_1}{1 + j\omega R_1 C_1}$$

$$= R_2 + \frac{R_1 (1 - j\omega R_1 C_1)}{1 + \omega^2 R_1^2 C_1^2}$$

which has a resistive part

$$R_o(\omega) = R_2 + \frac{R_1}{1 + \omega^2 R_1^2 C_1^2}$$

By applying (8.7-6) to the equivalent source, we have

$$\overline{e_n^2(t)} = 2k T_s \left[R_2 + \frac{R_1}{1 + \omega^2 R_1^2 C_1^2} \right] \frac{d\omega}{\pi}$$

Finally, we equate $\overline{e_n^2(t)}$ for the actual and equivalent networks to find T_s:

$$T_s = \frac{T_1 R_1 + T_2 R_2(1 + \omega^2 R_1^2 C_1^2)}{R_1 + R_2(1 + \omega^2 R_1^2 C_1^2)}$$

The preceding example shows that effective noise temperature may be a function of frequency. In this case, the available noise power is also frequency dependent.

Again we see that $T_s = T$ in the above example if $T_1 = T_2 = T$, as it must because it is a linear, passive, two-terminal network with only resistors and a capacitor, as noted previously.

An Antenna as a Noise Source

In practice, all antennas produce noise at their output because of reception of electromagnetic radiation from noise sources external to the antenna.† The amount of available noise power dN_{as} in an incremental band $d\omega$ depends in a rather complicated manner on all the space surrounding the antenna. However, it is possible to model the antenna in a simple way by assigning to it an *antenna temperature* T_a chosen so that dN_{as} and T_a are related by (8.7-4). Thus,

$$dN_{as} = kT_a \frac{d\omega}{2\pi} \tag{8.7-8}$$

In general, antenna temperature may vary with frequency. However, in many applications T_a can be considered constant (with respect to ω) because its variation with frequency over a frequency band comparable to that of the desired signal being received is often small.

Example 8.7-3 A very sensitive meter that is capable of measuring noise power in a (small) frequency band 1 kHz wide at any frequency $\omega/2\pi$ is attached to a microwave antenna used in a radio relay link. It registers 2.0 (10^{-18}) W when the meter's input impedance is matched to the antenna so that its reading is maximum. We find the antenna temperature T_a.

Since maximum power is extracted from the antenna, the power is its available power and (8.7-8) gives

$$T_a = \frac{2\pi \, dN_{as}}{k \, d\omega} = \frac{2\pi(2)10^{-18}}{1.38(10^{-23})2\pi(10^3)} = \frac{200}{1.38} \approx 144.9 \text{ K}$$

---

† There are many sources of external noise; several of these are described by Peebles (1976, pp. 463–464).

8.8 INCREMENTAL MODELING OF NOISY NETWORKS

In this section we shall show how a noisy network can be modeled as a noise-free network excited by a suitably chosen external noise source. We also develop some measures of the "noisiness" of a network. All our work is applicable to an incremental band $d\omega$.

Available Power Gain

Consider first a linear, noise-free, two-port (4-terminal) network having an input impedance Z_i when the output port is open-circuited. Its output impedance, found by looking back into its output port, is Z_o when being driven by a source with source impedance Z_s. The source open-circuit voltage is $e_s(t)$ and the network's open-circuit output voltage is $e_o(t)$. The applicable network is illustrated in Figure 8.8-1.

The available power, denoted dN_{as}, of the source is

$$dN_{as} = \frac{\overline{e_s^2(t)}}{4R_s} \tag{8.8-1}$$

where R_s is the real part of Z_s. This power is independent of Z_i. The available power, denoted dN_{aos}, in the output due to the source is

$$dN_{aos} = \frac{\overline{e_o^2(t)}}{4R_o} \tag{8.8-2}$$

where R_o is the real part of Z_o. This power does depend on Z_i through its influence on the generation of $e_o(t)$ but does not depend on the load impedance Z_L. We define the *available power gain* denoted G_a of the two-port network as the ratio of the available powers

$$G_a = \frac{dN_{aos}}{dN_{as}} = \frac{R_s \overline{e_o^2(t)}}{R_o \overline{e_s^2(t)}} \tag{8.8-3}$$

When a cascade of M noise-free networks is involved where $M = 1, 2, \ldots$, it is easy to see that the overall available power gain G_a is the product of available power gains G_m, $m = 1, 2, \ldots, M$, if G_m is the gain of stage m when all preceding stages are connected and treated as its source (see Problem 8-65). Thus,

$$G_a = \prod_{m=1}^{M} G_m \tag{8.8-4}$$

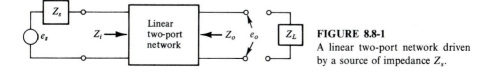

FIGURE 8.8-1
A linear two-port network driven by a source of impedance Z_s.

Equivalent Networks, Effective Input Noise Temperature

Consider next the case of a linear two-port network *with* internally generated noise. The network is assumed to be driven from a source with effective noise temperature T_s as shown in Figure 8.8-2a. If G_a is the network's available power gain, the available output noise power due to the source alone is

$$dN_{aos} = G_a dN_{as} = G_a k T_s \frac{d\omega}{2\pi} \tag{8.8-5}$$

from (8.8-3) and (8.7-7).

Total available output noise power dN_{ao} is larger than dN_{aos} because of internally generated noise. Let ΔN_{ao} represent the *excess available noise power* at the output. We shall imagine that ΔN_{ao} is generated by the source by defining *effective input noise temperature* T_e as the temperature *increase* that the source would require to account for all output available noise power. It therefore follows that

$$\Delta N_{ao} = G_a k T_e \frac{d\omega}{2\pi} \tag{8.8-6}$$

With this definition, the noisy network is replaced by a noise-free network driven by a source of temperature $T_s + T_e$ as shown in Figure 8.8-2b.

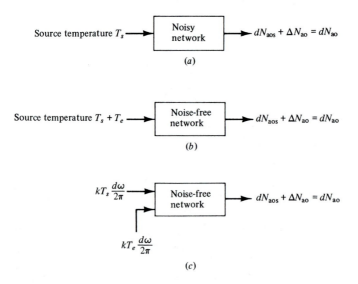

(a)

(b)

(c)

FIGURE 8.8-2
A network with internally generated noise driven from a noise source (a), and equivalent noise-free networks (b) and (c). [*Reproduced from Peebles (1976) with permission of publishers Addison-Wesley, Advanced Book Program.*]

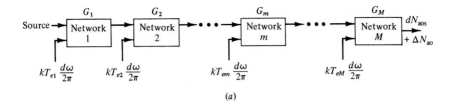

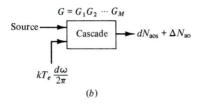

FIGURE 8.8-3
(a) M networks in cascade and (b) the equivalent network. [*Reproduced from Peebles (1976) with permission of publishers Addison-Wesley, Advanced Book Program.*]

It is somewhat helpful to model the available source noise power by use of two inputs, as shown in Figure 8.8-2c. The second input represents the internally generated noise due to the network. The representation is convenient in visualizing noise effects when networks are cascaded as illustrated in Figure 8.8-3. By equating expressions for output available noise powers in the cascade and equivalent network, the effective input noise temperature T_e of the cascade is determined to be

$$T_e = T_{e1} + \frac{T_{e2}}{G_1} + \frac{T_{e3}}{G_1 G_2} + \cdots + \frac{T_{eM}}{G_1 G_2 \cdots G_{M-1}} \qquad (8.8\text{-}7)$$

where T_{em} and G_m, $m = 1, 2, \ldots, M$, are the effective input noise temperature and available power gain, respectively, for the mth stage when all $m - 1$ previous stages are connected and form its source.

An especially useful application of (8.8-7) is to the cascade of stages in an amplifier. We develop an example.

Example 8.8-1 The stages in a three-stage amplifier have effective input noise temperatures $T_{e1} = 1350$ K, $T_{e2} = 1700$ K and $T_{e3} = 2600$ K. The respective available power gains are $G_1 = 16, G_2 = 10$, and $G_3 = 6$. We find the effective input noise temperature of the overall amplifier by use of (8.8-7):

$$T_e = 1350 + \frac{1700}{16} + \frac{2600}{16(10)} = 1350 + 106.25 + 16.25$$

$$= 1472.5 \text{ K}$$

We see that, even though T_{e2} and T_{e3} are larger than T_{e1}, the contributions to T_e by the second and third stages are much smaller than that of the first stage because of the gain of previous stages. In general, it is clear from (8.8-7) that an amplifier should have its lowest noise, highest gain stage first, followed by its next best stage, etc., for best noise performance.

Spot Noise Figures

Effective input noise temperature T_e of a network is a measure of its noise performance. Better performance corresponds to lower values of T_e. Another measure of performance is *incremental* or *spot noise figure* denoted by F and defined as the total incremental available output noise power dN_{ao} divided by the incremental available output noise power due to the source alone:

$$F = \frac{dN_{ao}}{dN_{aos}} = \frac{dN_{aos} + \Delta N_{ao}}{dN_{aos}} = 1 + \frac{\Delta N_{ao}}{dN_{aos}} \tag{8.8-8}$$

An alternative form derives from the substitution of (8.8-5) and (8.8-6):

$$F = 1 + \frac{T_e}{T_s} \tag{8.8-9}$$

In an ideal network, $T_e = 0$ so $F = 1$. For any real network, F is larger than unity.

In practice, a given network might be driven by a variety of sources. For example, an amplifier might be driven by an antenna, mixer, attenuator, other amplifier, etc. Its spot noise figure is therefore a function of the effective noise temperature of the source. However, by defining a *standard source* as having a *standard noise temperature* $T_0 = 290$ K and *standard spot noise figure* F_0, given by

$$F_0 = 1 + \frac{T_e}{T_0} \tag{8.8-10}$$

a network can be specified independent of its application.

When a network is used with the source for which it is intended to operate F will be called the *operating spot noise figure* and given the symbol F_{op}. From (8.8-9)

$$F_{op} = 1 + \frac{T_e}{T_s} \tag{8.8-11}$$

Operating and standard spot noise figures can also be developed for a cascade of networks (see Problems 8-66 and 8-68).

Example 8.8-2 An engineer purchases an amplifier that has a narrow bandwidth of 1 kHz and standard spot noise figure of 3.8 at its frequency of operation. The amplifier's available output noise power is 0.1 mW when its input is connected to a radio receiving antenna having an antenna temperature of 80 K. We find the amplifier's input effective noise temperature T_e, its operating spot noise figure F_{op}, and its available power gain G_a.

T_e derives from (8.8-10):

$$T_e = T_0(F_0 - 1) = 290(3.8 - 1) = 812 \text{ K}$$

We can now use (8.8-11) to obtain F_{op}:

$$F_{op} = 1 + \frac{812}{80} = 11.15$$

From (8.8-5) and (8.8-6) we add to get total available output noise power:

$$dN_{ao} = dN_{aos} + \Delta N_{ao} = \frac{k(T_s + T_e)G_a \, d\omega}{2\pi}$$

so

$$G_a = \frac{2\pi \, dN_{ao}}{k(T_s + T_e) \, d\omega} = \frac{2\pi(0.1)10^{-3}}{1.38(10^{-23})(812 + 80)2\pi(10^3)} \approx 8.12(10^{12})$$

8.9 MODELING OF PRACTICAL NOISY NETWORKS

In a realistic network, the frequency band of interest is not incremental. Therefore such quantities as available power gain, noise temperature, and noise figure are not necessarily constant but become frequency dependent, in general. In this section we extend the earlier concepts based on an incremental frequency band to include practical networks, by defining *average* noise temperatures and *average* noise figures.

Average Noise Figures

We define *average operating noise figure* $\bar{F}_{op}$ as the *total* output available noise power N_{ao} from a network divided by the *total* output available noise power N_{aos} due to the source alone. Thus,

$$\bar{F}_{op} = \frac{N_{ao}}{N_{aos}} \tag{8.9-1}$$

N_{aos} is found by integration of (8.8-5):

$$N_{aos} = \frac{k}{2\pi} \int_0^\infty T_s G_a \, d\omega \tag{8.9-2}$$

We may similarly use (8.8-8) with (8.8-5) to determine N_{ao}:

$$N_{ao} = \int_0^\infty dN_{ao} = \int_0^\infty F_{op} \, dN_{aos} = \frac{k}{2\pi} \int_0^\infty F_{op} T_s G_a \, d\omega \tag{8.9-3}$$

Thus, from (8.9-1)

$$\bar{F}_{op} = \frac{\int_0^\infty F_{op} T_s G_a \, d\omega}{\int_0^\infty T_s G_a \, d\omega} \tag{8.9-4}$$

In many cases the source's temperature is approximately constant. Operating average noise figure then becomes

$$\bar{F}_{op} = \frac{\int_0^\infty F_{op} G_a \, d\omega}{\int_0^\infty G_a \, d\omega} \qquad T_s \text{ constant} \tag{8.9-5}$$

An antenna is an example of a source having an approximately constant noise temperature (so long as the surroundings viewed by the antenna are fixed). Another example is a standard source for which $T_s = T_0 = 290$ K is constant. We define *average standard noise figure* $\bar{F}_0$ as that for which the source is standard. In this case

$$\bar{F}_0 = \frac{\int_0^\infty F_0 G_a \, d\omega}{\int_0^\infty G_a \, d\omega} \tag{8.9-6}$$

as can be shown by repeating the steps leading to (8.9-4).

Average Noise Temperatures

From the definition of effective input noise temperature T_e, it follows that the incremental available output noise power from a network with available power gain G_a that is driven by a source of temperature T_s is

$$dN_{ao} = G_a k (T_s + T_e) \frac{d\omega}{2\pi} \tag{8.9-7}$$

Total available power is therefore

$$N_{ao} = \int_0^\infty dN_{ao} = \frac{k}{2\pi} \int_0^\infty G_a (T_s + T_e) \, d\omega \tag{8.9-8}$$

Next, we define *average effective source temperature* $\bar{T}_s$ and *average effective input noise temperature* $\bar{T}_e$ as *constant* temperatures that produce the same total available power as given by (8.9-8). Hence

$$N_{ao} = \frac{k}{2\pi} (\bar{T}_s + \bar{T}_e) \int_0^\infty G_a \, d\omega \tag{8.9-9}$$

By equating (8.9-9) and (8.9-8) on a term-by-term basis, we get

$$\bar{T}_s = \frac{\int_0^\infty T_s G_a \, d\omega}{\int_0^\infty G_a \, d\omega} \tag{8.9-10}$$

and

$$\bar{T}_e = \frac{\int_0^\infty T_e G_a \, d\omega}{\int_0^\infty G_a \, d\omega} \tag{8.9-11}$$

If (8.8-10) and (8.8-11) are substituted into (8.9-6) and (8.9-4), respectively, we obtain the interrelationships

$$\bar{F}_0 = 1 + \frac{\bar{T}_e}{T_0} \tag{8.9-12}$$

$$\bar{F}_{op} = 1 + \frac{\bar{T}_e}{\bar{T}_s} \tag{8.9-13}$$

By equating $\bar{T}_e$ from these last two expressions, we obtain alternative interrelationships

$$\bar{F}_0 = 1 + \frac{\bar{T}_s}{T_0} (\bar{F}_{op} - 1) \tag{8.9-14}$$

$$\bar{F}_{op} = 1 + \frac{T_0}{\bar{T}_s} (\bar{F}_0 - 1) \tag{8.9-15}$$

Average effective noise temperature is a very useful concept for modeling network noise in a simple way. To demonstrate this fact, note that (8.9-9) can be written as

$$N_{ao} = \frac{k}{2\pi} (\bar{T}_s + \bar{T}_e) G_a(\omega_0) \frac{\int_0^\infty G_a(\omega) \, d\omega}{G_a(\omega_0)} \tag{8.9-16}$$

where ω_0 is the centerband angular frequency of the function $G_a(\omega)$. Since $G_a(\omega)$ is the available power gain (or power transfer function) of the network, we identify

$$W_N = \frac{\int_0^\infty G_a(\omega) \, d\omega}{G_a(\omega_0)} \tag{8.9-17}$$

as the *noise bandwidth* of the network, by analogy with (8.5-6). Equation (8.9-16) becomes

$$N_{ao} = G_a(\omega_0) k (\bar{T}_s + \bar{T}_e) \frac{W_N}{2\pi} \tag{8.9-18}$$

which says that actual available output noise power is that due to a source with *constant* temperature $\bar{T}_s + \bar{T}_e$ driving an equivalent noise-free network with an ideal rectangular transfer function of bandwidth W_N(rad/s) and midband available power gain $G_a(\omega_0)$. This result represents a very simple network model.

Modeling of Attenuators

Consider a source of average effective temperature $\bar{T}_s$ driving an impedance-matched lossy attenuator with power loss L (a number not less than one) at all frequencies. The attenuator has a physical temperature T_L. It can be shown (Peebles, 1976, p. 463; Mumford and Scheibe, 1968, p. 23) that the average effective input noise temperature of the attenuator is

$$\bar{T}_e = T_L(L - 1) \tag{8.9-19}$$

From (8.9-12) and (8.9-13) the applicable average noise figures are

$$\bar{F}_0 = 1 + \frac{T_L}{T_0}(L - 1) \tag{8.9-20}$$

$$\bar{F}_{op} = 1 + \frac{T_L}{\bar{T}_s}(L - 1) \tag{8.9-21}$$

Note that if $T_L = T_0$ or if $T_L = \bar{T}_s$, the average noise figure of the attenuator is just equal to its loss.

Model of Example System

One of the most important applications of the theory of this and the preceding two sections is in modeling receiving systems. As illustrated in Figure 8.9-1a, consider a receiving antenna that drives a receiver amplifier through various

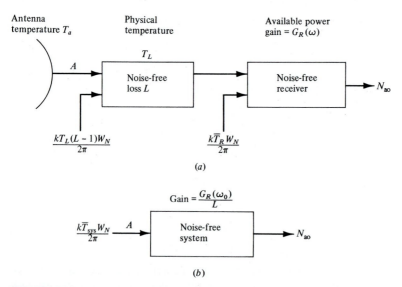

(a)

(b)

FIGURE 8.9-1
A model of a receiving system (a) and its equivalent (b). [*Reproduced from Peebles (1976), with permission of publishers Addison-Wesley, Advanced Book Program.*]

broad-band components having an overall loss L. These components (which may include microwave transmission lines, isolators, or other devices) are all assumed to have physical temperature T_L. The antenna temperature is T_a and the receiver average effective input noise temperature is $\bar{T}_R$. The receiver's noise bandwidth is W_N and it has a centerband available power gain $G_R(\omega_0)$. We demonstrate that the system is equivalent to that shown in Figure 8.9-1b.

The equivalent system has the same noise bandwidth as the actual system and has a centerband available power gain $G_R(\omega_0)/L$. It is driven by a simple source with *system noise temperature* $\bar{T}_{\text{sys}}$. The available output noise power in the actual system is the sum of the antenna's contribution plus those due to excess noises in the attenuator and receiver. By using earlier models, this noise power is

$$N_{\text{ao}} = k[T_a + T_L(L-1) + \bar{T}_R L] \frac{G_R(\omega_0)W_N}{L(2\pi)} \qquad (8.9\text{-}22)$$

For the equivalent system

$$N_{\text{ao}} = k\bar{T}_{\text{sys}} \frac{G_R(\omega_0)W_N}{L(2\pi)} \qquad (8.9\text{-}23)$$

By equating the above two expressions, we obtain

$$\bar{T}_{\text{sys}} = T_a + T_L(L-1) + \bar{T}_R L \qquad (8.9\text{-}24)$$

From (8.9-24), the average effective input noise temperature of the system taken at point A in Figure 8.9-1a is

$$\bar{T}_e = T_L(L-1) + \bar{T}_R L \qquad (8.9\text{-}25)$$

From (8.9-13) the average system operating noise figure is

$$\bar{F}_{\text{op}} = 1 + \frac{T_L}{T_a}(L-1) + \frac{\bar{T}_R}{T_a} L \qquad (8.9\text{-}26)$$

Example 8.9-1 An antenna with temperature $T_a = 150$ K is connected to a receiver by means of a waveguide that is at a physical temperature of 280 K and has a loss of 1.5 (1.76 dB).† The receiver has a noise bandwidth of $W_N/2\pi = 10^6$ Hz and an average effective input noise temperature $\bar{T}_R = 700$ K. We determine the system's noise temperature $\bar{T}_{\text{sys}}$, its operating average noise figure $\bar{F}_{\text{op}}$, and its available output noise power when $G_R(\omega_0) = 10^{12}$ (120 dB).

From (8.9-24)

$$\bar{T}_{\text{sys}} = 150 + 280(1.5 - 1) + 700(1.5) = 1340 \text{ K}$$

---

† A number L expressed in *decibels* (dB), denoted L_{dB}, is related to L as a numeric (power ratio) by $L_{\text{dB}} = 10 \log_{10}(L)$.

From (8.9-26)

$$\bar{F}_{op} = 1 + \frac{280}{150}(1.5 - 1) + \frac{700}{150}(1.5) \approx 8.93 \qquad \text{or} \qquad 9.51 \text{ dB}$$

Finally, we use (8.9-23) to find N_{ao}:

$$N_{ao} = 1.38(10^{-23})1340.0(10^{12})\frac{10^6}{1.5} \approx 12.3 \text{ mW}$$

PROBLEMS

8-1   A signal $x(t) = u(t) \exp(-\alpha t)$ is applied to a network having an impulse response $h(t) = Wu(t)\exp(-Wt)$. Here α and W are real positive constants and $u(\cdot)$ is the unit-step function. Find the system's response by use of (8.1-10).

8-2   Work Problem 8-1 by using (8.1-11) to find the spectrum $Y(\omega)$ of the response.

8-3   A rectangular pulse of amplitude A and duration T, defined by

$$x(t) = \begin{cases} A & 0 < t < T \\ 0 & \text{elsewhere} \end{cases}$$

is applied to the system of Problem 8-1.
(a) Find the time response $y(t)$.
(b) Sketch your response for $W = \pi/T$ and $W = 2\pi/T$.

8-4   A filter is called *gaussian* if it has a transfer function

$$H(\omega) = \frac{1}{\sqrt{2\pi}W_{rms}} e^{-\omega^2/2W_{rms}^2}$$

where W_{rms} is the root-mean-squared (rms) bandwidth.
(a) Sketch $H(\omega)$.
(b) How is W_{rms} related to the 3-dB bandwidth?

8-5   Two systems have transfer functions $H_1(\omega)$ and $H_2(\omega)$.
(a) Show that the transfer function $H(\omega)$ of the *cascade* of the two, which means that the output of the first feeds the input of the second system, is $H(\omega) = H_1(\omega)H_2(\omega)$.
(b) For a cascade of N systems with transfer functions $H_n(\omega)$, $n = 1, 2, \ldots, N$, show that

$$H(\omega) = \prod_{n=1}^{N} H_n(\omega)$$

*8-6   Work Problem 8-1 if the output of the given network is applied to a second identical network and the response is taken from the second network.

8-7 The impulse response of a system is

$$h(t) = \begin{cases} t^3 e^{-t^2} & 0 < t \\ 0 & t < 0 \end{cases}$$

By use of (8.1-8) or (8.1-10), find the response of the network to the pulse

$$x(t) = \begin{cases} A & 0 < t < T \\ 0 & \text{elsewhere} \end{cases}$$

where A and T are real positive constants.

8-8 Work Problem 8-7 if the network's impulse response is

$$h(t) = \begin{cases} t^3 e^{-t} & 0 < t \\ 0 & t < 0 \end{cases}$$

8-9 Given the network shown in Figure P8-9.
(*a*) Find the impulse response $h(t)$.
(*b*) By Fourier transforming $h(t)$, find $H(\omega)$.
(*c*) Sketch $h(t)$ and $H(\omega)$.

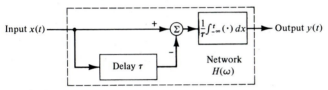

FIGURE P8-9
[*Reproduced from Peebles (1976), with permission of publishers Addison-Wesley, Advanced Book Program.*]

8-10 Find the transfer function of the network of Figure P8-9 by use of (8.1-13).

8-11 By using (8.1-13), find the transfer function of the network illustrated in Figure P8-11. Assume that no loading is present due to any output circuitry.

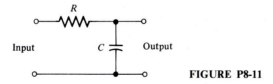

FIGURE P8-11

8-12 Work Problem 8-11 for the network of Figure P8-12.

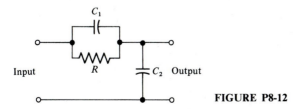

FIGURE P8-12

★**8-13**   (a) Work Problem 8-11 for the network of Figure P8-13.

(b) Under what conditions will the network behave approximately as a lowpass filter?

(c) Find a relationship between R_1, C_1, R_2, and C_2 such that the network behaves at all frequencies as a pure resistive attenuator.

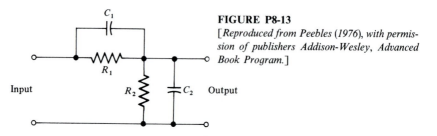

FIGURE P8-13

[*Reproduced from Peebles (1976), with permission of publishers Addison-Wesley, Advanced Book Program.*]

8-14   Given the network shown in Figure P8-14.

(a) If the output causes no loading on the network, find the transfer function $H(\omega)$.

(b) Define $\omega_0 = 1/\sqrt{LC}$ and $Q_0 = R/\omega_0 L$. Plot $|H(\omega)|^2$ as a function of $x = (\omega - \omega_0)Q_0/\omega_0$ for Q_0 large and ω near ω_0. (*Hint:* Use the approximation $\omega \approx \omega_0$ for the most significant values of ω when Q_0 is large.)

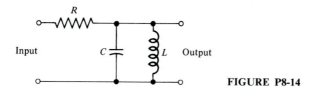

FIGURE P8-14

★**8-15**   (a) Find the transfer function $H(\omega)$ for the network shown in Figure P8-15.

(b) Define $\omega_0 = 1/\sqrt{LC}$ and $Q_0 = 1/\omega_0(R + R_L)C$ and assume $Q_0 \gg 1$, so that the values of ω for which $H(\omega)$ is significant correspond to $\omega \approx \omega_0$. Use these facts to obtain an approximation for $H(\omega)$.

(c) If an impulse is applied to the network, find an expression for the approximate energy absorbed by R_L. (*Hint:* Use Parseval's theorem.)

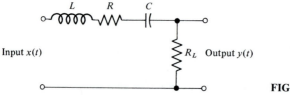

FIGURE P8-15

8-16 A class of filters called *Butterworth filters* has a power transfer function defined by

$$|H(\omega)|^2 = \frac{1}{1 + (\omega/W)^{2n}}$$

where $n = 1, 2, \ldots,$ is a number related to the number of circuit elements and W is the 3-dB bandwidth in radians per second. Sketch $|H(\omega)|^2$ for $n = 1, 2, 4,$ and 8 and note the behavior. As $n \to \infty$, what does $|H(\omega)|^2$ become?

8-17 Determine which of the following impulse responses do not correspond to a system that is stable, or realizable, or both, and state why.
(a) $h(t) = u(t + 3)$
(b) $h(t) = u(t)e^{-t^2}$
(c) $h(t) = e^t \sin(\omega_0 t)$ ω_0 a real constant
(d) $h(t) = u(t)e^{-3t} \sin(\omega_0 t)$ ω_0 a real constant.

8-18 Use (8.1-10) and prove (8.1-15).

8-19 Show that (8.1-16) must be true if a linear time-invariant system is to be stable.

8-20 A system is defined by

$$y(t) = \int_{-\infty}^{t} x(\xi)\, d\xi$$

for all $x(t)$ for which the integral exists. Show that the system is linear, time-invariant, and causal.

8-21 A random process

$$X(t) = A \sin(\omega_0 t + \Theta)$$

where A and ω_0 are real positive constants and Θ is a random variable uniformly distributed on the interval $(-\pi, \pi)$, is applied to the network of Problem 8-1. Find an expression for the network's response process using (8.2-3).

8-22 Work Problem 8-21 for a network with impulse response

$$h(t) = u(t)te^{-t}$$

8-23 A random process $X(t)$ is applied to a linear time-invariant system. A response $Y(t) = X(t) - X(t - \tau)$ occurs where τ is a real constant.
(a) Sketch a block diagram of the system.
(b) Find the system's transfer function.

8-24 Work Problem 8-23 if the response is

$$Y(t) = X(t - \tau) + \int_{t_1}^{t_2} X(t - \xi)\, d\xi$$

where t_1 and t_2 are real constants.

8-25 A random process $X(t)$ has an autocorrelation function

$$R_{XX}(\tau) = A^2 + Be^{-|\tau|}$$

where A and B are positive constants. Find the mean value of the response of a system having an impulse response

$$h(t) = \begin{cases} e^{-Wt} & 0 < t \\ 0 & t < 0 \end{cases}$$

where W is a real positive constant, for which $X(t)$ is its input.

8-26 Work Problem 8-25 for the system for which

$$h(t) = \begin{cases} te^{-Wt} & 0 < t \\ 0 & t < 0 \end{cases}$$

8-27 Work Problem 8-25 for the system for which

$$h(t) = \begin{cases} e^{-Wt} \sin(\omega_0 t) & 0 < t \\ 0 & t < 0 \end{cases}$$

where W and ω_0 are real positive constants.

8-28 White noise with power density 5 W/Hz is applied to the system of Problem 8-25. Find the mean-squared value of the response using (8.2-7).

8-29 Work Problem 8-28 for the system of Problem 8-26.

8-30 Work Problem 8-28 for the system of Problem 8-27.

8-31 Let jointly wide-sense stationary processes $X_1(t)$ and $X_2(t)$ cause responses $Y_1(t)$ and $Y_2(t)$, respectively, from a linear time-invariant system with impulse response $h(t)$. If the sum $X(t) = X_1(t) + X_2(t)$ is applied, the response is $Y(t)$. Find expressions, in terms of $h(t)$ and characteristics of $X_1(t)$ and $X_2(t)$, for
(a) $E[Y]$ (b) $R_{YY}(t, t + \tau)$

8-32 Show that the cross-correlation function for the output components $Y_1(t)$ and $Y_2(t)$ in Problem 8-31 is given by

$$R_{Y_1 Y_2}(t, t + \tau) = \int_{-\infty}^{\infty} \int_{-\infty}^{\infty} R_{X_1 X_2}(\tau + u - v) h(u) h(v) \, du \, dv$$

$$= R_{Y_1 Y_2}(\tau)$$

8-33 Two separate systems have impulse responses $h_1(t)$ and $h_2(t)$. A process $X_1(t)$ is applied to the first system and its response is $Y_1(t)$. Similarly, a process $X_2(t)$ invokes a response $Y_2(t)$ from the second system. Find the cross-correlation function of $Y_1(t)$ and $Y_2(t)$ in terms of $h_1(t)$, $h_2(t)$, and the cross-correlation function of $X_1(t)$ and $X_2(t)$. Assume $X_1(t)$ and $X_2(t)$ are jointly wide-sense stationary.

8-34 Two systems are cascaded. A random process $X(t)$ is applied to the input of the first system that has impulse response $h_1(t)$; its response $W(t)$ is the input to the second system having impulse response $h_2(t)$. The second system's output is $Y(t)$. Find the cross-correlation function of $W(t)$ and $Y(t)$

in terms of $h_1(t)$ and $h_2(t)$, and the autocorrelation function of $Y(t)$ if $X(t)$ is wide-sense stationary.

8-35 Let the two systems of Problem 8-34 be identical, each with the impulse response given in Problem 8-26. If $E[X(t)] = 2$ and $W = 3$ rad/s, find $E[Y(t)]$.

8-36 The random process $X(t)$ of Problem 8-21 (the signal) is added to white noise with power density $\mathcal{N}_0/2$, where $\mathcal{N}_0$ is a positive constant, and the sum is applied to the network of Example 8.1-1.
(a) Find the power spectrums of the output signal and output noise.
(b) Find the ratio of output signal average power to output noise average power.
(c) What value of $W = R/L$ will maximize the ratio of part (b)?

8-37 A random process $X(t)$ having autocorrelation function

$$R_{XX}(\tau) = Pe^{-\alpha|\tau|}$$

where P and α are real positive constants, is applied to the input of a system with impulse response

$$h(t) = \begin{cases} We^{-Wt} & 0 < t \\ 0 & t < 0 \end{cases}$$

where W is a real positive constant. Find the autocorrelation function of the network's response $Y(t)$.

8-38 Find the cross-correlation function $R_{XY}(\tau)$ for Problem 8-37.

8-39 For the processes and system of Problem 8-31, show that the power spectrum of $Y(t)$ is

$$\mathcal{S}_{YY}(\omega) = |H(\omega)|^2[\mathcal{S}_{X_1X_2}(\omega) + \mathcal{S}_{X_2X_2}(\omega) + \mathcal{S}_{X_1X_1}(\omega) + \mathcal{S}_{X_2X_1}(\omega)]$$

8-40 If $X_1(t)$ and $X_2(t)$ are statistically independent random processes in Problem 8-31, use the results of Problem 8-39 to show that the output power spectrum becomes

$$\mathcal{S}_{YY}(\omega) = |H(\omega)|^2[\mathcal{S}_{X_1X_1}(\omega) + \mathcal{S}_{X_2X_2}(\omega) + 4\pi\bar{X}_1\bar{X}_2\delta(\omega)]$$

8-41 Rework Example 8.4-1 when the network is replaced by two identical networks in cascade, that is, when $H(\omega) = [1 + (j\omega L/R)]^{-2}$.

8-42 Show that (8.4-7) and (8.4-8) are true.

8-43 A network with transfer function $H(\omega) = j\omega$ is a *differentiator*; its input is the wide-sense stationary random process $X(t)$ and its output is $\dot{X}(t) = dX(t)/dt$.
(a) By using (8.4-7), show that

$$R_{X\dot{X}}(\tau) = \frac{dR_{XX}(\tau)}{d\tau}$$

(b) By using (8.4-1), show that

$$R_{\dot{X}\dot{X}}(\tau) = -\frac{d^2R_{XX}(\tau)}{d\tau^2}$$

8-44   Given the random process

$$Y(t) = \frac{1}{2T} \int_{t-T}^{t+T} X(\xi)\, d\xi$$

where $X(t)$ is a wide-sense stationary process. Use (8.2-1) to show that the power spectrum of $Y(t)$ is

$$\mathscr{S}_{YY}(\omega) = \mathscr{S}_{XX}(\omega) \left[\frac{\sin(\omega T)}{\omega T} \right]^2$$

8-45   Prove (8.5-6).

8-46   A random process $X(t)$ has a power spectrum $\mathscr{S}_{XX}(\omega)$ that is nonzero only for $-W_X < \omega < W_X$, where W_X is a real positive constant. $X(t)$ is applied to a system with transfer function

$$H(\omega) = 1 + j(\omega/W_H) \qquad -W_X < \omega < W_X$$

Find the average power P_{YY} in the network's response $Y(t)$ in terms of the rms bandwidth of $\mathscr{S}_{XX}(\omega)$, the constant W_H, and the average power P_{XX} in $X(t)$. Discuss the effect of letting $W_X \to \infty$.

8-47   Find the noise bandwidth of the system having the power transfer function

$$|H(\omega)|^2 = \frac{1}{1 + (\omega/W)^4}$$

where W is a real positive constant.

8-48   Work Problem 8-47 for the function

$$|H(\omega)|^2 = \frac{1}{[1 + (\omega/W)^2]^2}$$

8-49   Work Problem 8-47 for the function

$$|H(\omega)|^2 = \frac{1}{[1 + (\omega/W)^2]^3}$$

8-50   White noise with power density $\mathscr{N}_0/2$ is applied to a lowpass network for which $|H(0)| = 2$; it has a noise bandwidth of 2 MHz. If the average output noise power is 0.1 W in a 1-Ω resistor, what is $\mathscr{N}_0$?

8-51   White noise with power density $\mathscr{N}_0/2$ is applied to an ideal lowpass filter with bandwidth W.
(a) Find and sketch the autocorrelation function of the response.
(b) If samples of the output noise taken at times $t_n = n\pi/W$, $n = 0, \pm 1, \pm 2, \ldots$, are considered as values of random variables, what can you say about these random variables?

8-52   Work Problem 8-51 for an ideal bandpass filter centered on a frequency $\omega_0/2\pi$ that has a bandwidth W. Assume sample times are now $t_n = n2\pi/W$, $n = 0, \pm 1, \pm 2, \ldots$.

★8-53   A band-limited random process $N(t)$ has the power density spectrum

$$\mathcal{S}_{NN}(\omega) = \begin{cases} P \cos\left[\pi(\omega - \omega_0)/W\right] & -W/2 \le \omega - \omega_0 \le W/2 \\ P \cos\left[\pi(\omega + \omega_0)/W\right] & -W/2 \le \omega + \omega_0 \le W/2 \\ 0 & \text{elsewhere} \end{cases}$$

where P, W, and $\omega_0 > W$ are real positive constants.
(a) Find the power in $N(t)$.
(b) Find the power spectrum $\mathcal{S}_{XX}(\omega)$ of $X(t)$ when $N(t)$ is represented by (8.6-2).
(c) Find the cross-correlation function $R_{XY}(\tau)$.
(d) Are $X(t)$ and $Y(t)$ orthogonal processes?

★8-54   A band-limited random process is given by (8.6-2) and has the power density spectrum shown in Figure P8-54.
(a) Sketch $\mathcal{S}_{XX}(\omega)$.
(b) Sketch $\mathcal{S}_{XY}(\omega)$, if a sketch is possible.

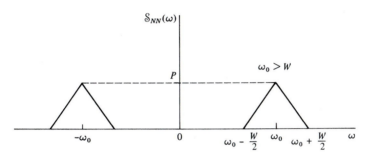

FIGURE P8-54

★8-55   Work Problem 8-54 for the power spectrum of Figure P8-55.

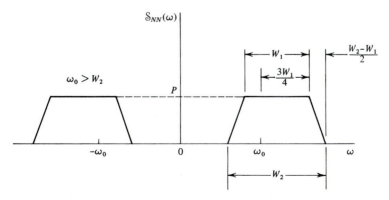

FIGURE P8-55

★8-56   Use (8.6-2) and derive (8.6-23).

8-57   A sonar echo system on a submarine transmits a random noise $n(t)$ to determine the distance to another "target" submarine. Distance R is given by $v\tau_R/2$ where v is the speed of the sound waves in water and τ_R is the time it takes the reflected version of $n(t)$ to return. Its block diagram is shown in Figure P8-57. Assume that $n(t)$ is a sample function of an ergodic random process $N(t)$ and T is very large.
(a) Find V in terms of a correlation function of $N(t)$.
(b) What value of the delay τ_T will cause V to be maximum?
(c) State in words how the submarine can determine the distance to the target.

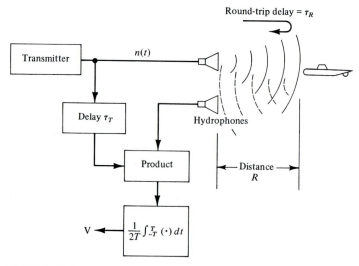

FIGURE P8-57

8-58   Two resistors with resistances R_1 and R_2 are connected in parallel and have physical temperatures T_1 and T_2, respectively.
(a) Find the effective noise temperature T_s of an equivalent resistor with resistance equal to the parallel combination of R_1 and R_2.
(b) If $T_1 = T_2 = T$, what is T_s?

8-59   Work Problem 8-58 for three resistances R_1, R_2, and R_3 in parallel when they have physical temperatures T_1, T_2, and T_3, respectively.

8-60   Work Example 8.7-2 if a second capacitor is placed across the resistance R_2. Is it possible to choose C_2 so that T_s is independent of frequency?

★8-61   Find the effective noise temperature of the network of Figure P8-61 if R_1 and R_2 are at physical temperatures T_1 and T_2, respectively.

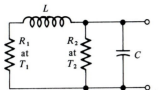

FIGURE P8-61

8-62 A two-port network is illustrated in Figure P8-62. Find its available power gain.

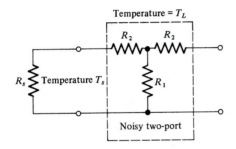

FIGURE P8-62

8-63 If the two-port network of Problem 8-62 has a physical temperature T_L and is driven by a source of resistance R_s and effective noise temperature T_s, what is the effective input noise temperature of the network?

8-64 If the output of the network of Problem 8-62 is connected to the input of a second identical network, what is the available power gain of the cascade if $R_1 = 5\Omega$, $R_2 = 3\Omega$ and $R_s = 7\Omega$?

8-65 Show that (8.8-4) is valid.

8-66 In a cascade of M network stages for which the mth stage has available power gain G_m and operating spot noise figure F_{opm} when driven by all previous stages as its source, show that the overall cascade's operating spot noise figure is

$$F_{op} = F_{op1} + \frac{T_{s1}(F_{op2} - 1)}{T_s G_1} + \cdots + \frac{T_{s(M-1)}(F_{opM} - 1)}{T_s G_1 G_2 \cdots G_{M-1}}$$

where $T_{s(m-1)}$ is the temperature of all stages prior to stage m treated as a source.

8-67 An amplifier has a standard spot noise figure $F_0 = 6.31$ (8.0 dB). An engineer uses the amplifier to amplify the output of an antenna that is known to have an antenna temperature of $T_a = 180$ K.
(a) What is the effective input noise temperature of the amplifier?
(b) What is the operating spot noise figure?

8-68   In a cascade of M stages for which F_{0m}, $m = 1, 2, \ldots, M$, is the standard spot noise figure of stage m which has available power gain G_m, show that the standard spot noise figure of the cascade of networks is

$$F_0 = F_{01} + \frac{F_{02} - 1}{G_1} + \frac{F_{03} - 1}{G_1 G_2} + \cdots + \frac{F_{0M} - 1}{G_1 G_2 \cdots G_{M-1}}$$

8-69   An amplifier has three stages for which $T_{e1} = 200$ K (first stage), $T_{e2} = 450$ K, and $T_{e3} = 1000$ K (last stage). If the available power gain of the second stage is 5, what gain must the first stage have to guarantee an effective input noise temperature of 250 K?

8-70   An amplifier has an operating spot noise figure of 10 dB when driven by a source of effective noise temperature 225 K.
(a) What is the standard spot noise figure of the amplifier?
(b) If a matched attenuator with a loss of 3.2 dB is placed between the source and the amplifier's input, what is the operating spot noise figure of the attenuator-amplifier cascade if the attenuator's physical temperature is 290 K?
(c) What is the standard spot noise figure of the cascade in (b)?

8-71   One manufacturer sells a microwave receiver having an operating spot noise figure of 10 dB when driven by a source with effective noise temperature 130 K. Another sells a receiver with a standard spot noise figure of 6 dB.
(a) Find the effective input noise temperatures of the two receivers.
(b) All other parameters, such as gain, cost, etc., being the same, which receiver would be the best to purchase?

8-72   What is the maximum average effective input noise temperature that an amplifier can have if its average standard noise figure is to not exceed 1.7?

8-73   An amplifier has an average standard noise figure of 2.0 dB and an average operating noise figure of 6.5 dB when used with a source of average effective source temperature $\bar{T}_s$. What is $\bar{T}_s$?

8-74   An antenna with average noise temperature 60 K connects to a receiver through various microwave elements that can be modeled as an impedance-matched attenuator with an overall loss of 2.4 dB and a physical temperature of 275 K. The overall system noise temperature is $\bar{T}_{sys} = 820$ K.
(a) What is the average effective input noise temperature of the receiver?
(b) What is the average operating noise figure of the attenuator-receiver cascade?
(c) What is the available output noise power of the receiver if it has an available power gain of 110 dB and a noise bandwidth of 10 MHz?

8-75   If the antenna-attenuator cascade of Problem 8-74 is considered as a noise source, what is its average effective noise temperature?

8-76   The loss L in Figure 8.9-1a is replaced by two cascaded matched attenuators, one with loss L_1 at temperature T_1 attached to the antenna output, and one with loss L_2 at temperature T_2 that connects to the receiver. Derive a new expression for $\bar{T}_{sys}$ analogous to (8.9-24).

ADDITIONAL PROBLEMS, SECOND EDITION

8-77 A network is driven by a resistive source as shown in Figure P8-77. Find: (a) Z_i, (b) Z_o, and (c) G_a. (d) Is the network a matched attenuator?

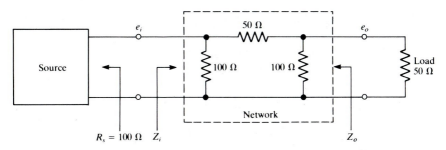

FIGURE P8-77

8-78 A network has the transfer function

$$H(\omega) = \frac{2e^{j\omega/20}}{(20 + j\omega)^3}$$

(a) Determine and sketch its impulse response. (*Hint:* Use Appendix E.)
(b) Is the network physically realizable?
(c) Determine if the network is stable by evaluating I in (8.1-16).

★8-79 Show that the impulse response of a cascade of N identical networks, each with transfer function

$$H_1(\omega) = 1/(\alpha + j\omega)$$

where $\alpha > 0$ is a constant, is given by

$$h_N(t) = u(t)\left[\frac{t^{N-1}}{(N-1)!}\right]\exp(-\alpha t)$$

8-80 A signal

$$x(t) = u(t)\exp(-\alpha t)$$

is applied to a network having an impulse response

$$h(t) = u(t)W^2 t \exp(-Wt)$$

Here $\alpha > 0$ and $W > 0$ are real constants. By use of (8.2-2) find the network's response $y(t)$.

8-81 Work Problem 8-80 assuming

$$h(t) = u(t)W^3 t^2 \exp(-Wt)$$

8-82 A stationary random process $X(t)$ is applied to the input of a system for which

$$h(t) = 3u(t)t^2 \exp(-8t)$$

If $E[X(t)] = 2$ what is the mean value of the system's response $Y(t)$?

8-83 Work Problem 8-28 for the system of Problem 8-82.

8-84 White noise with power density $\mathcal{N}_0/2$ is applied to a network with impulse response

$$h(t) = u(t)Wt \exp(-Wt)$$

where $W > 0$ is a constant. Find the cross-correlations of the input and output.

8-85 Work Problem 8-84 for a network with impulse response.

$$h(t) = u(t)Wt \sin(\omega_0 t) \exp(-Wt)$$

where ω_0 is a constant.

8-86 A random process $X(t)$ is applied to a network with impulse response

$$h(t) = u(t)t \exp(-bt)$$

where $b > 0$ is a constant. The cross-correlation of $X(t)$ with the output $Y(t)$ is known to have the same form:

$$R_{XY}(\tau) = u(\tau)\tau \exp(-b\tau)$$

(a) Find the autocorrelation of $Y(t)$.
(b) What is the average power in $Y(t)$?

8-87 Work Problem 8-86 except assume

$$h(t) = u(t)t^2 \exp(-bt)$$

and

$$R_{XY}(\tau) = u(\tau)\tau^2 \exp(-b\tau)$$

8-88 Two identical networks are cascaded. Each has impulse response

$$h(t) = u(t)3t \exp(-4t)$$

A wide-sense stationary process $X(t)$ is applied to the cascade's input.
(a) Find an expression for the response $Y(t)$ of the cascade.
(b) If $E[X(t)] = \bar{X} = 6$, find $E[Y(t)]$.

8-89 A stationary random process $X(t)$, having an autocorrelation function

$$R_{XX}(\tau) = 2 \exp(-4|\tau|)$$

is applied to the network of Figure P8-89. Find: (a) $\mathcal{S}_{XX}(\omega)$, (b) $|H(\omega)|^2$, and (c) $\mathcal{S}_{YY}(\omega)$.

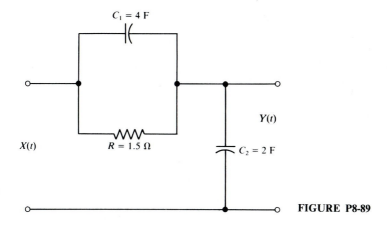

$C_1 = 4$ F

$Y(t)$

$X(t)$

$R = 1.5\ \Omega$

$C_2 = 2$ F

FIGURE P8-89

8-90 A wide-sense stationary process $X(t)$, with mean value 5 and power spectrum

$$\mathscr{S}_{XX}(\omega) = 50\pi\delta(\omega) + 3/[1 + (\omega/2)^2]$$

is applied to a network with impulse response

$$h(t) = 4 \exp\left(-4|t|\right)$$

(a) Find $H(\omega)$ for the network.
Determine: (b) the mean $\bar{Y}$, and (c) the power spectrum of the response $Y(t)$.

8-91 White noise, for which $R_{XX}(\tau) = 10^{-2}\delta(\tau)$, is applied to a network with impulse response

$$h(t) = u(t)3t \exp\left(-4t\right)$$

(a) Use (8.2-9) to obtain the network's output noise power (in a 1-ohm resistor).
(b) Obtain an expression for the output power spectrum.

8-92 White noise with power density $\mathscr{N}_0/2 = 6(10^{-6})$ W/Hz is applied to an ideal filter (gain = 1) with bandwidth W (rad/s). Find W so that the output's average noise power is 15 watts.

8-93 An ideal filter with a midband power gain of 8 and bandwidth of 4 rad/s has noise $X(t)$ at its input with power spectrum

$$\mathscr{S}_{XX}(\omega) = (50/\sqrt{8\pi}) \exp\left(-\omega^2/8\right)$$

What is the noise power at the network's output?

8-94 White noise with power density $\mathscr{N}_0/2$, $\mathscr{N}_0 > 0$ a constant, is applied to a lowpass network for which $H(0) = 8$ and its noise bandwidth is 12 MHz. If average output noise power is 0.5 W in a 1-ohm resistor, what is $\mathscr{N}_0$?

8-95 A system's power transfer function is

$$|H(\omega)|^2 = 16/[256 + \omega^4]$$

(a) What is its noise bandwidth?
(b) If white noise with power density $6(10^{-3})$ W/Hz is applied to the input, find the noise power in the system's output.

★8-96 Assume a band-limited random process $N(t)$ has a power spectrum

$$\mathscr{S}_{NN}(\omega) = B[u(\omega - \omega_0 + W_1) - u(\omega - \omega_0 - W_2)] \exp[-a(\omega - \omega_0 + W_1)]$$

$$+ B[u(-\omega - \omega_0 + W_1) - u(-\omega - \omega_0 - W_2)] \exp[-a(-\omega - \omega_0 + W_1)]$$

where B, ω_0, W_1, and W_2 are positive constants, and a is a constant.

Assume $2\omega_0 > W_1 + W_2$ and find analytical expressions for (a) the power spectrum $\mathscr{S}_{XX}(\omega)$ and (b) the cross-power spectrum $\mathscr{S}_{XY}(\omega)$ for the processes $X(t)$ and $Y(t)$ involved in the representation of (8.6-2) for $N(t)$.
(c) Sketch $\mathscr{S}_{XX}(\omega)$ and $\mathscr{S}_{XY}(\omega)$ for $W_1 = W_2/2$ and $a = 1/W_1$.
(d) Repeat part (c) except with $a = -1/W_1$.

★8-97 Find the functions $R_{XX}(\tau)$ and $R_{XY}(\tau)$ applicable in Problem 8-96.

8-98 Determine the effective noise temperature of the network of Figure P8-98 if resistors R_1 and R_2 are at different physical temperatures T_1 and T_2, respectively.

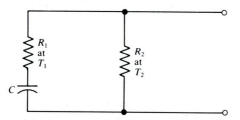

FIGURE P8-98

8-99 Two resistors in series have different physical temperatures as in Example 8.7-1. Let R_1 and R_2 be independent random variables uniformly distributed on (1000, 1500) and (2200, 2700), respectively. Their average resistances are then $\bar{R}_1 = 1250 \ \Omega$ and $\bar{R}_2 = 2450 \ \Omega$.
(a) What is the effective noise temperature of the two resistors as a source if $T_1 = 250$ K and $T_2 = 330$ K and average resistors are used?
(b) What is the mean effective noise temperature of the source for the same values of T_1 and T_2?

8-100 An amplifier has three stages for which $T_{e1} = 150$ K (first stage), $T_{e2} = 350$ K, and $T_{e3} = 600$ K (output stage). Available power gain of the first stage is 10 and overall input effective noise temperature is 190 K.
(a) What is the available power gain of the second stage?
(b) What is the cascade's standard spot noise figure?
(c) What is the cascade's operating spot noise figure when used with a source of noise temperature $T_s = 50$ K?

8-101 Three networks are cascaded. Available power gains are $G_1 = 8$ (input stage), $G_2 = 6$, and $G_3 = 20$ (output stage). Respective input effective spot noise temperatures are $T_{e1} = 40$ K, $T_{e2} = 100$ K, and $T_{e3} = 280$ K.

(a) What is the input effective spot noise temperature of the cascade?

(b) If the cascade is used with a source of noise temperature $T_s = 30$ K, find the percentage of total available output noise power (in a band $d\omega$) due to each of the following: (1) source, and the excess noises of (2) network 1, (3) network 2, and (4) network 3.

8-102 An antenna with effective noise temperature $T_a = 90$ K is connected to an attenuator that is at a physical temperature of 270 K and has a loss of 1.9. What is the effective spot noise temperature of the antenna-attenuator cascade if its output is considered as a noise source?

8-103 An amplifier, when used with a source of average noise temperature 60 K, has an average operating noise figure of 5.

(a) What is $\bar{T}_e$?

(b) If the amplifier is sold to the engineering public, what noise figure would be quoted in a catalog (give a numerical answer)?

(c) What average operating noise figure results when the amplifier is used with an antenna of temperature 30 K?

8-104 An engineer purchases an amplifier with average operating noise figure of 1.8 when used with a 50-Ω broadband source having average source temperature of 80 K. When used with a different 50-Ω source the average operating noise figure is 1.25. What is the average noise temperature of the source?

8-105 An amplifier with a noise bandwidth of at least 1.8 MHz is needed by an engineer. Two units from which he can choose are: unit 1—average standard noise figure = 3.98, noise bandwidth = 2.0 MHz, and available power gain = 10^6; unit 2—average standard noise figure = 2.82, noise bandwidth = 2.9 MHz, and available power gain = 10^6.

Find: (a) $\bar{T}_e$ for unit 1, (b) $\bar{T}_e$ for unit 2, (c) excess noise power of unit 1, and (d) excess noise power of unit 2.

(e) If the source's noise temperature $\bar{T}_s$ is very small, which unit is the best to purchase and why?

(f) If $\bar{T}_s \gg \bar{T}_e$, which is best and why?

★**8-106** A resistor is cooled to 75 K and serves as a noise source for a network with available power gain

$$G_a(\omega) = 10^{36}/(10^6 + \omega^2)^4$$

(a) Write an expression for the power spectrum of the network's output noise that is due to the source.

(b) Compute the available output noise power that is due to the source alone.

8-107 A broadband antenna, for which $T_a = 120$ K, connects through an attenuator with loss 2.5 to a receiver with average input effective noise temperature

80 K, available power gain 10^{12}, and noise bandwidth 20 MHz. The antenna and attenuator both have a physical temperature of 200 K.

(a) What is the attenuator's input effective noise temperature?

(b) What is the system's noise temperature?

(c) Find the average standard noise figure of the receiver by itself.

(d) What is the available noise power at the receiver's output (in system operation)?

(e) Determine the input effective noise temperature of the attenuator-receiver taken as a unit.

(f) What is the average operating noise figure of this system when the antenna is the source?

8-108 An antenna with average noise temperature 120 K connects to a receiver through an impedance-matched attenuator having a loss of 1.5 and physical temperature 75 K. For the overall system $\bar{T}_{sys} = 500$ K.

(a) What is the average effective input noise temperature of the receiver?

(b) What is the average operating noise figure of the attenuator-receiver cascade?

(c) What is the available output noise power of the receiver if its available power gain is 120 dB and its noise bandwidth is 20 MHz (system is connected)?

8-109 A receiving system consists of an antenna with noise temperature 80 K that feeds a matched attenuator with physical temperature 220 K and loss 2.6. The attenuator drives an amplifier with average effective noise temperature 170 K, noise bandwidth 4 MHz, and available power gain 10^8.

Find: (a) the overall system's average noise temperature $\bar{T}_{sys}$, (b) the available noise power N_{ao} at the system's output, (c) the total noise power available at the attenuator's output (within the noise bandwidth) and how much of the total (as a percentage) is due to the antenna alone, and (d) the average operating noise figure $\bar{F}_{op}$ of the system.

ADDITIONAL PROBLEMS, THIRD EDITION

8-110 If τ in the circuit of Figure P8-9 is changed to T, show that the circuit is equivalent to the operation

$$y(t) = \frac{1}{T} \int_{t-T}^{t} x(\xi) \, d\xi$$

8-111 Show that the network of Problem 8-110 is equivalent to a linear filter with impulse response

$$h(t) = \frac{1}{T} [u(t) - u(t - T)]$$

and find its transfer function.

8-112 Work Problem 8-11 for the network of Figure P8-112.

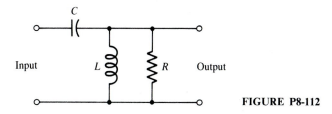

FIGURE P8-112

8-113 Work Problem 8-11 for the network of Figure P8-113.

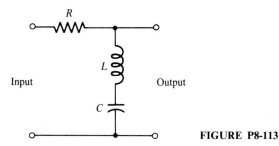

FIGURE P8-113

8-114 If a "time autocorrelation function" for the impulse response $h(t)$ of a linear filter is defined (for finite-energy impulse responses) by

$$\mathcal{R}_{hh}(\xi) = \int_{-\infty}^{\infty} h(t)h(t + \xi)\, dt$$

show that (8.2-9) can be written as

$$R_{YY}(\tau) = \int_{-\infty}^{\infty} R_{XX}(\alpha)\mathcal{R}_{hh}(\tau - \alpha)\, d\alpha = R_{XX}(\tau) * \mathcal{R}_{hh}(\tau)$$

8-115 Use the results of Problem 8-114 to find $R_{YY}(\tau)$ applicable to a system defined by the impulse response

$$h(t) = \frac{1}{T}\left[u(t) - u(t - T)\right]$$

where $T > 0$ is a constant.

8-116 Suppose the system of Figure 8.3-1 defined by $h(t)$ is in operation while the low-level white noise $X(t)$ is applied. That is, suppose the system's input is an operating (random) input signal $S(t)$ added to $X(t)$. $Y(t)$ will then contain a response, the operating output, due to $S(t)$, and a response, the output noise, due to $X(t)$. The cross-correlation measurement system's inputs are still $X(t)$ and $Y(t)$. Show that (8.3-4) still applies provided $S(t)$ is a process that is orthogonal to $X(t)$. Assume $X(t)$ and $S(t)$ are jointly wide-sense stationary.

8-117 A stationary random signal $X(t)$ has an autocorrelation function $R_{XX}(\tau) = 10 \exp(-|\tau|)$. It is added to white noise [independent of $X(t)$] for which $\mathcal{N}_0/2 = 10^{-3}$ and the sum is applied to a filter having a transfer function

$$H(\omega) = \frac{2}{(1 + j\omega)^3}$$

(a) Find the signal component of the output power spectrum and the average power in the output signal.

(b) Find the power spectrum of, and average power in, the output noise.

(c) What is the ratio of the output signal's power to the output average noise power?

8-118 A random noise $X(t)$, having a power spectrum

$$\mathcal{S}_{XX}(\omega) = \frac{3}{49 + \omega^2}$$

is applied to a differentiator that has a transfer function $H_1(\omega) = j\omega$. The differentiator's output is applied to a network for which

$$h_2(t) = u(t)t^2 \exp(-7t).$$

The network's response is a noise denoted by $Y(t)$.

(a) What is the average power in $X(t)$?

(b) Find the power spectrum of $Y(t)$.

(c) Find the average power in $Y(t)$.

8-119 Suppose

$$|H(\omega)|^2 = \frac{\omega^2}{[1 + (\omega/W)^2]^4}$$

for a network where $W > 0$ is a constant. Treat $|H(\omega)|^2$ as a bandpass function.

(a) Find ω_0, the value of ω where $|H(\omega)|^2$ is maximum.

(b) Find the network's noise bandwidth.

8-120 Work Problem 8-119 except for a network defined by

$$|H(\omega)|^2 = \frac{\omega^4}{[1 + (\omega/W)^2]^4}$$

★8-121 Work Problem 8-53 except assume $N(t)$ has the power density spectrum

$$\mathcal{S}_{NN}(\omega) = \begin{cases} K_1 + K_2 \left(\dfrac{\omega - \omega_0}{W}\right)^2 & -W/2 < \omega - \omega_0 < W/2 \\[2mm] K_1 + K_2 \left(\dfrac{\omega + \omega_0}{W}\right)^2 & -W/2 < \omega + \omega_0 < W/2 \\[2mm] 0 & \text{elsewhere in } \omega \end{cases}$$

where $K_1 > 0$, $K_2 > 0$ and $W > 0$ are real constants.

★**8-122** A bandpass bandlimited noise $N(t)$ has the power density spectrum of Problem 8-121. Find its autocorrelation function by using (8.6-11).

8-123 Find the effective noise temperature T_s of the network of Figure P8-123. What values does T_s assume for $\omega = 1/\sqrt{LC}$, $\omega = -\infty$ and $\omega = \infty$?

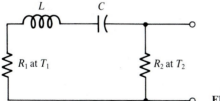

FIGURE P8-123

8-124 Work Problem 8-123, except replace the series L–C circuit by a parallel L–C circuit.

8-125 Three identical amplifiers, each having a spot effective input noise temperature of 125 K and available power gain G, are cascaded. The overall spot effective input noise temperature of the cascade is 155 K. What is G?

8-126 Three amplifiers that may be connected in any order in a cascade are defined as follows:

TABLE P8-126

Amplifier	Effective input noise temperature	Available power gain
A	110 K	4
B	120 K	6
C	150 K	12

What sequence of connections will give the lowest overall effective input noise temperature for the cascade?

8-127 In an amplifier the first stage in a cascade of 5 stages has $T_{e_1} = 75$ K and $G_1 = 0.5$. Each succeeding stage has an effective input noise temperature and an available power gain that are each 1.75 times that of the stage preceding it. What is the cascade's effective input noise temperature?

★**8-128** Generalize Problem 8-127 by letting T_{e_1} and G_1 be arbitrary and letting each succeeding stage have an effective input noise temperature and available power gain of K times that of the stage before it, where $K > 0$. Find a value of K that minimizes T_e for the cascade. Use the value of K found to determine the minimum value of T_e (for any G_1).

8-129 A designer requires an amplifier to give an operating spot noise figure of not more than 1.8 when operating with a 160-K source. What is the largest value of standard spot noise figure that will be acceptable in a purchased amplifier?

8-130 Two amplifiers have standard spot noise figures of $F_{01} = 1.6$ (unit 1) and $F_{02} = 1.4$ (unit 2). They have respective available power gains of $G_{a1} = 12$ and $G_{a2} = 8$. The two amplifiers are to be used in a cascade driven from an antenna to obtain an overall available power gain of $(8)12 = 96$.
(a) For best performance, which unit should be driven by the antenna?
(b) What is the standard spot noise figure of the best cascade?

8-131 An antenna with an effective noise temperature of 80 K drives a cascade of two amplifiers. The first (fed by the antenna) has an available power gain of 15 while the second has an input effective noise temperature of 600 K. The input effective noise temperature of the cascade is 140 K. The available power at the cascade's output in a small 1000-Hz band is $4.14(10^{-16})$ W.
(a) What is the input effective noise temperature of the first amplifier?
(b) What is the available power gain of the second stage?
(c) What is the cascade's operating spot noise figure?
(d) What is the cascade's standard spot noise figure?

8-132 Assume a source has an effective noise temperature of

$$T_s(\omega) = \frac{8000}{100 + \omega^2}$$

and feeds an amplifier that has an available power gain of

$$G_a(\omega) = \left| \frac{8}{10 + j\omega} \right|^2$$

(a) Find $\bar{T}_s$ for this source.
(b) Find the amplifier's noise bandwidth.
(c) What is the noise power available at the amplifier's output due to the source?

8-133 The available power gain of a network is

$$G_a(\omega) = \frac{K\omega^2}{(W^2 + \omega^2)^3}$$

where K and W are positive constants.
(a) At what value of ω, denoted by ω_0, does $G_a(\omega)$ reach a maximum?
(b) If $G_a(\omega)$ is considered to be a bandpass function with nominal (center) frequency ω_0, what is its noise bandwidth?

8-134 Work Problem 8-133, except assume an available power gain

$$G_a(\omega) = \frac{K\omega^4}{(W^2 + \omega^2)^4}$$

8-135 For the network of Problem 8-133, assume its input spot effective noise temperature varies as $T_e = 50 + (4\omega/W)^2$ and find its average input effective noise temperature.

8-136 A receiving system can be modeled as in Figure 8.9-1 if $T_a = 130$ K, $L = 1.6$, $T_L = 200$ K, $W_N/2\pi = 8$ MHz, $G_R(\omega_0) = 5(10^9)$, and $\bar{T}_{sys} = 558$ K. A sinusoidal signal with an angular frequency ω_0 is also being received that produces an available power of $55(10^{-12})$ W at the antenna's output. Find: (a) $\bar{T}_R$, (b) N_{ao}, (c) available output signal power S_{ao}, (d) the signal-to-noise ratio S_{ao}/N_{ao}, (e) $\bar{F}_0$ for the receiver, and (f) the effective input noise temperature of the loss, $\bar{T}_{e(loss)}$.

8-137 A receiving system has an antenna, for which $T_a = 120$ K, driving two broadband matched-impedance attenuators in cascade, which then drive a receiver for which $\bar{T}_R = 100$ K, $W_N/2\pi = 5$ MHz, and $G_R(\omega_0) = 10^{12}$. The attenuator to which the antenna is connected has a physical temperature of 70 K and a loss of 1.6. The other attenuator's physical temperature is 250 K and its loss is 1.9.

(a) What is the receiver's available output noise power?

(b) What available signal power at the antenna's output will produce a signal-to-noise power ratio of 1000 (or 30 dB) at the receiver's output?

(c) What is $\bar{T}_{sys}$?

8-138 An antenna, for which $T_a = 60$ K, feeds a cascade of two impedance-matched attenuators. The first, connected to the antenna, has a physical temperature of 75 K and a loss of 1.9. The second attenuator, at a physical temperature of 290 K and with a loss of 1.4, drives a broadband mixer that has an available power gain of 0.5 and $\bar{T}_e = 500$ K. Finally, the mixer drives an amplifier for which $G_a(\omega_0) = 10^7$, $\bar{F}_0 = 5$, and $W_N = 2\pi(10^6)$ rad/s.

(a) What is the input effective noise temperature of the attenuator that is at physical temperature 75 K?

(b) Repeat (a) for the second attenuator.

(c) What is the average input effective noise temperature of the whole cascade?

(d) What is $\bar{T}_{sys}$?

(e) What is the average operating noise figure of the cascade having the antenna as its source?

(f) What average noise power is available at the amplifier's output?

CHAPTER
9

OPTIMUM LINEAR SYSTEMS

9.0 INTRODUCTION

The developments of the preceding chapter related entirely to the *analysis* of a linear system. In this chapter we do an about-face and concentrate only on the *synthesis* of a linear system. In particular, we choose the system in such a way that it satisfies certain rules that make it *optimum*.

In designing any optimum system we must consider three things: *input specification, system constraints*, and *criterion of optimality*.

Input specification means that at least some knowledge must be available about the input to the system. For example, we might specify the input to consist of the sum of a random signal and a noise. Alternatively, the input could be the sum of a deterministic signal and a noise. In addition, we may be able to specify signal and noise correlation functions, power spectrums, or probability densities. Thus, we may know a great deal about the inputs in some cases or little in others. Regardless, however, there is some minimum knowledge required of the characteristics of the input for any given problem.

System constraints define the form of the resulting system. For example, we might allow the system to be linear, nonlinear, time-invariant, realizable, etc. In our work we shall be exclusively concerned with linear time-invariant systems but will not necessarily require that they be realizable. By relaxing the realizability constraint, we shall be able to introduce the most important topics of interest without undue mathematical complexity.

298

In principle, there is great latitude available in choosing the criterion of optimality. In a practical sense, however, it should be a meaningful measure of "goodness" for the problem at hand and should correspond to equations that are mathematically tractable. We shall be concerned with only two criteria. One will involve the minimization of a suitably defined error quantity. The other will relate to maximization of the ratio of a signal power to a noise power. This last criterion leads us to an optimum system often called a *matched filter*.

9.1 SYSTEMS THAT MAXIMIZE SIGNAL-TO-NOISE RATIO

An important class of systems involves the transmission of a deterministic signal of known form in noise. A digital communication system is one example† where, during a time interval T, a known signal may arrive at the receiver in the presence of additive noise. The presence of the signal corresponds to transmission of a digital "1," while absence of the signal occurs when a digital "0" is transmitted (noise is always present). It would seem reasonable that some system (or filter‡) could be found that would enhance its output signal power at some instant in time while reducing its output average noise power. Indeed, such a filter that maximizes this output *signal-to-noise ratio* can be found and it is called a *matched filter*. It can be shown that decisions made as to whether the signal was present or not during time interval T have the smallest probability of being in error if they are based on samples taken at the times of maximum signal-to-noise ratio. Although our comments here are directed toward a digital communication system, we shall find as we progress that the matched filter concept is a broad one, applying to many situations.

In this section we shall consider the optimization of a linear time-invariant system when the input consists of the sum of a Fourier-transformable deterministic signal $x(t)$ of known form and continuous noise $n(t)$. If we denote by $x_o(t)$ and $n_o(t)$ the output signal and noise, the criterion of optimality we choose is the maximization of the ratio of the output signal power at some time t_o to the output average noise power. Thus, with $n_o(t)$ assumed to be a sample function of a wide-sense stationary random process§ $N_o(t)$, we maximize

$$\left(\frac{\hat{S}_o}{N_o}\right) = \frac{|x_o(t_o)|^2}{E[N_o^2(t)]} \tag{9.1-1}$$

where

$$\hat{S}_o = |x_o(t_o)|^2 \tag{9.1-2}$$

---

† Although we discuss only this example, many systems such as radars, sonars, radio altimeters, ionospheric sounders, and automobile crash avoidance systems are other examples.

‡ We often use the words system, filter, or network in this chapter to convey the same meaning.

§ This assumption is equivalent to assuming the input noise is from a wide-sense stationary random process since the system is assumed to be linear and time-invariant (see Section 8.2).

is the output signal power at time t_o and

$$N_o = E[N_o^2(t)] \tag{9.1-3}$$

is the output average noise power.

Matched Filter for Colored Noise

Define $X(\omega)$ as the Fourier transform of $x(t)$, and $H(\omega)$ as the transfer function of the system. The output signal at any time t is

$$x_o(t) = \frac{1}{2\pi} \int_{-\infty}^{\infty} X(\omega)H(\omega)e^{j\omega t}\, d\omega \tag{9.1-4}$$

From (8.4-6), the output average noise power can be written in the form

$$N_o = E[N_o^2(t)] = \frac{1}{2\pi} \int_{-\infty}^{\infty} \mathscr{S}_{NN}(\omega)|H(\omega)|^2\, d\omega \tag{9.1-5}$$

where $\mathscr{S}_{NN}(\omega)$ is the power density spectrum of the random process, denoted $N(t)$, that represents the input noise $n(t)$. By use of (9.1-4) at time t_o and (9.1-5), we can write (9.1-1) as

$$\left(\frac{\hat{S}_o}{N_o}\right) = \frac{\left|\dfrac{1}{2\pi} \displaystyle\int_{-\infty}^{\infty} X(\omega)H(\omega)e^{j\omega t_o}\, d\omega\right|^2}{\dfrac{1}{2\pi} \displaystyle\int_{-\infty}^{\infty} \mathscr{S}_{NN}(\omega)|H(\omega)|^2\, d\omega} \tag{9.1-6}$$

To find $H(\omega)$ that maximizes (9.1-6), we shall apply the *Schwarz†* inequality. If $A(\omega)$ and $B(\omega)$ are two possibly complex functions of the real variable ω, the inequality states that

$$\left|\int_{-\infty}^{\infty} A(\omega)B(\omega)\, d\omega\right|^2 \leq \int_{-\infty}^{\infty} |A(\omega)|^2\, d\omega \int_{-\infty}^{\infty} |B(\omega)|^2\, d\omega \tag{9.1-7}$$

The equality holds only when $B(\omega)$ is proportional to the complex conjugate of $A(\omega)$; that is, when

$$B(\omega) = CA^*(\omega) \tag{9.1-8}$$

where C is any *arbitrary* real constant.

By making the substitutions

$$A(\omega) = \sqrt{\mathscr{S}_{NN}(\omega)}H(\omega) \tag{9.1-9}$$

$$B(\omega) = \frac{X(\omega)e^{j\omega t_o}}{2\pi\sqrt{\mathscr{S}_{NN}(\omega)}} \tag{9.1-10}$$

---

† Named for the German mathematician Hermann Amandus Schwarz (1843–1921).

in (9.1-7) we obtain

$$\left|\frac{1}{2\pi}\int_{-\infty}^{\infty} X(\omega)H(\omega)e^{j\omega t_o}\, d\omega\right|^2 \le \int_{-\infty}^{\infty}\mathscr{S}_{NN}(\omega)|H(\omega)|^2\, d\omega\, \frac{1}{(2\pi)^2}\int_{-\infty}^{\infty}\frac{|X(\omega)|^2}{\mathscr{S}_{NN}(\omega)}\, d\omega$$

(9.1-11)

With this last result, we write (9.1-6) as

$$\left(\frac{\hat{S}_o}{N_o}\right) \le \frac{1}{2\pi}\int_{-\infty}^{\infty}\frac{|X(\omega)|^2}{\mathscr{S}_{NN}(\omega)}\, d\omega$$

(9.1-12)

The maximum value of $(\hat{S}_o/N_o)$ occurs when the equality holds in (9.1-12), which implies that (9.1-8) is true. Denote the optimum filter transfer function by $H_{opt}(\omega)$. We find this function by solving (9.1-8) using (9.1-9) and (9.1-10); the result is

$$H_{opt}(\omega) = \frac{1}{2\pi C}\frac{X^*(\omega)}{\mathscr{S}_{NN}(\omega)}e^{-j\omega t_o}$$

(9.1-13)

From (9.1-13), we find that the optimum filter is proportional to the complex conjugate of the input signal's spectrum; we might say that the system is therefore *matched* to the specified signal since it depends so intimately on it. $H_{opt}(\omega)$ is also inversely proportional to the power spectrum of the input noise. In general, this noise has been assumed nonwhite; that is, colored. Because of these facts, an optimum filter given by (9.1-13) is called a *matched filter for colored noise*.

$H_{opt}(\omega)$ is also proportional to the inverse of the arbitrary constant C. In other words, $H_{opt}(\omega)$ has an arbitrary absolute magnitude. This fact allows the optimal system to have arbitrary gain. Intuitively, we feel that this should be true because gain affects both input signal and input noise in the same way, and, in the ratio of (9.1-1), gain cancels.

The time t_o at which the output ratio $(\hat{S}_o/N_o)$ is maximum enters into the optimum system transfer function only through the factor $\exp(-j\omega t_o)$. Such a factor only represents an ideal delay. Since t_o is a parameter that a designer may have some latitude in choosing, its value may be selected in some cases to make the optimum filter causal.

In general, the system defined by (9.1-13) may not be realizable. For certain forms of colored noise realizable filters may be found (Thomas, 1969, Chapter 5). In practice, one can always approximate (9.1-13) by a suitably chosen real filter.

Matched Filter for White Noise

If the input noise is white with power density $\mathscr{N}_0/2$, the optimum filter of (9.1-13) becomes

$$H_{opt}(\omega) = KX^*(\omega)e^{-j\omega t_o}$$

(9.1-14)

where $K = 1/\pi C\mathscr{N}_0$ is an arbitrary constant. Here the optimum filter is related only to the input signal's spectrum and the time that $(\hat{S}_o/N_o)$ is maximum. Thus, the name *matched filter* is very appropriate. Indeed, the name was originally attached to the filter in white noise; we have liberalized the name to include the preceding colored noise case.

The impulse response denoted $h_{opt}(t)$ of the optimum filter is the inverse Fourier transform of $H_{opt}(\omega)$. From (9.1-14), it is easily found that

$$h_{opt}(t) = Kx^*(t_o - t) \tag{9.1-15}$$

For real signals $x(t)$, (9.1-15) reduces to

$$h_{opt}(t) = Kx(t_o - t) \tag{9.1-16}$$

Equation (9.1-16) indicates that the impulse response is equal to the input signal displaced to a new origin at $t = t_o$ and folded about this point so as to "run backward."

Example 9.1-1 We shall find the matched filter for the signal of Figure 9.1-1*a* when received in white noise. From (9.1-16), the matched filter's impulse

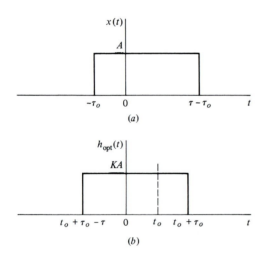

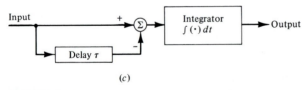

FIGURE 9.1-1
A matched filter and its related signals. (*a*) Input signal, (*b*) the filter's impulse response, and (*c*) the filter's block diagram. [*Reproduced from Peebles (1976), with permission of publishers Addison-Wesley, Advanced Book Program.*]

response is as shown in (b). By Fourier transformation of the waveform in (b), we readily obtain

$$H_{opt}(\omega) = KA\tau \frac{\sin(\omega\tau/2)}{(\omega\tau/2)} e^{-j\omega[t_0 + \tau_o - (\tau/2)]}$$

An alternative development consists of Fourier-transforming the input signal to get $X(\omega)$ and then using (9.1-14).

Whether or not any chance exists for the matched filter to be realizable may be determined from the impulse response of Figure 9.1-1b. Clearly, to be causal, and therefore realizable, the delay must be at least $\tau - \tau_o$; that is

$$t_o \geq \tau - \tau_o$$

If we assume this last condition is satisfied, the optimum filter is illustrated in (c) where the arbitrary constant K is set equal to $1/A$. This filter still requires that perfect integrators be possible. Of course, they are not. However, very good approximations are possible using modern operational amplifiers with feedback, so for all practical purposes matched filters for rectangular pulses in white noise may be constructed.†

9.2 SYSTEMS THAT MINIMIZE MEAN-SQUARED ERROR

A second class of optimum systems is concerned with causing the output to be a good estimate of some function of the input signal which arrives along with additive noise. One example corresponds to the output being a good estimate of the *derivative* of the input signal. In another case, the system could be designed so that its output is a good estimate of either the past, present, or future value of the input signal. We shall concern ourselves with only this last case. The optimum system or filter that results is called a *Wiener filter*.‡

Wiener Filters

The basic problem to be studied is depicted by Figure 9.2-1. The input signal $x(t)$ is now assumed to be *random*; it is therefore modeled as a sample function of a random process $X(t)$. It is applied to the input of the system along with additive noise $n(t)$ that is a sample function of a noise process $N(t)$. We assume $X(t)$ and $N(t)$ are jointly wide-sense stationary processes and that $N(t)$ has zero mean. The sum of signal and noise is denoted $W(t)$:

$$W(t) = X(t) + N(t) \tag{9.2-1}$$

---

† Other techniques using *integrate-and-dump* methods exist. See Peebles (1976), pp. 361–362.
‡ After Norbert Wiener (1894–1964), a great American mathematician whose work has tremendously affected many areas of science and engineering.

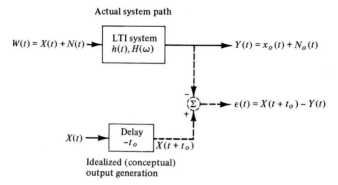

FIGURE 9.2-1
Operations that define the Wiener filter problem.

The system is assumed to be linear and time-invariant with a real impulse response $h(t)$ and a transfer function $H(\omega)$. The output of the system is denoted $Y(t)$.

In general, we shall select $H(\omega)$ so that $Y(t)$ is the best possible estimate of the input signal $X(t)$ at a time $t + t_o$; that is, the best estimate of $X(t + t_o)$. If $t_o > 0$, $Y(t)$ is an estimate of a *future* value of $X(t)$ corresponding to a *prediction filter*. If $t_o < 0$, $Y(t)$ is an estimate of a *past* value of $X(t)$ and we have a *smoothing filter*. If $t_o = 0$, $Y(t)$ is an estimate of the current value of $X(t)$.

Now if $Y(t)$ differs from the desired true value of $X(t + t_o)$, we make an error of

$$\varepsilon(t) = X(t + t_o) - Y(t) \tag{9.2-2}$$

This error is illustrated conceptually in Figure 9.2-1 by dashed lines. The optimum filter will be chosen so as to minimize the mean-squared value of $\varepsilon(t)$.† We shall not be concerned with obtaining a system that is realizable. Some information is given by Thomas (1969) on the more difficult problem where $H(\omega)$ must be realizable. Thus, we seek to find $H(\omega)$ that minimizes

$$
\begin{aligned}
E[\varepsilon^2(t)] &= E[\{X(t + t_o) - Y(t)\}^2] \\
&= E[X^2(t + t_o) - 2Y(t)X(t + t_o) + Y^2(t)] \\
&= R_{XX}(0) - 2R_{YX}(t_o) + R_{YY}(0) \tag{9.2-3}
\end{aligned}
$$

From the Fourier transform relationship between an autocorrelation function and a power spectrum, we have

$$R_{XX}(0) = \frac{1}{2\pi} \int_{-\infty}^{\infty} \mathscr{S}_{XX}(\omega)\, d\omega \tag{9.2-4}$$

---

† We could elect to minimize the average error, or even force such an error to be zero. This approach does not prevent large positive errors from being offset by large negative errors, however. By minimizing the squared error, we eliminate such possibilities.

where $\mathscr{S}_{XX}(\omega)$ is the power density spectrum of $X(t)$. From a similar relationship and (8.4-1) we have

$$R_{YY}(0) = \frac{1}{2\pi} \int_{-\infty}^{\infty} \mathscr{S}_{WW}(\omega)|H(\omega)|^2 \, d\omega \qquad (9.2\text{-}5)$$

where $\mathscr{S}_{WW}(\omega)$ is the power spectrum of $W(t)$. By substitution of (9.2-4) and (9.2-5) into (9.2-3), we have

$$E[\varepsilon^2(t)] = -2R_{YX}(t_o) + \frac{1}{2\pi} \int_{-\infty}^{\infty} [\mathscr{S}_{XX}(\omega) + \mathscr{S}_{WW}(\omega)|H(\omega)|^2] \, d\omega \qquad (9.2\text{-}6)$$

To reduce (9.2-6) further, we develop the cross-correlation function:

$$R_{YX}(t_o) = E[Y(t)X(t + t_o)] = E\left[X(t + t_o) \int_{-\infty}^{\infty} h(\xi)W(t - \xi) \, d\xi \right]$$

$$= \int_{-\infty}^{\infty} R_{WX}(t_o + \xi)h(\xi) \, d\xi \qquad (9.2\text{-}7)$$

where $R_{WX}(\cdot)$ is the cross-correlation function of $W(t)$ and $X(t)$. After replacing $R_{WX}(t_o + \xi)$ by its equivalent, the inverse Fourier transform of the cross-power spectrum $\mathscr{S}_{WX}(\omega)$, we obtain

$$R_{YX}(t_o) = \int_{-\infty}^{\infty} \frac{1}{2\pi} \int_{-\infty}^{\infty} \mathscr{S}_{WX}(\omega)e^{j\omega(t_o + \xi)} \, d\omega \, h(\xi) \, d\xi$$

$$= \frac{1}{2\pi} \int_{-\infty}^{\infty} \mathscr{S}_{WX}(\omega)e^{j\omega t_o}\left\{ \int_{-\infty}^{\infty} h(\xi)e^{j\omega\xi} \, d\xi \right\} d\omega$$

$$= \frac{1}{2\pi} \int_{-\infty}^{\infty} \mathscr{S}_{WX}(\omega)H(-\omega)e^{j\omega t_o} \, d\omega \qquad (9.2\text{-}8)$$

Substitution of this expression into (9.2-6) allows it to be written as

$$E[\varepsilon^2(t)] = \frac{1}{2\pi} \int_{-\infty}^{\infty} \{\mathscr{S}_{XX}(\omega) - 2\mathscr{S}_{WX}(\omega)H(-\omega)e^{j\omega t_o} + \mathscr{S}_{WW}(\omega)|H(\omega)|^2\} \, d\omega$$

$$(9.2\text{-}9)$$

The transfer function that minimizes $E[\varepsilon^2(t)]$ is now found. We may write $H(\omega)$ in the form

$$H(\omega) = A(\omega)e^{jB(\omega)} \qquad (9.2\text{-}10)$$

where $A(\omega)$ is the magnitude of $H(\omega)$, and $B(\omega)$ is its phase. Next we observe that $\mathscr{S}_{XX}(\omega)$ and $\mathscr{S}_{WW}(\omega)$ are real nonnegative functions, since they are power spectrums, while the cross-power spectrum $\mathscr{S}_{WX}(\omega)$ is complex in general and can be written as

$$\mathscr{S}_{WX}(\omega) = C(\omega)e^{jD(\omega)} \qquad (9.2\text{-}11)$$

After using (9.2-10) and (9.2-11) in (9.2-9) and invoking the fact that

$$H(-\omega) = H^*(\omega) \tag{9.2-12}$$

for filters having a real impulse response $h(t)$, we obtain

$$E[\varepsilon^2(t)] = \frac{1}{2\pi} \int_{-\infty}^{\infty} \{\mathcal{S}_{XX}(\omega) + \mathcal{S}_{WW}(\omega)A^2(\omega)\} \, d\omega$$

$$- \frac{1}{2\pi} \int_{-\infty}^{\infty} 2C(\omega)A(\omega)e^{j[\omega t_o + D(\omega) - B(\omega)]} \, d\omega \tag{9.2-13}$$

We minimize $E[\varepsilon^2(t)]$ by first selecting the phase of $H(\omega)$ to maximize the second integral in (9.2-13) and then, with the optimum phase substituted, minimize the resulting expression by choice of $A(\omega)$. Clearly, choosing

$$B(\omega) = \omega t_o + D(\omega) \tag{9.2-14}$$

will maximize the second integral and give the expression

$$E[\varepsilon^2(t)] = \frac{1}{2\pi} \int_{-\infty}^{\infty} \{\mathcal{S}_{XX}(\omega) - 2C(\omega)A(\omega) + \mathcal{S}_{WW}(\omega)A^2(\omega)\} \, d\omega$$

$$= \frac{1}{2\pi} \int_{-\infty}^{\infty} \left\{ \mathcal{S}_{XX}(\omega) - \frac{C^2(\omega)}{\mathcal{S}_{WW}(\omega)} + \mathcal{S}_{WW}(\omega)\left[A(\omega) - \frac{C(\omega)}{\mathcal{S}_{WW}(\omega)} \right]^2 \right\} \, d\omega \tag{9.2-15}$$

In writing the last form of (9.2-15), we have completed the square in $A(\omega)$. Finally, it is clear that choosing

$$A(\omega) = \frac{C(\omega)}{\mathcal{S}_{WW}(\omega)} \tag{9.2-16}$$

will minimize the right side of (9.2-15). By combining (9.2-16), (9.2-14), and (9.2-11) with (9.2-10) we have the optimum filter transfer function which we denote $H_{\text{opt}}(\omega)$:

$$H_{\text{opt}}(\omega) = \frac{\mathcal{S}_{WX}(\omega)}{\mathcal{S}_{WW}(\omega)} e^{j\omega t_o} \tag{9.2-17}$$

For the special case where input signal and noise are uncorrelated, it is easy to show that

$$\mathcal{S}_{WW}(\omega) = \mathcal{S}_{XX}(\omega) + \mathcal{S}_{NN}(\omega) \tag{9.2-18}$$

$$\mathcal{S}_{WX}(\omega) = \mathcal{S}_{XX}(\omega) \tag{9.2-19}$$

where $\mathcal{S}_{NN}(\omega)$ is the power spectrum of $N(t)$. Hence, for this special case

$$H_{\text{opt}}(\omega) = \frac{\mathcal{S}_{XX}(\omega)}{\mathcal{S}_{XX}(\omega) + \mathcal{S}_{NN}(\omega)} e^{j\omega t_o} \tag{9.2-20}$$

Example 9.2-1 We find the optimum filter for estimating $X(t + t_o)$ when there is no input noise. We let $\mathscr{S}'_{NN}(\omega) = 0$ in (9.2-20):

$$H_{\text{opt}}(\omega) = e^{j\omega t_o}$$

This expression corresponds to an ideal delay line with delay $-t_o$. If $t_o > 0$, corresponding to prediction, we require an unrealizable negative delay line. If $t_o < 0$, corresponding to a smoothing filter, the required delay is positive and realizable. Of course, $t_o = 0$ results in $H_{\text{opt}}(\omega) = 1$. In other words, the optimum filter for estimating $X(t)$ when no noise is present is just a direct connection from input to output, a result that is intuitively agreeable.

Minimum Mean-Squared Error

On substitution of (9.2-17) into (9.2-15), we readily find the mean-squared error of the optimum filter

$$E[\varepsilon^2(t)]_{\min} = \frac{1}{2\pi} \int_{-\infty}^{\infty} \frac{\mathscr{S}_{XX}(\omega)\mathscr{S}_{WW}(\omega) - |\mathscr{S}_{WX}(\omega)|^2}{\mathscr{S}_{WW}(\omega)} \, d\omega \qquad (9.2\text{-}21)$$

For the special case where input signal and noise are uncorrelated, this equation reduces to

$$E[\varepsilon^2(t)]_{\min} = \frac{1}{2\pi} \int_{-\infty}^{\infty} \frac{\mathscr{S}_{XX}(\omega)\mathscr{S}_{NN}(\omega)}{\mathscr{S}_{XX}(\omega) + \mathscr{S}_{NN}(\omega)} \, d\omega \qquad (9.2\text{-}22)$$

9.3 OPTIMIZATION BY PARAMETER SELECTION

We conclude our discussions of optimum linear systems by briefly considering a second approach that minimizes mean-squared error. The problem we undertake is identical to that of the last section up to (9.2-9), which defines the mean-squared error. Now, however, rather than seeking the filter that minimizes this error, we *specify* the *form* of the filter in terms of a number of unknown parameters and then determine the parameter values that minimize the mean-squared error. This procedure necessarily leads to a real filter so long as the form we choose corresponds to such a filter.

If we assume the special case where the input signal $X(t)$ and noise $N(t)$ are uncorrelated, (9.2-9) can be written as

$$E[\varepsilon^2(t)] = \frac{1}{2\pi} \int_{-\infty}^{\infty} \mathscr{S}_{\varepsilon\varepsilon}(\omega) \, d\omega \qquad (9.3\text{-}1)$$

where

$$\mathscr{S}_{\varepsilon\varepsilon}(\omega) = \mathscr{S}_{XX}(\omega) - 2\mathscr{S}_{XX}(\omega)H(-\omega)e^{j\omega t_o} + [\mathscr{S}_{XX}(\omega) + \mathscr{S}_{NN}(\omega)]|H(\omega)|^2 \qquad (9.3\text{-}2)$$

Since the imaginary part of $H(-\omega) \exp(j\omega t_o)$ is an odd function of ω when $h(t)$ is real (as assumed), the only contribution to the integral of (9.3-1) due to the middle term in (9.3-2) results from the real part of $H(-\omega) \exp(j\omega t_o)$. Thus, the error-contributing part of (9.3-2) can be written as†

$$\mathcal{S}_{\varepsilon\varepsilon}(\omega) = \mathcal{S}_{XX}(\omega)[1 - H(\omega)e^{-j\omega t_o} - H(-\omega)e^{j\omega t_o} + |H(\omega)|^2] + \mathcal{S}_{NN}(\omega)|H(\omega)|^2$$

$$= \mathcal{S}_{XX}(\omega)|1 - H(-\omega)e^{j\omega t_o}|^2 + \mathcal{S}_{NN}(\omega)|H(\omega)|^2 \qquad (9.3\text{-}3)$$

because $H(-\omega) = H^*(\omega)$.

We summarize the synthesis procedure. First, a filter form is chosen for a real filter. The applicable transfer function $H(\omega)$ will depend on a number of unknown parameters. $H(\omega)$ is next substituted into (9.3-3), to obtain $\mathcal{S}_{\varepsilon\varepsilon}(\omega)$, the power density spectrum of the error $\varepsilon(t)$. Finally, the error $E[\varepsilon^2(t)]$ is calculated from (9.3-1) and the parameters are then found by formally minimizing this error. Although this procedure is direct and conceptually simple to apply, the solution of the integral of (9.3-1) may be tedious. For the case where $\mathcal{S}_{XX}(\omega)$ and $\mathcal{S}_{NN}(\omega)$ are rational functions of ω and $H(\omega)$ corresponds to a real filter form, the resulting integral has been tabulated for a number of functions $\mathcal{S}_{\varepsilon\varepsilon}(\omega)$ involving orders of ω up to 14 (Thomas, 1969, pp. 249 and 636, and James, et al., 1947, p. 369).

All the preceding discussion has related to the special case where the input signal and input zero-mean noise are jointly wide-sense stationary and uncorrelated. For the more general case of correlated signal and noise, the choice of form for $H(\omega)$ must be substituted into (9.2-9) and the integral solved. The unknown filter coefficients are then determined that minimize $E[\varepsilon^2(t)]$.

PROBLEMS

9-1 A matched filter is to be found for a signal defined by

$$x(t) = \begin{cases} A(\tau + t)/\tau & -\tau < t < 0 \\ A(\tau - t)/\tau & 0 < t < \tau \\ 0 & \text{elsewhere} \end{cases} \quad \leftrightarrow \quad X(\omega) = A\tau\left[\frac{\sin(\omega\tau/2)}{\omega\tau/2}\right]^2$$

when added to noise having a power density spectrum

$$\mathcal{S}_{NN}(\omega) = \frac{W_2}{W_2^2 + \omega^2}$$

where A, τ, and W_2 are real positive constants.
(a) Find the matched filter's transfer function $H_{\text{opt}}(\omega)$.
(b) Find the filter's impulse response $h_{\text{opt}}(t)$. Plot $h_{\text{opt}}(t)$.
(c) Is there a value of t_0 for which the filter is causal? If so, find it.
(d) Sketch the block diagram of a network that has $H_{\text{opt}}(\omega)$ as its transfer function.

---

† In writing (9.3-3), we also use the fact that $2 \operatorname{Re}(z) = z + z^*$ for any complex number z.

9-2 Work Problem 9-1 (a), (b), and (c) for the signal

$$x(t) = u(t)[e^{-W_2 t} - e^{-\alpha W_2 t}]$$

if $\alpha > 1$ is a real constant.

9-3 Work Problem 9-1 (a), (b), and (c) for the signal

$$x(t) = u(-t)[e^{W_2 t} - e^{\alpha W_2 t}]$$

if $\alpha > 1$ is a real constant.

★**9-4** By proper inverse Fourier transformation of (9.1-13), show that the impulse response $h_{opt}(t)$ of the matched filter for signals in colored noise satisfies

$$\int_{-\infty}^{\infty} h_{opt}(\xi) R_{NN}(t - \xi) \, d\xi = x^*(t_o - t)$$

9-5 A signal $x(t)$ and colored noise $N(t)$ are applied to the network of Figure P9-5. We select $|H_1(\omega)|^2 = 1/\mathscr{S}_{NN}(\omega)$ so that the noise $N_1(t)$ is white. We also make $H_2(\omega)$ a matched filter for the signal $x_1(t)$ in the white noise $N_1(t)$. Show that the cascade is a matched filter for $x(t)$ in the noise $N(t)$.

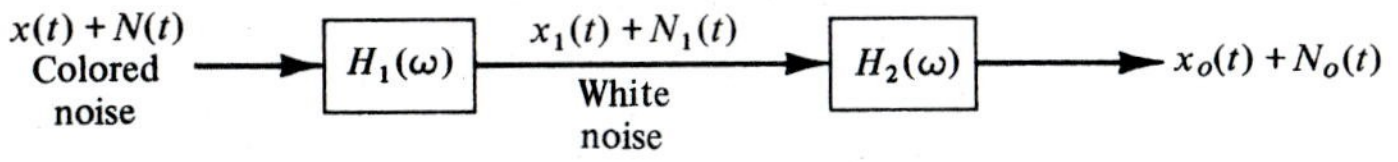

FIGURE P9-5

9-6 For the matched filter of Example 9.1-1, find and sketch the output signal. [*Hint:* Fourier-transform $x(t)$ and use a transform pair from Appendix E to obtain $x_o(t)$.]

9-7 Assume the power density of the white noise at the input to the matched filter of Example 9.1-1 is $\mathscr{N}_0/2$ with $\mathscr{N}_0 > 0$ a real constant. Find the output signal-to-noise ratio of the filter at time t_o.

9-8 Show that the maximum output signal-to noise ratio obtainable from a filter matched to a signal $x(t)$ in white noise with power density $\mathscr{N}_0/2$ is

$$\left(\frac{\hat{S}_o}{N_o}\right)_{max} = \frac{2}{\mathscr{N}_0} \int_{-\infty}^{\infty} |x(t)|^2 \, dt = \frac{2E}{\mathscr{N}_0}$$

where E is the energy in $x(t)$ and $\mathscr{N}_0 > 0$ is a real constant.

9-9 Let τ be a positive real constant. A pulse

$$x(t) = \begin{cases} A \cos(\pi t/\tau) & |t| < \tau/2 \\ 0 & |t| > \tau/2 \end{cases}$$

is added to white noise with a power density of $\mathscr{N}_0/2$. Find $(\hat{S}_o/N_o)_{max}$ for a filter matched to $x(t)$ by using the result of Problem 9-8.

9-10 Find the matched filter's transfer function applicable to Problem 9-9.

9-11 Show that the output signal $x_o(t)$ from a filter matched to a signal $x(t)$ in white noise is

$$x_o(t) = K \int_{-\infty}^{\infty} x^*(\xi) x(\xi + t - t_o) \, d\xi$$

That is, $x_o(t)$ is proportional to the *correlation integral* of $x(t)$.

9-12 Show that the output signal $x_o(t)$ from a filter matched to a signal in white noise reaches its maximum magnitude at $t = t_o$ if the filter impulse response is given by (9.1-15). (*Hint:* Use the result of Problem 9-11.)

9-13 Fourier-transform the signal of Figure 9.1-1a, and use (9.1-14) to verify the optimum system transfer function given in Example 9.1-1.

9-14 The signal

$$x(t) = u(t)e^{-Wt}$$

where $W > 0$ is a real constant, is applied to a filter along with white noise with power density $\mathcal{N}_0/2$, $\mathcal{N}_0 > 0$ being a real constant.
(a) Find the transfer function of the filter matched to $x(t)$ at time t_o.
(b) Find and sketch the filter's impulse response.
(c) Is there any value of t_o that will make the filter causal?
(d) Find the output maximum signal-to-noise ratio.

9-15 Work Problem 9-14 for the signal

$$x(t) = u(-t)e^{Wt}$$

9-16 Work Problem 9-14 for the signal

$$x(t) = u(t)te^{-Wt}$$

9-17 Work Problem 9-14 for the signal

$$x(t) = -u(-t)te^{Wt}$$

9-18 If a real signal $x(t)$ exists only in the interval $0 < t < T$, show that the *correlation receiver* of Figure P9-18 is a matched filter at time $t = T$; that is, show that the ratio of peak signal power to average noise power, both at time T, is the same as the ordinary matched filter. Assume white input noise.

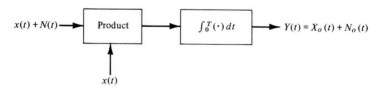

FIGURE P9-18

9-19 Find the matched filter for the signal

$$x(t) = Ae^{-\alpha t^2}$$

in white noise with power density $\mathcal{N}_0/2$ where $\mathcal{N}_0 > 0$, $\alpha > 0$, and A are real constants.

9-20 A random signal $X(t)$ and uncorrelated white noise $N(t)$ have autocorrelation functions

$$R_{XX}(\tau) = \frac{WP}{2} e^{-W|\tau|}$$

$$R_{NN}(\tau) = (\mathcal{N}_0/2)\delta(\tau)$$

where $W > 0$, $P > 0$, and $\mathcal{N}_0 > 0$ are real constants.
(a) Find the transfer function of the optimum Wiener filter.
(b) Find and sketch the impulse response of the filter when $t_o < 0$, $t_o > 0$, and $t_o = 0$.

9-21 Find the minimum mean-squared error of the filter in Problem 9-20.

9-22 Work Problem 9-20 for colored noise defined by

$$R_{NN}(\tau) = W_N e^{-W_N|\tau|}$$

where $W_N > 0$ is a real constant.

9-23 Work Problem 9-21 for the noise defined in Problem 9-22.

9-24 A random signal $X(t)$ and additive uncorrelated noise $N(t)$ have respective power spectrums

$$\mathcal{S}_{XX}(\omega) = \frac{9}{9 + \omega^4} \qquad \text{and} \qquad \mathcal{S}_{NN}(\omega) = \frac{3}{6 + \omega^4}$$

(a) Find the transfer function of the Wiener filter for the given signal and noise.
(b) Find the minimum value of the error in predicting $X(t + t_o)$.

9-25 Work Problem 9-24 for signal and uncorrelated white noise defined by

$$\mathcal{S}_{XX}(\omega) = \frac{A}{W^2 + \omega^4}$$

$$\mathcal{S}_{NN}(\omega) = \mathcal{N}_0/2$$

where $A > 0$, $W > 0$, and $\mathcal{N}_0 > 0$ are real constants.

9-26 A deterministic signal $x(t) = A \cos(\omega_0 t)$ and white noise with power density $\mathcal{N}_0/2$ are applied to a one-section lowpass filter with transfer function $H(\omega) = W/(W + j\omega)$. Here $W > 0$, $\mathcal{N}_0 > 0$, ω_0, and A are all real constants. What value of W will cause the ratio of output *average* signal power to average noise power to be maximum?

9-27 Work Problem 9-26 if the network consists of two identical one-section filters in cascade.

9-28 Work Problem 9-26 if $x(t) = A \cos(\omega_0 t + \Theta)$, where Θ is a random variable uniformly distributed on the interval $(0, 2\pi)$.

9-29 A random signal $X(t)$ having the autocorrelation function

$$R_{XX}(\tau) = W_X e^{-W_X|\tau|}$$

and uncorrelated noise with power density $\mathcal{N}_0/2$ are applied to a lowpass filter with transfer function

$$H(\omega) = \frac{W}{W + j\omega}$$

Here $W > 0$ and $W_X > 0$ are real constants.

(a) What value of W will minimize the mean-squared error if the output is to be an estimate of $X(t)$?

(b) Calculate the minimum mean-squared error.

★**9-30** Work Problem 9-29 by finding the real constants $G > 0$ and $W > 0$ for the filter defined by

$$H(\omega) = \frac{GW}{W + j\omega}$$

ADDITIONAL PROBLEMS, SECOND EDITION

9-31 A signal $x(t) = u(t)5t^2 \exp(-2t)$ is added to white noise for which $\mathcal{N}_0/2 = 10^{-2}$ W/Hz. The sum is applied to a matched filter.

(a) What is the filter's transfer function?

(b) What is $(\hat{S}_o/N_o)$?

(c) Sketch the impulse response of the filter.

(d) Is the filter realizable?

9-32 A signal

$$x(t) = u(t)t^2 \exp(-Wt)$$

is added to noise with power spectrum

$$\mathcal{S}_{NN}(\omega) = P/(W_N^2 + \omega^2)$$

where W, P, and W_N are positive constants. The sum is applied to a matched filter.

(a) Find the filter's transfer function.

(b) Find the filter's impulse response.

(c) What is the maximum signal-to-noise ratio at the output?

9-33 A pulse of amplitude $A > 0$ and duration $\tau > 0$ is $x(t) = A \operatorname{rect}(t/\tau)$. The pulse is added to white noise of power density $\mathcal{N}_0/2$ when it arrives at a receiver. For some practical reasons the receiver (filter) is not a matched filter but is a simple lowpass filter with transfer function

$$H(\omega) = W/(W + j\omega)$$

$W > 0$ a constant.

(a) Find the ratio of instantaneous output signal power $x_o^2(t)$ at any time t to average noise power $E[N_o^2(t)]$ at the filter's output. At what time, denoted by t_o, is the ratio maximum?

(b) At time t_o what bandwidth W will maximize signal-to-noise ratio?

(c) Plot the loss in output signal-to-noise ratio that results, compared to a matched filter, for various values of $0 < W \leq 5/\tau$. What is the minimum loss?

★9-34 Reconsider the system of Problem 9-33 except assume

$$H(\omega) = W^2/(W + j\omega)^2$$

(a) Find the time t_o at which output signal-to-noise ratio is largest.

(b) For the t_o found in (a) determine the output signal-to-noise ratio. Plot this result versus $W\tau$ for $0 < W\tau \leq 6$ and determine what value of W gives the best performance.

(c) What minimum loss in signal-to-noise ratio occurs compared to a matched filter?

9-35 A pulse

$$x(t) = A \; \text{rect} \; (t/2\tau)[1 - (t/\tau)^2]$$

where A and $\tau > 0$ are constants, is added to white noise.

(a) Find the output signal $x_o(t)$ of a filter matched to the pulse.

(b) Sketch $x(t)$ and $x_o(t)$.

(c) What is the matched filter's output signal-to-noise ratio?

(d) What is the transfer function if K in (9.1-16) is chosen so that $|H_{opt}(0)| = 1$? Is there a value of t_o that makes the filter causal?

★9-36 A deterministic waveform $\psi(t)$ is defined by

$$\psi(t) = a(t)e^{j\phi(t) + j\omega_o t} = v(t)e^{j\omega_o t}$$

where $a(t)$ and $\phi(t)$ are "slowly" varying amplitude and phase "modulation" functions and $\omega_0 > 0$ is a large constant. The white-noise matched filter for $\psi(t)$ is defined by

$$h_{opt}(t) = \psi^*(t_o - t)$$

if $K = 1$ in (9.1-15). Now let $\psi(t)$ be offset in frequency by an amount ω_d before being applied to the "matched filter" so that

$$\psi_R(t) = \psi(t) \exp{(-j\omega_d t)}$$

is applied with noise to the filter.

(a) Show that the filter's response to $\psi_R(t)$ is

$$\chi(t_o - t, \omega_d) = \int_{-\infty}^{\infty} \psi(\xi)\psi^*(t_o - t + \xi)e^{-j\omega_d \xi} \, d\xi$$

The function $|\chi(\alpha, \omega_d)|^2$ is called the *ambiguity function* of the waveform $\psi(t)$.

(b) Show that the volume under the ambiguity function does not depend on the form of $\psi(t)$ but only on $|\chi(0, 0)|^2$.

(c) Show that

$$\chi(t_o - t, \omega_d) = e^{j\omega_0(t - t_o)} \int_{-\infty}^{\infty} v(\xi)v^*(t_o - t + \xi)e^{-j\omega_d \xi} \, d\xi$$

*9-37 Reconsider the ambiguity function of Problem 9-36.
  (a) Show that $|\chi(\tau, \omega_d)|^2 \le |\chi(0, 0)|^2$.
  (b) Show that another form for $\chi(\tau, \omega_d)$ is

$$\chi(\tau, \omega_d) = \frac{1}{2\pi} \int_{-\infty}^{\infty} \Psi^*(\omega)\Psi(\omega + \omega_d)e^{-j\omega\tau} \, d\omega$$

  where $\Psi(\omega)$ is the Fourier transform of $\psi(t)$.
  (c) Show that

$$\chi(\tau, 0) = \int_{-\infty}^{\infty} \psi(\xi)\psi^*(\xi + \tau) \, d\xi$$

$$= \frac{1}{2\pi} \int_{-\infty}^{\infty} |\Psi(\omega)|^2 e^{-j\omega\tau} \, d\omega$$

$$\chi(0, \omega_d) = \int_{-\infty}^{\infty} |\psi(\xi)|^2 e^{-j\omega_d\xi} \, d\xi$$

$$= \frac{1}{2\pi} \int_{-\infty}^{\infty} \Psi^*(\omega)\Psi(\omega + \omega_d) \, d\omega$$

  (d) Show that the symmetry of $\chi(\tau, \omega_d)$ is given by

$$\chi(\tau, \omega_d) = e^{j\omega_d\tau}\chi^*(-\tau, -\omega_d)$$

9-38 The deterministic signal

$$x(t) = \text{rect}\,(t/T) \exp\,(j\omega_0 t + j\mu t^2/2)$$

is a pulse having a linearly varying frequency with time during the pulse's duration T. The nominal frequency is ω_0 (rad/s). The matched filter for white noise has the impulse response of (9.1-15) which, for $t_o = 0$, is

$$h_{opt}(t) = K \, \text{rect}\,(t/T) \exp\,(j\omega_0 t - j\mu t^2/2)$$

  (a) If instantaneous frequency is to increase by a total amount $\Delta\omega$ (rad/s) during the pulse's duration T, how is the constant μ related to $\Delta\omega$ and T?
  (b) Find the value of K such that $|H_{opt}(\omega_0)| = 1$ when μ is large. [*Hint:* Note that

$$C(x) = \int_0^x \cos\,(\pi\xi^2/2) \, d\xi$$

  and

$$S(x) = \int_0^x \sin\,(\pi\xi^2/2) \, d\xi$$

  called *Fresnel integrals*, approach $^1/_2$ as $x \to \infty$.]
  (c) For the K found in (b), determine the output $x_o(t)$ of the filter. Sketch the envelopes of the signals $x(t)$ and $x_o(t)$ for $\Delta\omega T = 80\pi$ using the same

time-voltage axes. What observations can you make about what has happened to $x(t)$ as it passes through the filter?

★**9-39** (a) Find the transfer function $H_{opt}(\omega)$ of the matched filter of Problem 9-38. (*Hint:* Put the expression in terms of Fresnel integrals having arguments

$$x_1 = \sqrt{\Delta\omega T/2\pi}\{1 - [2(\omega - \omega_0)/\Delta\omega]\}/\sqrt{2}$$

and

$$x_2 = \sqrt{\Delta\omega T/2\pi}\{1 + [2(\omega - \omega_0)/\Delta\omega]\}/\sqrt{2}$$

where $\mu = \Delta\omega/T$.)

(b) Sketch the approximate form of $|H_{opt}(\omega)|$ that results when $\Delta\omega T$ is large.

9-40 A random signal $X(t)$ and uncorrelated white noise have respective power spectrums.

$$\mathscr{S}_{XX}(\omega) = 2\sqrt{2}\,P_{XX}W_X\omega^2/(W_X^4 + \omega^4)$$

and

$$\mathscr{S}_{NN}(\omega) = \mathscr{N}_0/2$$

Here P_{XX} is the average power in $X(t)$, while W_X and $\mathscr{N}_0$ are positive constants.

(a) Find the transfer function of the Wiener filter for this signal and noise.

(b) What is the minimum mean-squared filter error?

(c) Evaluate the result of (b) for $P_{XX} = 2$ W, $W_X = 15$ rad/s, and $\mathscr{N}_0/2 = 0.1$ W/Hz. [*Hint:* Use the known integral (Thomas, 1969, p. 249)

$$I_2 = \frac{1}{2\pi}\int_{-\infty}^{\infty} \frac{(b_1 - b_0\omega^2)\,d\omega}{a_2^2 + (a_1^2 - 2a_0a_2)\omega^2 + a_0^2\omega^4} = \frac{a_0b_1 - a_2b_0}{2a_0a_1a_2}$$

where b_0, b_1, a_0, a_1, and a_2 are constants and $a_0\lambda^2 + a_1\lambda + a_2$ has no roots in the lower half-plane when $\lambda = \omega + j\sigma$.]

9-41 Work Problem 9-40 for the signal with the power spectrum

$$\mathscr{S}_{XX}(\omega) = A/(W_X^2 + \omega^2)^2$$

Put results in terms of the average power P_{XX} in $X(t)$.

9-42 The respective power spectrums of a random signal $X(t)$ and uncorrelated noise $N(t)$ are

$$\mathscr{S}_{XX}(\omega) = (1/20)/(10^2 + \omega^2)$$

and

$$\mathscr{S}_{NN}(\omega) = \omega^2/(16^2 + \omega^2)^2$$

(a) What is the transfer function of the Wiener filter?

(b) What is the minimum mean-squared prediction error? (*Hint:* Use results from problem 9-40.)

★**9-43** Generalize the random signal of Problem 9-42 by assuming its power spectrum is

$$\mathcal{S}_{XX}(\omega) = (W_X^2/2000)/(W_X^2 + \omega^2)$$

where W_X is the signal's 3-dB bandwidth. Find the minimum mean-squared prediction error and plot the result for $W_X > 9.5$. What does an increase in W_X mean in a physical sense?

9-44 A random signal $X(t)$ plus uncorrelated noise $N(t)$, having respective power spectrums

$$\mathcal{S}_{XX}(\omega) = 2P_{XX}W_X/(W_X^2 + \omega^2)$$

and

$$\mathcal{S}_{NN}(\omega) = 4P_{NN}W_N^3/(W_N^2 + \omega^2)^2$$

is applied to a Wiener filter. Here P_{XX} and P_{NN} are the average signal and noise powers, respectively, while W_X and W_N are positive constants.

(a) Use (9.2-22) and find the filter's minimum mean-squared prediction error.
(b) Show that as $P_{XX} \to \infty$, $E[\varepsilon^2(t)]_{\min} \to P_{NN}$, and that $E[\varepsilon^2(t)]_{\min} \to P_{XX}$ if $P_{NN} \to \infty$.
(c) From a graphical plot of $E[\varepsilon^2(t)]_{\min}/P_{NN}$ versus W_X/W_N, determine if there is a preferred bandwidth ratio when $P_{NN}/P_{XX} = 8$. Is there a ratio that should be avoided? Discuss. (*Hint:* Use the integral given in Problem 9-40.)

ADDITIONAL PROBLEMS, THIRD EDITION

9-45 A signal

$$x(t) = \begin{cases} \dfrac{1}{2}e^{-t/6} & 0 < t < 3/2 \\ 0 & \text{elsewhere in } t \end{cases}$$

is added to white noise of power density $\mathcal{N}_0/2$ and the sum is applied to the input of a matched filter. The output peak signal-to-noise power ratio is 14. What is $\mathcal{N}_0/2$? (*Hint:* Use the results of Problem 9-8.)

9-46 White noise, for which $\mathcal{N}_0/2 = 10^{-8}/(24\pi)$, and a signal

$$x(t) = \begin{cases} Wte^{-Wt} & 0 < t < 2/W \\ 0 & \text{elsewhere in } t \end{cases}$$

are applied to a matched filter. What ratio of output peak signal power to average noise power can be achieved if $W = 5(10^6)$ rad/s? (*Hint:* Use results of Problem 9-8.)

9-47 In trying to build the matched filter required in Problem 9-46 an engineer encounters difficulties and builds, instead, a filter matched to the signal

$$x_a(t) = u(t)Wte^{-Wt}$$

which is the unlimited-time version of the signal $x(t)$. What ratio of output peak signal power to average noise power can be achieved for the same values of W and $\mathcal{N}_0/2$ as assumed in Problem 9-46?

★**9-48** Assume the signal and noise of Problem 9-46 are applied to the filter used by the engineer in Problem 9-47. Since the filter is not matched, optimum performance is not achieved.

(a) Use convolution to find the output signal $x_o(t)$ of the filter at any time t.

(b) Find the value of t_o for which the output signal's amplitude is maximum at $t = 0$.

(c) Find the maximum peak power in the output signal.

(d) Find the average noise power and the maximum output signal-to-noise power ratio.

9-49 The sum of a signal

$$x(t) = \begin{cases} 0 & t < -3 \\ 6 + 2t & -3 < t < 5 \\ 0 & 5 < t \end{cases}$$

and white noise, for which $\mathcal{N}_0/2 = 0.1$ W/Hz, is applied to a matched filter.

(a) What is the smallest value of t_o required for the filter to be causal?

(b) For the value of t_0 found in (a), sketch the impulse response of the matched filter.

(c) Find the maximum output signal-to-noise ratio it provides. (*Hint:* Use the results of Problem 9-8.)

9-50 Work Problem 9-49 except assume the signal shown in Figure P9-50.

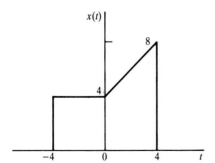

FIGURE P9-50

9-51 Find the transfer function of the white-noise matched filter corresponding to the signal

$$x(t) = (A + Bt)\left[u\left(t + \frac{A}{B}\right) - u\left(t - \frac{A}{B}\right)\right]$$

where $A > 0$ and $B > 0$ are constants.

9-52 Work Problem 9-40 except assume the signal $X(t)$ has a power spectrum

$$\mathcal{S}_{XX}(\omega) = \frac{P_{XX}4W_X\omega^2}{(W_X^2 + \omega^2)^2}$$

9-53 Use (9.2-20) and give arguments to justify that the Wiener filter emphasizes those frequencies where the ratio of signal power to noise power is largest.

9-54 A random signal $X(t)$ has a power density spectrum

$$\mathcal{S}_{XX}(\omega) = \frac{\mathcal{N}_X}{2} \operatorname{rect}\left(\frac{\omega}{W_X}\right)$$

where $\mathcal{N}_X > 0$ and $W_X > 0$ are constants.

(a) Find the average power P_{XX} in $X(t)$.

(b) Find the optimum (Wiener) filter's transfer function when input noise is independent of $X(t)$ and white with power density $\mathcal{N}_0/2$.

(c) Find the ratio of the minimum mean-squared error to the power P_{XX}. Evaluate the result for $\mathcal{N}_X/\mathcal{N}_0 = 16$.

9-55 Work Problem 9-33, except assume the input pulse is

$$x(t) = \frac{A}{\tau} t[u(t) - u(t - \tau)]$$

CHAPTER
10

SOME
PRACTICAL
APPLICATIONS
OF THE
THEORY

10.0   INTRODUCTION

The main purpose of this book has been to introduce the reader to the basic principles necessary to model random signals and noise. The principles were broad enough to include the descriptions of waveforms modified by passage through linear networks. In this chapter we shall apply the basic principles to a few practical problems that involve random signals, noise, and networks. Obviously, the list of practical applications is almost limitless and it is necessary to select only a finite few. Although the applications discussed here may not necessarily serve the main interests of all readers, they do represent important applications and do serve to illustrate the use of the book's theory.

In the following sections we shall describe two practical communication systems, two control systems (one with application to one of the communication systems), an application involving a computer-type signal, and two applications that relate to radar. In every case we are primarily interested in how these applications are affected by the presence of random noise. We begin by considering the common broadcast AM (amplitude modulation) communication system.

10.1 NOISE IN AN AMPLITUDE MODULATION COMMUNICATION SYSTEM

The communication system most familiar to the general public is probably the AM (amplitude modulation) system. In this system the amplitude of a high-frequency "carrier" is made to vary (be modulated) as a linear function of the message waveform, usually derived from music, speech, or other audio source. The carrier frequency assigned to a broadcast station in the United States is one of the values from 540 to 1600 kHz in 10-kHz steps. Each station must contain its radiated power to a 10-kHz band centered on its assigned frequency.

In this section we shall give a very brief introduction to the AM broadcast system and illustrate how the noise principles of the preceding chapters can be used to analyze the system's performance.

AM System and Waveforms

Figure 10.1-1 illustrates the basic *functions* that must be present in an AM system. In this figure we include only those functions necessary to the study of noise performance. A practical system would include many other devices such as amplifiers, mixers, oscillators, and antennas that do not directly affect our performance calculations.

The transmitted AM signal has the form

$$s_{AM}(t) = [A_0 + x(t)] \cos [\omega_0 t + \theta_0] \qquad (10.1\text{-}1)$$

where $A_0 > 0$, ω_0, and θ_0 are constants, while $x(t)$ represents a message that we model as a sample function of a random process $X(t)$. Note that the amplitude $[A_0 + x(t)]$ of the carrier $\cos(\omega_0 t + \theta_0)$ is a linear function of $x(t)$. Now, in general, one has no control over θ_0 because the turn-on time of a transmitter is random and the channel itself may introduce a phase angle that is random (which we presume is absorbed in the value of θ_0). Thus, we may properly model θ_0 as a value of a random variable Θ_0 independent of $X(t)$ and uniformly distributed on $(0, 2\pi)$. These considerations allow $s_{AM}(t)$ to be modeled as a sample function of a transmitted random process $S_{AM}(t)$ given by

$$S_{AM}(t) = [A_0 + X(t)] \cos(\omega_0 t + \Theta_0) \qquad (10.1\text{-}2)$$

The transmitted signal arrives at the receiver after passing through a channel with gain G_{ch}. The channel is assumed to add no signal distortion but does add zero-mean white gaussian noise of power density $\mathcal{N}_0/2$. A practical channel typically adds delay but this effect does not modify the noise performance. A receiver bandpass filter passes the received signal $s_R(t) = G_{ch}s_{AM}(t)$ with negligible distortion but has no wider bandwidth than necessary so as to not pass excessive

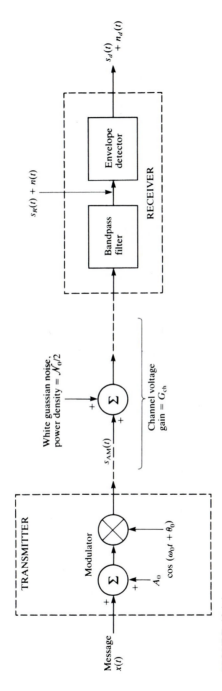

FIGURE 10.1-1
Functional block diagram of a broadcast AM system.

noise.† The noise $n(t)$ at the filter's output is a bandpass noise so the theory of Section 8.6 applies.

We model waveforms $s_R(t)$ and $n(t)$ as sample functions of processes $S_R(t)$ and $N(t)$, respectively. Thus, we may write

$$S_R(t) = G_{ch}S_{AM}(t)$$

$$= G_{ch}[A_0 + X(t)]\cos(\omega_0 t + \Theta_0) \tag{10.1-3}$$

$$N(t) = N_c(t)\cos(\omega_0 t + \Theta_0) - N_s(t)\sin(\omega_0 t + \Theta_0) \tag{10.1-4}$$

where $N_c(t)$ and $N_s(t)$ are lowpass noises with average powers $\overline{N_c^2(t)} = \overline{N_s^2(t)} = \overline{N^2(t)}$ from Section 8.6.

Noise Performance

A good measure of noise performance is the ratio of the average power in the output signal $s_d(t)$ of the system to the average power in the output noise $n_d(t)$. In the AM receiver an envelope detector is used to recover the transmitted message.

The total waveform applied to the envelope detector becomes

$$S_R(t) + N(t) = \{G_{ch}[A_0 + X(t)] + N_c(t)\}\cos(\omega_0 t + \Theta_0) - N_s(t)\sin(\omega_0 + \Theta_0)$$

$$= A(t)\cos[\omega_0 t + \Theta_0 + \psi(t)] \tag{10.1-5}$$

where‡

$$\psi(t) = \tan^{-1}\left\{\frac{N_s(t)}{G_{ch}[A_0 + X(t)] + N_c(t)}\right\} \tag{10.1-6}$$

$$A(t) = \langle\{G_{ch}[A_0 + X(t)] + N_c(t)\}^2 + N_s^2(t)\rangle^{1/2}$$

$$= G_{ch}[A_0 + X(t)]\left\langle 1 + \frac{2N_c(t)}{G_{ch}[A_0 + X(t)]} + \frac{N_c^2(t) + N_s^2(t)}{G_{ch}^2[A_0 + X(t)]^2}\right\rangle^{1/2} \tag{10.1-7}$$

Now only (10.1-7) is of interest because $A(t)$ is the envelope of $S_R(t) + N(t)$. The detector output is this envelope.

Since $N_c^2(t) + N_s^2(t)$ is the instantaneous envelope of the square of $N(t)$ (related to received noise power), while $G_{ch}^2[A_0 + X(t)]^2$ is the instantaneous envelope of the detector's input signal (related to received signal power), we make the assumption that input (received) signal-to-noise power ratio is large so that $[N_c^2(t) + N_s^2(t)]/G_{ch}^2[A_0 + X(t)]^2$ is small *most of the time*. The assumption allows

$$A(t) \approx G_{ch}[A_0 + X(t)] + N_c(t) \tag{10.1-8}$$

from (10.1-7). Only when this condition is true do we obtain quality performance anyway, so other situations are not usually of interest.

---

† The required bandwidth W_{rec} must be at least twice the spectral extent W_X of $X(t)$.

‡ Typically, *overmodulation* where $|X(t)|_{max}$, the maximum magnitude of $X(t)$, exceeds A_0 is undesirable in AM, so $[A_0 + X(t)] > 0$ is assumed in (10.1-7).

If we model $s_d(t)$ and $n_d(t)$ in Figure 10.1-1 as sample functions of processes $S_d(t)$ and $N_d(t)$, respectively, then (10.1-8) clearly gives

$$S_d(t) = G_{ch}[A_0 + X(t)] \tag{10.1-9}$$

$$N_d(t) = N_c(t) \tag{10.1-10}$$

The *useful* output signal average power, denoted by S_o, is that due to $X(t)$ in (10.1-9). If output average noise power is denoted by N_o then

$$S_o = G_{ch}^2 \overline{X^2(t)} \tag{10.1-11}$$

$$N_o = \overline{N_c^2(t)} = \overline{N^2(t)} \tag{10.1-12}$$

and performance is measured by

$$\left(\frac{S_o}{N_o}\right)_{AM} = \frac{G_{ch}^2 \overline{X^2(t)}}{\overline{N^2(t)}} \tag{10.1-13}$$

Next, we model the bandpass filter in Figure 10.1-1 as an ideal filter with bandwidth W_{rec}(rad/s). Noise power readily follows

$$\overline{N^2(t)} = \frac{1}{2\pi} 2 \int_{\omega_0 - (W_{rec}/2)}^{\omega_0 + (W_{rec}/2)} (\mathcal{N}_0/2)\, d\omega = \frac{\mathcal{N}_0 W_{rec}}{2\pi} \tag{10.1-14}$$

From (10.1-13) we have

$$\left(\frac{S_o}{N_o}\right)_{AM} = \frac{2\pi G_{ch}^2 \overline{X^2(t)}}{\mathcal{N}_0 W_{rec}} \tag{10.1-15}$$

Equation (10.1-15) is the principal result of this section. It describes the performance of the AM system. It is helpful to demonstrate the use of (10.1-15) by means of an example.

Example 10.1-1 Assume an AM system uses an unmodulated carrier of peak amplitude $A_0 = 10\sqrt{95}$ V and a message of power $\overline{X^2(t)} = 500$ W. Its channel has a gain $G_{ch} = \sqrt{32}/100$ with a noise density $\mathcal{N}_0/2 = (10^{-8})$ W/Hz. The receiver uses a filter with bandwidth $W_{rec} = 2\pi(10^4)$ rad/s. We compute various signal powers and system performance.

From Problem 10-1 the average power in the transmitted carrier is $A_0^2/2 = 4750$ W; the transmitted power due to message modulation is $R_{XX}(0)/2 = \overline{X^2(t)}/2 = 250$ W. Total average transmitted power is, therefore, 5000 W.

From (10.1-15) we compute

$$\left(\frac{S_o}{N_o}\right)_{AM} = \frac{2\pi(32)10^{-4}(500)}{2(10^{-8})2\pi(10^4)} = 8000 \qquad \text{(or 39.03 dB)}$$

This signal-to-noise ratio represents fairly good performance.

At the input to the envelope detector the received average signal power is 5000 W decreased by the loss incurred in passing over the channel: $5000(\sqrt{32}/100)^2 = 16$ W. From (10.1-14) and (10.1-12) the input average noise power is $10^{-8}2\pi(10^4)/\pi = 2(10^{-4})$ W. Input signal-to-noise ratio becomes $16/2(10^{-4}) = 80,000$ (or 49.03 dB). This value is well above the minimum for performance as required for (10.1-15) to be valid; in fact, if the performance of an AM system is satisfactory then (10.1-15) will always be valid (the reader should justify this fact by examining the *efficiency* of an AM system—see Problems 10-4 and 10-2.)

10.2 NOISE IN A FREQUENCY MODULATION COMMUNICATION SYSTEM

Another communication system with which the reader is familiar is the broadcast FM (frequency modulation) system. Here the instantaneous frequency of a sinusoidal "carrier" waveform is made to vary as a linear function of the message waveform. If $X(t)$ is a process representing the message, the FM transmitted waveform can be represented by the process

$$S_{FM}(t) = A \cos\left[\omega_0 t + \Theta_0 + k_{FM} \int X(t)\, dt\right] \qquad (10.2\text{-}1)$$

where A, ω_0, and $k_{FM} > 0$ are constants† and Θ_0 is a random variable independent of $X(t)$ and uniformly distributed on $(0, 2\pi)$. In a practical station $\omega_0/2\pi$ is the station's assigned frequency and is one of 100 possible frequencies from 88.1 to 107.9 MHz. Each station transmits power in a 200-kHz "channel" centered on its assigned frequency.

The constant k_{FM} in (10.2-1) is the transmitter's modulation constant. Its unit is rad/second per volt when $X(t)$ is a voltage. Transmitted signal bandwidth is difficult to compute in FM because FM is a nonlinear modulation. If k_{FM} is large enough, this bandwidth can readily be much larger than the bandwidth of the message process $X(t)$. If $X(t)$ is presumed to be bounded at $|X(t)|_{max}$ and have a crest-factor defined by (Problem 10-3)

$$K_{cr}^2 = \frac{|X(t)|_{max}^2}{E[X^2(t)]} = \frac{|X(t)|_{max}^2}{\overline{X^2(t)}} \qquad (10.2\text{-}2)$$

the bandwidth of $S_{FM}(t)$ for the broadband case is approximated by (Peebles, 1976)

$$W_{FM} \approx 2\Delta\omega = 2k_{FM}|X(t)|_{max}$$

$$= 2k_{FM}K_{cr}\sqrt{\overline{X^2(t)}} \qquad (10.2\text{-}3)$$

---

† If k_{FM} is negative its sign can be absorbed into the definition of $X(t)$.

Here

$$\Delta\omega = k_{FM}|X(t)|_{\max} \tag{10.2-4}$$

is the peak frequency deviation that instantaneous frequency can make from ω_0 (on either side).

Although difficult to prove, the average transmitted waveform power is

$$P_{FM} = E[S_{FM}^2(t)] = \frac{A^2}{2} \tag{10.2-5}$$

which is independent of the modulation.

FM System and Waveforms

Figure 10.2-1 illustrates the basic functions present in a typical FM system. The transmitted waveform passes over the channel modeled as a power gain G_{ch}^2 without distortion or delay (as also assumed in Section 10.1 above). The receiver's bandpass filter (BPF) is wide enough to pass $G_{ch}S_{FM}(t)$ with little distortion but not so wide as to pass excess noise. Its bandwidth is, therefore, $W_{FM} = 2\Delta\omega$.

The purpose of the limiter is to remove amplitude fluctuations in the received waveform. The limiter is necessary so that the receiver responds only to frequency variations (that contain the message) and not to amplitude variations that are mainly due to noise. The discriminator is the actual demodulation device; it produces a voltage proportional (constant of proportionality K_D) to instantaneous deviations of the frequency of its input waveform from a nominal value ω_0. Ideally, with no noise, the discriminator's output signal is $K_D k_{FM} X(t)$. The lowpass filter must pass this waveform with low distortion so that its output is proportional to $X(t)$

$$S_d(t) = K_D k_{FM} X(t) \tag{10.2-6}$$

It should have a bandwidth no wider than the spectral extent of $X(t)$, denoted by W_X, so as to not allow excessive output noise.

If the receiver's "input" is defined as the input to the limiter, the input signal's average power S_i is

$$S_i = G_{ch}^2 \frac{A^2}{2} \tag{10.2-7}$$

while the output signal power is

$$S_o = E[S_d^2(t)] = K_D^2 k_{FM}^2 \overline{X^2(t)} \tag{10.2-8}$$

By modeling the BPF in Figure 10.2-1 as an ideal filter the input noise power is readily found to be

$$N_i = \frac{1}{2\pi} 2 \int_{\omega_0 - \Delta\omega}^{\omega_0 + \Delta\omega} \frac{\mathcal{N}_0}{2} d\omega = \frac{\mathcal{N}_0 \Delta\omega}{\pi} \tag{10.2-9}$$

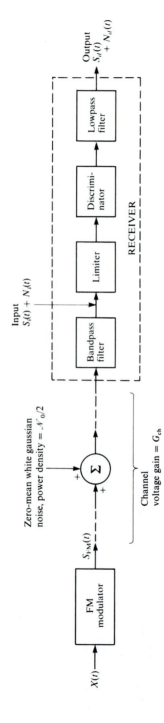

FIGURE 10.2-1
Functional block diagram of an FM communication system.

Input signal-to-noise power ratio is

$$\left(\frac{S_i}{N_i}\right)_{FM} = \frac{\pi G_{ch}^2 A^2}{2\mathcal{N}_0 \Delta\omega} \tag{10.2-10}$$

from (10.2-7) and (10.2-9).

Computation of output noise power is less straightforward than the preceding computations. However, its development forms the most interesting problem in computing system performance.

FM System Performance

Care must be exercised in finding output noise power because FM is a nonlinear operation. For relatively large $(S_i/N_i)_{FM}$ and wideband operation (developed above), signal and noise powers may be independently found. Signal power is found assuming noise zero (above). Noise power is found assuming the message is zero but carrier is still transmitted. In this latter case the waveform at the limiter is

$$G_{ch} A \cos[\omega_0 t + \Theta_0] + N_c(t) \cos(\omega_0 t + \Theta_o) - N_s(t) \sin(\omega_0 t + \Theta_0)$$

$$= A(t) \cos[\omega_0 t + \Theta_0 + \psi(t)] \tag{10.2-11}$$

where the bandpass noise $N_i(t)$ is modeled as in (10.1-4) (see also Section 8.6) and

$$A(t) = \{[G_{ch} A + N_c(t)]^2 + N_s^2(t)\}^{1/2} \tag{10.2-12}$$

$$\psi(t) = \tan^{-1}\left\{\frac{N_s(t)}{G_{ch} A + N_c(t)}\right\} \tag{10.2-13}$$

For large input signal-to-noise ratio we have $|G_{ch} A| \gg |N_c(t)|$ and $|G_{ch} A| \gg |N_s(t)|$ *most of the time*, so (10.2-13) becomes

$$\psi(t) \approx \tan^{-1}\left[\frac{N_s(t)}{G_{ch} A}\right] \approx \frac{N_s(t)}{G_{ch} A} \tag{10.2-14}$$

Equation (10.2-11) is now approximated by

$$A(t) \cos[\omega_0 t + \Theta_0 + \psi(t)] \approx A(t) \cos\left[\omega_0 t + \Theta_0 + \frac{N_s(t)}{G_{ch} A}\right] \tag{10.2-15}$$

Because the limiter removes $A(t)$ and the discriminator responds only to instantaneous frequency deviations from ω_0, the input to the lowpass filter is

$$\left(\frac{K_D}{G_{ch} A}\right) \frac{dN_s(t)}{dt} \tag{10.2-16}$$

If $\mathscr{S}_{N_sN_s}(\omega)$ is the power spectrum of $N_s(t)$ the power spectrum of (10.2-16) is

$$\left(\frac{K_D}{G_{ch}A}\right)^2 \omega^2 \mathscr{S}_{N_sN_s}(\omega) \tag{10.2-17}$$

However, we may use (8.6-17) and (8.6-16) to write this power spectrum as

$$\left(\frac{K_D}{G_{ch}A}\right)^2 \omega^2[\mathscr{S}_{N_iN_i}(\omega - \omega_0) + \mathscr{S}_{N_iN_i}(\omega + \omega_0)] \qquad |\omega| < \Delta\omega \tag{10.2-18}$$

where $\mathscr{S}_{N_iN_i}(\omega)$ is the power spectrum of $N_i(t)$; it is constant at $\mathscr{N}_0/2$ over bands of width $2\Delta\omega$ centered at ω_0 and $-\omega_0$.

Final output noise power results from the action of the lowpass filter on (10.2-18). We have

$$N_o = E[N_d^2(t)] = \frac{1}{2\pi}\int_{-W_X}^{W_X}\left(\frac{K_D}{G_{ch}A}\right)^2\omega^2[\mathscr{S}_{N_iN_i}(\omega - \omega_0) + \mathscr{S}_{N_iN_i}(\omega + \omega_0)]\,d\omega$$

$$= \frac{K_D^2}{2\pi G_{ch}^2 A^2}\int_{-W_X}^{W_X}\omega^2\left[\frac{\mathscr{N}_0}{2} + \frac{\mathscr{N}_0}{2}\right]d\omega = \frac{K_D^2\mathscr{N}_0 W_X^3}{3\pi G_{ch}^2 A^2} \tag{10.2-19}$$

Output performance is determined by

$$\left(\frac{S_o}{N_o}\right)_{FM} = \frac{3\pi G_{ch}^2 A^2 k_{FM}^2 \overline{X^2(t)}}{\mathscr{N}_0 W_X^3} \tag{10.2-20}$$

from (10.2-8) and (10.2-19). An alternative form of (10.2-20) is

$$\left(\frac{S_o}{N_o}\right)_{FM} = \frac{6}{K_{cr}^2}\left(\frac{\Delta\omega}{W_X}\right)^3\left(\frac{S_i}{N_i}\right)_{FM} \tag{10.2-21}$$

An important observation derives from (10.2-21). Since FM bandwidth is $2\Delta\omega$, we see that performance increases as the *cube* of bandwidth relative to $(S_i/N_i)_{FM}$. However, $(S_i/N_i)_{FM}$ decreases as the reciprocal of bandwidth from (10.2-10), so the *net* performance increases as the *square* of bandwidth. By simply increasing bandwidth at the transmitter, system performance rapidly increases. There is a limit to this procedure, unfortunately, that occurs when conditions under which the performance equations were derived are no longer valid. The break point, or *threshold*, occurs approximately where $(S_i/N_i)_{FM}$ drops below about 10 (or 10 dB). For a more detailed discussion of FM threshold the reader is referred to Peebles (1976). We shall emphasize FM system performance through an example.

Example 10.2-1 An FM system uses a message with crest factor 3 and bandwidth $W_X/2\pi = 3$ kHz. The FM modulator's bandwidth is $2\Delta\omega/2\pi = 20$ kHz and the receiver's input signal-to-noise ratio is 81. From (10.2-21) $(S_o/N_o)_{FM} = 2000$ (or 33.01 dB). We determine how much performance can be increased by raising $\Delta\omega$.

From (10.2-10) $(S_i/N_i)_{FM}$ decreases to 10 from 81 if $\Delta\omega$ increases by a factor of 8.1. Next, we again use (10.2-21) but now with $\Delta\omega/2\pi = 8.1(10)$ kHz and $(S_i/N_i)_{FM} = 10$:

$$\left(\frac{S_o}{N_o}\right)_{FM} = \frac{6}{9}\left(\frac{81}{3}\right)^3 (10) = 131,220$$

(or 51.18 dB). The bandwidth increase of 8.1 times has improved $(S_o/N_o)_{FM}$ by 65.61 times

10.3 NOISE IN A SIMPLE CONTROL SYSTEM

In this section we shall briefly consider the noise response of a simple control system modeled by the block diagram shown in Figure 10.3-1. The following section will then illustrate how a very practical network can be analyzed by applying the results developed here.

Transfer Function

Typical loop behavior in Figure 10.3-1 is to force the feedback signal F to approximate the command C so that the error C-F is small. The control loop's response R may be conveniently chosen. For example, if R in the time domain is to be derivative of the command then $H_2(\omega) = 1/j\omega$, the transfer function of an integrator. If R is to approximate C then $H_2(\omega) = 1$.

From Figure 10.3-1 it is clear that

$$R(\omega) = H_1(\omega)[C(\omega) - H_2(\omega)R(\omega)] \tag{10.3-1}$$

so

$$R(\omega) = C(\omega)\left[\frac{H_1(\omega)}{1 + H_1(\omega)H_2(\omega)}\right] \tag{10.3-2}$$

We define the *transfer function* of the control loop as

$$H(\omega) = \frac{R(\omega)}{C(\omega)} = \frac{H_1(\omega)}{1 + H_1(\omega)H_2(\omega)} \tag{10.3-3}$$

The transfer function (10.3-3) is not always stable. There are combinations of $H_1(\omega)$ and $H_2(\omega)$ that can cause instability. In general, if $H_1(\omega)$ and $H_2(\omega)$ are stable and $|H_1(\omega)H_2(\omega)|$ falls below unity, as a function of ω, before the phase of $H_1(\omega)H_2(\omega)$ becomes $-\pi$, and if the phase of $H_1(\omega)H_2(\omega)$ equals $-\pi$ at only one frequency, the transfer function $H(\omega)$ is stable. The product $H_1(\omega)H_2(\omega)$ is called the *open-loop transfer function* of the control system. Stability is a deep subject in control systems and we shall not develop it further because it detracts from the simple points to be made here.

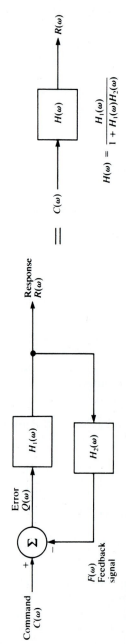

FIGURE 10.3-1
Block diagram of a simple control system.

Now suppose the command waveform in Figure 10.3-1 is the sum of a signal $S_c(t)$ and noise $N_c(t)$. Because the system is linear its responses to signal and noise may be computed separately. If $\mathcal{S}_{N_cN_c}(\omega)$ is the power spectrum of $N_c(t)$ then the power spectrum of the response noise $N_R(t)$ is

$$\mathcal{S}_{N_RN_R}(\omega) = \mathcal{S}_{N_cN_c}(\omega)\left|\frac{H_1(\omega)}{1 + H_1(\omega)H_2(\omega)}\right|^2 \tag{10.3-4}$$

whenever the network is stable.

An example serves to illustrate the use of (10.3-4).

Example 10.3-1 Let a signal

$$S_c(t) = Au(t)e^{-Wt}$$

plus white noise of power density $\mathcal{N}_0/2$ be applied to the control network where

$$H_1(\omega) = \frac{K_1W_1}{W_1 + j\omega} \qquad K_1 \gg 1$$

$$H_2(\omega) = 1$$

This choice means that we desire the response to equal the command. We find the output signal and the output noise power.

From (10.3-3)

$$H(\omega) = \frac{K_1W_1/(W_1 + j\omega)}{1 + [K_1W_1/(W_1 + j\omega)]} = \frac{K_1W_1}{(1 + K_1)W_1 + j\omega}$$

From pair 15 of Appendix E the inverse transform of $H(\omega)$ is

$$h(t) = K_1W_1u(t)e^{-(1 + K_1)W_1t}$$

The response signal becomes

$$S_R(t) = \int_{-\infty}^{\infty} h(\xi)S_c(t - \xi)\,d\xi$$

$$= K_1W_1A\int_{-\infty}^{\infty} u(\xi)u(t - \xi)e^{-[(1 + K_1)W_1 - W]\xi}\,d\xi\, e^{-Wt}$$

$$= K_1W_1Au(t)e^{-Wt}\int_0^t e^{-[(1 + K_1)W_1 - W]\xi}\,d\xi$$

$$= \frac{K_1W_1}{(1 + K_1)W_1 - W}\langle 1 - \exp\{-[(1 + K_1)W_1 - W]t\}\rangle S_c(t)$$

For $K_1 \gg 1$ so that $(1 + K_1)W_1 \gg W$ this result becomes

$$S_R(t) \approx S_c(t)$$

The approximation is more accurate as t becomes large. From (10.3-4) the output noise power spectrum is

$$\mathscr{S}_{N_R N_R}(\omega) = \frac{\mathscr{N}_0 (K_1 W_1)^2 / 2}{[(1 + K_1)W_1]^2 + \omega^2}$$

Output noise power is found using (C-25):

$$P_{N_R N_R} = \frac{1}{2\pi} \int_{-\infty}^{\infty} \mathscr{S}_{N_R N_R}(\omega) \, d\omega$$

$$= \frac{\mathscr{N}_0 K_1^2 W_1}{4(1 + K_1)} \approx \frac{\mathscr{N}_0 K_1 W_1}{4}$$

We observe in passing that this control loop is stable and its transfer function is equivalent to a simple lowpass filter of gain $K_1/(1 + K_1) \approx 1$ and 3-dB bandwidth $(1 + K_1)W_1 \approx K_1 W_1$. This unity-gain large-bandwidth filter resulted from a narrowband (bandwidth W_1) high gain filter (gain K_1) inside the loop.

Error Function

The error $Q \equiv C - F$ in Figure 10.3-1 is readily found. From

$$Q(\omega) = C(\omega) - F(\omega) = C(\omega) - H_2(\omega)H_1(\omega)Q(\omega) \tag{10.3-5}$$

we have

$$Q(\omega) = \frac{C(\omega)}{1 + H_1(\omega)H_2(\omega)} \tag{10.3-6}$$

Wiener Filter Application

By comparing (10.3-3) with the transfer function of a Wiener filter for uncorrelated signal and noise as given by (9.2-20) we see that the Wiener filter can be implemented as a loop. From (9.2-20)

$$H_{\text{opt}}(\omega) = \frac{e^{j\omega t_o}}{1 + [\mathscr{S}_{NN}(\omega)/\mathscr{S}_{XX}(\omega)]} \tag{10.3-7}$$

Thus

$$H(\omega) = H_{\text{opt}}(\omega) \qquad (10.3\text{-}8)$$

if

$$H_1(\omega) = e^{j\omega t_o} \qquad (10.3\text{-}9)$$

$$H_2(\omega) = [\mathscr{S}_{NN}(\omega)/\mathscr{S}_{XX}(\omega)]e^{-j\omega t_o} \qquad (10.3\text{-}10)$$

Of course these functions $H_1(\omega)$ and $H_2(\omega)$ may not be realizable even for realizable signal and noise power spectrums. Other choices for $H_1(\omega)$ and $H_2(\omega)$ are also possible (Problem 10-10).

10.4 NOISE IN A PHASE-LOCKED LOOP

The phase-locked loop (PLL) is a practical system to which the noise theory of this book can be applied as a good example. The PLL is also an example of the control system of the preceding section.

Figure 10.4-1 depicts the block diagram of a PLL. Broadly, the action of the loop is to force the phase of the output of the voltage-controlled oscillator (VCO) to closely follow the phase of the input signal. This action leads to one of the most important uses of the PLL, that of demodulating a frequency-modulated signal. If there is no input noise $N_i(t)$ and the VCO's phase follows that of the input FM signal, then the VCO's signal has the same FM as that transmitted. Since the VCO is just a frequency modulator, its input waveform (loop's output waveform) has to be proportional to the original message used at the transmitter. When input noise is present there is noise on the output signal. In this section we shall develop this output noise power and find the available output signal-to-noise power ratio.

Phase Detector

Consider first the phase detector. Although there are many forms of phase detector [Blanchard (1976) and Klapper et al. (1972)] they all provide an output response proportional to the difference between the phases of the two input waveforms for small difference phases. Thus

$$e_L(t) \approx K_P[\theta_1(t) - \theta_2(t)] \qquad (10.4\text{-}1)$$

if the two input waveform's phases are defined as $\theta_1(t)$ and $\theta_2(t)$. The constant K_p is the phase detector's sensitivity constant; its unit is volts per radian for $e_L(t)$ a voltage. In some phase detectors the response is also proportional to the amplitudes of the two input waveforms. Others depend only on one input amplitude because the other is large enough to saturate the device giving a type of limiting. Another type allows both inputs to limit in the detector and the output is not a function of either waveform's level. We shall assume either this last form of detector or that an actual limiter is in the path of the signal's input when a detector is used with limiting in the feedback path's input. Thus our phase detector is described by (10.4-1).

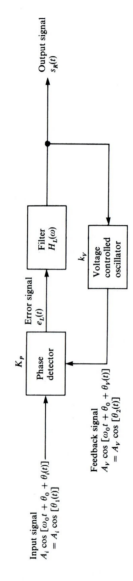

FIGURE 10.4-1
Block diagram of a phase-locked loop (PLL).

334

Loop Transfer Function

Since the VCO in Figure 10.4-1 acts like a frequency modulator for the "message" $s_R(t)$, its output can be written as

$$\text{VCO output} = A_V \cos\left[\omega_0 t + \theta_0 + \theta_V(t)\right]$$

$$= A_V \cos\left[\omega_0 t + \theta_0 + k_V \int s_R(t)\, dt\right]$$

$$= A_V \cos\left[\theta_2(t)\right] \tag{10.4-2}$$

where k_V is the VCO's modulation constant,

$$\theta_2(t) = \omega_0 t + \theta_0 + k_V \int s_R(t)\, dt \tag{10.4-3}$$

and

$$\theta_V(t) = k_V \int s_R(t)\, dt \tag{10.4-4}$$

The other phase detector input signal, from Figure 10.4-1, is the input waveform. If we define its phase as

$$\theta_1(t) = \omega_0 t + \theta_0 + \theta_i(t) \tag{10.4-5}$$

then the phase detector's response (10.4-1) becomes

$$e_L(t) = K_P\left[\omega_0 t + \theta_0 + \theta_i(t) - \omega_0 t - \theta_0 - k_V \int s_R(t)\, dt\right]$$

$$= K_P\left[\theta_i(t) - k_V \int s_R(t)\, dt\right] \tag{10.4-6}$$

Next, if we define Fourier transforms as follows

$$e_L(t) \leftrightarrow E_L(\omega) \tag{10.4-7}$$

$$\theta_i(t) \leftrightarrow \Theta_i(\omega) \tag{10.4-8}$$

$$s_R(t) \leftrightarrow S_R(\omega) \tag{10.4-9}$$

we may write (10.4-6) as

$$E_L(\omega) = K_P\left[\Theta_i(\omega) - \frac{k_V S_R(\omega)}{j\omega}\right] \tag{10.4-10}$$

From Figure 10.4-1

$$E_L(\omega) = \frac{S_R(\omega)}{H_L(\omega)} \tag{10.4-11}$$

On equating (10.4-10) and (10.4-11) we find the PLL's transfer function, denoted by $H_T(\omega)$, to be

$$H_T(\omega) = \frac{S_R(\omega)}{\Theta_i(\omega)} = \frac{K_P j\omega H_L(\omega)}{j\omega + K_P k_V H_L(\omega)} = \frac{j\omega}{k_V} H(\omega) \qquad (10.4\text{-}12)$$

where we also define†

$$H(\omega) = \frac{K_P k_V H_L(\omega)}{j\omega + K_P k_V H_L(\omega)} \qquad (10.4\text{-}13)$$

It should be noted that the above definition of transfer function relates the output *signal* to the input signal's *phase modulation* $\theta_i(t)$ according to

$$S_R(\omega) = H_T(\omega)\Theta_i(\omega) \qquad (10.4\text{-}14)$$

or

$$s_R(t) = \int_{-\infty}^{\infty} h_T(t - \xi)\theta_i(\xi)\,d\xi \qquad (10.4\text{-}15)$$

where $h_T(t)$ denotes the inverse transform of $H_T(\omega)$

$$h_T(t) \leftrightarrow H_T(\omega) \qquad (10.4\text{-}16)$$

The above developments show, in effect, that Figure 10.4-2 is an equivalent form for the loop of Figure 10.4-1.

Loop Noise Performance

We shall apply the preceding results to the case where the input to the PLL is the sum of an FM signal plus bandpass noise $N_i(t)$ modeled as

$$N_i(t) = N_c(t)\cos(\omega_0 t) - N_s(t)\sin(\omega_0 t) \qquad (10.4\text{-}17)$$

The representation (10.4-17) follows developments of Section 8.6 where $N_c(t)$ and $N_s(t)$ are lowpass random processes having the properties defined in (8.6-7) through (8.6-19). The actual input to the PLL is, therefore,

$$A_i \cos\left[\omega_0 t + \theta_0 + k_{FM}\int X(t)\,dt\right] + N_c(t)\cos(\omega_0 t) - N_s(t)\sin(\omega_0 t) \qquad (10.4\text{-}18)$$

where k_{FM} is the FM modulator's constant, $X(t)$ is the message process, and A_i, ω_0, and θ_0 are the input FM signal's peak amplitude, frequency, and phase, respectively.

---

† In many texts $H(\omega)$ is called the PLL transfer function but the loop's output is defined at a different point. (Where would it be?)

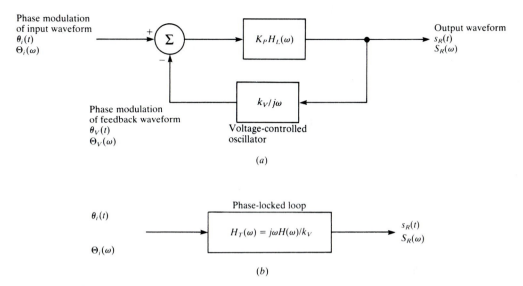

FIGURE 10.4-2
(a) Equivalent block diagram of the linear PLL of Figure 10.4-1, and (b) the transfer function equivalent of the loop in (a).

The exact analysis of the PLL's response to the waveform of (10.4-18) is very involved. However, it can be shown that the waveform of (10.4-18) can be put in the form (Problem 10-11)

$$R(t) \cos \left[\omega_0 t + \theta_0 + \theta_{\text{FM}}(t) + \theta_N(t) \right] \tag{10.4-19}$$

where

$$\theta_{\text{FM}}(t) = k_{\text{FM}} \int X(t) \, dt \tag{10.4-20}$$

and $\theta_N(t)$ is a phase angle caused by noise. For large-input signal-to-noise ratio $(A_i^2/2)/E[N_i^2(t)]$ and input noise $N_i(t)$ broadband relative to the FM signal, the autocorrelation function of $\theta_N(t)$ is approximately $1/A_i^2$ times the autocorrelation function of $N_c(t)$ (Problem 10-12). This fact means that, within a reasonable approximation, $\theta_N(t)$ can be replaced by the *equivalent* angle $N_c(t)/A_i$.

With the above noise equivalence used, the input phase modulation to the PLL from (10.4-19) is

$$\theta_i(t) = \theta_{\text{FM}}(t) + \theta_N(t)$$

$$= \theta_{\text{FM}}(t) + \frac{N_c(t)}{A_i} \tag{10.4-21}$$

The component $\theta_{FM}(t)$ is due to the signal. If $X(t)$ is a random process with power spectrum $\mathscr{S}_{XX}(\omega)$, we use (10.4-20) in (10.4-21) and find that the power spectrum of $\theta_i(t)$ is

$$\mathscr{S}_{\theta_i\theta_i}(\omega) = \frac{k_{FM}^2 \mathscr{S}_{XX}(\omega)}{\omega^2} + \frac{\mathscr{S}_{N_cN_c}(\omega)}{A_i^2} \tag{10.4-22}$$

After using the PLL's transfer function (10.4-12), the output waveform's power spectrum becomes

$$\mathscr{S}_{S_{RS_R}}(\omega) = \mathscr{S}_{\theta_i\theta_i}(\omega)|H_T(\omega)|^2$$

$$= \mathscr{S}_{XX}(\omega)\left(\frac{k_{FM}}{k_V}\right)^2 |H(\omega)|^2 + \mathscr{S}_{N_cN_c}(\omega)\frac{\omega^2}{A_i^2 k_V^2}|H(\omega)|^2 \tag{10.4-23}$$

The first right-side term in (10.4-23) is due to the desired message while the second is due to noise. Loop design is typically chosen so that $|H(\omega)|^2 \approx 1$ for all frequencies of interest in $\mathscr{S}_{XX}(\omega)$. In fact, if the message is to be preserved with very small distortion the bandwidth of the transfer function $H(\omega)$ may be significantly *larger* than the frequencies of interest in $\mathscr{S}_{XX}(\omega)$. Thus, if W_X is the spectral extent of the message $X(t)$ then the power in the output signal component is

$$S_o = \frac{1}{2\pi}\int_{-\infty}^{\infty} \mathscr{S}_{XX}(\omega)\left(\frac{k_{FM}}{k_V}\right)^2 |H(\omega)|^2 \, d\omega \approx \left(\frac{k_{FM}}{k_V}\right)^2 \frac{1}{2\pi}\int_{-\infty}^{\infty} \mathscr{S}_{XX}(\omega) \, d\omega$$

$$= \left(\frac{k_{FM}}{k_V}\right)^2 \overline{X^2(t)} \tag{10.4-24}$$

In some loops (see example to follow) $|H(\omega)|^2$ does not decrease rapidly enough to remove high-frequency noise due to the factor ω^2 in $\omega^2|H(\omega)|^2$ in (10.4-23). In these cases it may be necessary to follow the loop with a separate filter to better remove noise spectral components at frequencies $|\omega| > W_X$. As long as either the loop or a separate filter removes these components, the overall output noise power is approximately

$$N_o \approx \frac{1}{2\pi}\int_{-W_X}^{W_X} \mathscr{S}_{N_cN_c}(\omega)\frac{\omega^2}{A_i^2 k_V^2}|H(\omega)|^2 \, d\omega$$

$$\approx \frac{\mathcal{N}_0}{2\pi A_i^2 k_V^2}\int_{-W_X}^{W_X} \omega^2 \, d\omega = \frac{\mathcal{N}_0 W_X^3}{3\pi A_i^2 k_V^2} \tag{10.4-25}$$

Finally, we determine output signal-to-noise power ratio from (10.4-25) and (10.4-24). As in Section 10.2, we let A be the peak amplitude of the transmitted FM signal and let G_{ch} be the gain of the channel, so that

$$A_i = AG_{ch} \tag{10.4-26}$$

Thus,

$$\left(\frac{S_o}{N_o}\right)_{FM} = \frac{3\pi G_{ch}^2 A^2 k_{FM}^2 \overline{X^2(t)}}{\mathcal{N}_0 W_X^3} \tag{10.4-27}$$

On comparing (10.4-27) with (10.2-20) we find that both the discriminator and PLL forms of FM receiver have the same performance when the received (input) signal-to-noise ratio is large.

Example 10.4-1 As an example of a practical PLL's transfer function let the loop filter be a simple lowpass function with 3-dB bandwidth W_L where

$$H_L(\omega) = \frac{W_L}{W_L + j\omega}$$

The function $H(\omega)$, from (10.4-13), becomes

$$H(\omega) = \frac{1}{1 - \left(\dfrac{\omega}{\omega_n}\right)^2 + j2\zeta\left(\dfrac{\omega}{\omega_n}\right)}$$

where the quantities defined by

$$\omega_n = (K_P k_V W_L)^{1/2}$$

$$\zeta = \frac{1}{2}\sqrt{\frac{W_L}{K_P k_V}}$$

are called the *natural frequency* and *damping* factor, respectively, of the loop. Figure 10.4-3 illustrates how $|H(\omega)|$ behaves with ω/ω_n for ζ as a parameter. The curve for $\zeta = 1/\sqrt{2}$ is most flat in the sense that the largest number of derivatives of $|H(\omega)|$ are zero at $\omega = 0$.

For $\zeta = 1/\sqrt{2}$ and $\omega_n = W_X$, the signal's spectral extent, we have

$$|H(\omega)|^2 = \frac{W_X^4}{W_X^4 + \omega^4}$$

The more exact power in the noise term of (10.4-23) becomes

$$N_o = \frac{\mathcal{N}_0 W_X^4}{2\pi A_i^2 k_V^2} \int_{-\infty}^{\infty} \frac{\omega^2 \, d\omega}{W_X^4 + \omega^4} = \frac{\mathcal{N}_0 W_X^3}{2\sqrt{2} A_i^2 k_V^2}$$

after using (C-38). On comparing this result with (10.4-25) we see the noise in the loop output is $3\pi/2\sqrt{2} \approx 3.33$ times that of a broadband loop followed by an abrupt-cutoff filter of bandwidth W_X.

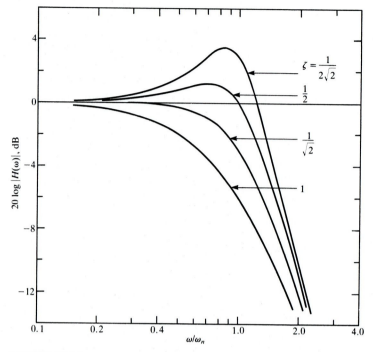

FIGURE 10.4-3
$|H(\omega)|$ for the loop of Example 10.4-1.

10.5 CHARACTERISTICS OF RANDOM COMPUTER-TYPE WAVEFORM

As another example of the practical application of the theory of this book we examine a waveform not unlike those encountered in binary computers. The waveform is shown in Figure 10.5-1; it consists of a sequence of rectangular

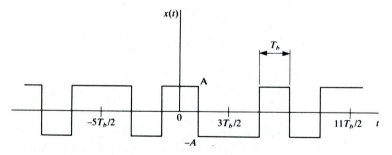

FIGURE 10.5-1
Typical waveform of a semirandom binary random process.

pulses of durations T_b having amplitudes that randomly may equal A or $-A$. Amplitudes A and $-A$ are assumed to occur with equal probability and the amplitude of any pulse interval is assumed to be statistically independent of the amplitudes of all other intervals. The random process from which this type of waveform is modeled as a sample function is called a *semirandom binary process* (see also Problem 6-4); in the remainder of this section we shall examine the description, power spectrum, and autocorrelation function of this process.

Process Description

The semirandom binary process $X(t)$ can be described by

$$X(t) = \sum_{k=-\infty}^{\infty} A_k \, \text{rect}\left[\frac{t - kT_b}{T_b}\right] \tag{10.5-1}$$

where $\{A_k\}$ is a set of statistically independent random variables and rect $(\cdot)$ is defined by (E-2). The A_k satisfy

$$E[A_k] = 0 \qquad k = 0, \pm 1, \pm 2, \ldots \tag{10.5-2}$$

$$E[A_k A_m] = \begin{cases} A^2 & k = m \\ 0 & k \neq m \end{cases} \tag{10.5-3}$$

The truncated version of $X(t)$ is needed in calculating power spectrum. We truncate to a time interval $2T$ centered on $t = 0$ that is a discrete multiple of T_b according to

$$2T = (2K + 1)T_b \tag{10.5-4}$$

Thus, the truncated process $X_T(t)$ is

$$X_T(t) = \sum_{k=-K}^{K} A_k \, \text{rect}\left[\frac{t - kT_b}{T_b}\right] \tag{10.5-5}$$

Power Spectrum

We compute the power spectrum $\mathcal{S}_{XX}(\omega)$ of $X(t)$ by use of (7.1-11). The Fourier transform of $X_T(t)$, denoted by $X_T(\omega)$, is

$$X_T(\omega) = T_b \sum_{k=-K}^{K} A_k \text{Sa}(\omega T_b/2) e^{-jk\omega T_b}$$

$$= T_b \text{Sa}(\omega T_b/2) \sum_{k=-K}^{K} A_k e^{-jk\omega T_b} \tag{10.5-6}$$

from (10.5-5) and pair 5 of Table E-1. Next,

$$\frac{E[|X_T(\omega)|^2]}{2T} = \frac{T_b \text{Sa}^2(\omega T_b/2)}{(2K + 1)} \sum_{k=-K}^{K} \sum_{m=-K}^{K} E[A_k A_m] e^{-j(k-m)\omega T_b}$$

$$= A^2 T_b \text{Sa}^2(\omega T_b/2) \tag{10.5-7}$$

Now because (10.5-7) does not depend on K, and therefore not on T through (10.5-4), we have

$$\mathcal{S}_{XX}(\omega) = \lim_{T \to \infty} \frac{E[|X_T(\omega)|^2]}{2T} = A^2 T_b \text{Sa}^2(\omega T_b/2) \tag{10.5-8}$$

The bandwidth of this power spectrum at its -3-dB point is $0.4429(2\pi/T_b) = 0.4429\omega_b$.

Autocorrelation Function

It follows from (10.5-1) through (10.5-3) that $E[X(t)X(t + \tau)]$ is zero unless both t and $t + \tau$ fall in the same pulse interval. The autocorrelation function is, therefore,

$$
\begin{aligned}
R_{XX}(t, t + \tau) &= E[X(t)X(t + \tau)] \\
&= \begin{cases} A^2 & (k - {}^1/_2)T_b < (t \text{ and } t + \tau) < (k + {}^1/_2)T_b \\ 0 & \text{elsewhere} \end{cases}
\end{aligned} \tag{10.5-9}
$$

Thus, the process $X(t)$ is not even wide-sense stationary since (10.5-9) depends on absolute time t.

The time-averaged autocorrelation function is readily obtained by inverse Fourier transforming (10.5-8) according to (7.2-9). After using pair 7 of Table E-1 we obtain

$$R_{XX}(\tau) = \lim_{T \to \infty} \frac{1}{2T} \int_{-T}^{T} R_{XX}(t, t + \tau)\, dt = A^2 \, \text{tri}\left(\frac{t}{T_b}\right) \tag{10.5-10}$$

The direct computation of $R_{XX}(\tau)$ by time-averaging $R_{XX}(t, t + \tau)$ is possible, but a bit more complicated than the inverse transform procedure used here (see Thomas, 1969, p. 107).

10.6 ENVELOPE AND PHASE OF A SINUSOIDAL SIGNAL PLUS NOISE

Many practical problems involve the probability density function of the envelope of the sum of a sinusoidal signal and noise. A radar, for example, may be interested in determining if a short segment (pulse) of a sinusoidal waveform is being received at some time or if only noise is being received. This problem is one of detection based on observing the received waveform's envelope; if the envelope is large enough (because of the signal's presence) the radar decides both the signal and the noise are present. We examine radar detection further in Section 10.7.

In this section we discuss probability densities involved in describing the envelope and phase of the sum of the sinusoidal signal and noise.

Waveforms

Let the signal be

$$s(t) = A_0 \cos(\omega_0 t + \theta_0) = A_0 \cos(\theta_0) \cos(\omega_0 t) - A_0 \sin(\theta_0) \sin(\omega_0 t) \quad (10.6\text{-}1)$$

where A_0, ω_0, and θ_0 are constants. We assume the noise $n(t)$ to be added to $s(t)$ is a sample function of a zero-mean, wide-sense stationary gaussian bandpass process $N(t)$ with power $E[N^2(t)] = \sigma^2$. From (8.6-2), the sum can be written as

$$s(t) + N(t) = [A_0 \cos(\theta_0) + X(t)] \cos(\omega_0 t) - [A_0 \sin(\theta_0) + Y(t)] \sin(\omega_0 t)$$

$$= R(t) \cos[\omega_0 t + \Theta(t)] \quad (10.6\text{-}2)$$

where $X(t)$ and $Y(t)$ are zero-mean, gaussian, lowpass processes having the same powers $E[X^2(t)] = E[Y^2(t)] = E[N^2(t)] = \sigma^2$. Other properties of $X(t)$ and $Y(t)$ are given in (8.6-7) through (8.6-19). The envelope and phase of the sum are $R(t)$ and $\Theta(t)$, respectively. We may think of $R(t)$ and $\Theta(t)$ as transformations of $X(t)$ and $Y(t)$ as follows:

$$R = T_1(X, Y) = \{[A_0 \cos(\theta_0) + X]^2 + [A_0 \sin(\theta_0) + Y]^2\}^{1/2} \quad (10.6\text{-}3a)$$

$$\Theta = T_2(X, Y) = \tan^{-1}\left[\frac{A_0 \sin(\theta_0) + Y}{A_0 \cos(\theta_0) + X}\right] \quad (10.6\text{-}3b)$$

Inverse transformations are:

$$X = T_1^{-1}(R, \Theta) = R \cos(\Theta) - A_0 \cos(\theta_0) \quad (10.6\text{-}4a)$$

$$Y = T_2^{-1}(R, \Theta) = R \sin(\Theta) - A_0 \sin(\theta_0) \quad (10.6\text{-}4b)$$

The functional dependence on t has been suppressed in writing (10.6-3) and (10.6-4) with the implied understanding that the quantities X, Y, R, and Θ are random variables defined from the respective processes at time t.

Probability Density of The Envelope

From (8.6-15), processes $X(t)$ and $Y(t)$ are statistically independent (at the same time t) because they are gaussian and uncorrelated. The joint density of random variables X and Y is, therefore,

$$f_{X,Y}(x, y) = \frac{e^{-(x^2+y^2)/2\sigma^2}}{2\pi\sigma^2} \quad (10.6\text{-}5)$$

From (5.4-4) the jacobian of the transformations (10.6-4) is readily found to be R. We next apply (5.4-6) to obtain the joint density of random variables R and Θ:

$$f_{R,\Theta}(r, \theta) = \frac{u(r)r}{2\pi\sigma^2} \exp\left\{-\frac{1}{2\sigma^2}[r^2 - 2rA_0 \cos(\theta - \theta_0) + A_0^2]\right\} \quad (10.6\text{-}6)$$

The density of R alone is obtained by integrating over all values of Θ:

$$f_R(r) = \int_0^{2\pi} f_{R,\Theta}(r, \theta)\, d\theta$$

$$= \frac{u(r)r}{\sigma^2} e^{-(r^2 + A_0^2)/2\sigma^2} \frac{1}{2\pi} \int_0^{2\pi} e^{rA_0 \cos(\theta - \theta_0)/\sigma^2}\, d\theta \tag{10.6-7}$$

The integral is known to equal the modified Bessel function of order zero

$$I_0(\beta) = \frac{1}{2\pi} \int_0^{2\pi} e^{\beta \cos(\theta)}\, d\theta \tag{10.6-8}$$

Thus,

$$f_R(r) = \frac{u(r)}{\sigma^2} r I_0\left(\frac{rA_0}{\sigma^2}\right) e^{-(r^2 + A_0^2)/2\sigma^2} \tag{10.6-9}$$

which is known as the *Rice* probability density.

Equation (10.6-9) is our principal result; it is the density of the envelope $R(t)$ at any time t. Figure 10.6-1 illustrates the behavior of (10.6-9). For $A_0/\sigma = 0$, the case of no signal, the density is Rayleigh. For A_0/σ large the density becomes

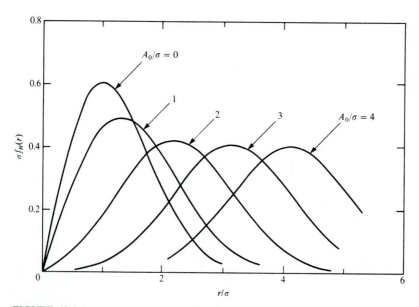

FIGURE 10.6-1
Probability densities of the envelope of a sinusoidal signal (amplitude A_0) plus noise (power σ^2) for various ratios A_0/σ.

gaussian. To show this last fact we note that

$$I_0(\beta) \approx \frac{e^\beta}{\sqrt{2\pi\beta}} \qquad \beta \gg 1 \qquad (10.6\text{-}10)$$

so for rA_0/σ^2 large

$$f_R(r) \approx u(r)\sqrt{\frac{r}{2\pi A_o\sigma^2}}\, \exp\left[\frac{-(r-A_0)^2}{2\sigma^2}\right] \qquad (10.6\text{-}11)$$

This function peaks for r near A_0, and since $A_0 \gg \sigma$, the most significant values of r exist only near A_0. Therefore, with $r \approx A_0$ (10.6-11) becomes

$$f_R(r) \approx \frac{e^{-(r-A_0)^2/2\sigma^2}}{\sqrt{2\pi\sigma^2}} \qquad (10.6\text{-}12)$$

which is a gaussian function with mean A_0 and variance σ^2.

Although difficult to derive, the mean and variance of R as found from (10.6-9) are known (Appendix F).

Probability Density of Phase

The density of the phase Θ of (10.6-2) derives by integrating (10.6-6) over all values of R. We shall leave the detailed steps for the reader as an exercise (Problem 10-16). The procedure is to first complete the square in r in the exponent, and, after a suitable variable change, integrate the sum of two terms. The result becomes (Middleton, 1960, p. 417)

$$\begin{aligned} f_\Theta(\theta) &= (1/2\pi)\exp\left(-A_0^2/2\sigma^2\right) \\ &+ \frac{A_0\cos(\theta-\theta_0)}{\sqrt{2\pi}\sigma}\exp\left[\frac{-A_0^2\sin^2(\theta-\theta_0)}{2\sigma^2}\right] \\ &\cdot F\left[\frac{A_0\cos(\theta-\theta_0)}{\sigma}\right] \end{aligned} \qquad (10.6\text{-}13)$$

where the function $F(\cdot)$ is given by (B-3). Figure 10.6-2 illustrates the behavior of $f_\Theta(\theta)$ for various values of A_0/σ when $\theta_0 = 3\pi/4$.

For noise only, which is the case of $A_0/\sigma = 0$, Figure 10.6-2 shows that the density of Θ is uniform on $(0, 2\pi)$. As A_0/σ becomes large the density approaches an impulse function located at the signal's phase (at $\theta = \theta_0$). Thus,

$$\lim_{A_0/\sigma \to \infty} [f_\Theta(\theta)] = \delta(\theta - \theta_0) \qquad (10.6\text{-}14)$$

(Problem 10-17).

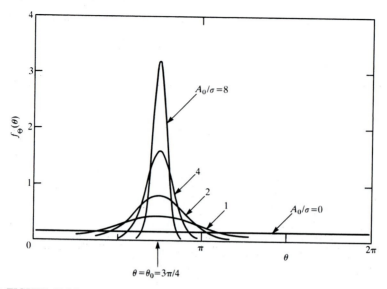

FIGURE 10.6-2
Probability density function of the phase of the sum of a sinusoidal signal and gaussian noise. Curves are plotted for a signal phase of $\theta_0 = 3\pi/4$.

10.7 RADAR DETECTION USING A SINGLE OBSERVATION

Radar can be used to detect the presence (and distance) of a nearby object (called the radar *target*). A representative problem might be to detect the presence of an aircraft approaching an airport. Here the airport's radar radiates a pulse of radio frequency (RF) energy. The pulse propagates outward until it strikes the target (aircraft), whereupon some of the energy is reflected back toward the radar. The target's presence can be detected at the radar simply by detecting the presence of the reflected RF pulse. Once the received pulse is detected the delay between the time of the radiated pulse and the received pulse is proportional to the target's distance from the radar. After a sufficient time interval (called the *pulse repetition frequency*, or PRF, *interval*, chosen for the most distant detection of interest) the radar transmits another RF pulse and the entire "detection" process is repeated.

A straightforward implementation within the radar receiver to achieve detection is depicted in Figure 10.7-1. During any PRF interval noise is always being received (mainly due to the radar's own self-generated noise). A reflected pulse is received with this noise only when a target is present. The envelope detector produces an output $W(t)$ that is some monotonic function $g(\cdot)$ of the envelope $R(t)$ of the received signal-plus-noise waveform. The first-order probability density function of $R(t)$ was developed in the preceding Section 10.6. On the average $R(t)$, and therefore $W(t)$, with a target present will be larger than $R(t)$ when only noise is being received. A suitable detection logic compares $W(t)$ to a *threshold* W_T; if

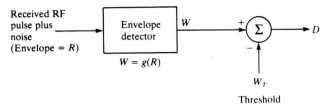

FIGURE 10.7-1
Simple radar detection network.

$W(t) > W_T$ the receiver decides that a target is present; if $W(t) \le W_T$ it assumes only noise is being received. These tests amount to determining when $D > 0$ in Figure 10.7-1; when $D > 0$ a target is declared to be present.

On the *average* the detection logic is valid. On any one PRF interval, however, it is possible for the receiver to make mistakes. For example, if no target is truly present it may occur that noise could become large enough at some time to make $W(t)$ exceed W_T and cause a false detection; this type of detection is called a *false alarm*. The probability of a false alarm, denoted by P_{fa}, is

$$P_{fa} = \int_{W_T}^{\infty} f_0(w)\, dw \tag{10.7-1}$$

where $f_0(w)$ is the probability density of $W(t)$ given that there is no target present. Generally, a radar wants P_{fa} to be small.

Another type of error occurs when a target is actually present but noise is such as to cancel its effect during the signal's duration and force $W(t) < W_T$. The radar usually is designed such that the probability of this event, called the *probability of a miss*, is small; it equals one minus the *detection* probability, denoted by P_d, given by

$$P_d = \int_{W_T}^{\infty} f_1(w)\, dw \tag{10.7-2}$$

Here $f_1(w)$ is the probability density of $W(t)$ when a target is present.

In most radars P_d and P_{fa} are parameters of greatest importance. W_T is usually chosen to give a prescribed value of P_{fa}. P_d then depends on the amplitude of the target's returned signal. In this section we shall develop expressions for P_{fa} and P_d when the radar makes detection decisions based on a single observation (uses only one PRF interval). Our results can be extended to multiple observations but the details are complicated and we only refer the reader to the literature (Difranco and Rubin, 1968).

False Alarm Probability and Threshold

When there is no target only noise is present at the input to the envelope detector. From (10.6-9) the density of the envelope of the noise is

$$f_R(r) = \frac{u(r)}{\sigma^2}\, re^{-r^2/2\sigma^2} \tag{10.7-3}$$

where σ^2 is the power in the input noise. Because the detector characteristic $g(R)$ is assumed monotonic, there is an *equivalent threshold* R_T on R that is related to W_T by

$$W_T = g(R_T) \tag{10.7-4}$$

$$R_T = g^{-1}(W_T) \tag{10.7-5}$$

where $g^{-1}(\cdot)$ is the inverse function of $g(\cdot)$. We may then compute P_{fa} from the envelope as follows:

$$P_{fa} = \int_{W_T}^{\infty} f_0(w)\, dw = \int_{R_T}^{\infty} f_R(r)\, dr$$

$$= \int_{R_T}^{\infty} \frac{r}{\sigma^2} e^{-r^2/2\sigma^2}\, dr = e^{-R_T^2/2\sigma^2} \tag{10.7-6}$$

Thus,

$$R_T = \left\{ 2\sigma^2 \ln\left(\frac{1}{P_{fa}}\right) \right\}^{1/2} \tag{10.7-7}$$

and

$$W_T = g\left[\left\{ 2\sigma^2 \ln\left(\frac{1}{P_{fa}}\right) \right\}^{1/2} \right] \tag{10.7-8}$$

where $\ln(\cdot)$ represents the natural logarithm.

Equation (10.7-8) gives the threshold W_T that is to be used to realize a specified value of P_{fa} when the noise power level is σ^2 at the detector's input.

Example 10.7-1 A radar receiver uses a square-law envelope detector defined by $W = 3R^2$. We find what threshold is required when noise power at the detector's input is $\sigma^2 = 0.025$ W and $P_{fa} = 10^{-6}$ is required. From (10.7-8)

$$W_T = 3\left[2(0.025) \ln\left(\frac{1}{10^{-6}}\right) \right] \approx 2.07 \text{ V}$$

Detection Probability

When a target signal is present the density of the received waveform's envelope is given by (10.6-9). Again using the idea of an equivalent threshold R_T on the envelope R we expand (10.7-2) to get

$$P_d = \int_{W_T}^{\infty} f_1(w)\, dw = \int_{R_T}^{\infty} f_R(r)\, dr$$

$$= \int_{\sqrt{2\sigma^2 \ln(1/P_{fa})}}^{\infty} \frac{r}{\sigma^2} I_0\left(\frac{rA_0}{\sigma^2}\right) e^{-(r^2 + A_0^2)/2\sigma^2}\, dr$$

$$= Q\left[\sqrt{\frac{A_0^2}{\sigma^2}},\ \sqrt{2 \ln\left(\frac{1}{P_{fa}}\right)} \right] \tag{10.7-9}$$

where

$$Q(\alpha, \beta) = \int_\beta^\infty \xi I_0(\alpha\xi)e^{-(\xi^2 + \alpha^2)/2} \, d\xi \qquad (10.7\text{-}10)$$

is called Marcum's Q-function (Marcum, 1950, 1960). Figure 10.7-2 illustrates P_d for various values of $A_0^2/2\sigma^2$ with P_{fa} as a parameter. Generally, the smaller P_{fa} is required to be the larger is the necessary signal strength to achieve a given value of P_d.

When P_{fa} is small while P_d is relatively large so that the threshold W_T is large and signal strength is relatively large, the approximation of (10.6-12)

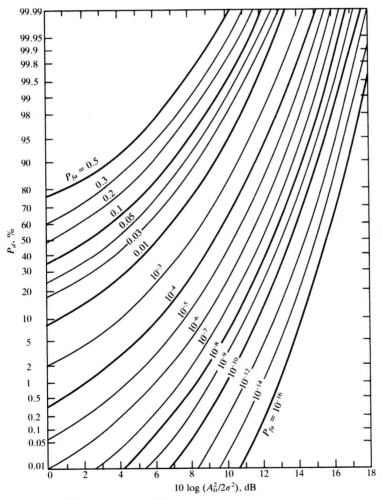

FIGURE 10.7-2
Radar detection probabilities for various false alarm probabilities when detection is based on a single observation. [*Adapted from Barton (1964) with permission.*]

can be used in (10.7-9) to obtain

$$P_d \approx F\left[\frac{A_0}{\sigma} - \sqrt{2 \ln\left(\frac{1}{P_{fa}}\right)}\right]$$ (10.7-11)

where $F(\cdot)$ is given by (B-3).

Example 10.7-2 We find the value of P_d in a receiver having $P_{fa} = 10^{-10}$ when the received signal-to-noise power ratio at the detector's input is 16.0 dB. Here $A_0^2/2\sigma^2 = 39.811$ (16 dB). Thus, $(A_0/\sigma) - \sqrt{2 \ln(1/P_{fa})} \approx 2.137$. From Table B-1 and (10.7-11), $P_d \approx F(2.137) \approx 0.9837$ or 98.37%, which is in agreement with Figure 10.7-2.

PROBLEMS

10-1   Show that (a) the time-averaged autocorrelation function of $S_{AM}(t)$, as given by (10.1-2) is

$$R_{AM}(\tau) = {}^1/_2[A_0^2 + R_{XX}(\tau)] \cos(\omega_0 \tau)$$

if $X(t)$ is a zero-mean process, and (b) the power spectrum is

$$\mathcal{S}_{AM}(\omega) = \frac{A_0^2 \pi}{2} [\delta(\omega - \omega_0) + \delta(\omega + \omega_0)]$$

$$+ {}^1/_4[\mathcal{S}_{XX}(\omega - \omega_0) + \mathcal{S}_{XX}(\omega + \omega_0)]$$

where $\mathcal{S}_{XX}(\omega)$ is the power spectrum of $X(t)$.

10-2   Define transmitter efficiency η_{AM} in an amplitude modulation communication system as the ratio of transmitted power due to the message to the total power. For a zero-mean stationary random message show that

$$\eta_{AM} = \frac{R_{XX}(0)}{A_0^2 + R_{XX}(0)} = \frac{\int_{-\infty}^{\infty} \mathcal{S}_{XX}(\omega)\, d\omega}{2\pi A_0^2 + \int_{-\infty}^{\infty} \mathcal{S}_{XX}(\omega)\, d\omega} = \frac{\overline{X^2(t)}}{A_0^2 + \overline{X^2(t)}}$$

where $R_{XX}(\tau)$ and $\mathcal{S}_{XX}(\omega)$ are the autocorrelation function and power spectrum, respectively, of the message $X(t)$.

10-3   Define *crest factor* K_{cr} for a zero-mean, bounded, random signal by

$$K_{cr}^2 = |X(t)|_{max}^2 / \overline{X^2(t)}$$

If no *overmodulation* is to occur, such that $|X(t)|_{max} \leq A_0$ in the transmitted signal of an amplitude modulation system, show that the transmitter efficiency (Problem 10-2) is

$$\eta_{AM} \leq \frac{1}{1 + K_{cr}^2}$$

What is the maximum efficiency for a message $X(t) = A_m \cos(\omega_m t + \Theta_m)$, where A_m and ω_m are constants while Θ_m is a random variable uniform on $(0, 2\pi)$?

10-4 Use (10.1-3), (10.1-4), and (10.1-14) to show that the input signal-to-noise power ratio at the envelope detector of Figure 10.1-1 is

$$\left(\frac{S_i}{N_i}\right)_{AM} = \frac{\overline{S_R^2(t)}}{\overline{N^2(t)}} = \frac{\pi G_{ch}^2 [A_0^2 + \overline{X^2(t)}]}{\mathcal{N}_0 W_{rec}}$$

Use this result to show that (10.1-15) can be written in the form

$$\left(\frac{S_o}{N_o}\right)_{AM} = 2\eta_{AM}\left(\frac{S_i}{N_i}\right)_{AM}$$

where η_{AM} is defined in Problem 10-2.

10-5 In an AM broadcast system the total average transmitted power is 1 kW. The channel gain is $G_{ch} = 3\sqrt{2}(10^{-3})$. Average noise power at the envelope detector's input is 10^{-5} W and the output signal-to-noise power ratio of the receiver is 180 (or 22.55 dB).
(a) What is the average signal power at the input to the envelope detector?
(b) Find $(S_i/N_i)_{AM}$.
(c) What is the transmitter's efficiency?
(*Hint:* Use results of Problem 10-4.)

10-6 When the message in an FM system is a sinusoid, such as $x(t) = A_m \cos(\omega_m t)$ where $A_m > 0$ and ω_m are constants, *modulation index* β_{FM} is defined by $\beta_{FM} = \Delta\omega/\omega_m$.
(a) Write an expression for the instantaneous frequency (rad/s) of the FM waveform in terms of β_{FM}.
(b) What is the approximate bandwidth of the FM signal in terms of β_{FM} if $\Delta\omega$ is large relative to ω_m?
(c) For the specific waveform $x(t) = 0.1 \cos(10^3 t)$, what are β_{FM} and the transmitter's constant k_{FM} if the approximate bandwidth is to be 200 kHz?

10-7 Find an expression for the autocorrelation function of $S_{FM}(t)$, as given by (10.2-1), when $X(t)$ is a gaussian, zero-mean process. Formulate the expression in terms of the correlation coefficient and variance of the process

$$\Gamma(t) = k_{FM} \int X(t)\, dt$$

[*Hint:* Note that the expectation involving $X(t)$ leads to a characteristic function.]

10-8 In an FM system the transmitted signal has 10 kW of average power and a bandwidth of approximately 150 kHz when a random message with a crest factor of 4 is used (Problem 10-3). The signal passes over a channel for which $G_{ch} = 10^{-6}$ and $\mathcal{N}_0/2 = 5(10^{-15})/3$.

(a) Find the signal and noise average powers and the signal-to-noise ratio at the receiver's input.

(b) What is the message's spectral extent if the output signal-to-noise power ratio of the receiver is found to be 25,000?

10-9 Let $H_1(\omega) = K_1 W_1/(W_1 + j\omega)$ and $H_2(\omega) = 1/j\omega$ in (10.3-3) where $K_1 > 0$ and $W_1 > 0$ are constants.

(a) Are there any values of K_1 and/or W_1 that will make the loop of Figure 10.3-1 unstable?

(b) If $W_1 = 200$ and $K_1 = 40$ find the loop's output noise power if white noise of power density $\mathcal{N}_0/2 = 10^{-4}$ W/Hz is applied at the input. (*Hint:* Use the integral given in Problem 9-40.)

10-10 Show that the transfer function of the control system of Figure 10.3-1 is the same as the Wiener filter of (9.2-20) if

$$H_1(\omega) = \left[\frac{\mathscr{S}_{XX}(\omega)}{\mathscr{S}_{NN}(\omega)}\right] e^{j\omega t_o}$$

and

$$H_2(\omega) = e^{-j\omega t_o}$$

★10-11 Show that the sum of an FM waveform plus noise as given by (10.4-18) can be written in the form

$$R(t) \cos\left[\omega_0 t + \theta_0 + \theta_{FM}(t) + \theta_N(t)\right]$$

where

$$\theta_{FM}(t) = k_{FM} \int X(t)\, dt$$

and

$$R(t) = \langle\{N_c(t) + A_i \cos[\theta_0 + \theta_{FM}(t)]\}^2 + \{N_s(t) + A_i \sin[\theta_0 + \theta_{FM}(t)]\}^2\rangle^{1/2}$$

$$\theta_N(t) = \tan^{-1}\left\{\frac{N_s(t)\cos[\theta_0 + \theta_{FM}(t)] - N_c(t)\sin[\theta_0 + \theta_{FM}(t)]}{A_i + N_c(t)\cos[\theta_0 + \theta_{FM}(t)] + N_s(t)\sin[\theta_0 + \theta_{FM}(t)]}\right\}$$

★10-12 Assume the bandpass noise $N_i(t)$ in Problem 10-11 is wide-sense stationary and gaussian and note that if $|A_i| \gg |N_c(t)|$ and $|A_i| \gg N_s(t)|$ *most of the time*, then

$$\theta_N(t) \approx \frac{N_s(t)}{A_i}\cos[\theta_0 + \theta_{FM}(t)] - \frac{N_c(t)}{A_i}\sin[\theta_0 + \theta_{FM}(t)]$$

(a) Show that the autocorrelation function of the process $\Theta_N(t)$, for which $\theta_N(t)$ is a sample function, is

$$R_{\Theta_N \Theta_N}(t, t + \tau) = \frac{1}{A_i^2} R_{N_c N_c}(\tau) E\left[\cos\left\{k_{FM} \int_t^{t+\tau} X(\xi)\, d\xi\right\}\right]$$
$$+ \frac{1}{A_i^2} R_{N_s N_s}(\tau) E\left[\sin\left\{k_{FM} \int_t^{t+\tau} X(\xi)\, d\xi\right\}\right]$$

where $R_{N_c N_c}(\tau)$ and $R_{N_s N_s}(\tau)$ are the correlation functions of $N_c(t)$ and $N_s(t)$, and the expectations are with respect to the message process $X(t)$ assumed statistically independent of the noises. (*Hint:* Use the results of Section 8.6.)

(b) If noises $N_c(t)$ and $N_s(t)$ are broadband relative to the FM signal, justify that

$$R_{\Theta_N \Theta_N}(t, t + \tau) \approx \frac{1}{A_i^2} R_{N_c N_c}(\tau) = R_{\Theta_N \Theta_N}(\tau)$$

(c) If the message process varies slowly enough for values of τ that are important to $R_{N_c N_c}(\tau)$ such that

$$k_{FM} \int_t^{t+\tau} X(\xi)\, d\xi \approx k_{FM} X(t)\tau$$

is valid, show that the expression of part (a) reduces to

$$R_{\Theta_N \Theta_N}(t, t + \tau) \approx \frac{1}{A_i^2} \exp\left[\frac{-\sigma_X^2 k_{FM}^2 \tau^2}{2}\right] R_{N_c N_c}(\tau)$$

if $X(t)$ is a zero-mean, wide-sense stationary gaussian message of power σ_X^2. (*Hint:* Make use of characteristic functions.)

10-13 In Example 10.4-1 let $\zeta = {}^1\!/_2$ instead of $1/\sqrt{2}$ and recompute the loop's output noise power N_o. Compare the result with that of (10.4-25). Is there any improvement over the case where $\zeta = 1/\sqrt{2}$? (*Hint:* Make use of the integral given in Problem 9-40.)

10-14 Assume white noise is added to an FM signal and the sum is applied to a phase-locked loop for message recovery. Thus, $\mathscr{S}_{N_c N_c}(\omega) = \mathscr{N}_0$ in (10.4-23).

(a) If

$$H_L(\omega) = \frac{W_1 W_3 (W_2 + j\omega)}{W_2 (W_1 + j\omega)(W_3 + j\omega)}$$

where W_1, W_2, and W_3 are positive constants, find an expression for the power contained in the noise part of (10.4-23).

(b) Assume the loop is designed so that $W_3 = 2\omega_0$, $W_2 = \omega_0/5$, and $W_1 = \omega_0^2/5K$, where $K = K_P k_V$ and ω_0 is called the loop's *crossover frequency* (rad/s); it is the frequency where $|KH_L(\omega)/j\omega| = 1$. Evaluate the result found in part (a) when ω_0 equals the message's spectral extent W_X.

(c) If K is very large, to what does the evaluation of part (b) approach? [*Hint:* Use the known integral

$$I_3 = \frac{1}{2\pi} \int_{-\infty}^{\infty} \frac{(b_0\omega^4 - b_1\omega^2 + b_2)\,d\omega}{a_0^2\omega^6 + (a_1^2 - 2a_0a_2)\omega^4 + (a_2^2 - 2a_1a_3)\omega^2 + a_3^2}$$

$$= \frac{a_0b_1 - a_2b_0 - (a_0a_1b_2/a_3)}{2a_0(a_0a_3 - a_1a_2)}$$

where a_0, a_1, a_2, a_3, b_0, b_1, and b_2 are constants and $a_0\lambda^3 + a_1\lambda^2 + a_2\lambda + a_3$ has no roots in the lower half-plane when $\lambda = \omega + j\sigma$ (Thomas, 1969, p. 249).]

10-15 A sample function of a semirandom binary process is to be passed through a lowpass filter with transfer function $H(\omega) = W_L/(W_L + j\omega)$ where W_L is its 3-dB bandwidth. If the rise and fall times of the pulses in the output waveform are not to exceed 5% of the pulse duration T_b what minimum value of W_L is required? (*Hint:* Assume the input waveform has been at level $-A$ for many pulse intervals and suddenly makes a transition to level A; determine rise time as that required for the output to rise from $-A$ to $0.9A$.)

★10-16 Carry out the steps suggested in the text and show that (10.6-13) derives from (10.6-6).

★10-17 If $A_0/\sigma \to \infty$ in (10.6-13) show that (10.6-14) is true.

10-18 A radar receiver uses a linear envelope detector where $W = R$. Find an expression for false alarm probability P_{fa} in terms of W_T, the threshold voltage level.

10-19 Work Problem 10-18 for a square-law detector defined by $W = KR^2$, where $K > 0$ is a constant.

10-20 A radar uses a linear envelope detector defined by $W = R/4$. The threshold voltage is $W_T = 0.7$ volt. Measurements show that $P_{fa} = 4(10^{-7})$. What is the noise power at the envelope detector's input?

10-21 Work Problem 10-20 for a square-law detector with characteristic $W = R^2/4$.

10-22 False alarm probability is 10^{-8} in a radar that must have a detection probability of 0.9901. When target is present what signal-to-noise power ratio is necessary at the envelope detector's input? [*Hint:* Assume (10.7-11) applies.]

★10-23 A radar receiver as shown in Figure 10.7-1 uses a square-law detector defined by $W = KR^2$ where $K > 0$ is a constant. Find an expression for the probability density of W.

★10-24 A radar receiver uses a binary detection logic based on observing N PRF intervals (multiple observations). If the observations in the N intervals are statistically independent and the detection and false alarm probabilities on any one observation are P_{d1} and P_{fa1}, respectively, find P_d and P_{fa} that correspond to an overall detection logic based on obtaining at least n detections in N intervals.

ADDITIONAL PROBLEMS, THIRD EDITION

10-25 In an AM system the message's power is $\overline{X^2(t)} = 0.1$ W. The modulator's efficiency is $\eta_{AM} = 0.159$. Noise power at the receiver's envelope detector is $N_i = 10^{-4}$ W, and the signal-to-noise power ratio at the output is known to be $(S_o/N_o)_{AM} = 5000$. If $|X(t)|_{max} = A_0$, find: (a) K_{cr} (defined in Problem 10-3), (b) A_0, (c) $(S_i/N_i)_{AM}$, and (d) G_{ch}.

10-26 An AM communication system transmits an average power of 2 kW when using a message having a crest factor (defined in Problem 10-3) of $\sqrt{24}$ and a peak amplitude equal to A_0. The channel's voltage gain is $3(10^{-6})$ and in the receiver $(S_i/N_i)_{AM} = 5(10^5)$.

(a) What is the system's efficiency as defined in Problem 10-2?

(b) What is S_i?

(c) Find $(S_o/N_o)_{AM}$.

10-27 A random message has spectral extent $W_X = \pi(10^4)$ rad/s, a crest factor of 4.2, and average power of $\overline{X^2(t)} = 0.02$ W. The message is transmitted over a FM system for which $k_{FM} = 1.06(10^6)$ rad/s per volt. At the receiver $(S_i/N_i)_{FM} = 10$. Find: (a) $\Delta\omega$, and (b) $(S_o/N_o)_{FM}$.

10-28 In an FM system $\Delta\omega = 8\pi(10^4)$ rad/s, $(S_i/N_i)_{FM} = 14$ and $(S_o/N_o)_{FM} = 4200$ when the message has a crest factor of 3.2 and $\mathcal{N}_0 = 10^{-11}$ W/Hz.

(a) Find W_X.

(b) What is the peak voltage of the FM signal at the input to the receiver?

(c) Is the system operating above threshold?

10-29 An FM signal of peak amplitude 0.1 V at the input to an FM demodulator results in an input signal-to-noise power ratio of 20. If $\Delta\omega = \pi(10^5)$ rad/s in the FM signal and the effective transmitted signal voltage is $A = 2$ kV, find: (a) G_{ch} and (b) $\mathcal{N}_0$. If the transmitted message is an audio signal for which $|X(t)|_{max} = 1.4$ V, $W_X = \pi(10^4)$ rad/s, and $K_{cr} = 3$, find: (c) $(S_o/N_o)_{FM}$ and (d) k_{FM}.

10-30 A signal and white noise of power density $\mathcal{N}_0/2 = 10^{-3}$ are applied to the input of a simple linear control system for which

$$H_1(\omega) = \frac{Kj\omega}{(W_1 + j\omega)(W_2 + j\omega)}$$

$$H_2(\omega) = 1$$

Here K, W_1 and W_2 are positive constants.

(a) Find an expression for the noise power at the loop's output. (*Hint:* Use results of Problem 9-40.)

(b) Evaluate the result found in (a) for $K = 10$, $W_1 = 5$, and $W_2 = 25$.

10-31 A sinusoidal signal plus gaussian bandpass noise are applied to an envelope detector having an output R defined by (10.6-9). If the input signal-to-noise power ratio is $A_0^2/(2\sigma^2) = 2$, find the ratio of the mean of R to σ. Also find the variance of R relative to σ^2. (*Hint:* Use results from Appendix F.)

10-32 In a simple radar that uses a single observation for detection, the threshold voltage is $W_T = 0.92$ V. The rms noise voltage at the detector's input is $\sigma = 0.33$ V and the detector's characteristic is defined by $W = R^2/3$. When a target is present $P_d = 0.9015$.
(*a*) Find P_{fa}.
(*b*) What is the target's signal-to-noise ratio at the detector's input when expressed in dB?

10-33 A radar's envelope detector has the characteristic $g(R) = 0.4R^3$. False alarm probability is 10^{-8} for a single pulse when the noise power at the detector's input is $\sigma^2 = 0.01$ W.
(*a*) What is the threshold voltage W_T?
(*b*) What peak signal amplitude A_0 is needed at the detector's input if the detection probability is to be 0.998 on one pulse?

10-34 A radar uses a square-law envelope detector for which $g(R) = 0.4R^2$. It is known that $P_{fa} = 10^{-4}$ when the input noise power is $\sigma^2 = 0.03$ W. When signal is present, $P_d = 0.92$.
(*a*) Find the threshold voltage W_T.
(*b*) What is A_0, the received signal's peak amplitude?

REVIEW
OF THE
IMPULSE
FUNCTION

There are several ways of defining what is known as the impulse function (Papoulis, 1962) denoted $\delta(x)$. The most mathematically sound approach is to define $\delta(x)$ on the basis of its integral property. If $\phi(x)$ is any arbitrary function of x,† $x_1 < x_2$ are two values of x, and x_0 is the point of "occurrence" of the impulse, then $\delta(x)$ satisfies (Korn and Korn, 1961, p. 742)

$$\int_{x_1}^{x_2} \phi(x)\delta(x - x_0)\,dx = \begin{cases} 0 & x_2 < x_0 \quad \text{or} \quad x_0 < x_1 \\ \frac{1}{2}\left[\phi(x_0^+) + \phi(x_0^-)\right] & x_1 < x_0 < x_2 \\ \frac{1}{2}\phi(x_0^+) & x_0 = x_1 \\ \frac{1}{2}\phi(x_0^-) & x_0 = x_2 \end{cases} \tag{A-1}$$

---

† The function is also assumed to have *bounded variation* in the neighborhood of $x = x_0$ (see footnote, page 369).

It can be shown, using (A-1), that $\delta(x)$ behaves as a function having even symmetry, an area of unity, a vanishingly small "duration," and an infinite "amplitude" (Peebles, 1976, pp. 34–35).

A simpler form of (A-1) is often applicable to many practical situations. If $x_1 = -\infty$, $x_2 = \infty$, and $\phi(x)$ is arbitrary except that it is continuous at $x = x_0$, then

$$\int_{-\infty}^{\infty} \phi(x)\delta(x - x_0)\, dx = \phi(x_0) \tag{A-2}$$

A useful fact that is easily obtained from (A-1) is

$$\int_{-\infty}^{x} \delta(\xi - x_0)\, d\xi = u(x - x_0) \tag{A-3}$$

or, equivalently

$$\frac{du(x)}{dx} = \delta(x) \tag{A-4}$$

where $u(x)$ is the unit-step function defined by

$$u(x) = \begin{cases} 1 & 0 < x \\ 0 & x < 0 \end{cases} \tag{A-5}$$

The impulse function can be generalized to N-dimensional space (Korn and Korn, 1961, p. 745). If we assume a cartesian coordinate system with axes $\xi_1, \xi_2, \ldots, \xi_N$, and a function $\phi(\xi_1, \xi_2, \ldots, \xi_N)$ that is continuous at the point $(\xi_1 = x_1, \xi_2 = x_2, \ldots, \xi_N = x_n)$, then an *N-dimensional impulse function* $\delta(\xi_1, \xi_2, \ldots, \xi_N)$ is defined by

$$\int_{-\infty}^{\infty} \cdots \int_{-\infty}^{\infty} \phi(\xi_1, \xi_2, \ldots, \xi_N)\delta(\xi_1 - x_1, \xi_2 - x_2, \ldots, \xi_N - x_N)\, d\xi_1 \cdots d\xi_N$$

$$= \phi(x_1, x_2, \ldots, x_N) \tag{A-6}$$

Of special interest is the two-dimensional case; it is known that $\delta(\xi_1, \xi_2)$ can be written as (Bracewell, 1965, p. 85)

$$\delta(\xi_1, \xi_2) = \delta(\xi_1)\delta(\xi_2) \tag{A-7}$$

so (A-6) becomes

$$\int_{-\infty}^{\infty} \int_{-\infty}^{\infty} \phi(\xi_1, \xi_2)\delta(\xi_1 - x_1)\delta(\xi_2 - x_2)\, d\xi_1\, d\xi_2 = \phi(x_1, x_2) \tag{A-8}$$

By using (A-7) with an appropriate choice of $\phi(\xi_1, \xi_2)$ we readily find that, for $N = 2$, (A-6) can be written as

$$\int_{-\infty}^{y} \int_{-\infty}^{x} \delta(\xi_1 - x_0, \xi_2 - y_0)\, d\xi_1\, d\xi_2$$

$$= \int_{-\infty}^{y} \delta(\xi_2 - y_0)\, d\xi_2 \int_{-\infty}^{x} \delta(\xi_1 - x_0)\, d\xi_1$$

$$= u(x - x_0)u(y - y_0) \tag{A-9}$$

If $u(x - x_0)u(y - y_0)$ is interpreted as a *two-dimensional unit-step function*

$$u(x - x_0, y - y_0),$$

we have

$$\frac{\partial^2 u(x - x_0, y - y_0)}{\partial x \, \partial y} = \delta(x - x_0, y - y_0) \tag{A-10}$$

where

$$\delta(x - x_0, y - y_0) = \delta(x - x_0)\delta(y - y_0) \tag{A-11}$$

$$u(x - x_0, y - y_0) = u(x - x_0)u(y - y_0) \tag{A-12}$$

APPENDIX
B

GAUSSIAN DISTRIBUTION FUNCTION

The general gaussian or normal probability density and distribution functions are:

$$f_X(x) = \frac{1}{\sqrt{2\pi\sigma_X^2}} e^{-(x-a_X)^2/2\sigma_X^2} \tag{B-1}$$

$$F_X(x) = \int_{-\infty}^{x} f_X(\xi)\, d\xi = F\left(\frac{x-a_X}{\sigma_X}\right) \tag{B-2}$$

where $-\infty < a_X < \infty, 0 < \sigma_X$ are constants and $F(\cdot)$ is the "normalized" distribution function for $a_X = 0$ and $\sigma_X = 1$; that is

$$F(x) = \int_{-\infty}^{x} \frac{1}{\sqrt{2\pi}} e^{-\xi^2/2}\, d\xi \tag{B-3}$$

$F(x)$ is listed in the following table. When $a_X \neq 0$ and $\sigma_X \neq 1$, $F_X(x)$ can be found from $F(x)$ by use of (B-2). For negative values of x, use

$$F(-x) = 1 - F(x) \tag{B-4}$$

A function closely related to $F(x)$ is the Q-function defined by

$$Q(x) = \frac{1}{\sqrt{2\pi}} \int_{x}^{\infty} e^{-\xi^2/2}\, d\xi \tag{B-5}$$

TABLE B-1
Values of $F(x)$ for $0 \leq x \leq 3.89$ in steps of 0.01

x	.00	.01	.02	.03	.04	.05	.06	.07	.08	.09
0.0	.5000	.5040	.5080	.5120	.5160	.5199	.5239	.5279	.5319	.5359
0.1	.5398	.5438	.5478	.5517	.5557	.5596	.5636	.5675	.5714	.5753
0.2	.5793	.5832	.5871	.5910	.5948	.5987	.6026	.6064	.6103	.6141
0.3	.6179	.6217	.6255	.6293	.6331	.6368	.6406	.6443	.6480	.6517
0.4	.6554	.6591	.6628	.6664	.6700	.6736	.6772	.6808	.6844	.6879
0.5	.6915	.6950	.6985	.7019	.7054	.7088	.7123	.7157	.7190	.7224
0.6	.7257	.7291	.7324	.7357	.7389	.7422	.7454	.7486	.7517	.7549
0.7	.7580	.7611	.7642	.7673	.7704	.7734	.7764	.7794	.7823	.7852
0.8	.7881	.7910	.7939	.7967	.7995	.8023	.8051	.8078	.8106	.8133
0.9	.8159	.8186	.8212	.8238	.8264	.8289	.8315	.8340	.8365	.8389
1.0	.8413	.8438	.8461	.8485	.8508	.8531	.8554	.8577	.8599	.8621
1.1	.8643	.8665	.8686	.8708	.8729	.8749	.8770	.8790	.8810	.8830
1.2	.8849	.8869	.8888	.8907	.8925	.8944	.8962	.8980	.8997	.9015
1.3	.9032	.9049	.9066	.9082	.9099	.9115	.9131	.9147	.9162	.9177
1.4	.9192	.9207	.9222	.9236	.9251	.9265	.9279	.9292	.9306	.9319
1.5	.9332	.9345	.9357	.9370	.9382	.9394	.9406	.9418	.9429	.9441
1.6	.9452	.9463	.9474	.9484	.9495	.9505	.9515	.9525	.9535	.9545
1.7	.9554	.9564	.9573	.9582	.9591	.9599	.9608	.9616	.9625	.9633
1.8	.9641	.9649	.9656	.9664	.9671	.9678	.9686	.9693	.9699	.9706
1.9	.9713	.9719	.9726	.9732	.9738	.9744	.9750	.9756	.9761	.9767
2.0	.9773	.9778	.9783	.9788	.9793	.9798	.9803	.9808	.9812	.9817
2.1	.9821	.9826	.9830	.9834	.9838	.9842	.9846	.9850	.9854	.9857
2.2	.9861	.9864	.9868	.9871	.9875	.9878	.9881	.9884	.9887	.9890
2.3	.9893	.9896	.9898	.9901	.9904	.9906	.9909	.9911	.9913	.9916
2.4	.9918	.9920	.9922	.9925	.9927	.9929	.9931	.9932	.9934	.9936
2.5	.9938	.9940	.9941	.9943	.9945	.9946	.9948	.9949	.9951	.9952
2.6	.9953	.9955	.9956	.9957	.9959	.9960	.9961	.9962	.9963	.9964
2.7	.9965	.9966	.9967	.9968	.9969	.9970	.9971	.9972	.9973	.9974
2.8	.9974	.9975	.9976	.9977	.9977	.9978	.9979	.9979	.9980	.9981
2.9	.9981	.9982	.9982	.9983	.9984	.9984	.9985	.9985	.9986	.9986
3.0	.9987	.9987	.9987	.9988	.9988	.9989	.9989	.9989	.9990	.9990
3.1	.9990	.9991	.9991	.9991	.9992	.9992	.9992	.9992	.9993	.9993
3.2	.9993	.9993	.9994	.9994	.9994	.9994	.9994	.9995	.9995	.9995
3.3	.9995	.9995	.9996	.9996	.9996	.9996	.9996	.9996	.9996	.9997
3.4	.9997	.9997	.9997	.9997	.9997	.9997	.9997	.9997	.9998	.9998
3.5	.9998	.9998	.9998	.9998	.9998	.9998	.9998	.9998	.9998	.9998
3.6	.9998	.9999	.9999	.9999	.9999	.9999	.9999	.9999	.9999	.9999
3.7	.9999	.9999	.9999	.9999	.9999	.9999	.9999	.9999	.9999	.9999
3.8	.9999	.9999	.9999	.9999	.9999	.9999	.9999	1.0000	1.0000	1.0000

For negative values of x, use

$$Q(-x) = 1 - Q(x) \qquad \text{(B-6)}$$

$Q(x)$ is related to $F(x)$ by

$$F(x) = 1 - Q(x) \qquad \text{(B-7)}$$

Although a closed-form solution for $Q(x)$ is not known, an excellent approximation is

$$Q(x) \approx \left[\frac{1}{0.661x + 0.339\sqrt{x^2 + 5.51}} \right] \frac{e^{-x^2/2}}{\sqrt{2\pi}} \qquad x \geq 0 \qquad \text{(B-8)}$$

which is due to Börjesson and Sundberg, 1979. The maximum absolute relative error in the approximation for $Q(x)$ is given as 0.27 percent for any $x \geq 0$. By using the approximation (B-8) for $Q(x)$ in (B-7), an excellent approximation for $F(x)$ is realized.

APPENDIX
C

USEFUL
MATHEMATICAL
QUANTITIES

TRIGONOMETRIC IDENTITIES

$$\cos (x \pm y) = \cos (x) \cos (y) \mp \sin (x) \sin (y) \qquad \text{(C-1)}$$

$$\sin (x \pm y) = \sin (x) \cos (y) \pm \cos (x) \sin (y) \qquad \text{(C-2)}$$

$$\cos \left(x \pm \frac{\pi}{2} \right) = \mp \sin (x) \qquad \text{(C-3)}$$

$$\sin \left(x \pm \frac{\pi}{2} \right) = \pm \cos (x) \qquad \text{(C-4)}$$

$$\cos (2x) = \cos^2 (x) - \sin^2 (x) \qquad \text{(C-5)}$$

$$\sin (2x) = 2 \sin (x) \cos (x) \qquad \text{(C-6)}$$

$$2 \cos (x) = e^{jx} + e^{-jx} \qquad \text{(C-7)}$$

$$2j \sin (x) = e^{jx} - e^{-jx} \qquad \text{(C-8)}$$

$$2 \cos (x) \cos (y) = \cos (x - y) + \cos (x + y) \qquad \text{(C-9)}$$

$$2 \sin (x) \sin (y) = \cos (x - y) - \cos (x + y) \qquad \text{(C-10)}$$

$$2 \sin (x) \cos (y) = \sin (x - y) + \sin (x + y) \qquad \text{(C-11)}$$

$$2 \cos^2 (x) = 1 + \cos (2x) \qquad \text{(C-12)}$$

$$2 \sin^2(x) = 1 - \cos(2x) \tag{C-13}$$

$$4 \cos^3(x) = 3 \cos(x) + \cos(3x) \tag{C-14}$$

$$4 \sin^3(x) = 3 \sin(x) - \sin(3x) \tag{C-15}$$

$$8 \cos^4(x) = 3 + 4 \cos(2x) + \cos 4x) \tag{C-16}$$

$$8 \sin^4(x) = 3 - 4 \cos(2x) + \cos(4x) \tag{C-17}$$

$$A \cos(x) - B \sin(x) = R \cos(x + \theta) \tag{C-18}$$

where

$$R = \sqrt{A^2 + B^2} \tag{C-19a}$$

$$\theta = \tan^{-1}(B/A) \tag{C-19b}$$

$$A = R \cos(\theta) \tag{C-19c}$$

$$B = R \sin(\theta) \tag{C-19d}$$

INDEFINITE INTEGRALS

Rational Algebraic Functions

$$\int (a + bx)^n \, dx = \frac{(a + bx)^{n+1}}{b(n + 1)} \qquad 0 < n \tag{C-20}$$

$$\int \frac{dx}{a + bx} = \frac{1}{b} \ln |a + bx| \tag{C-21}$$

$$\int \frac{dx}{(a + bx)^n} = \frac{-1}{(n - 1)b(a + bx)^{n-1}} \qquad 1 < n \tag{C-22}$$

$$\int \frac{dx}{c + bx + ax^2} = \frac{2}{\sqrt{4ac - b^2}} \tan^{-1}\left(\frac{2ax + b}{\sqrt{4ac - b^2}}\right) \qquad b^2 < 4ac$$

$$= \frac{1}{\sqrt{b^2 - 4ac}} \ln \left| \frac{2ax + b - \sqrt{b^2 - 4ac}}{2ax + b + \sqrt{b^2 - 4ac}} \right| \qquad b^2 > 4ac$$

$$= \frac{-2}{2ax + b} \qquad b^2 = 4ac \tag{C-23}$$

$$\int \frac{x \, dx}{c + bx + ax^2} = \frac{1}{2a} \ln |ax^2 + bx + c| - \frac{b}{2a} \int \frac{dx}{c + bx + ax^2} \tag{C-24}$$

$$\int \frac{dx}{a^2 + b^2x^2} = \frac{1}{ab} \tan^{-1}\left(\frac{bx}{a}\right) \tag{C-25}$$

$$\int \frac{x\,dx}{a^2 + x^2} = \frac{1}{2} \ln (a^2 + x^2) \tag{C-26}$$

$$\int \frac{x^2\,dx}{a^2 + x^2} = x - a \tan^{-1} \left(\frac{x}{a}\right) \tag{C-27}$$

$$\int \frac{dx}{(a^2 + x^2)^2} = \frac{x}{2a^2(a^2 + x^2)} + \frac{1}{2a^3} \tan^{-1} \left(\frac{x}{a}\right) \tag{C-28}$$

$$\int \frac{x\,dx}{(a^2 + x^2)^2} = \frac{-1}{2(a^2 + x^2)} \tag{C-29}$$

$$\int \frac{x^2\,dx}{(a^2 + x^2)^2} = \frac{-x}{2(a^2 + x^2)} + \frac{1}{2a} \tan^{-1} \left(\frac{x}{a}\right) \tag{C-30}$$

$$\int \frac{dx}{(a^2 + x^2)^3} = \frac{x}{4a^2(a^2 + x^2)^2} + \frac{3x}{8a^4(a^2 + x^2)} + \frac{3}{8a^5} \tan^{-1} \left(\frac{x}{a}\right) \tag{C-31}$$

$$\int \frac{x^2\,dx}{(a^2 + x^2)^3} = \frac{-x}{4(a^2 + x^2)^2} + \frac{x}{8a^2(a^2 + x^2)} + \frac{1}{8a^3} \tan^{-1} \left(\frac{x}{a}\right) \tag{C-32}$$

$$\int \frac{x^4\,dx}{(a^2 + x^2)^3} = \frac{a^2x}{4(a^2 + x^2)^2} - \frac{5x}{8(a^2 + x^2)} + \frac{3}{8a} \tan^{-1} \left(\frac{x}{a}\right) \tag{C-33}$$

$$\int \frac{dx}{(a^2 + x^2)^4} = \frac{x}{6a^2(a^2 + x^2)^3} + \frac{5x}{24a^4(a^2 + x^2)^2} + \frac{5x}{16a^6(a^2 + x^2)} + \frac{5}{16a^7} \tan^{-1} \left(\frac{x}{a}\right) \tag{C-34}$$

$$\int \frac{x^2\,dx}{(a^2 + x^2)^4} = \frac{-x}{6(a^2 + x^2)^3} + \frac{x}{24a^2(a^2 + x^2)^2} + \frac{x}{16a^4(a^2 + x^2)} + \frac{1}{16a^5} \tan^{-1} \left(\frac{x}{a}\right) \tag{C-35}$$

$$\int \frac{x^4\,dx}{(a^2 + x^2)^4} = \frac{a^2x}{6(a^2 + x^2)^3} - \frac{7x}{24(a^2 + x^2)^2} + \frac{x}{16a^2(a^2 + x^2)} + \frac{1}{16a^3} \tan^{-1} \left(\frac{x}{a}\right) \tag{C-36}$$

$$\int \frac{dx}{a^4 + x^4} = \frac{1}{4a^3\sqrt{2}} \ln \left(\frac{x^2 + ax\sqrt{2} + a^2}{x^2 - ax\sqrt{2} + a^2}\right) + \frac{1}{2a^3\sqrt{2}} \tan^{-1} \left(\frac{ax\sqrt{2}}{a^2 - x^2}\right) \tag{C-37}$$

$$\int \frac{x^2\,dx}{a^4 + x^4} = -\frac{1}{4a\sqrt{2}} \ln \left(\frac{x^2 + ax\sqrt{2} + a^2}{x^2 - ax\sqrt{2} + a^2}\right) + \frac{1}{2a\sqrt{2}} \tan^{-1} \left(\frac{ax\sqrt{2}}{a^2 - x^2}\right) \tag{C-38}$$

Trigonometric Functions

$$\int \cos (x)\,dx = \sin (x) \tag{C-39}$$

$$\int x \cos(x)\, dx = \cos(x) + x \sin(x) \tag{C-40}$$

$$\int x^2 \cos(x)\, dx = 2x \cos(x) + (x^2 - 2) \sin(x) \tag{C-41}$$

$$\int \sin(x)\, dx = -\cos(x) \tag{C-42}$$

$$\int x \sin(x)\, dx = \sin(x) - x \cos(x) \tag{C-43}$$

$$\int x^2 \sin(x)\, dx = 2x \sin(x) - (x^2 - 2) \cos(x) \tag{C-44}$$

Exponential Functions

$$\int e^{ax}\, dx = \frac{e^{ax}}{a} \qquad a \text{ real or complex} \tag{C-45}$$

$$\int x e^{ax}\, dx = e^{ax}\left[\frac{x}{a} - \frac{1}{a^2}\right] \qquad a \text{ real or complex} \tag{C-46}$$

$$\int x^2 e^{ax}\, dx = e^{ax}\left[\frac{x^2}{a} - \frac{2x}{a^2} + \frac{2}{a^3}\right] \qquad a \text{ real or complex} \tag{C-47}$$

$$\int x^3 e^{ax}\, dx = e^{ax}\left[\frac{x^3}{a} - \frac{3x^2}{a^2} + \frac{6x}{a^3} - \frac{6}{a^4}\right] \qquad a \text{ real or complex} \tag{C-48}$$

$$\int e^{ax} \sin(x)\, dx = \frac{e^{ax}}{a^2 + 1}[a \sin(x) - \cos(x)] \tag{C-49}$$

$$\int e^{ax} \cos(x)\, dx = \frac{e^{ax}}{a^2 + 1}[a \cos(x) + \sin(x)] \tag{C-50}$$

DEFINITE INTEGRALS

$$\int_{-\infty}^{\infty} e^{-a^2 x^2 + bx}\, dx = \frac{\sqrt{\pi}}{a} e^{b^2/(4a^2)} \qquad a > 0 \tag{C-51}$$

$$\int_{0}^{\infty} x^2 e^{-x^2}\, dx = \sqrt{\pi}/4 \tag{C-52}$$

$$\int_{0}^{\infty} \mathrm{Sa}(x)\, dx = \int_{0}^{\infty} \frac{\sin(x)}{x}\, dx = \frac{\pi}{2} \tag{C-53}$$

$$\int_0^\infty \mathrm{Sa}^2(x)\, dx = \pi/2 \tag{C-54}$$

FINITE SERIES

$$\sum_{n=1}^N n = \frac{N(N+1)}{2} \tag{C-55}$$

$$\sum_{n=1}^N n^2 = \frac{N(N+1)(2N+1)}{6} \tag{C-56}$$

$$\sum_{n=1}^N n^3 = \frac{N^2(N+1)^2}{4} \tag{C-57}$$

$$\sum_{n=0}^N x^n = \frac{x^{N+1}-1}{x-1} \tag{C-58}$$

$$\sum_{n=0}^N \frac{N!}{n!(N-n)!}\, x^n y^{N-n} = (x+y)^N \tag{C-59}$$

$$\sum_{n=0}^N e^{j(\theta+n\phi)} = \frac{\sin\left[(N+1)\phi/2\right]}{\sin(\phi/2)}\, e^{j[\theta+(N\phi/2)]} \tag{C-60}$$

$$\sum_{n=0}^N \binom{N}{n} = \sum_{n=0}^N \frac{N!}{n!(N-n)!} = 2^N \tag{C-61}$$

INFINITE SERIES

$$e^x = 1 + x + \frac{x^2}{2!} + \frac{x^3}{3!} + \cdots = \sum_{n=0}^\infty \frac{x^n}{n!} \tag{C-62}$$

APPENDIX
D

REVIEW
OF
FOURIER
TRANSFORMS

The *Fourier transform*† or spectrum $X(\omega)$ of a signal $x(t)$ is given by

$$X(\omega) = \int_{-\infty}^{\infty} x(t)e^{-j\omega t}\, dt \tag{D-1}$$

The *inverse Fourier transform* allows the recovery of $x(t)$ from its spectrum $X(\omega)$. It is given by

$$x(t) = \frac{1}{2\pi} \int_{-\infty}^{\infty} X(\omega)e^{j\omega t}\, d\omega \tag{D-2}$$

Together, (D-1) and (D-2) form a *Fourier transform pair*. Extensive tables of transform pairs exist (Campbell and Foster, 1948). A transform pair is often symbolized by use of a double-ended arrow:

$$x(t) \leftrightarrow X(\omega) \tag{D-3}$$

The Fourier transform $X(\omega)$ is valid for real or complex signals, and, in general, is a complex function of ω even for real signals $x(t)$. $X(\omega)$ describes the

---

† Named for the great French mathematician and physicist Baron Jean Baptiste Joseph Fourier (1768–1830).

368

relative complex voltages (amplitudes and phases) as a function of ω that are present in a waveform $x(t)$. From (D-1), we see that the unit of $X(\omega)$ is volts per hertz if $x(t)$ is a voltage-time waveform. Thus, $X(\omega)$ can be considered as the *density of voltage* in $x(t)$ as a function of angular frequency ω.

EXISTENCE

Conditions that guarantee the existence of the Fourier transform of a waveform $x(t)$ are:

1. that $x(t)$ be bounded with at most a finite number of maxima and minima and a finite number of discontinuities in any finite time interval,† and

2.
$$\int_{-\infty}^{\infty} |x(t)| \, dt < \infty \tag{D-4}$$

These conditions are only *sufficient* for $X(\omega)$ to exist; they are *not necessary*. Many signals of practical interest do not satisfy these conditions but do have transforms. Examples are: the unit-impulse function $\delta(t)$ that has the transform $X(\omega) = 1$; and the unit-step function $u(t)$, defined by $u(t) = 1$ for $0 < t$ and $u(t) = 0$ for $t < 0$, that has the transform $X(\omega) = \pi\delta(\omega) + (1/j\omega)$.

PROPERTIES

A number of extremely useful properties of Fourier transforms may be stated. We give these without proofs since the proofs may readily be found in the literature (Peebles, 1976, p. 29; Papoulis, 1962, p. 14). In these properties, we assume the Fourier transform of some signal $x(t)$ is $X(\omega)$, while the notation $X_n(\omega)$ implies the transform of a signal $x_n(t)$ with $n = 1, 2, \ldots, N$.

Linearity

For constants α_n (that may be complex):

$$x(t) = \sum_{n=1}^{N} \alpha_n x_n(t) \leftrightarrow \sum_{n=1}^{N} \alpha_n X_n(\omega) = X(\omega) \tag{D-5}$$

Time and Frequency Shifting

With t_0 and ω_0 real constants:

$$x(t - t_0) \leftrightarrow X(\omega)e^{-j\omega t_0} \tag{D-6}$$

$$x(t)e^{j\omega_0 t} \leftrightarrow X(\omega - \omega_0) \tag{D-7}$$

---

† These are known as the *Dirichlet conditions*, after the German mathematician Peter Gustov Lejeune Dirichlet (1805–1859). A signal satisfying them is said to have *bounded variation* (Thomas, 1969, p. 579).

Scaling

With α a real constant:

$$x(\alpha t) \leftrightarrow \frac{1}{|\alpha|} X\left(\frac{\omega}{\alpha}\right) \tag{D-8}$$

Duality

$$X(t) \leftrightarrow 2\pi x(-\omega) \tag{D-9}$$

Differentiation

$$\frac{d^n x(t)}{dt^n} \leftrightarrow (j\omega)^n X(\omega) \tag{D-10}$$

$$(-jt)^n x(t) \leftrightarrow \frac{d^n X(\omega)}{d\omega^n} \tag{D-11}$$

Integration

$$\int_{-\infty}^{t} x(\tau) \, d\tau \leftrightarrow \pi X(0)\delta(\omega) + \frac{X(\omega)}{j\omega} \tag{D-12}$$

$$\pi x(0)\delta(t) - \frac{x(t)}{jt} \leftrightarrow \int_{-\infty}^{\omega} X(\xi) \, d\xi \tag{D-13}$$

Conjugation

$$x^*(t) \leftrightarrow X^*(-\omega) \tag{D-14}$$

$$x^*(-t) \leftrightarrow X^*(\omega) \tag{D-15}$$

Convolution

$$x(t) = \int_{-\infty}^{\infty} x_1(\tau)x_2(t-\tau) \, d\tau \leftrightarrow X_1(\omega)X_2(\omega) = X(\omega) \tag{D-16}$$

$$x(t) = x_1(t)x_2(t) \leftrightarrow \frac{1}{2\pi} \int_{-\infty}^{\infty} X_1(\xi)X_2(\omega - \xi) \, d\xi = X(\omega) \tag{D-17}$$

Correlation

$$x(t) = \int_{-\infty}^{\infty} x_1^*(\tau)x_2(\tau + t) \, d\tau \leftrightarrow X_1^*(\omega)X_2(\omega) = X(\omega) \tag{D-18}$$

$$x(t) = x_1^*(t)x_2(t) \leftrightarrow \frac{1}{2\pi} \int_{-\infty}^{\infty} X_1^*(\xi)X_2(\xi + \omega) \, d\xi = X(\omega) \tag{D-19}$$

Parseval's† Theorem

$$\int_{-\infty}^{\infty} x_1^*(\tau)x_2(\tau)\,d\tau = \frac{1}{2\pi}\int_{-\infty}^{\infty} X_1^*(\omega)X_2(\omega)\,d\omega \tag{D-20}$$

An alternative form occurs when $x_1(t) = x_2(t) = x(t)$:

$$\int_{-\infty}^{\infty} |x(t)|^2\,dt = \frac{1}{2\pi}\int_{-\infty}^{\infty} |X(\omega)|^2\,d\omega \tag{D-21}$$

MULTIDIMENSIONAL FOURIER TRANSFORMS

The Fourier transform $X(\omega_1, \omega_2)$ of a function $x(t_1, t_2)$ of two "time" variables t_1 and t_2 is defined as the iterated double transform. Upon Fourier transforming $x(t_1, t_2)$ first with respect to t_1 we have

$$X(\omega_1, t_2) = \int_{-\infty}^{\infty} x(t_1, t_2)e^{-j\omega_1 t_1}\,dt_1 \tag{D-22}$$

$X(\omega_1, \omega_2)$ results from Fourier transformation of $X(\omega_1, t_2)$ with respect to t_2:

$$X(\omega_1, \omega_2) = \int_{-\infty}^{\infty} X(\omega_1, t_2)e^{-j\omega_2 t_2}\,dt_2 \tag{D-23}$$

or

$$X(\omega_1, \omega_2) = \int_{-\infty}^{\infty}\int_{-\infty}^{\infty} x(t_1, t_2)e^{-j\omega_1 t_1 - j\omega_2 t_2}\,dt_1\,dt_2 \tag{D-24}$$

By use of similar logic, the two-dimensional inverse Fourier transform is

$$x(t_1, t_2) = \frac{1}{(2\pi)^2}\int_{-\infty}^{\infty}\int_{-\infty}^{\infty} X(\omega_1, \omega_2)e^{j\omega_1 t_1 + j\omega_2 t_2}\,d\omega_1\,d\omega_2 \tag{D-25}$$

The extension of the above procedures to an N-dimensional function is direct; we obtain the Fourier transform pair

$$X(\omega_1, \ldots, \omega_N) = \int_{-\infty}^{\infty}\cdots\int_{-\infty}^{\infty} x(t_1, \ldots, t_N)e^{-j\omega_1 t_1 - \cdots - j\omega_N t_N}\,dt_1\cdots dt_N \tag{D-26}$$

$$x(t_1, \ldots, t_N) = \frac{1}{(2\pi)^N}\int_{-\infty}^{\infty}\cdots\int_{-\infty}^{\infty} X(\omega_1, \ldots, \omega_N)e^{j\omega_1 t_1 + \cdots + j\omega_N t_N}\,d\omega_1\cdots d\omega_N$$

$$\tag{D-27}$$

---

† Named for M. A. Parseval (1755–1836), a French mathematician.

PROBLEMS

D-1   Find the Fourier transform of a pulse $x(t)$ defined by

$$x(t) = \begin{cases} A & -\tau/2 < t < \tau/2 \\ 0 & \text{elsewhere} \end{cases}$$

where $\tau > 0$ and A are real constants.

D-2   If a signal $y(t)$ is the product of $x(t)$ of Problem D-1 with a cosine wave, that is, if

$$y(t) = x(t) \cos(\omega_0 t + \theta_0)$$

where ω_0 and θ_0 are real constants, what is the Fourier transform of $y(t)$?

D-3   Find the Fourier transform of the waveform

$$x(t) = \begin{cases} A\left(1 - \dfrac{|t|}{\tau}\right) & |t| \le \tau \\ 0 & |t| > \tau \end{cases}$$

where $\tau > 0$ and A are real constants.

D-4   By direct use of (D-1), find the Fourier transform of the waveform

$$x(t) = \begin{cases} A \cos(\pi t/2\tau) & |t| \le \tau \\ 0 & |t| > \tau \end{cases}$$

where $\tau > 0$ and A are real constants.

D-5   The waveform of Problem D-4 can be written in the form

$$x(t) = A \, \text{rect} \, (t/2\tau) \cos(\pi t/2\tau)$$

where rect $(t/2\tau)$ is defined by (E-2). By using (D-19), find the Fourier transform of $x(t)$.

D-6   The complex form of the *Fourier series* of an arbitrary periodic signal $y(t)$ of period T is

$$y(t) = \sum_{n=-\infty}^{\infty} C_n e^{jn2\pi t/T}$$

where the *Fourier series coefficients* are given by

$$C_n = \frac{1}{T} \int_{-T/2}^{T/2} y(t) e^{-jn2\pi t/T} \, dt$$

for $n = 0, \pm 1, \pm 2, \ldots$. Show that the Fourier transform of this arbitrary periodic signal is

$$Y(\omega) = 2\pi \sum_{n=-\infty}^{\infty} C_n \delta\left(\omega - \frac{n2\pi}{T}\right)$$

where $\delta(\cdot)$ is the unit-impulse function of Appendix A.

★D-7 Prove the Fourier transform pair

$$\sum_{n=-\infty}^{\infty} \delta(t - nT) \leftrightarrow \frac{2\pi}{T} \sum_{n=-\infty}^{\infty} \delta\left(\omega - \frac{n2\pi}{T}\right)$$

where $T > 0$ is a real constant and $\delta(\cdot)$ is the impulse function of Appendix A. (*Hint:* Represent the time function by a complex Fourier series as in Problem D-6, find the Fourier coefficients of the series, and then Fourier-transform the series.)

★D-8 From the expression in Problem D-7, it is readily shown that

$$\sum_{n=-\infty}^{\infty} e^{-jn\omega T} = \frac{2\pi}{T} \sum_{n=-\infty}^{\infty} \delta\left(\omega - \frac{n2\pi}{T}\right)$$

Use this result to prove that the periodic signal

$$y(t) = \sum_{n=-\infty}^{\infty} x(t - nT)$$

comprised of repetitions in each period T of a basic waveform $x(t)$, has the Fourier transform $Y(\omega)$ given by

$$Y(\omega) = \frac{2\pi}{T} \sum_{n=-\infty}^{\infty} X\left(\frac{n2\pi}{T}\right) \delta\left(\omega - \frac{n2\pi}{T}\right)$$

where $X(\omega)$ is the Fourier transform of $x(t)$. By using the result of Problem D-6, we see that the coefficient C_n of the Fourier series of $y(t)$ is related to the Fourier transform of its component waveform $x(t)$ by

$$C_n = \frac{1}{T} X\left(\frac{n2\pi}{T}\right)$$

D-9 Find the Fourier transform of the waveform

$$x(t) = u(t)e^{j\omega_0 t}$$

where $u(\cdot)$ is the unit-step function of (A-5) and ω_0 is a real constant.

D-10 Find the Fourier transform of a sequence of $2N + 1$ pulses of the form given in Problem D-1, where $N = 0, 1, 2, \ldots$. That is, find the transform of

$$y(t) = \sum_{n=-N}^{N} x(t - nT)$$

with $T > 0$ a real constant and $\tau < T$.

D-11 Determine the Fourier transform of the signal

$$x(t) = \begin{cases} At^2 & 0 < t < \tau \\ 0 & \text{elsewhere} \end{cases}$$

where $\tau > 0$ and A are real constants.

D-12 Show that the inverse Fourier transform of the function

$$X(\omega) = \begin{cases} K & -W < \omega < W \\ 0 & \text{elsewhere} \end{cases}$$

is

$$x(t) = (KW/\pi)\, \text{Sa}\,(Wt)$$

where $W > 0$ and K are real constants and Sa $(\cdot)$ is the *sampling function* defined by (E-3).

D-13 The transfer function $H(\omega)$ of a lowpass filter can be approximated by

$$H(\omega) = \begin{cases} K_0 + 2 \sum_{n=1}^{N} K_n \cos(n\pi\omega/W) & -W < \omega < W \\ 0 & \text{elsewhere} \end{cases}$$

Here $W > 0, K_0, K_1, \ldots, K_N$ are real constants and $N \geq 0$ is an integer. Find the inverse Fourier transform $h(t)$ of $H(\omega)$ which is the *impulse response* of the network, in terms of sampling functions (see Problem D-12).

D-14 Let $x(t)$ have the Fourier transform $X(\omega)$. Find the transforms of the following functions in terms of $X(\omega)$:

(a) $x(t-2) \exp(j\omega_0 t)$ (b) $\dfrac{dx(t)}{dt} \exp[j\omega_0(t-3)]$ (c) $x(t-3) - 3x(2t)$

Here ω_0 is a real constant.

D-15 If $x(t) \leftrightarrow X(\omega)$, find the inverse transforms of the following functions in terms of $x(t)$:

(a) $X(\omega)X^*(\omega + \omega_0)$ (b) $X(\omega - \omega_0) \dfrac{dX(\omega)}{d\omega}$ (c) $X^*(-\omega) + X(\omega)$

Here * represents complex conjugation and ω_0 is a real constant.

D-16 A voltage $x(t)$ exists across a resistor of resistance R. Show that the real energy E expended in the resistance is

$$E = \frac{1}{2\pi R} \int_{-\infty}^{\infty} |X(\omega)|^2 \, d\omega$$

where $X(\omega)$ is the Fourier transform of $x(t)$.

D-17 It is known that

$$x(t) = e^{-\alpha|t|} \leftrightarrow \frac{2\alpha}{\alpha^2 + \omega^2} = X(\omega)$$

where $\alpha > 0$ is a real constant. Find the Fourier transform $Y(\omega)$ of

$$y(t) = \frac{6}{4 + t^2}$$

D-18 Use the definition (A-2) of an impulse function to prove that the impulse has the Fourier transform 1. That is, show that

$$\delta(t) \leftrightarrow 1$$

D-19 By use of various Fourier transform properties, show that the following are true:

(a) $A \leftrightarrow A(2\pi)\delta(\omega)$ where A is a constant

(b) $\cos(\omega_0 t) \leftrightarrow \pi[\delta(\omega - \omega_0) + \delta(\omega + \omega_0)]$ where ω_0 is a real constant

D-20 Use the facts that

$$u(t)e^{-\alpha t} \leftrightarrow \frac{1}{\alpha + j\omega}$$

and

$$\cos(\omega_0 t) \leftrightarrow \pi[\delta(\omega - \omega_0) + \delta(\omega + \omega_0)]$$

where $\alpha > 0$ and ω_0 are real constants, to prove that

$$u(t)e^{-\alpha t}\cos(\omega_0 t) \leftrightarrow \frac{\alpha + j\omega}{(\alpha^2 + \omega_0^2 - \omega^2) + j(2\alpha\omega)}$$

D-21 Prove (D-6) and (D-10).

★**D-22** Prove (D-12). [*Hint:* Use (D-16).]

D-23 Prove (D-18).

D-24 Find the Fourier transform of the signal

$$x(t_1, t_2) = \begin{cases} A & -\tau_1 < t_1 < \tau_1 \quad \text{and} \quad -\tau_2 < t_2 < \tau_2 \\ 0 & \text{elsewhere} \end{cases}$$

where $\tau_1 > 0$, $\tau_2 > 0$, and A are real constants.

ADDITIONAL PROBLEMS, THIRD EDITION

D-25 By direct transformation, find the Fourier transform of

$$x(t) = \begin{cases} At & 0 < t < \tau \\ 0 & t < 0 \text{ and } t > \tau \end{cases}$$

D-26 Show that a frequency-doman impulse can be represented by

$$\delta(\omega) = \frac{1}{2\pi} \int_{-\infty}^{\infty} e^{-j\omega t}\, dt$$

D-27 Show that a time-domain impulse can be represented by

$$\delta(t) = \frac{1}{2\pi} \int_{-\infty}^{\infty} e^{j\omega t}\, d\omega$$

D-28 First find the spectrum of the signal $x(t) = A \exp[-W|t|]$, where $A > 0$ and $W > 0$ are constants, and then use the result with the frequency shifting property of Fourier transforms to determine the spectrum of $y(t) = A \exp[-W|t|] \cos(\omega_0 t)$, where $\omega_0 > 0$ is a constant.

D-29 A waveform $x(t)$ and its Fourier transform are defined by the pair

$$u(t)t^3 e^{-\alpha t} \leftrightarrow \frac{6}{(\alpha + j\omega)^4}$$

where $\alpha > 0$ is a constant. Use the duality property to develop a dual transform pair.

D-30 A waveform $x(t)$ has a derivative $y(t) = dx(t)/dt$ and spectrum $Y(\omega)$ defined by the Fourier transform pair

$$y(t) = \left\{ \begin{array}{l} \delta(t + 3\tau) + \delta(t + \tau) \\ -\delta(t - 3\tau) - \delta(t - \tau) \end{array} \right\} \leftrightarrow Y(\omega) = \left\{ \begin{array}{l} e^{j3\omega\tau} + e^{j\omega\tau} \\ -e^{-j3\omega\tau} - e^{-j\omega\tau} \end{array} \right\}$$

where τ is a positive constant. (a) Sketch $x(t)$. (b) Find $X(\omega)$, the spectrum of $x(t)$, by use of the integral property of Fourier transforms.

D-31 A waveform $x(t)$ has a Fourier transform

$$X(\omega) = A \operatorname{rect}\left[\frac{\omega - \omega_0}{W}\right] \cos^2\left[\frac{\pi(\omega - \omega_0)}{W}\right]$$

$$+ A \operatorname{rect}\left[\frac{\omega + \omega_0}{W}\right] \cos^2\left[\frac{\pi(\omega + \omega_0)}{W}\right]$$

where A, W, and $\omega_0 > W/2$ are all positive constants. (a) Find $x(t)$. (b) Find the energy in $x(t)$ by use of Parseval's theorem.

TABLE
OF
USEFUL
FOURIER
TRANSFORMS

In the following table of Fourier transform pairs, we define

$$u(\xi) = \begin{cases} 1 & \xi > 0 \\ 0 & \xi < 0 \end{cases} \tag{E-1}$$

$$\text{rect}\,(\xi) = \begin{cases} 1 & |\xi| < {}^1\!/_2 \\ 0 & |\xi| > {}^1\!/_2 \end{cases} \tag{E-2}$$

$$\text{Sa}\,(\xi) = \frac{\sin\,(\xi)}{\xi} \tag{E-3}$$

$$\text{tri}\,(\xi) = \begin{cases} 1 - |\xi| & |\xi| < 1 \\ 0 & |\xi| > 1 \end{cases} \tag{E-4}$$

$$x(t) \leftrightarrow X(\omega) \tag{E-5}$$

and let α, τ, σ, ω_0, and W be real constants.

TABLE E-1
Fourier Transform Pairs

Pair	$x(t)$	$X(\omega)$	Notes
1	$\alpha\delta(t)$	α	
2	$\alpha/2\pi$	$\alpha\delta(\omega)$	
3	$u(t)$	$\pi\delta(\omega) + (1/j\omega)$	
4	$\frac{1}{2}\delta(t) - \dfrac{1}{j2\pi t}$	$u(\omega)$	
5	$\text{rect}\,(t/\tau)$	$\tau\,\text{Sa}\,(\omega\tau/2)$	$\tau > 0$
6	$(W/\pi)\,\text{Sa}\,(Wt)$	$\text{rect}\,(\omega/2W)$	$W > 0$
7	$\text{tri}\,(t/\tau)$	$\tau\,\text{Sa}^2\,(\omega\tau/2)$	$\tau > 0$
8	$(W/\pi)\,\text{Sa}^2\,(Wt)$	$\text{tri}\,(\omega/2W)$	$W > 0$
9	$e^{j\omega_0 t}$	$2\pi\delta(\omega - \omega_0)$	
10	$\delta(t - \tau)$	$e^{-j\omega\tau}$	
11	$\cos(\omega_0 t)$	$\pi[\delta(\omega - \omega_0) + \delta(\omega + \omega_0)]$	
12	$\sin(\omega_0 t)$	$-j\pi[\delta(\omega - \omega_0) - \delta(\omega + \omega_0)]$	
13	$u(t)\cos(\omega_0 t)$	$\dfrac{\pi}{2}[\delta(\omega - \omega_0) + \delta(\omega + \omega_0)] + \dfrac{j\omega}{\omega_0^2 - \omega^2}$	
14	$u(t)\sin(\omega_0 t)$	$-j\dfrac{\pi}{2}[\delta(\omega - \omega_0) - \delta(\omega + \omega_0)] + \dfrac{\omega_0}{\omega_0^2 - \omega^2}$	
15	$u(t)e^{-\alpha t}$	$\dfrac{1}{\alpha + j\omega}$	$\alpha > 0$
16	$u(t)te^{-\alpha t}$	$\dfrac{1}{(\alpha + j\omega)^2}$	$\alpha > 0$
17	$u(t)t^2 e^{-\alpha t}$	$\dfrac{2}{(\alpha + j\omega)^3}$	$\alpha > 0$
18	$u(t)t^3 e^{-\alpha t}$	$\dfrac{6}{(\alpha + j\omega)^4}$	$\alpha > 0$
19	$e^{-\alpha|t|}$	$\dfrac{2\alpha}{\alpha^2 + \omega^2}$	$\alpha > 0$
20	$e^{-t^2/(2\sigma^2)}$	$\sigma\sqrt{2\pi}\,e^{-\sigma^2\omega^2/2}$	$\sigma > 0$

SOME PROBABILITY DENSITIES AND DISTRIBUTIONS

For convenience of reference we list below the probability density $f_X(x)$ and distribution function $F_X(x)$ for some well-known distributions. Where appropriate, we also give the mean $\bar{X}$, variance σ_X^2, and characteristic function $\Phi_X(\omega)$.

A number of constants and functions are used as defined below:†

$$a, a_1, a_2, b, b_1, b_2, \sigma, \text{ and } p \text{ are real constants} \tag{F-1a}$$

$$N \text{ is a positive integer} \tag{F-1b}$$

$$\delta(\xi) = \text{impulse function of (2.3-2)} \tag{F-1c}$$

$$u(\xi) = \text{unit step function of (2.2-4)} \tag{F-1d}$$

$$\text{rect}(\xi) = \text{rectangular function of (E-2)} \tag{F-1e}$$

$$\Gamma(x) = \int_0^\infty \xi^{x-1} e^{-\xi} d\xi \qquad \text{Re}(x) > 0$$

$$= \text{gamma function} \tag{F-1f}$$

---

† Re (z) denotes the real part of z.

$$P(\alpha, \beta) = \frac{1}{\Gamma(\alpha)} \int_0^\beta \xi^{\alpha-1} e^{-\xi} d\xi \qquad \mathrm{Re}\,(\alpha) > 0$$

$$= \text{incomplete gamma function} \tag{F-1g}$$

$$P(x|N) = \frac{1}{2^{N/2}\Gamma(N/2)} \int_0^x \xi^{(N/2)-1} e^{-\xi/2} d\xi$$

$$= \text{chi-square probability function}$$

$$= P\left(\frac{N}{2}, \frac{x}{2}\right) \tag{F-1h}$$

$$I(u, p) = \frac{1}{\Gamma(p+1)} \int_0^{u\sqrt{p+1}} \xi^p e^{-\xi} d\xi$$

$$= \text{Pearson's form of incomplete gamma function (Pearson, 1934)}$$

$$= P(p+1, u\sqrt{p+1}) \tag{F-1i}$$

$$I_x(a, b) = \frac{\Gamma(a+b)}{\Gamma(a)\Gamma(b)} \int_0^x \xi^{a-1} (1-\xi)^{b-1} d\xi$$

$$= \text{incomplete beta function} \tag{F-1j}$$

$$F(x) = \text{gaussian distribution of (B-3)} \tag{F-1k}$$

$$I_n(x) = (x/2)^n \sum_{k=0}^{\infty} \frac{(x/2)^{2k}}{k!(n+k)!}$$

$$= \frac{1}{\pi} \int_0^\pi e^{x\cos(\theta)} \cos(n\theta)\, d\theta$$

$$= \text{modified Bessel function of first kind of order } n = 0, 1, 2, \ldots \tag{F-1l}$$

$$Q(\alpha, \beta) = \int_\beta^\infty \xi I_0(\alpha\xi) \exp\left[\frac{-(\xi^2 + \alpha^2)}{2}\right] d\xi \tag{F-1m}$$

The functions of (F-1f) through (F-1j) and that of (F-1l) are discussed in detail in Abramowitz and Stegun, editors (1964). $Q(\alpha, \beta)$ is Marcum's Q-function; it is tabulated in Marcum (1950).

DISCRETE FUNCTIONS

Bernoulli

For $0 < p < 1$

$$f_X(x) = (1-p)\delta(x) + p\delta(x-1) \tag{F-2}$$

$$F_X(x) = (1-p)u(x) + pu(x-1) \tag{F-3}$$

$$\bar{X} = p \tag{F-4}$$

$$\sigma_X^2 = p(1 - p) \tag{F-5}$$

$$\Phi_X(\omega) = 1 - p + pe^{j\omega} \tag{F-6}$$

Binomial

For $0 < p < 1$ and $N = 1, 2, \ldots$

$$f_X(x) = \sum_{k=0}^{N} \binom{N}{k} p^k (1 - p)^{N-k} \delta(x - k) \tag{F-7}$$

$$F_X(x) = \sum_{k=0}^{N} \binom{N}{k} p^k (1 - p)^{N-k} u(x - k) \tag{F-8}$$

$$\bar{X} = Np \tag{F-9}$$

$$\sigma_X^2 = Np(1 - p) \tag{F-10}$$

$$\Phi_X(\omega) = [1 - p + pe^{j\omega}]^N \tag{F-11}$$

Pascal†

For $0 < p < 1$ and $N = 1, 2, \ldots$

$$f_X(x) = \sum_{k=N}^{\infty} \binom{k - 1}{N - 1} p^N (1 - p)^{k-N} \delta(x - k) \tag{F-12}$$

$$F_X(x) = \sum_{k=N}^{\infty} \binom{k - 1}{N - 1} p^N (1 - p)^{k-N} u(x - k) \tag{F-13}$$

$$\bar{X} = \frac{N}{p} \tag{F-14}$$

$$\sigma_X^2 = \frac{N(1 - p)}{p^2} \tag{F-15}$$

$$\Phi_X(\omega) = p^N e^{jN\omega} [1 - (1 - p)e^{j\omega}]^{-N} \tag{F-16}$$

Poisson

For $b > 0$

$$f_X(x) = e^{-b} \sum_{k=0}^{\infty} \frac{b^k}{k!} \delta(x - k) \tag{F-17}$$

---

† Blaise Pascal (1623–1662) was a French mathematician.

$$F_X(x) = e^{-b} \sum_{k=0}^{\infty} \frac{b^k}{k!} u(x - k) \tag{F-18}$$

$$\bar{X} = b \tag{F-19}$$

$$\sigma_X^2 = b \tag{F-20}$$

$$\Phi_X(\omega) \doteq \exp\left[b(e^{j\omega} - 1)\right] \tag{F-21}$$

CONTINUOUS FUNCTIONS

Arcsine

For $a > 0$

$$f_X(x) = \frac{\text{rect}\,(x/2a)}{\pi\sqrt{a^2 - x^2}} \tag{F-22}$$

$$F_X(x) = \begin{cases} 0 & -\infty < x < -a \\ \dfrac{1}{2} + \dfrac{1}{\pi} \sin^{-1}\left(\dfrac{x}{a}\right) & -a \le x < a \\ 1 & a \le x < \infty \end{cases} \tag{F-23}$$

$$\bar{X} = 0 \tag{F-24}$$

$$\sigma_X^2 = \frac{a^2}{2} \tag{F-25}$$

Beta

For $a > 0$ and $b > 0$

$$f_X(x) = \frac{\Gamma(a + b)}{\Gamma(a)\Gamma(b)} [u(x) - u(x - 1)]x^{a-1}(1 - x)^{b-1} \tag{F-26}$$

$$F_X(x) = \begin{cases} I_x(a, b)u(x) & x < 1 \\ 1 & x \ge 1 \end{cases} \tag{F-27}$$

$$\bar{X} = \frac{a}{a + b} \tag{F-28}$$

$$\sigma_X^2 = \frac{ab}{(a + b)^2(a + b + 1)} \tag{F-29}$$

Cauchy

For $b > 0$ and $-\infty < a < \infty$

$$f_X(x) = \frac{(b/\pi)}{b^2 + (x-a)^2} \tag{F-30}$$

$$F_X(x) = \frac{1}{2} + \frac{1}{\pi}\tan^{-1}\left(\frac{x-a}{b}\right) \tag{F-31}$$

$$\bar{X} = \text{is undefined} \tag{F-32}$$

$$\sigma_X^2 = \text{is undefined} \tag{F-33}$$

$$\Phi_X(\omega) = e^{ja\omega - b|\omega|} \tag{F-34}$$

Chi-Square with N Degrees of Freedom

For $N = 1, 2, \ldots$

$$f_X(x) = \frac{x^{(N/2)-1}}{2^{N/2}\Gamma(N/2)}e^{-x/2}u(x) \tag{F-35}$$

$$F_X(x) = P(x|N) = P\left(\frac{N}{2},\frac{x}{2}\right) \tag{F-36}$$

$$\bar{X} = N \tag{F-37}$$

$$\sigma_X^2 = 2N \tag{F-38}$$

$$\Phi_X(\omega) = (1 - j2\omega)^{-N/2} \tag{F-39}$$

Erlang

For $N = 1, 2, \ldots$ and $a > 0$

$$f_X(x) = \frac{a^N x^{N-1} e^{-ax}}{(N-1)!}u(x) \tag{F-40}$$

$$F_X(x) = \left[1 - e^{-ax}\sum_{n=0}^{N-1}\frac{(ax)^n}{n!}\right]u(x) \tag{F-41}$$

$$\bar{X} = \frac{N}{a} \tag{F-42}$$

$$\sigma_X^2 = \frac{N}{a^2} \tag{F-43}$$

$$\Phi_X(\omega) = \left(\frac{a}{a - j\omega}\right)^N \tag{F-44}$$

Exponential

For $a > 0$

$$f_X(x) = ae^{-ax}u(x) \tag{F-45}$$

$$F_X(x) = [1 - e^{-ax}]u(x) \tag{F-46}$$

$$\bar{X} = \frac{1}{a} \tag{F-47}$$

$$\sigma_X^2 = \frac{1}{a^2} \tag{F-48}$$

$$\Phi_X(\omega) = \frac{a}{a - j\omega} \tag{F-49}$$

Gamma

For $a > 0$ and $b > 0$

$$f_X(x) = \frac{a^b x^{b-1} e^{-ax}}{\Gamma(b)}\, u(x) \tag{F-50}$$

$$F_X(x) = I\left(\frac{ax}{\sqrt{b}}, b - 1\right)u(x) \tag{F-51}$$

$$\bar{X} = \frac{b}{a} \tag{F-52}$$

$$\sigma_X^2 = \frac{b}{a^2} \tag{F-53}$$

$$\Phi_X(\omega) = \left(\frac{a}{a - j\omega}\right)^b \tag{F-54}$$

Note that if b is a positive integer the gamma density becomes the Erlang density. Also if $b = N/2$, for $N = 1, 2, \ldots$, and $a = \frac{1}{2}$ the gamma density becomes the chi-square density.

Gaussian-Univariate

For $b > 0$ and $-\infty < a < \infty$

$$f_X(x) = (\pi b)^{-1/2} e^{-(x-a)^2/b} \tag{F-55}$$

$$F_X(x) = F\left(\frac{x - a}{\sqrt{b/2}}\right) \tag{F-56}$$

$$\bar{X} = a \tag{F-57}$$

$$\sigma_X^2 = \frac{b}{2} \tag{F-58}$$

$$\Phi_X(\omega) = e^{j\omega a - (\omega^2 b/4)} \tag{F-59}$$

Gaussian-Bivariate

For $-\infty < a_1 < \infty$, $-\infty < a_2 < \infty$, $b_1 > 0$, $b_2 > 0$ and $-1 \le \rho \le 1$

$$f_{X_1, X_2}(x_1, x_2) = [\pi^2 b_1 b_2 (1 - \rho^2)]^{-1/2}$$

$$\cdot \exp\left\{ \frac{-1}{(1 - \rho^2)} \left[\frac{(x_1 - a_1)^2}{b_1} \right.\right.$$

$$\left.\left. - \frac{2\rho(x_1 - a_1)(x_2 - a_2)}{\sqrt{b_1 b_2}} + \frac{(x_2 - a_2)^2}{b_2} \right] \right\} \tag{F-60}$$

$$F_{X_1, X_2}(x_1, x_2) = L\left(-\left[\frac{x_1 - a_1}{\sqrt{b_1/2}} \right], -\left[\frac{x_2 - a_2}{\sqrt{b_2/2}} \right], \rho \right) \tag{F-61}$$

where $L(x_1, x_2, \rho)$ is a probability function discussed extensively and graphed in Abramowitz and Stegun, editors (1964), p. 936. Also

$$\bar{X}_1 = a_1 \tag{F-62}$$

$$\bar{X}_2 = a_2 \tag{F-63}$$

$$\sigma_{X_1}^2 = b_1/2 \tag{F-64}$$

$$\sigma_{X_2}^2 = b_2/2 \tag{F-65}$$

$$\Phi_{X_1, X_2}(\omega_1, \omega_2) = \exp\left\{ j\omega_1 a_1 + j\omega_2 a_2 - \frac{1}{4}[\omega_1^2 b_1 + 2\rho\omega_1\omega_2\sqrt{b_1 b_2} + \omega_2^2 b_2] \right\} \tag{F-66}$$

Laplace

For $b > 0$ and $-\infty < a < \infty$

$$f_X(x) = \frac{b}{2} e^{-b|x - a|} \tag{F-67}$$

$$F_X(x) = \begin{cases} \frac{1}{2}e^{b(x - a)} & -\infty < x < a \\ 1 - \frac{1}{2}e^{-b(x - a)} & a \le x < \infty \end{cases} \tag{F-68}$$

$$\bar{X} = a \tag{F-69}$$

$$\sigma_X^2 = \frac{2}{b^2} \tag{F-70}$$

$$\Phi_X(\omega) = b^2 \frac{e^{ja\omega}}{b^2 + \omega^2} \tag{F-71}$$

Log-Normal

For $-\infty < a < \infty$, $-\infty < b < \infty$, and $\sigma > 0$

$$f_X(x) = \frac{u(x - b)e^{-[\ln(x-b)-a]^2/2\sigma^2}}{\sqrt{2\pi}(x - b)\sigma} \tag{F-72}$$

$$F_X(x) = u(x - b)F\{\sigma^{-1}[\ln(x - b) - a]\} \tag{F-73}$$

$$\bar{X} = b + \exp\left(a + \frac{\sigma^2}{2}\right) \tag{F-74}$$

$$\sigma_X^2 = [\exp(\sigma^2) - 1]\exp(2a + \sigma^2) \tag{F-75}$$

Rayleigh

For $-\infty < a < \infty$ and $b > 0$

$$f_X(x) = \frac{2}{b}(x - a)e^{-(x-a)^2/b}u(x - a) \tag{F-76}$$

$$F_X(x) = [1 - e^{-(x-a)^2/b}]u(x - a) \tag{F-77}$$

$$\bar{X} = a + \sqrt{\frac{\pi b}{4}} \tag{F-78}$$

$$\sigma_X^2 = \frac{b(4 - \pi)}{4} \tag{F-79}$$

Rice [Thomas (1969), Middleton (1960)]

For $a > 0$ and $b > 0$

$$f_X(x) = \frac{x}{b^2}e^{-(a^2+x^2)/2b^2}I_0\left(\frac{ax}{b^2}\right)u(x) \tag{F-80}$$

$$F_X(x) = \left[1 - Q\left(\frac{a}{b}, \frac{x}{b}\right)\right]u(x) \tag{F-81}$$

$$\bar{X} = b\sqrt{\frac{\pi}{2}}e^{-k^2/4}\left[\left(1 + \frac{k^2}{2}\right)I_0\left(\frac{k^2}{4}\right) + \frac{k^2}{2}I_1\left(\frac{k^2}{4}\right)\right] \tag{F-82}$$

$$\sigma_X^2 = b^2(2 + k^2) - (\bar{X})^2 \tag{F-83}$$

$$k^2 = \frac{a^2}{b^2} \tag{F-84}$$

Uniform

For $-\infty < a < b < \infty$

$$f_X(x) = \frac{u(x - a) - u(x - b)}{b - a} \tag{F-85}$$

$$F_X(x) = \begin{cases} \dfrac{(x - a)u(x - a)}{b - a} & x < b \\ 1 & x \geq b \end{cases} \tag{F-86}$$

$$\bar{X} = \frac{a + b}{2} \tag{F-87}$$

$$\sigma_X^2 = \frac{(b - a)^2}{12} \tag{F-88}$$

$$\Phi_X(\omega) = \frac{e^{j\omega b} - e^{j\omega a}}{j\omega(b - a)} \tag{F-89}$$

Weibull

For $a > 0$ and $b > 0$

$$f_X(x) = abx^{b-1}e^{-ax^b}u(x) \tag{F-90}$$

$$F_X(x) = [1 - e^{-ax^b}]u(x) \tag{F-91}$$

$$\bar{X} = \frac{\Gamma(1 + b^{-1})}{a^{1/b}} \tag{F-92}$$

$$\sigma_X^2 = \frac{\Gamma(1 + 2b^{-1}) - [\Gamma(1 + b^{-1})]^2}{a^{2/b}} \tag{F-93}$$

Note that if $b = 2$ the Weibull density becomes a Rayleigh density.

BIBLIOGRAPHY

Abramowitz, M., and I. Stegun, editors (1964): *Handbook of Mathematical Functions with Formulas, Graphs, and Mathematical Tables*, National Bureau of Standards Applied Mathematics Series 55, U.S. Government Printing Office, Washington, D.C.

Barton, D. K. (1964): *Radar System Analysis*, Prentice-Hall, Englewood Cliffs, New Jersey.

Bendat, J. S., and A. G. Piersol (1986): *Random Data: Analysis and Measurement Procedures*, 2d ed., Wiley Interscience, New York.

Blackman, R. B., and J. W. Tukey (1958): *The Measurement of Power Spectra*, Dover, New York.

Blanchard, A. (1976): *Phase-Locked Loops, Application to Coherent Receiver Design*, John Wiley & Sons, New York.

Börjesson, P. O., and C.-E. W. Sundberg (1979): "Simple Approximations of the Error Function $Q(x)$ for Communications Applications," *IEEE Transactions on Communications*, vol. COM-27, no. 3, March, 1979, pp. 639–643.

Bracewell, R. (1965): *The Fourier Transform and Its Applications*, McGraw-Hill, New York.

Campbell, G. A., and R. M. Foster (1948): *Fourier Integrals for Practical Applications*, Van Nostrand, Princeton, New Jersey.

Carlson, A. B. (1975): *Communication Systems, An Introduction to Signals and Noise in Electrical Communication*, 2d ed., McGraw-Hill, New York.

Clarke, A. B., and R. L. Disney (1970): *Probability and Random Processes for Engineers and Scientists*, Wiley, New York.

Cooper, G. R., and C. D. McGillem (1971): *Probabilistic Methods of Signal and System Analysis*, Holt, Rinehart and Winston, New York. See also 2d ed., 1986.

Cramér H. (1946): *Mathematical Methods of Statistics*, Princeton University Press, Princeton, New Jersey.

Davenport, W. B., Jr., and W. L. Root (1958): *An Introduction to the Theory of Random Signals and Noise*, McGraw-Hill, New York.

Davenport, W. B., Jr. (1970): *Probability and Random Processes, An Introduction for Applied Scientists and Engineers*, McGraw-Hill, New York.

DiFranco, J. V., and W. L. Rubin (1968): *Radar Detection*, Prentice-Hall, Englewood Cliffs, New Jersey.

Dillard, G. M. (1967): "Generating Random Numbers Having Probability Distributions Occurring in Signal Detection Problems," *Transactions of IEEE*, vol. IT-13, no. 4, October, 1967, pp. 616–617.

Dubes, R. C. (1968): *The Theory of Applied Probability*, Prentice-Hall, Englewood Cliffs, New Jersey.

Dwight, H. B. (1961): *Tables of Integrals and other Mathematical Data*, 4th ed., Macmillan, New York.

Gardner, W. A. (1990): *Introduction to Random Processes with Applications to Signals and Systems*, 2d ed., McGraw-Hill, New York.

Gray, R. M., and L. D. Davisson (1986): *Random Processes: A Mathematical Approach for Engineers*, Prentice-Hall, Englewood Cliffs, New Jersey.

Helstrom, C. W. (1984): *Probability and Stochastic Processes for Engineers*, Macmillan, New York. See also 2d ed., 1991.

James, H. M., N. B. Nichols, and R. S. Phillips (1947): *Theory of Servomechanisms*, M.I.T. Radiation Laboratory Series, vol. 25, McGraw-Hill, New York.

Kay, S. M. (1986): *Modern Spectral Estimation—Theory and Applications*, Prentice-Hall, Englewood Cliffs, New Jersey.

Kennedy, J. B., and A. M. Neville, (1986): *Basic Statistical Methods for Engineers and Scientists*, 3d ed., Harper & Row, New York.

Klapper, J., and J. T., Frankle (1972): *Phase-Locked and Frequency-Feedback Systems*, Academic Press, New York.

Korn, G. A., and T. M. Korn (1961): *Mathematical Handbook for Scientists and Engineers*, McGraw-Hill, New York.

Lathi, B. P. (1968): *An Introduction to Random Signals and Communication Theory*, International Textbook, Scranton, Pennsylvania.

Leon-Garcia, A. (1989): *Probability and Random Processes for Electrical Engineering*, Addison-Wesley, Reading, Massachusetts.

Marcum, J. I., "Studies of Target Detection by Pulsed Radar," Special Monograph Issue *IRE Transactions on Information Theory*, vol. IT-6, no. 2, April, 1960.

Marcum, J. I., "Table of Q Functions," U.S. Air Force Project RAND Research Memorandum RM-339, January 1, 1950 (ASTIA Document AD116551).

McFadden, M. (1963): *Sets, Relations, and Functions*, McGraw-Hill, New York.

Melsa, J. L., and A. P. Sage (1973): *An Introduction to Probability and Stochastic Processes*, Prentice-Hall, Englewood Cliffs, New Jersey.

Middleton, D. (1960): *An Introduction to Statistical Communication Theory*, McGraw-Hill, New York.

Miller, K. S. (1974): *Complex Stochastic Processes, An Introduction to Theory and Application*, Addison-Wesley, Reading, Massachusetts.

Milton, J. S., and C. P. Tsokos (1976): *Probability Theory with the Essential Analysis*, Addison-Wesley, Reading, Massachusetts.

Mumford, W. W., and E. H. Scheibe (1968): *Noise Performance Factors in Communication Systems*, Horizon House-Microwave, Dedham, Massachusetts.

Papoulis, A. (1962): *The Fourier Integral and its Applications*, McGraw-Hill, New York.

Papoulis, A. (1965): *Probability, Random Variables, and Stochastic Processes*, McGraw-Hill, New York. See also the 2d ed., 1984.

Parzen, E. (1962): *Stochastic Processes*, Holden-Day, San Francisco, California.

Pearson, K., editor (1934): *Tables of the Incomplete Gamma Functions*, Cambridge University Press, Cambridge, England.

Peebles, P. Z., Jr. (1976): *Communication System Principles*, Addison-Wesley, Reading, Massachusetts.

Peebles, P. Z., Jr., and T. A. Giuma (1991): *Principles of Electrical Engineering*, McGraw-Hill, New York.

Prabhu, N. U. (1965): *Stochastic Processes, Basic Theory and its Applications*, Macmillan, New York.

Ralston, A., and H. S. Wilf (1967): *Mathematical Methods for Digital Computers*, vol. II, Wiley, New York.

Rosenblatt, M. (1974): *Random Processes*, 2d ed., Springer-Verlag, New York.

Ross, S. M. (1972): *Introduction to Probability Models*, Academic Press, New York.

Shanmugan, K. S., and A. M. Breipohl (1988): *Random Signals: Detection, Estimation and Data Analysis*, John Wiley, New York.

Spiegel, M. R. (1963): *Theory and Problems of Advanced Calculus*, Schaum, New York.

Thomas, J. B. (1969): *An Introduction to Statistical Communication Theory*, Wiley, New York.

van der Ziel, A. (1970): *Noise: Sources, Characterization, Measurement*, Prentice-Hall, Englewood Cliffs, New Jersey.

Wilks, S. S. (1962): *Mathematical Statistics*, Wiley, New York.

Wozencraft, J. M., and I. M. Jacobs (1965): *Principles of Communication Engineering*, Wiley, New York.

Ziemer, R. E., and W. H. Tranter (1976): *Principles of Communications Systems, Modulation, and Noise*, Houghton Mifflin, Boston, Massachusetts.

INDEX